BEGINNING MICROSOFT® SQL SERVER® 2012 PROGRAMMING

BEGINNING

Microsoft® SQL Server® 2012
Programming

BEGINNING

Microsoft® SQL Server® 2012 Programming

Paul Atkinson
Robert Vieira

WILEY

John Wiley & Sons, Inc.

Beginning Microsoft® SQL Server® 2012 Programming

Published by
John Wiley & Sons, Inc.
10475 Crosspoint Boulevard
Indianapolis, IN 46256
www.wiley.com

ISBN: 978-1-118-10228-2   5 0 H1   7 7 7 2   1/13
ISBN: 978-1-118-22388-8 (ebk)
ISBN: 978-1-118-23621-5 (ebk)
ISBN: 978-1-118-26216-0 (ebk)

Manufactured in the United States of America

10 9 8 7 6 5 4 3 2 1

For general information on our other products and services please contact our Customer Care Department within the United States at (877) 762-2974, outside the United States at (317) 572-3993 or fax (317) 572-4002.

Wiley publishes in a variety of print and electronic formats and by print-on-demand. Some material included with standard print versions of this book may not be included in e-books or in print-on-demand. If this book refers to media such as a CD or DVD that is not included in the version you purchased, you may download this material at http://booksupport.wiley.com. For more information about Wiley products, visit www.wiley.com.

Library of Congress Control Number: 2012933622

This book is dedicated to my parents, and to the unique perspective they provide from the union of the often professorial Atkinsons and the utterly hilarious Walshes. If any fraction of their wit has leaked through into its pages, this book will have succeeded.

CREDITS

EXECUTIVE EDITOR
Robert Elliott

PROJECT EDITOR
Maureen Spears

TECHNICAL EDITOR
Eric Aldinger

PRODUCTION EDITOR
Daniel Scribner

COPY EDITOR
Gayle Johnson

EDITORIAL MANAGER
Mary Beth Wakefield

FREELANCER EDITORIAL MANAGER
Rosemarie Graham

ASSOCIATE DIRECTOR OF MARKETING
David Mayhew

MARKETING MANAGER
Ashley Zurcher

BUSINESS MANAGER
Amy Knies

PRODUCTION MANAGER
Tim Tate

VICE PRESIDENT AND EXECUTIVE GROUP PUBLISHER
Richard Swadley

VICE PRESIDENT AND EXECUTIVE PUBLISHER
Neil Edde

ASSOCIATE PUBLISHER
Jim Minatel

PROJECT COORDINATOR, COVER
Katie Crocker

PROOFREADER
Louise Watson, Word One

INDEXER
Ron Strauss

COVER DESIGNER
Ryan Sneed

COVER IMAGE
© Arthur S. Aubry / Getty Images

ABOUT THE AUTHORS

PAUL ATKINSON has been working with database technology since his days at Microsoft in the early 1990s, where he learned Microsoft Access first as a side project and later as a support rep. From there he went on to get a degree in Computer Science from Portland State University, rode the dot-com wave as a DBA, and came out of the dot-com bust as a contractor primarily in the health care industry. Currently, Paul works for Huron Healthcare as a BI Architect and Team Lead developing both traditional and real-time BI solutions. His training classes in high-performance T-SQL programming are among the most popular course offerings available at Huron. Paul, his wife Kristin, and their daughter Maureen love living in Portland, Oregon. When he's not working or writing Paul plays on multiple soccer teams, and otherwise keeps busy as a mountain biker, snowboarder, hasher, bicycle commuter, chairman of the school site council, proud member of the Timbers Army, and semi-professional chocolatier. As Robert Heinlein wrote, specialization is for insects.

ROBERT VIEIRA is a Software Architect with Huron Consulting Group and is considered one of the leading authorities on Microsoft SQL Server. He speaks at conferences nationally and is well known for his unique tutorial approach in his teaching and writing.

ABOUT THE TECHNICAL EDITOR

ERIC ALDINGER is a quality assurance engineer working out of Portland, Oregon. He spends much of his time working on thorny data integration and data warehousing issues on green field development projects. Editing this text proves the improbable axiom that a University of California, Riverside, literature degree is good for something outside of academia, given enough time. Eric has many hobbies, none of which are of interest to readers of this book.

ACKNOWLEDGMENTS

NOBODY COMPLETES A PROJECT like this alone. Crafting a technical book that's readable despite the fairly dry material found therein takes an enormous amount of time and dedication, and that's not from the author — it's from those who support, guide, and encourage him. While there are many who helped with this, my first foray, there are a few without whom I'd never have gotten through it.

Rob Vieira, whose efforts early on helped create the genre of the developer-centric SQL Server book, has probably contributed more to this title than anyone — even me. Besides laying down a framework, Rob has also been a mentor and a friend, and without him, I'd never have started on this effort at all. That said, I'm sure he'll be pleased when I've finished, since he's probably bored of my escaping work before 6:00 to come home and write.

Bob Elliott, for giving me the chance based on nothing but a recommendation (albeit a good one).

Kristin Atkinson, my wife of more than 15 years now; you have carried the house on your shoulders since I picked up this project. Each night I come home and sit down to write, and you've taken care of every other thing. Not only have you cleared the path, but you've made an excellent sounding board. This book is as much yours as it is anyone's, and by now you probably know more about SQL Server than any other artisan chocolatier I know.

Maureen Spears, you have phenomenal tolerance for my first-timer mistakes and questions, not to mention delays. Your help, attitude, and feedback have kept my enthusiasm up long after it could have flagged.

Eric Aldinger, by stepping up and enthusiastically accepting the role of technical editor, you've ensured the errata section on this title will be ridiculously clean. Once we're done here we need to spend less time on technical books and more on bikes.

CONTENTS

INTRODUCTION

OUT OF EVERY ENDING COMES the beginning of something new. This title has been Rob Vieira's for many years, and now he's wrapping up that chapter of his life while I begin a new chapter of my own — and the first chapter of this text. Likewise, you, as a reader, are also entering something of a transition; you know something about programming, probably, but you're about to begin a completely new experience as a programmer of relational databases in general and Microsoft SQL Server 2012 in particular.

Database programming is a pretty big shift from most other kinds of software engineering. If you're at all like me, something brought you from your early programming experience (6502-based machines in BASIC for me) to databases. For me it happened at Microsoft in the early '90s, supporting a beta product that flew under the radar; I was asked to track certain aspects of the work I was doing in Access (2.0 at that time). Once I learned to do that, I was hooked, and a couple years on the Access support queue (learning SQL Server 4.2 and beyond as well) sealed the deal.

Working with SQL Server is a whole different animal from ordinary procedural programming. You get to think in mathematical and set-based terms, and learn how to ask carefully for what you want without spelling out how to actually accomplish the work. Transitioning from procedural programming to this kind of thinking without help is like trying to make a paradigm shift without a clutch. And yet this language, SQL, has a certain simplicity to it sometimes that makes it a pleasure to work with, once you learn how to think like it thinks.

I learned from immersion, from Microsoft's internal trainers, and from peers; what I wished for at the time was a book I could read that would give me the concepts and the functional knowledge to understand what I was seeing and know what was out there that I didn't know about yet. This book is the book I wanted, which means if you're in that early learning phase with T-SQL, it's probably the book you need as well.

This is a step-by-step tutorial, providing you the concepts you need in bite-sized pieces presented in an orderly way, each building on the last. The whole reason it exists is that you'd likely have a terrible time picking up such a completely new set of concepts by choosing topics out of an online help database. Books are still, in 2012, a great way to learn new ideas.

My hope is that, in this book, you find something that covers all of the core elements of SQL Server with the same success that we had in the original *Professional SQL Server Programming* titles. When you're done, you should be set to be a highly functional SQL Server 2012 programmer and, with any luck, you'll enjoy the unique challenges of database programming for years to come.

WHO THIS BOOK IS FOR

It is almost sad that the word "beginner" is in the title of this book. Don't get me wrong; if you are a beginner, this title is for you. But it is designed to last you well beyond your beginning days. What is covered in this book is necessary for the beginner, but there is simply too much information for you to remember all of it all the time, and so it is laid out in a fashion that should make a solid review and reference book even for the more intermediate, and, yes, even advanced user.

The beginning user will want to start right at the beginning. Things are designed such that just about everything in this book is a genuine "need to know" sort of thing. With the possible exception of the chapters on XML, Reporting Services, and Integration Services, every item in this book is fundamental to you having the breadth of understanding you need to make well-informed choices on how you approach your SQL Server problems. Even these three topics are increasingly fundamental to being a serious SQL Server developer.

For the intermediate user, you can probably skip perhaps as far as Chapter 7 or 8 to start. Although I still recommend scanning the prior chapters for holes in your skills or general review, you can probably skip ahead with little harm done and get to something that might be a bit more challenging for you.

Advanced users, in addition to utilizing this as an excellent reference resource, will probably want to focus on Chapter 12 and beyond. Virtually everything from that point forward should be of some interest (the new debugging, transactions, XML, BI, Reporting Services, Integration Services, and more!).

WHAT THIS BOOK COVERS

Well, if you've read the title, you're probably not shocked to hear that this book covers SQL Server 2012 with a definite bent toward the developer's perspective.

SQL Server 2012 is the latest incarnation of a database management system that has now been around for more than two decades. It builds on the base redesign that was done to the product in version 7.0 — this time adding some brilliant analysis and reporting functionality, among other things. This book focuses on core development needs of every developer, regardless of skill level. The focus is highly oriented to just the 2012 version of the product, but there is regular mention of backward-compatibility issues, as they may affect your design and coding choices.

HOW THIS BOOK IS STRUCTURED

The book is designed to become increasingly more advanced as you progress through it, but, from the very beginning, I'm assuming that you are already an experienced developer — just not necessarily with databases. In order to make it through this book, you do need to already have understanding of programming basics such as variables, data types, and procedural programming. You do not have to have seen a query before in your life (though I suspect you have).

The focus of the book is highly developer-oriented. This means that it will, for the sake of both brevity and sanity, sometimes gloss over or totally ignore items that are more the purview of the database administrator than the developer. You will, however, be reminded of administration issues either as they affect the developer or as they need to be thought of during the development process — you'll also take a brief look at several administration-related issues in Chapter 21.

The book makes a very concerted effort to be language independent in terms of your client-side development. VB, C#, C++, Java, and other languages are generally ignored (it focuses on the server side of the equation) and treated equally where addressed.

In terms of learning order, you'll start by learning the foundation objects of SQL, and then move on to basic queries and joins. From there, you can begin adding objects to your database and discuss items that are important to the physical design — then it is on to the more robust code aspects of SQL Server scripting, stored procedures, user-defined functions, and triggers. After a short tutorial on business intelligence, you'll have a look at a few of the relatively peripheral features of SQL Server. Last but not least, you can wrap things up with a bit of important material on administration meant to help you keep the databases you develop nice and healthy.

 NOTE *This book is a tutorial, but there's reference material online you might want to refer to even after you're done. This bonus material, including a full reference containing system functions and a document of very simple connectivity examples, is available at* www.wrox.com. *Once at the site, search for the book by its ISBN, which is 978-1-118-102282.*

WHAT YOU NEED TO USE THIS BOOK

In order to make any real, viable use of this book, you will need an installation of SQL Server. The book makes extensive use of the actual SQL Server 2012 management tools, so I highly recommend that you have a version that contains the full product, rather than just using SQL Server Express. That said, the book is focused on the kind of scripting required for developers, so even SQL Server Express users should be able to get the lion's share of learning out of most of the chapters. You will also need the AdvenureWorks sample database, the AdventureWorks database for BI and reporting, and a few custom databases installed. Instructions for accessing these databases can be found in the ReadMe file on this book's website (www.wrox.com).

A copy of Visual Studio is handy for working with this book, but most of the Visual Studio features needed are included in the Business Intelligence Studio that comes along with the SQL Server product.

CONVENTIONS

To help you get the most from the text and keep track of what's happening, I've used a number of conventions throughout the book.

TRY IT OUT

The *Try It Out* is an exercise you should work through, following the text in the book.

1.   The exercises usually consist of a set of steps.

2. Each step has a number.

3. Follow the steps through with your copy of the database.

How It Works

After each *Try It Out*, the code you've typed will be explained in detail.

 WARNING *Boxes with a warning icon like this one hold important, not-to-be-forgotten information that is directly relevant to the surrounding text.*

 NOTE *The pencil icon indicates notes, tips, hints, tricks, and asides to the current discussion.*

➤ We *italicize* new terms and important words when we introduce them.

➤ We show keyboard strokes like this: Ctrl+A.

➤ We show filenames, URLs, and code within the text like so: `persistence.properties`.

➤ We present code in two different ways:

```
We use a monofont type with no highlighting for most code examples.
```

```
We use bold to emphasize code that's particularly important in the present
context.
```

SOURCE CODE

As you work through the examples in this book, you may choose either to type in all the code manually or to use the source code files that accompany the book. All the source code used in this book is available for download at www.wrox.com. When at the site, simply locate the book's title (use the Search box or one of the title lists) and click the Download Code link on the book's detail page to obtain all the source code for the book. Code that is included on the website is highlighted by the following icon:

**Available for
download on
Wrox.com**

Listings include the filename in the title. If it is just a code snippet, you'll find the filename in a code note such as this:

Code snippet filename

NOTE *Because many books have similar titles, you may find it easiest to search by ISBN; this book's ISBN is 978-1-118-10228-2.*

Once you download the code, just decompress it with your favorite compression tool. Alternately, you can go to the main Wrox code download page at www.wrox.com/dynamic/books/download .aspx to see the code available for this book and all other Wrox books.

ERRATA

We make every effort to ensure that there are no errors in the text or in the code. However, no one is perfect, and mistakes do occur. If you find an error in one of our books, like a spelling mistake or faulty piece of code, we would be very grateful for your feedback. By sending in errata you may save another reader hours of frustration and at the same time you will be helping us provide even higher quality information.

To find the errata page for this book, go to www.wrox.com and locate the title using the Search box or one of the title lists. Then, on the book details page, click the Book Errata link. On this page you can view all errata that has been submitted for this book and posted by Wrox editors. A complete book list including links to each book's errata is also available at www.wrox.com/misc-pages/ booklist.shtml.

If you don't spot "your" error on the Book Errata page, go to www.wrox.com/contact/ techsupport.shtml and complete the form there to send us the error you have found. We'll check the information and, if appropriate, post a message to the book's errata page and fix the problem in subsequent editions of the book.

P2P.WROX.COM

For author and peer discussion, join the P2P forums at p2p.wrox.com. The forums are a web-based system for you to post messages relating to Wrox books and related technologies and interact with other readers and technology users. The forums offer a subscription feature to e-mail you topics of interest of your choosing when new posts are made to the forums. Wrox authors, editors, other industry experts, and your fellow readers are present on these forums.

At http://p2p.wrox.com you will find a number of different forums that will help you not only as you read this book, but also as you develop your own applications. To join the forums, just follow these steps:

1. Go to p2p.wrox.com and click the Register link.

2. Read the terms of use and click Agree.

3. Complete the required information to join as well as any optional information you wish to provide and click Submit.

4. You will receive an e-mail with information describing how to verify your account and complete the joining process.

 NOTE *You can read messages in the forums without joining P2P but in order to post your own messages, you must join.*

Once you join, you can post new messages and respond to messages other users post. You can read messages at any time on the web. If you would like to have new messages from a particular forum e-mailed to you, click the Subscribe to this Forum icon by the forum name in the forum listing.

For more information about how to use the Wrox P2P, be sure to read the P2P FAQs for answers to questions about how the forum software works as well as many common questions specific to P2P and Wrox books. To read the FAQs, click the FAQ link on any P2P page.

1

RDBMS Basics: What Makes Up a SQL Server Database?

WHAT YOU WILL LEARN IN THIS CHAPTER:

➤ Understand what the objects are that make up a SQL Server database

➤ Learn the data types available for use in SQL Server 2012

➤ Discover how to name objects

What makes up a database? Data for sure. (What use is a database that doesn't store anything?) But a *Relational Database Management System (RDBMS)* is actually much more than data. Today's advanced RDBMSs not only store your data, they also manage that data for you, restricting the kind of data that can go into the system, and facilitating getting data out of the system. If all you want is to tuck the data away somewhere safe, you could use just about any data storage system. RDBMSs allow you to go beyond the storage of the data into the realm of defining what that data should look like, or the *business rules* of the data.

Don't confuse what I'm calling the "business rules of the data" with the more generalized business rules that drive your entire system (for example, preventing someone from seeing anything until they've logged in, or automatically adjusting the current period in an accounting system on the first of the month). Those types of rules can be enforced at virtually any level of the system (these days, it's usually in the middle or client tier of an n-tier system). Instead, what I'm talking about here are the business rules that specifically relate to the data. For example, you can't have a sales order with a negative amount. With an RDBMS, you can incorporate these rules right into the integrity of the database itself.

The notion of the database taking responsibility for the data within, as well as the best methods to input and extract data from that database, serves as the foundation for this book. This chapter provides an overview of the rest of the book. Most items discussed in this chapter are covered again in later chapters, but this chapter is intended to provide you with a road map or plan to bear in mind as you progress through the book. With this in mind, I'll give you a high-level look into:

➤ Database objects

➤ Data types

➤ Other database concepts that ensure data integrity

AN OVERVIEW OF DATABASE OBJECTS

An instance of an RDBMS such as SQL Server contains many *objects*. Object purists out there may quibble with whether Microsoft's choice of what to (and what not to) call an object actually meets the normal definition of an object, but, for SQL Server's purposes, the list of some of the more important database objects can be said to contain such things as:

➤ The database itself

➤ The transaction log

➤ Tables

➤ Indexes

➤ Filegroups

➤ Diagrams

➤ Views

➤ Stored procedures

➤ User-defined functions

➤ Sequences

➤ Users

➤ Roles

➤ Assemblies

➤ Reports

➤ Full-text catalogs

➤ User-defined data types

The Database Object

The database is effectively the highest-level object that you can refer to within a given SQL Server. (Technically speaking, the server itself can be considered to be an object, but not from any real "programming" perspective, so I'm not going there.) Most, but not all, other objects in a SQL Server are children of the database object.

NOTE *If you are already familiar with SQL Server you may now be saying, "What? What happened to logins or SQL Agent tasks?" SQL Server has several other objects (as listed previously) that exist in support of the database. With the exception of linked servers, and perhaps Integration Services packages, these are primarily the domain of the database administrator and, as such, you generally won't give them significant thought during the design and programming processes. (They are programmable via something called the SQL Management Objects [SMO], which is beyond the scope of this book.) Although there are some exceptions to this rule, I generally consider them to be advanced in nature, and thus they are not covered in the beginner version of this book.*

A database is typically a group of constructs that include at least a set of table objects and, more often than not, other objects, such as stored procedures and views that pertain to the particular grouping of data stored in the database's tables.

What types of tables do you store in just one database, and what goes in a separate database? I'll discuss that in some detail later in the book, but for now I'll take the simple approach of saying that any data that is generally thought of as belonging to just one system, or is significantly related, will be stored in a single database. An RDBMS, such as SQL Server, may have multiple databases on just one server, or it may have only one. The number of databases that reside on an individual SQL Server depends on such factors as capacity (CPU power, disk I/O limitations, memory, and so on), autonomy (you want one person to have management rights to the server this system is running on, and someone else to have admin rights to a different server), and just how many databases your company or client has. Some servers have only one production database; others have many. Also, any version of SQL Server that you're likely to find in production these days has multiple instances of SQL Server — complete with separate logins and management rights — all on the same physical server. (SQL Server 2000 was already five years old by the time it was replaced, so I'll assume most shops have that or higher.)

 NOTE *I'm sure many of you are now asking, "Can I have different versions of SQL Server on the same box — say, SQL Server 2008 and SQL Server 2012?" The answer is yes. You can mix SQL Server 2008 and 2012 on the same box. Personally, I am not at all trusting of this configuration, even for migration scenarios, but if you have the need, yes, it can be done.*

When you first load SQL Server, you start with at least four system databases:

➤ `master`

➤ `model`

➤ `msdb`

➤ `tempdb`

All of these need to be installed for your server to run properly. (Indeed, without some of them, it won't run at all.) From there, things vary depending on which installation choices you made. Examples of some of the databases you may see include the following:

➤ **ReportServer:** The database that serves Reporting Server configuration and model storage needs

➤ **ReportServerTempDB:** The working database for Reporting Server

➤ **AdventureWorks:** The sample database

➤ **AdventureWorksDW:** Sample for use with Analysis Services

In addition to the system-installed examples, you may, when searching the web or using other tutorials, find reference to a couple of older samples:

➤ `pubs`

➤ `Northwind`

Because these examples were no longer used in the prior edition of this book, I won't deal with them further here, but I still mention them mostly because they carry fond memories from simpler times, and partly because you might find them out there somewhere.

 NOTE *For this edition, the examples will either be homegrown or else come from the newer AdventureWorks samples. The AdventureWorks database is certainly a robust example and does a great job of providing examples of just about every little twist and turn you can make use of in SQL Server 2012. There is, however, a problem with that — complexity. The AdventureWorks database can sometimes be excessively complex for a training database. It takes features that are likely to be used only in exceptional cases and uses them as a dominant feature. So, with that said, let me make the point now that AdventureWorks should not necessarily be used as a template for what to do in other similar applications.*

The master Database

Every SQL Server, regardless of version or custom modifications, has the `master` database. This database holds a special set of tables (system tables) that keeps track of the system as a whole. For example, when you create a new database on the server, an entry is placed in the `sysdatabases` table in the `master` database. All extended and system-stored procedures, regardless of which database they are intended for use with, are stored in this database. Obviously, since almost everything that describes your server is stored in here, this database is critical to your system and cannot be deleted.

The system tables, including those found in the `master` database, were, in the past, occasionally used in a pinch to provide system configuration information, such as whether certain objects existed before you performed operations on them. Microsoft warned developers for years not to use the system tables directly, but, because there were few other options, most developers ignored that advice. Happily, Microsoft began providing other options in the form of system and information schema views; you can now utilize these views to get at the systems' metadata as necessary, with

Microsoft's full blessing. For example, if you try to create an object that already exists in any particular database, you get an error. If you want to force the issue, you could test to see whether the table already has an entry in the `sys.objects` table for that database. If it does, you would delete that object before re-creating it.

 WARNING *If you're quite cavalier, you may be saying to yourself, "Cool, I can't wait to mess around in those system tables!"* Don't go there! *Using the system tables in any form is fraught with peril. Microsoft makes absolutely no guarantees about compatibility in the* `master` *database between versions. Indeed, they virtually guarantee that they will change. Fortunately, several alternatives (for example, system functions, system-stored procedures, and* `information_schema` *views) are available for retrieving much of the metadata that is stored in the system tables.*

All that said, there are still times when nothing else will do, but, in general, you should consider them to be evil cannibals from another tribe and best left alone.

The model Database

The `model` database is aptly named, in the sense that it's the model on which a copy can be based. The `model` database forms a template for any new database that you create. This means that you can, if you want, alter the `model` database if you want to change what standard, newly created databases look like. For example, you could add a set of audit tables that you include in every database you build. You could also include a few user groups that would be cloned into every new database that was created on the system. Note that because this database serves as the template for any other database, it's a required database and must be left on the system; you cannot delete it.

There are several points to keep in mind when altering the `model` database:

➤ **Any database you create has to be at least as large as the** **model** **database.** That means that if you alter the `model` database to be 100MB in size, you can't create a database smaller than 100MB.

➤ **Similar pitfalls apply when adding objects or changing settings, which can lead to unintended consequences.** As such, for 90 percent of installations, I strongly recommend leaving this one alone.

The msdb Database

`msdb` is where the SQL Agent process stores any system tasks. If you schedule backups to run on a database nightly, there is an entry in `msdb`. Schedule a stored procedure for one-time execution, and yes, it has an entry in `msdb`. Other major subsystems in SQL Server make similar use of `msdb`. SSIS packages and policy-based management definitions are examples of other processes that make use of `msdb`.

The tempdb Database

`tempdb` is one of the key working areas for your server. Whenever you issue a complex or large query that SQL Server needs to build interim tables to solve, it does so in `tempdb`. Whenever you create a temporary table of your own, it is created in tempdb, even though you think you're creating it in the current database. (An alias is created in the local database for you to reference it by, but the physical table is created in tempdb.) Whenever there is a need for data to be stored temporarily, it's probably stored in tempdb.

tempdb is very different from any other database. Not only are the objects within it temporary, the database itself is temporary. It has the distinction of being the only database in your system that is rebuilt from scratch every time you start your SQL Server.

 NOTE *Technically speaking, you can actually create objects yourself in* tempdb. *I strongly recommend against this practice. You can create temporary objects from within any database to which you have access in your system — they will be stored in* tempdb. *Creating objects directly in* tempdb *gains you nothing, but adding the confusion of referring to things across databases. This is another of those "Don't go there!" kind of things.*

ReportServer

This database will exist only if you installed ReportServer. (It does not necessarily have to be the same server as the database engine, but note that if it is a different server, it requires a separate license.) The ReportServer database stores any persistent metadata for your Reporting Server instance. Note that this is purely an operational database for a given Reporting Server instance, and should not be modified (and only rarely accessed) other than through the Reporting Server.

ReportServerTempDB

This serves the same basic function as the ReportServer database, except that it stores nonpersistent data (such as working data for a report that is running). Again, this is a purely operational database, and you should not access or alter it in any way except through the Reporting Server.

AdventureWorks

SQL Server included samples long before this one came along. The old samples had their shortcomings, though. For example, they contained a few poor design practices. In addition, they were simplistic and focused on demonstrating certain database concepts rather than on SQL Server as a product, or even databases as a whole. I'll hold off the argument of whether AdventureWorks has the same issues. Let's just say that AdventureWorks was, among other things, an attempt to address this problem.

From the earliest stages of development of SQL Server 2005, Microsoft knew it wanted a far more robust sample database that would act as a sample for as much of the product as possible. AdventureWorks is the outcome of that effort. As much as you will hear me complain about its overly complex nature for the beginning user, it is a masterpiece in that it shows it *all* off. Okay, so it's not really *everything*, but it is a fairly complete sample, with more realistic volumes of data, complex structures, and sections that show samples for the vast majority of product features. In this sense, it's truly terrific.

AdventureWorks will be something of your home database — you'll use it extensively as you work through the examples in this book.

AdventureWorksDW

This is the Analysis Services sample. The DW stands for Data Warehouse, which is the type of database over which most Analysis Services projects are built. Perhaps the greatest thing about this sample is that Microsoft had the foresight to tie the transaction database sample with the analysis sample, providing a whole set of samples that show the two of them working together.

Decision support databases are discussed in more detail in Chapters 17 and 18 of this book, and you will be using this database, so keep that in mind as you fire up Analysis Services and play around. Take a look at the differences between the two databases. They are meant to serve the same fictional company, but they have different purposes: learn from it.

The pubs Database

Ahhhh, pubs! It's almost like an old friend. pubs is one of the original example databases and was supplied with SQL Server as part of the install prior to SQL Server 2005. It is now available only as a separate download from the Microsoft website. You still find many training articles and books that refer to pubs, but Microsoft has made no promises regarding how long they will continue to make it available. pubs has absolutely nothing to do with the operation of SQL Server. It is merely there to provide a consistent place for your training and experimentation. You do not need pubs to work the examples in this book, but you may want to download and install it to work with other examples and tutorials you may find on the web.

The Northwind Database

If your past programming experience has involved Access or Visual Basic, you should already be somewhat familiar with the Northwind database. Northwind was added to SQL Server beginning in version 7.0, but was removed from the basic installation as of SQL Server 2005. Much like pubs, it can, for now, be downloaded separately from the base SQL Server install. (Fortunately, it is part of the same sample download and install as pubs is.) Like pubs, you do not need the Northwind database to work the examples in this book, but it is handy to have it available for work with various examples and tutorials you will find on the web.

> **USING NORTHWIND AND PUBS WITH SQL SERVER 2012**
>
> These sample databases are getting a bit long in the tooth, and support has dwindled. You can still use them, but you'll need to go through a conversion process that I'm not going to detail here. If you really want to locate and use these samples, you can do it, but it's going to take a little extra effort.

The Transaction Log

Believe it or not, the database file itself isn't where most things happen. Although the data is certainly read in from there, any changes you make don't initially go to the database itself. Instead, they are written serially to the *transaction log*. At some later point in time, the database is issued a *checkpoint*; it is at that point in time that all the changes in the log are propagated to the actual database file.

The database is in a random access arrangement, but the log is serial in nature. While the random nature of the database file allows for speedy access, the serial nature of the log allows things to be tracked in the proper order. The log accumulates changes that are deemed as having been committed, and then writes several of them at a time to the physical database file(s).

You'll take a much closer look at how things are logged in Chapter 14, but for now, remember that the log is the first place on disk that the data goes, and it's propagated to the actual database at a later time. You need both the database file and the transaction log to have a functional database.

The Most Basic Database Object: Table

Databases are made up of many things, but none is more central to the make-up of a database than tables are. A table can be thought of as equating to an accountant's ledger or an Excel spreadsheet and consists of *domain* data (columns) and *entity* data (rows). The actual data for the database is stored in the tables.

Each table definition also contains the *metadata* (descriptive information about data) that describes the nature of the data it is to contain. Each column has its own set of rules about what can be stored in that column. A violation of the rules of any one column can cause the system to reject an inserted row, an update to an existing row, or the deletion of a row.

Take a look at the Production.Location table in the AdventureWorks database. (The view presented in Figure 1-1 is from the SQL Server Management Studio. This is a fundamental tool and you will see how to make use of it in the next chapter.)

	LocationID	Name	CostRate	Availability	ModifiedDate
1	1	Tool Crib	0.00	0.00	1998-06-01 00:00:00.000
2	2	Sheet Metal Racks	0.00	0.00	1998-06-01 00:00:00.000
3	3	Paint Shop	0.00	0.00	1998-06-01 00:00:00.000
4	4	Paint Storage	0.00	0.00	1998-06-01 00:00:00.000
5	5	Metal Storage	0.00	0.00	1998-06-01 00:00:00.000
6	6	Miscellaneous Storage	0.00	0.00	1998-06-01 00:00:00.000
7	7	Finished Goods Storage	0.00	0.00	1998-06-01 00:00:00.000
8	10	Frame Forming	22.50	96.00	1998-06-01 00:00:00.000
9	20	Frame Welding	25.00	108.00	1998-06-01 00:00:00.000
10	30	Debur and Polish	14.50	120.00	1998-06-01 00:00:00.000
11	40	Paint	15.75	120.00	1998-06-01 00:00:00.000
12	45	Specialized Paint	18.00	80.00	1998-06-01 00:00:00.000
13	50	Subassembly	12.25	120.00	1998-06-01 00:00:00.000
14	60	Final Assembly	12.25	120.00	1998-06-01 00:00:00.000

FIGURE 1-1

The table in Figure 1-1 is made up of five columns of data. The number of columns remains constant regardless of how much data (even zero) is in the table. Currently, the table has 14 records. The number of records will go up and down as you add or delete data, but the nature of the data in each record (or row) is described and restricted by the *data type* of the column.

Indexes

An *index* is an object that exists only within the framework of a particular table or view. An index works much like the index does in the back of an encyclopedia. There is some sort of lookup (or "key") value that is sorted in a particular way, and once you have that, you are provided another key with which you can look up the actual information you were after.

An index provides you ways of speeding the lookup of your information. Indexes fall into two categories:

- ➤ **Clustered:** You can have only one of these per table. If an index is *clustered*, it means that the table on which the clustered index is based is physically sorted according to that index. If you were indexing an encyclopedia, the clustered index would be the page numbers (the information in the encyclopedia is stored in the order of the page numbers).

- ➤ **Non-clustered:** You can have many of these for every table. This is more along the lines of what you probably think of when you hear the word "index." This kind of index points to some other value that will let you find the data. For the encyclopedia, this would be the keyword index at the back of the book.

Note that views that have indexes — or *indexed views* — must have at least one clustered index before they can have any non-clustered indexes.

Triggers

A *trigger* is an object that exists only within the framework of a table. Triggers are pieces of logical code that are automatically executed when certain things (such as inserts, updates, or deletes) happen to your table.

Triggers can be used for a great variety of things, but are mainly used for either copying data as it is entered or checking the update to make sure that it meets some criteria.

Constraints

A *constraint* is yet another object that exists only within the confines of a table. Constraints are much like they sound; they confine the data in your table to meet certain conditions. Constraints, in a way, compete with triggers as possible solutions to data integrity issues. They are not, however, the same thing: Each has its own distinct advantages.

Filegroups

By default, all your tables and everything else about your database (except the log) are stored in a single file. That file is, by default, a member of what's called the *primary filegroup*. However, you are not stuck with this arrangement.

SQL Server allows you to define a little over 32,000 *secondary files*. (If you need more than that, perhaps it isn't SQL Server that has the problem.) These secondary files can be added to the primary filegroup or created as part of one or more *user-defined filegroups*. Although there is only one primary filegroup (and it is actually called "Primary"), you can have up to 255 user-defined filegroups. A user-defined filegroup is created as an option to a CREATE DATABASE or ALTER DATABASE command.

Diagrams

I will discuss database diagramming in some detail when I discuss normalization and database design. For now, suffice it to say that a database diagram is a visual representation of the database design, including the various tables, the column names in each table, and the relationships between tables. In your travels as a developer, you may have heard of an *entity-relationship diagram (ERD)*. In an ERD, the database is divided into two parts: entities (such as "supplier" and "product") and relations (such as "supplies" and "purchases").

 NOTE *The included database design tools are, unfortunately, a bit sparse. Indeed, the diagramming methodology the tools use does not adhere to any of the accepted standards in ER diagramming. Still, these diagramming tools really do provide all the "necessary" things, so they are at least something of a start.*

Figure 1-2 is a diagram that shows some of the various tables in the AdventureWorks database. The diagram also describes many other properties about the database (although it may be a bit subtle since this is new to you). Notice the tiny icons for keys and the infinity sign. These depict the nature of the relationship between two tables. I'll talk about relationships extensively in Chapters 6 and 8, and I'll delve further into diagrams later in the book.

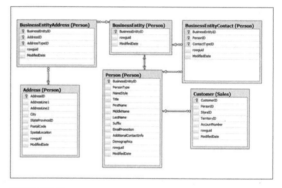

FIGURE 1-2

Views

A *view* is something of a virtual table. A view, for the most part, is used just like a table, except that it doesn't contain any data of its own. Instead, a view is merely a preplanned mapping and representation of the data stored in tables. The plan is stored in the database in the form of a query. This query calls for data from some, but not necessarily all, columns to be retrieved from one or more tables. The data retrieved might not (depending on the view definition) have to meet special criteria in order to be shown as data in that view.

Until SQL Server 2000, the primary purpose of views was to control what the user of the view saw. This has two major impacts: security and ease of use. With views you can control what the users see, so if there is a section of a table that should be accessed by only a few users (for example, salary details), you can create a view that includes only those columns to which everyone is allowed access. In addition, the view can be tailored so that the user doesn't have to search through any unneeded information.

In addition to these most basic uses for views, you also have the ability to create what is called an *indexed view*. This is the same as any other view, except that one or more indexes have been created against the view. This results in a couple of performance impacts (some positive, one negative):

➤ Views that reference multiple tables generally have *much* better read performance with an indexed view, because the join between the tables is preconstructed.

➤ Aggregations performed in the view are precalculated and stored as part of the index; again, this means that the aggregation is performed one time (when the row is inserted or updated), and then can be read directly from the index information.

➤ Inserts and deletes have higher overhead because the index on the view has to be updated immediately; updates also have higher overhead if the key column or the cluster key of the index is affected by the update.

You will learn more about these performance issues more deeply in Chapter 10.

Stored Procedures

Stored procedures (or *sprocs*) are the bread and butter of programmatic functionality in SQL Server. Stored procedures are generally an ordered series of Transact-SQL (the language used to query Microsoft SQL Server) statements bundled up into a single logical unit. They allow for variables and parameters, as well as selection and looping constructs. Sprocs offer several advantages over just sending individual statements to the server in the sense that they:

➤ Are referred to using short names, rather than a long string of text, therefore less network traffic is required in order to run the code within the sproc.

➤ Are pre-optimized and precompiled, saving a small amount of time each time the sproc is run.

➤ Encapsulate a process, usually for security reasons or just to hide the complexity of the database.

➤ Can be called from other sprocs, making them reusable in a somewhat limited sense.

Although sprocs are the core of programmatic functionality in SQL Server, be careful in their use. They are often a solution, but they are also frequently not the only solution. Make sure they are the right choice before selecting a sproc as the option you go with.

User-Defined Functions

User-defined functions (UDFs) have a tremendous number of similarities to sprocs, except that they:

➤ **Can return a value of most SQL Server data types.** Excluded return types include text, ntext, image, cursor, and timestamp.

➤ **Can't have side effects.** Basically, they can't do anything that reaches outside the scope of the function, such as changing tables, sending e-mails, or making system or database parameter changes.

UDFs are similar to the functions that you would use in a standard programming language such as VB.NET or C++. You can pass more than one variable in and get a value out. SQL Server's UDFs vary from the functions found in many procedural languages, in that all variables (except table variables used as parameters) passed into the function are passed in by value. If you're familiar with passing in variables `By Ref` or passing in pointers, sorry, there is no equivalent here. There is, however, some good news in that you can return a special data type called a `table`. I'll examine the impact of this in Chapter 13.

Sequences

Sequences are a new type of object introduced in SQL Server 2012. The job of a sequence is to provide a source of sequential numbers that can be accessed by any number of processes, guaranteeing that no two will retrieve the same next value at the same time. Because they are objects existing on their own — not bound to any table — sequences have a variety of uses that you'll get to look at more closely in Chapter 7.

Users and Roles

These two go hand in hand. *Users* are pretty much the equivalent of logins. In short, this object represents an identifier for someone to log in to the SQL Server. Anyone logging in to SQL Server has to map (directly or indirectly, depending on the security model in use) to a user. Users, in turn, belong to one or more *roles*. Rights to perform certain actions in SQL Server can then be granted directly to a user or to a role to which one or more users belong.

Rules

Rules and constraints provide restriction information about what can go into a table. If an updated or inserted record violates a rule, that insertion or update will be rejected. In addition, a rule can be used to define a restriction on a *user-defined data type*. Unlike constraints, rules aren't bound to a particular table. Instead they are independent objects that can be bound to multiple tables or even to specific data types (which are, in turn, used in tables).

Rules have been considered deprecated by Microsoft for several releases now. They should be considered for backward compatibility only, and you should avoid them in new development.

 NOTE *Given that Microsoft introduced some new deprecation-management functionality in SQL Server 2008, I suspect that features (such as rules) that have been deprecated for several versions may finally be removed in the next version of SQL Server. As such, I feel the need to stress again that rules should not be utilized for new development. Indeed, it is probably long past time to actively migrate away from them.*

Defaults

There are two types of defaults. There is the default that is an object unto itself, and the default that is not really an object, but rather metadata describing a particular column in a table (in much the same way that there are rules, which are objects, and constraints, which are not objects, but metadata). They serve the same purpose. If, when inserting a record, you don't provide the value of a column and that column has a default defined, a value will be inserted automatically as defined in the default. You will examine both types of defaults in Chapter 6.

User-Defined Data Types

User-defined data types are either extensions to the system-defined data types or complex data types defined by a method in a .NET assembly. The possibilities here are almost endless. Although SQL Server 2000 and earlier had the idea of user-defined data types, they were really limited to different filtering of existing data types. With releases since SQL Server 2005, you have the ability to bind .NET assemblies to your own data types, meaning you can have a data type that stores (within reason) about anything you can store in a .NET object. Indeed, the spatial data types (Geographic and Geometric) that were added in SQL Server 2008 are implemented using a user-defined type based on a .NET assembly. .NET assemblies are definitely an advanced topic and beyond the scope of this book.

> **NOTE** *Careful with this! The data type that you're working with is pretty fundamental to your data and its storage. Although being able to define your own thing is very cool, recognize that it will almost certainly come with a large performance cost. Consider it carefully, be sure it's something you need, and then, as with everything like this, TEST, TEST, TEST!!!*

Full-Text Catalogs

Full-text catalogs are mappings of data that speed the search for specific blocks of text within columns that have full-text searching enabled. Prior to SQL Server 2008, full-text catalogs were stored external to the database (thus creating some significant backup and recovery issues). As of SQL Server 2008, full-text catalogs have been integrated into the main database engine and storage mechanisms. Due to their complex nature, full-text indexes are beyond the scope of this text.

SQL SERVER DATA TYPES

Now that you're familiar with the base objects of a SQL Server database, take a look at the options that SQL Server has for one of the fundamental items of any environment that handles data — data types. Note that since this book is intended for developers, and that no developer could survive for 60 seconds without an understanding of data types, I'm going to assume that you already know how data types work, and just need to know the particulars of SQL Server data types.

SQL Server 2012 has the intrinsic data types shown in the following Table 1-1:

TABLE 1-1: Data Types

DATA TYPE NAME	CLASS	SIZE IN BYTES	NATURE OF THE DATA
Bit	Integer	1	The size is somewhat misleading. The first `bit` data type in a table takes up 1 byte; the next 7 make use of the same byte. Allowing nulls causes an additional byte to be used.
Bigint	Integer	8	This just deals with the fact that we use larger and larger numbers on a more frequent basis. This one allows you to use whole numbers from -2^{63} to $2^{63}-1$. That's plus or minus about 92 quintillion.
Int	Integer	4	Whole numbers from −2,147,483,648 to 2,147,483,647.
SmallInt	Integer	2	Whole numbers from −32,768 to 32,767.
TinyInt	Integer	1	Whole numbers from 0 to 255.
Decimal or Numeric	Decimal/ Numeric	Varies	Fixed precision and scale from $-10^{38}-1$ to $10^{38}-1$. The two names are synonymous.
Money	Money	8	Monetary units from -2^{63} to 2^{63} plus precision to four decimal places. Note that this could be any monetary unit, not just dollars.
SmallMoney	Money	4	Monetary units from −214,748.3648 to +214,748.3647.
Float (also a synonym for ANSI Real)	Approximate Numerics	Varies	Accepts an argument (from 1-53, for example, `Float(20)`) that determines size and precision. Note that the argument is in bits, not bytes. Ranges from −1.79E + 308 to 1.79E + 308.
DateTime	Date/Time	8	Date and time data from January 1, 1753, to December 31, 9999, with an accuracy of three hundredths of a second.
DateTime2	Date/Time	Varies (6–8)	Updated incarnation of the more venerable `DateTime` data type. Supports larger date ranges and large time-fraction precision (up to 100 nanoseconds). Like `DateTime`, it is not time zone aware but does align with the .NET `DateTime` data type.

DATA TYPE NAME	CLASS	SIZE IN BYTES	NATURE OF THE DATA
SmallDateTime	Date/Time	4	Date and time data from January 1, 1900, to June 6, 2079, with an accuracy of one minute.
DateTimeOffset	Date/Time	Varies (8–10)	Similar to the DateTime data type, but also expects an offset designation of –14:00 to +14:00 offset from UTC time. Time is stored internally as UTC time, and any comparisons, sorts, or indexing will be based on that unified time zone.
Date	Date/Time	3	Stores only date data from January 1, 0001, to December 31, 9999, as defined by the Gregorian calendar. Assumes the ANSI standard date format (YYYY-MM-DD), but will implicitly convert from several other formats.
Time	Date/Time	Varies (3–5)	Stores only time data in user-selectable precisions as granular as 100 nanoseconds (which is the default).
Cursor	Special Numeric	1	Pointer to a cursor. While the pointer takes up only a byte, keep in mind that the result set that makes up the actual cursor also takes up memory. Exactly how much will vary depending on the result set.
Timestamp/ rowversion	Special Numeric (binary)	8	Special value that is unique within a given database. Value is set by the database itself automatically every time the record is either inserted or updated, even though the timestamp column wasn't referred to by the UPDATE statement (you're actually not allowed to update the timestamp field directly).
UniqueIdentifier	Special Numeric (binary)	16	Special Globally Unique Identifier (GUID) is guaranteed to be unique across space and time.
Char	Character	Varies	Fixed-length character data. Values shorter than the set length are padded with spaces to the set length. Data is non-Unicode. Maximum specified length is 8,000 characters.

continues

TABLE 1-1 *(continued)*

DATA TYPE NAME	CLASS	SIZE IN BYTES	NATURE OF THE DATA
VarChar	Character	Varies	Variable-length character data. Values are not padded with spaces. Data is non-Unicode. Maximum specified length is 8,000 characters, but you can use the `max` keyword to indicate it as essentially a very large character field (up to 2^31 bytes of data).
Text	Character	Varies	Legacy support as of SQL Server 2005. Use `varchar(max)` instead!
NChar	Unicode	Varies	Fixed-length Unicode character data. Values shorter than the set length are padded with spaces. Maximum specified length is 4,000 characters.
NVarChar	Unicode	Varies	Variable-length Unicode character data. Values are not padded. Maximum specified length is 4,000 characters, but you can use the `max` keyword to indicate it as essentially a very large character field (up to 2^31 bytes of data).
Ntext	Unicode	Varies	Variable-length Unicode character data. Like the `Text` data type, this is legacy support only. In this case, use `nvarchar(max)`.
Binary	Binary	Varies	Fixed-length binary data with a maximum length of 8,000 bytes.
VarBinary	Binary	Varies	Variable-length binary data with a maximum specified length of 8,000 bytes, but you can use the `max` keyword to indicate it as essentially a BLOB field (up to 2^31 bytes of data).
Image	Binary	Varies	Legacy support only as of SQL Server 2005. Use `varbinary(max)` instead!
Table	Other	Special	This is primarily for use in working with result sets, typically passing one out of a User-Defined Function or as a parameter for stored procedures. Not usable as a data type within a table definition (you can't nest tables).

DATA TYPE NAME	CLASS	SIZE IN BYTES	NATURE OF THE DATA
HierarchyID	Other	Special	Special data type that maintains hierarchy-positioning information. Provides special functionality specific to hierarchy needs. Comparisons of depth, parent/child relationships, and indexing are allowed. Exact size varies with the number and average depth of nodes in the hierarchy.
Sql_variant	Other	Special	This is loosely related to the Variant in VB and C++. Essentially, it is a container that allows you to hold most other SQL Server data types in it. That means you can use this when one column or function needs to be able to deal with multiple data types. Unlike VB, using this data type forces you to *explicitly* cast it in order to convert it to a more specific data type.
XML	Character	Varies	Defines a character field as being for XML data. Provides for the validation of data against an XML Schema, as well as the use of special XML-oriented functions.
CLR	Other	Varies	Varies depending on the specific nature of the CLR object supporting a CLR-based custom data type. The spatial data types GEOMETRY and GEOGRAPHY that ship with SQL Server 2012 are implemented as CLR types.

Most of these have equivalent data types in other programming languages. For example, an int in SQL Server is equivalent to a Long in Visual Basic and, for most systems and compiler combinations in C++, is equivalent to a signed int.

 NOTE *SQL Server has no concept of unsigned numeric data types.*

In general, SQL Server data types work much as you would expect given experience in most other modern programming languages. Adding numbers yields a sum, but adding strings concatenates them. When you mix the usage or assignment of variables or fields of different data types, a number of types convert *implicitly* (or automatically). Most other types can be converted explicitly. (You specifically say what type you want to convert to.) A few can't be converted between at all. Figure 1-3 contains a chart that shows the various possible conversions.

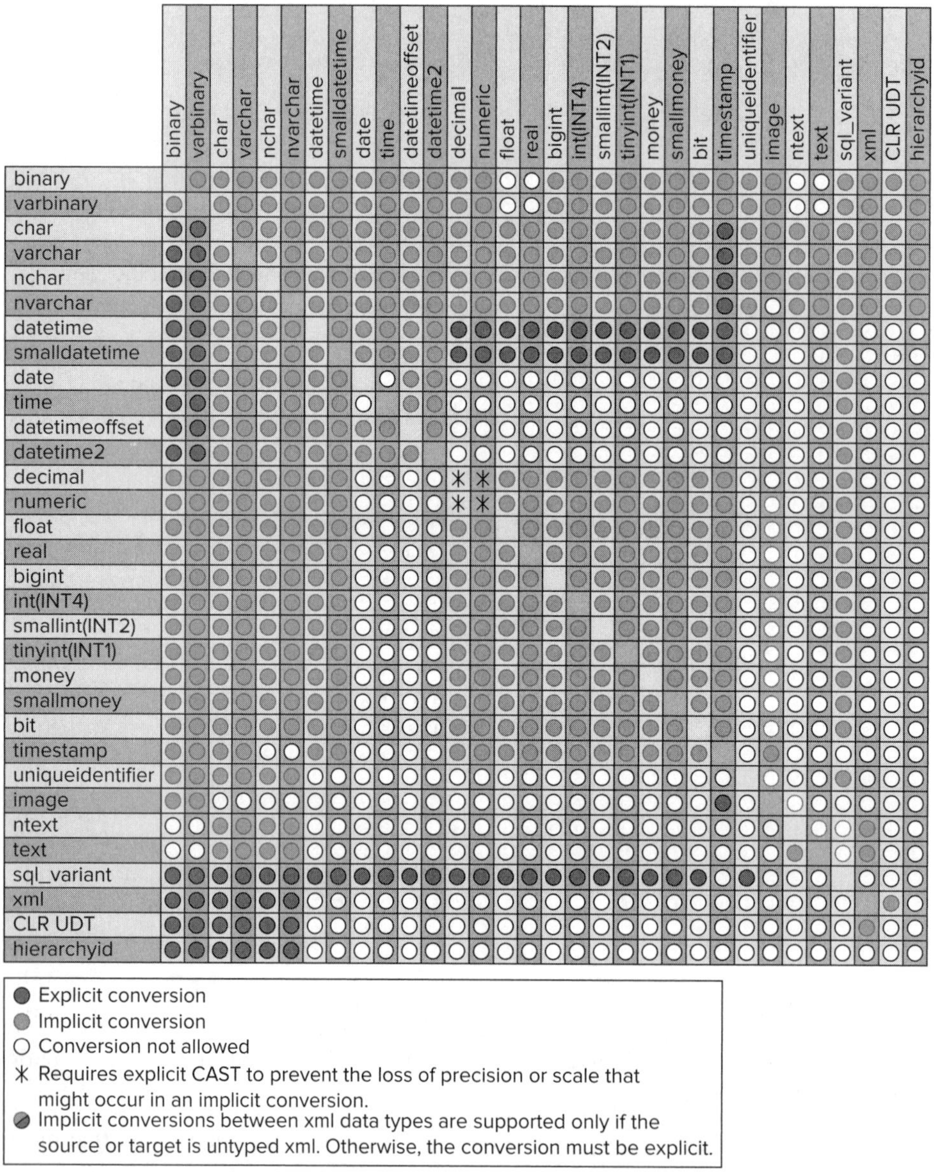

Legend:

- ● Explicit conversion
- ◐ Implicit conversion
- ○ Conversion not allowed
- ✳ Requires explicit CAST to prevent the loss of precision or scale that might occur in an implicit conversion.
- ◑ Implicit conversions between xml data types are supported only if the source or target is untyped xml. Otherwise, the conversion must be explicit.

FIGURE 1-3

Why would you have to convert a data type? Well, let me show you a simple example. If you wanted to output the phrase Today's date is ##/##/####, where ##/##/#### is the current date, you might write it like this:

Available for download on Wrox.com

```
SELECT 'Today''s date is ' + GETDATE()
```

Code snippet Chap01.SQL

NOTE *I will discuss Transact-SQL statements such as this in much greater detail later in the book, but the expected result of the previous example should be fairly obvious to you.*

The problem is that this statement would yield the following result:

```
Msg 241, Level 16, State 1, Line 1
Conversion failed when converting date and/or time from character string.
```

Not exactly what you were after, is it? Now try it with the CONVERT() function:

```
SELECT 'Today''s date is ' + CONVERT(varchar(12), GETDATE(),101)
```

Using CONVERT like this yields something like:

```
---------------------------------
Today's date is 01/01/2012

(1 row(s) affected)
```

Date and time data types, such as the output of the GETDATE() function, aren't implicitly convertible to a string data type, such as Today's date is, yet you'll run into these conversions on a regular basis. Fortunately, the CAST and CONVERT() functions enable you to convert between many SQL Server data types. I will discuss the CAST and CONVERT() functions more in a later chapter.

In short, data types in SQL Server perform much the same function that they do in other programming environments. They help prevent programming bugs by ensuring that the data supplied is of the same nature that the data is supposed to be (remember 1/1/1980 means something different as a date than as a number) and ensures that the kind of operation performed is what you expect.

NULL Data

What if you have a row that doesn't have any data for a particular column — that is, what if you simply don't know the value? For example, let's say that you have a record that is trying to store the company performance information for a given year. Now, imagine that one of the fields is a percentage growth over the prior year, but you don't have records for the year before the first record in your database. You might be tempted to just enter a zero in the PercentGrowth column. Would that provide the right information though? People who didn't know better might think that meant you had zero percent growth, when the fact is that you simply don't know the value for that year.

Values that are indeterminate are said to be NULL. It seems that every time I teach a class in programming, at least one student asks me to define the value of NULL. Well, that's a tough one, because by definition a NULL value means that you don't know what the value is. It could be 1. It could be 347. It could be –294 for all you know. In short, it means *I don't know, undefined,* or perhaps *not applicable.*

SQL SERVER IDENTIFIERS FOR OBJECTS

Now you've heard all sorts of things about objects in SQL Server. It's time to take a closer look at naming objects in SQL Server.

What Gets Named?

Basically, everything has a name in SQL Server. Here's a partial list:

➤ Stored procedures

➤ Tables

➤ Columns

➤ Views

➤ Rules

➤ Constraints

➤ Defaults

➤ Indexes

➤ Filegroups

➤ Triggers

➤ Databases

➤ Servers

➤ User-defined functions

➤ Sequences

➤ Logins

➤ Roles

➤ Full-text catalogs

➤ Files

➤ User-defined types

And the list goes on. Most things I can think of except rows (which aren't really objects) have a name. The trick is to make every name both useful and practical.

Rules for Naming

As I mentioned earlier in the chapter, the rules for naming in SQL Server are fairly relaxed, allowing things like embedded spaces and even keywords in names. Like most freedoms, however, it's easy to make some bad choices and get yourself into trouble.

Here are the main rules:

➤ The name of your object must start with any letter, as defined by the specification for Unicode 3.2. This includes the letters most Westerners are used to: A–Z and a–z. Whether "A" is different from "a" depends on the way your server is configured, but either makes for a valid beginning to an object name. After that first letter, you're pretty much free to run wild; almost any character will do.

➤ The name can be up to 128 characters for normal objects and 116 for temporary objects.

➤ Any names that are the same as SQL Server keywords or contain embedded spaces must be enclosed in double quotes ("") or square brackets ([]). Which words are considered keywords varies depending on the compatibility level to which you have set your database.

 NOTE *Note that double quotes are acceptable as a delimiter for column names only if you have* SET QUOTED_IDENTIFIER ON. *Using square brackets (* [*and*] *) avoids the chance that your users will have the wrong setting.*

These rules are generally referred to as the rules for identifiers and are in force for any objects you name in SQL Server, but may vary slightly if you have a localized version of SQL Server (one adapted for certain languages, dialects, or regions). Additional rules may exist for specific object types.

 NOTE *I'm going to take this as my first opportunity to launch into a diatribe on the naming of objects. SQL Server has the ability to embed spaces in names and, in some cases, to use keywords as names. Resist the temptation to do either of these things! Columns with embedded spaces in their names have nice headers when you make a* SELECT *statement, but there are other ways to achieve the same result. Using embedded spaces and keywords for column names is begging for bugs, confusion, and other disasters. I'll discuss later why Microsoft has elected to allow this, but for now, just remember to associate embedded spaces or keywords in names with evil empires, torture, and certain death. (This won't be the last time you hear from me on this one.)*

SUMMARY

Like most things in life, the little things do matter when thinking about an RDBMS. Sure, almost anyone who knows enough to even think about picking up this book has an idea of the *concept* of storing data in columns and rows, even if they don't know that these groupings of columns and rows should be called tables. But a few tables seldom make a real database. The things that make today's RDBMSs great are the extra things — the objects that enable you to place functionality and business rules that are associated with the data right into the database with the data.

Database data has *type*, just as most other programming environments do. Most things that you do in SQL Server are going to have at least some consideration of type. Review the types that are available, and think about how these types map to the data types in any programming environment with which you are familiar.

EXERCISES

1. What is the purpose of the master database?

2. What are two differences between the datetime and datetime2 data types?

▶ **WHAT YOU LEARNED IN THIS CHAPTER**

TOPIC	CONCEPT
Types of Objects	A new installation of SQL Server creates system databases and permits creation of many types of objects both within and external to those databases.
Data Types	SQL Server provides a variety of data types that can be used to efficiently and correctly store information.
Identifiers	You can give your objects names up to 128 characters (116 for temporary objects) that start with a letter.

2

Learning the Tools of the Trade

WHAT YOU WILL LEARN IN THIS CHAPTER:

➤ Which tools are provided with SQL Server

➤ What each tool does, and how to access it

➤ How to configure and connect to a SQL Server instance

➤ About the development environments for developing in different SQL Server components

Now that you know something about the many types of objects that exist in SQL Server, you probably should get to know something about how to find these objects and how to monitor your system in general.

In this chapter, you look into the tools that serve SQL Server's base functionality, mostly having to do with the relational database engine. The tools for managing the add-on service are covered in more detail in the chapters where each of those services is the main topic. Some of them offer only a small number of highly specialized tasks; others do many different things. Most of them have been around in SQL Server in one form or another for a long time.

The tools you see in this chapter include:

➤ SQL Server Books Online

➤ SQL Server Configuration Manager

➤ SQL Server Management Studio

➤ Business Intelligence Developer Studio

➤ SQL Server Integration Services (SSIS) and the Import/Export Wizard

➤ SQL Server Reporting Services

➤ Reporting Services Configuration Manager

➤ Bulk Copy Program (bcp)

➤ Profiler

➤ sqlcmd

➤ PowerShell

GETTING HELP WITH BOOKS ONLINE

Is Books Online (BOL) a tool? I think so. Let's face it, it doesn't matter how many times you read this or any other book on SQL Server; you're not going to remember everything you'll ever need to know about SQL Server. SQL Server is one of my mainstay products, and I still can't remember it all. Books Online is simply one of the most important tools you're going to find in SQL Server.

> **NOTE** My general philosophy about books or any other reference materials related to programming is that I can't have enough of them. I first began programming in 1990 or so, and back then it was possible to remember most things (but not everything). Today it's simply impossible. If you have any diversification at all (something that is, in itself, rather difficult these days), there are just too many things to remember, and the things you don't use every day get lost in dying brain cells.
>
> Here's a simple piece of advice: don't even try to remember it all. Remember that what you've seen is possible. Remember what is an integral foundation to what you're doing. Remember what you work with every day. With regard to relational databases, remember the theory. Then remember to build a good reference library (starting with this book) and keep a healthy list of good SQL Server sites in your favorites list to fill in information on subjects you don't work with every day and may not remember the details of.

As you see in Figure 2-1, Books Online in SQL Server uses the updated .NET online help interface, which is replacing the older standard online help interface used among the Microsoft technical product line (such as MSDN and Visual Studio).

Everything works pretty much as one would expect here, so I'm not going to go into the details of how to operate a help system. Suffice it to say that SQL Server Books Online is a great quick reference that follows you to whatever machine you're working on at the time.

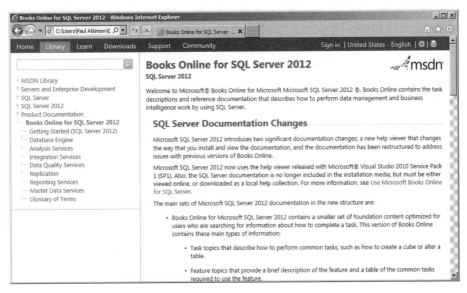

FIGURE 2-1

NOTE *When you first access help, you'll have the option of using help live from the Internet or installing the content locally. At this point I don't have a strong recommendation either way, but I can offer a consideration. Installing locally really doesn't take up all that much space when you consider cost per megabyte these days; having that quick reference available wherever you are running SQL Server can save you a fortune in time. When you need a syntax reference, the last thing you want to do is start a pitched battle against Internet Explorer's Enhanced Security Configuration to get help from* microsoft.com. *On the other hand, getting your content online means you're guaranteed to see the most recent information. It's completely up to you.*

SQL SERVER CONFIGURATION MANAGER

Administrators who configure computers for database access are the main users of this tool, but it's still important to understand what this tool is about.

The SQL Server Configuration Manager combines some settings that were, in earlier releases, spread across multiple tools into one spot. The items managed in the Configuration Manager fall into two areas:

> ➤ Service Management

> ➤ Network Configuration

NOTE *Note that while I'm showing only two major areas here, the Configuration Manager splits the Network Configuration side of things up into multiple nodes.*

Service Management

SQL Server is a large product and the various pieces of it utilize a host of services that run in the background on your server. A full installation will encompass nine services, and seven of these can be managed from this part of the SQL Server Configuration Manager (the other two are services that act as background support).

The services available for management here include:

➤ **Integration Services:** This powers the Integration Services engine that you look at in Chapter 20.

➤ **Analysis Services:** This powers the Analysis Services engine, which is touched on briefly in Chapters 17 and 18.

➤ **Reporting Services:** The underlying engine that supports Reporting Services (Chapter 19).

➤ **SQL Server Agent:** The main engine behind anything in SQL Server that is scheduled. Utilizing this service, you can schedule jobs to run on a variety of different schedules. These jobs can have multiple tasks to them and can even branch into different tasks depending on the outcome of some previous task. Examples of things run by the SQL Server Agent include backups, as well as routine import and export tasks.

➤ **SQL Server:** The core database engine that works on data storage, queries, and system configuration for SQL Server.

➤ **SQL Server Browser:** This supports advertising your server so those browsing your local network can identify that your system has SQL Server installed.

Network Configuration

A fair percentage of the time, any connectivity issues discovered are the result of client network configuration, or how that configuration matches with that of the server.

SQL Server provides several of what are referred to as *Net-Libraries* (network libraries), or *NetLibs*. These are dynamic-link libraries (DLLs) that SQL Server uses to communicate with certain network protocols. NetLibs serve as something of an insulator between your client application and the network protocol, which is essentially the language that one network card uses to talk to another, that is to be used. They serve the same function at the server end, too. The NetLibs supplied with SQL Server 2012 include:

➤ Named Pipes

➤ TCP/IP (the default)

➤ Shared Memory

➤ VIA (a special virtual interface that your storage-hardware vendor may support)

NOTE *VIA is a special network library that is made for use with some very special (and expensive) hardware. If you're running in a VIA environment, you'll know about the special requirements associated with it. For those of you that aren't running in that environment, it suffices to say that VIA offers a very fast but expensive solution to high-speed communication between servers. It would not usually be used for a normal client, but the client protocol is still included.*

The same NetLib must be available on both the client and server computers so that they can communicate with each other via the network protocol. Choosing a client NetLib that is not also supported on the server will result in your connection attempt failing with a `Specified SQL Server Not Found` error.

Regardless of the data access method and kind of driver used (SQL Native Client, ODBC, OLE DB), it will always be the driver that talks to the NetLib. The process works as shown in Figure 2-2.

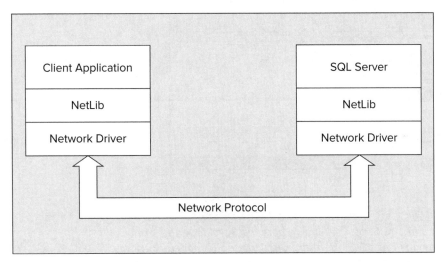

FIGURE 2-2

The steps in order are:

1. The client app talks to the driver (SQL Native Client, ODBC).

2. The driver calls the client NetLib.

3. This NetLib calls the appropriate network protocol and transmits the data to a server NetLib.

4. The server NetLib then passes the requests from the client to SQL Server.

Replies from SQL Server to the client follow the same sequence, only in reverse.

NOTE *In case you're familiar with TCP/IP, the default port that the IP NetLib will listen on is 1433. A port can be thought of as being like a channel on the radio — signals are bouncing around on all sorts of different frequencies, but they help only when you're listening on the right channel. Note that this is the default, so there is no guarantee that the particular server you're trying to connect to is listening to that particular port — indeed, most security experts recommend changing it to something nonstandard.*

The Protocols

Let's start off with that "What are the available choices?" question. If you run the Configuration Management utility and open the Server Network Configuration tree, you'll see something like Figure 2-3.

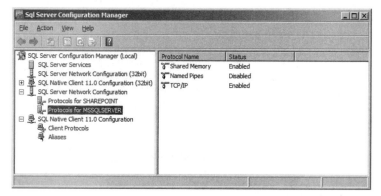

FIGURE 2-3

 NOTE *How many nodes are shown here will vary depending on your installation. In Figure 2-3, there are duplicate nodes for Network and Client configuration to allow for separate treatment of 32-bit versus 64-bit libraries. There will be only one node for each if you're running a 32-bit installation.*

 WARNING *For security reasons, only Shared Memory is enabled at installation time.*

You'll want to leave Shared Memory enabled for when you're accessing the machine locally. (It works only when the client is on the same physical server as the SQL Server installation.) But you need to enable at least one other NetLib if you want to be able to contact your SQL Server remotely (say, from a web server or from different clients on your network).

In order for your client to gain a connection to the server, the server has to be listening for the protocol with which the client is trying to communicate and, in the case of TCP/IP, on the same port.

> **NOTE** At this point, you might be tempted to say, "Hey, why don't I just enable every NetLib? Then I won't have to worry about it." This situation is like anything you add onto your server — more overhead. In this case, it would slow down your server (not terribly, but every little bit counts) and expose you to unnecessary openings in your security. (Why leave an extra door open if nobody is supposed to be using that door?)

Okay, now let's take a look at what SQL Server can support and why you would want to choose a particular protocol.

Named Pipes

Named Pipes can be very useful when TCP/IP is not available, or there is no Domain Name Service (DNS) server to allow the naming of servers under TCP/IP.

> **NOTE** Technically speaking, you can connect to a SQL Server running TCP/IP by using its IP address in the place of the name. This works all the time, even if there is no DNS service, as long as you have a route from the client to the server. (If it has the IP address, it doesn't need the name.) Keep in mind, however, that if your IP address changes for some reason, you'll need to change which IP address you're accessing (a real pain if you have a bunch of config files you need to change!).

TCP/IP

TCP/IP has become something of the de facto standard networking protocol and is also the only option if you want to connect directly to your SQL Server via the Internet, which, of course, uses only IP.

> **NOTE** Don't confuse the need to have your database server available to a web server with the need to have your database server directly accessible to the Internet. You can have a web server that is exposed to the Internet, but also has access to a database server that is not directly exposed to the Internet. (The only way for an Internet connection to see the data server is through the web server.)
>
> Connecting your data server directly to the Internet is a security hazard in a big way. If you insist on doing it (and there can be valid reasons for doing so, rare though they may be), pay particular attention to security precautions. Here's a quick sanity check: if you're using this beginner book, the decision to open your database server to the Internet is probably not one you should be making by yourself just yet.

Shared Memory

Shared memory removes the need for interprocess marshaling — a way of packaging information before transferring it across process boundaries — between the client and the server, if they are running on the same box. The client has direct access to the same memory-mapped file where the server is storing data. This removes a substantial amount of overhead and is *very* fast. It's useful only when accessing the server locally (say, from a web server installed on the same server as the database), but it can be quite a boon performance-wise.

On to the Client

Now you've seen all the possible protocols and you know how to choose which ones to offer. Once you know what your server is offering, you can configure the client. Most of the time, the defaults are going to work just fine, but let's take a look at what you've got. Expand the Client Network Configuration tree and select the Client Protocols node, as shown in Figure 2-4.

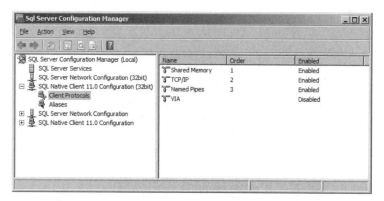

FIGURE 2-4

SQL Server enables the client to start with one protocol, then, if that doesn't work, move on to another. In Figure 2-4, I am first using Shared Memory, then trying TCP/IP, and finally going to Named Pipes if TCP/IP doesn't work as defined by the Order column. Unless you change the default (changing the priority by using the up and down arrows), Shared Memory is the NetLib that is used first for connections to any server not listed in the aliases list (the next node under Client Network Configuration), followed by TCP/IP and so on.

 NOTE *If you have TCP/IP support on your network (and today, that's virtually guaranteed), configure your server to use it for any remote access. IP has less overhead than Named Pipes and just plain runs faster; there is no reason not to use it, unless your network doesn't support it. It's worth noting, however, that for local servers (where the server is on the same physical system as the client), the Shared Memory NetLib will be quicker, as you do not need to go through the network stack to view your local SQL Server.*

The Aliases list is a listing of all the servers on which you have defined a specific NetLib to be used when contacting that particular server. This means that you can contact one server using IP and another using Named Pipes — whatever you need to get to that particular server. Figure 2-5 shows a client configured to use the Named Pipes NetLib for requests from the server named BEGINNINGTSQL2012 and to use whatever is set up as the default for contact with any other SQL Server.

FIGURE 2-5

Again, remember that the Client Network Configuration setting on the network machine must have a default protocol that matches one supported by the server, or it must have an entry in the Aliases list to specifically choose a NetLib supported by that server.

 NOTE *If you are connecting to your SQL Server over the Internet (which is a very bad idea from a security standpoint, but people do it), you'll probably want to use the server's actual IP address, rather than the name of the server. This gets around some name resolution issues that may occur when dealing with SQL Server and the Internet. Keep in mind, however, that you'll need to change the IP address manually if the server gets a new IP; you won't be able to count on DNS to take care of it for you.*

SQL SERVER MANAGEMENT STUDIO

The *SQL Server Management Studio* is pretty much home base when administering a SQL Server. It provides a variety of functionality for managing your server using a relatively easy-to-use graphical user interface. Branched off of the Visual Studio IDE environment's code base, it combines a myriad of functionality that used to be in separate tools.

For the purposes of this book, I'm not going to cover everything that the Management Studio has to offer, but here's a quick rundown of the things you can do:

➤ Create, edit, and delete databases and database objects

➤ Query your database using T-SQL

➤ Manage scheduled tasks, such as backups and the execution of SSIS package runs

➤ Display current activity, such as who is logged on, what objects are locked, and from which client they are running

➤ Manage security, including such items as roles, logins, and remote and linked servers

➤ Initiate and manage the Database Mail Service

➤ Create and manage full-text search catalogs

➤ Manage configuration settings for the server

➤ Initiate an instance of the new PowerShell console

➤ Create and manage publishing and subscribing databases for replication

➤ Manage data processing in cubes or tabular databases for SQL Server Analysis Services (SSAS)

➤ Create queries against a multidimensional SSAS database in MDX, or against a tabular SSAS database in DAX

You will be seeing a great deal of the Management Studio throughout this book, so let's take a closer look at some of the key functions Management Studio serves.

Getting Started with the Management Studio

When you first start the Management Studio, you are presented with a Connection dialog box similar to the one in Figure 2-6.

Your login screen may look a little bit different from this, depending on whether you've logged in before, what machine you logged into, and what login name you used. Most of the options on the login screen are pretty self-explanatory, but let's look at a couple in more depth.

FIGURE 2-6

Server Type

This relates to which of the various subsystems of SQL Server you are logging in to (the normal database server, Analysis Services, Report Server, or Integration Services). Because these different types of servers can share the same name, pay attention to this to make sure you're logging in to what you think you're logging in to. Except in the chapters specifically targeting those other components, you'll be connecting to the database engine more or less exclusively throughout this book.

Server Name

As you might guess, this is the SQL Server in to which you're asking to be logged. In Figure 2-6, I have chosen " . ". This doesn't mean that there is a server named period, but rather that I want to log in to the default instance of SQL Server that is on this same machine, regardless of what this machine is named. Selecting " . " (local) not only automatically identifies which server (and instance) you want to use, but also how you're going to get there. You can also use `"(local)"` as another option that has the same meaning as `"."`.

> **NOTE** *SQL Server allows multiple instances of SQL Server to run at one time. These are just separate loads into memory of the SQL Server engine running independently from each other.*

Note that the default instance of your server will have the same name as your machine on the network. There are ways to change the server name after the time of installation, but they are problematic at best and deadly to your server at worst. Additional instances of SQL Server will be named the same as the default (BEGINNINGSQL2012 in many of the examples in this book) followed by a dollar sign, and the instance name, for example, SIDDARTHA$SHRAMANA.

If you select `"."` or `(local)`, your system uses the Shared Memory NetLib regardless of which NetLib you selected for contacting other servers. This is a bad news/good news story. The bad news is that you give up a little bit of control. (SQL Server will always use Shared Memory to connect; you can't choose anything else.) The good news is that you don't have to remember which server you're on, and you get a high-performance option for work on the same machine. If you use your local PC's actual server name, SQL Server versions later than 2005 will still use the shared memory connection, so you don't have to worry about incurring the additional overhead of the network stack.

Now what if you can't remember what the server's name is? Just click the down arrow to the right of the server box to get a list of recently connected servers. If you scroll down, you'll see a Browse for More option. If you choose this option, SQL Server will poll the network for any servers that are advertising to the network; essentially, this is a way for a server to let itself be known to other systems on the network. You can see from Figure 2-7 that you get two tabs: one that displays local servers (all of the instances of SQL Server on the same system you're running on) and another that shows other SQL Servers on the network.

FIGURE 2-7

You can select one of these servers and click OK.

> **NOTE** *Watch out when using the Server Selection dialog box. Although it's usually pretty reliable, there are ways of configuring a SQL Server so that it doesn't broadcast. When a server has been configured this way, it won't show up in the list (but you can still connect if you know its name or address). Also, servers that are only listening on the TCP/IP NetLib and don't have a DNS entry will not show up. You must, in this case, already know your IP address and refer to the server using it.*

Authentication

You can choose between Windows Authentication and SQL Server Authentication. Windows Authentication will always be available, even if you configured it as SQL Server Authentication. Logins using usernames and passwords that are local to SQL Server (not part of a larger Windows network) are acceptable to the system only if you specifically turn on SQL Server Authentication.

Windows Authentication

Windows Authentication is just as it sounds. You have Windows users and groups. Those Windows users are mapped into SQL Server logins in their Windows user profile. When they attempt to log in to SQL Server, they are validated through the Windows domain and mapped to roles according to the login. These roles identify what the user is allowed to do.

The best part of this model is that you have only one password. (If you change it in the Windows domain, it's changed for your SQL Server logins, too.) You don't have to fill in anything to log in; it just takes the login information from the way you're currently logged in to the Windows network. Additionally, the administrator has to administer users in only one place. The downside is that mapping this process can get complex, and to administer the Windows user side of things, you must be a domain administrator.

SQL Server Authentication

The security does not care at all about what the user's rights to the network are, but it does care about what you explicitly set up in SQL Server. The authentication process doesn't take into account the current network login at all; instead, the user provides a SQL Server — specific login and password.

This can be nice because the administrator for a given SQL Server doesn't need to be a domain administrator (or even have a username on your network, for that matter) to give rights to users on the SQL Server. It even works across domains, or where domain trust relationships don't exist. The process also tends to be somewhat simpler than under Windows Authentication. Finally, it means that one user can have multiple logins that give different rights to different things.

TRY IT OUT **Making the Connection**

Let's get you logged in. How this works will depend on whether your server was installed with Windows Authentication or Mixed Mode, and what access you have to it, so there are two paths here.

If you installed with Mixed Mode enabled, follow these steps:

1. Choose the (local) option for the SQL Server.

2. Select SQL Server Authentication.

3. Select a login name of sa, which stands for System Administrator. Alternatively, you may log in as a different user, as long as that user has system administrator privileges.

4. Enter the same password that you set when you installed SQL Server. On case-sensitive servers, the login is also case sensitive, so make sure you enter it in lowercase.

5. Click Connect.

NOTE *Be careful with the password for the* sa *user. This and any other user who is a sysadmin is a superuser with full access to everything.*

If your installation was with Windows Authentication only, follow these steps:

1. Choose the (local) option for the SQL Server.

2. Select Windows Authentication.

3. Click Connect.

If you're connecting to a server that has been installed by someone else, or where you have changed the default information, you need to provide login information that matches those changes. After you click OK, you should see the Object Explorer window screen shown in Figure 2-8.

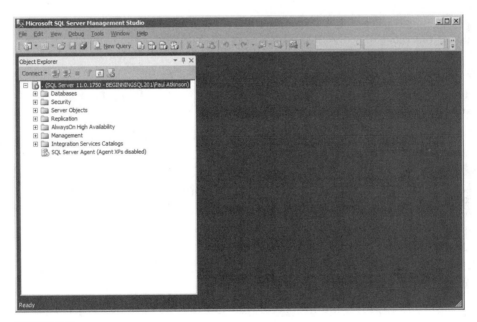

FIGURE 2-8

How It Works

The Login dialog box gathers all the information needed to create the connection. Once it has that, it assembles the connection information into a single connection string and sends that to the server. The connection is then either accepted or rejected, and if it is accepted, a connection handle is given to the Query window so that the connection information can be used over and over again for many queries, as long as you do not disconnect.

Again, many of the items here (New, Open, Save, Cut, Paste, and so on) are things that you have seen plenty of times in other Windows applications and should be familiar with, but there's also a fair amount that's specific to SQL Server. The main thing to notice, for now, is that the menus in the Management Studio are context sensitive — that is, different menus are available, and what they contain changes based on which window is active in the Studio. Be sure to explore the different contextual menus you get as you explore different parts of the Management Studio.

Interacting Through the Query Window

This part of the Management Studio takes the place of what was, at one time, a separate tool that was called *Query Analyzer*. The Query window is your tool for interactive sessions with a given SQL Server. It's where you can execute statements using *Transact-SQL* (T-SQL). I lovingly pronounce it "Tee-Squeal," but it's supposed to be "Tee-Sequel." T-SQL is the native language of SQL Server. It's a dialect of Structured Query Language (SQL), and is largely compliant with modern ANSI/ISO SQL standards. You'll find that most RDBMS products support basic ANSI/ISO SQL compatibility.

Because the Query window is where you will spend a fair amount of time in this book, let's take a more in-depth look at this tool and get familiar with how to use it.

Getting Started

Well, I've been doing plenty of talking about things in this book, and it's high time I give you the opportunity to start doing something. To that end, follow these steps:

1. Open a new Query window by clicking the New Query button toward the top-left of the Management Studio or choosing File ➪ New ➪ New Query With Current Connection from the File menu.

    When the Query window opens, you'll get context-sensitive menus and toolbar buttons designed for T-SQL. Before you look at the specifics, let's get your very first query out of the way.

2. Select AdventureWorks in the database dropdown box on the SQL Editor toolbar.

3. Type the following code into the main window of the Query window:

    ```
    SELECT * FROM Person.Address;
    ```

Code snippet Chap02.sql

Notice that several things happen as you type:

➤ The coloring of words and phrases changes as you type.

➤ The Management Studio guesses as to what you're trying to do (as shown in Figure 2-9). Utilizing *IntelliSense*, much like Visual Studio, SQL Server will give you hints as to what probably should come next in your code.

FIGURE 2-9

Statement keywords should appear in blue. Unidentifiable items, such as column and table names (these vary with every table in every database on every server), are in black. Statement arguments and connectors are in red. Pay attention to how these work and learn them. They can help you catch many bugs before you've even run the statement (and seen the resulting error).

> **NOTE** *There is a long-standing tradition of typing SQL keywords, such as* SELECT *or* FROM *in this example, in all caps. Although there is nothing that mandates this, I'd like to encourage you to continue this practice from the start; it makes reading code substantially easier and keeps things consistent with code written by us older folks.*

The check-mark icon (Parse) on the SQL Editor toolbar represents another simple debugging item that quickly parses the query for you without actually attempting to run the statement. If there are any syntax errors, this should catch them before you see error messages. A debugger is available as another way to find errors. You'll look at that in depth in Chapter 12.

IntelliSense

Since SQL Server 2008, programmers writing T-SQL within Management Studio have had the benefit of IntelliSense to smooth their coding. IntelliSense is a technology, available for years in Microsoft's other development environments, that gives real-time context-sensitive suggestions while you type.

Although Microsoft has done a terrific job with it, it is not without some peculiarities created by the nature of SQL versus other languages. Of particular importance is what help you can get when you're adding columns to be selected. You'll see more about the syntax of this in later chapters, but SQL syntax calls for column names before the names of the tables those columns are sourced from. The result is problematic for IntelliSense as, when you are typing your column names, the tool has no way of knowing which tables you're trying to get those columns from (and therefore no way of giving you appropriate hints). I generally get around this by skipping ahead to add the table names and then coming back to fill in the column names; you can easily do the same.

REFRESHING THE INTELLISENSE CACHE

One other important aspect of IntelliSense is how it keeps the menu of available suggestions up to date. Within the object-oriented programming model often used in Visual Studio, objects and methods in the IntelliSense menus are updated as often as files are changed; that is, if you alter an object or get the latest code from source control, that's enough to keep IntelliSense in sync. Not so in T-SQL. Because database objects exist outside the file system and can be altered by anyone with access, updating is a bit more haphazard unless you manage it manually. If you ever see IntelliSense failing to recognize objects that you know exist or failing to suggest columns you've recently added, pressing Control+Shift+R (or selecting Edit ⇨ IntelliSense ⇨ Refresh Local Cache) will bring it up to date with your current schema.

Now click the Execute button (with the red exclamation point next to it) on the toolbar. The Query window changes a bit, as shown in Figure 2-10.

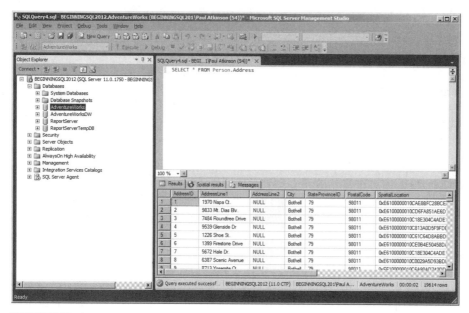

FIGURE 2-10

Notice that the main window has been automatically divided into two panes. The top is your original query text; the bottom is called the *results pane*. In addition, notice that the results pane has a tab at the top of it. Later on, after you've run queries that return multiple sets of data, you'll see that you can get each of these results on separate tabs; this can be rather handy, because you often don't know how long each set of data, or *result set*, is.

 NOTE *The terms result set and recordset are frequently used to refer to a set of data that is returned as a result of some command being run. You can think of these words as interchangeable.*

Now change a setting or two and see how the result varies. Take a look at the toolbar above the Query window and check out a set of three icons, highlighted in Figure 2-11.

Results to Text, Results to Grid, and Results to File buttons

FIGURE 2-11

These control the way you receive output. From the left, they are Results to Text, Results to Grid, and Results to File. The same choices can also be made from the Query menu under the Results To submenu.

Results to Text

The Results to Text option takes all the output from your query and puts it into one page of text results. The page can be of virtually infinite length (limited only by the available memory in your system).

Before discussing this further, rerun that previous query using this option and see what you get. Choose the Results to Text option and rerun the previous query by clicking Execute, as shown in Figure 2-12.

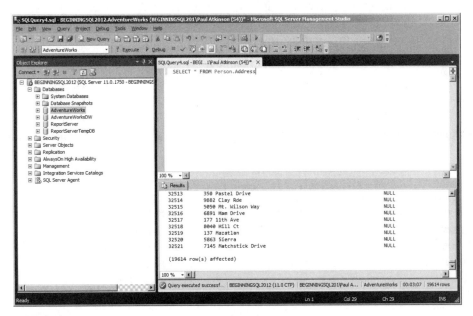

FIGURE 2-12

The data that you get back is exactly the same as before. It's just given to you in a different format. I use this output method in several scenarios:

➤ When I'm getting only one result set and the results have only fairly narrow columns

➤ When I want to be able to save my results in a single text file

➤ When I'm going to have multiple result sets, but the results are expected to be small, and I want to be able to see more than one result set on the same page without dealing with multiple scrollbars

➤ When I'm interested in not only the data output, but also the output of performance measures, error messages, or debugging information

Results to Grid

This option divides the columns and rows into a grid arrangement. Following is a list of specific things that this option gives you that the Results to Text doesn't:

➤ You can resize the column by hovering your mouse pointer on the right border of the column header, and then clicking and dragging the column border to its new size. Double-clicking the right border results in the autofit for the column.

➤ If you select several cells, and then cut and paste them into another grid (say, Microsoft Excel), they will be treated as individual cells. (Under the Results to Text option, the cut data is pasted all into one cell.) Also, right-clicking to copy allows you the option of Copy with Headers, which includes the column header row when you paste it in. This behavior can be defaulted in settings.

➤ You can select just one or two columns of multiple rows. (Under Results to Text, if you select several rows, all the inner rows have every column selected; you can select only in the middle of the row for the first and last row selected.)

I use this option for almost everything because I find that I usually want one of the benefits I just listed.

Results to File

Think of this one as largely the same as Results to Text, but it routes the output directly to a file instead of to screen. I use this one to generate files I intend to parse using some utility or that I want to easily e-mail.

SETTING DEFAULT BEHAVIORS

Management Studio has a wide variety of settings you can adjust to make the environment comfortable for you. Once you've been using it for a while, you'll start to have an opinion about how you like your output, whether you use Copy with Headers all the time, or any of a host of other things. You can adjust these by selecting Options on the Tools menu.

DATA SECURITY

When you're gathering query output for any reason, consider whether your work environment has applicable security standards. When you're in control of a database, you often have access to sensitive data, and the whole copy-and-paste thing (or even worse, Results to File) can represent an insidious security violation.

Insert Snippet

SQL snippets are a great way to get you started on many of the commands you're going to learn throughout this book. As I said at the start of the chapter, it's unlikely you're ever going to remember all the syntax for everything you're ever going to want to do, and usually your best bet is to be ready with some kind of reference. *Snippets* are references (of sorts) that actually help you to accomplish a lot of common tasks right out of the box, and also present a framework for you to add your own.

The idea behind Insert Snippet is related to the Template Explorer that's existed within SSMS for years. Each snippet is a bit of code designed to contain all the common parts of some T-SQL task, with the various bits and pieces all stubbed out so you can replace them with your own. Most out-of-the-box snippets are for the various CREATE statements you're going to learn, but you can also create your own. Using snippets, you can work from a template when you can't remember all the keywords or the order of all the elements in a statement...which can be often. Using snippets could scarcely be easier. When you want to place a snippet in your code, right-click where you'd like to insert it and choose Insert Snippet.

Explore the available snippets by going to the Tools menu and selecting Code Snippets Manager. For now, just browse around, because I'm not going into the code yet that you'll find here, but as you learn about creating objects, do remember to return to the snippets.

sqlcmd Mode

This chapter will discuss sqlcmd a bit more shortly. For now, suffice it to say that it is a tool that helps you run queries from a Windows command line. It has some special scripting abilities that are meant specifically for command-line scripting. By default, these special script commands are not available in the Query window. Turning sqlcmd mode on activates the special sqlcmd scripting options even in the Query window.

> **NOTE** *Be aware that the Query window always utilizes the* SQLNativeClient *connection method (even when operating in sqlcmd mode), whereas the actual sqlcmd utility uses an OLE DB connection. The result is that you may see slight differences in behavior between running a script using sqlcmd and using sqlcmd from the Query window. These tend to be corner case differences, and are rarely seen and generally innocuous.*

Show Execution Plan

Every time you run a query, SQL Server parses your query into its component parts and then sends it to the *query optimizer*. The query optimizer is the part of SQL Server that figures out the best way to run your query to balance fast results with minimum impact to other users. When you use the Show Estimated Execution Plan option, you receive a graphical representation and additional information about how SQL Server plans to run your query. Similarly, you can turn on the Include Actual Execution Plan option. Most of the time, this is the same as the estimated execution plan, but you will occasionally see differences here due to changes that the optimizer decides to make while running the query, as well as changes in the actual cost of running the query versus what the optimizer *thinks* is going to happen.

QUERY OPTIMIZATION

I've always felt that, although it's a generally accepted industry term, query *optimizer* is a bit optimistic. That name sure makes it sound like SQL Server is going to exhaustively search for the best possible, or optimal, plan, and it's just not going to. For very simple queries that might be possible, but as your code gets more involved, the query optimizer will simply do its best to come up with a reasonable plan, and never mind perfection.

The thing to take away here is that, although SQL is very good at coming up with an optimal plan, it's not all-powerful; making things easy for the optimizer is a knack you'll want to learn as you go. The best way to do that is to do just what you're reading about here...look at the plan.

Let's see what a query plan looks like in the simple query from earlier. Click the Include Actual Execution Plan option, and execute the query again, as shown in Figure 2-13.

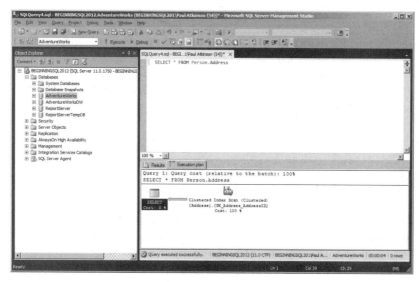

FIGURE 2-13

Note that you have to actually click the Execution Plan tab for it to come up and that your query results are still displayed in the way you selected. The Show Estimated Execution plan option gives you the same output as an Include Actual Execution Plan does, with two exceptions:

➤ You get the plan immediately rather than after your query executes.

➤ Although what you see is the actual *plan* for the query, all the cost information is estimated and the query is not actually run. Under Include Actual Execution, the query is physically executed and the cost information you get is actual rather than estimated.

> **NOTE** *Note that the plan in Figure 2-13 is an extremely simple execution plan. More complex queries may show a variety of branching and parallel operations.*

The Available Databases Combo Box

Finally, take another look at the Available Databases combo box. In short, this is where you select the default database that you want your queries to run against for the current window (you changed AdventureWorks to be your default database earlier if you've been playing along at home). Initially, the Query window will start with whatever the default database is for the user that's logged in (for sa, that is the master database unless someone has changed it on your system). You can then change it to any other database that the current login has permission to access. Because you're probably using the sa user ID, every database on the current server should have an entry in the Available Databases combo box.

The Object Explorer

This useful little tool enables you to navigate your database, look up object names, and even perform actions like scripting and looking at the underlying data.

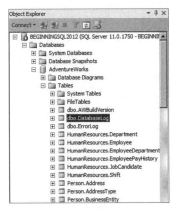

In the example in Figure 2-14, I've expanded the database node all the way down to the listing of tables in the AdventureWorks database. You can drill down even farther to see individual columns (including data type and similar properties) of the tables — a very handy tool for browsing your database.

SQL SERVER DATA TOOLS (FORMERLY BIDS)

FIGURE 2-14

Throughout most of this book, SQL Server Management Studio will be your primary tool. Using SSMS gets you through all those things you've just read about and more, and it will be your comfortable home for most of your SQL Server career. However, if you've been developing software in other languages, you might already be happy working in Visual Studio or a similar IDE. For you, and for some other SQL-related development that doesn't neatly fit into SSMS, there's SQL Server Data Tools (SSDT).

To begin with, SSDT looks an awful lot like Visual Studio, and that's for a good reason: it *is* Visual Studio. In this case, it's a lightweight version with tools designed expressly to support T-SQL development and the SQL Server Business Intelligence suite, including SQL Server Integration Services (SSIS), SQL Server Reporting Services (SSRS), and SQL Server Analysis Services (SSAS). You'll get a quick introduction to those next, with more complete coverage later in the book.

SSDT replaces the venerable Business Intelligence Developer Studio (BIDS), which was just for the BI tool suite. With SSDT, you have a lot more ability to do T-SQL development and tie in with other

Visual Studio add-ons and capabilities, such as database projects. For this book, though, I'm going to stick with SSMS for T-SQL development and go to SSDT when we get to the BI stuff.

SSDT doesn't require a great deal more introduction as an environment; however, it's worth noting that the interface is pure Visual Studio, using projects as a paradigm. You can create a solution that holds several projects, but each project has a particular type — a database project or one of the BI types — that tells SSDT what tools to display, what the coding window should look like, and how it should compile and deploy the output. This project infrastructure, and the complexity (such as it is) that comes with it, is why this book will use SSDT only where it's required.

When you get to Chapters 17–20 and start using Integration Services, Reporting Services, and Analysis Services, you'll see a lot more of SSDT.

SQL SERVER INTEGRATION SERVICES (SSIS)

Your friend and mine — that's what *SSIS* (formerly known as *Data Transformation Services* or *DTS*) is. I simply sit back in amazement every time I look at this feature of SQL Server. To give you a touch of perspective here, I've done a couple of Business Intelligence projects over the years. (These are usually systems that don't have online data going in and out, but instead pull data together to help management make decisions.) A BI project gathers data from a variety of sources and pumps it into one centralized database — called a *data warehouse* — to be used for centralized reporting.

These projects can get very expensive very quickly, as they attempt to deal with the fact that not every system calls what is essentially the same data by the same name. There can be an infinite number of issues to be dealt with. These can include data integrity (what if the field has a NULL and you don't allow NULLs?) or differences in business rules (one system deals with credits by allowing a negative order quantity, another doesn't allow this and has a separate set of tables to deal with credits). The list can go on and on, and so can the expense.

With SSIS a tremendous amount of the coding — usually in some client-side language — that had to be done to handle these situations can be eliminated or, at least, simplified. SSIS enables you to take data from any data source that has an OLE DB or .NET data provider and pump it into a SQL Server table.

 NOTE *Be aware that there is a special OLE DB provider for ODBC. This provider allows you to map your OLE DB access directly to an ODBC driver. That means anything that ODBC can access can also be accessed by OLE DB (and, therefore, SSIS).*

While we're at it, it's also worth pointing out that SSIS, although part of SQL Server, can work against any OLE DB source and any OLE DB destination. That means that SQL Server doesn't need to be involved in the process at all other than to provide the data pump. You could, for example, push data from Oracle to Excel, or even DB/2 to MySQL.

While transferring your data, you can also apply what are referred to as transformations to that data. *Transformations* essentially alter the data according to some logical rule(s). The alteration can be as simple as changing a column name, or as complex as an analysis of the integrity of the data and application of rules to change it if necessary. To think about how this is applied, consider the example I gave earlier of taking data from a field that allows NULLs and moving it to a table that doesn't allow NULLs. With SSIS you can automatically change any NULL values to some other value you choose during the transfer process. (For a number, that might be zero, or for a character, it might be something like unknown.)

SQL SERVER REPORTING SERVICES (SSRS)

In my early experience with SQL Server, reporting was something left to other applications; this was a database product, and if you wanted to do layout then you needed to get something else. Back then we used Crystal Reports, or Microsoft Access, or if the layout wasn't all that important then you could drop a result set into Excel and pass that around. Since then, report consumers have become a great deal more sophisticated, as have products designed to make sophisticated reporting easier to produce. Voilà — *SQL Server Reporting Services (SSRS)*.

SSRS has a few different ways to interact, depending on who's using it. As a developer, you need to decide early on how you're planning to present reports to your users, so that you know what you want to start with. If you're going to present a static set of reports that they can run at will, you can build those in SSDT and deploy them to the report server. If you want to give your users the ability to construct their own reports on an ad hoc basis, you can create SSAS tabular models and hand the Report Builder over to your users so that they can do it themselves. If all some users need is a regularly e-mailed report, you can do that, too, without giving them access to the server at all.

Reporting Services has a few major components. It all begins with SQL Server Data Tools (or the full version of Visual Studio, if you've got it), where you can build reports. You'll get a chance to really dig into SSRS in Chapter 19.

SQL SERVER ANALYSIS SERVICES (SSAS)

SQL Server Analysis Services is a tool that's designed to help you get quick access to the information contained in your data, even if your data comprises millions or billions of rows. The primary way it does this is by helping you to create new models of your data, either as a cube (which you'll get to try in Chapter 18) or as a highly optimized tabular model (part of what you'll get to do in Chapter 19). Working in concert with reporting tools such as SSRS, Power View, or PowerPivot, Analysis Services lets you analyze huge datasets very, very fast.

The primary task you'll engage in directly with SSAS is model development; once you've created an appropriate cube or tabular model, and set up a job to keep it populated, you'll interact through one of the reporting tools. Model development is handled through SQL Server Data Tools, just like SSRS and SSIS.

BULK COPY PROGRAM (BCP)

If SSIS is your friend and mine, the *Bulk Copy Program*, or *bcp*, would be that old friend that we may not see that much anymore, but really appreciate when we do.

bcp is a command-line program whose sole purpose in life is to move formatted data in and out of SQL Server en masse. It was around long before what has now become SSIS was thought of, and while SSIS is replacing bcp for most import/export activity, bcp still has a certain appeal for people who like command-line utilities. In addition, you'll find an awful lot of SQL Server installations out there that still depend on bcp to move data around fast.

SQL SERVER PROFILER

I can't tell you how many times this one has saved my bacon by telling me what was going on with my server when nothing else would. It's not something a developer (or even a DBA, for that matter) tends to use every day, but it's extremely powerful and can be your salvation when you're sure nothing can save you.

SQL Server Profiler is, in short, a real-time tracing tool. Whereas Performance Monitor is all about tracking what's happening at the macro level — system configuration stuff — the Profiler is concerned with tracking specifics. This is both a blessing and a curse. The Profiler can, depending on how you configure your trace, give you the specific syntax of every statement executed on your server. Now imagine that you are doing performance tuning on a system with 1,000 users. I'm sure you can imagine the reams of paper that would be used to print the statements executed by so many people in just a minute or two. Fortunately, the Profiler has a vast array of filters to help you narrow things down and track more specific problems, such as long-running queries, or the exact syntax of a query being run within a stored procedure. This is nice when your procedure has conditional statements that cause it to run different things under different circumstances.

SQLCMD

As I mentioned back when I was talking about the Management Console, SQL Server has a tool to use when you want to include SQL commands and management tasks in command-line batch files — sqlcmd. You won't see sqlcmd in your SQL Server program group. Indeed, it's amazing how many people don't even know that this utility is around; that's because it's a console application rather than a Windows program.

Prior to version 7.0 and the advent of what was then called DTS (now SSIS), sqlcmd was often used in conjunction with the Bulk Copy Program (bcp) to manage the import of data from external systems. This type of use is decreasing as administrators and developers everywhere learn the power and simplicity of SSIS. Even so, there are occasionally items that you want to script into a larger command-line process. sqlcmd gives you that capability.

sqlcmd can be very handy, particularly if you use files that contain scripts. Keep in mind, however, that there are tools that can more effectively accomplish much of what sqlcmd can and with a user interface that is more consistent with the other things you're doing with your SQL Server. I'll touch on sqlcmd lightly later in this book, and that should be enough to carry you through the majority of what you'll want to use it for.

 NOTE *Once again, just for history and being able to understand if people you talk SQL Server with use a different lingo, sqlcmd is yet another new name for this tool of many names. Originally, it was referred to as ISQL. In SQL Server 2000 and 7.0, it was known as osql.*

POWERSHELL

PowerShell integration has been with us since SQL Server 2008. PowerShell serves as an extremely robust scripting and server-navigation engine. Using PowerShell, the user can navigate all objects on the server as though they were part of a directory structure in the file system. (You even use the `dir-` and `cd`-style commands you use in a command window.)

Given the advanced nature of PowerShell scripting, and the fact that this is a beginning book, I'll go into it only to a limited extent. On the flip side, it's so useful that you really ought to have at least some exposure to it, so you'll find an introduction to PowerShell scripting in Chapter 21.

SUMMARY

Most of the tools that you've been exposed to here aren't ones you'll use every day. Indeed, for the average developer, only SQL Server Management Studio will get daily use. Nevertheless, it's important to have some idea of the role that each one can play. Each has something significant to offer you. You will see each of these tools again in your journey through this book.

Note that there are some other utilities available that don't have shortcuts on your Start menu (connectivity tools, server diagnostics, and maintenance utilities), which are mostly admin related.

EXERCISES

1. Which SQL Server components require you to do your development in SSDT?

2. How can you find out what the query optimizer plans to do with your code? Can you see what it actually did? How?

▶ **WHAT YOU LEARNED IN THIS CHAPTER**

TOPIC	CONCEPT
Books Online	The SQL Server help and documentation you can install locally or access online. Whether you're a beginner or a seasoned professional, you'll continue to use Books Online to answer syntax questions, research exception cases, and locate just the right commands.
Configuration Manager	With Configuration Manager, you can set up which services are available on your server, the network protocols you'll answer on. Set up services and protocols only when you expect clients to use them.
SQL Server Management Studio	This will be your home during the vast majority of your SQL Server career. SSMS not only provides you with access to write code in T-SQL directly against your database (and thus has been the primary development environment) but also lists server objects and properties and gives access to many server management tasks.
SQL Server Data Tools	Based on Visual Studio, this is the primary development environment for all the non-T-SQL development. Here you'll build SSIS packages, SSAS models, and SSRS reports. It's also where you'll do T-SQL development when you want to work within a database project.
SQL Server Integration Services	A SQL Server component made to move data among a wide variety of sources and destinations.
SQL Server Reporting Services	Where you'll build reports against SQL Server and SSAS data sources, among others. SSRS manages reports on the server, delivers them to users on a schedule, caches them, and otherwise helps you control their distribution.
SQL Server Analysis Services	Where you'll create high-performance data models for analytical reporting. In SSAS, you can create cubes for complex analysis, or use tabular models for simple, user-driven analysis.
Profiler	Gives you a window into what's happening on your server. Using Profiler can help with troubleshooting, index tuning, deadlock detection, and many other sleuthing tasks.
Command Line Tools	SQL Server includes sqlcmd, which allows you to execute T-SQL and return results from the command line.
PowerShell	SQL Server 2012 has much more integration into the Windows PowerShell scripting language. Using PowerShell, you can automate virtually any SQL-related task.

3

The Foundation Statements of T-SQL

WHAT YOU WILL LEARN IN THIS CHAPTER:

- ➤ How to retrieve data from your database
- ➤ How to insert data into tables
- ➤ How to update data in place

At last! You've finally ingested the most boring stuff. It doesn't get any worse than basic objects and tools, does it? As it goes, you have to lay down a foundation before you can build a house. The nice thing is that the foundation is now down. Having used the clichéd example of building a house, I'm going to turn it all upside down by talking about the things that let you enjoy living in the house before you've even talked about the plumbing. You see, when working with databases, you have to get to know how data is going to be accessed before you can learn all that much about the best ways to store it.

This chapter covers the most fundamental *Transact-SQL (T-SQL)* statements. T-SQL is SQL Server's own dialect of Structured Query Language (SQL). The T-SQL statements that you learn about in this chapter are:

- ➤ SELECT
- ➤ INSERT
- ➤ UPDATE
- ➤ DELETE

These four statements are the bread and butter of T-SQL. You'll learn plenty of other statements as you go along, but these statements make up the basis of T-SQL's *Data Manipulation Language* (DML). Because you'll generally issue far more commands meant to manipulate (that is, read and modify) data than other types of commands (such as those to grant user rights or create a table), you'll find that these will become like old friends in no time at all.

In addition, SQL provides many operators and keywords that help refine your queries. You'll learn some of the most common of these in this chapter.

 NOTE *While T-SQL is unique to SQL Server, the statements you use most of the time are not. T-SQL is largely ANSI/ISO compliant. (The standard was originally governed by ANSI, and was later taken over by the ISO. It was ANSI long enough that people generally still refer to it as ANSI compliance.) This means that, by and large, T-SQL complies with a very wide open standard. What this means to you as a developer is that much of the SQL you're going to learn in this book is directly transferable to other SQL-based database servers, such as Sybase (which long ago used to share the same code base as SQL Server), Oracle, DB2, and MySQL. Be aware, however, that every RDBMS has different extensions and performance enhancements that it uses, above and beyond the ANSI/ISO standard. I will try to point out the ANSI versus non-ANSI ways of doing things where applicable. In some cases, you'll have a choice to make — performance versus portability to other RDBMS systems. Most of the time, however, the ANSI way is as fast as any other option. In such a case, the choice should be clear: stay ANSI compliant.*

GETTING STARTED WITH A BASIC SELECT STATEMENT

If you haven't used SQL before, or don't feel like you've really understood it yet, pay attention here! The SELECT statement and the structures used within it are the lion's share of all the commands you will perform with SQL Server. Let's look at the basic syntax rules for a SELECT statement:

```
SELECT [ALL|DISTINCT] [TOP (<expression>) [PERCENT] [WITH TIES]]
                                            <column list>
 [FROM <source table(s)/view(s)>]
 [WHERE <restrictive condition>]
 [GROUP BY <column name or expression using a column in the SELECT list>]
 [HAVING <restrictive condition based on the GROUP BY results>]
 [ORDER BY <column list>]
 [[FOR XML {RAW|AUTO|EXPLICIT|PATH [(<element>)]}][, XMLDATA
                                    [, ELEMENTS][, BINARY base 64]]
  [OPTION (<query hint>, [, ...n])]
```

Wow — that's a lot to decipher. Let's look at the parts.

> **NOTE** *Note that the parentheses around the* TOP *expression are, technically speaking, optional. Microsoft refers to them as "required," and then points out that a lack of parentheses is actually supported, but for backward compatibility only. This means that Microsoft may pull support for that in a later release, so if you do not need to support older versions of SQL Server, I strongly recommend using parentheses to delimit a* TOP *expression in your queries.*

The SELECT Statement and FROM Clause

The verb — in this case a SELECT — is the part of the overall statement that tells SQL Server what you are doing. A SELECT indicates that you are merely reading information, as opposed to modifying it. What you are selecting is identified by an expression or column list immediately following the SELECT. You'll see what I mean by this in a moment.

Next, you add in more specifics, such as where SQL Server can find this data. The FROM statement specifies the name of the table or tables from which you want to get your data. With these, you have enough to create a basic SELECT statement. Fire up the SQL Server Management Studio and take a look at a simple SELECT statement:

```
SELECT * FROM INFORMATION_SCHEMA.TABLES;
```

Code snippet Chap03.sql

Let's look at what you've asked for here. You've asked to SELECT information; when you're working in SQL Server Management Studio, you can also think of this as requesting to display information. The * may seem odd, but it actually works pretty much as * does everywhere: it's a wildcard. When you write SELECT *, you're telling T-SQL that you want to select every column from the table. Next, the FROM indicates that you've finished writing which items to output and that you're about to indicate the source of the information — in this case, INFORMATION_SCHEMA.TABLES.

> **NOTE** INFORMATION_SCHEMA *is a special access path that is used for displaying metadata about your system's databases and their contents.* INFORMATION_SCHEMA *has several parts that can be specified after a period, such as* INFORMATION_SCHEMA.SCHEMATA *or* INFORMATION_SCHEMA.VIEWS. *These special access paths to the metadata of your system are there so you don't have to use system tables.*

TRY IT OUT Using the SELECT Statement

Let's play around with this some more. Change the current database to be the AdventureWorks database. Recall that to do this, you need only select the AdventureWorks entry from the combo box in the toolbar at the top of the Query window in the Management Studio, as shown in Figure 3-1.

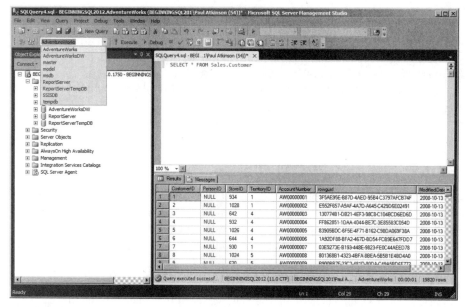

FIGURE 3-1

 NOTE *If you're having difficulty finding the combo box that lists the various databases, try clicking once in the Query window. The SQL Server Management Studio toolbars are context sensitive — that is, they change by whatever the Query window thinks is the current thing you are doing. If you don't have a Query window as the currently active window, you may have a different set of toolbars up (one that is more suitable to some other task). As soon as a Query window is active, it should switch to a set of toolbars that are suitable to query needs.*

Now that you have the AdventureWorks database selected, let's start looking at some real data from your database. Try this query:

```
SELECT * FROM Sales.Customer;
```

Code snippet Chap03.sql

After you have that in the Query window, just click Execute on the toolbar (the F5 key is a shortcut for Execute and becomes a reflex for you) and watch SQL Server give you your results. This query lists every row of data in every column of the `Sales.Customer` table in the current database (in this case, AdventureWorks). If you didn't alter any of the settings on your system or the data in the AdventureWorks database before you ran this query, you should see the following information if you click the Messages tab:

```
(19820 row(s) affected)
```

For a SELECT statement, the number shown here is the number of rows that your query returned. You can also find the same information on the right side of the status bar (found below the results pane), with some other useful information, such as the login name of the user you're logged in as, the current database as of when the last query was run (this will persist, even if you change the database in the database dropdown box, until you run your next query in this query window), and the time it took for the query to execute.

How It Works

Let's look at a few specifics of your SELECT statement. Notice that I capitalized SELECT and FROM. This is not a requirement of SQL Server — you could run them as SeLeCt and frOM and they would work just fine. I capitalized them purely for purposes of convention and readability. You'll find that many SQL coders use the convention of capitalizing all commands and keywords, and then use mixed case for table, column, and non-constant variable names. The standards you choose or have forced upon you may vary, but live by at least one rule: be consistent.

> **NOTE** One characteristic I share with Rob, who wrote the last edition of this book, is a tendency to get up on a soapbox from time to time; I'm standing on one now, and it's for a good reason. Nothing is more frustrating for a person who has to read your code or remember your table names than lack of consistency. When someone looks at your code or, more important, uses your column and table names, it shouldn't take him or her long to guess most of the way you do things just by experience with the parts that he or she has already worked with. Being consistent is one of those incredibly simple rules that has been broken to at least some degree in almost every database I've ever worked with. Break the trend: be consistent.

The SELECT is telling the Query window what you are doing, and the * is saying what you want (remember that * = every column). Then comes the FROM.

A FROM clause does just what it says — that is, it defines the place from which your data should come. Immediately following the FROM is the names of one or more tables. In your query, all the data came from a table called Customer.

Now let's try taking a little bit more specific information. Let's say all you want is a list of all your customers by last name:

```
SELECT LastName FROM Person.Person;
```

Code snippet Chap03.sql

Your results should look something like:

```
Abbas
Abel
Abercrombie
```

```
. . .
Zukowski
Zwilling
Zwilling
```

Note that I've snipped rows out of the middle for brevity. You should have 19,972 rows. Because the last name of each customer is all that you want, that's all that you've selected.

> **NOTE** *Many SQL writers have the habit of cutting their queries short and always selecting every column by using an * in their selection criteria. This is another one of those habits to resist. While typing in an * saves you a few moments of typing the column names that you want, it also means that more data has to be retrieved than is really necessary. In addition, SQL Server must figure out just how many columns "*" amounts to and what specifically they are. You would be surprised at just how much this can drag down your application's performance and that of your network.*
>
> *In the old days, we had to completely spell out — and therefore perfectly remember — every column name that we wanted. Nowadays you've got IntelliSense built into SSMS, so all you have to remember are the first few characters. You see, there's really no good argument for using * just out of laziness anymore. In short, a good rule to live by is to select what you need — no more, no less.*

Let's try another simple query. How about:

```sql
SELECT Name FROM Production.Product;
```

Code snippet Chap03.sql

Again, assuming that you haven't modified the data that came with the sample database, SQL Server should respond by returning a list of 504 products that are available in the AdventureWorks database:

```
Name
----------------------------------------
Adjustable Race
Bearing Ball
BB Ball Bearing
. . .
. . .
Road-750 Black, 44
Road-750 Black, 48
Road-750 Black, 52
```

The columns that you have chosen right after your SELECT clause are known as the SELECT list. In short, the SELECT list is made up of the columns that you have requested be output from your query.

> **NOTE** *The columns that you have chosen right after your* SELECT *clause are known as the SELECT list.*

The WHERE Clause

Well, things are starting to get boring again, aren't they. So let's add in the WHERE clause. The WHERE clause allows you to place conditions on what is returned to you. What you have seen thus far is unrestricted information, in the sense that every row in the table specified has been included in your results. Unrestricted queries such as these are very useful for populating things like list boxes and combo boxes and in other scenarios when you are trying to provide a *domain listing*.

> **NOTE** *For the purposes here, don't confuse a domain listing with that of a Windows domain. A domain listing is an exclusive list of choices. For example, if you want someone to provide you with information about a state in the United States, you might provide him or her with a list that limits the domain of choices to just the 50 states. That way, you can be sure that the option selected will be a valid one. You will see this concept of domains further when you begin learning about database design, as well as entity versus domain constraints.*

Now you'll want to try to look for more specific information. This time you don't want a complete listing of product names; you want information on a specific product. Try this: see if you can come up with a query that returns the name, product number, and reorder point for a product with the ProductID 356.

Let's break it down and build the query one piece at a time. First, you're asking for information to be returned, so you know that you're looking at a SELECT statement. The statement of what you want indicates that you would like the product name, product number, and reorder point, so you have to know the column names for these pieces of information. You're also going to need to know from which table or tables you can retrieve these columns.

If you haven't memorized the database schema yet, you'll want to explore the tables that are available. Because you've already used the Production.Product table once before, you know that it's there. The Production.Product table has several columns. To give you a quick listing of the column options, you can study the Object Explorer tree of the Production.Product table from Management Studio. To open this screen in the Management Studio, click Tables underneath the AdventureWorks database, and then expand the Production.Product and Columns nodes. As in Figure 3-2, you will see each of the columns along with its data type and nullability options. Again, you'll see some other methods of finding this information a little later in the chapter.

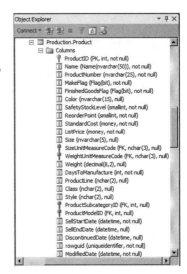

FIGURE 3-2

You don't have a column called `product name`, but you do have one that's probably what you're looking for: `Name`. (Original eh?) The other two columns are, save for the missing space between the two words, just as easy to identify.

Therefore, the `Products` table is going to be the place you get your information FROM, and the `Name`, `ProductNumber`, and `ReorderPoint` columns will be the specific columns from which you'll get your information:

```
SELECT Name, ProductNumber, ReorderPoint
FROM Production.Product
```

Code snippet Chap03.sql

This query, however, still won't give you the results that you're after; it will still return too much information. Run it and you'll see that it still returns every record in the table rather than just the one you want.

If the table has only a few records and all you want to do is take a quick look at it, this might be fine. After all, you can look through a small list yourself, right? But that's a pretty big if. In any significant system, very few of your tables will have small record counts. You don't want to have to go scrolling through 10,000 records. What if you had 100,000 or 1,000,000? Even if you felt like scrolling through them all, the time before the results were back would be increased dramatically. Finally, what do you do when you're designing this into your application and you need a quick result that gets straight to the point?

What you're going to need (not just here, but pretty much all the time) is a conditional statement that will limit the results of your query to exactly what you want: in this case, product identifier 356. That's where the WHERE clause comes in. The WHERE clause immediately follows the FROM clause and defines which conditions a record has to meet before it will be returned. For your query, you want the row in which the `ProductID` is equal to 356. You can now finish your query:

```
SELECT Name, ProductNumber, ReorderPoint
FROM Production.Product
WHERE ProductID = 356
```

Code snippet Chap03.sql

Run this query against the AdventureWorks database, and you should come up with the following:

```
Name                            ProductNumber        ReorderPoint
----------------------------    ------------------   ------------
LL Grip Tape                    GT-0820                      600

(1 row(s) affected)
```

This time you've received precisely what you wanted — nothing more, nothing less. In addition, this query runs much faster than the first one.

Table 3-1 shows all the operators you can use with the WHERE clause:

TABLE 3-1: WHERE Clause Operators

OPERATOR	EXAMPLE USAGE	EFFECT
`=, >, <, >=, <=, <>, !=, !>, !<`	`<Column Name> = <Other Column Name>` `<Column Name> = 'Bob'`	These standard comparison operators work as they do in pretty much any programming language, with a couple of notable points: 1. What constitutes "greater than," "less than," and "equal to" can change depending on the collation order you have selected. (For example, `"ROMEY" = "romey"` in places where case-insensitive sort order has been selected, but `"ROMEY" < > "romey"` in a case-sensitive situation.) 2. `!=` and `<>` both mean "not equal." `!<` and `!>` mean "not less than" and "not greater than," respectively.
`AND, OR, NOT`	`<Column1> = <Column2> AND <Column3> >= <Column 4>` `<Column1> != "MyLiteral" OR <Column2> = "MyOtherLiteral"`	Standard Boolean logic. You can use these to combine multiple conditions into one WHERE clause. NOT is evaluated first, then AND, then OR. If you need to change the evaluation order, you can use parentheses. Note that XOR is not supported.
`BETWEEN`	`<Column1> BETWEEN 1 AND 5`	Comparison is TRUE if the first value is between the second and third values, inclusive. It is the functional equivalent of A>=B AND A<=C. Any of the specified values can be column names, variables, or literals.
`LIKE`	`<Column1> LIKE "ROM%"`	Uses the % and _ characters for wildcarding. % indicates a value of any length can replace the % character. _ indicates any one character can replace the _ character. Enclosing characters in [ ] symbols indicates any single character within the [ ] is OK. ([a-c] means a, b, and c are OK. [ab] indicates a or b are OK.) ^ operates as a NOT operator, indicating that the next character is to be excluded.
`IN`	`<Column1> IN (List of Numbers)` `<Column1> IN ("A", "b", "345")`	Returns TRUE if the value to the left of the IN keyword matches any of the values in the list provided after the IN keyword. This is frequently used in subqueries, which you will look at in Chapter 7.

continues

TABLE 3-1 *(continued)*

OPERATOR	EXAMPLE USAGE	EFFECT
`ALL, ANY, SOME`	`<column|expression> (comparison operator) <ANY|SOME> (subquery)`	These return TRUE if any or all (depending on which you choose) values in a subquery meet the comparison operator's (for example, <, >, =, >=) condition. ALL indicates that the value must match all the values in the set. ANY and SOME are functional equivalents and will evaluate to TRUE if the expression matches any value in the set.
`EXISTS`	`EXISTS (subquery)`	Returns TRUE if at least one row is returned by the subquery. Again, you'll look into this one further in Chapter 7.

> **NOTE** *Note that these are not the only operators in SQL Server. These are just the ones that apply to the* WHERE *clause. There are a few operators that apply only as assignment operators (rather than comparison). These are inappropriate for a* WHERE *clause.*

ORDER BY

In the queries that you've run thus far, most have come out in something resembling alphabetical order. Is this by accident? It will probably come as somewhat of a surprise to you, but the answer to that is yes, it's been purely dumb luck so far. If you don't say you want a specific sorting on the results of a query, you get the data in the order that SQL Server decides to give it to you. This will always be based on what SQL Server decided was the lowest-cost way to gather the data. It will usually be based either on the physical order of a table or on one of the indexes SQL Server used to find your data.

> **NOTE** *Microsoft's samples have a nasty habit of building themselves in a manner that happen to lend themselves to coming out in alphabetical order. It's a long story as to why, but I wish they wouldn't do that, because most data won't work that way. The short rendition as to why has to do with the order in which Microsoft inserts its data. Because Microsoft typically inserts it in alphabetical order, the ID columns are ordered the same as alphabetical order (just by happenstance). Because most of these tables happen to be physically sorted in ID order (you'll learn more about physical sorting of the data in Chapter 9), the data wind up appearing alphabetically sorted. If Microsoft inserted the data in a more random name order — as would likely happen in a real-life scenario — the names would tend to come out more mixed up unless you specifically asked for them to be sorted by name.*

Think of an ORDER BY clause as being a sort by. It gives you the opportunity to define the order in which you want your data to come back. You can use any combination of columns in your ORDER BY clause, as long as they are columns (or derivations of columns) found in the tables within your FROM clause.

Let's look at this query:

```
SELECT Name, ProductNumber, ReorderPoint
FROM Production.Product;
```

This will produce the following results:

```
Name                            ProductNumber       ReorderPoint
-----------------------------   ----------------    ------------
Adjustable Race                 AR-5381                      750
Bearing Ball                    BA-8327                      750
...
...
Road-750 Black, 48              BK-R19B-48                    75
Road-750 Black, 52              BK-R19B-52                    75

(504 row(s) affected)
```

As it happened, the query result set was sorted in ProductID order. Why? Because SQL Server decided that the best way to look at this data was by using an index that sorts the data by ProductID. That just happened to be what created the lowest-cost (in terms of CPU and I/O) query. Were you to run this exact query when the table has grown to a much larger size, SQL Server might choose an entirely different execution plan and therefore might sort the data differently. You could force this sort order by changing your query to this:

**Available for
download on
Wrox.com**

```
SELECT Name, ProductNumber, ReorderPoint
FROM Production.Product
ORDER BY Name;
```

Code snippet Chap03.sql

Note that the WHERE clause isn't required. It can either be there or not be there depending on what you're trying to accomplish. Just remember that if you do have a WHERE clause, it goes before the ORDER BY clause.

Unfortunately, that previous query doesn't really give you anything different, so you don't see what's actually happening. Let's change the query to sort the data differently — by the ProductNumber:

**Available for
download on
Wrox.com**

```
SELECT Name, ProductNumber, ReorderPoint
FROM Production.Product
ORDER BY ProductNumber;
```

Code snippet Chap03.sql

Now your results are quite different. It's the same data, but it's been substantially rearranged:

```
Name                                    ProductNumber          ReorderPoint
------------------------------------    --------------------   ------------
Adjustable Race                         AR-5381                750
Bearing Ball                            BA-8327                750
LL Bottom Bracket                       BB-7421                375
ML Bottom Bracket                       BB-8107                375
...
...
Classic Vest, L                         VE-C304-L              3
Classic Vest, M                         VE-C304-M              3
Classic Vest, S                         VE-C304-S              3
Water Bottle - 30 oz.                   WB-H098                3

(504 row(s) affected)
```

SQL Server still chose the least-cost method of giving you your desired results, but the particular set of tasks it actually needed to perform changed somewhat because the nature of the query changed.

You can also do your sorting using numeric fields (note that you're querying a new table):

Available for download on Wrox.com

```
SELECT Name, SalesPersonID
FROM Sales.Store
WHERE Name BETWEEN 'g' AND 'j'
    AND SalesPersonID > 283
ORDER BY SalesPersonID, Name DESC;
```

Code snippet Chap03.sql

This one results in:

```
Name                                                SalesPersonID
--------------------------------------------------  -------------
Inexpensive Parts Shop                              286
Ideal Components                                    286
Helpful Sales and Repair Service                    286
Helmets and Cycles                                  286
Global Sports Outlet                                286
Gears and Parts Company                             286
Irregulars Outlet                                   288
Hometown Riding Supplies                            288
Good Bicycle Store                                  288
Global Bike Retailers                               288
Instruments and Parts Company                       289
Instant Cycle Store                                 290
Impervious Paint Company                            290
Hiatus Bike Tours                                   290
Getaway Inn                                         290

(15 row(s) affected)
```

Notice several things in this query. You've made use of many of the things that have been covered up to this point. You've combined multiple WHERE clause conditions and also have an ORDER BY clause in place. In addition, you've added some new twists in the ORDER BY clause.

➤ You now have an ORDER BY clause that sorts based on more than one column. To do this, you simply comma-delimited the columns you wanted to sort by. In this case, you've sorted first by SalesPersonID and then added a sub-sort based on Name.

➤ The DESC keyword tells SQL Server that the ORDER BY should work in descending order for the Name sub-sort rather than using the default of ascending. (If you want to explicitly state that you want it to be ascending, use ASC.)

 NOTE *While you'll usually sort the results based on one of the columns that you are returning, it's worth noting that the* ORDER BY *clause can be based on any column in any table used in the query, regardless of whether it is included in the* SELECT *list.*

Aggregating Data Using the GROUP BY Clause

With ORDER BY, I have kind of taken things out of order compared with how the SELECT statement reads at the top of the chapter. Let's review the overall statement structure:

```
SELECT [TOP (<expression>) [PERCENT] [WITH TIES]] <column list>
[FROM <source table(s)/view(s)>]
[WHERE <restrictive condition>]
[GROUP BY <column name or expression using a column in the SELECT list>]
[HAVING <restrictive condition based on the GROUP BY results>]
[ORDER BY <column list>]
[[FOR XML {RAW|AUTO|EXPLICIT|PATH [(<element>)]}][, XMLDATA]
                              [, ELEMENTS][, BINARY base 64]]
 [OPTION (<query hint>, [, ...n])]
```

Why, if ORDER BY is the sixth line, did I look at it before the GROUP BY? There are two reasons:

➤ ORDER BY is used far more often than GROUP BY, so I want you to have more practice with it.

➤ I want to make sure that you understand that you can mix and match all of the clauses after the FROM clause, as long as you keep them in the order that SQL Server expects them (as defined in the syntax definition).

The GROUP BY clause is used to aggregate information. Let's look at a simple query without a GROUP BY. Let's say that you want to know how many parts were ordered in a given set of orders:

```
SELECT SalesOrderID, OrderQty
FROM Sales.SalesOrderDetail
WHERE SalesOrderID IN (43660, 43670, 43672);
```

Code snippet Chap03.sql

This yields a result set of:

```
SalesOrderID OrderQty
------------ --------
43660        1
43660        1
43670        1
43670        2
43670        2
43670        1
43672        6
43672        2
43672        1

(9 row(s) affected)
```

Even though you've only asked for three orders, you're seeing each individual line of detail from the orders. You can either get out your adding machine, or you can make use of the GROUP BY clause with an aggregator. In this case, you can use SUM():

```
SELECT SalesOrderID, SUM(OrderQty)
FROM Sales.SalesOrderDetail
WHERE SalesOrderID IN (43660, 43670, 43672)
GROUP BY SalesOrderID;
```

Code snippet Chap03.sql

This gets you what you were really looking for:

```
SalesOrderID
------------ -----------
43660        2
43670        6
43672        9

(3 row(s) affected)
```

As you would expect, the SUM function returns totals — but totals of what? That blank column header is distinctly unhelpful. You can easily supply an *alias* for your result to make that easier to consume. Let's modify the query slightly to provide a column name for the output:

```
SELECT SalesOrderID, SUM(OrderQty) AS TotalOrderQty
FROM Sales.SalesOrderDetail
WHERE SalesOrderID IN (43660, 43670, 43672)
GROUP BY SalesOrderID;
```

Code snippet Chap03.sql

This gets you the same basic output, but also supplies a header to the grouped column:

```
SalesOrderID TotalOrderQty
------------ -------------
43660        2
43670        6
43672        9

(3 row(s) affected)
```

> **NOTE** *If you're just trying to get some quick results, there really is no need to alias the grouped column as you've done here, but many of your queries are going to be written to supply information to other elements of a larger program. The code that's utilizing your queries will need some way of referencing your grouped column; aliasing your column to some useful name can be critical in that situation. You'll examine aliasing a bit more shortly.*

If you didn't supply the GROUP BY clause, the SUM would have been of all the values in all of the rows for the named column. In this case, however, you did supply a GROUP BY, and so the total provided by the SUM function is the total in each group.

> **NOTE** *Note that when you use a GROUP BY clause, all the columns in the SELECT list must either be aggregates (SUM, MIN/MAX, AVG, and so on) or columns included in the GROUP BY clause. Likewise, if you are using an aggregate in the SELECT list, your SELECT list must only contain aggregates, or there must be a GROUP BY clause.*

You can also group based on multiple columns. To do this you just add a comma and the next column name. Let's say, for example, that you're looking for the number of orders each salesperson has taken for the first 10 customers. You can use both the SalesPersonID and CustomerID columns in your GROUP BY. (I'll explain how to use the COUNT() function shortly.)

```
SELECT CustomerID, SalesPersonID, COUNT(*)
FROM Sales.SalesOrderHeader
WHERE CustomerID <= 11010
GROUP BY CustomerID, SalesPersonID
ORDER BY CustomerID, SalesPersonID;
```

This gets you counts, but the counts are pulled together based on how many orders a given salesperson took from a given customer:

```
CustomerID  SalesPersonID
----------- ------------- -----------
11000       NULL          3
11001       NULL          3
11002       NULL          3
11003       NULL          3
```

```
11004      NULL          3
11005      NULL          3
11006      NULL          3
11007      NULL          3
11008      NULL          3
11009      NULL          3
11010      NULL          3

(11 row(s) affected)
```

Aggregates

When you consider that aggregates usually get used with a GROUP BY clause, it's probably not surprising that they are functions that work on groups of data. For example, in one of the previous queries, you got the sum of the OrderQty column. The sum is calculated and returned on the selected column for each group defined in the GROUP BY clause — in the case of your SUM, it was just SalesOrderID. A wide range of aggregates is available, but let's play with the most common.

> **NOTE** *While aggregates show their power when used with a* GROUP BY *clause, they are not limited to grouped queries. If you include an aggregate without a* GROUP BY, *the aggregate will work against the entire result set (all the rows that match the* WHERE *clause). The catch here is that, when not working with a* GROUP BY, *some aggregates can only be in the* SELECT *list with other aggregates — that is, they can't be paired with a column name in the* SELECT *list unless you have a* GROUP BY. *For example, unless there is a* GROUP BY, AVG *can be paired with* SUM, *but not with a specific column.*

AVG

This one is for computing averages. Let's try running the order quantity query that ran before, but now you'll modify it to return the average quantity per order, rather than the total for each order:

```
SELECT SalesOrderID, AVG(OrderQty)
FROM Sales.SalesOrderDetail
WHERE SalesOrderID IN (43660, 43670, 43672)
GROUP BY SalesOrderID;
```

Code snippet Chap03.sql

Notice that the results changed substantially:

```
SalesOrderID
------------ -------------
43660        1
43670        1
43672        3

(3 row(s) affected)
```

You can check the math — on order number 43672 there were three line items totaling nine altogether (9 / 3 = 3).

MIN/MAX

Bet you can guess these two. Yes, these grab the minimum and maximum amounts for each grouping for a selected column. Again, let's use that same query modified for the MIN function:

```sql
SELECT SalesOrderID, MIN(OrderQty)
FROM Sales.SalesOrderDetail
WHERE SalesOrderID IN (43660, 43670, 43672)
GROUP BY SalesOrderID;
```

Code snippet Chap03.sql

This gives the following results:

```
SalesOrderID
------------ -----------
43660          1
43670          1
43672          1

(3 row(s) affected)
```

Modify it one more time for the MAX function:

```sql
SELECT SalesOrderID, MAX(OrderQty)
FROM Sales.SalesOrderDetail
WHERE SalesOrderID IN (43660, 43670, 43672)
GROUP BY SalesOrderID;
```

Code snippet Chap03.sql

And you come up with this:

```
SalesOrderID
------------ -----------
43660          1
43670          2
43672          6

(3 row(s) affected)
```

What if, however, you wanted both the MIN and the MAX? Simple! Just use both in your query:

```sql
SELECT SalesOrderID, MIN(OrderQty), MAX(OrderQty)
FROM Sales.SalesOrderDetail
WHERE SalesOrderID IN (43660, 43670, 43672)
GROUP BY SalesOrderID;
```

Code snippet Chap03.sql

Now, this will yield an additional column and a bit of a problem:

```
SalesOrderID
------------ ----------- -----------
43660          1           1
43670          1           2
43672          1           6

(3 row(s) affected)
```

Can you spot the issue here? You've gotten back everything that you asked for, but now that you have more than one aggregate column, you have a problem identifying which column is which. Sure, in this particular example you can be sure that the columns with the largest numbers are the columns generated by the MAX and the smallest are generated by the MIN. The answer to which column is which is not always so apparent, so let's make use of an *alias*. An alias allows you to change the name of a column in the result set, and you can create it by using the AS keyword:

Available for
download on
Wrox.com

```
SELECT SalesOrderID, MIN(OrderQty) AS MinOrderQty, MAX(OrderQty) AS
MaxOrderQty
FROM Sales.SalesOrderDetail
WHERE SalesOrderID IN (43660, 43670, 43672)
GROUP BY SalesOrderID;
```

Code snippet Chap03.sql

Now your results are somewhat easier to make sense of:

```
SalesOrderID MinOrderQty MaxOrderQty
------------ ----------- -----------
43660          1           1
43670          1           2
43672          1           6

(3 row(s) affected)
```

It's worth noting that the AS keyword is actually optional. Indeed, there was a time (prior to version 6.5 of SQL Server) when it wasn't even a valid keyword. If you like, you can execute the same query as before, but remove the two AS keywords from the query — you'll see that you wind up with exactly the same results. It's also worth noting that you can alias any column (and even, as you'll see in the next chapter, table names), not just aggregates.

Let's re-run this last query, but this time skip using the AS keyword in some places, and alias every column:

Available for
download on
Wrox.com

```
SELECT SalesOrderID AS 'Order Number',
    MIN(OrderQty) MinOrderQty, MAX(OrderQty) MaxOrderQty
FROM Sales.SalesOrderDetail
WHERE SalesOrderID IN (43660, 43670, 43672)
GROUP BY SalesOrderID;
```

Code snippet Chap03.sql

Despite the AS keyword being missing in some places, you've still changed the name output for every column:

```
Order Number MinOrderQty MaxOrderQty
------------ ----------- -----------
43660        1           1
43670        1           2
43672        1           6

(3 row(s) affected)
```

> **NOTE** *I must admit that I usually don't include the* AS *keyword in my aliasing, but I would also admit that it's a bad habit on my part. I've been working with SQL Server since before the* AS *keyword was available and have, unfortunately, become set in my ways about it (I simply forget to use it). I would, however, strongly encourage you to go ahead and make use of this extra word. Why? Well, first, because it reads somewhat more clearly and, second, because it's the ANSI/ISO standard way of doing things.*
>
> *So then, why did I even tell you about it? Well, I got you started doing it the right way — with the* AS *keyword — but I want you to be aware of alternate ways of doing things, so you aren't confused when you see something that looks a little different.*

COUNT(Expression|*)

The COUNT(*) function is about counting the rows in a query. To begin with, let's go with one of the most common varieties of queries:

```sql
SELECT COUNT(*)
FROM HumanResources.Employee
WHERE HumanResources.Employee.BusinessEntityID = 5;
```

Code snippet Chap03.sql

The record set you get back looks a little different from what you're used to in earlier queries:

```
-----------
1

(1 row(s) affected)
```

Let's look at the differences. First, as with all columns that are returned as a result of a function call, there is no default column name. If you want there to be a column name, you need to supply an alias. Next, you'll notice that you haven't really returned much of anything. So what does this record set represent? It is the number of rows that matched the WHERE condition in the query for the table(s) in the FROM clause.

Just for fun, try running the query without the WHERE clause:

```
SELECT COUNT(*)
FROM HumanResources.Employee;
```

Code snippet Chap03.sql

If you haven't done any deletions or insertions into the Employee table, you should get a record set that looks something like this:

```
-----------
290

(1 row(s) affected)
```

What is that number? It's the total number of rows in the Employee table. This is another one to keep in mind for future use.

Now, you're just getting started! If you look back at the header for this section (the COUNT section), you'll see that there are two ways of using COUNT. I've already discussed using COUNT with the * option. Now it's time to look at it with an expression — usually a column name.

First, try running the COUNT the old way, but against a new table:

```
SELECT COUNT(*)
FROM Person.Person;
```

Code snippet Chap03.sql

This is a slightly larger table, so you get a higher COUNT:

```
-----------
19972

(1 row(s) affected)
```

Now alter your query to select the count for a specific column:

```
SELECT COUNT(AdditionalContactInfo)
FROM Person.Person;
```

Code snippet Chap03.sql

You'll get a result that is a bit different from the one before:

```
-----
10
Warning: Null value is eliminated by an aggregate or other SET operation.

(1 row(s) affected)
```

This new result brings with it a question. Why, since the `AdditionalContactInfo` column exists for every row, is there a different `COUNT` for `AdditionalContactInfo` than there is for the row count in general? The answer is fairly obvious when you stop to think about it — there isn't a value, as such, for the `AdditionalContactInfo` column in every row. In short, the `COUNT`, when used in any form other than `COUNT(*)`, ignores `NULL` values. Let's verify that `NULL` values are the cause of the discrepancy:

```
SELECT COUNT(*)
FROM Person.Person
WHERE AdditionalContactInfo IS NULL;
```

Code snippet Chap03.sql

This should yield the following record set:

```
-----------
19962

(1 row(s) affected)
```

Now let's do the math:

10 + 19,962 = 19,972

That's 10 records with a defined value in the `AdditionalContactInfo` field and 19,962 rows where the value in the `AdditionalContactInfo` field is `NULL`, making a total of 19,972 rows.

> **NOTE** *Actually, all aggregate functions ignore NULLs except for* `COUNT(*)`. *Think about this for a minute — it can have a very significant impact on your results. Many users expect NULL values in numeric fields to be treated as zero when performing averages, but a NULL does not equal zero, and as such shouldn't be used as one. If you perform an AVG or other aggregate function on a column with NULLs, the NULL values will not be part of the aggregation unless you manipulate them into a non-NULL value inside the function (using* `COALESCE()` *or* `ISNULL()`, *for example). You'll explore this further in Chapter 7, but beware of this when coding in T-SQL and when designing your database.*
>
> *Why does it matter in your database design? Well, it can have a bearing on whether or not you decide to allow NULL values in a field because of the way that queries are likely to be run against the database and how you want your aggregates to work.*

Before leaving the COUNT function, you had better see it in action with the GROUP BY clause.

> **NOTE** *For this next example, you'll need to load and execute the* `BuildAndPopulateEmployee2.sql` *file included with the downloadable source code (you can get that from the* `wrox.com` *website).*
>
> *All references to employees in the following examples should be aimed at the new* `Employees2` *table rather than* `Employees`.

Let's say your boss has asked you to find out the number of employees who report to each manager. The statements that you've done thus far would count up either all the rows in the table (COUNT(*)) or all the rows in the table that didn't have null values (COUNT(ColumnName)). When you add a GROUP BY clause, these aggregators perform exactly as they did before, except that they return a count for each grouping rather than the full table. You can use this to get your number of reports:

Available for
download on
Wrox.com

```
SELECT ManagerID, COUNT(*)
FROM HumanResources.Employee2
GROUP BY ManagerID;
```

Code snippet Chap03.sql

Notice that you are grouping only by the ManagerID — the COUNT() function is an aggregator and, therefore, does not have to be included in the GROUP BY clause.

```
ManagerID
----------- -----------
NULL        1
1           3
4           3
5           4

(4 row(s) affected)
```

Your results tell us that the manager with ManagerID 1 has three people reporting to him or her, and that three people report to the manager with ManagerID 4, as well as four people reporting to ManagerID 5. You are also able to tell that one Employee record had a NULL value in the ManagerID field. This employee apparently doesn't report to anyone (hmmm, president of the company I suspect?).

It's probably worth noting that you, technically speaking, could use a GROUP BY clause without any kind of aggregator, but this wouldn't make sense. Why not? Well, SQL Server is going to wind up doing work on all the rows in order to group them, but functionally speaking you would get the same result with a DISTINCT option (which you'll look at shortly), and it would operate much faster.

Now that you've seen how to operate with groups, let's move on to one of the concepts that a lot of people have problems with. Of course, after reading the next section, you'll think it's a snap.

Placing Conditions on Groups with the HAVING Clause

Up to now, all of the conditions have been against specific rows. If a given column in a row doesn't have a specific value or isn't within a range of values, the entire row is left out. All of this happens before the groupings are really even thought about.

What if you want to place conditions on what the groups themselves look like? In other words, what if you want every row to be added to a group, but then you want to say that only after the groups are fully accumulated are you ready to apply the condition. Well, that's where the HAVING clause comes in.

The HAVING clause is used only when there is also a GROUP BY in your query. Whereas the WHERE clause is applied to each row before it even has a chance to become part of a group, the HAVING clause is applied to the aggregated value for that group.

Let's start off with a slight modification to the GROUP BY query you used at the end of the previous section — the one that tells you the number of employees assigned to each manager's EmployeeID:

Available for
download on
Wrox.com

```
SELECT ManagerID AS Manager, COUNT(*) AS Reports
FROM HumanResources.Employee2
GROUP BY ManagerID;
```

Code snippet Chap03.sql

In the next chapter, you'll learn how to put names on the EmployeeIDs that are in the Manager column. For now though, just note that there appear to be three different managers in the company. Apparently, everyone reports to these three people, except for one person who doesn't have a manager assigned — that is probably the company president (you could write a query to verify that, but instead just trust in the assumption for now).

This query doesn't have a WHERE clause, so the GROUP BY was operating on every row in the table and every row is included in a grouping. To test what would happen to your COUNTs, try adding a WHERE clause:

Available for
download on
Wrox.com

```
SELECT ManagerID AS Manager, COUNT(*) AS Reports
FROM HumanResources.Employee2
WHERE EmployeeID != 5
GROUP BY ManagerID;
```

Code snippet Chap03.sql

This yields one slight change that may be somewhat different than expected:

```
Manager      Reports
-----------  -----------
NULL         1
1            3
4            2
5            4
(4 row(s) affected)
```

No rows were eliminated from the result set, but the result for `ManagerID` 4 was decreased by one (what the heck does this have to do with `ManagerID` 5?). You see, the `WHERE` clause eliminated the one row where the `EmployeeID` was 5. As it happens, `EmployeeID` 5 reports to `ManagerID` 4, so the total for `ManagerID` 4 is one less (`EmployeeID` 5 is no longer counted for this query). `ManagerID` 5 is not affected, as you eliminated him or her as a report (as an `EmployeeID`) rather than as a manager. The key thing here is to realize that `EmployeeID` 5 is eliminated *before* the `GROUP BY` was applied.

I want to look at things a bit differently though. See if you can work out how to answer the following question: Which managers have more than three people reporting to them? You can look at the query without the `WHERE` clause and tell by the `COUNT`, but how do you tell programmatically? That is, what if you need this query to return only the managers with more than three people reporting to them? If you try to work this out with a `WHERE` clause, you'll find that there isn't a way to return rows based on the aggregation. The `WHERE` clause is already completed by the system before the aggregation is executed. That's where the `HAVING` clause comes in:

```
SELECT ManagerID AS Manager, COUNT(*) AS Reports
FROM HumanResources.Employee2
WHERE EmployeeID != 5
GROUP BY ManagerID
HAVING COUNT(*) > 3;
```

Code snippet Chap03.sql

Try it out and you'll come up with something a little bit more like what you were after:

```
Manager     Reports
-----------  -----------
5           4

(1 row(s) affected)
```

There is only one manager who has more than three employees reporting to him or her.

Outputting XML Using the FOR XML Clause

SQL Server has a number of features to natively support XML. From being able to index XML data effectively to validating XML against a schema document, SQL Server is very robust in meeting XML data storage and manipulation needs.

One of the oldest features in SQL Server's XML support arsenal is the `FOR XML` clause you can use with the `SELECT` statement. Use of this clause causes your query output to be supplied in an XML format, and a number of options are available to allow fairly specific control of exactly how that XML output is styled. I'm going to shy away from the details of this clause for now because XML is a discussion unto itself, and you'll spend extra time with XML in Chapter 16. So for now, just trust me that it's better to learn the basics first.

Making Use of Hints Using the OPTION Clause

The OPTION clause is a way of overriding some of SQL Server's ideas of how best to run your query. Because SQL Server really does usually know what's best for your query, using the OPTION clause will more often hurt you than help you. Still, it's nice to know that it's there, just in case.

This is another one of those "I'll get there later" subjects. I'll talk about query hints extensively when I talk about locking later in the book, but until you understand what you're affecting with your hints, there is little basis for understanding the OPTION clause. As such, I'll defer discussion of it for now.

The DISTINCT and ALL Predicates

There's just one more major concept to get through and you'll be ready to move from the SELECT statement on to action statements. It has to do with repeated data.

Let's say, for example, that you wanted a list of the IDs for all of the products that you have sold at least 30 of in an individual sale (more than 30 at one time). You can easily get that information from the SalesOrderDetail table with the following query:

Available for
download on
Wrox.com

```
SELECT ProductID
FROM Sales.SalesOrderDetail
WHERE OrderQty > 30;
```

Code snippet Chap03.sql

What you get back is one row matching the ProductID for every row in the SalesOrderDetail table that has an order quantity that is more than 30:

```
ProductID
-----------
709
863
863
863
863
863
863
863
715
863
...
...
869
869
867

(31 row(s) affected)
```

Although this meets your needs from a technical standpoint, it doesn't really meet your needs from a reality standpoint. Look at all those duplicate rows! While you could look through and see which products sold more than 30 at a time, the number of rows returned and the number of duplicates can quickly become overwhelming. As with the problems discussed before, SQL has an answer. It comes in the form of the DISTINCT predicate on your SELECT statement.

Try re-running the query with a slight change:

```
SELECT DISTINCT ProductID
FROM Sales.SalesOrderDetail
WHERE OrderQty > 30;
```

Code snippet Chap03.sql

Now you come up with a true list of the ProductIDs that sold more than 30 at one time:

```
ProductID
-----------
863
869
709
864
867
715

(6 row(s) affected)
```

As you can see, this cut down the size of your list substantially and made the contents of the list more relevant. Another side benefit of this query is that it will actually perform better than the first one. Why? Well, I go into that later in the book when I discuss performance issues further, but for now, suffice it to say that not having to return every single row means that SQL Server may not have to do quite as much work in order to meet the needs of this query.

As the old commercials on television go, "But wait! There's more!" You're not done with DISTINCT yet. Indeed, the next example is one that you might be able to use as a party trick to impress your programmer friends. You see, this is one that an amazing number of SQL programmers don't even realize you can do. DISTINCT can be used as more than just a predicate for a SELECT statement. It can also be used in the expression for an aggregate. What do I mean? Let's compare three queries.

First, grab a row count for the SalesOrderDetail table in AdventureWorks:

```
SELECT COUNT(*)
FROM Sales.SalesOrderDetail;
```

Code snippet Chap03.sql

If you haven't modified the SalesOrderDetail table, this should yield you around 121,317 rows.

Now run the same query using a specific column to COUNT:

```
SELECT COUNT(SalesOrderID)
FROM Sales.SalesOrderDetail;
```

Code snippet Chap03.sql

Because the `SalesOrderID` column is part of the key for this table, it can't contain any `NULL`s (more on this in Chapter 9). Therefore, the net count for this query is always going to be the same as the `COUNT(*)` — in this case, it's 121,317.

> **NOTE** *Key is a term used to describe a column or combination of columns that can be used to identify a row within a table. There are actually several kinds of keys (you'll see much more on these in Chapters 6, 8, and 9), but when the word "key" is used by itself, it is usually referring to a table's primary key. A primary key is a column (or group of columns) that is (are) effectively the unique name for that row. When you refer to a row using its primary key, you can be certain that you will get back only one row, because no two rows are allowed to have the same primary key within the same table.*

Now for the fun part. Modify the query again:

Available for
download on
Wrox.com

```sql
SELECT COUNT(DISTINCT SalesOrderID)
FROM Sales.SalesOrderDetail;
```

Code snippet Chap03.sql

Now you get a substantially different result:

```
-----------
31465

(1 row(s) affected)
```

All duplicate rows were eliminated before the aggregation occurred, so you have substantially fewer rows.

> **NOTE** *Note that you can use `DISTINCT` with any aggregate function, although I question whether many of the functions have any practical use for it. For example, I can't imagine why you would want an average of just the `DISTINCT` rows.*

That takes us to the `ALL` predicate. With one exception, it is a very rare thing indeed to see someone actually including an `ALL` in a statement. `ALL` is perhaps best understood as being the opposite of `DISTINCT`. Where `DISTINCT` is used to filter out duplicate rows, `ALL` says to include every row. `ALL` is the default for any `SELECT` statement, except for situations where there is a `UNION`. You will read about the impact of `ALL` in a `UNION` situation in the next chapter, but for now, realize that `ALL` is happening any time you don't ask for a `DISTINCT`.

ADDING DATA WITH THE INSERT STATEMENT

By now you should pretty much have the hang of basic SELECT statements. You would be doing well to stop here, save for a pretty major problem. You wouldn't have very much data to look at if you didn't have some way of getting it into the database in the first place. That's where the INSERT statement comes in.

The full syntax for INSERT has several parts:

```
INSERT [TOP ( <expression> ) [PERCENT] ] [INTO] <tabular object>
  [(<column list>)]
  [ OUTPUT <output clause> ]
{ VALUES (<data values>) [,(<data values>)] [, ...n]
    | <table source>
    | EXEC <procedure>
    | DEFAULT VALUES
```

This is a bit wordy to worry about now, so let's simplify it a bit. The more basic syntax for an INSERT statement looks like this:

```
INSERT [INTO] <table>
  [(<column list>)]
  VALUES (<data values>) [,(<data values>)] [, ...n]
```

Let's look at the parts.

INSERT is the action statement. It tells SQL Server what it is that you're going to be doing with this statement; everything that comes after this keyword is merely spelling out the details of that action.

The INTO keyword is pretty much just fluff. Its sole purpose in life is to make the overall statement more readable. It is completely optional, but I highly recommend its use for the very reason that it was added to the statement: it makes things much easier to read. As you go through this section, try a few of the statements both with and without the INTO keyword. It's a little less typing if you leave it out, but it's also quite a bit stranger to read. It's up to you, but settle on one way or the other.

Next comes the table (technically table, view, or a common table expression, but you're just going to worry about tables for now) into which you are inserting.

Until this point, things have been pretty straightforward. Now comes the part that's a little more difficult: the column list. An explicit column list (where you specifically state the columns to receive values) is optional, but not supplying one means that you have to be extremely careful. If you don't provide an explicit column list, each value in your INSERT statement will be assumed to match up with a column in the same ordinal position of the table in order (first value to first column, second value to second column, and so on). Additionally, a value must be supplied for every column, in order, until you reach the last column that both does not accept NULLs and has no default. (You'll see more about what I mean shortly.) The exception is an IDENTITY column, which should be skipped when supplying values (SQL Server will fill that in for you). In summary, this will be a list of one or more columns that you are going to be providing data for in the next part of the statement.

Finally, you'll supply the values to be inserted. There are two ways of doing this, but for now, focus on single line inserts that use data that you explicitly provide. To supply the values, you can start with the VALUES keyword, and then follow that with a list of values separated by commas and enclosed in parentheses. The number of items in the value list must exactly match the number of columns in the column list. The data type of each value must match or be implicitly convertible to the type of the column with which it corresponds (they are taken in order).

> **NOTE** *On the issue of whether or not to specifically state a value for all columns, I really recommend naming every column every time, even if you just use the* DEFAULT *keyword or explicitly state* NULL. DEFAULT *will tell SQL Server to use whatever the default value is for that column (if there isn't one, you'll get an error).*
>
> *What's nice about this is the readability of code; this way it's really clear what you are doing. In addition, I find that explicitly addressing every column leads to fewer bugs. If someone adds a column to that table, an* INSERT *that lists every column may still work, but one that doesn't is broken. Worse, if columns are reordered (which is uncommon but possible), you could see data loaded into the wrong fields if you weren't explicit.*

Whew! That's confusing, so let's practice with this some.

To get started with INSERTs, UPDATEs, and DELETEs, you'll want to create a couple of tables to work with. (AdventureWorks is a bit too bulky for just starting out.) To be ready to try these next few examples, you'll need to run a few statements that you haven't really learned about yet. Try not to worry about the contents of this yet; I'll get to discussing them fully in Chapter 5.

You can either type these and execute them, or use the file called Chap3CreateExampleTables.sql included with the downloadable files for this book.

> **NOTE** *This next block of code is what is called a* script. *This particular script is made up of one batch. You will be examining batches at length in Chapter 11.*

Available for
download on
Wrox.com

```
/* This script creates a couple of tables for use with
** several examples in Chapter 3 of Beginning SQL Server
** 2012 Programming
*/

CREATE TABLE Stores
(
    StoreCode      char(4)       NOT NULL PRIMARY KEY,
    Name           varchar(40)   NOT NULL,
    Address        varchar(40)   NULL,
    City           varchar(20)   NOT NULL,
    State          char(2)       NOT NULL,
    Zip            char(5)       NOT NULL
);


CREATE TABLE Sales
(
    OrderNumber    varchar(20)   NOT NULL PRIMARY KEY,
```

```
    StoreCode    char(4)      NOT NULL
      FOREIGN KEY REFERENCES Stores(StoreCode),
    OrderDate    date         NOT NULL,
    Quantity     int          NOT NULL,
    Terms        varchar(12)  NOT NULL,
    TitleID      int          NOT NULL
);
```

Code snippet Chap03.sql

Most of the inserts you're going to do in this chapter
will be to the `Stores` table you just created, so let's
review the properties for that table. To do this, expand
the Tables node of whichever database was current when
you ran the preceding script (probably AdventureWorks
given the other examples you've been running) in the
Object Explorer within the Management Studio.
Then expand the Columns node, as shown in Figure 3-3.
Note that you're looking for the dbo.Stores table you
just created, not the Sales.Store table that came with
AdventureWorks.

In this table, every column happens to be a `char` or
`varchar`.

For your first insert, you can eliminate the optional column list
and allow SQL Server to assume you're providing something
for every column:

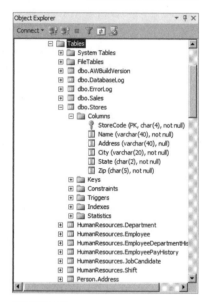

FIGURE 3-3

```
INSERT INTO Stores
VALUES
    ('TEST', 'Test Store', '1234 Anywhere Street', 'Here', 'NY', '00319');
```

Code snippet Chap03.sql

As stated earlier, unless you provide a different column list (I'll cover how to provide a column list
shortly), all the values have to be supplied in the same order as the columns are defined in the table.
After executing this query, you should see a statement that tells you that one row was affected by your
query. Now, just for fun, try running the exact same query a second time. You'll get the following error:

```
Msg 2627, Level 14, State 1, Line 1
Violation of PRIMARY KEY constraint 'PK__Stores__1387E197'.
Cannot insert duplicate key in object 'dbo.Stores'.
The statement has been terminated.
```

 NOTE *The system-generated name you see for the previous primary key constraint
will likely differ on your instance of SQL Server. Let this be a reminder to take the
extra 10 seconds to put descriptive names on your keys when you create them.*

Why did it work the first time and not the second? Because this table has a primary key that does not allow duplicate values for the StoreCode field. If you had changed that one field, you could have left the rest of the columns alone, and it would have taken the new row. You'll see more of primary keys in the chapters on design and constraints.

So let's see what you just inserted:

Available for download on Wrox.com

```
SELECT *
FROM Stores
WHERE StoreCode = 'TEST';
```

Code snippet Chap03.sql

This query yields exactly what you inserted:

```
StoreCode Name          Address                 City              State  Zip
--------- ------------  ----------------------- ----------------  -----  ---
TEST      Test Store    1234 Anywhere Street    Here              NY     00319

(1 row(s) affected)
```

Note that I've trimmed a few spaces off the end of each column to help it fit on a page neatly, but the true data is just as you expected it to be.

Now let's try it again with modifications for inserting into specific columns:

Available for download on Wrox.com

```
INSERT INTO Stores
    (StoreCode, Name, City, State, Zip)
VALUES
    ('TST2', 'Test Store', 'Here', 'NY', '00319');
```

Code snippet Chap03.sql

Note that on the line with the data values this example changed just two things. First, the value you are inserting into the primary key column is different so it won't generate an error. Second, this query has eliminated the value that was associated with the Address column, because it has omitted that column in the column list. There are a few different instances where you can skip a column in a column list and not provide any data for it in the INSERT statement. For now, you're just taking advantage of the fact that the Address column is not a required column — that is, it accepts NULLs. Because you're not providing a value for this column and because it has no default (you'll see more on defaults later on), this column is set to NULL when you perform your INSERT. You could verify that by rerunning your test SELECT statement with one slight modification:

Available for download on Wrox.com

```
SELECT *
FROM Stores
WHERE StoreCode = 'TST2';
```

Code snippet Chap03.sql

Now you see something a little different:

```
StoreCode    Name             Address          City     State     Zip
---------    ----------       ---------------  -------  --------  -----
TST2         Test Store       NULL             Here     NY        00319

(1 row(s) affected)
```

Notice that a NULL was inserted for the column that you skipped.

Note that the columns have to be *nullable* in order to do this. What does that mean? Pretty much what it sounds like: It means that you are allowed to have NULL values for that column. Believe me, you will be learning about the nullability of columns at great length in this book, but for now, just realize that some columns allow NULLs and some don't. You can always skip providing information for columns that allow NULLs.

If, however, the column is not nullable, one of three conditions must exist, or you will receive an error and the INSERT will be rejected:

➤ The column has been defined with a *default value*. A default is a constant value that is inserted if no other value is provided. You will learn how to define defaults in Chapter 7.

➤ The column is defined to receive some form of system-generated value. The most common of these is an IDENTITY value (covered more in the design chapter), where the system typically starts counting first at one row, increments to two for the second, and so on. These aren't really row numbers, as rows may be deleted later on and numbers can, under some conditions, get skipped, but they serve to make sure each row has its own identifier. Other less common defaults may include SYSDATETIME() or a value retrieved from a SEQUENCE (more on the SEQUENCE object in Chapter 11).

➤ You supply a value for the column.

Just for completeness, go ahead and perform one more INSERT statement. This time, insert a new sale into the Sales table. To view the properties of the Sales table, you can either open its Properties dialog box as you did with the Stores table, or you can run a system-stored procedure called sp_help. sp_help reports information about any database object, user-defined data type, or SQL Server data type. The syntax for using sp_help is as follows:

```
EXEC sp_help <name>
```

To view the properties of the Sales table, you just have to type the following into the Query window:

```
EXEC sp_help Sales;
```

Code snippet Chap03.sql

Which returns (among other things):

```
Column_name        Type         Computed     Length    Prec  Scale  Nullable
-----------------  -----------  -----------  --------  -----  -----  --------
OrderNumber        varchar      no           20                      no
StoreCode          char         no           4                       no
OrderDate          date         no           3         10     0      no
Quantity           int          no           4         10     0      no
Terms              varchar      no           12                      no
TitleID            int          no           4         10     0      no
```

The Sales table has six columns in it, but pay particular attention to the Quantity, OrderDate, and TitleID columns; they are of types that you haven't done INSERTs with up to this point.

What you need to pay attention to in this query is how to format the types as you're inserting them. You do *not* use quotes for numeric values as you have with character data. However, the date data type does require quotes. (Essentially, it goes in as a string and it then gets converted to a date.)

```sql
INSERT INTO Sales
    (StoreCode, OrderNumber, OrderDate, Quantity, Terms, TitleID)
VALUES
    ('TEST', 'TESTORDER', '01/01/1999', 10, 'NET 30', 1234567);
```

Code snippet Chap03.sql

This gets back the now familiar (1 row(s) affected) message. Notice, however, that I moved around the column order in my insert. The data in the VALUES portion of the insert needs to match the column list, but the column list can be in any order you choose to make it; it does not have to be in the order the columns are listed in the physical table.

 NOTE *Note that while I've used the MM/DD/YYYY format that is popular in the United States, you can use a wide variety of other formats (such as the internationally more popular YYYY-MM-DD) with equal success. The default for your server will vary depending on whether you purchase a localized copy of SQL Server or if the setting has been changed on the server.*

Multirow Inserts

Starting with SQL Server 2008, you have the ability to insert multiple rows at one time. To do this, just keep tacking on additional comma-delimited insertion values. For example:

```sql
INSERT INTO Sales
    (StoreCode, OrderNumber, OrderDate, Quantity, Terms, TitleID)
VALUES
    ('TST2', 'TESTORDER2', '01/01/1999', 10, 'NET 30', 1234567),
    ('TST2', 'TESTORDER3', '02/01/1999', 10, 'NET 30', 1234567);
```

Code snippet Chap03.sql

This inserts both sets of values using a single statement. To check what you have, go ahead and look in the `Sales` table:

```
SELECT *
FROM Sales;
```

Code snippet Chap03.sql

And sure enough, you get back the one row you inserted earlier along with the two rows you just inserted:

```
OrderNumber          StoreCode OrderDate  Quantity    Terms    TitleID
-------------------- --------- ---------- ----------- -------- ------
TESTORDER            TEST      1999-01-01 10          NET 30   1234567
TESTORDER2           TST2      1999-01-01 10          NET 30   1234567
TESTORDER3           TST2      1999-02-01 10          NET 30   1234567

(3 row(s) affected)
```

> **NOTE** *This feature has the potential to really boost performance in situations where you are performing multiple* INSERT*s. Previously, your client application would have to issue a completely separate* INSERT *statement for each row of data you wanted to insert (there were some ways around this, but they required extra thought and effort that it seems few developers were willing to put in). Using this method can eliminate many round trips to your server; just keep in mind that it also means that your application will not be backward compatible with prior versions of SQL Server.*

The INSERT INTO . . . SELECT Statement

What if you have a block of data that you want to INSERT? As you have just seen, you can perform multirow INSERTs explicitly, but what if you want to INSERT a block of data that can be selected from another source, such as:

➤   Another table in your database

➤   A totally different database on the same server

➤   A heterogeneous query from another SQL Server or other data

➤   The same table (usually you're doing some sort of math or other adjustment in your SELECT statement, in this case)

The INSERT INTO . . . SELECT statement can INSERT data from any of these. The syntax for this statement comes from a combination of the two statements you've seen thus far — the INSERT statement and the SELECT statement. It looks something like this:

```
INSERT INTO <table name>
[<column list>]
<SELECT statement>
```

The result set created from the SELECT statement becomes the data that is added in your INSERT statement.

Let's check this out by doing something that, if you get into advanced coding, you'll find yourself doing all too often — SELECTing some data into some form of temporary table. In this case, I'll show you how to declare a variable of type table and fill it with rows of data from your Orders table:

> **NOTE** *Like the prior database-creation example, this next block of code is what is called a script. Again, you will be examining scripts and batches at length in Chapter 11.*

Available for download on Wrox.com

```sql
/* This next statement is going to use code to
** change the "current" database to AdventureWorks.
** This makes certain, right in the code, that you are going
** to the correct database.
*/

USE AdventureWorks;

/* This next statement declares your working table.
** This particular table is actually a variable you are declaring
** on the fly.
*/

DECLARE @MyTable Table
(
    SalesOrderID    int,
    CustomerID      char(5)
);

/* Now that you have your table variable, you're ready
** to populate it with data from your SELECT statement.
** Note that you could just as easily insert the
** data into a permanent table (instead of a table variable).
*/
INSERT INTO @MyTable
    SELECT SalesOrderID, CustomerID
    FROM AdventureWorks.Sales.SalesOrderHeader
    WHERE SalesOrderID BETWEEN 44000 AND 44010;

-- Finally, make sure that the data was inserted like you think
SELECT *
FROM @MyTable;
```

Code snippet Chap03.sql

This should yield results that look like this:

```
(11 row(s) affected)
SalesOrderID CustomerID
------------ ----------
44000        27918
44001        28044
44002        14572
44003        19325
44004        28061
44005        26629
44006        16744
44007        25555
44008        27678
44009        27759
44010        13680

(11 row(s) affected)
```

The first instance of `(11 row(s) affected)` you see is the effect of the `INSERT...SELECT` statement at work. Your `SELECT` statement returned 11 rows, so that's what got `INSERT`ed into your table. You then used a straight `SELECT` statement to verify the `INSERT`.

 NOTE *Note that if you try running a* `SELECT` *against* `@MyTable` *by itself (that is, outside this script), you're going to get an error.* `@MyTable` *is a declared variable, and it exists only as long as it remains in scope within the running batch. After that, it is automatically destroyed.*

It's also worth noting that you could have used what's called a temporary table. *This is similar in nature, but it doesn't work in quite the same way. You'll discover a lot more about temp tables and table variables in Chapters 11 through 13.*

CHANGING WHAT YOU'VE GOT WITH THE UPDATE STATEMENT

The `UPDATE` statement, like most SQL statements, does pretty much what it sounds like it does — it updates existing data. The structure is a little bit different from a `SELECT`, although you'll notice definite similarities. Like the `INSERT` statement, it has a fairly complex set of options, but a more basic version that will meet the vast majority of your needs.

The full syntax supports the same `TOP` and similar predicates that were supported under `SELECT` and `INSERT`:

```
UPDATE [TOP ( <expression> ) [PERCENT] ] <tabular object>
  SET <column> = <value>[.WRITE(<expression>, <offset>, <length>)]
    [,<column> = <value>[.WRITE(<expression>, <offset>, <length>)]]
  [ OUTPUT <output clause> ]
[FROM <source table(s)>]
[WHERE <restrictive condition>]
```

Let's look at the more basic syntax:

```
UPDATE <table name>
SET <column> = <value> [,<column> = <value>]
[FROM <source table(s)>]
[WHERE <restrictive condition>]
```

An UPDATE can be created from multiple tables, but can affect only one table. What do I mean by that? Well, you can build a condition, or retrieve values from any number of different tables, but only one table at a time can be the subject of the UPDATE action. Don't sweat this one too much. I haven't even started talking about joining multiple tables yet (next chapter folks!), so I won't get into complex UPDATE statements here. For now, you'll look at simple updates.

Let's start by doing some updates to the data that you inserted in the INSERT statement section. Try to rerun that query to look at one row of inserted data. (Don't forget to switch back to the pubs database.)

```
SELECT *
FROM Stores
WHERE StoreCode = 'TEST';
```

Code snippet Chap03.sql

This returns the following:

```
StoreCode    Name          Address               City    State  Zip
----------   ------------  --------------------  ------  -----  -----
TEST         Test Store    1234 Anywhere Street  Here    NY     00319
```

Here's how to update the value in the City column:

```
UPDATE Stores
SET City = 'There'
WHERE StoreCode = 'TEST';
```

Code snippet Chap03.sql

Much like when you ran the INSERT statement, you don't get much back from SQL Server:

```
(1 row(s) affected)
```

Yet when you run your SELECT statement again, you see that the value has indeed changed:

```
StoreCode    Name          Address               City    State  Zip
----------   ------------  --------------------  ------  -----  -----
TEST         Test Store    1234 Anywhere Street  There   NY     00319
```

Note that you could have changed more than one column just by adding a comma and the additional column expression. For example, the following statement would have updated both columns:

```
UPDATE Stores
SET City = 'There', State = 'NY'
WHERE StoreCode = 'TEST';
```

Code snippet Chap03.sql

If you choose, you can use an expression for the SET clause instead of the explicit values you've used thus far. For example, you could add a suffix on all of the store names by concatenating the existing store name with a suffix:

```
UPDATE Stores
SET Name = Name + ' - ' + StoreCode;
```

Code snippet Chap03.sql

After executing that UPDATE, run a SELECT statement on Stores:

```
SELECT *
FROM Stores
```

Code snippet Chap03.sql

You should see the Name suffixed by the StoreCode:

StoreCode	Name	Address	City	State	Zip
TEST	Test Store - TEST	1234 Anywhere Street	There	NY	00319
TST2	Test Store - TST2	NULL	Here	NY	00319

As you can see, a single UPDATE statement can be fairly powerful. Even so, this is really just the beginning. You'll see even more advanced updates in later chapters.

NOTE *While SQL Server is nice enough to let you* UPDATE *pretty much any column (there are a few that we can't, such as* timestamp*), be very careful about updating primary keys. Doing so puts you at very high risk of orphaning other data (data that has a reference to the data you're changing).*

For example, the StoreCode *field in the* Stores *table is a primary key. If you decide to change* StoreCode *10 to 35 in* Stores*, any data in the* Sales *table that relates to that store may be orphaned and lost if the* StoreCode *value in all of the records relating to* StoreCode *10 is not also updated to 35. As it happens, there is a constraint that references the* Stores *table, so SQL Server would prevent such an orphaning situation in this case (you'll investigate constraints in Chapter 7), but updating primary keys is risky at best.*

THE DELETE STATEMENT

The version of the DELETE statement that's covered in this chapter may be one of the easiest statements of them all. Even in the more complex syntax, there's no column list, just a table name and (usually) a WHERE clause. The full version looks like this:

```
DELETE [TOP ( <expression> ) [PERCENT] ] [FROM] <tabular object>
   [ OUTPUT <output clause> ]
[FROM <table or join condition>]
[WHERE <search condition> | CURRENT OF [GLOBAL] <cursor name>]
```

The basic syntax couldn't be much easier:

```
DELETE <table name>
[WHERE <condition>]
```

The WHERE clause works just like all the WHERE clauses you've seen thus far. You don't need to provide a column list because you are deleting the entire row. (You can't DELETE half a row, for example; that would be an UPDATE.)

Because this is so easy, you can master this by performing only a couple of quick DELETEs that are focused on cleaning up the INSERTs that you performed earlier in the chapter. First, run a SELECT to make sure the first of those rows is still there:

Available for download on Wrox.com

```
SELECT *
FROM Stores
WHERE StoreCode = 'TEST';
```

Code snippet Chap03.sql

If you haven't already deleted it, you should come up with a single row that matches what you added with your original INSERT statement. Now let's get rid of it:

Available for download on Wrox.com

```
DELETE Stores
WHERE StoreCode = 'TEST';
```

Code snippet Chap03.sql

Note that you've run into a situation where SQL Server is refusing to DELETE this row because of referential integrity violations:

```
Msg 547, Level 16, State 0, Line 1
The DELETE statement conflicted with the REFERENCE constraint
 "FK__Sales__StoreCode__1B29035F". The conflict occurred in
database "AdventureWorks", table "dbo.Sales", column 'StoreCode'.
The statement has been terminated.
```

SQL Server won't let you delete a row if it is referenced as part of a foreign key constraint. You'll see much more on foreign keys in Chapter 7, but for now, just keep in mind that if one row references another row (either in the same or in a different table — it doesn't matter) using a foreign key, the referencing row must be deleted before the referenced row can be deleted. One of your `INSERT` statements inserted a record into the `Sales` table that had a `StoreCode` of `TEST` — this record is referencing the record you have just attempted to delete.

Before you can delete the record from the `Stores` table, you must delete the record it is referencing in the `Sales` table:

```
DELETE Sales
WHERE StoreCode = 'TEST';
```

Code snippet Chap03.sql

Now you can successfully rerun the first `DELETE` statement:

```
DELETE Stores
WHERE StoreCode = 'TEST';
```

Code snippet Chap03.sql

You can do two quick checks to verify that the data was indeed deleted. The first happens automatically when the `DELETE` statement is executed; you should get a message telling you that one row was affected. The other quick check is to rerun the `SELECT` statement; you should get zero rows back.

For one more easy practice `DELETE`, you can also kill that second row by making just a slight change:

```
DELETE Sales
WHERE StoreCode = 'TST2';
```

Code snippet Chap03.sql

That's it for simple `DELETE`s! As with the other statements in this chapter, you'll come back to the `DELETE` statement when you learn about more complex search conditions.

SUMMARY

T-SQL is SQL Server's own brand of ANSI/ISO SQL or Structured Query Language. T-SQL is largely ANSI/ISO compliant, but it also has a number of its own extensions to the language. You'll see more of those in later chapters.

Even though, for backward compatibility, SQL Server has a number of different syntax choices that are effectively the same, wherever possible you ought to use the ANSI form. Where there are different choices available, I will usually show you all of the choices, but again, stick with the ANSI/ISO version wherever possible. This is particularly important for situations where you think your backend — or database server — might change at some point. Your ANSI code will more than likely run on the new database server; however, code that is only T-SQL definitely will not.

In this chapter, you have gained a solid taste of making use of single table statements in T-SQL, but the reality is that you often need information from more than one table. In the next chapter, you will learn how to make use of JOINs to allow you to use multiple tables.

EXERCISES

1. Write a query that outputs all of the columns and all of the rows from the Product table (in the Production schema) of the AdventureWorks database.

2. Modify the query in Exercise 1 so it filters down the result to just the products that have no ProductSubcategoryID. (HINT: There are 209, and you will need to be looking for NULL values.)

3. Add a new row into the Location (in the Production schema) table in the AdventureWorks database.

4. Remove the row you just added.

▶ **WHAT YOU LEARNED IN THIS CHAPTER**

TOPIC	CONCEPT
SELECT	The most fundamental of all SQL DML (Data Manipulation Language) statements, SELECT is used to retrieve data from a table. You will commonly SELECT fields FROM tables WHERE some conditions are met.
GROUP BY	You may aggregate data in your SELECT statements, rather than simply return the rows exactly as they appear in the table, by using aggregators such as SUM, MAX, MIN, and AVG on the fields you want to aggregate and adding a GROUP BY clause to group by the other fields.
Filtering	Filtering with WHERE occurs before aggregation, and filtering with HAVING happens after. Filtering is done with Boolean tests.
DISTINCT	To remove duplicate rows from your results, you may use SELECT DISTINCT. Duplicates are checked across all fields returned.
INSERT	To put data into a table, INSERT it. INSERT takes a list of the fields you want to insert into, the table you want to load the data into, and either a list of literal values using VALUES, or a SELECT statement that produces a compatible field list.
UPDATE	To alter data in a table, you use UPDATE table_name. Specify which values you want to change with SET field_name = value, and add a WHERE condition to limit the table rows updated.
DELETE	You can remove rows from your tables (permanently) with DELETE FROM table_name. Use a WHERE clause to limit the rows deleted.

4

JOINs

WHAT YOU WILL LEARN IN THIS CHAPTER:

➤ How to combine data from multiple tables into a single result set

➤ How to select rows with matching keys

➤ Including unmatched rows in your JOIN

➤ How to generate massive amounts of data with a Cartesian product

➤ What JOIN syntax might look like in older code

➤ How to stack multiple result sets together

Feel like a seasoned professional yet? Let me dash that feeling right away (just kidding)! While you now have the basic statements under your belt, they are only a small part of the bigger picture of the statements you will run. To put it simply, there is often not that much you can do with just one table — especially in a highly normalized database.

A *normalized* database is one where the data has been broken out from larger tables into many smaller tables for the purpose of eliminating repeating data, saving space, improving performance, and increasing data integrity. It's great stuff and vital to relational databases; however, it also means that you wind up getting your data from here, there, and everywhere.

> **NOTE** *You'll look into the concepts of normalization extensively in Chapter 8. For now, though, just keep in mind that the more normalized your database is, the more likely you're going to have to join multiple tables together in order to get all the data you want.*

This chapter introduces you to the process of combining tables into one result set by using the various forms of the JOIN clause. These include:

➤ INNER JOIN

➤ OUTER JOIN (both LEFT and RIGHT)

➤ FULL JOIN

➤ CROSS JOIN

You'll also learn that there is more than one syntax available to use for joins and that one particular syntax is the right choice. In addition, you'll see the UNION operator, which allows you to combine the results of two queries into one.

COMBINING TABLE DATA WITH JOINS

When you're operating in a normalized environment, you'll frequently run into situations in which not all of the information that you want is in one table. In other cases, all the information you want returned is in one table, but the information you want to place conditions on is in another table. This is where the JOIN clause comes in.

A JOIN does just what it sounds like — it joins the information from two tables together into one result set. You can think of a result set as being a *virtual table*. It has both columns and rows, and the columns have data types. Indeed, in Chapter 7, I'll show you how to treat a result set as if it were a table and use it for other queries.

How exactly does a JOIN put the information from two tables into a single result set? Well, that depends on how you tell it to put the data together — that's why there are four kinds of JOINs. The thing that all JOINs have in common is that they match one record up with one or more other records to make a record that is a superset created by the combined columns of both records.

For example, take a look at a record from a table called Films:

FILMID	FILMNAME	YEARMADE
1	My Fair Lady	1964

Now follow that up with a record from a table called Actors:

FILMID	FIRSTNAME	LASTNAME
1	Rex	Harrison

With a JOIN, you can create one record from these two records found in totally separate tables:

FILMID	FILMNAME	YEARMADE	FIRSTNAME	LASTNAME
1	My Fair Lady	1964	Rex	Harrison

This JOIN (at least apparently) joins records in a *one-to-one* relationship. One Films record joins to exactly one Actors record.

Let's expand things just a bit and see if you can see what's happening. I've added another record to the Actors table:

FILMID	FIRSTNAME	LASTNAME
1	Rex	Harrison
1	Audrey	Hepburn

Now let's see what happens when you join that to the very same (only one record) Films table:

FILMID	FILMNAME	YEARMADE	FIRSTNAME	LASTNAME
1	My Fair Lady	1964	Rex	Harrison
1	My Fair Lady	1964	Audrey	Hepburn

As you can see, the result has changed a bit — you are no longer seeing things as being one-to-one, but rather one-to-two or, more appropriately, what is called *one-to-many*. You can use that single record in the Films table as many times as necessary to have complete (joined) information about the matching records in the Actors table.

Have you noticed how they are matching up? It is, of course, by matching up the FilmID field from the two tables to create one record out of two.

The examples I've used here with such a limited dataset would actually yield the same results no matter what kind of JOIN was used. Let's move on now and look at the specifics of the different JOIN types.

SELECTING MATCHING ROWS WITH INNER JOIN

INNER JOINs are far and away the most common kind of JOIN. They match records together based on one or more common fields, as do most JOINs, but an INNER JOIN returns only the records where there are matches for whatever field(s) you have said are to be used for the JOIN. In the previous examples, every record was included in the result set at least once, but this situation — while it illustrates the concept — covers only a small slice of what you'll encounter in the real world.

To illustrate the far more common case of an INNER JOIN, I've added to the Films table:

FILMID	FILMNAME	YEARMADE
1	My Fair Lady	1964
2	Unforgiven	1992

And to the `Actors` table:

FILMID	FIRSTNAME	LASTNAME
1	Rex	Harrison
1	Audrey	Hepburn
2	Clint	Eastwood
5	Humphrey	Bogart

Using an `INNER JOIN`, the result set would look like this:

FILMID	FILMNAME	YEARMADE	FIRSTNAME	LASTNAME
1	My Fair Lady	1964	Rex	Harrison
1	My Fair Lady	1964	Audrey	Hepburn
2	Unforgiven	1992	Clint	Eastwood

Notice that Bogey was left out of this result set. That's because his `FilmID` didn't have a matching record in the `Films` table. If there isn't a match in both tables, the record isn't returned. Enough theory — it's time to try this out in code.

The preferred code for an `INNER JOIN` looks something like this:

```
SELECT <select list>
FROM <first_table>
<join_type> <second_table>
       [ON <join_condition>]
```

This is the ANSI syntax, and you'll have much better luck with it on non-SQL Server database systems than you will if you use the proprietary syntax required prior to version 6.5 (and still used by many developers today). You'll take a look at the other syntax later in the chapter.

> **NOTE** It is probably worth noting that the term ANSI syntax is there because the original foundations of it were created as part of an ANSI standard in the mid-1980s. That standard has since been taken over by the International Standards Organization (ISO), so you may hear it referred to based on either standards organization.

Fire up the Management Studio and take a test drive of `INNER JOIN`s using the following code against AdventureWorks:

```
SELECT *
FROM Person.Person
INNER JOIN HumanResources.Employee
    ON Person.Person.BusinessEntityID =
    HumanResources.Employee.BusinessEntityID
```

Code snippet Chap04.sql

The results of this query are too wide to print in this book, but if you run this, you should get something on the order of 290 rows back. There are several things worth noting about the results:

➤ The `BusinessEntityID` column appears twice, but there's nothing to say which one is from which table.

➤ All columns were returned from both tables.

➤ The first columns listed were from the first table listed.

You can figure out which `BusinessEntityID` is which just by looking at what table you selected first and matching it with the first `BusinessEntityID` column that shows up, but this is tedious at best, and at worst prone to errors. That's one of many reasons why using the plain * operator in JOINs is ill-advised. In the case of an INNER JOIN, however, it's not really that much of a problem because you know that both `BusinessEntityID` columns, even though they came from different tables, will be exact duplicates of each other. How do you know that? Think about it — since you're doing an INNER JOIN on those two columns, they have to match or the record wouldn't have been returned! Don't get in the habit of counting on this, however. When you look at other JOIN types, you'll find that you can't depend on the JOIN values being equal.

As for all columns being returned from both tables, that is as expected. You used the * operator, which as you've learned before is going to return all columns to you. As I mentioned earlier, the use of the * operator in joins is a bad habit. It's quick and easy, but it's also dirty — it is error-prone and can result in poor performance.

> **NOTE** *As I indicated back in Chapter 3, one good principle to adopt early on is to select what you need and need what you select. What I'm getting at here is that every additional record or column that you return takes up additional network bandwidth and often additional query processing on your SQL Server. The upshot is that selecting unnecessary information hurts performance not only for the current user, but also for every other user of the system and for users of the network on which the SQL Server resides.*
>
> *Select only the columns that you are going to be using and make your WHERE clause as restrictive as possible.*

If you insist on using the * operator, you should use it only for the tables from which you need all the columns. That's right — the * operator can be used on a per-table basis. For example, if you wanted all of the base information for a contact, but only needed the `Employee` table to figure out the contact's `JobTitle`, you could have changed your query to read:

Available for download on Wrox.com

```
SELECT Person.BusinessEntity.*, JobTitle
FROM Person.BusinessEntity
INNER JOIN HumanResources.Employee
    ON Person.BusinessEntity.BusinessEntityID =
    HumanResources.Employee.BusinessEntityID
```

Code snippet Chap04.sql

If you scroll over to the right in the results of this query, you'll see that most of the Employee-related information is now gone. Indeed, you also only have one instance of the `BusinessEntityID` column. What you get in your result set contains all the columns from the `BusinessEntity` table (since you used the `*` qualified for just that table — your one instance of `BusinessEntityID` came from this part of the `SELECT` list) and the only column that had the name `JobTitle` (which happened to be from the `Employee` table). Now let's try it again, with only one slight change:

Available for download on Wrox.com

```
SELECT Person.BusinessEntity.*, BusinessEntityID
FROM Person.BusinessEntity
INNER JOIN HumanResources.Employee
    ON Person.BusinessEntity.BusinessEntityID =
    HumanResources.Employee.BusinessEntityID
```

Code snippet Chap04.sql

Uh, oh — this is a problem. You get an error back:

```
Msg 209, Level 16, State 1, Line 1
Ambiguous column name 'BusinessEntityID'.
```

Why did `JobTitle` work and `BusinessEntityID` not work? For just the reason SQL Server has indicated — the column name is ambiguous. While `JobTitle` exists only in the `Employee` table, `BusinessEntityID` appears in both tables. SQL Server has no way of knowing which one you want. All the instances where you've returned `BusinessEntityID` up to this point have been resolvable: that is, SQL Server could figure out which column was which. In the first query (where you used a plain `*` operator), you asked SQL Server to return everything — that includes *both* `BusinessEntityID` columns, so no name resolution was necessary. In the second example (where you qualified the `*` to be only for `BusinessEntity`), you again said nothing specifically about which `BusinessEntityID` column to use — instead, you said to pull everything from the `Contact` table, and `BusinessEntityID` just happened to be in that list. `JobTitle` was resolvable because there was only one `JobTitle` column, so that was the one you wanted.

When you want to refer to a column where the column name exists more than once in your `JOIN` result, you must *fully qualify* the column name. You can do this in one of two ways:

- Provide the name of the table that the desired column is from, followed by a period and the column name (`Table.ColumnName`)

➤ Alias the tables, and provide that alias, followed by a period and the column name (`Alias.ColumnName`), as shown in the previous example

The task of providing the names is straightforward enough — you've already seen how that works with the qualified * operator, but now try the `BusinessEntityID` query again with a qualified column name:

```
SELECT Person.BusinessEntity.*,
    HumanResources.Employee.BusinessEntityID
FROM Person. BusinessEntity
INNER JOIN HumanResources.Employee
    ON Person. BusinessEntity. BusinessEntityID =
    HumanResources.Employee. BusinessEntityID
```

Code snippet Chap04.sql

Now things are working again, and the `BusinessEntityID` from the `Employee` table is added to the far right side of the result set.

Aliasing the table is only slightly trickier, but can cut down on the wordiness and help the readability of your query. It works almost exactly the same as aliasing a column in the simple `SELECT`s that you did in the previous chapter — right after the name of the table, you simply state the alias you want to use to refer to that table. Note that, just as with column aliasing, you can use the AS keyword (but for some strange reason, this hasn't caught on as much in practice):

```
SELECT pbe.*, hre.BusinessEntityID
FROM Person.BusinessEntity pbe
INNER JOIN HumanResources.Employee hre
    ON pbe.BusinessEntityID = hre.BusinessEntityID
```

Code snippet Chap04.sql

Run this code and you'll see that you receive the exact same results as in the previous query.

Be aware that using an alias is an all-or-nothing proposition. Once you decide to alias a table, you must use that alias in every part of the query. This is on a table-by-table basis, but try running some mixed code and you'll see what I mean:

```
SELECT pbe.*, HumanResources.Employee.BusinessEntityID
FROM Person.BusinessEntity pbe
INNER JOIN HumanResources.Employee hre
    ON pbe.BusinessEntityID = hre.BusinessEntityID
```

Code snippet Chap04.sql

This may seem like it should run fine, but it will give you an error:

```
Msg 4104, Level 16, State 1, Line 1
The multi-part identifier "HumanResources.Employee.BusinessEntityID" could not be bound.
```

Again, you can mix and match which tables you choose to use aliasing on and which you don't, but once you make a decision for a given table, you have to be consistent in how you reference that table.

Think back to those bullet points you saw a few pages earlier; the columns from the first table listed in the JOIN were the first columns returned. Take a break for a moment and think about why that is, and what you might be able to do to control it.

SQL Server always uses a column order that is the best guess it can make at how you want the columns returned. In the first query, you used one global * operator, so SQL Server didn't have much to go on. In that case, it goes on the small amount that it does have — the order of the columns as they exist physically in the table and the order of tables that you specified in your query. The nice thing is that it is extremely easy to reorder the columns — you just have to be explicit about it.

TRY IT OUT   **A Simple JOIN**

Let's try a small query to demonstrate the point. The simplest way to reorder the columns is to change which table is mentioned first, but you can actually mix and match your column order by simply explicitly stating the columns that you want (even if it is every column), and the order in which you want them.

Available for download on Wrox.com

```
SELECT pbe.BusinessEntityID, hre.JobTitle, pp.FirstName, pp.LastName
FROM Person.BusinessEntity pbe
INNER JOIN HumanResources.Employee hre
    ON pbe.BusinessEntityID = hre.BusinessEntityID
INNER JOIN Person.Person pp
    ON pbe.BusinessEntityID = pp.BusinessEntityID
WHERE hre.BusinessEntityID < 4
```

Code snippet Chap04.sql

This yields a pretty simple result set:

```
BusinessEntityID  JobTitle                          FirstName    LastName
----------------  --------------------------------  -----------  -----------
1                 Chief Executive Officer           Ken          Sánchez
2                 Vice President of Engineering      Terri        Duffy
3                 Engineering Manager                Roberto      Tamburello

(3 row(s) affected)
```

How It Works

Unlike when you were vague about which columns you wanted (when you just used the *), this time you were specific about what you wanted. Thus SQL Server knew exactly what to give you — the columns have come out in exactly the order that you specified in the SELECT list. Indeed, even when adding a table, you were able to mix columns from among all tables in the order desired.

How an **INNER JOIN** Is Like a **WHERE** Clause

In the `INNER JOIN`s that you've done so far, you've really been looking at the concepts that will work for any `JOIN` type — the column ordering and aliasing is exactly the same for any `JOIN`. The part that makes an `INNER JOIN` different from other `JOIN`s is that it is an exclusive `JOIN` — that is, it excludes all records that don't have a value in both tables (the first named, or left table, and the second named, or right table).

You saw the first example of this in the imaginary `Films` and `Actors` tables. Bogey was left out because he didn't have a matching movie in the `Films` table. Let's look at another example or two to show how this works.

While you probably didn't realize it in the previous examples, you've already been working with the exclusionary nature of the `INNER JOIN`. You see, the `BusinessEntity` table has many, many more rows than the 290 or so that you've been working with. Indeed, the `BusinessEntity` table has information on virtually any individual the AdventureWorks company works with. They can be individuals associated with a particular customer or vendor, or they can be employees. Let's check this out by seeing how many rows exist in the `BusinessEntity` table:

Available for download on Wrox.com

```
SELECT COUNT(*)
FROM Person.BusinessEntity
```

Code snippet Chap04.sql

Run this and, assuming you haven't added any new rows or deleted some, you should come up with approximately 20,777 rows; that's a lot more rows than the 290 that the Employee-related queries have been showing you!

So where did those other 20,487 rows go? As expected, they were excluded from the `Employee` query result set because there were no corresponding records in the `Employee` table. It is for this reason that an `INNER JOIN` is comparable to a `WHERE` clause. Just as the `WHERE` clause limits the rows returned to those that match the criteria specified, an `INNER JOIN` excludes rows because they have no corresponding match in the other table.

Just for a little more proof and practice, let's say you've been asked to produce a list of names associated with at least one customer and the account number of the customers they are associated with. Consider the following tables:

PERSON.PERSON	SALES.CUSTOMER
BusinessEntityID	CustomerID
PersonType	PersonID
NameStyle	StoreID
Title	TerritoryID
FirstName	AccountNumber

continues

(continued)

PERSON.PERSON	SALES.CUSTOMER
MiddleName	rowguid
LastName	ModifiedDate
Suffix	
EmailPromotion	
AdditionalContactInfo	
Demographics	
Rowguid	
ModifiedDate	

Try coming up with this query on your own for a few minutes before continuing. Once you've taken a fair bash at it, read on to see the attempt dissected.

The first thing to do is to figure out what data you need to return. The question calls for two different pieces of information to be returned: the person's name and the account number(s) of the customer they are associated with. The contact's name is available (in parts) from the Person .Person table. The customer's account number is available in the Sales.Customer table, so you can write the first part of your SELECT statement. For brevity's sake, just worry about the first and last names of the contact:

```
SELECT LastName + ', ' + FirstName AS Name, AccountNumber
```

Available for
download on
Wrox.com

Code snippet Chap04.sql

> **NOTE** *As in many development languages, the + operator can be used for concatenation of strings as well as for the addition of numbers. In this case, it is just connecting the last name to the first name with a comma separator in between.*

What you need now is something to join the two tables on, and that's where you run into your first problem — there doesn't appear to be one. The tables don't seem to have anything in common on which you can base the JOIN — fortunately, looks can be deceiving.

If you were to look more closely at the definition of the Sales.Customer table, you would find that the Customer.PersonID column has a *foreign key* (an indicator that a given column is dependent on information from another column). Indeed, the PersonID ties back to the BusinessEntityID in the Person.Person table.

This is probably not a bad time to point out that the AdventureWorks database serves as a very complete example, even going so far as to include some very questionable design for you to puzzle through. While this kind of design — a foreign key relationship with no kind of naming convention applying — would be frowned upon in many real-world development environments, AdventureWorks proudly displays it for your confusion. This is either shoddy architecture or a brilliant effort on Microsoft's part to prepare you for dealing with poorly built code in the field. I'll leave it to you to judge.

The good news is that there is no requirement that the columns that you join share the same name, so you can just join the columns specifying the appropriate names for each table.

TRY IT OUT **More Complex JOINs**

Using this mismatched pair of names in your JOIN is no problem — you just keep on going with your FROM clause and JOIN keywords (don't forget to switch the database to AdventureWorks):

```
SELECT CAST(LastName + ', ' + FirstName AS varchar(35)) AS Name, AccountNumber
FROM Person.Person pp
JOIN Sales.Customer sc
    ON pp.BusinessEntityID = sc.PersonID
```

Code snippet Chap04.sql

Your SELECT statement is now complete! If you execute, you get something like:

```
Name                      AccountNumber
------------------------- -------------
Robinett, David           AW00011377
Robinson, Rebecca         AW00011913
Robinson, Dorothy         AW00011952
Rockne, Carol Ann         AW00020164
Rodgers, Scott            AW00020211
Rodman, Jim               AW00020562
...
...
He, Crystal               AW00024634
Zheng, Crystal            AW00021127
Hu, Crystal               AW00027980

(19119 row(s) affected)
```

> **NOTE** *Note that your sort order and, therefore, the actual names you see at the top and bottom of your results may differ from what you see here. Remember, SQL Server makes no promises about the order your results will arrive in unless you use an* ORDER BY *clause — since you didn't use* ORDER BY, *the old adage "actual results may vary" comes into play.*

How It Works

If you were to compare this result against a simple SELECT * against the Person table, you would find that several contacts have been left out because although they are considered people, they apparently aren't customers (they may be employees, vendor contacts, or perhaps just potential customers). Once again, the key to INNER JOINs is that they are exclusive.

> **NOTE** Notice that you did not use the INNER keyword in the query. That is because an INNER JOIN is the default JOIN type. Schools of thought vary on this, but I believe that because leaving the INNER keyword out has dominated the way code has been written for so long, it is almost more confusing to put it in — that's why you won't see me use it again in this book. I think of optional keywords a lot like fields in the SELECT clause: include only the ones you need for clarity's sake, and otherwise save your typing.

RETRIEVING MORE DATA WITH OUTER JOIN

This type of JOIN is something of the exception rather than the rule. This is definitely not because it doesn't have its uses but rather because:

➤ More often than not, you'll want the kind of exclusiveness that an inner join provides.

➤ Many SQL writers learn inner joins and never go any further — they simply don't understand the outer variety.

➤ There are often other ways to accomplish the same thing.

➤ They are often simply forgotten about as an option.

Whereas inner joins are exclusive in nature, outer and, as you'll see later in this chapter, full joins are inclusive. It's a tragedy that people don't get to know how to make use of outer joins because they make seemingly difficult questions simple. They can also often speed performance when used instead of nested subqueries (which you'll get a chance to look at in Chapter 7).

Earlier in this chapter, I introduced the concept of a join having sides — a left and a right. The first named table is considered to be on the left and the second named table is considered to be on the right. With inner joins these don't even rate a passing thought, because both sides are always treated equally. With outer joins, however, understanding your left from your right is absolutely critical. When you look at it, it seems very simple because it is very simple, yet many query mistakes involving outer joins stem from not thinking through your left from your right.

To learn how to construct outer joins correctly, I'm going to show you two syntax illustrations. The first deals with the simple scenario of a two-table outer join. The second deals with the more complex scenario of mixing outer joins with any other join.

The Simple OUTER JOIN

The first syntax situation is the easy part — most people get this part just fine:

```
SELECT <SELECT list>
FROM <the table you want to be the "LEFT" table>
<LEFT|RIGHT> [OUTER] JOIN <table you want to be the "RIGHT" table>
                    ON <join condition>
```

> **NOTE** In the examples, you'll find that I tend to use the full syntax — that is, I include the OUTER keyword (for example, LEFT OUTER JOIN). Note that the OUTER keyword is optional — you need to include only the LEFT or RIGHT (for example, LEFT JOIN). In practice, I find that the OUTER keyword is rarely used.

What I'm trying to get across here is that the table that comes before the JOIN keyword is considered to be the LEFT table, and the table that comes after the JOIN keyword is considered to be the RIGHT table.

OUTER JOINs are, as I've said, inclusive in nature. What specifically gets included depends on which side of the join you have emphasized. A LEFT OUTER JOIN includes all the information from the table on the left, and a RIGHT OUTER JOIN includes all the information from the table on the right. I'll show you an example from AdventureWorks with a small query so that you can see what I mean.

Let's say you want to know what all the special offers are, the amount of each discount, and which products, if any, can have them applied. Looking over the AdventureWorks database, you have a table called SpecialOffer in the Sales schema. You also have an associate table called SpecialOfferProduct that lets you know which special offers are associated with which products:

SALES.SPECIALOFFER	SALES.SPECIALOFFERPRODUCT
SpecialOfferID	SpecialOfferID
Description	ProductID
DiscountPct	rowguid
Type	ModifiedDate
Category	
StartDate	
EndDate	
MinQty	
MaxQty	
rowguid	
ModifiedDate	

You can directly join these tables based on the `SpecialOfferID`. If you did this using a common `INNER JOIN`, it would look something like:

Available for
download on
Wrox.com

```
SELECT sso.SpecialOfferID, Description, DiscountPct, ProductID
FROM Sales.SpecialOffer sso
JOIN Sales.SpecialOfferProduct ssop
    ON sso.SpecialOfferID = ssop.SpecialOfferID
WHERE sso.SpecialOfferID != 1
```

Code snippet Chap04.sql

Note that I'm deliberately eliminating the rows with no discount (that's `SpecialOfferID` 1). This query yields 243 rows — each with an associated `ProductID`:

```
SpecialOfferID Description                     DiscountPct    ProductID
-------------- ------------------------------- -------------- -----------
2              Volume Discount 11 to 14        0.02           707
2              Volume Discount 11 to 14        0.02           708
2              Volume Discount 11 to 14        0.02           709
2              Volume Discount 11 to 14        0.02           711
...
...


...
...
16             Mountain-500 Silver Clearance   0.40           986
16             Mountain-500 Silver Clearance   0.40           987
16             Mountain-500 Silver Clearance   0.40           988

(243 row(s) affected)
```

Think about this, though. You wanted to see what all the special offers were — not just which ones were actually in use. This query only gives you special offers that have products utilizing the offer — it doesn't answer the question!

What you need is something that's going to return every special offer and the product IDs where applicable.

TRY IT OUT   Outer JOINs

In order to return every special offer and the products where applicable, you need to change only the `JOIN` type in the query:

Available for
download on
Wrox.com

```
SELECT sso.SpecialOfferID, Description, DiscountPct, ProductID
FROM Sales.SpecialOffer sso
LEFT JOIN Sales.SpecialOfferProduct ssop
    ON sso.SpecialOfferID = ssop.SpecialOfferID
WHERE sso.SpecialOfferID != 1
```

Code snippet Chap04.sql

This yields similar results, but with one rather important difference:

```
SpecialOfferID Description                    DiscountPct   ProductID
-------------- ------------------------------ ------------- ----------
2              Volume Discount 11 to 14       0.02          707
2              Volume Discount 11 to 14       0.02          708
2              Volume Discount 11 to 14       0.02          709
2              Volume Discount 11 to 14       0.02          711
...
...
6              Volume Discount over 60        0.20          NULL
...
...
16             Mountain-500 Silver Clearance  0.40          986
16             Mountain-500 Silver Clearance  0.40          987
16             Mountain-500 Silver Clearance  0.40          988

(244 row(s) affected)
```

If you were to perform a SELECT * against the discounts table, you'd quickly find that you have included every row from that table except for SpecialOfferID 1, which you explicitly excluded from the results.

How It Works

You are doing a LEFT JOIN, and the SpecialOffer table is on the left side of the JOIN. But what about the SpecialOfferProduct table? If you are joining and you don't have a matching record for the SpecialOfferProduct table, what happens? Since it is not on the inclusive side of the JOIN (in this case, the LEFT side), SQL Server will fill in a NULL for any value that comes from the opposite side of the join if there is no match with the inclusive side of the JOIN. In this case, all but one of the rows have ProductIDs. What you can discern from that is that all of the SpecialOffers are associated with at least one product except one (SpecialOfferID 6).

You've answered the question then; of the 16 SpecialOffers available, only one is not being used (Volume Discount over 60).

In this case, switching to a RIGHT JOIN would yield the same thing as the INNER JOIN, as the SpecialOfferProduct table contains only rows where there is an active link between a special offer and a product. The concept is, however, exactly the same. You could, for example, switch the order that you reference the tables and then use a RIGHT JOIN.

TRY IT OUT RIGHT OUTER JOINs

Now, let's see what happens if you change the question to a RIGHT OUTER JOIN:

Available for
download on
Wrox.com

```
SELECT sso.SpecialOfferID, Description, DiscountPct, ProductID
FROM Sales.SpecialOfferProduct ssop
RIGHT JOIN Sales.SpecialOffer sso
    ON ssop.SpecialOfferID = sso.SpecialOfferID
WHERE sso.SpecialOfferID != 1
```

Code snippet Chap04.sql

How It Works

If you tried the preceding query with a LEFT JOIN, you would get just the 243 rows you got with the INNER JOIN. Run it as presented here, and you get the unused special offer you wanted.

Finding Orphan or Non-Matching Records

One very common use for the inclusive nature of OUTER JOINs is finding unmatched records in the exclusive table. What do I mean by that? Let's look at an example.

I'm going to change that special offer question. This time I want to know the special offer names for all the special offers that are not associated with any products. Can you come up with a query to perform this based on what you know thus far? Actually, the very last query you ran has you 90 percent of the way there. Think about it for a minute: an OUTER JOIN returns a NULL value in the ProductID column wherever there is no match. What you are looking for is pretty much the same result set you received in the previous query, except that you want to filter out any records that do have a ProductID, and you want only the special offer name. To do this, you simply change the SELECT list and add an extra condition to the WHERE clause:

```
SELECT Description
FROM Sales.SpecialOfferProduct ssop
RIGHT OUTER JOIN Sales.SpecialOffer sso
    ON ssop.SpecialOfferID = sso.SpecialOfferID
WHERE sso.SpecialOfferID != 1
    AND ssop.SpecialOfferID IS NULL
```

Code snippet Chap04.sql

As expected, you have exactly the same discounts that had NULL values before:

```
Description
----------------------------
Volume Discount over 60

(1 row(s) affected)
```

There is one question you might be thinking at the moment that I want to answer in anticipation, so that you're sure you understand why this will always work. The question is: "What if the discount record really has a NULL value?" Well, that's why I suggested you build a WHERE clause on the same field that was part of your JOIN condition. If you are joining based on the SpecialOfferID columns in both tables, only three conditions can exist:

> ➤ If the SpecialOfferProduct.SpecialOfferID column has a non-NULL value, then, according to the ON operator of the JOIN clause, if a special offer record exists, SpecialOffer.SpecialOfferID must also have the same value as SpecialOfferProduct.SpecialOfferID (look at the ON ssop.SpecialOfferID = sso.SpecialOfferID).

➤ If the `SpecialOfferProduct.SpecialOfferID` column has a non-`NULL` value, then, according to the `ON` operator of the `JOIN` clause, if a special offer record does not exist, `SpecialOffer.SpecialOfferID` will be returned as `NULL`.

➤ If the `SpecialOfferProduct.SpecialOfferID` happens to have a `NULL` value, and `SpecialOffer.SpecialOfferID` also has a `NULL` value, there will be no join (NULL does not equal NULL), and `SpecialOffer.SpecialOfferID` will return `NULL` because there is no matching record.

A value of `NULL` does not join to a value of `NULL`. Why? Think about what I've already said about comparing `NULL`s — a `NULL` does not equal `NULL`. Be extra careful of this when coding. One of the more common questions I am asked is, "Why isn't this working?" in a situation where people are using an "equal to" operation on a `NULL` — it simply doesn't work because they are not equal. If you want to test this, try executing some simple code:

Available for download on Wrox.com

```
IF (NULL=NULL)
    PRINT 'It Does'
ELSE
    PRINT 'It Doesn''t'
```

Code snippet Chap04.sql

If you execute this, you'll get the answer to whether your SQL Server thinks a `NULL` equals a `NULL` — that is, it doesn't.

> **NOTE** Is the thing in this box (which I can't see into) the same as whatever is in that other opaque box? Understanding `NULL` values is a key milestone in learning how to write and debug SQL. What `NULL` really means is "I don't know," rather than some idea of "empty," so if the following comparisons confuse you, try mentally replacing `NULL` with "I don't know."
>
> `NULL` means the value could be anything or nothing, making any kind of comparison moot. Does `NULL` = `NULL`? No. So, does `NULL` != `NULL`? No, you can't conclude that either. In fact, while SQL Server will answer any comparison to `NULL` with `FALSE`, the best answer to the question of whether `NULL` = `NULL` is...`NULL`. Fortunately, Microsoft realized that implementing three-valued logic throughout SQL Server would be even more confusing than just dealing with `NULL` values. For more on dealing with `NULL`, see Chapter 7.

Let's use this notion of being able to identify non-matching records to locate some of the missing records from one of the earlier `INNER JOIN`s. Remember these two queries, which you ran against AdventureWorks?

Available for download on Wrox.com

```
SELECT pbe.BusinessEntityID, hre.JobTitle, pp.FirstName, pp.LastName
FROM Person.BusinessEntity pbe
INNER JOIN HumanResources.Employee hre
    ON pbe.BusinessEntityID = hre.BusinessEntityID
```

```
INNER JOIN Person.Person pp
    ON pbe.BusinessEntityID = pp.BusinessEntityID
WHERE hre.BusinessEntityID < 4
```

And . . .

```
SELECT COUNT(*)

FROM Person.BusinessEntity
```

Code snippet Chap04.sql

The first was one of the queries where you explored the INNER JOIN. You discovered by running the second query that the first had excluded (by design) some rows. Now I'll show you how to identify the excluded rows by using an OUTER JOIN.

You know from the SELECT COUNT(*) query that the first query is missing thousands of records from the BusinessEntity table. (It could conceivably be missing records from the Employee table, but you're not interested in that at the moment.) The implication is that there are records in the BusinessEntity table that do not have corresponding Employee records. This makes sense, of course, because you know that some of the persons are customers or vendor contacts. While the manager's first question was about all the employee contact information, it would be very common to ask just the opposite: "Which persons are not employees?" That question is answered with the same result obtained by asking, "Which records exist in Person that don't have corresponding records in the Employee table?" The solution has the same structure as the query to find special offers that aren't associated with any products:

Available for
download on
Wrox.com

```
SELECT  pp.BusinessEntityID, pp.FirstName, pp.LastName
FROM Person.Person pp
LEFT JOIN HumanResources.Employee hre
    ON pp.BusinessEntityID = hre.BusinessEntityID
WHERE hre.BusinessEntityID IS NULL
```

Code snippet Chap04.sql

Just that quickly you have a list of contacts that is somewhat cleaned up to contain just customers:

```
BusinessEntityID FirstName            LastName
---------------- -------------------- --------------------------------
293              Catherine            Abel
295              Kim                  Abercrombie
2170             Kim                  Abercrombie
...

...
2088             Judy                 Zugelder
12079            Jake                 Zukowski
2089             Michael              Zwilling

(19682 row(s) affected)
```

NOTE *Note that whether you use a* LEFT *or a* RIGHT JOIN *doesn't matter as long as the correct table or group of tables is on the corresponding side of the* JOIN. *For example, you could have run the preceding query using a* RIGHT JOIN *as long as you also switched which sides of the* JOIN *the* Person *and* Employee *tables were on. Here's what that looks like, and of course it will yield exactly the same results:*

Available for
download on
Wrox.com

```
SELECT  pp.BusinessEntityID, pp.FirstName, pp.LastName
FROM HumanResources.Employee hre
RIGHT JOIN Person.Person pp
    ON pp.BusinessEntityID = hre.BusinessEntityID
WHERE hre.BusinessEntityID IS NULL
```

Code snippet Chap04.sql

When I start to show you even more advanced queries, you'll run into a slightly more popular way of finding records that exist in one table without there being corresponding records in another table. Allow me to preface that by saying that using JOINs is usually the best bet in terms of performance — the more popular way isn't necessarily better. There are exceptions to the rule that I will cover as I come across them, but in general, the use of JOINs will be best when faced with multiple options.

Dealing with More Complex OUTER JOINs

Let's move on to the second illustration and how to make use of it. This scenario is all about dealing with an OUTER JOIN mixed with some other JOIN (no matter what the variety).

It is when combining an OUTER JOIN with other JOINs that the concept of sides becomes even more critical. What's important to understand here is that everything to the "left" — or before — the JOIN in question will be treated just as if it were a single table for the purposes of inclusion or exclusion from the query. The same is true for everything to the "right" — or after — the JOIN. The frequent mistake here is to perform a LEFT OUTER JOIN early in the query and then use an INNER JOIN late in the query. The OUTER JOIN includes everything up to that point in the query, but the INNER JOIN may still create a situation where something is excluded! My guess is that you will, like most people (including me for a while), find this exceptionally confusing at first, so let me show you what I mean with some examples. Because none of the databases that come along with SQL Server has any good scenarios for demonstrating this, you're going to have to create a database and sample data of your own.

If you want to follow along with the examples, the example database called Chapter4DB can be created by running `Chapter4DB.sql` from the downloadable source code. Simply open the file in the Management Studio query window and execute it.

 NOTE *Again, in order to utilize the next several examples, you must execute the* `Chapter4DB.sql` *script included in the downloadable code for this book.*

What I'm going to help you do is to build up a query step-by-step and watch what happens. The query you're looking for will return a vendor name and the address of that vendor. The example database only has a few records in it, so start out by selecting all the choices from the central item of the query — the vendor. I definitely want you to go ahead and start aliasing from the beginning, since you'll want to do this in the end (and it's a good habit in any case):

```
USE Chapter4DB

SELECT v.VendorName
FROM Vendors v
```

Code snippet Chap04.sql

This yields a scant three records:

```
VendorName
---------------------------------------
Don's Database Design Shop
Dave's Data
The SQL Sequel

(3 row(s) affected)
```

These are the names of every vendor that I've provided you at this time. Now add the address information — there are two issues here. First, you want the query to return every vendor no matter what, so you'll want to make use of an OUTER JOIN. Next, a vendor can have more than one address and vice versa, so the database design has made use of an associate table. This means that you don't have anything to directly join the Vendors and Address tables — you must instead join both of these tables to a linking table, which is called VendorAddress. Understanding that, you can start out with the logical first piece of this join:

```
SELECT v.VendorName
FROM Vendors v
LEFT JOIN VendorAddress va
    ON v.VendorID = va.VendorID
```

Code snippet Chap04.sql

Because VendorAddress doesn't itself have the address information, you don't need to include any columns from that table in your SELECT list. VendorAddress's sole purpose in life is to be the connection point of a many-to-many relationship (one vendor can have many addresses and, as I've set it up here, an address can be the home of more than one vendor). Running this, as you should expect, gives you the same results as before:

```
VendorName
-----------------------------------
Don's Database Design Shop
Dave's Data
The SQL Sequel

(3 row(s) affected)
```

Now is a good time to take a break from this particular query to check on the table against which you just joined. Try selecting all the data from the `VendorAddress` table:

```
SELECT *
FROM VendorAddress
```

Code snippet Chap04.sql

Just two records are returned:

```
VendorID        AddressID
--------        -------------
1               1
2               3

(2 row(s) affected)
```

You know, therefore, that your OUTER JOIN is working. Since there are only two records in the `VendorAddress` table and three vendors are returned, you must be returning at least one row from the `Vendors` table that didn't have a matching record in the `VendorAddress` table. While you're here, just verify that by briefly adding one more column back to your vendors query:

```
SELECT v.VendorName, va.VendorID
FROM Vendors v
LEFT JOIN VendorAddress va
    ON v.VendorID = va.VendorID
```

Code snippet Chap04.sql

Sure enough, you wind up with a NULL in the `VendorID` column from the `VendorAddress` table:

```
VendorName                VendorID
--------------------      -------------
Don's Database Design Shop  1
Dave's Data                 2
The SQL Sequel              NULL

(3 row(s) affected)
```

The vendor named `The SQL Sequel` would not have been returned if you were using an INNER or RIGHT JOIN. Using a LEFT JOIN has ensured that you get all vendors in your query result.

Now that you've tested things out a bit, it's time to return to your original query and then add the second JOIN to get the actual address information. Because you don't care if you get all addresses, no special JOIN is required — at least, it doesn't appear that way at first . . .

```
SELECT v.VendorName, a.Address
FROM Vendors v
LEFT JOIN VendorAddress va
    ON v.VendorID = va.VendorID
JOIN Address a
    ON va.AddressID = a.AddressID
```

Code snippet Chap04.sql

You get the address information as expected, but there's a problem:

```
VendorName                      Address
--------------------------      ---------------
Don's Database Design Shop      1234 Anywhere
Dave's Data                     567 Main St.

(2 row(s) affected)
```

Somehow, you've lost one of your vendors. That's because SQL Server is applying the rules in the order that you've stated them. You started with an OUTER JOIN between Vendors and VendorAddress. SQL Server does just what you want for that part of the query — it returns all vendors. The issue comes when it applies the next set of instructions. You have a result set that includes all the vendors, but you now apply that result set as part of an INNER JOIN. Because an INNER JOIN is exclusive to both sides of the JOIN, only records where the result of the first JOIN has a match with the second JOIN will be included. Since only two records match up with a record in the Address table, only two records are returned in the final result set.

➤ There are always multiple ways to solve a problem in SQL Server, and this is no exception. Bearing that in mind I'm not going to give you one way to solve this; I'm going to give you three: add yet another OUTER JOIN

➤ Change the order of the JOINs

➤ Group the JOINs together

Try this each way, starting by adding another OUTER JOIN first:

```
SELECT v.VendorName, a.Address
FROM Vendors v
LEFT JOIN VendorAddress va
            ON v.VendorID = va.VendorID
LEFT JOIN Address a
            ON va.AddressID = a.AddressID
```

Code snippet Chap04.sql

And now you get your expected result:

```
VendorName                           Address
--------------------------           -------------
Don's Database Design Shop           1234 Anywhere
Dave's Data                          567 Main St.
The SQL Sequel                       NULL

(3 row(s) affected)
```

In this case, that's sufficient. However, the logic is subtly different from what you had before. If there were rows in `VendorAddress` that didn't have matching rows in `Address`, the earlier query used to exclude those (with its `INNER JOIN` syntax), and now they're permitted. For right now, though, that's not a worry. You've got your result.

Now do something slightly more dramatic and reorder your original query:

Available for download on Wrox.com

```
SELECT v.VendorName, a.Address
FROM VendorAddress va
JOIN Address a
    ON va.AddressID = a.AddressID
RIGHT JOIN Vendors v
    ON v.VendorID = va.VendorID
```

Code snippet Chap04.sql

And you still get your desired result, this time without the subtle logic change:

```
VendorName                           Address
--------------------------           -------------
Don's Database Design Shop           1234 Anywhere
Dave's Data                          567 Main St.
The SQL Sequel                       NULL

(3 row(s) affected)
```

Now try this one more way: by grouping the joins. Remember from before that the result of a join, a result set, is effectively a table and can be used as one? You're going to take advantage of that now. You can group joins together by putting the join *conditions* in the order you want the joins executed.

Available for download on Wrox.com

```
SELECT v.VendorName, a.Address
FROM Vendors v
LEFT JOIN (
VendorAddress va
JOIN Address a
    ON va.AddressID = a.AddressID
)
ON v.VendorID = va.VendorID
```

Code snippet Chap04.sql

NOTE *The key to grouping joins is the order of the join conditions, not the parentheses in the example. In fact, the parentheses are completely optional, but in this case I take an exception to my own guideline of saving keystrokes by omitting unnecessary keywords or symbols. I find the additional punctuation makes this much easier for the programmer who follows you to grok what you've done.*

And yet again, you get your desired result:

```
VendorName                        Address
-------------------------         --------------
Don's Database Design Shop        1234 Anywhere
Dave's Data                       567 Main St.
The SQL Sequel                    NULL

(3 row(s) affected)
```

The question you should be asking now is, "Which way is best?" Quite often in SQL, as I said previously, there are several ways of executing a query without one having any significant advantage over the other — this is *not* one of those times. However, the first solution does (as mentioned) potentially provide a different result than the second or third, which are equivalent.

In general, I would steer you to the second of the two solutions where it works. It's certainly the easiest to read and follow, and the results are consistent with the original intent. More complex applications involving more tables might push you toward the third solution, though, so remember you can do this many ways.

NOTE *The rule of thumb is to get all of the* INNER JOINs *you can out of the way first; you will then find yourself using the minimum number of* OUTER JOINs *and decreasing the number of errors in your data.*

The reason has to do with navigating as quickly as possible to your data. If you keep adding OUTER JOINs not because of what's happening with the current table you're trying to add, but because you're trying to carry through an earlier JOIN result, you are much more likely to include something you don't intend, or to make some sort of mistake in your overall logic. The second and third solutions address this by using only the OUTER JOIN where necessary — just once. You can't always create a situation where the JOINs can be moved around to this extent, but you often can; when you can't, the third option is flexible enough to accommodate virtually any need.

> **NOTE** *I can't stress enough how often I see errors with* JOIN *order. It is one of those areas that just seems to give even some fairly seasoned developers fits. Time after time I get called in to look over a query that someone has spent hours verifying each section of, and it seems that at least half the time I get asked whether I know about this SQL Server "bug." The bug isn't in SQL Server — it's with the developer. If you take anything away from this section, I hope it is that* JOIN *order is one of the first places to look for errors when the results aren't coming up as you expect.*

SEEING BOTH SIDES WITH FULL JOINS

Like many things in SQL, a FULL JOIN (also known as a FULL OUTER JOIN) is basically what it sounds like — it is a matching up of data on both sides of the JOIN with everything included, no matter what side of the JOIN it is on.

FULL JOINs seem really cool when you learn them and then almost never get used. You'll find an honest politician more often than you'll find a FULL JOIN in use. Their main purpose in life is to look at the complete relationship between data without giving preference to one side or the other. You want to know about every record on both sides of the equation — with nothing left out.

A FULL JOIN is perhaps best described as what you would get if you could do a LEFT JOIN and a RIGHT JOIN in the same JOIN. You get all the records that match, based on the JOIN field(s). You also get any records that exist only on the left side, with NULLs being returned for columns from the right side. Finally, you get any records that exist only on the right side, with NULLs being returned for columns from the left side. Note that when I say finally, I don't mean to imply that they'll be last in the query. The result order you get (unless you use an ORDER BY clause) depends entirely on what SQL Server thinks is the least costly way to retrieve your records.

TRY IT OUT Full JOINs

Let's just get right to it by looking back at the previous query from the section on OUTER JOINs:

Available for download on Wrox.com

```
SELECT v.VendorName, a.Address
FROM VendorAddress va
JOIN Address a
    ON va.AddressID = a.AddressID
RIGHT JOIN Vendors v
    ON v.VendorID = va.VendorID
```

Code snippet Chap04.sql

What you want to do here is take it a piece at a time again and add some fields to the SELECT list that will let you see what's happening. First, take the first two tables using a FULL JOIN:

```
SELECT a.Address, va.AddressID
FROM VendorAddress va
FULL JOIN Address a
    ON va.AddressID = a.AddressID
```

Code snippet Chap04.sql

As it happens, a FULL JOIN on this section doesn't yield any more than a RIGHT JOIN would have:

```
Address          AddressID
-------------    -------------
1234 Anywhere    1
567 Main St.     3
999 1st St.      NULL
1212 Smith Ave   NULL
364 Westin       NULL

(5 row(s) affected)
```

But wait — there's more! Now add the second JOIN:

```
SELECT a.Address, va.AddressID, v.VendorID, v.VendorName
FROM VendorAddress va
FULL JOIN Address a
    ON va.AddressID = a.AddressID
FULL JOIN Vendors v
    ON va.VendorID = v.VendorID
```

Code snippet Chap04.sql

Now you have everything:

```
Address          AddressID    VendorID    VendorName
-------------    ----------   ----------   ------------------------------
1234 Anywhere    1            1            Don's Database Design Shop
567 Main St.     3            2            Dave's Data
999 1st St.      NULL         NULL         NULL
1212 Smith Ave   NULL         NULL         NULL
364 Westin       NULL         NULL         NULL
NULL             NULL         3            The SQL Sequel

(6 row(s) affected)
```

How It Works

As you can see, you have the same two rows that you would have had with an INNER JOIN clause. Those are then followed by the three Address records that aren't matched with anything in either table. Last, but not least, you have the one record from the Vendors table that wasn't matched with anything.

Again, use a FULL JOIN when you want all records from both sides of the JOIN — matched where possible, but included even if there is no match.

UNDERSTANDING CROSS JOINS

CROSS JOINs are very strange critters indeed. A CROSS JOIN differs from other JOINs in that there is no ON operator and that it joins every record on one side of the JOIN with every record on the other side of the JOIN. In short, you wind up with a Cartesian product of all the records on both sides of the JOIN. The syntax is the same as any other JOIN, except that it uses the keyword CROSS (instead of INNER, OUTER, or FULL) and that it has no ON operator. Here's a quick example from Chapter4DB:

Available for download on Wrox.com

```
SELECT v.VendorName, a.Address
FROM Vendors v
CROSS JOIN Address a
```

Code snippet Chap04.sql

Think back now — you had three records in the Vendors table and five records in the Address table (assuming you didn't insert or delete any). If you're going to match every record in the Vendors table with every record in the Address table, you should end up with 3 * 5 = 15 records in the CROSS JOIN:

```
VendorName                      Address
------------------------        --------------------
Don's Database Design Shop      1234 Anywhere
Don's Database Design Shop      567 Main St.
Don's Database Design Shop      999 1st St.
Don's Database Design Shop      1212 Smith Ave
Don's Database Design Shop      364 Westin
Dave's Data                     1234 Anywhere
Dave's Data                     567 Main St.
Dave's Data                     999 1st St.
Dave's Data                     1212 Smith Ave
Dave's Data                     364 Westin
The SQL Sequel                  1234 Anywhere
The SQL Sequel                  567 Main St.
The SQL Sequel                  999 1st St.
The SQL Sequel                  1212 Smith Ave
The SQL Sequel                  364 Westin

(15 row(s) affected)
```

Indeed, that's exactly what you get.

Every time I teach a SQL class, I get asked the same question about CROSS JOINs: "Why in the world would you use something like this?" I'm told there are scientific uses for it — this makes sense to me since I know there are a number of high-level mathematical functions that make use of Cartesian products. I presume that you could read a large number of samples into table structures, and then perform your CROSS JOIN to create a Cartesian product of your sample. There is, however, a much more frequently occurring use for CROSS JOINs — the creation of test data.

When you are building up a database, that database is quite often part of a larger-scale system that will need substantial testing. A recurring problem in testing of large-scale systems is the creation of large amounts of test data. By using a CROSS JOIN, you can do smaller amounts of data entry to create your test data in two or more tables, and then perform a CROSS JOIN against the tables to produce a much larger set of test data. You have a great example in the previous query — if you needed to match a group of addresses up with a group of vendors, that simple query yields 15 records from 8. Of course, the numbers can become far more dramatic. For example, if you created a table with 50 first names and then created a table with 250 last names, you could CROSS JOIN them together to create a table with 12,500 unique first name/last name combinations. By investing in keying in 300 names, you suddenly get a set of test data with 15,000 names.

EXPLORING ALTERNATIVE SYNTAX FOR JOINS

What you're going to look at in this section is what many people still consider to be the "normal" way of coding joins. Until SQL Server 6.5, the alternative syntax you'll look at here was the only join syntax in SQL Server, and what is today called the "standard" way of coding joins (that is, everything you've read here so far) wasn't even an option.

Until now, you have been using the ANSI/ISO syntax for all of your SQL statements. SQL Server 2012 requires that you use the ANSI method, which is just fine since it has much better portability between systems and is also much more readable. It is worth noting that the old syntax still has some support across platforms at the current time.

> **NOTE** *The old* OUTER JOIN *syntax you're about to see is no longer supported by SQL Server as of this version. Nevertheless it's good to know it's out there, because sooner or later, you will run into it in legacy code. I don't want you staring at that code saying, "What the heck is this?" Much to my surprise, Microsoft has actually followed through on its long-standing hint that it might remove this feature. It won't really be missed, because the ANSI syntax is actually more functional. Under old syntax, it was actually possible to create ambiguous query logic — where there was more than one way to interpret the query. The new syntax eliminates this problem.*

Remember when I compared a JOIN to a WHERE clause earlier in this chapter? Well, there was a reason. The old syntax expresses all of the JOINs within the WHERE clause.

The old syntax supports all of the JOINs that you've done using ANSI with the exception of a FULL JOIN. If you need to perform a FULL JOIN, I'm afraid you'll have to stick with the ANSI version.

An Alternative INNER JOIN

Let's do a déjà vu thing and look back at the first INNER JOIN you did in this chapter:

```
USE AdventureWorks

SELECT *
FROM Person.Person
```

```
JOIN HumanResources.Employee
    ON Person.Person.BusinessEntityID =
    HumanResources.Employee.BusinessEntityID
```

Code snippet Chap04.sql

This got you approximately 290 rows back. Instead of using the JOIN, however, you can rewrite it using a WHERE-clause–based join syntax. It's actually quite easy — just eliminate the JOIN keyword, replace it with a comma, and replace the ON operator with a WHERE clause:

```
SELECT *
FROM Person.Person, HumanResources.Employee
WHERE Person.Person.BusinessEntityID =
      HumanResources.Employee.BusinessEntityID
```

Code snippet Chap04.sql

It's a piece of cake and it yields the same 290 rows you got with the other syntax.

> **NOTE** *This syntax is supported by virtually all major SQL systems (Oracle, DB2, MySQL, and so on) in the world today, but it can create some ambiguity as to what point in the query processing the restriction should be applied. It is very rare to run into such an ambiguity, but it can happen, so use the JOIN syntax for any new queries and edit old queries to the new syntax as you are able.*

An Alternative OUTER JOIN

> **NOTE** *Note that the alternative syntax for OUTER joins is available only on SQL Server 2008R2 and earlier, and then only if you tell SQL Server you want to run in SQL Server 2000 compatibility mode (setting the compatibility level to 80 in the ALTER DATABASE command). SQL Server 2012 does not support compatibility level 80.*

The alternative syntax for OUTER JOINs works pretty much the same as the INNER JOIN, except that, because you don't have the LEFT or RIGHT keywords (and no OUTER or JOIN for that matter), your WHERE clause will need some special operators especially built for the task. These look like this:

ALTERNATIVE	ANSI
*=	LEFT JOIN
=*	RIGHT JOIN

To see an example of this syntax, start by looking at the first OUTER JOIN you did in this chapter. It made use of the AdventureWorks database and looked something like this:

```
SELECT sso.SpecialOfferID, Description, DiscountPct, ProductID
FROM Sales.SpecialOffer sso
LEFT JOIN Sales.SpecialOfferProduct ssop
    ON sso.SpecialOfferID = ssop.SpecialOfferID
WHERE sso.SpecialOfferID != 1
```

Code snippet Chap04.sql

In the older form, you would just lose the words LEFT JOIN (replacing them with a comma) and replace the ON operator with a WHERE clause, or, in this case, add the ON condition to the existing WHERE clause:

```
--NOTE: The statement below cannot be run on SQL Server 2012.
--If you have an earlier version and can set the compatibility
--level to 80, it can be run.
SELECT sso.SpecialOfferID, Description, DiscountPct, ProductID
FROM Sales.SpecialOffer sso,
    Sales.SpecialOfferProduct ssop
WHERE sso.SpecialOfferID *= ssop.SpecialOfferID
    AND sso.SpecialOfferID != 1
```

Code snippet Chap04.sql

If you could run this (again, this syntax no longer works on SQL 2012, but I want you to know that this kind of code is out there), you would get the same results you did in the original OUTER JOIN query. A RIGHT JOIN would function in much the same way. If you ever encounter this, you'll know what it does so you can update the syntax.

An Alternative CROSS JOIN

This is far and away the easiest of the bunch. To create a CROSS JOIN using the old syntax, you just do nothing. That is, you don't put anything in the WHERE clause of the form TableA.ColumnA = TableB.ColumnA.

So, for an ultra quick example, let's take the first example from the CROSS JOIN section earlier in the chapter. The ANSI syntax looked like this:

```
USE Chapter4DB

SELECT v.VendorName, a.Address
FROM Vendors v
CROSS JOIN Address a
```

Code snippet Chap04.sql

To convert it to the old syntax, you just strip out the CROSS JOIN keywords and add a comma:

Available for
download on
Wrox.com

```
USE Chapter4DB

SELECT v.VendorName, a.Address
FROM Vendors v, Address a
```

Code snippet Chap04.sql

As with the other examples in this section, you get the same results that you got with the ANSI syntax:

```
VendorName                      Address
--------------------------      --------------------
Don's Database Design Shop      1234 Anywhere
Don's Database Design Shop      567 Main St.
Don's Database Design Shop      999 1st St.
Don's Database Design Shop      1212 Smith Ave
Don's Database Design Shop      364 Westin
Dave's Data                     1234 Anywhere
Dave's Data                     567 Main St.
Dave's Data                     999 1st St.
Dave's Data                     1212 Smith Ave
Dave's Data                     364 Westin
The SQL Sequel                  1234 Anywhere
The SQL Sequel                  567 Main St.
The SQL Sequel                  999 1st St.
The SQL Sequel                  1212 Smith Ave
The SQL Sequel                  364 Westin

(15 row(s) affected)
```

This is supported across all versions and across most other database management systems, and is the most common use of the older forms that you're likely to see.

STACKING RESULTS WITH UNION

Okay, enough with all the "old syntax" versus "new syntax" stuff. Now you're into something that's the same regardless of what other join syntax you prefer — the UNION operator. UNION is a special operator you can use to cause two or more queries to generate one result set.

A UNION isn't really a JOIN, like the previous options you've been looking at — instead it's more of an appending of the data from one query right onto the end of another query (functionally, it works a little differently than this, but this is the easiest way to look at the concept). Where a JOIN combined information horizontally (adding more columns), a UNION combines data vertically (adding more rows), as illustrated in Figure 4-1.

When dealing with queries that use a UNION, there are just a few key points:

➤ All the UNIONed queries must have the same number of columns in the SELECT list. If your first query has three columns in the SELECT list, the second (and any subsequent queries being UNIONed) must also have three columns. If the first has five, the second must have five, too. Regardless of how many columns are in the first query, there must be the same number in the subsequent query(s).

➤ The headings returned for the combined result set will be taken only from the first of the queries. If your first query has a SELECT list that looks like SELECT Col1, Col2 AS Second, Col3 FROM..., regardless of how your columns are named or aliased in the subsequent queries, the headings on the columns returned from the UNION will be Col1, Second, and Col3 respectively.

➤ The data types of each column in a query must be implicitly compatible with the data type in the same relative column in the other queries. Note that I'm *not* saying they have to be the same data type — they just have to be implicitly convertible (a conversion table that shows implicit versus explicit conversions can be found in Figure 1-3 of Chapter 1). If the second column in the first query were of type char(20), it would be fine if the second column in the second query were varchar(50). However, because things are based on the first query, any rows longer than 20 would be truncated for data from the second result set.

➤ Unlike non-UNION queries, the default return option for UNIONs is DISTINCT rather than ALL. This can really be confusing to people. In your other queries, all rows were returned regardless of whether they were duplicated with another row, but the results of a UNION do not work that way. Unless you use the ALL keyword in your query, only one of any repeating rows will be returned.

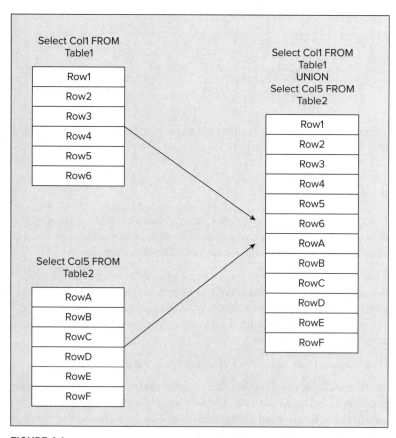

FIGURE 4-1

As always, it's best to take a look at this with an example or two.

TRY IT OUT **UNION**

First, I'll give you a look at a UNION that has some practical use to it. (It's something I could see happening in the real world — albeit not all that often.) For this example, you're going to assume that AdventureWorks is moving to a new facility, and I want you to send out an e-mail to all of the customers and vendors. You want to return a list of names and e-mail addresses for the address update. You can do this in just one query with something like this:

Available for
download on
Wrox.com

```
USE AdventureWorks

SELECT FirstName + ' ' + LastName AS Name,
    pe.EmailAddress EmailAddress
FROM Person.Person pp
JOIN Person.EmailAddress pe
    ON pp.BusinessEntityID = pe.BusinessEntityID
JOIN Sales.Customer sc
    ON pp.BusinessEntityID = sc.CustomerID

UNION

SELECT FirstName + ' ' + LastName AS VendorName,
    pe.EmailAddress VendorEmailAddress
FROM Person.Person pp
JOIN Person.EmailAddress pe
    ON pp.BusinessEntityID = pe.BusinessEntityID
JOIN Purchasing.Vendor pv
    ON pp.BusinessEntityID = pv.BusinessEntityID
```

Code snippet Chap04.sql

This gets back just one result set:

```
Name                   EmailAddress
-------------------    ----------------------------------------
A. Scott Wright        ascott0@adventure-works.com
Aaron Adams            aaron48@adventure-works.com
Aaron Allen            aaron55@adventure-works.com
...

...
Zachary Wilson         zachary36@adventure-works.com
Zainal Arifin          zainal0@adventure-works.com
Zheng Mu               zheng0@adventure-works.com

(10274 row(s) affected)
```

How It Works

You have your one result set from what would have been two.

SQL Server has run both queries and essentially stacked the results one on top of the other to create one combined result set. Again, notice that the headings for the returned columns all came from the SELECT list of the first of the queries.

Moving on to a second example, it's important to take a look at how a UNION deals with duplicate rows — it's actually just the inverse of a normal query in that it assumes you want to throw out duplicates. In your previous queries, the assumption was that you wanted to keep everything unless you used the DISTINCT keyword, but with UNION you must explicitly say you want ALL rows in order to see duplicates.

I want to be clear on what a duplicate means here, because that's just the sort of idea that's so perfectly simple it can trip up the unwary. Two (or more) rows are duplicates if every selected field value matches. Any difference in any selected field will cause both rows to appear regardless of whether you use UNION or UNION ALL. Differences in columns that you don't include in the SELECT list won't count, so as always you should SELECT only what you need. What's more, in this case — despite what I wrote earlier about NULL values not being equal — SQL Server will treat rows with identical NULL columns as duplicates.

In this example, a manager at AdventureWorks wants to clear out some shelf stock, and so she's asked you to produce a list of all the products that either have fewer than 100 units in stock, or are on a special promotion right now. The first attempt at a query like this is straightforward:

```
SELECT P.ProductNumber
FROM Production.Product P
JOIN Production.ProductInventory I
    ON I.ProductID = P.ProductID
WHERE I.Quantity < 100
UNION
SELECT P.ProductNumber
FROM Production.Product P
JOIN Sales.SpecialOfferProduct O
    ON P.ProductID = O.ProductID
WHERE O.SpecialOfferID > 1
```

Code snippet Chap04.sql

If your AdventureWorks database looks like mine, you'll see about 189 product IDs come back. However, there are multiple special offers in play, and having seen your initial report, your manager would like to add that information to it. Adding the special offer name to the query will look something like this:

```
SELECT P.ProductNumber, 'Less than 100 left' AS SpecialOffer
FROM Production.Product P
JOIN Production.ProductInventory I
    ON I.ProductID = P.ProductID
WHERE I.Quantity < 100
UNION
SELECT P.ProductNumber, SO.Description
```

```
FROM Production.Product P
JOIN Sales.SpecialOfferProduct O
    ON P.ProductID = O.ProductID
JOIN Sales.SpecialOffer SO
    ON SO.SpecialOfferID = O.SpecialOfferID
WHERE O.SpecialOfferID > 1
```

Code snippet Chap04.sql

The second return changed things a bit. Not only do you see the additional column you requested, but instead of 189 rows this query returns 355. 189 represents the number of distinct products that fit the request, while 355 represents the number of distinct product/offer combinations (including Less than 100 left as an offer). That's not the same as UNION ALL, though, which includes rows where the differences extend beyond what's selected:

Available for download on Wrox.com

```
SELECT P.ProductNumber, 'Less than 100 left' AS SpecialOffer
FROM Production.Product P
JOIN Production.ProductInventory I
    ON I.ProductID = P.ProductID
WHERE I.Quantity < 100
UNION ALL
SELECT P.ProductNumber, SO.Description
FROM Production.Product P
JOIN Sales.SpecialOfferProduct O
    ON P.ProductID = O.ProductID
JOIN Sales.SpecialOffer SO
    ON SO.SpecialOfferID = O.SpecialOfferID
WHERE SO.SpecialOfferID > 1
```

Code snippet Chap04.sql

In this final example, you'll see 422 rows come back, including many products that have multiple instances of the same special offer (presumably with different dates or some other distinction).

SUMMARY

In an RDBMS, the data you want is quite frequently spread across more than one table. JOINs allow you to combine the data from multiple tables in a variety of ways:

➤ Use an INNER JOIN when you want to exclude non-matching fields.

➤ Use an OUTER JOIN when you want to retrieve matches wherever possible, but also want a fully inclusive dataset on one side of the JOIN.

➤ Use a FULL JOIN when you want to retrieve matches wherever possible, but also want a fully inclusive dataset on both sides of the JOIN.

➤ Use a CROSS JOIN when you want a Cartesian product based on the records in two tables. This is typically used in scientific environments and when you want to create test data.

➤ Use a UNION when you want the combination of the result of a second query appended to the first query.

There are two forms of JOIN syntax available for INNER and OUTER JOINS. I provided the legacy syntax here to help you deal with legacy code, but the newer ANSI format presented through most of this chapter is highly preferable, as it is more readable, is not prone to the ambiguities of the older syntax, and will be supported in SQL Server for the indefinite future.

Over the course of the next few chapters, you will be learning how to build your own tables and how to *relate* them to each other. As you do this, the concepts of what columns to join on will become even clearer.

EXERCISES

1. Write a query against the AdventureWorks database that returns one column called Name and contains the last name of the employee with NationalIDNumber 112457891.

2. Write a query against the AdventureWorks database that returns all products (ID and Name) and including both all products that have no special offers, and all products that have the No Discount offer.

▶ **WHAT YOU LEARNED IN THIS CHAPTER**

TOPIC	CONCEPT
INNER JOIN	The most common type of join, the `INNER JOIN` selects only rows where the join conditions match on both sides.
OUTER JOIN	Allows you to select all data from one table and only those rows that match from another. The inclusive table is determined by designating the join as either a `LEFT JOIN` or a `RIGHT JOIN`.
FULL JOIN	A join that combines a `LEFT JOIN` and a `RIGHT JOIN`.
CROSS JOIN	Returns a Cartesian product containing all possible combinations of rows between the tables.
Alternative JOIN syntax	Recognizing the `JOIN` operators from early versions of SQL Server is important if you encounter them.
UNION, UNION ALL	`UNION` returns one dataset containing all the distinct rows from two datasets with compatible columns. `UNION ALL` removes the implicit `DISTINCT` qualifier.

5

Creating and Altering Tables

WHAT YOU WILL LEARN IN THIS CHAPTER:

➤ SQL object naming rules and conventions

➤ How to create a database using a script

➤ How to create a table using a script

➤ How to alter and drop objects

➤ Ways to create and alter objects using the GUI

➤ Script creation through the GUI

Every time I teach the T-SQL code for creating databases, tables, keys, and constraints, I am asked the same question, "Can't you just do this in the GUI tool?" The answer is an unequivocal "Yes!" Therefore, the next question usually follows quite shortly behind, "Then why are we spending all this time learning stuff I'll never use?" The answer is just as unequivocal — you will use the regular syntax on a quasi-regular basis. The reality is you probably won't actually write the code from scratch that often, but you'll verify and edit it on the majority of all larger database projects you work on — that means that you had better know how it works.

In this chapter, you'll study the syntax for creating your own tables. You'll also take a look at how to make use of the SQL Management Studio to help with this (after you know how to do it for yourself).

However, before you learn too much about the actual statements that create tables and other objects, I need to digress far enough to deal with the convention for a fully qualified object name and, to a lesser extent, object ownership.

OBJECT NAMES IN SQL SERVER

In all the queries that you've been performing so far in this book, you've seen simple naming at work. I've had you switch the active database in the Query Analyzer before running any queries, and that has helped your queries to work. How? Well, SQL Server looks at only a very narrow scope when trying to identify and locate the objects you name in your queries and other statements. For example, you've been providing only the names of tables without any additional information, but there are actually four levels in the naming convention for any SQL Server table (and any other SQL Server object for that matter). A fully qualified name is as follows:

```
[ServerName.[DatabaseName.[SchemaName.]]]ObjectName
```

You must provide an object name whenever you are performing an operation on that object, but all parts of the name to the left of the object name are optional. Indeed, most of the time, they are not needed and are therefore left off. Still, before you start creating objects, it's a good idea to get a solid handle on each part of the name. So let's move from the object name left.

Schema Name (aka Ownership)

If you want to separate your database objects into logical groups, you can create schemas to house them. For small databases this is rarely necessary, but for more complicated systems it's sometimes desirable either from an organizational perspective or to simplify security. Either way, it's completely up to the architect whether you're going to use them.

If you're utilizing schemas (most older databases do not, but their use on newer databases is somewhat more common), you may need to indicate which schema your object is in. It is entirely possible to have two objects with the same name that reside in different schemas. If you want to access an object that is not in your default schema (set on a login-by-login basis), you'll need to specifically state the schema name of your object. For example, let's look at what has to be one of the worst uses of schemas I've ever seen — the AdventureWorks database you've already been using — and take a look at a query that gets a list of employees and what city they live in:

```
SELECT
  e.NationalIDNumber, p.FirstName,p.LastName, City
FROM
  HumanResources.Employee e
INNER JOIN
  Person.Person p on p.BusinessEntityID = e.BusinessEntityID
INNER JOIN
  Person.BusinessEntityAddress a on p.BusinessEntityID = a.BusinessEntityID
INNER JOIN
  Person.Address pa on pa.AddressID = a.AddressID
```

Code snippet Chap05.sql

This example makes use of four tables spread across two schemas. If one of the two schemas involved — HumanResources and Person — happened to be the default schema, you could have left that schema name off when naming tables in that schema. In this case, all schemas were specifically named to be on the safe side.

NOTE *This is another time I'm going to get on the consistency soapbox. If you're going to use the schema features at all, I highly recommend using two-part naming (schema and table name) in all of your queries. It is far too easy for a change to be made to a user's default schema or to some other alias that would make assumptions about the default invalid. If you're not utilizing different schemas in your database design, it's fine to leave them off (and make your code a fair amount more readable in the process), but keep in mind there may be a price to pay if later you start using schemas and suddenly have to update all your old code to two-part naming.*

A Little More About Schemas

The ANSI/ISO standard for SQL has had the notion of what has been called a schema for quite some time now. SQL Server has had that same concept in place all along, but used to refer to it differently (and, indeed, had a different intent for it even if it could be used the same way). So, what you see referred to in SQL Server 2012 and other databases such as Oracle as "schema" was usually referred to as "owner" in SQL Server 2000 and prior.

The notion of the schema used to be a sticky one. While the problems of schema are still non-trivial, Microsoft has added some new twists to make them much easier to deal with. If, however, you need to deal with backward compatibility to prior versions of SQL Server, you'll need to either avoid the new features or use pretty much every trick they have to offer — and that means ownership (as it was known in prior versions) remains a significant hassle.

There were always some people who liked using ownership in their older designs, but I was definitely not one of them. For now, the main thing to know is that what is now "schema" is something that overlaps with an older concept called "ownership," and you may see both terms in use. Schema also becomes important in dealing with some other facets of SQL Server such as Notification Services.

Let's focus, for now, on what a schema is and how it works.

For prior releases, ownership (as it was known then) was actually a great deal like what it sounds — it was recognition, right within the fully qualified name, of who "owned" the object. Usually, this was either the person who created the object or the database owner (more commonly referred to as the dbo — I'll get to describing the dbo shortly). Things still work in a similar fashion, but the object is assigned to a schema rather than an owner. Whereas an owner related to one particular login, a schema can now be shared across multiple logins, and one login can have rights to multiple schemas. The schema feature in SQL Server 2012 is now purely organizational and shouldn't be confused with ownership any longer. Users can still own schemas or have a default schema, but the schema is not the same thing as the owner.

By default, only users who are members of the sysadmin system role, or the db_owner or db_ddladmin database roles, can create objects in a database.

NOTE *The roles mentioned here are just a few of many system and database roles that are available in SQL Server 2012. Roles have a logical set of permissions granted to them according to how that role might be used. When you assign a particular role to someone, you are giving that person the ability to have all the permissions that the role has.*

Individual users can also be given the right to create certain types of database and system objects. If such individuals do indeed create an object, then, by default, that object will be assigned to whatever schema is listed as default for that login.

NOTE *Just because a feature is there doesn't mean it should be used! Giving* CREATE *authority to individual users is nothing short of nightmarish. Trying to keep track of who created what, when, and for what reason becomes nearly impossible. In short, keep* CREATE *access limited to the members of the* sysadmins *or* db_owner *security roles.*

The Default Schema: dbo

Whoever creates the database is considered to be the "database owner," or dbo. Any objects that a dbo creates within that database shall be listed with a schema of dbo rather than that person's individual username.

To explain, let me begin with a counterexample. Say that I am an everyday user of a database, my login name is MySchema, and I have been granted CREATE TABLE authority to a given database. If I create a table called MyTable, the owner-qualified object name would be MySchema.MyTable. Note that, because the table has a specific owner, any user other than me (remember, I'm MySchema here) of MySchema.MyTable would need to provide the two part (schema-qualified) name in order for SQL Server to resolve the table name.

To continue, another user whose login is Group1Member is using the system. Group1Member is a member of a Windows domain group called Group1, which has a default schema of Group1. Using exactly the same CREATE TABLE script as I used (under MySchema), Group1Member creates a new table. The new table is called Group1.MyTable, and is distinct from MySchema.MyTable.

NOTE *Until SQL Server 2012, a Windows group could not be assigned a default schema, so don't look for that in previous versions. Use this feature when you want a schema to follow group membership rather than individual users.*

Now, let's say that there is also a user with a login name of Fred. Fred is the database owner (as opposed to just any member of db_owner). If Fred creates a table called MyTable using an identical CREATE statement to that used by MySchema and Group1Member, the two-part table name will be dbo.MyTable. In addition, as dbo also happens to be the default owner, any user could just refer to Fred's table as MyTable.

It's worth pointing out that members of the sysadmin role (including the sa login) always alias to the dbo. That is, no matter who actually owns the database, a member of sysadmin will always have full access as if it were the dbo, and any objects created by a member of sysadmin will, unless explicitly defined otherwise, show ownership belonging to the dbo. In contrast, objects created by members of the db_owner database role do *not* default to dbo as the default schema — they will be assigned to whatever that particular user has set as the default schema (it could be anything). Weird but true!

> **NOTE** *Microsoft keeps making the use of schemas easier and more consistent, and that's perfectly in keeping with both ANSI standards and user requests (including mine). Anything that makes a feature easier to deal with is okay in my book, but it doesn't change the considerations about when you'd actually want to use different schemas in your design. Rather, it just lowers the price of admission.*
>
> *The addition of schemas adds complexity to your database no matter what you do. While they can address organizational problems in your design, those problems can usually be dealt with in other ways that produce a much more user-friendly database. In addition, schemas, while an ANSI/ISO-compliant notion, are not supported in the same way across every major RDBMS product. This means using schemas is going to have an impact on you if you're trying to write code that can support multiple platforms.*

The Database Name

The next item in the fully qualified naming convention is the database name. Sometimes you want to retrieve data from a database other than the default, or current, database. Indeed, you may actually want to JOIN data from across databases. A database-qualified name gives you that ability. For example, if you were logged in with AdventureWorks as your current database, and you wanted to refer to the Orders table in the Accounting database you'll be building later in the chapter, you could refer to it by Accounting.dbo.Orders. Because dbo is the default schema, you could also use Accounting..Orders. If a schema named MySchema owns a table named MyTable in MyDatabase, you could refer to that table as MyDatabase.MySchema.MyTable. Remember that the current database (as determined by the USE command or in the dropdown box if you're using the SQL Server Management Studio) is always the default, so, if you want data from only the current database, you do not need to include the database name in your fully qualified name.

Naming by Server

In addition to naming other databases on the server you're connected to, you can also "link" to another server. Linked servers give you the capability to perform a JOIN across multiple servers — even different types of servers (SQL Server, Oracle, DB2, Access — just about anything with an OLE DB provider). You'll see a bit more about linked servers later in the book, but for now, just realize that there is one more level in the naming hierarchy, that it lets you access different servers, and that it works pretty much like the database and ownership levels work.

Now, let's add to the previous example. While creating a linked server is a bit advanced (you'll see that in Chapter 21), let's take it as read that there's a linked server called MyServer. If you want to retrieve information from that server, from a database called MyDatabase, and a table called `MyTable` owned by `MySchema`, the fully qualified name would be `MyServer.MyDatabase.MySchema.MyTable`.

Reviewing the Defaults

So let's look one last time at how the defaults work at each level of the naming hierarchy from right to left:

➤ **Object Name:** There isn't a default — you must supply an object name.

➤ **Ownership:** You can leave this off, in which case it will resolve first using the current user's name, and then, if the object name in question doesn't exist with the current user as owner, it will try the `dbo` as the owner.

➤ **Database Name:** This can also be left off unless you are providing a Server Name — in which case you must provide the Database Name for SQL Servers (other server types vary depending on the specific kind of server).

➤ **Server Name:** You can provide the name of a linked server here, but most of the time you'll just leave this off, which will cause SQL Server to default to the server you are logged in to.

If you want to skip the schema name, but still provide information regarding the database or server, you must still provide the extra ". " for the position where the owner would be. For example, if you are logged in using the AdventureWorks database on your local server, but want to refer to the `Sales.Customer` table in the AdventureWorks database on a linked server called `MyOtherServer`, you could refer to that table by using `MyOtherServer.AdventureWorks..Customer`. Because you didn't provide a specific schema name, it will assume that either the default schema for the user ID that is used to log on to the linked server or the `dbo` (in that order) is the schema of the object you want (in this case, `Customer`). Since the `Customer` table is not part of the `dbo` schema, the users would need to have a default schema of `Sales` or they would get an error that the object was not found. In general, I recommend explicitly naming the schema of the object you want to reference.

THE CREATE STATEMENT

It would be pretty nifty if you could just wave a wand, mumble some pseudo-Latin, and have your database spring into being exactly as you want it to. Unfortunately, creating things isn't quite that simple. You need to provide a well-defined syntax in order to create the objects in your database (and any wand-waving is entirely optional). To do that, you'll make use of the CREATE statement.

Let's look at the full structure of a CREATE statement, starting with the utmost in generality. You'll find that all the CREATE statements start out the same, and then get into the specifics. The first part of the CREATE statement will always look like this:

```
CREATE <object type> <object name>
```

This will be followed by the details that vary by the nature of the object you're creating.

CREATE DATABASE

For this part of things, I'm going to introduce you to a database called Accounting that you will use when you start to create tables. You and Accounting are going to become acquainted over the next several chapters, and you can start by creating that database here. The most basic syntax for the CREATE DATABASE statement looks like this:

```
CREATE DATABASE <database name>
```

> **NOTE** It's worth pointing out that when you create a new object, no one can access it except for the person who created it, the system administrator, and the database owner (which, if the object created was a database, is the same as the person who created it). This allows you to create things and make whatever adjustments you need to make before you explicitly allow access to your object.
>
> It's also worth noting that you can use the CREATE statement only to create objects on the local server (adding a specific server name doesn't work).

This yields a database that looks exactly like your model database (the model database was discussed in Chapter 1). In reality, what you want is almost always different, so let's look at a fuller (though still not entirely complete) syntax listing:

```
CREATE DATABASE <database name>
[ON [PRIMARY]
    ([NAME = <'logical file name'>,]
     FILENAME = <'file name'>
     [, SIZE = <size in kilobytes, megabytes, gigabytes, or terabytes>]
     [, MAXSIZE = size in kilobytes, megabytes, gigabytes, or terabytes>]
     [, FILEGROWTH = <kilobytes, megabytes, gigabytes, or
                                terabytes|percentage>])]
  [LOG ON
    ([NAME = <'logical file name'>,]
     FILENAME = <'file name'>
     [, SIZE = <size in kilobytes, megabytes, gigabytes, or terabytes>]
     [, MAXSIZE = size in kilobytes, megabytes, gigabytes, or terabytes>]
     [, FILEGROWTH = <kilobytes, megabytes, gigabytes, or terabytes|percentage>])]
[ CONTAINMENT = OFF|PARTIAL ]
[ COLLATE <collation name> ]
[ FOR ATTACH [WITH <service broker>]| FOR ATTACH_REBUILD_LOG|
    WITH DB_CHAINING ON|OFF | TRUSTWORTHY ON|OFF]
[AS SNAPSHOT OF <source database name>]
[;]
```

Keep in mind that some of the preceding options are mutually exclusive (for example, if you're creating for attaching, most of the options other than file locations are invalid). There's a lot there, so let's break down the parts.

CONTAINMENT

Contained databases are a new feature in SQL Server 2012. They allow you to deploy a database with fewer dependencies on the target SQL instance. For example, you can assign permissions to a Windows user without creating a SQL Server login for that user, granting you more independence when it comes time to move your database from server to server. Because this is a fairly advanced concept, it's beyond the scope of this book to cover it in its entirety. Suffice it to say it's out there and that the default setting for CONTAINMENT is OFF.

ON

ON is used in two places: to define the location of the file where the data is stored, and to define the same information for where the log is stored. You'll notice the PRIMARY keyword there — this means that what follows is the primary (or main) filegroup in which to physically store the data. You can also store data in what are called secondary filegroups — the use of which is outside the scope of this title. For now, stick with the default notion that you want everything in one file.

 NOTE *SQL Server allows you to store your database in multiple files; furthermore, it allows you to collect those files into logical groupings called filegroups. The use of filegroups is a fairly advanced concept and is outside the scope of this book.*

NAME

This one isn't quite what it sounds like. It is a name for the file you are defining, but only a logical name — that is, the name that SQL Server will use internally to refer to that file. You use this name when you want to resize (expand or shrink) the database and/or file.

FILENAME

This one *is* what it sounds like — the physical name on the disk of the actual operating system file in which the data and log (depending on what section you're defining) will be stored. The default here (assuming you used the simple syntax you looked at first) depends on whether you are dealing with the database itself or the log. By default, your file will be located in the \Data subdirectory under your main \Program Files\Microsoft SQL Server\MSSQL11.MSSQLSERVER\MSSQL directory (or whatever you called your main SQL Server directory if you changed it at install). If you're dealing with the physical database file, it will be named the same as your database with an .mdf extension. If you're dealing with the log, it will be named the same as the database file but with a suffix of _Log and an .ldf extension. You are allowed to specify other extensions if you explicitly name the files, but I strongly encourage you to stick with the defaults of mdf (database) and ldf (log file). As a side note, secondary files have a default extension of .ndf.

Keep in mind that while FILENAME is an optional parameter, it is optional only as long as you go with the extremely simple syntax (the one that creates a new database based on the model database) that I introduced first. If you provide any of the additional information, you must include an explicit file name — be sure to provide a full path.

SIZE

No mystery here. It is what it says — the size of the database. By default, the size is in megabytes, but you can make it kilobytes by using KB instead of MB after the numeric value for the size, or go bigger by using GB (gigabytes) or even TB (terabytes). Keep in mind that this value must be at least as large as the model database is and must be a whole number (no decimals) or you will receive an error. If you do not supply a value for SIZE, the database will initially be the same size as the model database.

MAXSIZE

This one is still pretty much what it sounds like, with only a slight twist compared to the SIZE parameter. SQL Server has a mechanism to allow your database to automatically allocate additional disk space (to grow) when necessary. MAXSIZE is the maximum size to which the database can grow. Again, the number is, by default, in megabytes, but like SIZE, you can use KB, GB, or TB to use different increment amounts. The slight twist is that there is no firm default. If you don't supply a value for this parameter, there is considered to be no maximum — the practical maximum becomes when your disk drive is full.

If your database reaches the value set in the MAXSIZE parameter, your users will start getting errors back saying that their INSERTs can't be performed. If your log reaches its maximum size, you will not be able to perform any logged activity (which is most activities) in the database. Personally, I recommend setting up what is called an *alert*. You can use alerts to tell you when certain conditions exist (such as a database or log that's almost full). You'll see how to create alerts in Chapter 21.

WHAT VALUE SHOULD MAXSIZE BE?

I recommend that you always include a value for MAXSIZE, and that you make it at least several megabytes smaller than would fill up the disk. I suggest this because a completely full disk can cause situations where you can't commit any information to permanent storage. If the log was trying to expand, the results could potentially be disastrous. In addition, even the operating system can occasionally have problems if it runs completely out of disk space — be aware of this if your file shares a disk with your OS.

This brings up a larger point about disk usage. You'll hear more from me later on this topic when you read about performance, but the disk is your biggest bottleneck most of the time. You should place your files wisely for more reasons than just filling space. Best practices suggest that, if at all possible, you should keep your database files on a separate volume than your OS files. Furthermore, for performance reasons, it's a good idea (again, in an ideal world) to keep any files with lots of concurrent usage on different disks. Indexes can be stored separately from their tables, logs from database files, and any other time you see contention for disk resources.

One more thing — if you decide to follow my advice on this issue, be sure to keep in mind that you may have multiple databases on the same system. If you size each of them to take up the full size of the disk less a few megabytes, you will still have the possibility of a full disk (if they all expand). There really isn't any one "right" answer for this scenario — you just need to prioritize your space according to likely usage, monitor your database sizes more closely, and set up alerts in Windows Server to notify you of low disk space situations.

FILEGROWTH

Whereas SIZE sets the initial size of the database, and MAXSIZE determines just how large the database file could get, FILEGROWTH essentially determines just how fast it gets to that maximum. You provide a value that indicates by how many bytes (in KB, MB, GB, or TB) at a time you want the file to be enlarged. Alternatively, you can provide a percentage value by which you want the database file to increase. With this option, the size will go up by the stated percentage of the current database file size. Therefore, if you set a database file to start out at 1GB with a FILEGROWTH of 20 percent, the first time it expands it will grow to 1.2GB, the second time to 1.44, and so on.

LOG ON

The LOG ON option allows you to establish that you want your log to go to a specific set of files and where exactly those files are to be located. If this option is not provided, SQL Server creates the log in a single file and defaults it to a size equal to 25 percent of the data file size. In most other respects, it has the same file specification parameters as the main database file does.

> **NOTE** *It is highly recommended that you store your log files on a different drive than your main data files. Doing so prevents the log and main data files from competing for I/O off the disk and provides additional safety should one hard drive fail.*

COLLATE

This one has to do with the issue of sort order, case sensitivity, and sensitivity to accents. When you installed your SQL Server, you decided on a default collation, but you can override this at the database level (and, as you'll see later, also at the column level).

FOR ATTACH

You can use this option to attach an existing set of database files to the current server. The files in question must be part of a database that was, at some point, properly detached using sp_detach_db. This deprecates the older sp_attach_db functionality and has the advantage of access to as many as 32,000 files — sp_attach_db is limited to 16.

If you use FOR ATTACH, you must complete the ON PRIMARY portion of the file location information. Other parts of the CREATE DATABASE parameter list can be left off as long as you are attaching the database to the same file path they were in when they were originally detached.

WITH DB CHAINING ON|OFF

Hmmm. How to address this one in a beginning-type way. . . . Well, suffice it to say this is a toughie, and is in no way a "beginning" kind of concept. With that in mind, here's the abridged version of what this relates to.

As previously mentioned, the concept of "schemas" didn't really exist in early versions of SQL Server. Instead, there was the notion of "ownership." One of the bad things that could happen with ownership was an *ownership chain*. This was a situation in which person A was the owner of an object, and then person B became the owner of an object that depended on person A's object. You could have person after person create objects depending on other people's objects, and there was a complex weave of permission issues based on this. An ownership chain that gets too complicated can make it difficult to implement any kind of sensible security model, as the weave of rights required to grant permissions on an object becomes a Gordian knot.

This switch is about respecting such ownership chains when they cross databases (person A's object is in DB1, and person B's object is in DB2). Turn it on, and cross database ownership chains work — turn it off, and they don't. Avoid such ownership chains as if they were the plague — if you find yourself thinking ownership chaining is a good idea, imagine unraveling that knot later, and reconsider.

TRUSTWORTHY

This switch adds an extra layer of security around access to system resources and files outside of the SQL Server context. For example, you may run a .NET assembly that touches files on your network — if so, you must identify the database that the assembly is part of as being trustworthy.

By default, this is turned off for security reasons — be certain you understand exactly what you're doing and why before you set this to on.

Building a Database

At this point, you should be ready to begin building your database. The following is the statement to create it, but keep in mind that the database itself is only one of many objects that you'll create on your way to a fully functional database:

Available for download on Wrox.com

```
CREATE DATABASE Accounting
ON
   (NAME = 'Accounting',
    FILENAME = 'C:\Program Files\Microsoft SQL
Server\MSSQL11.MSSQLSERVER\MSSQL\DATA\AccountingData.mdf',
    SIZE = 10,
    MAXSIZE = 50,
    FILEGROWTH = 5)
LOG ON
   (NAME = 'AccountingLog',
    FILENAME = 'C:\Program Files\Microsoft SQL
Server\MSSQL11.MSSQLSERVER\MSSQL\DATA\AccountingLog.ldf',
    SIZE = 5MB,
    MAXSIZE = 25MB,
    FILEGROWTH = 5MB);

GO
```

Code snippet Chap05.sql

Now is a good time to start learning about some of the informational utilities that are available with SQL Server. You saw `sp_help` in Chapter 4, but in this case, you'll try running a command called `sp_helpdb`. This one is especially tailored for database structure information, and often provides better information if you're more interested in the database itself than in the objects it contains. `sp_helpdb` takes one parameter — the database name:

```
EXEC sp_helpdb 'Accounting'
```

Code snippet Chap05.sql

This actually yields you two separate result sets. The first, shown in the following table, is based on the combined (data and log) information about your database:

```
Name     db_ size
Owner    dbid
```

NAME	DB_SIZE	OWNER	DBID	CREATED	STATUS	COMPATI-BILITY _LEVEL
Account-ing	15.00MB	BEGINNING SQL201\ Paul Atkinson	9	Dec 5 2011	Status=ONLINE, Updateability= READ_WRITE, UserAccess= MULTI_USER, Recovery=FULL, Version=705, Collation= SQL_Latin1_ General_CP1_ CI_AS, SQLSortOrder=52, IsAutoCreate Statistics, IsAutoUpdate Statistics, IsFullText Enabled	110

> **NOTE** *The actual values you receive for each of these fields may vary somewhat from mine. For example, the* DBID *value will vary depending on how many databases you've created and in what order you've created them. The various status messages will vary depending on what server options were in place at the time you created the database, as well as any options you changed for the database along the way.*

Note that the `db_size` property is the *total* of the size of the database and the size of the log.

The second provides specifics about the various files that make up your database — including their current size and growth settings (shown in Table 5-1):

TABLE 5-1: Files That Make Up the Database

NAME	FILEID	FILENAME	FILEGROUP	SIZE	MAXSIZE	GROWTH	USAGE
Accounting	1	C:\Program Files\ Microsoft SQL Server\ MSSQL11. MSSQLSERVER\ MSSQL\DATA\ Accounting Data.mdf	PRIMARY	10240 KB	51200 KB	5120 KB	data only
AccountingLog	2	C:\Program Files\ Microsoft SQL Server\ MSSQL11. MSSQLSERVER\ MSSQL\DATA\ Accounting-Log.ldf	NULL	5120 KB	25600 KB	5120 KB	log only

After you create tables and insert data, the database will begin to grow automatically on an as-needed basis.

CREATE TABLE

The first part of creating a table is pretty much the same as creating any object — remember that line I showed you? Well, here it is again:

```
CREATE <object type> <object name>
```

Because a table is what you want, you can be more specific:

```
CREATE TABLE Customers
```

With CREATE DATABASE, you could have stopped with just these first three keywords, and it would have built the database based on the guidelines established in the model database. With tables, however, there is no model, so you need to provide some more specifics in the form of columns, data types, and special operators.

Let's look at more extended syntax:

```
CREATE TABLE [database_name.[owner].]table_name
(<column name> <data type>
[[DEFAULT <constant expression>]
    |[IDENTITY [(seed, increment) [NOT FOR REPLICATION]]]]
    [ROWGUIDCOL]
    [COLLATE <collation name>]
    [NULL|NOT NULL]
    [<column constraints>]
    |[column_name AS computed_column_expression]
    |[<table_constraint>]
    [,...n]
)
[ON {<filegroup>|DEFAULT}]
[TEXTIMAGE_ON {<filegroup>|DEFAULT}]
```

Now that's a handful — and it still has sections taken out of it for simplicity's sake! As usual, let's look at the parts, starting with the second line (you've already seen the top line).

Table and Column Names

What's in a name? Frankly — a lot. You may recall that one of my first soapbox diatribes was back in Chapter 2 and was about names. I promised then that it wouldn't be the last you heard from me on the subject, and this won't be either.

The rules for naming tables and columns are, in general, the same rules that apply to all database objects. The SQL Server documentation will refer to these as the *rules for identifiers*, and they are the same rules you observed at the end of Chapter 1. The rules are actually pretty simple; what I want to touch on here, though, are some notions about how exactly to name your objects — not specific rules governing what SQL Server will and won't accept for names, but how to go about naming your tables and columns so that they are useful and make sense.

There are a ton of different "standards" out there for naming database objects — particularly tables and columns. My rules are pretty simple:

➤ **Capitalization:** For each word in the name, capitalize the first letter and use lowercase for the remaining letters.

➤ **Name length:** Keep the name short, but make it long enough to be descriptive.

➤ **Limit the use of abbreviations:** The only acceptable use of abbreviations is when the chosen abbreviation is recognized by everyone. Examples of abbreviations I use include "ID" to take the place of identification, "No" or "Num" (pick one) to take the place of number, and "Org" to take the place of organization. Keeping your names of reasonable length requires you to be more cavalier about your abbreviations sometimes, but keep in mind that, first and foremost, you want clarity in your names.

➤ **Linking tables:** When building tables based on other tables (usually called linking or associate tables), you should include the names of all parent tables in your new table name. For example, say you have a movie database where many stars can appear in many movies. If you have a `Movies` table and a `Stars` table, you may want to tie them together using a table called `MoviesStars`.

➤ **Eliminate spacing between words:** When you have two words in the name, do not use any separators (run the words together) — use the fact that you capitalize the first letter of each new word to determine how to separate words.

I can't begin to tell you the battles I've had with other database people about naming issues. For example, you'll find that a good many people believe that you should separate the words in your names with an underscore (_). Why don't I do it that way? Well, it's an ease of use issue. Underscores present a couple of different problems:

➤ First, many people have a difficult time typing an underscore without taking their hand away from the proper keyboard position — this leads to lots of typos.

➤ Second, in documentation it is not uncommon to run into situations where the table or column name is underlined. Underscores are, depending on the font, impossible to see when the text is underlined — this leads to confusion and more errors.

➤ Finally (and this is a nit-pick), it's just more typing.

NOTE *You also have the option to separate the words in the name using a regular space. If you recall my very first soapbox diatribe back in Chapter 1, you'll know that isn't really much of an option — it is extremely bad practice and creates an unbelievable number of errors. It was added to facilitate Access upsizing, and I continue to curse the people who decided to put it in — I'm sure they were well-meaning, but they are now part of the cause of much grief in the database world.*

This list is certainly not set in stone; rather it is just a *Reader's Digest* version of the rules I use when naming tables. I find that they save me a great deal of grief. I hope they'll do the same for you.

NOTE *Consistency, consistency, consistency. Every time I teach, I always warn my class that it's a word I'm going to repeat over and over, and in no place is it more important than in naming. If you have to pick one rule to follow, pick a rule that says that whatever your standards are, make them just that: standard. If you decide to abbreviate for some reason, abbreviate that word every time (the same way). Regardless of what you're doing in your naming, make it apply to the entire database consistently — consider having a standards document or style guide to make sure other developers utilize the same rules you do. This will save a ton of mistakes, and it will save your users time in terms of how long it takes for them to get to know the database.*

Data Types

There isn't much to this — the data types are as I described them in Chapter 2. You just need to provide a data type immediately following the column name — there is no default data type.

DEFAULT

I'll cover this in much more detail in the chapter on constraints, but for now, suffice to say that this is the value you want to use for any rows that are inserted without a user-supplied value for this particular column. The default, if you use one, should immediately follow the data type.

IDENTITY

The concept of an *identity* value is very important in database design. I will cover how to use identity columns in some detail in the chapters on design. What is an identity column? Well, when you make a column an identity column, SQL Server automatically assigns a sequenced number to this column with every row you insert. The number that SQL Server starts counting from is called the *seed* value, and the amount that the value increases or decreases by with each row is called the *increment*. The default is for a seed of 1 and an increment of 1, and most designs call for it to be left that way. As an example, however, you could have a seed of 3 and an increment of 5. In this case, you would start counting from 3, and then add 5 each time for 8, 13, 18, 23, and so on.

An identity column must be numeric, and, in practice, it is almost always implemented with an `integer` or `bigint` data type.

The usage is pretty simple; you simply include the `IDENTITY` keyword right after the data type for the column. An identity option cannot be used in conjunction with a default constraint. This makes sense if you think about it — how can there be a constant default if you're counting up or down every time?

> **NOTE** *It's worth noting that an identity column works sequentially. That is, once you've set a seed (the starting point) and the increment, your values only go up (or down if you set the increment to a negative number). There is no automatic mechanism to go back and fill in the numbers for any rows you may have deleted. If you want to fill in blank spaces like that, you need to use* SET IDENTITY_INSERT ON, *which allows you to turn off the identity process for inserts from the current connection. (Yes, turning it "on" turns it off — that is, you are turning on the ability to insert your own values, which has the effect of turning off the automatic value.) This can, however, create havoc if you're not careful or if people are still trying to use the system as you do this, so tread carefully.*

The most common use for an identity column is to generate a new value for use as an identifier for each row — that is, you commonly utilize identity columns to create a primary key for a table. Keep in mind, however, that an `IDENTITY` column and a `PRIMARY KEY` are completely separate notions — that is, just because you have an `IDENTITY` column doesn't mean that the value is unique (for example, you can reset the seed value and count back up through values you've used before). IDENTITY values are *typically* used as the PRIMARY KEY column, but they don't *have* to be used that way.

> **NOTE** *If you've come from the Access world, you'll notice that an* IDENTITY *column is much like an* AutoNumber *column. The major difference is that you have a bit more control over it in SQL Server.*

NOT FOR REPLICATION

This one is very tough to deal with at this point, so I am, at least in part, going to skip most of the details. Replication is a notion that's not covered in this book, so "not for replication" is going to lack context.

> **NOTE** *Briefly, replication is the process of automatically doing what, in a very loose sense, amounts to copying some or all of the information in your database to some other database. The other database may be on the same physical machine as the original, or it may be located remotely.*

The NOT FOR REPLICATION parameter determines whether a new identity value for the new database is assigned when the column is published to another database (via replication), or whether it keeps its existing value. There is a lot more to this when you start learning about SQL Server 2012's "Always On" capabilities, but that's more of an administrative than a programming topic. If you want to learn more, I suggest *Professional Microsoft SQL Server 2012 Administration* by Adam Jorgensen.

ROWGUIDCOL

This is also replication related and, in many ways, is the same in purpose to an identity column. You've already seen how using an identity column can provide you with an easy way to make sure that you have a value that is unique to each row and can, therefore, be used to identify that row. However, this can be a very error-prone solution when you are dealing with replicated or other distributed environments.

Think about it for a minute — while an identity column will keep counting upward from a set value, what's to keep the values from overlapping on different databases? Now, think about when you try to replicate the values such that all the rows that were previously in separate databases now reside in one database — uh oh! You now have duplicate values in the column that is supposed to uniquely identify each row!

Over the years, the common solution for this was to use separate seed values for each database you were replicating to and from. For example, you may have database A that starts counting at 1, database B starts at 10,000, and database C starts at 20,000. You can now publish them all into the same database safely — for a while. As soon as database A has more than 9,999 records inserted into it, you're in big trouble.

"Sure," you say, "why not just separate the values by 100,000 or 500,000?" If you have tables with a large amount of activity, you're still just delaying the inevitable — that's where a ROWGUIDCOL comes into play.

What is a ROWGUIDCOL? Well, it's quite a bit like an identity column in that it is usually used to uniquely identify each row in a table. The difference is to what lengths the system goes to make sure that the value used is truly unique. Instead of using a numerical count, SQL Server instead uses what is known as a *unique identifier* (in fact, GUID stands for Globally Unique Identifier). While an identity value is usually (unless you alter something) unique across time, it is not unique across space. Therefore, you can have two copies of your table running, and can have them both assigned identical identity values for what are different rows. While this is just fine to start with, it causes big problems when you try to bring the rows from both tables together as one replicated table. A unique identifier, sometimes still referred to as a *GUID*, is unique across both space and time.

> **NOTE** GUIDs (or, more commonly today, UUIDs — which look the same and do a better job at performing the same task) are in widespread use in computing today. For example, if you check the registry, you'll find tons of them. A GUID is a 128-bit value — for you math types, that's 38 zeros in decimal form. If I generated a GUID every second, it would, theoretically speaking, take me millions of years to generate a duplicate given a number of that size.
>
> GUIDs are generated using a combination of information — each of which is designed to be unique in either space or time. When you combine them, you come up with a value that is guaranteed, statistically speaking, to be unique across space and time.

There is a Windows API call to generate a GUID in normal programming, but, in addition to the ROWGUIDCOL option on a column, SQL has a special function to return a GUID — it is called the NEWID() function, and can be called at any time.

COLLATE

This works pretty much just as it did for the CREATE DATABASE command, with the primary difference being in terms of scope (here, you define at the column level rather than the database level).

NULL/NOT NULL

This one is pretty simple — it states whether or not the column in question accepts NULL values. The default, when you first install SQL Server, is to set a column to NOT NULL if you don't specify nullability. There is, however, a very large number of settings that can affect this default and change its behavior. For example, setting a value by using the sp_dbcmptlevel stored procedure or setting ANSI-compliance options can change this value.

TIP *I highly recommend explicitly stating the* NULL *option for every column in every table you ever build. Why? As I mentioned, there is a large number of settings that can affect what the system uses for a default for the nullability of a column. If you rely on these defaults, you may find later that your scripts don't seem to work right (because you or someone else has changed a relevant setting without realizing its full effect).*

Column Constraints

There's a whole chapter coming up on constraints, so I won't spend that much time on them here. Still, it seems like a good time to review the question of what column constraints are — in short, they are restrictions and rules that you place on individual columns about the data that can be inserted into that column.

For example, if you have a column that's supposed to store the month of the year, you might define that column as being of type `tinyint` — but that wouldn't prevent someone from inserting the number 54 in that column. Because 54 would give you bad data (it doesn't refer to a month), you might provide a constraint that says that data in that column must be between 1 and 12. You'll see how to do this in the next chapter.

Computed Columns

You can also have a column that doesn't have any data of its own, but whose value is derived on the fly from other columns in the table. If you think about it, this may seem odd because you could just figure it out at query time, but really, this is something of a boon for many applications.

For example, let's say that you're working on an invoicing system. You want to store information about the quantity of an item you have sold, and at what price. It used to be fairly commonplace to go ahead and add columns to store this information, along with another column that stored the extended value (price times quantity). However, that leads to unnecessary wasting of disk space and maintenance hassles when the totals and the base values get out of synch. With a computed column, you can get around that by defining the value of the computed column as price multiplied by quantity.

Let's look at the specific syntax:

```
<column name> AS <computed column expression>
```

The first item is a little different; it provides a column name to go with the value. This is simply the alias that you're going to use to refer to the value that is computed, based on the expression that follows the AS keyword.

Next comes the computed column expression. The expression can be any normal expression that uses either literals or column values from the same tables. Therefore, in the example of price and quantity, you might define this column as:

```
ExtendedPrice AS Price * Quantity
```

For an example using a literal, let's say that you always charge a fixed markup on your goods that is 20 percent over your cost. You could simply keep track of cost in one column, and then use a computed column for the `ListPrice` column:

```
ListPrice AS Cost * 1.2
```

Pretty easy, eh? There are a few caveats and provisos though:

➤ You cannot use a subquery, and the values cannot come from a different table.

➤ You cannot directly specify the data type of a computed column; it is implicitly of whatever type the expression produces. That said, you can use CAST or CONVERT as part of your expression to explicitly impose a type on the result.

➤ In SQL Server 2000 and earlier, you could not use a computed column as any part of any key (primary, foreign, or unique) or with a default constraint. For SQL Server 2005 and later, you can now use a computed column in constraints (you must flag the computed column as persisted if you do this, however).

➤ Special steps must be taken if you want to create indexes on computed columns. You'll learn about these steps when you explore indexing in Chapter 9.

There will be plenty of specific examples of how to use computed columns a little later in this chapter.

> **NOTE** *Even years after computed columns were added to the product, I'm still rather surprised that I don't hear much debate about the use of them. Rules for normalization of data say that we should not have a column in our table for information that can be derived from other columns — that's exactly what a computed column is!*
>
> *I'm glad the religious zealots of normalization haven't weighed in on this one much, as I like computed columns as something of a compromise. By default, you aren't storing the data twice, and you don't have issues with the derived values not agreeing with the base values because they are calculated on the fly directly from the base values. However, you still get the end result you wanted. Note that if you index the computed column, you are indeed actually storing the data (you have to for the index). This, however, has its own benefits when it comes to read performance.*
>
> *This isn't the way to do everything related to derived data, but it sure is an excellent helper for many situations.*

Table Constraints

Table constraints are quite similar to column constraints, in that they place restrictions on the data that can be inserted into the table. What makes them a little different is that they may be based on more than one column.

Again, I will be covering these in the constraints chapter (Chapter 6), but examples of table-level constraints include PRIMARY and FOREIGN KEY constraints, as well as CHECK constraints.

NOTE *Okay, so why is a* CHECK *constraint a table constraint? Isn't it a column constraint because it affects what you can place in a given column? The answer is that it's both. If it is based on solely one column, it meets the rules for a column constraint. If, however (as* CHECK *constraints can be), it is dependent on multiple columns, you have what would be referred to as a table constraint.*

ON

Remember when you were dealing with database creation, and I said you could create different filegroups? Well, the ON clause in a table definition is a way of specifically stating on which filegroup (and, therefore, physical device) you want the table located. You can place a given table on a specific physical device or, as you will want to do in most cases, just leave the ON clause out, and it's placed on whatever the default filegroup is (which is the PRIMARY unless you've set it to something else). You will be looking at this usage extensively in the Chapter 9, which deals with indexes and performance tuning.

TEXTIMAGE_ON

This one is basically the same as the ON clause you just looked at, except that it lets you move a very specific part of the table to yet a different filegroup. This clause is valid only if your table definition has large column(s) in it, including the following:

➤ text or ntext

➤ image

➤ xml

➤ varchar(max) or nvarchar(max)

➤ varbinary(max)

➤ Any CLR user-defined type columns (including geometry and geography)

When you use the TEXTIMAGE_ON clause, you move only the BLOB information into the separate filegroup — the rest of the table stays either on the default filegroup or with the filegroup chosen in the ON clause.

TIP *There can be some serious performance increases to be had by splitting your database into multiple files, and then storing those files on separate physical disks. When you do this, it means you get the I/O from both drives. Major discussion of this is outside the scope of this book, but keep this in mind as something to gather more information about should you run into I/O performance issues.*

Creating a Table

All right, you've seen plenty; you're ready for some action, so now you can build a few tables.

When you started this section, you looked at the standard CREATE syntax of:

```
CREATE <object type> <object name>
```

And then you moved on to a more specific start (indeed, it's the first line of the statement that creates the table) and created a table called Customers:

```
CREATE TABLE Customers
```

Your Customers table is going to be the first table in a database you will be putting together to track your company's accounting. You'll be looking at designing a database in a couple of chapters, but you can go ahead and get started on your database by building a couple of tables to learn the CREATE TABLE statement. You'll look at most of the concepts of table construction in this section, but I'll save a few for later on in the book. That being said, let's get started building the first of several tables.

You'll want to add in a USE *<database name>* line prior to the CREATE code to ensure that when you run the script, the table is created in the proper database. You can then follow up that first line, which you've already seen, with a few columns.

> **NOTE** *Any script you create for regular use with a particular database should include a* USE *command with the name of that database. This ensures that you really are creating, altering, and dropping the objects in the database you intend. More than once, I've been the victim of my own stupidity when I blindly opened a script and executed it only to find that the wrong database was current, and any tables with the same name had been dropped (thus losing all data) and replaced by a new layout. You can also tell when other people have done this by taking a look around the master database — you'll often find several extraneous tables in that database from people running* CREATE *scripts that were meant to go somewhere else.*

```
USE Accounting
CREATE TABLE Customers
(
    CustomerNo      int           IDENTITY  NOT NULL,
    CustomerName    varchar(30)             NOT NULL,
    Address1        varchar(30)             NOT NULL,
    Address2        varchar(30)             NOT NULL,
    City            varchar(20)             NOT NULL,
    State           char(2)                 NOT NULL,
    Zip             varchar(10)             NOT NULL,
```

```
Contact        varchar(25)              NOT NULL,
Phone          char(15)                 NOT NULL,
FedIDNo        varchar(9)               NOT NULL,
DateInSystem   date            NOT NULL
)
```

This is a somewhat simplified table compared to what you would probably use in real life, but there's plenty of time to change it later (and you will).

Once you've built the table, you'll want to verify that it was indeed created, and that it has all the columns and types that you expect. To do this, you can make use of several commands, but perhaps the best is one that will seem like an old friend before you're done with this book: sp_help. The syntax is simple:

```
EXEC sp_help <object name>
```

To specify the table object that you just created, try executing the following code:

```
EXEC sp_help Customers
```

Available for download on Wrox.com

Code snippet Chap05.sql

You use the EXEC command in two different ways. This rendition executes a stored procedure — in this case, a system stored procedure. You'll see the second version later when you are dealing with advanced query topics and stored procedures in Chapters 11 and 12.

> **NOTE** *Technically speaking, you can execute a stored procedure by simply calling it (without using the EXEC keyword). The problem is that this works only if the sproc being called is the first statement of any kind in the batch. Just having sp_help Customers would have worked in the place of the previous code, but if you tried to run a SELECT statement before it — it would blow up on you. Not using EXEC leads to very unpredictable behavior and should be avoided.*

Try executing the command, and you'll find that you get back several result sets, one after another. The information retrieved includes separate result sets for:

➤ Table name, schema, type of table (system versus user), and creation date

➤ Column names, data types, nullability, size, and collation

➤ The identity column (if one exists), including the *initial* seed and increment values

➤ The ROWGUIDCOL (if one exists)

➤ Filegroup information

➤ Index names (if any exist), types, and included columns

➤ Constraint names (if any), types, and included columns

➤ Foreign key (if any) names and columns

➤ The names of any schema-bound views (more on this in Chapter 10) that depend on the table

Now that you're certain that your table was created, let's take a look at creating yet another table — the Employees table. This time, let's talk about what you want in the table first, and then you can try to code the CREATE script for yourself.

The Employees table is another fairly simple table. It should include information on:

➤ The employee's ID — this should be automatically generated by the system

➤ First name

➤ Optionally, middle initial

➤ Last name

➤ Title

➤ Social Security number

➤ Salary

➤ The previous salary

➤ The amount of the last raise

➤ Date of hire

➤ Date terminated (if there is one)

➤ The employee's manager

➤ Department

Start by trying to figure out a layout for yourself.

Before we start looking at this together, let me tell you not to worry too much if your layout isn't exactly like mine. There are as many database designs as there are database designers — and that all begins with table design. We all can have different solutions to the same problem. What you want to look for is whether you have all the concepts that need to be addressed. That being said, let's take a look at one way to build this table.

There is at least one special column here. The EmployeeID is to be generated by the system and therefore is an excellent candidate for either an identity column or a ROWGUIDCOL. There are several reasons you might want to go one way or the other between these two, but I'll go with an identity column for a couple of reasons:

➤ It's going to be used by an average person. (Would you want to have to remember a GUID?)

➤ It incurs lower overhead.

You're now ready to start constructing your script. Here's the start of mine:

```
CREATE TABLE Employees
(
    EmployeeID        int             IDENTITY  NOT NULL,
```

For this column, the NOT NULL option has essentially been chosen by virtue of using an IDENTITY column. You cannot allow NULL values in an IDENTITY column. Note that, depending on your server settings, you will, most likely, still need to include NOT NULL explicitly (if you leave it to the default you may get an error depending on whether the default allows NULLs).

Next up, you want to add in your name columns. I usually allow approximately 25 characters for names. Most names are far shorter than that, but I've bumped into enough that were rather lengthy (especially because hyphenated names have become so popular) that I allow for the extra room. In addition, I make use of a variable-length data type for two reasons:

➤ To recapture the space of a column that is defined somewhat longer than the actual data usually is (retrieve blank space)

➤ To simplify searches in the WHERE clause — fixed-length columns are padded with spaces, which requires extra planning when performing comparisons against fields of this type

The exception in this case is the middle initial. Because you really need to allow for only one character here, recapture of space is not an issue. Indeed, a variable-length data type would actually use more space in this case, because a varchar needs not only the space to store the data, but also a small amount of overhead space to keep track of how long the data is. In addition, ease of search is not an issue because if you have any value in the field at all, there isn't enough room left for padded spaces.

> **NOTE** For the code that you write directly in T-SQL, SQL Server automatically adjusts to the padded spaces issue — that is, an xx placed in a char(5) is treated as being equal (if compared) to an xx placed in a varchar(5) — this is not, however, true in your client APIs such as SqlNativeClient and ADO.NET. If you connect to a char(5) in ADO.NET, an xx will evaluate to xx with three spaces after it — if you compare it to xx, it will evaluate to False. An xx placed in a varchar(5), however, will automatically have any trailing spaces trimmed, and comparing it to xx in ADO.NET will evaluate to True.

Because a name for an employee is a critical item, I will not allow any NULL values in the first and last name columns. The middle initial is not nearly so critical (indeed, some people in the United States don't have a middle name at all, while my wife has two, and I hear that it's not uncommon for Brits to have several), so let's allow a NULL for that field only:

```
    FirstName        varchar(25)        NOT NULL,
    MiddleInitial    char(1)            NULL,
    LastName         varchar(25)        NOT NULL,
```

> **NOTE** NOT NULL *does not mean not empty. Were you to encounter a fellow with no last name — let's take the musician, Sting, for example — you could add an entry with an empty string (' ') for a last name if you wished. This is a normal situation, where you design for the rule and handle the exception. You could build in enough flexibility to perfectly handle every possible situation, but is this unwieldy design worth it, given the rarity of the case? As always with SQL, it depends on your exact situation, but in general I'll repeat — design for the rule and handle the exception.*

Next up is the employee's title. You must know what they are doing if you're going to be cutting them a paycheck, so you can also make this a required field:

```
Title           varchar(25)         NOT NULL,
```

In that same paycheck vein, you must know their Social Security number (or similar identification number outside the United States) in order to report for taxes. In this case, you can use a `varchar` and allow up to 11 characters, as these identification numbers are different lengths in different countries. If you know your application is going to require only SSNs from the United States, you'll probably want to make it `char(11)` instead:

```
SSN             varchar(11)         NOT NULL,
```

You must know how much to pay the employees — that seems simple enough — but what comes next is a little different. When you add in the prior salary and the amount of the last raise, you get into a situation where you could use a computed column. The new salary is the sum of the previous salary and the amount of the last raise. The `Salary` amount is something that you might use quite regularly — indeed you might want an index on it to help with ranged queries, but for various reasons I don't want to do that here (I'll talk about the ramifications of indexes on computed columns in Chapter 9), so I'm going to use `LastRaise` as my computed column:

```
Salary          money               NOT NULL,
PriorSalary     money               NOT NULL,
LastRaise AS Salary - PriorSalary,
```

If you hired them, you must know the date of hire — so that will also be required:

```
HireDate        date                NOT NULL,
```

Note that I've chosen to use a `date` data type rather than the older standard `datetime` to save space. The `datetime` data type stores both date and time information down to fractions of a second. However, because you're primarily interested in the date of hire, not the time, the `date` will meet your needs and take up half the space.

NOTE *Be aware that the* date, time, *and* datetime2 *data types (as opposed to the more venerable* datetime *and* smalldatetime *data types) were new with SQL Server 2008. If you need to remain backward compatible with previous versions, you'll need to stick with the* datetime *and* smalldatetime *data types.*

The date of termination is something you may not know (I'd like to think that some employees are still working for you), so you'll need to leave it nullable:

```
TerminationDate   date                    NULL,
```

You absolutely want to know who the employees are reporting to (somebody must have hired them!) and what department they are working in:

```
    ManagerEmpID      int                     NOT NULL,
    Department        varchar(25)             NOT NULL
)
```

So, just for clarity, let's look at the entire script required to create this table:

```
USE Accounting

CREATE TABLE Employees
(
    EmployeeID        int             IDENTITY  NOT NULL,
    FirstName         varchar(25)               NOT NULL,
    MiddleInitial     char(1)                   NULL,
    LastName          varchar(25)               NOT NULL,
    Title             varchar(25)               NOT NULL,
    SSN               varchar(11)               NOT NULL,
    Salary            money                     NOT NULL,
    PriorSalary       money                     NOT NULL,
    LastRaise AS Salary - PriorSalary,
    HireDate          date                      NOT NULL,
    TerminationDate   date                      NULL,
    ManagerEmpID      int                       NOT NULL,
    Department        varchar(25)               NOT NULL
)
```

Again, I would recommend executing sp_help on this table to verify that the table was created as you expected.

THE ALTER STATEMENT

Okay, so now you have a database and a couple of nice tables — isn't life grand? If only things always stayed the same, but they don't. Sometimes (actually, far more often than you would like), you'll get requests to *change* a table rather than re-create it. Likewise, you may need to change the size, file locations, or some other feature of your database. That's where the ALTER statement comes in.

Much like the CREATE statement, the ALTER statement almost always starts out the same:

```
ALTER <object type> <object name>
```

This is totally boring so far, but it won't stay that way. You'll see the beginnings of issues with this statement right away, and things will get really interesting (read: convoluted and confusing!) when you deal with this even further in the next chapter (when you deal with constraints).

ALTER DATABASE

Let's get right into it by taking a look at changing your database. You'll actually make a couple of changes just so you can see the effects of different things and how their syntax can vary.

Perhaps the biggest trick with the ALTER statement is to remember what you already have. With that in mind, let's take a look again at what you already have:

```
EXEC sp_helpdb Accounting
```

Notice that I didn't put the quotation marks in this time as I did when you used this stored proc earlier. That's because this system procedure, like many of them, accepts a special data type called sysname. As long as what you pass in is a name of a valid object in the system, the quotes are optional for this data type.

So, the results should be just like they were when you created the database (see the next two tables):

NAME	DB_ SIZE	OWNER	DBID	CREATED	STATUS	COMPATI-BILITY_ LEVEL
Account-ing	15.00MB	BEGINNING SQL201\ Paul Atkinson	9	Dec 5 2011	Status=ONLINE, Updateability= READ_WRITE, UserAccess= MULTI_USER, Recovery=FULL, Version=705, Collation= SQL_Latin1_ General_CP1_ CI_AS, SQLSortOrder=52, IsAutoCreate Statistics, IsAutoUpdate Statistics, IsFullTextEnabled	110

And . . .

NAME	FILEID	FILENAME	FILE-GROUP	SIZE	MAXSIZE	GROWTH	USAGE
Account-ing	1	c:\Program Files\ Microsoft SQL Server\ MSSQL11. MSSQLSERVER\ MSSQL\DATA\ Accounting Data.mdf	PRI-MARY	10240BK	51200KB	5120KB	data only
Account-ingLog	2	c:\Program Files\ Microsoft SQL Server\ MSSQL11. MSSQLSERVER\ MSSQL\DATA\ Accounting-Log.ldf	NULL	5120KB	25600KB	5120KB	log only

Let's say you want to change things a bit. For example, let's say that you know that you are going to be doing a large import into your database. Currently, your database is only 15MB in size — that doesn't hold much these days. Because you have Autogrow turned on, you could just start your import, and SQL Server would automatically enlarge the database 5MB at a time. Keep in mind, however, that it's actually a fair amount of work to reallocate the size of the database. If you were inserting 100MB worth of data, the server would have to deal with that reallocation at least 16 times (at 20MB, 25MB, 30MB, and so on). Because you know that you're going to be getting up to 100MB of data, why not just do it in one shot? To do this, you would use the ALTER DATABASE command.

The general syntax looks like this:

```
ALTER DATABASE <database name>
    ADD FILE
        ([NAME = <'logical file name'>,]
        FILENAME = <'file name'>
```

```
        [, SIZE = <size in KB, MB, GB or TB>]
        [, MAXSIZE = < size in KB, MB, GB or TB >]
        [, FILEGROWTH = <No of KB, MB, GB or TB |percentage>]) [,...n]
              [ TO FILEGROUP filegroup_name]
  [, OFFLINE ]

    |ADD LOG FILE
        ([NAME = <'logical file name'>,]
         FILENAME = <'file name'>
         [, SIZE = < size in KB, MB, GB or TB >]
         [, MAXSIZE = < size in KB, MB, GB or TB >]
         [, FILEGROWTH = <No KB, MB, GB or TB |percentage>])
    |REMOVE FILE <logical file name> [WITH DELETE]
    |ADD FILEGROUP <filegroup name>
    |REMOVE FILEGROUP <filegroup name>
    |MODIFY FILE <filespec>
    |MODIFY NAME = <new dbname>
    |MODIFY FILEGROUP <filegroup name> {<filegroup property>|NAME =
              <new filegroup name>}
    |SET <optionspec> [,...n ][WITH <termination>]
    |COLLATE <collation name>
```

The reality is that you will very rarely use all that stuff — sometimes I think Microsoft just puts it there for the sole purpose of confusing the heck out of us (just kidding!).

So, after looking at all that gobbledygook, let's just worry about what you need to expand your database to 100MB:

```
ALTER DATABASE Accounting
    MODIFY FILE
    (NAME = Accounting,
     SIZE = 100MB)
```

Code snippet Chap05.sql

Note that, unlike when you created your database, you don't get any information about the allocation of space — instead, you get the rather non-verbose:

```
The command(s) completed successfully.
```

Gee — how informative. . . . So, you'd better check on things for yourself (see the text two tables):

```
EXEC sp_helpdb Accounting
```

NAME	DB_ SIZE	OWNER	DBID	CREATED	STATUS	COMPATIB-ILITY_ LEVEL
Accounting	105.00 MB	BEGINNING SQL201 \Paul Atkinson	9	Dec 5 2011	Status=ONLINE, Updateability= READ_WRITE, UserAccess= MULTI_USER, Recovery=FULL, Version=705, Collation= SQL_Latin1_ General_ CP1_CI_AS, SQLSortOrder=52, IsAutoCreate Statistics, IsAutoUpdate Statistics, IsFullTextEnabled	110

And

NAME	FILEID	FILENAME	FILE-GROUP	SIZE	MAXSIZE	GROWTH	USAGE
Accounting	1	c:\Program Files\ Microsoft SQL Server\ MSSQL11. MSSQLSERVER\ MSSQL\DATA\ Accounting-Data.mdf	PRIMARY	102400 KB	102400 KB	5120 KB	data only
AccountingLog	2	c:\Program Files\ Microsoft SQL Server\ MSSQL11. MSSQLSERVER\ MSSQL\DATA\ Accounting-Log.ldf	NULL	5120 KB	25600 KB	5120 KB	log only

Things pretty much work the same for any of the more common database-level modifications you'll make. The permutations are, however, endless. The more complex filegroup modifications and the like are outside the scope of this book, but if you need more information on them, I recommend one of the more administrator-oriented books out there (and there are a ton of them).

Option and Termination Specs

SQL Server has a few options that can be set with an ALTER DATABASE statement. Among these are database-specific defaults for most of the SET options that are available (such as ANSI_PADDING, ARITHABORT — handy if you're dealing with indexed or partitioned views), state options (for example, single user mode or read-only), and recovery options. The effects of the various SET options are discussed where they are relevant throughout the book. This new ALTER functionality simply gives you an additional way to change the defaults for any particular database.

SQL Server also has the ability to control the implementation of some of the changes you are trying to make on your database. Many changes require that you have exclusive control over the database — something that can be hard to deal with if other users are already in the system. SQL Server gives you the ability to gracefully force other users out of the database so that you can complete your database changes. The strength of these actions ranges from waiting a number of seconds (you decide how long) before kicking other users out, all the way up to immediate termination of any option transactions (automatically rolling them back). Relatively uncontrolled (from the client's perspective) termination of transactions is not something to be taken lightly. Such an action is usually in the realm of the database administrator. As such, I will consider further discussion out of the scope of this book.

ALTER TABLE

A far, far more common need is the situation where you need to change the makeup of one of your tables. This can range from simple things like adding a new column to more complex issues such as changing a data type.

Let's start by taking a look at the basic syntax for changing a table:

```
ALTER TABLE table_name
    {[ALTER COLUMN <column_name>
        { [<schema of new data type>].<new_data_type>
            [(precision [, scale])] max |
<xml schema collection>
        [COLLATE <collation_name>]
        [NULL|NOT NULL]
        |[{ADD|DROP} ROWGUIDCOL] | PERSISTED}]
    |ADD
        <column name> <data_type>
        [[DEFAULT <constant_expression>]
        |[IDENTITY [(<seed>, <increment>) [NOT FOR REPLICATION]]]]
        [ROWGUIDCOL]
        [COLLATE <collation_name>]
            [NULL|NOT NULL]
        [<column_constraints>]
        |[<column_name> AS <computed_column_expression>]
    |ADD
```

```
                   [CONSTRAINT <constraint_name>]
                   {[{PRIMARY KEY|UNIQUE}
                       [CLUSTERED|NONCLUSTERED]
                       {(<column_name>[ ,...n ])}
                       [WITH FILLFACTOR = <fillfactor>]
                       [ON {<filegroup> | DEFAULT}]
                       ]
                       |FOREIGN KEY
                          [(<column_name>[ ,...n])]
                          REFERENCES <referenced_table> [(<referenced_column>[ ,...n])]
                          [ON DELETE {CASCADE|NO ACTION}]
                          [ON UPDATE {CASCADE|NO ACTION}]
                          [NOT FOR REPLICATION]
                       |DEFAULT <constant_expression>
                          [FOR <column_name>]
                       |CHECK [NOT FOR REPLICATION]
                          (<search_conditions>)
                     [,...n][ ,...n]
                       |[WITH CHECK|WITH NOCHECK]
              | { ENABLE | DISABLE } TRIGGER
                  { ALL | <trigger name> [ ,...n ] }

          |DROP
              {[CONSTRAINT] <constraint_name>
                  |COLUMN <column_name>}[ ,...n]
              |{CHECK|NOCHECK} CONSTRAINT
                  {ALL|<constraint_name>[ ,...n]}
              |{ENABLE|DISABLE} TRIGGER
                  {ALL|<trigger_name>[ ,...n]}
          | SWITCH [ PARTITION <source partition number expression> ]
              TO [ schema_name. ] target_table
              [ PARTITION <target partition number expression> ]
      }
```

As with the CREATE TABLE command, there's quite a handful there to deal with.

So let's start an example of using this by looking back at the Employees table in the Accounting database:

```
EXEC sp_help Employees
```

Code snippet Chap05.sql

For the sake of saving a few trees, I'm going to edit the results that I show here in the next table to just the part you care about — you'll actually see much more than this:

COLUMN_NAME	TYPE	COMPUTED	LENGTH	PREC	SCALE	NULLABLE
EmployeeID	int	no	4	10	0	no
FirstName	varchar	no	25			no
MiddleInitial	char	no	1			yes

continues

(continued)

COLUMN_NAME	TYPE	COMPUTED	LENGTH	PREC	SCALE	NULLABLE
LastName	varchar	no	25			no
Title	varchar	no	25			no
SSN	varchar	no	11			no
Salary	money	no	8	19	4	no
PriorSalary	money	no	8	19	4	no
LastRaise	money	yes	8	19	4	yes
HireDate	date	no	3		no	
TerminationDate	date	no	3			yes
ManagerEmpID	int	no	4	10	0	no
Department	varchar	no	25			no

Let's say that you've decided you'd like to keep previous employer information on your employees (probably so you know who will be trying to recruit the good ones back!). That just involves adding another column, and really isn't all that tough. The syntax looks much like it did with the CREATE TABLE statement except that it has obvious alterations to it:

```
ALTER TABLE Employees
    ADD
        PreviousEmployer    varchar(30)    NULL
```

Not exactly rocket science — is it? Indeed, you could have added several additional columns at one time if you had wanted to. It would look something like this:

```
ALTER TABLE Employees
    ADD
        DateOfBirth     date        NULL,
        LastRaiseDate   date        NOT NULL
            DEFAULT '2008-01-01'
```

Code snippet Chap05.sql

NOTE *Notice the* DEFAULT *I slid in here. You haven't really looked at these yet (they are in the next chapter), but I wanted to use one here to point out a special case.*

If you want to add a NOT NULL *column after the fact, you have the issue of what to do with rows that already have* NULL *values. I have shown one solution to that here by providing a default value. The default is then used to populate the new column for any row that is already in your table.*

Before you go away from this topic for now, take a look at what you've added:

```
EXEC sp_help Employees
```

Code snippet Chap05.sql

COLUMN_NAME	TYPE	COMPUTED	LENGTH	PREC	SCALE	NULLABLE
EmployeeID	int	no	4	10	0	no
FirstName	varchar	no	25			no
MiddleInitial	char	no	1			yes
LastName	varchar	no	25			no
Title	varchar	no	25			no
SSN	varchar	no	11			no
Salary	money	no	8	19	4	no
PriorSalary	money	no	8	19	4	no
LastRaise	money	yes	8	19	4	yes
HireDate	date	no	3			no
TerminationDate	date	no	3			yes
ManagerEmpID	int	no	4	10	0	no
Department	varchar	no	25			no
PreviousEmployer	varchar	no	30			yes
DateOfBirth	date	no	3			yes
LastRaiseDate	date	no	3			no

As you can see, all of your columns have been added. The thing to note, however, is that they all went to the end of the column list. There is no way to add a column to a specific location in SQL Server. If you want to move a column to the middle, you need to create a completely new table (with a different name), copy the data over to the new table, DROP the existing table, and then rename the new one.

NOTE *This issue of moving columns around can get very sticky indeed. Even some of the tools that are supposed to automate this often have problems with it. Why? Well, any foreign key constraints you have that reference this table must first be dropped before you are allowed to delete the current version of the table. That means that you have to drop all your foreign keys, make the changes, and then add all your foreign keys back. It doesn't end there, however; any indexes you have defined on the old table are automatically dropped when you drop the existing table — that means that you must remember to re-create your indexes as part of the build script to create your new version of the table — yuck!*

But wait! There's more! While you haven't really looked at views yet, I feel compelled to make a reference here to what happens to your views when you add a column. You should be aware that even if your view is built using a SELECT * *as its base statement, your new column will not appear in your view until you rebuild the view. Column names in views are resolved at the time the view is created for performance reasons. That means any views that have already been created when you add your columns have already resolved using the previous column list — you must either* DROP *and re-create the view or use an* ALTER VIEW *statement to rebuild it.*

THE DROP STATEMENT

Performing a DROP is the same as deleting whatever object(s) you reference in your DROP statement. It's very quick and easy, and the syntax is exactly the same for all of the major SQL Server objects (tables, views, sprocs, triggers, and so on). It goes like this:

```
DROP <object type> <object name> [, ...n]
```

Actually, this is about as simple as SQL statements get. You could drop both of your tables at the same time if you wanted:

Available for download on Wrox.com

```
USE Accounting

DROP TABLE Customers, Employees
```

Code snippet Chap05.sql

This deletes them both.

TIP *Be very careful with this command. There is no "Are you sure?" kind of question that goes with this — it just assumes you know what you're doing and deletes the object(s) in question.*

The syntax is very much the same for dropping the entire database. Now go ahead and drop the Accounting database:

```
USE master

DROP DATABASE Accounting
```

Code snippet Chap05.sql

You should see the following in the Results pane:

```
Command(s) completed successfully.
```

You may run into a situation where you get an error that says that the database cannot be deleted because it is in use. If this happens, check a couple of things:

➤ Make sure that the database that you have as current in the Management Studio is something other than the database you're trying to drop (that is, make sure you're not using the database as you're trying to drop it).

➤ Ensure you don't have any other connections open (using the Management Studio or sp_who) that are showing the database you're trying to drop as the current database.

I usually solve the first one just as I did in the code example — I switch to using the master database. The second issue you have to check manually — I usually close other sessions down entirely just to be sure. Of course, if one of those other sessions belongs to someone else, you may want to discuss things before dropping the database.

USING THE GUI TOOL

You've just spent a lot of time learning (or perhaps slogging through) perfect syntax for creating a database and a couple of tables — that's enough of that for a while. Let's take a look at the graphical tool in the Management Studio that allows you to build and relate tables. From this point on, you'll not only be dealing with code, but with the tool that can generate much of that code for you.

Creating a Database Using the Management Studio

If you run the SQL Server Management Studio and expand the Databases node, you should see something like Figure 5-1.

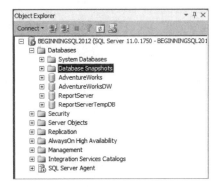

FIGURE 5-1

NOTE *If you look closely at Figure 5-1, you'll see that my Accounting database is still showing even though I dropped it in the previous example (just as you did yours). You might not wind up seeing this, depending on whether you already had the Management Studio open when you dropped the database or you opened it after you dropped the database in the Query window.*

Why the difference? Well, in earlier versions of SQL Server, the tools that are now the Management Studio refreshed information, such as the available databases, regularly. Now it updates only when it knows it has a reason to (for example, you deleted something by using the Management Studio Object Explorer instead of a Query window, or perhaps you explicitly chose to refresh). The reason for the change was performance. The old 6.5 Enterprise Manager used to be a slug performance-wise because it was constantly making round trips to "poll" the server. The newer approach performs much better, but doesn't necessarily have the most up-to-date information.

The bottom line on this is that if you see something in the Management Studio Object Explorer that you don't expect to, try clicking in there and pressing F5 (refresh). It should then update things for you.

Now follow these steps to create a database using Management Studio:

1. Right-click the Databases node, and choose the New Database option. This pulls up the Database Properties dialog box.

2. You can fill in the information on how you want your database created. Use the same choices that you did when you created the Accounting database at the beginning of the chapter. You need to fill in:

   ➤ **The basic name and size info:** This is shown in Figure 5-2. As far as the name goes — this is pretty basic. You called it Accounting before, and because you dropped the first one you created, there's no reason not to call it that again.

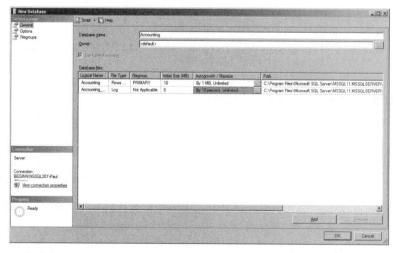

FIGURE 5-2

➤ The file name, size, and growth information.

NOTE *I've expanded the dialog box manually to make sure you can see everything. You may see less than what's pictured here, as the default size of the dialog box is not nearly enough to show it all — just grab a corner of the dialog box and expand it to see the additional information.*

3. Click Options tab, which contains a host of additional settings, as shown in Figure 5-3.

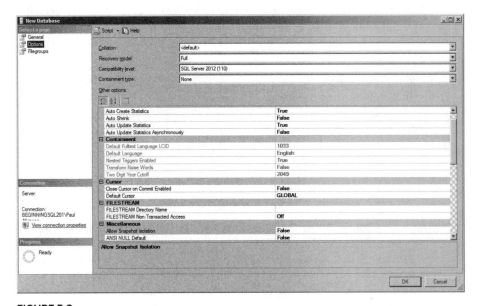

FIGURE 5-3

➤ **Collation name:** You have the choice of having each database (and, indeed, individual columns if you wish) have its own collation. For the vast majority of installs, you'll want to stick with whatever the server default was set to when the server was installed (presumably, someone had already thought this out fairly well, although if you weren't involved in the installation, it never hurts to ask). However, you can change it for just the current database by setting it here.

NOTE *"Why," you may ask, "would I want a different collation?" Well, in the English-speaking world, a common need for specific collations would be that some applications are written expecting an "a" to be the same as an "A" — while others are expecting case sensitivity ("a" is not the same as "A"). In the old days, you would have to have separate servers set up in order to handle this. Another, non-English example would be dialect differences that are found within many countries of the world — even where they speak the same general language.*

> ➤ **Compatibility level:** This controls whether certain SQL Server 2012 syntax and keywords are supported. As you might expect from the name of this setting, the goal is to allow you to roll back to keywords and functional behavior that more closely matches older versions if your particular application happens to need that. For example, as you roll it back to earlier versions, some words that are keywords in later versions revert to being treated as non-keywords, and certain behaviors that have had their defaults changed in recent releases will revert to the older default.

> ➤ **Containment:** As I said before, containment allows you to deploy a database with fewer dependencies on the target SQL instance. For this example, leave Containment set to None, the default.

4. The remaining properties will vary from install to install, but work as I described them earlier in the chapter. Okay, given that the other settings are pretty much standard fare, go ahead and try it out. Click OK, and after a brief pause during which the database is created, you'll see it added to the tree.

5. Expand the tree to show the various items underneath the Accounting node, and select the Database Diagrams node. Right-click it, and you'll get a dialog indicating that the database is missing some objects it needs to support database diagramming, as shown in Figure 5-4. Click Yes.

FIGURE 5-4

  NOTE *You should only see Figure 5-4 the first time a diagram is being created for that database. SQL Server keeps track of diagrams inside special tables that it creates in your database only if you are going to actually create a diagram that will use them.*

With that, you'll get an Add Table dialog, as shown in Figure 5-5. This lets you decide which tables you want to include in your diagram — you can create multiple diagrams if you wish, potentially each covering some subsection — or *submodel* — of the overall database schema. In this case, you have an empty list because you just created your database and it has no tables in it yet.

6. For now, just click Close (you can't add tables if there are no tables to add!), and you should get an empty diagram screen.

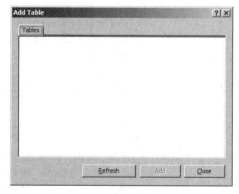

FIGURE 5-5

7. You can add a table either by right-clicking and choosing the appropriate option, or by clicking the New Table icon in the toolbar. When you choose New Table, SQL Server asks you for the name you want to give your new table. You then get a mildly helpful dialog box

that lets you fill in your table one piece at a time — complete with labels for what you need to fill out, as shown in Figure 5-6.

8. I've gone ahead and filled in the columns as they were in the original Customers table, but you also need to define your first column as being an identity column. Unfortunately, you don't appear to have any way of doing that with the default grid here. To change which items you can define for your table, you need to right-click in the editing dialog box, and select Table View ⇨ Modify Custom.

    You then get a list of items from which you can choose, as shown in Figure 5-7. For now, just select the extra item you need — Identity and its associated elements, Seed and Increment.

FIGURE 5-6

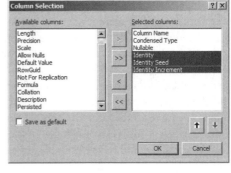

FIGURE 5-7

9. Go back to the editing dialog box and select Table View ⇨ Custom to view the identity column (see Figure 5-8). You're ready to fill in your table definition.

> **NOTE** Okay, so SQL Server can be a bit temperamental on this. If you do not check the box to make this the default, SQL Server changes what your "custom" view looks like, but it does not make the custom view the active one — the result is that you won't see the changes you made as you exit the dialog box. So, again, make sure that after changing the view, you right-click and select Table View ⇨ Custom again. It should then look like Figure 5-8.

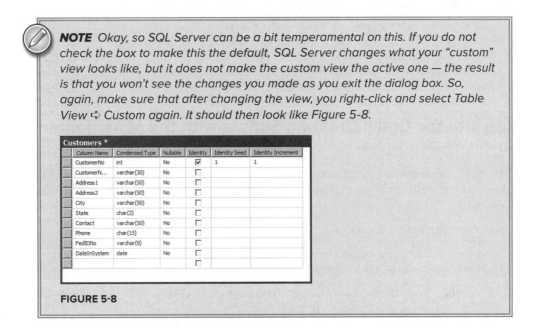

FIGURE 5-8

10.   Once you have the table filled out, you can save the changes, and that creates your table for you.

 NOTE *This is really a point of personal preference, but I prefer to set the view down to just column names at this point. You can do this by clicking the Show icon on the toolbar or, as I prefer, by right-clicking the table and choosing Table View ⇨ Column Names. I find that this saves a lot of screen real estate and makes more room for me to work on additional tables.*

Now try to add in the `Employees` table as it was defined earlier in the chapter. The steps should be pretty much as they were for the `Customers` table, with just one little hitch — you have a computed column. To deal with the computed column, just select Modify Custom again (from the right-click menu), and add the Formula column. Then, simply add the proper formula (in this case, Salary-PriorSalary). When you have all the columns entered, save your new table (accepting the confirmation dialog box). Your diagram should have two tables in it (see Figure 5-9).

FIGURE 5-9

 NOTE *It's very important to understand that the diagramming tool that is included with SQL Server is not designed to be everything to everyone.*

Presumably, because you are reading this part of this book, you are just starting out on your database journey — this tool will probably be adequate for you for a while. Eventually, you may want to take a look at some more advanced (and far more expensive) tools to help you with your database design.

Backing into the Code: Creating Scripts with the Management Studio

One last quick introduction before you exit this chapter — you'll read about the basics of having the Management Studio write your scripts for you. For now, I'm going to do this as something of a quick-and-dirty introduction.

To generate scripts, follow these steps:

1.   Go into the Management Studio and right-click the database for which you want to generate scripts. (In this case, you're going to generate scripts on the Accounting database.)

2.   From the pop-up menu, choose Script Database As ⇨ CREATE To ⇨ New Query Editor Window, as shown in Figure 5-10.

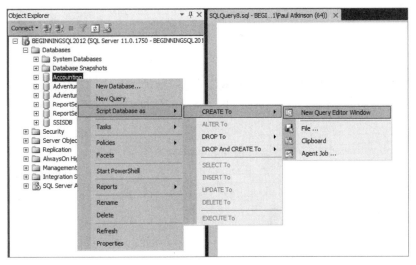

FIGURE 5-10

Whoa! SQL Server generates a heck of a lot more code than you saw when you created your database to begin with. Don't panic, however — all it is doing is being very explicit in scripting major database settings rather than relying on defaults as you did when you scripted it yourself.

Note that you are not limited to scripting the database — if you want to script other objects in the database, just navigate and right-click them much the way that you right-clicked the Accounting database and, boom!, you've got yourself a SQL Script.

As you can see, scripting couldn't be much easier. Once you get a complex database put together, it won't be quite as easy as it seems in this particular demonstration, but it is a lot easier than writing it all out by hand. The reality is that it really is pretty simple once you learn what the scripting options are, and you'll learn much more about those later in the book.

SUMMARY

This chapter covered the basics of the CREATE, ALTER, and DROP statements as they relate to creating a database and tables. There are, of course, many other renditions of these that I will cover as you continue through the book. You have also taken a look at the wide variety of options that you can use in databases and tables to have full control over your data. Finally, you have begun to see the many things that you can use the Management Studio for in order to simplify your life, and make design and scripting simpler.

At this point, you're ready to start getting into some hardcore details about how to lay out your tables, and a discussion on the concepts of normalization and more general database design. I am, however, actually going to make you wait another chapter before you get there, so that you know about constraints and keys somewhat before hitting the design issues.

EXERCISES

1.   Using the Management Studio's script generator, generate SQL for both the `Customers` and the `Employees` tables.

2.   Without using the Management Studio, script a database called MyDB with a starting database size of 17MB and a starting log size of 5MB — set both the log and the database to grow in 5MB increments.

3.   Create a table called `Foo` with a single variable length character field called `Col1` — limit the size of `Col1` to 50 characters.

▶ **WHAT YOU LEARNED IN THIS CHAPTER**

TOPIC	CONCEPT
`CREATE DATABASE`	The container for all your data, the database object is created using the `CREATE DATABASE` statement. You can specify the size and location of the data and log files, spread the data across multiple files, and set up a data growth strategy.
`CREATE TABLE`	Tables are the basic unit of data storage. `CREATE TABLE` starts similarly to `CREATE DATABASE`, but the rest of the syntax centers on specifying column names and their data types, keys, and constraints, as well as some storage options.
`ALTER DATABASE`	Functions similarly to `CREATE DATABASE`, but applies its changes to a database that already exist. `ALTER DATABASE` will throw an error if it's run against a nonexistent database.
`ALTER TABLE`	Can be used to add or change columns, constraints, or storage on an existing table.
`DROP DATABASE,` `DROP TABLE`	Used to remove an object entirely from the system. Dropping a database or table results in loss of any data stored within.
Using SSMS to create objects	Using Management Studio, a simple dialog can be used to create a database. Creating tables can also be done through the designer GUI.
Using SSMS to generate scripts	Using SSMS, you can have SQL Server generate and save a `CREATE` script for any object in your database. This is extremely useful for source control or deployment scenarios.

Keys and Constraints

➤ What kinds of constraints are available to enforce data integrity

➤ Uses and syntax for entity constraints, including primary keys and unique constraints

➤ Uses and syntax for domain constraints, including CHECK and DEFAULT constraints

➤ How to create and use foreign key constraints as referential integrity constraints

➤ How to temporarily disable constraints

➤ Uses of rules and defaults

➤ How to choose among all these options

You've heard me talk about them, but now it's time to look at them seriously — it's time to deal with constraints. I've talked a couple of times already about what constraints are, but here's a review in case you decided to skip straight to this chapter.

 NOTE *A constraint is a restriction. Placed at either column or table level, a constraint ensures that your data meets certain data integrity rules.*

This goes back to the notion that I talked about back in Chapters 1 and 2, that ensuring data integrity is not the responsibility of the programs that use your database, but rather the responsibility of the database itself. If you think about it, this is really cool. Data is inserted, updated, and deleted from the database by many sources. Even in standalone applications (situations where only one program accesses the database), the same table may be accessed from many different places in the program. It doesn't stop there though. Your database administrator (that might mean you if you're a dual-role kind of person) may be altering data occasionally to deal with problems that arise. In more complex scenarios, you can actually run into situations where literally hundreds of different access paths exist for altering just one piece of data, let alone your entire database.

Moving the responsibility for data integrity into the database itself has been revolutionary to database management. There are still many things that can go wrong when you are attempting to insert data into your database, but your database is now *proactive* rather than *reactive* to problems. Many problems with what programs allow into the database are now caught much earlier in the development process because, although the client program allowed the data through, the database knows to reject it. How does it do it? Primarily with constraints (data types and triggers are among the other worker bees of data integrity).

In this chapter, you'll be looking at the three types of constraints at a high level:

➤ Entity constraints

➤ Domain constraints

➤ Referential integrity constraints

At a more specific level, you'll be looking at the methods of implementing each of these types of constraints, including:

➤ Primary key constraints

➤ Foreign key constraints

➤ Unique constraints (also known as alternate keys)

➤ Check constraints

➤ Default constraints

➤ Rules

➤ Defaults (similar to default constraints)

You'll also take a very cursory look at triggers and stored procedures (there will be much more on these later) as methods of implementing data integrity rules.

TYPES OF CONSTRAINTS

There are a number of ways to implement constraints, but each of them falls into one of three categories — domain, entity, or referential integrity constraints, as illustrated in Figure 6-1.

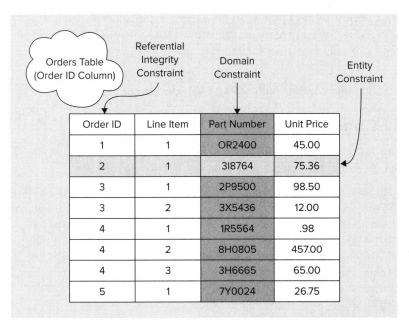

FIGURE 6-1

Domain Constraints

Domain constraints deal with one or more columns. What I'm talking about here is ensuring that a particular column or set of columns meets particular criteria. When you insert or update a row, the constraint is applied without respect to any other row in the table — it's the column's data you're interested in.

For example, if you want to confine the `Unit Price` column to include only values that are greater than or equal to zero, that would be a domain constraint. Although any row that had a `Unit Price` that didn't meet the constraint would be rejected, you're actually enforcing integrity to make sure that the entire column (for *every* row, no matter how many rows) meets the constraint. The domain is the column, and the constraint is a domain constraint.

You'll see this kind of constraint when dealing with check constraints, rules, defaults, and default constraints.

Entity Constraints

Entity constraints are all about comparing rows. This form of constraint doesn't really care about what the data in the column looks like; it's interested in a particular row, and how that row compares to other rows in the table. Entity constraints are best exemplified by a constraint that requires every row to have a unique value for a column or combination of columns (for example, refer back to Figure 6-1 and observe the `Order ID` and `Line Item` columns).

"What," you say, "a unique column? Doesn't that mean it's a domain constraint?" No, it doesn't. I'm not saying that a column has to meet any particular format, or that the value has to be greater or less than anything. What I'm saying is that for *each* row, the same value can't already exist in *some other* row.

You'll see this kind of constraint when dealing with primary key and unique constraints.

Referential Integrity Constraints

Referential integrity constraints are created when a value in one column must match the value in another column — in either the same table or, far more typically, a different table.

Let's say that you are taking orders for a product and that you accept credit cards. In order to be paid by the credit card company, you need to have some form of merchant agreement with that company. You don't want your employees to take credit cards from companies that aren't going to pay you back. That's where referential integrity comes in — it allows you to build what you would call a *domain* or *lookup table*. This table's sole purpose in life is to provide a limited list (often called a *domain list*) of acceptable values. In your case, you might build a table that looks something like this:

CREDITCARDID	CREDITCARD
1	VISA
2	MasterCard
3	Discover Card
4	American Express

You can then build one or more tables that *reference* the `CreditCardID` column of your domain table. With referential integrity, any table (such as the `Orders` table) that is defined as referencing the `CreditCard` table must have a column that matches up to the `CreditCardID` column. For each row that you insert into the referencing table, it must have a value that is in your domain list (it must have a corresponding row in the `CreditCard` table).

You'll see more of this as you learn about foreign key constraints later in this chapter.

CONSTRAINT NAMING

Before I get down to the nitty-gritty of constraints, I'll digress for a moment and address the issue of naming constraints yourself or letting the system generate names.

 NOTE *For each of the different types of constraints that you will be dealing with in this chapter, you can elect not to supply a name — that is, you can have SQL Server provide a name for you. Resist the temptation to do this. You'll quickly find that when SQL Server creates its own name, it isn't particularly useful.*

An example of a system-generated name might be something like PK__Employees__145C0A3F. This is a SQL Server–generated name for a primary key on the Employees table of the Accounting database, which you will create later in the chapter. The "PK" is for primary key (which is the most useful naming element), the Employees is for the Employees table that it is on, and the rest is a randomly generated value to ensure uniqueness. You get this type of naming only if you create the primary key through script. If you created this table through Management Studio, it would have a name of PK_Employees.

That one isn't too bad, but you get less help on other constraints; for example, a CHECK constraint used later in the chapter might generate something like CK__Customers__22AA2996. From this, you know that it's a CHECK constraint, but you know nothing about the nature of CHECK.

Because you can have multiple CHECK constraints on a table, you could wind up with all of these as names of constraints on the same table:

➤ CK__Customers__22AA2996

➤ CK__Customers__25869641

➤ CK__Customers__267ABA7A

Needless to say, if you needed to edit one of these constraints, it would be a pain to figure out which was which.

Personally, I use either a combination of constraint types with a phrase to indicate what it does or the name(s) of the column(s) it affects. For example, I might use CKPriceExceedsCost if I have a constraint to ensure that my users can't sell a product at a loss, or perhaps something as simple as CKCustomerPhoneNo on a column that ensures that phone numbers are formatted properly.

As with the naming of anything that you'll use in this book, how exactly you name things is really not all that important. What is important is that you:

➤ Be consistent.

➤ Make it something that everyone can understand.

➤ Keep it as short as you can while still meeting the preceding rules.

➤ Did I mention to be consistent?

KEY CONSTRAINTS

There are four types of common keys that you may hear about in your database endeavors. These are primary keys, foreign keys, alternate keys, and inversion keys. For this chapter, I'll take a look at only the first three of these, as they provide constraints on a database.

 NOTE *An inversion key is basically just any index (I'll cover indexes in Chapter 9) that does not apply some form of constraint to the table (primary key, foreign key, unique). Inversion keys, rather than enforcing data integrity, are merely an alternative way of sorting the data.*

Keys are one of the cornerstone concepts of database design and management, so fasten your seatbelt and hold on tight. This will be one of the most important concepts you'll read about in this book, and will become absolutely critical as you move on to normalization in Chapter 8.

Primary Key Constraints

Before I define what a primary key actually is, I'm going to digress slightly into a brief discussion of relational databases. Relational databases are constructed on the idea of being able to "relate" data. Therefore, it becomes critical in relational databases for most tables (there are exceptions, but they are very rare) to have a unique identifier for each row. A unique identifier allows you to accurately reference a record from another table in the database, thereby forming a relation between those two tables.

 NOTE *This is a wildly different concept from the one used with old mainframe environments or the ISAM databases (dBase, FoxPro, and so on) of the '80s and early '90s. In those environments, you dealt with one record at a time. You would generally open the entire table, and go one record at a time until you found what you were looking for. If you needed data from a second table, you had to open that table separately and fetch that table's data, and then mix the data programmatically yourself.*

Primary keys are the unique identifiers for each row. They must contain unique values (and hence cannot be NULL*)*. Because of their importance in relational databases, primary keys are the most fundamental of all keys and constraints.

 NOTE *Don't confuse the primary key, which uniquely identifies each row in a table, with a GUID, which is a more specific tool, typically used to identify something (it could be anything, really) across all space and time. Although a GUID can certainly be used as a primary key, it incurs some overhead, and is usually not called for when you're only dealing with the contents of a table. Indeed, the only common place that a GUID becomes particularly useful in a database environment is as a primary key when dealing with replicated or other distributed data.*

A table can have a maximum of one primary key. As I mentioned earlier, it is rare to have a table in which you don't want a primary key.

NOTE *When I say "rare" here, I mean very rare. A table that doesn't have a primary key severely violates the concept of relational data — it means that you can't guarantee that you can relate to a specific record. The data in your table no longer has anything that gives it distinction.*

Situations in which you can have multiple rows that are logically identical are actually not that uncommon, but that doesn't mean that you don't want a primary key. In these instances, you'll want to take a look at fabricating some sort of key. This approach has most often been implemented using an identity column, although using a GUID is now an appropriate alternative in some situations. Sequences, a new object in SQL Server 2012, provide an additional option.

Let's look at what happens when you don't have a primary key. Imagine you're in the Accounting database, and an order is accidentally keyed twice.

```
CustomerNo    OrderDate     EmployeeID
1             04/25/2011    6
1             04/25/2011    6
```

Now, the order entry clerk is diligent — immediately, he wants to delete the duplicate entry. How can a SQL statement be constructed to accomplish this? Without a primary key, there is no combination of fields that can identify one row and not the other! You need some way of uniquely identifying the row to be deleted.

```
ALTER TABLE Orders ADD OrderID INT IDENTITY
```

By adding the `OrderID` column, you can now distinguish the second order from the first. `OrderID` is not yet a primary key — it has no constraint guaranteeing its uniqueness yet — but it is certainly a candidate.

```
CustomerNo    OrderDate     EmployeeID    OrderID
1             04/25/2011    6             1
1             04/25/2011    6             2
```

A primary key ensures uniqueness within the columns declared as being part of that primary key, and that unique value serves as an identifier for each row in that table. How do you create a primary key? Actually, there are two ways. You can create the primary key either in your CREATE TABLE command or with an ALTER TABLE command.

NOTE *Much of the rest of this chapter makes use of the Accounting database you created in Chapter 5. The assumption is that the Accounting database is as it was at the end of Chapter 5 after using the Management Studio to create tables in the database.*

Creating the Primary Key at Table Creation

Let's review one of the CREATE TABLE statements from the previous chapter:

```
CREATE TABLE Customers
(
    CustomerNo      int   IDENTITY    NOT NULL,
    CustomerName    varchar(30)       NOT NULL,
    Address1        varchar(30)       NOT NULL,
    Address2        varchar(30)       NOT NULL,
    City            varchar(20)       NOT NULL,
    State           char(2)           NOT NULL,
    Zip             varchar(10)       NOT NULL,
    Contact         varchar(25)       NOT NULL,
    Phone           char(15)          NOT NULL,
    FedIDNo         varchar(9)        NOT NULL,
    DateInSystem    smalldatetime     NOT NULL
);
```

This CREATE statement should seem old hat by now, but it's missing a very important piece — a PRIMARY KEY constraint. You want to identify CustomerNo as your primary key. Why CustomerNo? Well, I'll give you a look into what makes a good primary key in the next chapter, but for now just think about it a bit. Do you want two customers to have the same CustomerNo? Definitely not. It makes perfect sense for a CustomerNo to be used as an identifier for a customer. Indeed, such a system has been used for years, so there's really no sense in reinventing the wheel here.

> **NOTE** *Before starting the examples in this chapter, download and run the* Chap06AccountingDB.sql *file. This will create a clean copy of the Accounting database, regardless of whether you have worked through the examples in Chapter 5.*

Code snippet Chap06AccountingDB.sql

To alter your CREATE TABLE statement to include a PRIMARY KEY constraint, just add the constraint information right after the column(s) that you want to be part of your primary key. In this case, you would use:

```
USE Accounting;

CREATE TABLE Customers
(
    CustomerNo      int    IDENTITY    NOT NULL
        PRIMARY KEY,
    CustomerName    varchar(30)        NOT NULL,
    Address1        varchar(30)        NOT NULL,
    Address2        varchar(30)        NOT NULL,
    City            varchar(20)        NOT NULL,
```

```
    State           char(2)          NOT NULL,
    Zip             varchar(10)      NOT NULL,
    Contact         varchar(25)      NOT NULL,
    Phone           char(15)         NOT NULL,
    FedIDNo         varchar(9)       NOT NULL,
    DateInSystem    smalldatetime    NOT NULL
);
```

Code snippet Chap06.sql

Notice that you just have to alter one line (just remove the comma) and add some code on a second line for that column. It was easy! Again, you just need to add one simple keyword (okay, so it's two words, but they operate as one) and you have yourself a primary key.

Creating a Primary Key on an Existing Table

Now, what if you already have a table and you want to set the primary key? That's also easy. You'll do that for the Employees table:

```
USE Accounting

ALTER TABLE Employees
    ADD CONSTRAINT PK_Employees
    PRIMARY KEY (EmployeeID);
```

Code snippet Chap06.sql

The ALTER command tells SQL Server:

➤ That you are adding something to the table (you could also be dropping something from the table if you so chose)

➤ What it is that you're adding (a constraint)

➤ What you want to name the constraint (to allow you to address the constraint directly later)

➤ The type of constraint (primary key)

➤ The column(s) that the constraint applies to

Foreign Key Constraints

Foreign keys are both a method of ensuring data integrity and a manifestation of the relationships between tables. When you add a foreign key to a table, you are creating a dependency between the table for which you define the foreign key (the *referencing* table) and the table your foreign key references (the *referenced* table). After adding a foreign key, any record you insert into the referencing table must have a matching record in the referenced column(s) of the referenced table, or the value of the foreign key column(s) must be set to NULL. This can be a little confusing, so let's take a look at an example.

> **NOTE** *When I say that a value must be "set to* NULL*," I'm referring to how the actual* INSERT *statement looks. As you'll learn in a moment, the data may actually look slightly different once it gets in the table, depending on what options you've set in your* FOREIGN KEY *declaration.*

For this example, create another table in the Accounting database called Orders. One thing you'll notice in this CREATE script is that you're going to use both a primary key and a foreign key. A primary key, as you will see as you continue through the design, is a critical part of a table. Your foreign key is added to the script in almost exactly the same way as your primary key was, except that you must say what you are referencing. The syntax goes on the column or columns that you are placing your FOREIGN KEY constraint on, and looks something like this:

```
<column name> <data type> <nullability>
FOREIGN KEY REFERENCES <table name>(<column name>)
    [ON DELETE {CASCADE|NO ACTION|SET NULL|SET DEFAULT}]
    [ON UPDATE {CASCADE|NO ACTION|SET NULL|SET DEFAULT}]
```

TRY IT OUT   Creating a Table with a Foreign Key

For the moment, I'm going to ignore the ON clause. That leaves a script that looks something like this for the Orders table:

```
USE Accounting

CREATE TABLE Orders
(
    OrderID     int     IDENTITY    NOT NULL
        PRIMARY KEY,
    CustomerNo  int                 NOT NULL
        FOREIGN KEY REFERENCES Customers(CustomerNo),
    OrderDate   date                NOT NULL,
    EmployeeID  int                 NOT NULL
);
```

Code snippet Chap06.sql

Note that the actual column being referenced must have either a PRIMARY KEY or a UNIQUE constraint defined on it (I'll discuss UNIQUE constraints later in the chapter).

> **NOTE** *It's also worth noting that primary and foreign keys can exist on the same column. You can see an example of this in the AdventureWorks database with the* Sales.SalesOrderDetail *table. The primary key is composed of both the* SalesOrderID *and the* SalesOrderDetailID *columns — the former is also the foreign key and references the* Sales.SalesOrderHeader *table. You'll actually create a table later in the chapter that has a column that is both a primary key and a foreign key.*

How It Works

Once you have successfully run the preceding code, run `sp_help`, and you should see your new constraint reported under the constraints section of the `sp_help` information. If you want to get even more to the point, you can run `sp_helpconstraint`. The syntax is easy:

```
EXEC sp_helpconstraint <table name>
```

Run `sp_helpconstraint` on your new `Orders` table, and you'll get information back giving you the names, criteria, and status for all the constraints on the table. At this point, your `Orders` table has one `FOREIGN KEY` constraint and one `PRIMARY KEY` constraint.

 NOTE *When you run* `sp_helpconstraint` *on this table, the word "clustered" will appear right after the reporting of the* `PRIMARY KEY`. *This just means it has a clustered index. You can explore the meaning of this further in Chapter 9.*

Your new foreign key has been referenced in the physical definition of your table, and is now an integral part of your table. As I discussed in Chapter 1, the database is in charge of its own integrity. Your foreign key enforces one constraint on the data and makes sure your database integrity remains intact.

Unlike primary keys, foreign keys are not limited to just one per table. You can have between 0 and 253 foreign keys in each table. The only limitation is that a given column can reference only one foreign key. However, you can have more than one column participate in a single foreign key. A given column that is the target of a reference by a foreign key can also be referenced by many tables. You'll see a lot more about how to choose foreign keys in Chapter 8.

Adding a Foreign Key to an Existing Table

Just like with primary keys, or any constraint for that matter, there are situations when you will want to add a foreign key to a table that already exists. This process is similar to creating a primary key.

TRY IT OUT Adding a Foreign Key to an Existing Table

You can add another foreign key to your `Orders` table to restrict the `EmployeeID` field (which is intended to have the ID of the employee who entered the order) to valid employees as defined in the `Employees` table. To do this, you need to be able to uniquely identify a target record in the referenced table. As I've already mentioned, you can do this by referencing either a primary key or a column with a `UNIQUE` constraint. In this case, you'll make use of the existing primary key that you placed on the `Employees` table earlier in the chapter:

Available for download on Wrox.com

```
ALTER TABLE Orders
    ADD CONSTRAINT FK_EmployeeCreatesOrder
    FOREIGN KEY (EmployeeID) REFERENCES Employees(EmployeeID);
```

Code snippet Chap06.sql

Now execute `sp_helpconstraint` again against the `Orders` table, and you'll see that your new constraint has been added.

How It Works

Your latest constraint works just as the last one did — the physical table definition is aware of the rules placed on the data it is to contain. Just as it would not allow string data to be inserted into a numeric column, now it will not allow a row to be inserted into the `Orders` table where the referenced employee in charge of that order is not a valid `EmployeeID`. If someone attempts to add a row that doesn't match with an employee record, the insertion into `Orders` will be rejected in order to maintain the integrity of the database.

> **NOTE** Note that while you've added two foreign keys, there is still a line down at the bottom of your `sp_helpconstraint` results (or under the Messages tab if you have Results in Grid selected) that says `No foreign keys reference this table`. This is telling you that, although you do have foreign keys in this table that reference other tables, there are no other tables out there that reference this table. If you want to see the difference, just run `sp_helpconstraint` on the `Customers` or `Employees` tables at this point, and you'll see that each of these tables is now referenced by your new `Orders` table.

Making a Table Self-Referencing

What if the column you want to refer to isn't in another table, but is actually right within the table in which you are building the reference? Can a table be both the referencing and the referenced table? You bet! Indeed, while this is far from the most common of situations, it is actually used with regularity.

> **NOTE** Before you actually create this self-referencing constraint that references a required (non-nullable) field that's based on an identity column, it's rather critical that you get at least one row in the table prior to the foreign key being added. Why? Well, the problem stems from the fact that the identity value is chosen and filled in after the foreign key has already been checked and enforced. That means that you don't have a value yet for that first row to reference when the check happens. If you're committed to using an identity column, the only other option here is to go ahead and create the foreign key but then disable it when adding the first row. You'll learn about disabling constraints a little later in this chapter.

Okay, because this is a table that's referencing a column based on an identity column, you need to get a primer row into the table before you add your constraint:

```
INSERT INTO Employees
    (
    FirstName,
    LastName,
    Title,
    SSN,
    Salary,
    PriorSalary,
    HireDate,
    ManagerEmpID,
    Department
    )
VALUES
    (
    'Billy Bob',
    'Boson',
    'Head Cook & Bottle Washer',
    '123-45-6789',
    100000,
    80000,
    '1990-01-01',
    1,
    'Cooking and Bottling'
    );
```

Now that you have a primer row, you can add your foreign key. In an ALTER situation, this works just the same as any other foreign key definition. You can now try this out:

```
ALTER TABLE Employees
    ADD CONSTRAINT FK_EmployeeHasManager
    FOREIGN KEY (ManagerEmpID) REFERENCES Employees(EmployeeID);
```

Code snippet Chap06.sql

There is one difference with a CREATE statement. You can (but you don't have to) leave out the FOREIGN KEY phrasing and just use the REFERENCES clause. You already have your Employees table set up at this point, but if you were creating it from scratch, the script would appear as follows (pay particular attention to the foreign key on the ManagerEmpID column):

```
CREATE TABLE Employees (
    EmployeeID        int    IDENTITY   NOT NULL
        PRIMARY KEY,
    FirstName         varchar (25)      NOT NULL,
    MiddleInitial     char (1)          NULL,
    LastName          varchar (25)      NOT NULL,
    Title             varchar (25)      NOT NULL,
    SSN               varchar (11)      NOT NULL,
    Salary            money             NOT NULL,
    PriorSalary       money             NOT NULL,
    LastRaise AS Salary -PriorSalary,
    HireDate          smalldatetime     NOT NULL,
    TerminationDate   smalldatetime     NULL,
    ManagerEmpID      int               NOT NULL
```

```
        REFERENCES Employees(EmployeeID),
    Department          varchar (25)      NOT NULL
);
```

Code snippet Chap06.sql

 NOTE *It's worth noting that, if you try to* DROP *the* Employees *table at this point (to run the second example), you're going to get an error. Why? Well, when you established the reference in your* Orders *table to the* Employees *table, the two tables became "schema-bound;" that is, the* Employees *table now knows that it has what is called a dependency on it. SQL Server will not let you drop a table that is referenced by another table. You have to drop the foreign key in the* Orders *table before SQL Server will allow you to delete the* Employees *table (or the* Customers *table, for that matter).*

In addition, doing the self-referencing foreign key in the constraint doesn't allow you to get your primer row in, so it's important that you do it this way only when the column the foreign key constraint is placed on allows NULLs*. That way, the first row can have a* NULL *in that column and avoid the need for a primer row.*

Cascading Actions

One important difference between foreign keys and other kinds of keys is that foreign keys are *bidirectional*; that is, they not only restrict the child table to values that exist in the parent, but they also check for child rows whenever you do something to the parent (thus preventing orphans). The default behavior is for SQL Server to "restrict" the parent row from being deleted if any child rows exist. Sometimes, however, you would rather automatically delete any dependent records rather than prevent the deletion of the referenced record. The same notion applies to updates to records where you would like the dependent record to automatically reference the newly updated record. Somewhat more rare is the instance where you want to alter the referencing row to some sort of known state. For this, you have the option to set the value in the dependent row to either NULL or whatever the default value is for that column.

The process of making such automatic deletions and updates is known as *cascading*. This process, especially for deletes, can actually run through several layers of dependencies (where one record depends on another, which depends on another, and so on). So, how do you implement cascading actions in SQL Server? All you need is a modification to the syntax you use when declaring your foreign key. You just add the ON clause that I skipped at the beginning of this section.

Check this out by adding a new table to your Accounting database. You'll make this a table to store the individual line items in an order, so you'll call it OrderDetails:

```
CREATE TABLE OrderDetails
(
    OrderID      int          NOT NULL,
    PartNo       varchar(10)  NOT NULL,
    Description  varchar(25)  NOT NULL,
    UnitPrice    money        NOT NULL,
```

```
    Qty           int               NOT NULL,
    CONSTRAINT    PK_OrderDetails
        PRIMARY KEY   (OrderID, PartNo),
    CONSTRAINT    FK_OrderContainsDetails
        FOREIGN KEY   (OrderID)
            REFERENCES Orders(OrderID)
            ON UPDATE   NO ACTION
            ON DELETE   CASCADE
);
```

Code snippet Chap06.sql

This time there's a whole lot going on, so let's take it apart piece by piece.

> **NOTE** *Before you get too far into looking at the foreign key aspects of this, notice something about how the primary key was done here. Instead of placing the declaration immediately after the key, I decided to declare it as a separate constraint item. This helps facilitate the multicolumn primary key (which therefore could not be declared as a column constraint) and the clarity of the overall* CREATE TABLE *statement. Likewise, I could have declared the foreign key either immediately following the column or, as I did here, as a separate constraint item. I'll touch on this a little bit later in the chapter.*

First, notice that your foreign key is also part of your primary key. This is not at all uncommon in child tables, and is actually almost always the case for associate tables (more on this in the next chapter). Just remember that each constraint stands alone — you add, change, or delete each of them independently.

Next, look at the FOREIGN KEY declaration:

```
    FOREIGN KEY   (OrderID)
    REFERENCES    Orders(OrderID)
```

You've declared the OrderID as being dependent on a "foreign" column. In this case, it's for a column (also called OrderID) in a separate table (Orders), but as you saw earlier in the chapter, it could just as easily have been in the same table.

> **NOTE** *There is something of a "gotcha" when creating foreign keys that reference the same table the foreign key is being defined on. Foreign keys of this nature are not allowed to have declarative* CASCADE *actions. The reason for this restriction is to avoid cyclical updates or deletes; that is, situations in which the first update causes another, which in turn tries to update the first. The result could be a never-ending loop.*

Now, to get to the heart of the cascading issue, you need to look at the ON clauses:

```
ON UPDATE    NO ACTION
ON DELETE    CASCADE
```

You've defined two *referential integrity actions*. As you might guess, a referential integrity action is what you want to have happen whenever the referential integrity rule you've defined is invoked. For situations where the parent record (in the Orders table) is updated, you've said that you do not want that update to be cascaded to the child table (OrderDetails). For illustration purposes, however, I've chosen a CASCADE for deletes.

 NOTE *Note that* NO ACTION *is the default, and so specifying this in your code is optional. While the "typical" way of coding this is to leave out the* NO ACTION, *I would encourage you to include the* NO ACTION *explicitly (whenever you add the* ON *clause) to make your intent clear.*

Now try an insert into the OrderDetails table:

Available for download on Wrox.com

```
INSERT INTO OrderDetails
VALUES
    (1, '4X4525', 'This is a part', 25.00, 2);
```

Code snippet Chap06.sql

Unless you've been playing around with your data some, this generates an error:

```
Msg 547, Level 16, State 0, Line 1
The INSERT statement conflicted with the FOREIGN KEY constraint
    "FK_OrderContainsDetails". The conflict occurred in database
    "Accounting", table "dbo.Orders", column 'OrderID'.
The statement has been terminated.
```

Why? Well, you haven't inserted anything into your Orders table yet, so how can you refer to a record in the Orders table if there isn't anything there?

 NOTE *This is going to expose you to one of the hassles of relational database work — dependency chains. A dependency chain exists when you have something that is, in turn, dependent on something else, which may yet be dependent on something else, and so on. There's really nothing you can do about this. It's just something that comes along with database work. You have to start at the top of the chain and work your way down to what you need inserted. Fortunately, the records you need are often already there, save one or two dependency levels.*

Okay, so in order to get your row into the `OrderDetails` table, you must also have a record already in the `Orders` table. Unfortunately, getting a row into the `Orders` table requires that you have one in the `Customers` table (remember that foreign key you built on `Orders`?). So, let's take care of it a step at a time:

```
INSERT INTO Customers  -- Our Customer.
                       -- Remember that CustomerNo is
                       -- an Identity column
VALUES
   ('Billy Bob''s Shoes',
   '123 Main St.',
   ' ',
   'Vancouver',
   'WA',
   '98685',
   'Billy Bob',
   '(360) 555-1234',
   '931234567',
   GETDATE()
   );
```

Code snippet Chap06.sql

Now you have a customer, so select against the record you just inserted to be sure:

CUSTOMER NO	1
Customer Name	Billy Bob's Shoes
Address 1	123 Main Street
Address 2	
City	Vancouver
State	WA
Zip	98685
Contact	Billy Bob
Phone	(360) 555-1234
FedIDNo	931234567
DateInSystem	2000-07-10 21:17:00

So you have a `CustomerID` of 1 (your number may be different depending on what experimentation you've done). You can take that number and use it in the next `INSERT` (into `Orders`, finally). Try inserting an order for `CustomerID` 1:

```
INSERT INTO Orders
    (CustomerNo, OrderDate, EmployeeID)
VALUES --Assuming the CustomerID of the row you just entered was 1
    (1, GETDATE(), 1);
```

Code snippet Chap06.sql

This time, things should work fine.

> **NOTE** *It's worth noting that the reason you don't still get an error here is that you already inserted that primer row in the* Employees *table; otherwise, you would have needed to get a row into that table before SQL Server would have allowed the insert into* Orders *(remember that* Employees *foreign key?). Dependency chains are easy to forget about when everything just works.*

At this point, you're ready for the insert into the `OrderDetails` table. Just to help with a `CASCADE` example you're going to be doing in a moment, you're actually going to insert not one, but two rows:

```
INSERT INTO OrderDetails
VALUES
    (1, '4X4525', 'This is a part', 25.00, 2)

INSERT INTO OrderDetails
VALUES
    (1, '0R2400', 'This is another part', 50.00, 2);
```

Code snippet Chap06.sql

You can verify things by running a `SELECT`:

```
SELECT OrderID, PartNo FROM OrderDetails;
```

This gets you back to the expected two rows:

```
OrderID      PartNo
---------    ---------
1            0R2400
1            4X4525

(2 row(s) affected)
```

Now that you have entered the data, take a look at the effect a CASCADE has on that data. Go ahead and delete a row from the Orders table, and then see what happens in OrderDetails:

```
USE Accounting

-- First, look at the rows in both tables
SELECT *
FROM Orders;

SELECT *
FROM OrderDetails;

-- Now delete the Order record
DELETE Orders
WHERE OrderID = 1;

-- Finally, look at both sets of data again
-- and see the CASCADE effect
SELECT *
FROM Orders;

SELECT *
FROM OrderDetails;
```

Code snippet Chap06.sql

This yields some interesting results:

```
OrderID        CustomerNo      OrderDate                 EmployeeID
---------      ------------    --------------------      --------------
1              1               2000-07-13 22:18:00       1

(1 row(s) affected)
OrderID        PartNo       Description             UnitPrice       Qty
---------      -------      --------------------    -----------     ----
1              0R2400       This is another part    50.0000         2
1              4X4525       This is a part          25.0000         2

(2 row(s) affected)

(1 row(s) affected)
OrderID        CustomerNo      OrderDate         EmployeeID
--------       -----------     ------------      -----------------------

(0 row(s) affected)
OrderID        PartNo       Description        UnitPrice       Qty
---------      -----------  --------------     -----------     --------

(0 row(s) affected)
```

Notice that even though you issued a DELETE against the Orders table only, the DELETE also cascaded to your matching records in the OrderDetails table. Records in both tables were deleted.

If you had defined your table with a CASCADE update and updated a relevant record, that, too, would have been propagated to the child table.

> **NOTE** *It's worth noting that there is no limit to the depth that a* CASCADE *action can reach. For example, if you had a* ShipmentDetails *table that referenced rows in* OrderDetails *with a* CASCADE *action, those, too, would have been deleted just by your one* DELETE *in the* Orders *table.*
>
> *This is actually one of the danger areas of cascading actions. It's very, very easy to not realize all the different things that one* DELETE *or* UPDATE *statement can do in your database. For this and other reasons, I'm not a huge fan of cascading actions. They allow people to get lazy, and that's something that's not usually a good thing when doing something like deleting data!*

Those Other CASCADE Actions …

So, those were examples of cascading updates and deletes, but what about the other two types of cascade actions I mentioned? What of SET NULL and SET DEFAULT?

These were added with SQL Server 2005, so avoid them if you want backward compatibility with SQL Server 2000, but their operation is very simple: If you perform an update that changes the parent values for a row, the child row will be set to either NULL or whatever the default value for that column is (whichever you chose — SET NULL or SET DEFAULT). It's just that simple.

Other Things to Think About with Foreign Keys

There are some other things to think about before you're done with foreign keys. I will be coming back to this subject over and over again throughout the book, but for now, I just want to get in a couple of finer points:

➤ What makes values in foreign keys required versus optional

➤ How foreign keys are bi-directional

What Makes Values in Foreign Keys Required versus Optional

The nature of a foreign key provides you two possible choices regarding how to fill in a column or columns that have a foreign key defined for them:

➤ Fill the column in with a value that matches the corresponding column in the referenced table.

➤ Do not fill in a value at all and leave the value NULL.

You can make the foreign key completely required (limit your users to just the first option in the preceding list) by simply defining the referencing column as NOT NULL. Since a NULL value won't be valid in the column and the foreign key requires any non-NULL value to have a match in the referenced table, you know that every row will have a match in your referenced table. In other words, the reference is required.

> **NOTE** *Creating a non-*NULL *foreign key constraint delivers a bonus: any join between the referenced and referencing tables can be written as an* INNER JOIN *without any risk of missing data. SQL Server has a variety of means of making such a join fast. If your business rules allow it, this is the way to go.*

Allowing the referencing column to have NULLs will create the same requirement, except that the user will also have the option of supplying no value — even if there is not a match for NULL in the referenced table, the insert will still be allowed.

How Foreign Keys Are Bi-Directional

I touched on this some when I discussed CASCADE actions, but when defining foreign keys, I can't stress enough that they effectively place restrictions on *both* tables. Up to this point, I've been talking about things in terms of the referencing table; however, once the foreign key is defined, the referenced table must also live by the following rule.

> **NOTE** *By default, you cannot delete a record or update the referenced column in a referenced table if that record is referenced from the dependent table. If you want to be able to delete or update such a record, you need to set up a* CASCADE *action for the delete and/or update.*

Consider this "You can't delete or update a referenced record" idea for a minute.

You just defined a couple of foreign keys for the Orders table. One of those references the EmployeeID columns of the Employees table. Let's say, for instance, that you have an employee with an EmployeeID of 10 who takes many orders for a year or two, and then decides to quit and move on to another job. Your tendency would probably be to delete the record in the Employees table for that employee, but that would create a rather large problem — you would get what are called *orphaned* records in the Orders table. Your Orders table would have a large number of records that still have an EmployeeID of 10. If you are allowed to delete EmployeeID 10 from the Employees table, you will no longer be able to tell which employee entered in all those orders. The value for the EmployeeID column of the Orders table will become worthless!

Now let's take this example one step further. Let's say that the employee did not quit. Instead, for some unknown reason, you wanted to change that employee's ID number. If you made the change (via an UPDATE statement) to the Employees table, but did not make the corresponding update to the Orders table, you would again have orphaned records. You would have records with a value of 10 in the EmployeeID column of the Orders table with no matching employee.

Now, let's take it one more step further! Imagine that someone comes along and inserts a new record with an EmployeeID of 10. You would now have a number of records in your Orders table that will be related to an employee who didn't take those orders. You would have bad data (yuck!).

Instead of allowing orphaned records, SQL Server, by default, restricts you from deleting or updating records from the referenced table (in this case, the `Employees` table) unless any dependent records have already been deleted from or updated in the referencing (in this case, `Orders`) table.

> **NOTE** *This is actually not a bad segue into a brief discussion about when a* `CASCADE` *action makes sense and when it doesn't. Data-integrity-wise, you probably wouldn't want to allow the deletion of an employee if there are dependent rows in the* `Orders` *table. Not being able to trace back to the employee would degrade the value of your data. On the other hand, it may be perfectly valid (for some very strange reason) to change an employee's ID. You could* `CASCADE` *that update to the* `Orders` *table with little ill effect. Another moral to the story here is that you don't need the same* `CASCADE` *decision for both* `UPDATE` *and* `DELETE` *— think about each separately (and carefully).*

As you can see, although the foreign key is defined on one table, it actually placed restrictions on both tables (if the foreign key is self-referenced, both sets of restrictions are on the one table).

UNIQUE Constraints

These are relatively easy. `UNIQUE` constraints are essentially the younger sibling of primary keys in that they require a unique value throughout the named column (or combination of columns) in the table. You will often hear `UNIQUE` constraints referred to as *alternate keys*. The major differences are that they are not considered to be *the* unique identifier of a record in a table (even though you could effectively use it that way) and that you *can* have more than one `UNIQUE` constraint (remember that you can only have one primary key per table).

Once you establish a `UNIQUE` constraint, every value in the named columns must be unique. If you try to update or insert a row with a value that already exists in a column with a `UNIQUE` constraint, SQL Server will raise an error and reject the record.

> **NOTE** *Unlike a primary key, a* `UNIQUE` *constraint does not automatically prevent you from having a* `NULL` *value. Whether* `NULL`s *are allowed or not depends on how you set the* `NULL` *option for that column in the table. Keep in mind, however, that if you do allow* `NULL`s, *you will be able to insert only one of them (although a* `NULL` *doesn't equal another* `NULL`, *they are still considered to be duplicate from the perspective of a* `UNIQUE` *constraint). To effectively create a* `UNIQUE` *constraint that only affects non-*`NULL` *values, refer to the section on filtered indexes in Chapter 9.*

Because there is nothing novel about this (you've pretty much already seen it with primary keys), let's get right to the code. It's time to create yet another table in the Accounting database. This time, it will be the `Shippers` table:

Available for
download on
Wrox.com

```
CREATE TABLE Shippers
(
    ShipperID       int     IDENTITY    NOT NULL
        PRIMARY KEY,
    ShipperName     varchar(30)         NOT NULL,
    Address         varchar(30)         NOT NULL,
    City            varchar(25)         NOT NULL,
    State           char(2)             NOT NULL,
    Zip             varchar(10)         NOT NULL,
    PhoneNo         varchar(14)         NOT NULL
        UNIQUE
);
```

Code snippet Chap06.sql

Now run `sp_helpconstraint` against the `Shippers` table, and verify that your `Shippers` table has been created with the proper constraints.

Creating UNIQUE Constraints on Existing Tables

Again, this works pretty much the same as with primary and foreign keys. You can go ahead and create a `UNIQUE` constraint on the `Employees` table:

Available for
download on
Wrox.com

```
ALTER TABLE Employees
    ADD CONSTRAINT AK_EmployeeSSN
    UNIQUE (SSN);
```

Code snippet Chap06.sql

A quick run of `sp_helpconstraint` verifies that your constraint was created as planned, and tells you on which columns the constraint is active.

 NOTE *In case you're wondering, the* AK *I used in the constraint name here is for alternate key — much like* PK *and* FK *for primary and foreign keys, respectively. You will also often see a* UQ *or just* U *prefix used for* UNIQUE *constraint names.*

CHECK CONSTRAINTS

The nice thing about CHECK constraints is that they are not restricted to a particular column. They can be related to a column, but they can also be essentially table related in that they can check one column against another, as long as all the columns are within a single table and the values are for the same row being updated or inserted. They can also check that any combination of column values meets a criterion.

The constraint is defined using the same rules that you would use in a WHERE clause. Examples of the criteria for a CHECK constraint include:

GOAL	SQL
Limit Month column to appropriate numbers	BETWEEN 1 AND 12
Proper SSN formatting	LIKE '[0-9][0-9][0-9]-[0-9][0-9]-[0-9][0-9][0-9][0-9]'
Limit to a specific list of Shippers	IN ('UPS', 'Fed Ex', 'USPS')
Price must be positive	UnitPrice >= 0
Reference another column in the same row	ShipDate >= OrderDate

This really only scratches the surface, and the possibilities are virtually endless. Almost anything you could put in a WHERE clause, you can also put in your constraint. What's more, CHECK constraints are very fast performance-wise as compared to the alternatives (rules and triggers).

Still building on the Accounting database, try adding a modification to the Customers table to check for a valid date in the DateInSystem field (you can't have a date in the system that's in the future):

Available for download on Wrox.com

```
ALTER TABLE Customers
    ADD CONSTRAINT CN_CustomerDateInSystem
    CHECK
    (DateInSystem <= GETDATE ());
```

Now try to insert a record that violates the CHECK constraint; you'll get an error:

```
INSERT INTO Customers
    (CustomerName, Address1, Address2, City, State, Zip, Contact,
     Phone, FedIDNo, DateInSystem)
VALUES
    ('Customer1', 'Address1', 'Add2', 'MyCity', 'NY', '55555',
     'No Contact', '553-1212', '930984954', '12-31-2049');
```

Code snippet Chap06.sql

```
Msg 547, Level 16, State 0, Line 1
The INSERT statement conflicted with the CHECK constraint
    "CN_CustomerDateInSystem". The conflict occurred in database
    "Accounting", table "dbo.Customers", column 'DateInSystem'.
The statement has been terminated.
```

Now if you change things to use a `DateInSystem` that meets the criterion used in the CHECK (anything with today's date or earlier), the INSERT works fine.

DEFAULT CONSTRAINTS

This will be the first of two types of data integrity tools that will be called something to do with "default." This is, unfortunately, very confusing, but I'll do my best to make it clear (and I think it will become so).

> **NOTE** *You'll see the other type of default when you look at rules and defaults later in the chapter.*

A DEFAULT constraint, like all constraints, becomes an integral part of the table definition. It defines what to do when a new row is inserted that doesn't include data for the column on which you have defined the DEFAULT constraint. You can define it either as a literal value (say, setting a default salary to zero or "UNKNOWN" for a string column) or as one of several system values such as GETDATE().

The main points to understand about a DEFAULT constraint are that:

➤ Defaults are used only in INSERT statements. They are ignored for UPDATE and DELETE statements.

➤ If any value is supplied in the INSERT, the default is not used.

➤ If no value is supplied, the default will always be used.

Defaults are made use of only in INSERT statements. I cannot express enough how much this confuses many SQL Server beginners. Think about it this way: When you are first inserting the record, SQL Server doesn't have any kind of value for your column except what you supplied (if anything) or the default. If neither of these is supplied, SQL Server either inserts a NULL (essentially amounting to "I don't know") or, if your column definition says NOT NULL, rejects the record. After that first insert, however, SQL Server already has some value for that column. If you are updating that column, it has your new value. If the column in question isn't part of an UPDATE statement, SQL Server just leaves what is already in the column — even if it's NULL.

If a value was provided for the column, there is no reason to use the default. The supplied value is used.

If no value is supplied, the default will always be used. Now this seems simple enough until you think about the circumstance where a NULL value is what you actually want to go into that column for a record. If you don't supply a value on a column that has a default defined, the default will be used. What do you do if you really wanted it to be NULL? Say so — insert NULL as part of your INSERT statement.

> **NOTE** *Under the heading of "One more thing," it's worth noting that there is an exception to the rule about an UPDATE command not using a default. The exception happens if you explicitly say that you want a default to be used. You do this by using the keyword DEFAULT as the value you want the column updated to.*

Defining a DEFAULT Constraint in Your CREATE TABLE Statement

At the risk of sounding repetitious, this works pretty much like all the other column constraints you've dealt with thus far. You just add it to the end of the column definition.

To work an example, start by dropping the existing `Shippers` table that you created earlier in the chapter. This time, you'll create a simpler version of that table, including a default:

Available for download on Wrox.com

```
CREATE TABLE Shippers
(
    ShipperID      int    IDENTITY    NOT NULL
        PRIMARY KEY,
    ShipperName    varchar(30)        NOT NULL,
    DateInSystem   smalldatetime      NOT NULL
        DEFAULT GETDATE ()
);
```

After you run your CREATE script, you can again make use of `sp_helpconstraint` to see what you have done. You can then test how your default works by inserting a new record:

```
INSERT INTO Shippers
    (ShipperName)
VALUES
    ('United Parcel Service');
```

Then run a SELECT statement on your `Shippers` table:

```
SELECT * FROM Shippers;
```

Code snippet Chap06.sql

The default value has been generated for the `DateInSystem` column since you didn't supply a value yourself:

```
ShipperID      ShipperName                DateInSystem
-----------    --------------------------  ---------------------------
1              United Parcel Service       2011-04-25 19:05:00

(1 row(s) affected)
```

Adding a DEFAULT Constraint to an Existing Table

Although this one is still pretty much more of the same, there is a slight twist. You'll make use of the ALTER statement to ADD the constraint as before, but you must also add a FOR operator to tell SQL Server which column is the target for the DEFAULT:

Available for download on Wrox.com

```
ALTER TABLE Customers
    ADD CONSTRAINT CN_CustomerDefaultDateInSystem
        DEFAULT GETDATE() FOR DateInSystem;
```

And an extra example:

```
ALTER TABLE Customers
   ADD CONSTRAINT CN_CustomerAddress
      DEFAULT 'UNKNOWN' FOR Address1;
```

Code snippet Chap06.sql

As with all constraints except for a PRIMARY KEY, you are able to add more than one per table.

 NOTE *You can mix and match any and all of these constraints as you choose — just be careful not to create constraints that have mutually exclusive conditions. For example, don't have one constraint that says that* col1 > col2 *and another one that says that* col2 > col1. *SQL Server will let you do this, and you wouldn't see the issues with it until runtime.*

DISABLING CONSTRAINTS

Sometimes you want to eliminate constraints, either just for a time or permanently. It probably doesn't take much thought to realize that SQL Server must give you some way of deleting constraints, but SQL Server also allows you to just deactivate a FOREIGN KEY or CHECK constraint while otherwise leaving it intact.

The concept of turning off a data integrity rule might seem rather ludicrous at first. I mean, why would you want to turn off the thing that makes sure you don't have bad data? First, realize that any reason for turning off a data integrity rule is going to be a temporary thing (otherwise you would be dropping it entirely). The usual reason to disable a data integrity rule is because you already have bad data. This data usually falls into two categories:

➤ Data that's already in your database when you create the constraint

➤ Data that you want to add after the constraint is already built

SQL Server allows you to turn the integrity check off long enough to deal with the bad data you want to make an exception for, and then re-enable the integrity check later — all without physically removing the data integrity check.

 NOTE *You cannot disable* PRIMARY KEY *or* UNIQUE *constraints.*

Ignoring Bad Data When You Create the Constraint

All this syntax has been just fine for the circumstances in which you create the constraint at the same time as you create the table. Quite often, however, data rules are established after the fact. Let's say, for instance, that you missed something when you were designing your database, and you now have some records in an `Invoicing` table that show a negative invoice amount. You might want to add a rule that won't let any more negative invoice amounts into the database, but at the same time, you want to preserve the existing records in their original state — someone can deal with those later.

To add a constraint that won't apply to existing data, you make use of the `WITH NOCHECK` option when you perform the `ALTER TABLE` statement that adds your constraint. As always, take a look at an example.

The `Customers` table you created in the Accounting database has a field called `Phone`. The `Phone` field was created with a data type of `char` because you expected all of the phone numbers to be of the same length. You also set it with a length of 15 in order to ensure that you have enough room for all the formatting characters. However, you have not done anything to make sure that the records inserted into the database do indeed match the formatting criteria that you expect. To test this out, try to insert a record in a format that is not what you're expecting, but might be a very honest mistake in terms of how someone might enter a phone number:

```
INSERT INTO Customers
    (CustomerName,
     Address1,
     Address2,
     City,
     State,
     Zip,
     Contact,
     Phone,
     FedIDNo,
     DateInSystem)
VALUES
    ('MyCust',
     '123 Anywhere',
     '',
     'Reno',
     'NV',
     80808,
     'Joe Bob',
     '555-1212',
     '931234567',
     GETDATE());
```

Now add a constraint to control the formatting of the `Phone` field:

```
ALTER TABLE Customers
    ADD CONSTRAINT CN_CustomerPhoneNo
    CHECK
    (Phone LIKE '([0-9][0-9][0-9]) [0-9][0-9][0-9]-[0-9][0-9][0-9][0-9]');
```

Code snippet Chap06.sql

When you run this, you'll see that you have a problem:

```
Msg 547, Level 16, State 0, Line 1
The ALTER TABLE statement conflicted with the CHECK constraint
"CN_CustomerPhoneNo". The conflict occurred in database
    "Accounting", table "dbo.Customers", column 'Phone'.
```

SQL Server does not create the constraint unless the existing data meets the constraint criteria. To get around this long enough to install the constraint, you need to correct the existing data or you must make use of the WITH NOCHECK option in the ALTER statement. To do this, just add WITH NOCHECK to the statement as follows:

```
ALTER TABLE Customers
    WITH NOCHECK
ADD CONSTRAINT CN_CustomerPhoneNo
CHECK
(Phone LIKE '([0-9][0-9][0-9]) [0-9][0-9][0-9]-[0-9][0-9][0-9][0-9]');
```

Now if you run the same INSERT statement again (remember it inserted without a problem last time), the constraint works and the data is rejected:

```
Msg 547, Level 16, State 0, Line 1
The ALTER TABLE statement conflicted with the CHECK constraint
"CN_CustomerPhoneNo". The conflict occurred in database
        "Accounting", table "dbo.Customers", column 'Phone'.
```

However, if you modify the INSERT statement to adhere to the constraint and then re-execute it, the row will be inserted normally:

```
INSERT INTO Customers
    (CustomerName,
    Address1,
    Address2,
    City,
    State,
    Zip,
    Contact,
    Phone,
    FedIDNo,
    DateInSystem)
VALUES
    ('MyCust',
    '123 Anywhere',
    '',
    'Reno',
    'NV',
    80808,
    'Joe Bob',
    '(800) 555-1212',
    '931234567',
    GETDATE());
```

Code snippet Chap06.sql

Try running a SELECT on the Customers table at this point. You'll see data that both does and does not adhere to your CHECK constraint criterion:

```
SELECT CustomerNo, CustomerName, Phone FROM Customers;
```

Code snippet Chap06.sql

```
CustomerNo          CustomerName                    Phone
-----------         --------------------            --------------
1                   Billy Bob's Shoes               (360) 555-1234
2                   Customer1                       553-1212
3                   MyCust                          555-1212
5                   MyCust                          (800) 555-1212

(2 row(s) affected)
```

The old data is retained for back reference, but any new data is restricted to meeting the new criteria.

Temporarily Disabling an Existing Constraint

All right, so you understand why you need to add new constraints that do not check old data, but why would you want to temporarily disable an existing constraint? Why would you want to let data that you know is bad be added to the database? Actually, the most common reason is basically the same reason for which you make use of the WITH NOCHECK option — old data.

Old data doesn't just come in the form of data that has already been added to your database. It may also be data that you are importing from a legacy database or some other system. Whatever the reason, the same issue still holds: You have some existing data that doesn't match up with the rules, and you need to get it into the table.

Certainly one way to do this would be to drop the constraint, add the desired data, and then add the constraint back using a WITH NOCHECK. But what a pain! Fortunately, you don't need to do that. Instead, you can run an ALTER statement with an option called NOCHECK that turns off the constraint in question. Here's the code that disables the CHECK constraint that you just added in the previous section:

```
ALTER TABLE Customers
    NOCHECK
        CONSTRAINT CN_CustomerPhoneNo;
```

Now you can run that INSERT statement again — the one you proved wouldn't work if the constraint were active:

```
INSERT INTO Customers
    (CustomerName,
     Address1,
     Address2,
     City,
     State,
     Zip,
```

```
          Contact,
          Phone,
          FedIDNo,
          DateInSystem)
      VALUES
          ('MyCust',
          '123 Anywhere',
          '',
          'Reno',
          'NV',
          80808,
          'Joe Bob',
          '555-1212',
          '931234567',
          GETDATE());
```

Code snippet Chap06.sql

Once again, you are able to INSERT non-conforming data to the table.

By now, you may be asking how you know whether you have the constraint turned on. It would be pretty tedious if you had to create a bogus record to try to insert in order to test whether your constraint is active. As with most (but not all) of these kinds of dilemmas, SQL Server provides a procedure to indicate the status of a constraint, and it's a procedure you've already seen: sp_helpconstraint. To execute it against your Customers table is easy:

```
      EXEC sp_helpconstraint Customers;
```

Code snippet Chap06.sql

The results are a little too verbose to fit into the pages of this book, but the second result set this procedure generates includes a column called status_enabled. Whatever this column says the status is can be believed. In this case, it should currently be Disabled.

When you are ready for the constraint to be active again, you simply turn it back on by issuing the same command with a CHECK in the place of the NOCHECK:

```
      ALTER TABLE Customers
        CHECK
          CONSTRAINT CN_CustomerPhoneNo;
```

Code snippet Chap06.sql

If you run the INSERT statement to verify that the constraint is again functional, you will see a familiar error message:

```
      Msg 547, Level 16, State 0, Line 1
      The INSERT statement conflicted with the CHECK constraint
      "CN_CustomerDateInSystem". The conflict occurred in database
          "Accounting", table "dbo.Customers", column 'DateInSystem'.
      The statement has been terminated.
```

The other option, of course, is to run sp_helpconstraint again, and check out the status_enabled column. If it shows as Enabled, your constraint must be functional again.

RULES AND DEFAULTS — COUSINS OF CONSTRAINTS

Rules and *defaults* have been around much longer than CHECK and DEFAULT constraints have been. They are something of an old SQL Server standby, and are definitely not without their advantages.

That being said, I'm going to digress from explaining them long enough to recommend that you look them over for backward compatibility and legacy-code familiarity only. Rules and defaults are not ANSI compliant (which creates portability issues), and they do not perform as well as constraints do. Microsoft has listed rules and defaults only for backward compatibility since version 7.0 — that's five versions and nearly 15 years — not an encouraging thing if you're asking yourself whether this feature is going to continue to be supported in the future. I wouldn't go so far as to suggest that you start sifting through and replacing any old code that you may come across (you probably have better uses for your time), but you should use constraints for any new code you generate.

The primary thing that sets rules and defaults apart from constraints is in their very nature; constraints are features of a table — they have no existence on their own — whereas rules and defaults are actual objects in and of themselves. Whereas a constraint is defined in the table definition, rules and defaults are defined independently and are then "bound" to the table after the fact.

The independent-object nature of rules and defaults gives them the ability to be reused without being redefined. Indeed, rules and defaults are not limited to being bound to just tables; they can also be bound to data types, providing the ability to make highly functional user-defined data types on versions of SQL Server that didn't allow CLR data types.

Rules

A rule is incredibly similar to a CHECK constraint. The only difference beyond those I've already described is that rules are limited to working with just one column at a time. You can bind the same rule separately to multiple columns in a table, but the rule will work independently with each column and will not be aware of the other columns at all. A constraint defined as (QtyShipped <= QtyOrdered) would not work for a rule (it refers to more than one column), whereas LIKE ([0-9][0-9][0-9]) would (it applies only to whatever column the rule is bound to).

Let's define a rule so that you can see the differences firsthand:

Available for
download on
Wrox.com

```
CREATE RULE SalaryRule
    AS @Salary > 0;
```

Notice that what you are comparing is shown as a variable. Whatever the value is of the column being checked, that is the value that will be used in the place of @Salary. Thus, in this example, you're saying that any column your rule is bound to would have to have a value greater than zero.

If you want to go back and see what your rule looks like, you can make use of sp_helptext:

```
EXEC sp_helptext SalaryRule;
```

Code snippet Chap06.sql

And it will show you your exact rule definition:

```
Text
-----------------------------------
CREATE RULE SalaryRule
      AS @Salary > 0
```

Now you've got a rule, but it isn't doing anything. If you tried to insert a record in your Employees table, you could still insert any value right now without any restrictions beyond data type.

To activate the rule, you need to make use of a special stored procedure called sp_bindrule. You want to bind your SalaryRule to the Salary column of your Employees table. The syntax looks like this:

```
sp_bindrule <''rule''>, <''object_name''>, [<''futureonly_flag''>]
```

The rule part is simple enough; that's the rule you want to bind. The object_name is also simple; it's the object (column or user-defined data type) to which you want to bind the rule. The only odd parameter is the futureonly_flag, and it applies only when the rule is bound to a user-defined data type. The default is for this to be off. However, if you set it to True or pass in a 1, the binding of the rule will apply only to new columns to which you bind the user-defined data type. Any columns that already have the data type in its old form will continue to use that form.

Because you're just binding this rule to a column, your syntax requires only the first two parameters:

```
EXEC sp_bindrule 'SalaryRule', 'Employees.Salary';
```

Code snippet Chap06.sql

Take a close look at the object_name parameter. You have Employees and Salary separated by a ". " Why is that? Because the rule isn't associated with any particular table until you bind it, you need to state the table and column to which the rule is bound. If you do not use the tablename .column naming structure, SQL Server assumes that what you're naming must be a user-defined data type. If it doesn't find one, you'll get an error message that's a bit confusing if you hadn't intended to bind the rule to a data type:

```
Msg 15148, Level 16, State 1, Procedure sp_bindrule, Line 190
The data type or table column 'Salary' does not exist or you
      do not have permission.
```

In this case, trying to insert or update an Employees record with a negative value violates the rule and generates an error.

If you want to remove the rule from use with this column, you can make use of `sp_unbindrule`:

```
EXEC sp_unbindrule 'Employees.Salary';
```

Code snippet Chap06.sql

The `futureonly_flag` parameter is usually an option, but it doesn't apply to this particular example. If you use `sp_unbindrule` with the `futureonly_flag` turned on, and it is used against a user-defined data type (rather than a specific column), the unbinding will apply only to future uses of that data type — existing columns using that data type will still make use of the rule.

Dropping Rules

If you want to completely eliminate a rule from your database, you use the same DROP syntax that you've already become familiar with for tables:

```
DROP RULE <rule name>
```

Defaults

Defaults are even more similar to their cousin — a DEFAULT constraint — than a rule is to a CHECK constraint. Indeed, they work identically, with the only real differences being in the way that they are attached to a table and the default's (the object, not the constraint) support for a user-defined data type.

> **NOTE** *The concept of defaults versus* DEFAULT *constraints is wildly difficult for a lot of people to grasp. After all, they have almost the same name. If I refer to "default," I am referring to either the object-based default (what I'm talking about in this section), or a shorthand to the actual default value (that will be supplied if you don't provide an explicit value). If I refer to a "*DEFAULT *constraint," I am talking about the non-object-based solution — the solution that is an integral part of the table definition.*

The syntax for defining a default works much as it did for a rule:

```
CREATE DEFAULT <default name>
AS <default value>
```

Therefore, to define a default of zero for `Salary`, use this syntax:

```
CREATE DEFAULT SalaryDefault
    AS 0;
```

Again, a default is worthless without being bound to something. To bind it, you'll make use of `sp_bindefault`, which is, other than the procedure name, identical in syntax to the `sp_bindrule` procedure:

```
EXEC sp_bindefault 'SalaryDefault', 'Employees.Salary';
```

To unbind the default from the table, you'd use `sp_unbindefault`:

```
EXEC sp_unbindefault 'Employees.Salary';
```

Code snippet Chap06.sql

Keep in mind that the `futureonly_flag` also applies to this stored procedure; it is just not used here.

Dropping Defaults

If you want to completely eliminate a default from your database, you use the same DROP syntax that you've already become familiar with for tables and rules:

```
DROP DEFAULT <default name>
```

Determining Which Tables and Data Types Use a Given Rule or Default

If you ever go to delete or alter your rules or defaults, you may first want to take a look at which tables and data types are using them. Again, SQL Server comes to the rescue with a system-stored procedure. This one is called `sp_depends`. Its syntax looks like this:

```
EXEC sp_depends <object name>
```

`sp_depends` provides a listing of all the objects that depend on the object you've requested information about.

 NOTE *Unfortunately,* `sp_depends` *is not a sure bet to tell you about every object that depends on a parent object. SQL Server supports something called "deferred name resolution." Basically, deferred name resolution means that you can create objects (primarily stored procedures) that depend on another object — even before the second (target of the dependency) object is created. For example, SQL Server will now allow you to create a stored procedure that refers to a table even before the said table is created. In this instance, SQL Server isn't able to list the table as having a dependency on it. Even after you add the table, it will not have any dependency listing if you use* `sp_depends`.

TRIGGERS FOR DATA INTEGRITY

There's an entire chapter coming up (Chapter 15) on triggers, but any discussion of constraints, rules, and defaults would not be complete without at least a mention of triggers.

One of the most common uses of triggers is to implement data integrity rules. Because you have that chapter coming up, I'm not going to get into it very deeply here, other than to say that triggers have a very large number of things they can do data integrity-wise that a constraint or rule could never hope to do. The downside (and you knew there had to be one) is that they incur substantial additional overhead and are, therefore, much (very much) slower in almost any circumstance. They are procedural in nature (which is where they get their power), but they also happen after everything else is done and should be used only as a relatively last resort.

CHOOSING WHAT TO USE

Wow. Here you are with all these choices, and now how do you figure out which is the right one to use? Some of the constraints are fairly independent (primary and foreign keys, UNIQUE constraints) — you are using either them or nothing. The rest have some level of overlap with each other, and it can be rather confusing when deciding what to use. You've learned a bit about the strengths and weaknesses each of the options in this chapter, but it will probably make a lot more sense if you look at them all together for a bit. Here they are, compiled into Table 6-1.

TABLE 6-1: Data Integrity Decision Matrix

RESTRICTION	PROS	CONS
Constraints	Fast. Can reference other columns. Happen before the command occurs. ANSI-compliant.	Must be redefined for each table. Can't reference other tables. Can't be bound to data types.
Rules, Defaults	Independent objects. Reusable. Can be bound to data types. Happen before the command occurs.	Slightly slower. Can't reference across columns. Can't reference other tables. Really meant for backward compatibility only!!!
Triggers	Ultimate flexibility. Can reference other columns and other tables. Can even use .NET to reference information that is external to your SQL Server.	Happen after the command occurs. High overhead.

The main time to use rules and defaults is if you are implementing a rather robust logical model and are making extensive use of user-defined data types without the benefit of CLR. In this instance, rules and defaults can provide a lot of functionality and ease of management without much programmatic overhead. You just need to be aware that they may go away someday. Probably not soon, but someday.

Triggers should be used only when a constraint is not an option. Like constraints, they are attached to the table and must be redefined with every table you create. On the bright side, they can do most things that you are likely to want to do data integrity-wise. Indeed, they used to be the common method of enforcing foreign keys (before FOREIGN KEY constraints were added). I will cover these in some detail later in the book.

That leaves constraints, which should become your data integrity solution of choice. They are fast and not that difficult to create. Their downfall is that they can be limiting (they can't reference other tables except for a foreign key), and they can be tedious to redefine over and over again if you have a common constraint logic.

 NOTE *Regardless of what kind of integrity mechanism you're putting in place (keys, triggers, constraints, rules, or defaults), the thing to remember can best be summed up in just one word — balance.*

Every new thing that you add to your database adds more overhead, so you need to make sure that whatever you're adding has value before you stick it in your database. Avoid things like redundant integrity implementations (for example, I can't tell you how often I've come across a database that has foreign keys defined for referential integrity and triggers to do the same thing). Make sure you know what constraints you have before you put the next one on, and make sure you know exactly what you hope to accomplish with it.

SUMMARY

The different types of data integrity mechanisms described in this chapter are part of the backbone of a sound database. Perhaps the biggest power of RDBMSs is that the database can now take responsibility for data integrity rather than depend on the application. This means that even ad hoc queries are subject to the data rules and that multiple applications are all treated equally with regard to data integrity issues.

In the chapters to come, you will see the tie between some forms of constraints and indexes. You'll also look at the advanced data integrity rules that can be implemented using triggers. You'll also begin looking at how the choices between these different mechanisms affect your design decisions.

1. In the Accounting database, create a constraint making the FedIDNo column of the Customers table an alternate key.

2. In your business, an employee can never be her own manager. Create a constraint on the Employees table to prevent this.

▶ **WHAT YOU LEARNED IN THIS CHAPTER**

TOPIC	CONCEPT
Types of constraints	SQL Server provides entity constraints (which refer to columns within a single row), domain constraints (which compare columns across different rows), and referential integrity constraints (which compare columns between related tables).
Key constraints	Primary keys, foreign keys, and unique constraints form the building blocks of referential integrity.
CHECK constraints	Prevent bad data from entering your database from any source by placing CHECK constraints to reject rows that violate the rules.
DEFAULT constraints	Replace values not specified on INSERT with a given default.
Disabling constraints	Allow non-compliant data that either predates the constraint or must be inserted later.
Rules and defaults	Older way of constraining data; mostly to be avoided. Do not confuse defaults with DEFAULT constraints.
Choosing what to use	Constraints are limited but great for what they do; rules and defaults are less limited but nearing obsolescence; triggers are ultimately flexible but much slower than other options.

7

Adding More to Your Queries

WHAT YOU WILL LEARN IN THIS CHAPTER:

➤ How to create and use nested and correlated subqueries

➤ Syntax and purpose of derived tables

➤ Several ways to use Common Table Expressions (CTEs)

➤ How to make use of the `EXISTS` operator

➤ Data manipulation with `MERGE`

➤ Ranking output rows with windowing functions

➤ Ad hoc paging with `OFFSET` and `FETCH`

➤ Tips on optimizing query performance

There are a number of topics in SQL Server that depend on other knowledge, which is a challenge in organizing a book like this. For example, there are things you're about to learn how to do in queries that would be easier if you knew about user-defined functions, or scripting, or variables, but at the same time it's difficult to teach about functions without knowing a few T-SQL statements to put in there. Besides, some of these statements are things that might help a beginning user see some real possibilities, so I'm going to start in on some more interesting things here in an effort to whet your appetite.

Some of the concepts in this chapter are going to challenge you with a new way of thinking. You already had a taste of this just dealing with joins, but you haven't had to deal with the kind of depth that I want to challenge you with in this chapter. Even if you don't have that much procedural programming experience, the fact is that your brain has a natural tendency to break complex problems down into their smaller subparts (sub-procedures, logical steps) as opposed to solving them whole (the "set," or SQL way).

While SQL Server 2012 supports procedural language concepts now more than ever, my challenge to you is to try to see the question as a whole first. Be certain that you can't get it in a single query. Even if you can't think of a way, quite often you can break it up into several small queries and then combine them one at a time back into a larger query that does it all in one task. You should first try to see it as a whole but, if you can't, go ahead and break it down, then combine it into the whole again to the largest extent that makes sense.

This is really what's at the heart of my challenge of a new way of thinking — conceptualizing the question as a whole rather than in steps. When you program in most languages, you usually work in a linear fashion. With SQL, however, you need to think more in terms of set theory. You can liken this to math class and the notion of A union B, or A intersect B. You need to think less in terms of steps to resolve the data and more about how the data fits together.

In this chapter, you'll use this concept of data fit to ask what amounts to multiple questions in just one query. Essentially, you're going to look at ways of taking what seems like multiple queries and placing them into something that will execute as a complete unit. In addition, you'll also be looking at query performance and what you can do to get the most out of queries.

You'll see how, using subqueries, you can make the seemingly impossible completely possible, and how an odd tweak here and there can make a big difference in your query performance.

WHAT IS A SUBQUERY?

A *subquery* is a normal T-SQL query that is nested inside another query. Subqueries are created using parentheses when you have a SELECT statement that serves as the basis for either part of the data or the condition in another query.

Subqueries are generally used to fill one of a few needs:

➤ To break a query into a series of logical steps

➤ To provide a listing to be the target of a WHERE clause together with [IN|EXISTS|ANY|ALL]

➤ To provide a lookup driven by each individual record in a parent query

Some subqueries are very easy to think of and build, but some are extremely complex — it usually depends on the complexity of the relationship between the inner (the sub) and the outer (the top) queries.

It's also worth noting that most subqueries (but definitely not all) can also be written using a join. In places where you can use a join instead, the join is usually the preferable choice for a variety of reasons that you will continue to explore over the remainder of the book.

 NOTE *I have seen spirited debates among experienced developers over the joins versus subqueries (or CTEs, as you'll see later in this chapter) issue.*

In general, the common wisdom has said to always use the join, and that's what I've generally advocated (because of experience rather than traditional logic — you've already seen several places in this book where I've pointed out how traditional thinking can be bogus). In battling some thorny performance issues over the last year, I've had the opportunity to explore this a fair amount.

What I've found was essentially that the right answer depends entirely upon circumstances. You will explore these circumstances fully toward the end of the chapter after you have a bit more background.

Now that you know what a subquery theoretically is, let's look at some specific types and examples of subqueries.

Building a Nested Subquery

A *nested subquery* is one that goes in only *one* direction — returning either a single value for use in the outer query, or perhaps a full list of values to be used with the IN operator. In the event you want to use an explicit = operator, you'll use a query that returns a single value — that means one column from one row. If you are expecting a list back, you'll need to use the IN operator with your outer query.

In the loosest sense, your query syntax will look something like one of these two syntax templates:

```
SELECT <SELECT list>
FROM <SomeTable>
WHERE <SomeColumn> = (
        SELECT <single column>
        FROM <SomeTable>
        WHERE <condition that results in only one row returned>)
```

Or:

```
SELECT <SELECT list>
FROM <SomeTable>
WHERE <SomeColumn> IN (
        SELECT <single column>
        FROM <SomeTable>
        [WHERE <condition>)]
```

Obviously, the exact syntax will vary, not only because you will be substituting the select list and exact table names, but also because you may have a multitable join in either the inner or the outer queries — or both.

Nested Queries Using Single-Value SELECT Statements

Let's get down to the nitty-gritty with an explicit example. Let's say, for example, that you want to know the ProductIDs of every item sold on the first day any product was purchased from the system.

If you already know the first day that an order was placed in the system, it's no problem. The query would look something like this:

```
SELECT DISTINCT sod.ProductID
FROM Sales.SalesOrderHeader soh
JOIN Sales.SalesOrderDetail sod
    ON soh.SalesOrderID = sod.SalesOrderID
WHERE OrderDate = '07/01/2005';  --This is first OrderDate in the system
```

Code snippet Chap07.sql

This yields the correct results:

```
ProductID
-----------
707
708
709
...
...
776
777
778

(47 row(s) affected)
```

But let's say, just for instance, that you are regularly purging data from the system, and you still want to ask this same question as part of an automated report.

Because it's going to be automated, you can't run a query to find out what the first date in the system is and manually plug that into your query — or can you? Actually, the answer is: "Yes, you can," by putting it all into just one statement:

Available for download on Wrox.com

```
SELECT DISTINCT soh.OrderDate, sod.ProductID
FROM Sales.SalesOrderHeader soh
JOIN Sales.SalesOrderDetail sod
   ON soh.SalesOrderID = sod.SalesOrderID
WHERE OrderDate = (SELECT MIN(OrderDate) FROM Sales.SalesOrderHeader);
```

Code snippet Chap07.sql

It's just that quick and easy. The inner query (`SELECT MIN...`) retrieves a single value for use in the outer query. Because you're using an equal sign, the inner query absolutely must return only one column from one single row or you get a runtime error.

> **NOTE** Notice that I added the order date to this new query. While it did not have to be there for the query to report the appropriate ProductIDs, it does clarify what date those ProductIDs are from. Under the first query, you knew what date because you had explicitly said it, but under this new query, the date is data driven, so it is often worthwhile to provide it as part of the result.

Nested Queries Using Subqueries That Return Multiple Values

Perhaps the most common of all subqueries implemented in the world are those that retrieve some form of domain list and use it as criteria for a query.

For this one, let's revisit a problem you looked at in Chapter 4 when you were examining outer joins. What you want is a list of all the products that have special offers.

You might write something like this:

```
SELECT ProductID, Name
FROM Production.Product
WHERE ProductID IN (
    SELECT ProductID FROM Sales.SpecialOfferProduct);
```

Code snippet Chap07.sql

This returns 295 rows:

```
ProductID    Name
----------   -------------------------------------------------
680          HL Road Frame - Black, 58
706          HL Road Frame - Red, 58
707          Sport-100 Helmet, Red
...
...
997          Road-750 Black, 44
998          Road-750 Black, 48
999          Road-750 Black, 52

(295 row(s) affected)
```

While this works just fine, queries of this type almost always can be done using an inner join rather than a nested SELECT. For example, you could get the same results as the preceding subquery by running this simple join:

```
SELECT DISTINCT pp.ProductID, Name
FROM Production.Product pp
JOIN Sales.SpecialOfferProduct ssop
    ON pp.ProductID = ssop.ProductID;
```

Code snippet Chap07.sql

For performance reasons, you want to use the join method as your default solution if you don't have a specific reason for using the nested SELECT — there will be more about this before the chapter's done.

NOTE *SQL Server is actually pretty smart about this kind of thing. In the lion's share of situations, SQL Server actually resolves the nested subquery solution to the same query plan it would use on the join — indeed, if you checked the query plan for both the nested subquery and the previous join, you'd find it was the exact same plan. So, with that in mind, the truth is that most of the time, there really isn't that much difference. The problem, of course, is that I just said most of the time. When the query plans vary, the join is usually the better choice, and thus the recommendation to use that syntax by default.*

Using a Nested SELECT to Find Orphaned Records

This type of nested SELECT is nearly identical to the previous example, except that you add the NOT operator. The difference this makes when you are converting to join syntax is that you are equating to an outer join rather than an inner join.

Before you do the nested SELECT syntax, let's review one of the examples of an outer join from Chapter 4. In this query, you were trying to identify all the special offers that do not have matching products:

```
SELECT Description
FROM Sales.SpecialOfferProduct ssop
RIGHT OUTER JOIN Sales.SpecialOffer sso
    ON ssop.SpecialOfferID = sso.SpecialOfferID
WHERE sso.SpecialOfferID != 1
    AND ssop.SpecialOfferID IS NULL;
```

Code snippet Chap07.sql

This returned one row:

```
Description
--------------------
Volume Discount over 60

(1 row(s) affected)
```

This is the way that, typically speaking, things should be done (or as a LEFT JOIN). I can't say, however, that it's the way that things are usually done. The join usually takes a bit more thought, so you usually wind up with the nested SELECT instead. Why? Well, it comes back to thinking of data in steps rather than sets...the join is set-based thinking, which isn't as natural to many people.

See if you can write this nested SELECT on your own. Once you're done, come back and take a look.

It should wind up looking like this:

```
SELECT Description
FROM Sales.SpecialOffer sso
WHERE sso.SpecialOfferID != 1
    AND sso.SpecialOfferID NOT IN
        (SELECT SpecialOfferID FROM Sales.SpecialOfferProduct);
```

Code snippet Chap07.sql

This yields exactly the same record.

BUILDING CORRELATED SUBQUERIES

Two words for you on this section: Pay attention! This is another one of those little areas that, if you truly get it, can really set you apart from the crowd. By "get it," I don't just mean that you understand how it works, but also that you understand how important it can be.

Correlated subqueries are one of those things that make the impossible possible. What's more, they often turn several lines of code into one and can sometimes create a corresponding increase in performance. The problem with them is that they require a substantially different style of thought than what you're probably used to. Correlated subqueries are probably the single easiest concept in SQL to learn, understand, and then promptly forget, because the concept simply goes against the grain of how you think. If you're one of the few who choose to remember it as an option, you will be one of the few who figure out that hard-to-figure-out problem. You'll also be someone with a far more complete toolset when it comes to squeezing every ounce of performance out of your queries.

How Correlated Subqueries Work

What makes correlated subqueries different from the nested subqueries you've been looking at is that the information travels in *two* directions rather than one. In a nested subquery, the inner query is processed only once, and that information is passed out for the outer query, which will also execute just once — essentially providing the same value or list that you would have provided if you had typed it in yourself.

With correlated subqueries, however, the inner query runs on information provided by the outer query, and vice versa. That may seem a bit confusing (that chicken or the egg thing again), but it works in a three-step process:

1. The outer query obtains a record and passes it into the inner query.

2. The inner query executes based on the passed-in value(s).

3. The inner query then passes the values from its results back to the outer query, which uses them to finish its processing.

Correlated Subqueries in the WHERE Clause

I realize that this is probably a bit confusing, so let's look at it in an example.

Let's go back to the AdventureWorks database and look again at the query where you wanted to know the orders that happened on the first date that an order was placed in the system. However, this time let's add a new twist: you want to know the SalesOrderID(s) and OrderDate of the first order in the system for each customer. That is, you want to know the first day that a customer placed an order and the IDs of those orders. Let's look at it piece by piece.

First, you want the OrderDate, SalesOrderID, and CustomerID for each of your results. All that information can be found in the SalesOrderHeader table, so you know that your query is going to be based, at least in part, on that table.

Next, you need to know what the first date in the system was for each customer. That's where the tricky part comes in. When you did this with a nested subquery, you were looking only for the first date in the entire file — now you need a value that's by individual customer.

This wouldn't be that big a deal if you were to do it in two separate queries — you could just create a temporary table (or CTE) and then join back to it.

> **NOTE** *A temporary table is pretty much just what it sounds like — a table that is created for temporary use and will go away after processing is complete. Exactly how long it will stay around is variable and is outside the scope of this chapter. You will, however, read about temporary tables a bit more as you continue through the book.*
>
> *CTEs (Common Table Expressions) are coming up a little later in this chapter, and are another easy way to organize this type of query. I'll hold off on that example until you get there.*

The temporary table solution might look something like this:

```
USE AdventureWorks;

-- Get a list of customers and the date of their first order
SELECT soh.CustomerID, MIN(soh.OrderDate) AS OrderDate
INTO #MinOrderDates
FROM Sales.SalesOrderHeader soh
GROUP BY soh.CustomerID;

-- Do something additional with that information
SELECT soh.CustomerID, soh.SalesOrderID, soh.OrderDate
FROM Sales.SalesOrderHeader soh
JOIN #MinOrderDates t
  ON soh.CustomerID = t.CustomerID
  AND soh.OrderDate = t.OrderDate
ORDER BY soh.CustomerID;

DROP TABLE #MinOrderDates;
```

Code snippet Chap07.sql

This gets back a little over 19,000 rows:

```
(19119 row(s) affected)
CustomerID   SalesOrderID OrderDate
-----------  ------------ ------------------------
11000        43793        2001-07-22 00:00:00.000
11001        43767        2001-07-18 00:00:00.000
11002        43736        2001-07-10 00:00:00.000
...
...
30116        51106        2003-07-01 00:00:00.000
30117        43865        2001-08-01 00:00:00.000
30118        47378        2002-09-01 00:00:00.000

(19134 row(s) affected)
```

NOTE *As previously stated, don't worry if your results are slightly different from those shown here — it just means you've been playing around with the AdventureWorks data a little more or a little less than I have.*

The fact that you are building two completely separate result sets here is emphasized by the fact that you see two different `row(s) affected` in the results. That, more often than not, has a negative impact on performance. You'll get a chance to explore this further after you explore your options some more.

Sometimes using this multiple-query approach is simply the only way to get things done without using a cursor — this is not one of those times.

Okay, so if you want this to run in a single query, you must find a way to look up each individual customer. You can do this by making use of an inner query that performs a lookup based on the current `CustomerID` in the outer query. You then must return a value back out to the outer query so it can match things up based on the earliest order date.

It looks like this:

```
SELECT soh1.CustomerID, soh1.SalesOrderID, soh1.OrderDate
FROM Sales.SalesOrderHeader soh1
WHERE soh1.OrderDate = (
    SELECT Min(soh2.OrderDate)
    FROM Sales.SalesOrderHeader soh2
    WHERE soh2.CustomerID = soh1.CustomerID)
ORDER BY CustomerID;
```

Code snippet Chap07.sql

With this, you get back the same 19,134 rows:

```
CustomerID  SalesOrderID OrderDate
----------- ------------ -----------------------
11000       43793        2001-07-22 00:00:00.000
11001       43767        2001-07-18 00:00:00.000
11002       43736        2001-07-10 00:00:00.000
. . .
. . .
30116       51106        2003-07-01 00:00:00.000
30117       43865        2001-08-01 00:00:00.000
30118       47378        2002-09-01 00:00:00.000

(19134 row(s) affected)
```

There are a few key things to notice in this query:

➤ **You see only one `row(s) affected` line.** This gives you a good clue that only one query plan had to be executed.

➤ **The outer query (in this example) looks pretty much just like a nested subquery.** The inner query, however, has an explicit reference to the outer query (notice the use of the `soh2` alias).

➤ **Aliases are used in both queries.** This is despite the fact that the outer query shouldn't look like it needs one. Aliases are used because they are required whenever you explicitly refer to a column from the other query (the inside query refers to a column on the outside or vice versa).

NOTE *The latter point concerning needing aliases is a big area of confusion. The fact is that sometimes you need them and sometimes you don't. Although I don't tend to use them in the types of very simple nested subqueries that you looked at in the early part of this chapter, I do alias everything when dealing with correlated subqueries.*

The hard-and-fast rule is that you must alias any table (and its related columns) that's going to be referred to by the other query. The problem is that this can quickly become very confusing. The way to be on the safe side is to alias everything — that way you're positive of which table in which query you're getting your information from.

Note that `19,134 row(s) affected` is displayed only once. That's because it affected 19,134 rows only one time. Just by observation, you might guess that this version probably runs faster than the two-query version and, in reality, it does. Again, you'll delve further into this shortly.

In this particular query, the outer query references only the inner query in the WHERE clause — it could also have requested data from the inner query to include in the select list.

Normally, it's up to you whether to use an alias, but with correlated subqueries they are often required. This particular query is a really great one for showing why, because the inner and outer queries are based on the same table. Because both queries are getting information from each other, how would they know which instance of the table data that you were interested in without aliasing?

Correlated Subqueries in the SELECT List

Subqueries can also be used to provide a different kind of answer in your selection results. This kind of situation is often found where the information you're after is fundamentally different from the rest of the data in your query (for example, you want an aggregation on one field, but you don't want all the baggage from that to affect the other fields returned).

To test this, I'll have you run a somewhat modified version of the query you used in the previous section. What I'm going to say you're after here is just the account number of the customer and the first date on which that customer ordered something.

This tweak creates a somewhat more significant change than is probably apparent at first. You're now asking for the customer's account number, which means that you have to bring the Customer table into play. In addition, you no longer need to build any kind of condition in — you're asking for all customers (no restrictions), and you just want to know when each customer's first order date was.

The query actually winds up being a bit simpler than the last one, and it looks like this:

Available for download on Wrox.com

```
SELECT sc.AccountNumber,
    (SELECT Min(OrderDate)
            FROM Sales.SalesOrderHeader soh
            WHERE soh.CustomerID = sc.CustomerID)
        AS OrderDate
FROM Sales.Customer sc;
```

Code snippet Chap07.sql

This returns data that looks something like this:

```
AccountNumber OrderDate
------------- -----------------------
AW00000001    NULL
AW00000002    NULL
AW00000007    NULL
...
...
AW00030102    2002-12-01 00:00:00.000
AW00030104    2002-07-01 00:00:00.000
AW00030113    2002-09-01 00:00:00.000

(19820 row(s) affected)
```

Note that there are a couple of rows that have a NULL in the Order Date column. Why do you suppose that is? The cause is, of course, because there is no record in the Orders table that matches the then-current record in the Customer table (the outer query). If we weren't concerned about that row, a much simpler query would be possible.

This brings up a small digression, which will cover a useful function for this situation — ISNULL().

Dealing with NULL Data — the ISNULL Function

There are actually a few functions specifically meant to deal with NULL data, but the one of particular use to you at this point is ISNULL(). ISNULL() accepts a variable (which you'll read about in Chapter 11) or expression and tests it for a NULL value. If the value is indeed NULL, the function returns some other specified value. If the original value is not NULL, the original value is returned. This syntax is pretty straightforward:

```
ISNULL(<expression to test>, <replacement value if null>)
```

ISNULL VERSUS COALESCE

ISNULL is a very commonly used function in the realm of Microsoft SQL Server, but it's specific to that database product. The ANSI equivalent, which is also supported in SQL Server, is COALESCE. In any of these examples, COALESCE works exactly the same as ISNULL (I've avoided edge cases where there are some differences); you can try replacing one with the other, if you like, and the results will be identical.

So, why have both? ISNULL stays because it's in common usage and because of the way it handles some edge cases. COALESCE stays because it's ANSI compliant, and also it's a bit more powerful. COALESCE can take more than just two arguments: it can take practically any number (over a thousand), and it will choose the first non-NULL value and return it. If you ever find yourself nesting ISNULL functions, think of using COALESCE instead.

So, for example:

ISNULL EXPRESSION	VALUE RETURNED
ISNULL(NULL, 5)	5
ISNULL(5, 15)	5
ISNULL(MyColumnName, 0) where MyColumnName IS NULL	0
ISNULL(MyColumnName, 0) where MyColumnName = 3	3
ISNULL(MyColumnName, 0) where MyColumnName ='Fred Farmer'	Fred Farmer

Now let's see this at work in your query:

```
SELECT sc.AccountNumber,
   ISNULL(CAST((SELECT Min(OrderDate)
     FROM Sales.SalesOrderHeader soh
     WHERE soh.CustomerID = sc.CustomerID) AS varchar), 'NEVER ORDERED')
     AS OrderDate
FROM Sales.Customer sc;
```

Code snippet Chap07.sql

Now, some example lines that you had problems with. You go from:

```
. . .
. . .
AW00000696    NULL
```

```
AW00000697    NULL
AW00000698    NULL
AW00011012    2003-09-17 00:00:00.000
AW00011013    2003-10-15 00:00:00.000
AW00011014    2003-09-24 00:00:00.000
. . .
. . .
```

to something a bit more useful:

```
. . .
. . .
AW00000696    NEVER ORDERED
AW00000697    NEVER ORDERED
AW00000698    NEVER ORDERED
AW00011012    Sep 17 2003 12:00AM
AW00011013    Oct 15 2003 12:00AM
AW00011014    Sep 24 2003 12:00AM
. . .
. . .
```

NOTE *Notice that I also had to put the* CAST() *function into play to get this to work. The reason has to do with casting and implicit conversion. Because the column* Order Date *is of type* Date *there is an error generated since* NEVER ORDERED *can't be converted to the* Date *data type. Keep* CAST() *in mind — it can help you out of little troubles like this one. This is covered further later in this chapter.*

So, at this point, you've seen correlated subqueries that provide information for both the WHERE clause and the select list. You can mix and match these two in the same query if you wish.

DERIVED TABLES

Sometimes you need to work with the results of a query in a way that doesn't really lend itself to the kinds of subqueries that you've seen up to this point. An example would be where, for each row in a given table, you have multiple results in the subquery, but you're looking for an action more complex than the IN operator provides. Essentially, what I'm talking about here are situations where you wish you could use a JOIN operator on your subquery.

It's at times like these that you can turn to a somewhat lesser known construct in SQL — a *derived table*. A derived table is made up of the columns and rows of a result set from a query. (Heck, they have columns, rows, data types, and so on just like normal tables, so why not use them as such?)

Imagine for a moment that you want to get a list of account numbers and the associated territories for all accounts that ordered a particular product — say, an HL Mountain Rear Wheel. No problem! Your query might look something like this:

```
SELECT sc.AccountNumber, sst.Name
FROM Sales.SalesOrderHeader soh
JOIN Sales.SalesOrderDetail sod
  ON soh.SalesOrderID = sod.SalesOrderID
JOIN Production.Product pp
  ON sod.ProductID = pp.ProductID
JOIN Sales.Customer sc
  ON sc.CustomerID = soh.CustomerID
JOIN Sales.SalesTerritory sst
  ON sst.TerritoryID = sc.TerritoryID
WHERE pp.Name = 'HL Mountain Rear Wheel';
```

Code snippet Chap07.sql

Okay, so other than how many tables were required, that was easy. Now I'm going to throw you a twist — let's now say you want to know the account number and territory for all accounts that ordered not only an HL Mountain Rear Wheel, but also an HL Mountain Front Wheel. Notice that I said they have to have ordered both — now you have a problem. You're first inclination might be to write something like:

```
WHERE pp.Name = 'HL Mountain Rear Wheel'
   AND pp.Name = 'HL Mountain Front Wheel'
```

But that's not going to work at all — each row is for a single product, so how can it have both HL Mountain Rear Wheel and HL Mountain Front Wheel as the name at the same time? Nope — that's not going to get it at all (it will run, but you won't get any rows back).

What you really need here is to join the results of a query to find buyers of HL Mountain Rear Wheel with the results of a query to find buyers of HL Mountain Front Wheel. How do you join results, however? Well, as you might expect given the title of this section, through the use of derived tables.

To create a derived table, you need to do two things:

➤ Enclose the query that generates the result set in parentheses

➤ Alias the results of the query, so the alias can be referenced as a table

So, the syntax looks something like this:

```
SELECT <select list>
FROM (<query that returns a regular resultset>) AS <alias name>
JOIN <some other base or derived table>
```

So let's take this now and apply it to those requirements. Again, what you want are the account numbers and territories of all the companies that have ordered both HL Mountain Rear Wheel and HL Mountain Front Wheel. So your query could look something like this:

```
SELECT DISTINCT sc.AccountNumber, sst.Name
FROM Sales.Customer AS sc
JOIN Sales.SalesTerritory sst
    ON sc.TerritoryID = sst.TerritoryID
JOIN (
    SELECT CustomerID
    FROM Sales.SalesOrderHeader soh
    JOIN Sales.SalesOrderDetail sod
        ON soh.SalesOrderID = sod.SalesOrderID
    JOIN Production.Product pp
        ON sod.ProductID = pp.ProductID
    WHERE pp.Name = 'HL Mountain Rear Wheel') AS dt1
    ON sc.CustomerID = dt1.CustomerID
JOIN (
    SELECT CustomerID
    FROM Sales.SalesOrderHeader soh
    JOIN Sales.SalesOrderDetail sod
        ON soh.SalesOrderID = sod.SalesOrderID
    JOIN Production.Product pp
        ON sod.ProductID = pp.ProductID
    WHERE Name = 'HL Mountain Front Wheel') AS dt2
    ON sc.CustomerID = dt2.CustomerID;
```

Code snippet Chap07.sql

You wind up with 58 accounts:

```
AccountNumber Name
------------- -----------------------------
AW00029484    Southeast
AW00029490    Northwest
AW00029499    Canada
. . .
. . .
AW00030108    Canada
AW00030113    United Kingdom
AW00030118    Central

(58 row(s) affected)
```

If you want to check things out on this, just run the queries for the two derived tables separately and compare the results.

> **NOTE** *For this particular query, I needed to use the* DISTINCT *keyword. If I didn't, I would have potentially received multiple rows for each customer — for example, AW00029771 has ordered the HL Mountain Rear Wheel twice, so I would have gotten one record for each. I only asked which customers had ordered both, not how many had they ordered.*

As you can see, you were able to take a seemingly impossible query and make it both possible and even reasonably well performing.

Keep in mind that derived tables aren't the solutions for everything. For example, if the result set is going to be fairly large and you're going to have lots of joined records, you might want to look at using a temporary table and building an index on it (derived tables have no indexes). Every situation is different, but now you have one more weapon in your arsenal.

USING COMMON TABLE EXPRESSIONS (CTES)

One of the reasons I thought it would be a good idea to revise this book for SQL Server 2012 is that in a few cases the common ways of doing things are beginning to change. This is definitely one of those times. Until fairly recently, if you needed to somehow transform a table and use the result, you probably felt like you had plenty of options. You could use a subquery, or a derived table, or you could create a temporary table. Today, Common Table Expressions are often used for those same tasks.

On the surface, then, you might think, "We already have three ways of doing this . . . why do we need one more?" If this were only a kind of new syntax for derived tables, you'd surely be right. It turns out that CTEs offer some really cool new functionality — like recursion — along with their more simple applications. Let's start simple and work up to the fun stuff.

Using the WITH Keyword

In its simplest use, a CTE is like a derived table that's declared up front rather than inline. The small (but nifty) advantage this syntax provides is that it organizes your code so that it's a little easier to read. Rather than trying to arrange your derived table's indenting and parentheses so it's clearly set apart from the rest of your joins (or WHERE conditions, or however you're using it), the CTE way of doing this puts the derived table's definition at the top of your query. To begin a query with a CTE, you use the WITH keyword.

The syntax for this looks like:

```
WITH <expression_name> [ ( column_name [ ,...n ] ) ]
    AS
    ( CTE_query_definition )
    [, <another_expression>]
<query>
```

So you begin by giving your CTE a name, exactly like the alias you might have used for a derived table. You can then provide a list of column names that the CTE will return; if the CTE names all its own return columns, this is optional. Finally, within parentheses comes the CTE query definition, followed by the main query that uses the CTE.

TERMINATING STATEMENTS WITH A SEMICOLON

If you look back through the code examples in this book, you'll find that sometimes (but not all the time) I've ended my T-SQL statements with a semicolon. While you've heard me rail about consistency, this is one area that I haven't entirely achieved it yet myself. The semicolons are never harmful but rarely required, so using them is, on balance, a good habit to start.

The statement before a `WITH` is one of the rare situations in which a semicolon is required. You see, `WITH` is an overloaded keyword in T-SQL. Among its uses are declaring namespaces for XML-based queries, suggesting indexes or other optimizer hints, and now beginning a CTE. This ambiguity about the meaning of `WITH` means that the parser needs a bit of help to know for sure what you mean — is this `WITH` part of the statement you're just finishing (a hint), or part of the next (a CTE)? By terminating the prior statement, you give SQL server what it needs to know what you were doing.

TRY IT OUT | Using a CTE

The last example you looked at using a derived table did something interesting: it created two derived tables using identical tables, joins, and selected columns, and then it joined them. Give that one a try using a CTE.

Once you've defined a CTE, you can use it as many times as you like within the current statement. What you can do here, then, is to perform all your joins in the CTE to produce the people who've purchased a product, and then join two instances of that together to find those who have bought both products.

```
WITH MyCTE AS (
SELECT sc.CustomerID, sc.AccountNumber, sst.Name, pp.Name ProductName
    FROM Sales.SalesOrderHeader soh
    JOIN Sales.SalesOrderDetail sod
        ON soh.SalesOrderID = sod.SalesOrderID
    JOIN Production.Product pp
        ON sod.ProductID = pp.ProductID
    JOIN Sales.Customer sc
    ON sc.CustomerID = soh.CustomerID
    JOIN Sales.SalesTerritory sst
    ON sc.TerritoryID = sst.TerritoryID
)
SELECT DISTINCT Rear.AccountNumber, Rear.Name
FROM MyCTE Rear  --Rear Wheel
JOIN MyCTE Front --Front Wheel
    ON Rear.CustomerID = Front.CustomerID
WHERE Rear.ProductName = 'HL Mountain Rear Wheel'
AND Front.ProductName = 'HL Mountain Front Wheel';
```

Code snippet Chap07.sql

How It Works

MyCTE functions very much like a derived table, but because it's defined at the start of the statement, it can be used as many times during the statement as you like. MyCTE retrieves all the combinations of products purchased by customers. The normal-looking SELECT query that follows uses that as if it were a table (or view, or derived table, or however you're most comfortable thinking about that), choosing which rows to display in the WHERE clause. It's easy to see that if you wanted to compare a third product, you could simply join the CTE in again — say if you wanted to see whether those wheels were purchased along with a frame.

Using a CTE can also help with one of the problems you solved in Chapter 4, about combining inner and outer joins. If you recall, there was an example showing how to create an outer join to an inner joined combination of tables, which could be resolved either by reordering joins or by grouping them as follows:

Available for download on Wrox.com

```
USE Chapter4DB

SELECT v.VendorName, a.Address
FROM Vendors v
LEFT JOIN (
    VendorAddress va
    JOIN Address a
        ON va.AddressID = a.AddressID
)
ON v.VendorID = va.VendorID
```

Code snippet Chap07.sql

NOTE To run this example, you'll need the Chapter4DB database you downloaded and created back in Chapter 4 (joins).

This kind of logic can be a great deal simpler by embedding the inner join in a CTE, and then outer joining to that in the main query.

```
WITH a AS (
    SELECT va.VendorID, a.Address
    FROM VendorAddress va
    JOIN Address a
        ON va.AddressID = a.AddressID
)
SELECT v.VendorName, a.Address
FROM Vendors v
LEFT JOIN a
    ON v.VendorID = a.VendorID;
```

Code snippet Chap07.sql

Using Multiple CTEs

Having started your statement with WITH lets you define not just one, but many CTEs without repeating the WITH keyword. What's more, each one can use (as a part of its definition) any CTE defined earlier in the statement. All you have to do is finish your CTE with a comma and start the next definition.

Working this way can build up a final result with a bit more procedural thinking ("first I need a complete customer made up of these things, then I need an order made up of those . . . ") while still allowing the query optimizer to have a decent chance to work things out efficiently using set theory. For example, let's try that sales query again, but build it up one step at a time.

```sql
USE AdventureWorks

WITH CustomerTerritory AS (
    SELECT sc.CustomerID, sc.AccountNumber, sst.Name TerritoryName
    FROM Sales.Customer sc
    JOIN Sales.SalesTerritory sst
        ON sc.TerritoryID = sst.TerritoryID
), MyCTE AS (
SELECT sc.CustomerID, sc.AccountNumber, sc.TerritoryName, pp.Name ProductName
    FROM Sales.SalesOrderHeader soh
    JOIN Sales.SalesOrderDetail sod
        ON soh.SalesOrderID = sod.SalesOrderID
    JOIN Production.Product pp
        ON sod.ProductID = pp.ProductID
    JOIN CustomerTerritory sc
        ON sc.CustomerID = soh.CustomerID
)
SELECT DISTINCT Rear.AccountNumber, Rear.TerritoryName
FROM MyCTE Rear  --Rear Wheel
JOIN MyCTE Front --Front Wheel
    ON Rear.CustomerID = Front.CustomerID
WHERE Rear.ProductName = 'HL Mountain Rear Wheel'
AND Front.ProductName = 'HL Mountain Front Wheel';
```

Code snippet Chap07.sql

Not only does organizing the query this way produce exactly the same 58 rows as in the prior example, but the query optimizer executes it in exactly the same way.

Recursive CTEs

CTEs can refer to prior CTEs, but if you structure them right they can also call themselves recursively.

Huh?

Recursion is a topic that, for most programmers, is a dangerous brain-bender right up until the point where it becomes second nature. If you're not familiar with the concept, there's a brief but more complete introduction to the idea of recursion in Chapter 12, but for now I'm going to leave it at this: a recursive program calls itself, eventually hitting a base or anchor instance that returns without the recursive call.

A detailed description of recursive CTE behavior is hardly beginner matter, so I'm not going to go further into it in this book, but it's important to know what's possible.

USING THE EXISTS OPERATOR

I call EXISTS an operator, but Books Online calls it a keyword. That's probably because it defies description in some senses. It's an operator much like the IN keyword is, but it also looks at things just a bit differently.

When you use EXISTS, you don't really return data — instead, you return a simple TRUE/FALSE regarding the existence of data that meets the criteria established in the query that the EXISTS statement is operating against.

Filtering with EXISTS

Let's go right to an example, so you can see how this is applied. What you'll see how to query here is a list of people who are employees:

Available for download on Wrox.com

```
SELECT BusinessEntityID, LastName + ', ' + FirstName AS Name
FROM Person.Person pp
WHERE EXISTS
    (SELECT BusinessEntityID
    FROM HumanResources.Employee hre
    WHERE hre.BusinessEntityID = pp.BusinessEntityID);
```

Code snippet Chap07.sql

As you might expect, this returns a relatively small subset of the Person table — 290 of them:

```
BusinessEntityID Name
---------------- ---------------------------------------
263              Trenary, Jean
78               D'sa, Reuben
242              Poe, Deborah
...
...
95               Scardelis, Jim
215              Harrington, Mark
112              Evans, John

(290 row(s) affected)
```

You could have easily done this same thing with a join:

```
SELECT pp.BusinessEntityID, LastName + ', ' + FirstName AS Name
FROM Person.Person pp
JOIN HumanResources.Employee hre
  ON pp.BusinessEntityID = hre.BusinessEntityID;
```

Code snippet Chap07.sql

This join-based syntax, for example, would have yielded exactly the same results (subject to possible sort differences). So why, then, would you want to use this new syntax? Performance — plain and simple.

When you use the EXISTS keyword, SQL Server doesn't have to perform a full row-by-row join. Instead, it can look through the records until it finds the first match and stop right there. As soon as there is a single match, the EXISTS is TRUE, so there is no need to go further.

Let's take a brief look at things the other way around — that is, what if your query wanted the persons who were *not* employees? Under the join method that you looked at in Chapter 4, you would have had to make some significant changes in the way you went about getting your answer. First, you would have to use an outer join. Then you would perform a comparison to see whether any of the Employee records were NULL.

It would look something like this:

```
SELECT pp.BusinessEntityID, LastName + ', ' + FirstName AS Name
FROM Person.Person pp
LEFT JOIN HumanResources.Employee hre
    ON pp.BusinessEntityID = hre.BusinessEntityID
WHERE hre.BusinessEntityID IS NULL;
```

Code snippet Chap07.sql

Which returns 19,682 rows:

```
BusinessEntity    ID Name
---------------   ------------------------------
293               Abel, Catherine
295               Abercrombie, Kim
2170              Abercrombie, Kim
...
...
2088              Zugelder, Judy
12079             Zukowski, Jake
2089              Zwilling, Michael

(19682 row(s) affected)
```

To do the same change over using EXISTS instead of JOIN, you add only one word to the original EXISTS query — NOT:

```
SELECT BusinessEntityID, LastName + ', ' + FirstName AS Name
FROM Person.Person pp
WHERE NOT EXISTS
    (SELECT BusinessEntityID
    FROM HumanResources.Employee hre
    WHERE hre.BusinessEntityID = pp.BusinessEntityID);
```

Code snippet Chap07.sql

And you get back those exact same 19,682 rows.

The performance difference here is, in most cases, even more marked than with the inner join. SQL Server just applies a little reverse logic versus the straight EXISTS statement. In the case of the NOT you're now using, SQL can still stop looking as soon as it finds one matching record — the only difference is that it knows to return FALSE for that lookup rather than TRUE. Performance-wise, everything else about the query is the same.

Using EXISTS in Other Ways

One common use of EXISTS is to check for the existence of a table before running a CREATE statement. You may want to drop an existing table, or you just may want to change to an ALTER statement or some other statement that adjusts the existing table, if there is one. One of the most common ways you'll see this done looks something like this:

Available for
download on
Wrox.com

```
IF EXISTS
    (SELECT *
    FROM sys.objects
    WHERE OBJECT_NAME(object_id) = 'foo'
        AND SCHEMA_NAME(schema_id) = 'dbo'
        AND OBJECTPROPERTY(object_id, 'IsUserTable') = 1)
BEGIN
    DROP TABLE dbo.foo;
    PRINT 'Table foo has been dropped';
END
GO

CREATE TABLE dbo.foo
(
  Column1 int IDENTITY(1,1) NOT NULL,
  Column2 varchar(50)NULL
);
```

Code snippet Chap07.sql

Because EXISTS returns nothing but TRUE or FALSE, it works as an excellent conditional expression. The preceding example runs the DROP TABLE code only if the table exists; otherwise, it skips over that part and moves right into the CREATE statement. This avoids one of two errors showing up when you run the script:

➤ **The script can't run the CREATE statement because the object already exists.** You would probably create other problems if you were running this in a script where other tables were depending on this being done first.

➤ **The script can't DROP the table because the table didn't exist yet.** This pretty much just creates a message that might be confusing to a customer who installs your product.

You're covered for both.

As an example of this, you can try writing your own CREATE script for something that's often skipped in the automation effort — the database. But creation of the database is often left as part of some cryptic directions that say something like "create a database called 'xxxx'." The fun part is when the people who are actually installing it (who often don't know what they're doing) start including the quotes, or creating a database that is too small, or making a host of other possible and very simple errors. This is the point where I hope you have a good tech support department.

Instead of leaving that in questionably capable hands, you can just build a little script to create the database object that could go with AdventureWorks. For safety's sake, let's call it AdventureWorksCreate. In this example you should keep the statement to a minimum because you're interested in the EXISTS rather than the CREATE command:

```
USE MASTER;
GO

IF NOT EXISTS
    (SELECT 'True'
    FROM sys.databases
    WHERE name = 'AdventureWorksCreate')
BEGIN
    CREATE DATABASE AdventureWorksCreate;
END
ELSE
BEGIN
    PRINT 'Database already exists. Skipping CREATE DATABASE Statement';
END
GO
```

Code snippet Chap07.sql

The first time you run this, there won't be any database called AdventureWorksCreate (unless by sheer coincidence you created something called that before you got to this point), so you'll get a response that looks like this:

```
Command(s) completed successfully.
```

This was unhelpful in terms of telling you what exactly was done, but at least you know it thinks it did what you asked.

Now run the script a second time and you'll see a change:

```
Database already exists. Skipping CREATE DATABASE Statement
```

So, without much fanfare or fuss, you've added a rather small script that makes things much more usable for the installers of your product. That may be an end user who bought your off-the-shelf product, or it may be you — in which case it's even better that it's fully scripted.

The long and the short of it is that EXISTS is a very handy keyword indeed. It can make some queries run much faster, and it can also simplify some queries and scripts.

> **NOTE** *A word of caution here — this is another one of those places where it's easy to get trapped in "traditional thinking." While* EXISTS *blows other options away in a large percentage of queries where* EXISTS *is a valid construct, that's not always the case. For example, the query used as a derived table example can also be written with a couple of* EXISTS *operators (one for each product), but the derived table happens to run more than twice as fast. That's definitely the exception, not the rule —* EXISTS *normally smokes a derived table for performance. Just remember that rules are sometimes made to be broken.*

MIXING DATA TYPES: CAST AND CONVERT

You'll see both CAST and CONVERT used frequently. Indeed, you've seen both of these very briefly already in this chapter. Considering how often you'll use these two functions, this seems like a good time to look a little closer at what they can do for you.

Both CAST and CONVERT perform data type conversions for you. In most respects, they both do the same thing, with the exception that CONVERT also does some date-formatting conversions that CAST doesn't offer.

> **NOTE** *So, the question probably quickly rises in your mind, "Hey, if* CONVERT *does everything that* CAST *does, and* CONVERT *also does date conversions, why would I ever use* CAST*?" I have a simple answer for that — ANSI/ISO compliance.* CAST *is ANSI/ISO-compliant, but* CONVERT *isn't — it's that simple.*

Let's take a look for the syntax for each.

```
CAST (expression AS data_type)

CONVERT(data_type, expression[, style])
```

With a little flip-flop on which goes first and the addition of the formatting option on CONVERT (with the `style` argument), they have basically the same syntax.

CAST and CONVERT can deal with a wide variety of data type conversions that you'll need to do when SQL Server won't do it implicitly for you. For example, converting a number to a string is a very common need. To illustrate:

```
SELECT 'The Customer has an Order numbered ' + SalesOrderID
FROM Sales.SalesOrderHeader
WHERE CustomerID = 29825;
```

will yield an error:

```
Msg 245, Level 16, State 1, Line 1
Conversion failed when converting the varchar value 'The Customer has an
Order numbered ' to data type int.
```

But change the code to convert the number first:

```
SELECT 'The Customer has an Order numbered ' + CAST(SalesOrderID AS
varchar)
FROM Sales.SalesOrderHeader
WHERE CustomerID = 29825;
```

Code snippet Chap07.sql

And you get a much different result:

```
----------------------------------------------------------------
The Customer has an Order numbered 43659
The Customer has an Order numbered 44305
The Customer has an Order numbered 45061
The Customer has an Order numbered 45779
The Customer has an Order numbered 46604
The Customer has an Order numbered 47693
The Customer has an Order numbered 48730
The Customer has an Order numbered 49822
The Customer has an Order numbered 51081
The Customer has an Order numbered 55234
The Customer has an Order numbered 61173
The Customer has an Order numbered 67260

(12 row(s) affected)
```

The conversions can actually get a little less intuitive. For example, what if you wanted to convert a `timestamp` column into a regular number? A `timestamp` is just a binary number, so the conversion isn't any really big deal:

Available for download on Wrox.com

```
CREATE TABLE ConvertTest
(
    ColID    int     IDENTITY,
    ColTS    timestamp
);
GO

INSERT INTO ConvertTest
    DEFAULT VALUES;

SELECT ColTS AS Uncoverted, CAST(ColTS AS int) AS Converted
FROM ConvertTest;
```

Code snippet Chap07.sql

This yields something like (your exact numbers will vary):

```
(1 row(s) affected)
Uncoverted          Converted
-----------------   -------------
0x00000000000000C9  201

(1 row(s) affected)
```

You can also convert dates:

```
SELECT OrderDate, CAST(OrderDate AS varchar) AS Converted
FROM Sales.SalesOrderHeader
WHERE SalesOrderID = 43663;
```

Code snippet Chap07.sql

This yields something similar to (your exact format may change depending on system date configuration):

```
OrderDate               Converted
----------------------  -----------------------------
2001-07-01 00:00:00.000 Jul  1 2001 12:00AM

(1 row(s) affected)
```

Notice that CAST can still do date conversion; you just don't have any control over the formatting as you do with CONVERT. For example:

Available for download on Wrox.com

```
SELECT OrderDate, CONVERT(varchar(12), OrderDate, 111) AS Converted
FROM Sales.SalesOrderHeader
WHERE SalesOrderID = 43663;
```

Code snippet Chap07.sql

This yields:

```
OrderDate               Converted
----------------------  ------------
2001-07-01 00:00:00.000 2001/07/01

(1 row(s) affected)
```

Which is quite a bit different from what CAST did. Indeed, you could have converted to any one of 34 two-digit- or four-digit-year formats.

```
SELECT OrderDate, CONVERT(varchar(12), OrderDate, 5) AS Converted
FROM Sales.SalesOrderHeader
WHERE SalesOrderID = 43663;
```

Code snippet Chap07.sql

This returns:

```
OrderDate               Converted
----------------------- ------------
2001-07-01 00:00:00.000 01-07-01

(1 row(s) affected)
```

All you need is to supply a code at the end of the CONVERT function (111 in the preceding example gave us the Japan standard, with a four-digit year, and 5 the Italian standard, with a two-digit year) that tells which format you want. Anything in the 100s is a four-digit year; anything less than 100, with a few exceptions, is a two-digit year. The available formats can be found in Books Online under the topic of CONVERT or CASE.

 NOTE *Keep in mind that you can set a* split point *that SQL Server will use to determine whether a two-digit year should have a 20 added on the front or a 19. The default breaking point is 49/50 — a two-digit year of 49 or less will be converted using a 20 on the front. Anything higher will use a 19. These can be changed in the database server configuration (administrative issues are discussed in Chapter 21).*

SYNCHRONIZING DATA WITH THE MERGE COMMAND

The MERGE command was new with SQL Server 2008 and provides a somewhat different way of thinking about DML statements. With MERGE, you have the prospect of combining multiple DML action statements (INSERT, UPDATE, and DELETE) into one overall action, improving performance (they can share many of the same physical operations) and simplifying transactions. MERGE makes use of a special USING clause that winds up working somewhat like a CTE. The result set in the USING clause can then be used to conditionally apply your INSERT, UPDATE, and DELETE statements. The basic syntax looks something like this:

```
MERGE [ TOP ( <expression> ) [ PERCENT ] ]
  [ INTO ] <target table> [ WITH ( <hint> ) ] [ [ AS ] <alias> ]
  USING <source query>
    ON <condition for join with target>
  [ WHEN MATCHED [ AND <clause search condition> ]
      THEN <merge matched> ]
  [ WHEN NOT MATCHED [ BY TARGET ] [ AND <clause search condition> ]
      THEN <merge not matched> ]
  [ WHEN NOT MATCHED BY SOURCE [ AND <clause search condition> ]
      THEN <merge matched> ]
  [ <output clause> ]
  [ OPTION ( <query hint> [ ,...n ] ) ];
```

The Merge Command in Action

Let's use the example of receiving a shipment for inventory. Assume that you're keeping a special roll up table of your sales for reporting purposes. You want to run a daily query that will add any new sales to your monthly roll up. On the first night of the month, this is pretty much a no-brainer, as, because there are no other roll up records for the month, any sales for the day are just rolled up and inserted. On the second day, however, you have a different scenario: You need to roll up and insert new records as you did the first day, but you must update existing records (for products that have already sold that month).

Let's take a look at how MERGE can manage both actions in one step. Before you get going on this, however, you need to create your roll up table:

Available for download on Wrox.com

```
USE AdventureWorks

CREATE TABLE Sales.MonthlyRollup
(
    Year       smallint    NOT NULL,
    Month      tinyint     NOT NULL,
    ProductID int         NOT NULL
    FOREIGN KEY
        REFERENCES Production.Product(ProductID),
    QtySold    int         NOT NULL,
    CONSTRAINT PKYearMonthProductID
      PRIMARY KEY
      (Year, Month, ProductID)
);
```

Code snippet Chap07.sql

This is a pretty simple example of a monthly roll up table making it very easy to get sales totals by product for a given year and month. To make use of this, however, you need to regularly populate it with rolled up values from your detail table. To do this, you'll use MERGE.

First, you need to start by establishing a result set that will figure out from what rows you need to be sourcing data for your roll up. For purposes of this example, focus on August 2007 and start with a query for the first day of the month:

Available for download on Wrox.com

```
SELECT soh.OrderDate, sod.ProductID, SUM(sod.OrderQty) AS QtySold
FROM Sales.SalesOrderHeader soh
JOIN Sales.SalesOrderDetail sod
    ON soh.SalesOrderID = sod.SalesOrderID
WHERE soh.OrderDate >= '2007-08-01'
    AND soh.OrderDate < '2007-08-02'
GROUP BY soh.OrderDate, sod.ProductID;
```

Code snippet Chap07.sql

This gets you the total sales, by ProductID, for every date in your range (your range just happens to be limited to one day).

NOTE *There is a bit of a trap built into how this has been done this up to this point. I've set the* GROUP BY *to use the* OrderDate, *but* OrderDate *is a datetime data type as opposed to just a* date *data type. If orders were to start coming in with actual times on them, it would mess with the assumption of the orders all grouping nicely into one date. If this were a production environment, you would want to cast the* OrderDate *to a* date *data type or use* DATEPART *to ensure that the grouping was by day rather than by time.*

With this, you're ready to build your merge:

```
Figure          [FILENAME]
MERGE Sales.MonthlyRollup AS smr
USING
(
    SELECT soh.OrderDate, sod.ProductID, SUM(sod.OrderQty) AS QtySold
    FROM Sales.SalesOrderHeader soh
    JOIN Sales.SalesOrderDetail sod
        ON soh.SalesOrderID = sod.SalesOrderID
    WHERE soh.OrderDate >= '2007-08-01' AND soh.OrderDate < '2007-08-02'
    GROUP BY soh.OrderDate, sod.ProductID
) AS s
ON (s.ProductID = smr.ProductID)
WHEN MATCHED THEN
    UPDATE SET smr.QtySold = smr.QtySold + s.QtySold
WHEN NOT MATCHED THEN
    INSERT (Year, Month, ProductID, QtySold)
    VALUES (DATEPART(yy, s.OrderDate),
        DATEPART(m, s.OrderDate),
        s.ProductID,
        s.QtySold);
```

Code snippet Chap07.sql

Note that the semicolon is required at the end of the MERGE statement. Although the semicolon remains optional on most SQL statements for backward-compatibility reasons, you'll find it working its way into more and more statements as a required delimiter of the end of the statement (or before, for CTEs). This is particularly true for multipart statements such as MERGE.

When you run this, you should get 192 rows affected, assuming you haven't been altering the data in AdventureWorks. Now, because your Sales.MonthlyRollup table was empty, there wouldn't have been any matches, so all rows were inserted. You can verify that by querying the Sales .MonthlyRollup table:

```
SELECT *
FROM Sales.MonthlyRollup;
```

Code snippet Chap07.sql

This returns the expected 192 rows:

```
Year   Month  ProductID    QtySold
------ -----  -----------  -----------
2003   8      707          242
2003   8      708          281
2003   8      711          302
...
...
2003   8      997          43
2003   8      998          138
2003   8      999          103

(192 row(s) affected)
```

Every row that was in the basic SELECT that powered your MERGE wound up being inserted into your table. Let's move on, however, to the second day of the month:

Available for download on Wrox.com

```
MERGE Sales.MonthlyRollup AS smr
USING
(
    SELECT soh.OrderDate, sod.ProductID, SUM(sod.OrderQty) AS QtySold
    FROM Sales.SalesOrderHeader soh
    JOIN Sales.SalesOrderDetail sod
        ON soh.SalesOrderID = sod.SalesOrderID
    WHERE soh.OrderDate >= '2007-08-02' AND soh.OrderDate < '2007-08-03'
    GROUP BY soh.OrderDate, sod.ProductID
) AS s
ON (s.ProductID = smr.ProductID)
WHEN MATCHED THEN
    UPDATE SET smr.QtySold = smr.QtySold + s.QtySold
WHEN NOT MATCHED THEN
    INSERT (Year, Month, ProductID, QtySold)
    VALUES (DATEPART(yy, s.OrderDate),
        DATEPART(m, s.OrderDate),
        s.ProductID,
        s.QtySold);
```

Code snippet Chap07.sql

You update the date you're running this for (simulating running it on the second day of the month), and running it should get you 38 rows:

```
(38 row(s) affected)
```

But something is different this time — you already had rows in the table that your new batch of sales may have matched up with. You know you affected 38 rows, but *how* did you affect them? Rerun the SELECT on your table:

Available for download on Wrox.com

```
SELECT *
FROM Sales.MonthlyRollup;
```

Code snippet Chap07.sql

And instead of 230 rows (the 192 plus the 38), you get only 194 rows. Indeed, 36 of your 38 rows were repeat sales and were therefore treated as updates, rather than insertions. Two rows (`ProductIDs` 882 and 928) were sales of products that had not been previously sold in that month and thus needed to be inserted as new rows — one pass over the data, but the equivalent of two statements ran.

You could perform similar actions that decide to delete rows based on matched or not matched conditions.

A Brief Look at BY TARGET versus BY SOURCE

In the previous examples, I've largely ignored the issue of what table you must match when you're determining the action to perform. The default is BY TARGET, and thus all of the examples (which haven't used the BY keyword) have been analyzed on whether there is or isn't a match in the target table (the table named immediately after the MERGE keyword). The comparison, from a matching perspective, is similar to a full outer join. As the join is analyzed, there can be a match on the source side, the target side, or both. If you have specified BY TARGET (or not used the BY keyword at all because matching by target is the default), the action (INSERT, UPDATE, or DELETE) is applied only if the target side of the join has a match. Likewise, if you have specified BY SOURCE, the merge action is applied only if the source side of the join has a match.

Most of the time, you can map a particular merge action to a specific match scenario:

➤ **NOT MATCHED [BY TARGET]:** This typically maps to a scenario where you insert rows into a table based on data you found in the source.

➤ **MATCHED [BY TARGET]:** This implies that the row already exists in the target, and thus it is likely you will perform an update action on the target table row.

➤ **NOT MATCHED BY SOURCE:** This is typically utilized to deal with rows that are missing (and likely deleted) from the source table, and you will usually be deleting the row in the target under this scenario (although you may also just update the row to set an inactive flag or similar marker).

There are other possible mixes, but these easily cover the bulk of things that most any SQL developer will see.

GATHERING AFFECTED ROWS WITH THE OUTPUT CLAUSE

Sometimes when you perform a DML operation, there's more you want to do with the affected rows. The INSERT, DELETE, and MERGE commands provide you the option of outputting what amounts to a SELECT statement with the details of what actions were actually performed. The OUTPUT keyword is essentially a substitute for SELECT, but brings along several special operators to allow you to match up to the merged data. These include:

➤ **$action:** Used with MERGE only. Returns INSERTED, UPDATED, or DELETED, as appropriate, to indicate the action taken for that particular row.

➤ **inserted:** Used with MERGE, INSERT, or UPDATE. A reference to an internal working table that contains a reference to any data inserted for a given row. Note that this includes the current values for data that has been updated.

➤ **deleted:** Used with MERGE, DELETE, or UPDATE. A reference to an internal working table that contains a reference to any data deleted from a given row. Note that this includes the previous values for data that has been updated.

 NOTE *You will visit the* inserted *and* deleted *tables in much more detail when you explore triggers in Chapter 15.*

Let's try these by resetting your MonthlyRollup table, and executing your MERGE statements again with the OUTPUT clause included. Start by truncating the MonthlyRollup table to clear out your previous work:

```
USE AdventureWorks
TRUNCATE TABLE Sales.MonthlyRollup;
```

This clears all data out of the table and resets everything about the table to a state as though it had just been created using the CREATE command. You're now ready to execute your first MERGE statement again, but this time including the OUTPUT clause:

```
MERGE Sales.MonthlyRollup AS smr
USING
(
  SELECT soh.OrderDate, sod.ProductID, SUM(sod.OrderQty) AS QtySold
  FROM Sales.SalesOrderHeader soh
  JOIN Sales.SalesOrderDetail sod
    ON soh.SalesOrderID = sod.SalesOrderID
  WHERE soh.OrderDate >= '2007-08-01' AND soh.OrderDate < '2007-08-02'
  GROUP BY soh.OrderDate, sod.ProductID
) AS s
ON (s.ProductID = smr.ProductID)
WHEN MATCHED THEN
  UPDATE SET smr.QtySold = smr.QtySold + s.QtySold
WHEN NOT MATCHED THEN
  INSERT (Year, Month, ProductID, QtySold)
  VALUES (DATEPART(yy, s.OrderDate),
          DATEPART(m, s.OrderDate),
          s.ProductID,
          s.QtySold)
OUTPUT $action,
        inserted.Year,
        inserted.Month,
        inserted.ProductID,
        inserted.QtySold,
```

```
        deleted.Year,
        deleted.Month,
        deleted.ProductID,
        deleted.QtySold;
```

Code snippet Chap07.sql

This, of course, performs exactly the same action it did the first time you ran it (inserting 192 rows), but this time you get a result set back that provides information about the action taken:

```
$action Year Month ProductID QtySold Year Month ProductID QtySold
------- ---- ----- --------- ------- ---- ----- --------- -------
INSERT  2007 8     707       242     NULL NULL  NULL      NULL
INSERT  2007 8     708       281     NULL NULL  NULL      NULL
INSERT  2007 8     711       302     NULL NULL  NULL      NULL
......
......
INSERT  2007 8     997       43      NULL NULL  NULL      NULL
INSERT  2007 8     998       138     NULL NULL  NULL      NULL
INSERT  2007 8     999       103     NULL NULL  NULL      NULL
(192 row(s) affected)
```

Notice that, because you had only inserted rows in this particular query, all the data from the deleted table is null. Things change quickly though when you run the second MERGE statement (with the same OUTPUT clause added):

```
MERGE Sales.MonthlyRollup AS smr
USING
(
  SELECT soh.OrderDate, sod.ProductID, SUM(sod.OrderQty) AS QtySold
  FROM Sales.SalesOrderHeader soh
  JOIN Sales.SalesOrderDetail sod
    ON soh.SalesOrderID = sod.SalesOrderID
  WHERE soh.OrderDate >= '2007-08-02' AND soh.OrderDate < '2007-08-03'
  GROUP BY soh.OrderDate, sod.ProductID
) AS s
ON (s.ProductID = smr.ProductID)
WHEN MATCHED THEN
  UPDATE SET smr.QtySold = smr.QtySold + s.QtySold
WHEN NOT MATCHED THEN
  INSERT (Year, Month, ProductID, QtySold)
  VALUES (DATEPART(yy, s.OrderDate),
          DATEPART(m, s.OrderDate),
          s.ProductID,
          s.QtySold)
OUTPUT $action,
        inserted.Year,
        inserted.Month,
        inserted.ProductID,
        inserted.QtySold,
        deleted.Year,
```

```
        deleted.Month,
        deleted.ProductID,
        deleted.QtySold;
```

Code snippet Chap07.sql

This time you see more than one action and, in the case of UPDATED results, you have data for both the inserted (the new values) and the deleted (the old values) tables:

```
$action Year Month ProductID QtySold Year   Month ProductID QtySold
------- ---- ----- --------- ------- ------ ----- --------- -------
INSERT  2003 8     928       2       NULL   NULL  NULL      NULL
INSERT  2003 8     882       1       NULL   NULL  NULL      NULL
UPDATE  2003 8     707       249     2007   8     707       242
...

...
UPDATE  2003 8     963       32      2007   8     963       31
UPDATE  2003 8     970       54      2007   8     970       53
UPDATE  2003 8     998       139     2007   8     998       138
(38 row(s) affected)
```

THROUGH THE LOOKING GLASS: WINDOWING FUNCTIONS

By now you've learned a lot that can be done in SQL Server, and if you've gone through the examples and understood them, you're probably starting to feel pretty competent. Very likely this feeling is accurate, but of course there's always something more. Ranking or windowing functions can show how truly deep the rabbit hole goes.

Using the windowing functions ROW_NUMBER, RANK, DENSE_RANK, and NTILE, you can have SQL count off your results to determine where each row falls within the result set (or a partition thereof).

Let's look more closely at a couple of these now and see ways they can be used.

ROW_NUMBER

On its surface, ROW_NUMBER is the simplest of these functions. It simply outputs a unique, incrementing value for each returned row.

To start digging into the usefulness of this, imagine the HR department at AdventureWorks has formed a compensation committee to work out bonuses for the sales staff. The department managers have a few questions for you while they try to come up with an equitable split, beginning with a relatively simple question — how do the sales staff rank, first to last, with respect to sales year-to-date?

Using only the ROW_NUMBER function and specifying that its order should be over the sales amount in descending order, you can answer this first exploratory question easily.

```
SELECT p.LastName,
    ROW_NUMBER() OVER (ORDER BY s.SalesYTD DESC) AS 'Row Number',
    CAST(s.SalesYTD AS INT) SalesYTD, a.PostalCode
FROM Sales.SalesPerson s
```

```
      INNER JOIN Person.Person p
          ON s.BusinessEntityID = p.BusinessEntityID
      INNER JOIN Person.Address a
          ON a.AddressID = p.BusinessEntityID
  WHERE TerritoryID IS NOT NULL
      AND SalesYTD <> 0;
```

Code snippet Chap07.sql

This ranks the salespeople in order of their sales, showing Mitchell as clearly #1.

LastName	Row Number	SalesYTD	PostalCode
Mitchell	1	4251369	98027
Pak	2	4116871	98055
Blythe	3	3763178	98027
Carson	4	3189418	98027
Varkey Chudukatil	5	3121616	98055
Saraiva	6	2604541	98055
Ito	7	2458536	98055
Reiter	8	2315186	98027
Valdez	9	1827067	98055
Mensa-Annan	10	1576562	98055
Campbell	11	1573013	98055
Vargas	12	1453719	98027
Tsoflias	13	1421811	98055
Ansman-Wolfe	14	1352577	98027

```
(14 row(s) affected)
```

Your work isn't done. The compensation committee quickly realizes that, given different conditions in the two sales regions (determined by their postal codes), they'd prefer to rank each region differently. Fortunately, you have the PARTITION BY clause available. PARTITION BY tells the function to reset its count when a column (or combination of columns) changes value. In this case, you'll start counting over when you change postal codes.

```
SELECT p.LastName,
    ROW_NUMBER() OVER
        (PARTITION BY PostalCode ORDER BY s.SalesYTD DESC) AS 'Row Number',
    CAST(s.SalesYTD AS INT) SalesYTD, a.PostalCode
FROM Sales.SalesPerson s
    INNER JOIN Person.Person p
        ON s.BusinessEntityID = p.BusinessEntityID
    INNER JOIN Person.Address a
        ON a.AddressID = p.BusinessEntityID
WHERE TerritoryID IS NOT NULL
    AND SalesYTD <> 0;
```

Code snippet Chap07.sql

And now you have the rows numbered within each postal code, but still ranked in sales order.

LastName	Row Number	SalesYTD	PostalCode
Mitchell	1	4251369	98027
Blythe	2	3763178	98027
Carson	3	3189418	98027
Reiter	4	2315186	98027
Vargas	5	1453719	98027
Ansman-Wolfe	6	1352577	98027
Pak	1	4116871	98055
Varkey Chudukatil	2	3121616	98055
Saraiva	3	2604541	98055
Ito	4	2458536	98055
Valdez	5	1827067	98055
Mensa-Annan	6	1576562	98055
Campbell	7	1573013	98055
Tsoflias	8	1421811	98055

```
(14 row(s) affected)
```

TRY IT OUT   Using ROW_NUMBER() to Choose a Related Row

When you combine ROW_NUMBER with a CTE, you get a very useful case — the ability to pick out the highest ranked row for a given group, based on an arbitrary ranking.

In the example you just tried, you could partition the output to determine the sales rank within each region. As in other places, however, this query perhaps returns more than you might want: how can you return only the top salesperson for each region? With only 14 rows, it's easy enough in this case to do things manually, but you'll rarely be dealing with datasets small enough to go through by hand.

If you're thinking ahead, you might be tempted to try something like this:

```
SELECT p.LastName,
    ROW_NUMBER() OVER
        (PARTITION BY PostalCode ORDER BY s.SalesYTD DESC) AS 'Row Number',
    CAST(s.SalesYTD AS INT) SalesYTD, a.PostalCode
FROM Sales.SalesPerson s
    INNER JOIN Person.Person p
        ON s.BusinessEntityID = p.BusinessEntityID
    INNER JOIN Person.Address a
        ON a.AddressID = p.BusinessEntityID
WHERE TerritoryID IS NOT NULL
    AND SalesYTD <> 0
        AND ROW_NUMBER() OVER
            (PARTITION BY PostalCode ORDER BY s.SalesYTD DESC) = 1;
```

But you'll see that produces an error.

```
Msg 4108, Level 15, State 1, Line 13
Windowed functions can only appear in the SELECT or ORDER BY clauses.
```

Sadly, it's true. What you can do, though, is place the windowed output within a CTE, and then filter that.

```
WITH Ranked AS (
SELECT p.LastName,
    ROW_NUMBER() OVER
        (PARTITION BY PostalCode ORDER BY s.SalesYTD DESC) AS 'Row Number',
    CAST(s.SalesYTD AS INT) SalesYTD, a.PostalCode
FROM Sales.SalesPerson s
    INNER JOIN Person.Person p
        ON s.BusinessEntityID = p.BusinessEntityID
    INNER JOIN Person.Address a
        ON a.AddressID = p.BusinessEntityID
WHERE TerritoryID IS NOT NULL
    AND SalesYTD <> 0
)
SELECT LastName, SalesYTD, PostalCode
FROM Ranked
WHERE [Row Number] = 1;
```

Code snippet Chap07.sql

Now you can see the output you were after.

```
LastName              SalesYTD    PostalCode
-------------------   ----------  ---------------
Mitchell              4251369     98027
Pak                   4116871     98055

(2 row(s) affected)
```

How It Works

These functions are computed after the WHERE clause has already filtered the rows, so it's too late to apply the output of the function as a filter. Until the WHERE clause has done its work, there's no way to number the output rows. The optimizer may have had other work to do as well, such as performing joins, that might change the cardinality of the result set and affect the function output.

Using this pattern, it's easy to grab the "top" row(s) within an arbitrary group and based on whatever ordering you've got in mind.

RANK, DENSE_RANK, and NTILE

Let's get back to the compensation committee's questions about salesperson bonuses. The value of ROW_NUMBER for the work so far has been that it generates, within each partition, a unique numbering. That's a problem now for the HR folks, who believe firmly in ties. Depending on how they wish to accommodate ties, you may want to use RANK, DENSE_RANK, or NTILE(x).

➤ **RANK:** Allows multiple rows to have the same value if their order value is the same, but resumes counting at the ROW_NUMBER value; for example, where the first rank is an n-way tie, the second rank starts with a RANK value of n+1.

➤ **DENSE_RANK:** Also keeps a matching value for matching order values, but the ranks always increment; for example, the second rank is always 2 regardless of an n-way tie for first.

➤ **NTILE(x):** Divides the total result into x categories, and ranks them from 1-x; thus NTILE(4) gives the first quarter of the results a 1, the second quarter a 2, and so on.

Here's a query that illustrates the four functions you've just learned. Note that each of the rankings is ordered by PostalCode and not partitioned when looking at the results.

```
SELECT p.LastName,
    ROW_NUMBER() OVER (ORDER BY a.PostalCode) AS 'Row Number',
    RANK() OVER (ORDER BY a.PostalCode) AS 'Rank',
    DENSE_RANK() OVER (ORDER BY a.PostalCode) AS 'Dense Rank',
    NTILE(4) OVER (ORDER BY a.PostalCode) AS 'Quartile',
    CAST(s.SalesYTD AS INT) SalesYTD, a.PostalCode
FROM Sales.SalesPerson s
    INNER JOIN Person.Person p
        ON s.BusinessEntityID = p.BusinessEntityID
    INNER JOIN Person.Address a
        ON a.AddressID = p.BusinessEntityID
WHERE TerritoryID IS NOT NULL
    AND SalesYTD <> 0;
```

Code snippet Chap07.sql

You can see the output in Table 7-1.

TABLE 7-1: Windowing Functions

LASTNAME	ROW NUMBER	RANK	DENSE RANK	QUARTILE	SALESYTD	POSTALCODE
Blythe	1	1	1	1	3763178	98027
Mitchell	2	1	1	1	4251369	98027
Carson	3	1	1	1	3189418	98027
Vargas	4	1	1	1	1453719	98027
Reiter	5	1	1	2	2315186	98027
Ansman-Wolfe	6	1	1	2	1352577	98027
Ito	7	7	2	2	2458536	98055
Saraiva	8	7	2	2	2604541	98055
Campbell	9	7	2	3	1573013	98055
Mensa-Annan	10	7	2	3	1576562	98055
Tsoflias	11	7	2	3	1421811	98055
Valdez	12	7	2	4	1827067	98055
Pak	13	7	2	4	4116871	98055
Varkey Chudukatil	14	7	2	4	3121616	98055

ONE CHUNK AT A TIME: AD HOC QUERY PAGING

There are a fair number of dedicated database programmers out there, and perhaps you're looking to join their ranks. For those who have specialized in this field, phrases like "UI design" generate a very fast response of "somebody else's problem." There's one aspect of UI design, though, that's been a pain point for a while: paging.

Wherever your query results are eventually going to be displayed, quite often that user interface has room for fewer than infinite results on a screen (particularly in web-based applications). UI designers have used paging as a common solution for some time, showing perhaps the top 20 results and allowing the user to fetch the next 20 with a click of a More button. What they don't want to do in many cases is cache the whole result set — it could have millions of rows!

Since their introduction in SQL 2005, it's been common to use the ranking functions above to help implement this kind of paging, but the SQL required to implement that solution has a little complexity to it. In SQL Server 2012, there's a new syntax designed to expressly solve this problem: OFFSET . . . FETCH. OFFSET tells a SELECT query how many rows to skip, and FETCH says how many rows to retrieve starting there.

In this example, your web designer has asked you to assist her with a product catalog page. In its simplest form, it simply has to show 20 products per page. The first page's results could easily be retrieved using the following SELECT TOP (20) query:

Available for download on Wrox.com

```
SELECT TOP 20 ProductID, ProductNumber, Name
FROM Production.Product
ORDER BY ProductNumber
```

The real challenge is how you're going to get the second page, third page, and beyond. You can do that with OFFSET ... FETCH:

```
SELECT ProductID, ProductNumber, Name
FROM Production.Product
ORDER BY ProductNumber
OFFSET 20 ROWS
FETCH NEXT 20 ROWS ONLY

SELECT ProductID, ProductNumber, Name
FROM Production.Product
ORDER BY ProductNumber
OFFSET 40 ROWS
FETCH NEXT 20 ROWS ONLY
```

Code snippet Chap07.sql

There are a couple minor restrictions with this syntax that I should warn you about.

➤ ORDER BY is required to use an OFFSET . . . FETCH clause.

➤ Although OFFSET can be used without FETCH, FETCH cannot be used without OFFSET.

➤ You can't use SELECT TOP with OFFSET ... FETCH.

➤ Although you can use arithmetic or variables to determine how many rows to offset or fetch, you cannot use a scalar subquery.

PERFORMANCE CONSIDERATIONS

You've already been exposed to some of the macro-level "what's the best thing to do" stuff as you've gone through the chapter, but, like most things in life, it's not as easy as all that. What I want to do here is provide something of a quick reference for performance issues for your queries. I'll try to steer you toward the right kind of query for the right kind of situation.

ON USING BLANKET RULES

Yes, it's time again folks for one of my now famous soapbox diatribes. At issue this time is the concept of blanket use of blanket rules.

What I'm going to be talking about in this section is the way that things *usually* work. The word "usually" is extremely operative here. There are very few rules in SQL that will be true 100 percent of the time. In a world full of exceptions, SQL has to be at the pinnacle of that — exceptions are a dime a dozen when you try to describe the performance world in SQL Server.

In short, you need to gauge just how important the performance of a given query is. If performance is critical, don't take these rules too seriously — instead, use them as a starting point, and then TEST, TEST, TEST!!!

Measuring Performance

I'm going to have a lot more to say about this later, but until you have some kind of way to see how your queries perform, the exhortation to test them can seem almost cruel. I can almost hear the urgent question, "How?!"

What I'm about to give you is just a couple tools. Remember, though, that to a man with only a hammer, every problem looks like a nail. I'm giving you a hammer and a screwdriver, but you'd do well to read up on other techniques before relying on these for every query.

 NOTE *When testing performance, simulating real-world conditions can be critical. You should always test on data as similar in variety and volume as possible to what you expect to find in real life, and do so on a hardware and software platform as much like the production server(s) that you plan to have live on game day as you can manage. This includes (where possible) any load balancing, replication, maintenance jobs, and the like.*

NOTE *Once, back in the days when a gig of memory cost a small fortune, I tested a new procedure on our test hardware. I used a backup of the actual live database, so I knew my data was genuinely identical to a real-life scenario, and the test hardware and OS were precisely identical but for one thing: the test server had 4GB of memory, while the live server had 8GB.*

You know I wouldn't be writing this note if there weren't a surprise, so it should be no surprise that when we went live, the test results didn't pan out. The new code, which took a few minutes on the test hardware, took hours on live — which was the server with more memory! The actual difference (with the additional memory, SQL used a parallel query plan that turned out to be really bad) is immaterial. The real point is if it's not identical, there's a risk, however slight.

Here are a few tools for evaluating the performance of your queries.

➤ **For rough numbers, just run the query.** Sometimes this is all it takes to know that something's wrong; if you expect it to come back instantly and it takes a few seconds (or minutes, or more), you've learned what you need to know.

➤ **Back in Chapter 2, you had a brief look at a query plan.** By checking the estimated cost shown in the mouseover text on the query root, you can get a very broad metric for how costly the query is likely to be.

➤ Using **SET STATISTICS TIME ON** and/or **SET STATISTICS IO ON**, you can get numeric values for time, disk reads, and other actual values. While these numbers are real, remember they can be affected by data in cache, so run each test a few times.

NOTE *One last word (for now) on performance: data from your tables costs a lot more to read from disk than from the buffer. The first time your query reads a table's data from disk, it'll be markedly slower than successive times. Remember this when comparing two versions of a query: make sure you're testing with either the data in cache for both or empty for both, or you may fool yourself into using the wrong version.*

JOINs versus Subqueries versus CTEs versus . . .

This is that area I mentioned earlier in the chapter that often causes heated debate. And, as you might expect when two people have such conviction in their points of view, both views are correct up to a point (and, it follows, wrong up to a point).

The long-standing, traditional viewpoint about subqueries has always been that you are much better off using joins if you can. This is absolutely correct — sometimes. In reality, it depends on a large number of factors. Table 7-2 discusses some of the issues that the performance balance will depend on and which side of the equation they favor.

TABLE 7-2: Choosing among Subqueries, Derived Tables, and CTEs

SITUATION	FAVORS
The value returned from a subquery is going to be the same for every row in the outer query.	Pre-query. Declaring a variable and then selecting the needed value into that variable will allow the would-be subquery to be executed just once, rather than once for every record in the outer table.
Both tables are relatively small (say 10,000 records or fewer).	Subqueries. I don't know the exact reasons, but I've run several tests on this and it held up pretty much every time. I suspect that the issue is the lower overhead of a lookup versus a join.
The match, after considering all criteria, is going to return only one value.	Subqueries. Again, there is much less overhead in going and finding just one record and substituting it than having to join the entire table.
The match, after considering all criteria, is going to return relatively few values, and there is no index on the lookup column.	Subqueries. A single lookup or even a few lookups will usually take less overhead than a hash join.
The lookup table is relatively small, but the base table is large.	Nested subqueries, if applicable; joins or CTEs if versus a correlated subquery. With subqueries, the lookup will happen only once and is relatively low overhead. With correlated subqueries, however, you will be cycling the lookup many times — in this case, the join is a better choice.
Correlated subquery versus join versus CTE	CTE or join, based on readability. Internally, a correlated subquery creates a nested-loop situation. This can create quite a bit of overhead. It is substantially faster than cursors in most instances, but slower than other options that might be available. Use a join if it's simple, or a CTE if the join obfuscates the query's meaning.
Derived tables versus whatever	Derived tables typically carry a fair amount of overhead to them, so proceed with caution. The thing to remember is that they are run (derived, if you will) once, and then they are in memory, so most of the overhead is in the initial creation and the lack of indexes (in larger result sets). They can be fast or slow — it just depends. Think before coding on these.
EXISTS versus whatever	EXISTS. EXIST does not have to deal with multiple lookups for the same match. Once it finds one match for that particular row, it is free to move on to the next lookup — this can seriously cut down on overhead.

These are just the highlights. The possibilities of different mixes and additional situations are positively endless.

 NOTE *I can't stress enough how important it is when in doubt — heck, even when you're not in doubt but performance is everything — to make reasonable tests of competing solutions to a problem. Most of the time the blanket rules will be fine, but not always. By performing reasonable tests, you can be certain you've made the right choice.*

SUMMARY

The query options you learned back in Chapters 3 and 4 cover perhaps 80 percent or more of the query situations that you run into, but it's that other 20 percent that can kill you. Sometimes the issue is whether you can even find a query that will give you the answers you need. Sometimes it's that you have a particular query or sproc that has unacceptable performance. Whatever the case, you'll run across plenty of situations where simple queries and joins just won't fit the bill. You need something more and, hopefully, the options covered in this chapter have given you a little extra ammunition to deal with these tough situations.

EXERCISES

1. Write a query that returns the hire dates of all AdventureWorks employees in MM/DD/YY format.

2. Write separate queries using a join, a subquery, a CTE, and then an `EXISTS` to list all AdventureWorks persons who have not placed an order.

3. Show the most recent five orders that were purchased from account numbers that have spent more than $70,000 with AdventureWorks.

▶ WHAT YOU LEARNED IN THIS CHAPTER

TOPIC	CONCEPT
Nested Subqueries	You can use this to return one or more values to a query from tables not necessarily otherwise addressed in that query. Often the same work can be accomplished more efficiently with a join, but not always.
Correlated Subqueries	Subqueries that refer back to fields in the outer query, and so get executed once per row returned by the outer query. Can have a significant impact on performance, either positive or negative depending on alternatives.
Derived Tables	A syntax for embedding a query within a query and giving it a table-like alias, so that it acts like a table.
Common Table Expressions	Declared at the beginning of a statement, CTEs are similar in purpose to derived tables but are somewhat more flexible and generally perform better. CTEs can refer back to earlier CTEs defined in the same statement, or even recursively to themselves.
`EXISTS`	Works like an operator on a subquery, looking for the first row that matches. It's a very efficient way to find that information (which could also be done through a join), because it can stop searching as soon as it finds the first matching row.
`MERGE`	Allows you to compare two datasets and to insert, update, and/or delete rows, based on matching rows in either dataset, within a single pass over the data.
Windowing Functions	You can rank data based on ordering not otherwise applied to the query, and even use multiple orderings for different functions. Different rankings include `ROW_NUMBER`, `RANK`, `DENSE_RANK`, and `NTILE`. Windowing functions are especially useful when combined with CTEs.
`OFFSET ... FETCH`	Permits ad hoc paging through a result set by allowing the use of an offset from the beginning and a number of rows to return. Useful for returning pages of data to a UI, among other things.
Measuring Performance	Looking at the query plan and measuring IO and time against actual runs are two good ways of measuring query performance. Because different plans may be used based on differences in hardware, data quantity, data profile, or other considerations, it is critical to measure performance in an environment as similar to real as possible.

Being Normal: Normalization and Other Basic Design Issues

WHAT YOU WILL LEARN IN THIS CHAPTER:

➤ How to organize your tables into third normal form, and what the other normal forms entail

➤ Which types of relationships can be defined between tables, and the mechanisms available to enforce them

➤ How to diagram your database using the tools provided with SQL Server

➤ Design issues beyond normalization, including denormalization

I can imagine you as being somewhat perplexed about the how and why of some of the tables you've constructed thus far. With the exception of a chapter or two, this book has tended to have an *Online Transaction Processing*, or *OLTP*, flair to the examples. Don't get me wrong; I will point out, from time to time, some of the differences between OLTP and its more analysis-oriented cousin *Online Analytical Processing (OLAP)*. My point is that you will, in most of the examples, be seeing a table design that is optimized for the most common kind of database — OLTP. As such, the table examples will typically have a database layout that is, for the most part, *normalized* to what is called the third normal form.

So what is "normal form"? You'll be taking a very solid look at that in this chapter, but, for the moment, let's just say that it means your data has been broken into a logical, non-repetitive format that can easily be reassembled into the whole. In addition to normalization (which is the process of putting your database into normal form), you'll also be examining the characteristics of OLTP and OLAP databases. And, as if you didn't have enough between those two topics, you'll also be looking at many examples of how the constraints you've already seen are implemented in the overall solution.

NOTE *This is probably going to be one of the toughest chapters in the book to grasp because of a paradox in what to learn first. Some of the concepts used in this chapter refer to topics I'll be covering later — such as triggers and stored procedures. On the other hand, it is difficult to relate those topics without giving you an understanding of their role in database design.*

I strongly recommend reading this chapter through, and then coming back to it again after you've read several of the subsequent chapters.

UNDERSTANDING TABLES

This is going to seem beyond basic, but let's briefly review what exactly a table is. I'm obviously not talking about the kind that sits in your kitchen, but, rather, the central object of any database.

A table is a collection of instances of data that have the same general *attributes*. These instances of data are organized into *rows* and *columns* of data. A table should represent a "real-world" collection of data (often referred to as an *entity*), and will have *relationships* with information in other tables. A drawing of the various entities (tables) and relationships (how they work together) is usually referred to as an entity-relationship diagram — or *ER diagram*. Sometimes the term "ER diagram" will even be shortened further to *ERD*.

By connecting two or more tables through their various relationships, you can temporarily create other tables as needed from the combination of the data in both tables (you've already seen this to some degree in Chapters 4 and 5). A collection of related entities are then grouped together into a database.

KEEPING YOUR DATA "NORMAL"

Normalization is something of the cornerstone model of modern OLTP database design. Normalization first originated along with the concept of relational databases. Both came from the work of E. F. Codd (IBM) in 1969. Codd put forth the notion that a database "consists of a series of unordered tables that can be manipulated using non-procedural operations that return tables."

Several things are key about this:

➤ Order must be unimportant.

➤ The tables need to "relate" to each other in a non-procedural way (indeed, Codd called tables "relations").

➤ By relating these base tables, you can create a virtual table to meet a new need.

Normalization was a natural offshoot of the design of a database of "relations."

UNDERSTANDING NORMALIZATION

The concept of normalization has to be one of most over-referenced and yet misunderstood concepts in programming. Everyone thinks they understand it, and many do in at least its academic form. Unfortunately, it also tends to be one of those things that many database designers wear like a cross — it is somehow their symbol that they are "real" database architects. What it really is, however, is a symbol that they know what the normal forms are — and that's all. Normalization is really just one piece of a larger database design picture. Sometimes you need to normalize your data — then again, sometimes you need to deliberately denormalize your data. Even within the normalization process, there are often many ways to achieve what is technically a normalized database.

My point in this latest soapbox diatribe is that normalization is a theory, and that's all it is. Once you choose whether to implement a normalized strategy, what you have is a database — hopefully the best one you could possibly design. Don't get stuck on what the books (including this one) say you're supposed to do — do what's right for the situation that you're in. As the author of this book, all I can do is relate concepts to you — I can't implement them for you, and neither can any other author (at least not with the written word). You need to pick and choose between these concepts in order to achieve the best fit and the best solution. Now, excuse me while I put that soapbox away and get on to talking about the normal forms and what they purportedly do for you.

Let's start off by saying that there are six normal forms. For those of you who have dealt with databases and normalization some before, that number may come as a surprise. You are very likely to hear that a fully normalized database is one that is normalized to the third normal form — doesn't it then follow that there must be only three normal forms? Perhaps it will make those same people who thought there were only three normal forms feel better that this book covers only the three forms you've heard about, as they are the only three that are put to any regular use in the real world. I will, however, briefly (very briefly) skim over the other three forms just for posterity.

You've already looked at how to create a primary key and some of the reasons for using one in tables — if you want to act on just one row, you need to uniquely identify that row. The concepts of normalization are highly dependent on issues surrounding the definition of the primary key and what columns are dependent on it. One phrase you might hear frequently in normalization is:

The key, the whole key, and nothing but the key.

The somewhat fun addition to this is:

The key, the whole key, and nothing but the key, so help me Codd!

This is a super-brief summarization of what normalization is about out to the third normal form. When you can say that all your columns are dependent only on the whole key and nothing more or less, you are at the third normal form.

Let's take a look at the various normal forms and what each does for you.

Before the Beginning

You actually need to begin by getting a few things in place even before you try to get your data into first normal form. The following guidelines must be in place before you can consider the table to be a true entity in the relational database sense of the word:

> ➤   The table should describe one and only one entity. (No trying to shortcut and combine things!)

> ➤   All rows must be unique, and there must be a primary key.

> ➤   The column and row order must not matter.

The place to start, then, is by identifying the right entities to have. Some of these are fairly obvious, others are not. Many of them are exposed and refined as you go through the normalization process. At the very least, go through and identify all the obvious entities.

 NOTE *If you're familiar with object-oriented programming, you can liken the most logical top-level entities to objects in an object model.*

Think about a simple model — the sales model — again. To begin with, you're not going to worry about the different variations possible, or even what columns you're going to have — instead, you're just going to worry about identifying the basic entities of your system.

First, think about the most basic process. What you want to do is create an entity for each atomic unit that you want to maintain data on in the process. Your process, then, looks like this:

> ➤   **Start with a business scenario:** A customer calls or comes in and talks to an employee who takes an order.

> ➤   **First pass at entities:** A first pass on this might have one entity: Orders.

 NOTE *As you become more experienced at normalization, your first pass at something like this is probably going to yield you quite a few more entities right from the beginning. For now though, let's just take this one and see how the normalization process shows you the others that you need.*

> ➤   **Primary key:** Assuming you have your concepts down of what you want your entities to be, the next place to go is to determine your beginning columns and, from there, a primary key.

Remember that a primary key provides a unique identifier for each row. You can peruse your list of columns and come up with *key candidates*. Your list of key candidates should include any column that can potentially be used to uniquely identify each row in your entity. There is, otherwise, no hard and fast rule as to which column has to be the primary key (this is one of many reasons you'll see such wide variation in how people design databases that are meant to contain the same basic information). In some cases, you will not be able to find even one candidate key, and you will need to make one up (remember the Identity and rowguid() columns?).

You already created an Orders table in the previous chapter, but for example purposes take a look at a very common implementation of an Orders table in the old flat file design:

ORDERS
OrderNo
CustomerNo
CustomerName
CustomerAddress
CustomerCity
CustomerState
CustomerZip
OrderDate
ItemsOrdered
Total

Because this is an Orders table, and logically, an order number is meant to be one to an order, I'm going to go with OrderNo as my primary key.

Okay, so now you have a basic entity. Nothing about this entity cares about the ordering of columns (tables are, by convention, usually organized as having the primary key as the first column(s), but, technically speaking, it doesn't have to be that way). Nothing in the basic makeup of this table cares about the ordering of the rows. The table, at least superficially, describes just one entity. In short, you're ready to begin your normalization process (actually, you sort of already have).

The First Normal Form

The first normal form (*1NF*) is all about eliminating repeating groups of data and guaranteeing *atomicity* (the data is self-contained and independent). At a high level, it works by creating a primary key (which you already have), and then moving any repeating data groups into new tables, creating new keys for those tables, and so on. In addition, you break out any columns that combine data into separate rows for each piece of data.

In the more traditional flat file designs, repeating data was commonplace — as was having multiple pieces of information in a column. This was rather problematic in a number of ways:

➤ **Expense:** At that time, disk storage was extremely expensive. Storing data multiple times means wasted space. Data storage has become substantially less expensive, so this isn't as big an issue as it once was.

➤ **Performance:** Repetitive data means more data to be moved, and larger I/O counts. This means that performance is hindered as large blocks of data must be moved through the data bus and or network. This, even with today's much faster technology, can have a substantial negative impact on performance.

➤ **Data integrity:** The data between rows of what should have been repeating data often did not agree, creating something of a data paradox and a general lack of data integrity.

➤ **Parsing data:** If you wanted to query information out of a column that has combined data, you had to first come up with a way to parse the data in that column (this was extremely slow).

Now, there are a lot of columns in your table (well, for a simple example anyway), and I probably could have easily tossed in a few more. Still, the nice thing about it is that I could query everything from one place when I want to know about orders.

Just to explore what this means, take a look at what some data in this table (as shown in Table 8-1) might look like. Note that I'm going to cut out a few columns here just to help things fit on a page, but I think you'll still be able to see the point:

TABLE 8-1: Orders before Normalization

ORDER NO	ORDER DATE	CUSTOMER NO	CUSTOMER NAME	CUSTOMER ADDRESS	ITEMSORDERED
100	1/1/99	54545	ACME Co	1234 1st St.	1A4536, Flange, 7lbs, $75;4-OR2400, Injector, .5lbs, $108;4-OR2403, Injector, .5lbs, $116;1-4I5436, Head, 63lbs, $750
101	1/1/99	12000	Sneed Corp.	555 Main Ave.	1-3X9567, Pump, 5lbs, $62.50
102	1/1/99	66651	ZZZ & Co.	4242 SW 2nd	7-8G9200; Fan, 3lbs, $84;1-8G5437, Fan, 3lbs, $15;1-3H6250, Control, 5lbs, $32
103	1/2/99	54545	ACME Co	1234 1st St.	40-8G9200, Fan, 3lbs, $480;1-2P5523, Housing, 1lb, $165;1-3X9567, Pump, 5lbs, $42

You have a number of issues to deal with in this table if you're going to normalize it. While you have a functional primary key (yes, these existed long before relational systems), you have problems with both of the main areas of the first normal form:

➤ Repeating groups of data (customer information) that need to be broken out into different tables.

➤ The `ItemsOrdered` column does not contain data that is atomic in nature.

You can start by moving several columns out of Table 8-2:

TABLE 8-2: Orders Table with Repeating Groups Removed

ORDERNO (PK)	ORDERDATE	CUSTOMERNO	ITEMSORDERED
100	1/1/1999	54545	1A4536, Flange, 7lbs, $75;4-OR2400, Injector, .5lbs, $108;4-OR2403, Injector, .5lbs, $116;1-4I5436, Head, 63lbs, $750
101	1/1/1999	12000	1-3X9567, Pump, 5lbs, $62.50
102	1/1/1999	66651	7-8G9200; Fan, 3lbs, $84;1-8G5437, Fan, 3lbs, $15;1-3H6250, Control, 5lbs, $32
103	1/2/1999	54545	40-8G9200, Fan, 3lbs, $480;1-2P5523, Housing, 1lbs, $165;1-3X9567, Pump, 5lbs, $42

And putting them into their own tables, as shown in Table 8-3:

TABLE 8-3: Customers Table from Repeating Groups

CUSTOMERNO (PK)	CUSTOMERNAME	CUSTOMERADDRESS
54545	ACME Co	1234 1st St.
12000	Sneed Corp.	555 Main Ave.
66651	ZZZ & Co.	4242 SW 2nd

There are several things to notice about the old and new tables:

➤ **Choosing a primary key:** You must have a primary key for your new table to ensure that each row is unique. For the `Customers` table, there are two candidate keys — `CustomerNo` and `CustomerName`. `CustomerNo` was actually created just to serve this purpose and seems the logical choice — after all, it's entirely conceivable that you could have more than one customer with the same name. (For example, there have to be hundreds of companies named ACME in the United States)

➤ **Maintaining data references to new table:** Although you've moved the data out of the `Orders` table, you still need to maintain a reference to the data in the new `Customers` table. This is why you still see the `CustomerNo` (the primary key) column in the `Orders` table. Later on, when you build your references, you'll create a foreign key constraint to force all orders to have valid customer numbers.

➤ **Removing duplicate information:** You were able to eliminate an instance of the information for ACME Co. That's part of the purpose of moving data that appears in repetitive groups — to just store it once. This saves you space and prevents conflicting values.

➤ **Moving only repeating *groups* of data:** You still see the same order date several times, but it doesn't really fit into a group — it's just a relatively random piece of data that has no relevance outside of this table.

So, you've dealt with the repeating data; next, you're ready to move on to the second violation of first normal form — atomicity. If you take a look at the `ItemsOrdered` column, you'll see that there are actually several different pieces of data there:

➤ Anywhere from one to many individual part numbers

➤ Quantity weight information on each of those parts

Part number, weight, and price are each atomic pieces of data if kept to themselves, and when they are combined into one lump grouping, you no longer have atomicity.

> **NOTE** *Believe it or not, things were sometimes really done this way. At first glance, it seemed the easy thing to do — paper invoices often had just one big block area for writing up what the customer wanted, and computer-based systems were often just as close to a clone of paper as someone could make it.*

You'll want to go ahead and break things up — and, while you're at it, add in a new piece of information in the form of a unit price, as shown in Figure 8-1. The problem is that, once you break up this information, your primary key no longer uniquely identifies your rows — your rows are still unique, but the primary key is now inadequate.

Order No (PK)	Order Date	Customer No	Part No	Description	Qty	Unit Price	Total Price	Wt.
100	1/1/2012	54545	1A4536	Flange	5	15	75	6
100	1/1/2012	54545	0R2400	Injector	4	27	108	.5
100	1/1/2012	54545	0R2403	Injector	4	29	116	.5
100	1/1/2012	54545	4I5436	Head	1	750	750	3
101	1/1/2012	12000	3X9567	Pump	1	62.50	62.50	5
102	1/1/2012	66651	8G9200	Fan	7	12	84	3
102	1/1/2012	66651	8G5437	Fan	1	15	15	3
102	1/1/2012	66651	3H6250	Control	1	32	32	5
103	1/2/2012	54545	8G9200	Fan	40	12	480	3
103	1/2/2012	54545	2P5523	Housing	1	165	165	1
103	1/2/2012	54545	3X9567	Pump	1	42	42	5

FIGURE 8-1

For now, you'll address this by adding a line item number to your table, as shown in Figure 8-2, so you can, again, uniquely identify your rows.

Order No (PK)	Line Item (PK)	Order Date	Customer No	Part No	Description	Qty	Unit Price	Total Price	Wt.
100	1	1/1/2012	54545	1A4536	Flange	5	15	75	6
100	2	1/1/2012	54545	0R2400	Injector	4	27	108	.5
100	3	1/1/2012	54545	0R2403	Injector	4	29	116	.5
100	4	1/1/2012	54545	4I5436	Head	1	750	750	3
101	1	1/1/2012	12000	3X9567	Pump	1	62.50	62.50	5
102	1	1/1/2012	66651	8G9200	Fan	7	12	84	3
102	2	1/1/2012	66651	8G5437	Fan	1	15	15	3
102	3	1/1/2012	66651	3H6250	Control	1	32	32	5
103	1	1/2/2012	54545	8G9200	Fan	40	12	480	3
103	2	1/2/2012	54545	2P5523	Housing	1	165	165	1
103	3	1/2/2012	54545	3X9567	Pump	1	42	42	5

FIGURE 8-2

NOTE *Rather than create another column as you did here, you also could have taken the approach of making* `PartNo` *part of your primary key. The fallout from this would have been that you could not have had the same part number appear twice in the same order. I'll briefly discuss keys based on more than one column — or composite keys — in the next chapter.*

At this point, you've met the criteria for first normal form. You have no repeating groups of data, and all columns are atomic. You do have issues with data having to be repeated within a column (because it's the same for all rows for that primary key), but you'll deal with that shortly. To sum up, your data is now dependent on the key, but not necessarily on the whole key or nothing but the key.

The Second Normal Form

The next phase in normalization is to go to the second normal form (*2NF*). Second normal form further reduces the incidence of repeated data (not necessarily groups).

Second normal form has two rules to it:

➤ The table must meet the rules for first normal form. (Normalization is a building block kind of process — you can't stack the third block on if you don't have the first two there already.)

➤ Each column must depend on the *whole* key.

The example you've been developing has a problem — actually, it has a couple of them — in this area. Look at the first normal form version of your `Orders` table again (Figure 8-2) — is every column dependent on the whole key? Are there any that need only part of the key?

The answers are no and yes, respectively. There are two columns that depend only on the `OrderNo` column — not the `LineItem` column. The columns in question are `OrderDate` and `CustomerNo`; both are the same for the entire order regardless of how many line items there are. Dealing with these requires that you introduce yet another table. At this point, you run across the concept of a *header* versus a *detail* table for the first time.

Sometimes what is, in practice, one entity still needs to be broken into two tables and, thus, two entities. The header is something of the parent table of the two tables in the relationship. It contains information that needs to be stored only once while the detail table stores the information that may exist in multiple instances. The header usually keeps the name of the original table, and the detail table usually has a name that starts with the header table name and adds on something to indicate that it is a detail table (for example, `OrderDetails`). For every one header record, you usually have at least one detail record and may have many, many more. This is one example of a kind of relationship (a one-to-many relationship) that you look at in the next major section.

So let's take care of this by splitting your table again. You'll actually start with the detail table because it's keeping the bulk of the columns. From this point forward, you'll call this table (as shown in Table 8-4) `OrderDetails`:

TABLE 8-4: The OrderDetails Table

ORDERNO (PK)	LINEITEM (PK)	PARTNO	DESCRIPTION	QTY	UNIT PRICE	TOTAL PRICE	WT
100	1	1A4536	Flange	5	15	75	6
100	2	OR2400	Injector	4	27	108	.5
100	3	OR2403	Injector	4	29	116	.5
100	4	4I5436	Head	1	750	750	3
101	1	3X9567	Pump	1	62.50	62.50	5
102	1	8G9200	Fan	7	12	84	3
102	2	8G5437	Fan	1	15	15	3
102	3	3H6250	Control	1	32	32	5
103	1	8G9200	Fan	40	12	480	3
103	2	2P5523	Housing	1	165	1	
103	3	3X9567	Pump	1	42	42	5

Then you move on to what, although you could consider it to be the new table of the two, will serve as the header table and thus will keep the `Orders` name (see Table 8-5):

TABLE 8-5: Orders as a Header Table

ORDERNO (PK)	ORDERDATE	CUSTOMERNO
100	1/1/1999	54545
101	1/1/1999	12000
102	1/1/1999	66651
103	1/2/1999	54545

So, now you have second normal form. All of your columns depend on the entire key. I'm sure you won't be surprised to hear that you still have a problem or two, though — you'll deal with them next. As it happens, while your columns are dependent on the key, and in fact the whole key, there remain dependencies you haven't yet resolved.

The Third Normal Form

This is the relative end of the line. There are levels of normalization beyond this, but none that get much attention outside of academic circles. I'll give you an extremely brief look at those next, but first you need to finish the business at hand.

I mentioned at the end of the discussion of the second normal form that the example still had problems — you still haven't reached the third normal form (*3NF*). The third normal form deals with the issue of having all the columns in your tables not just be dependent on something — but dependent on the right thing. The third normal form has three rules to it:

➤ The table must be in 2NF (I told you this was a building block thing).

➤ No column can have any dependency on any other non-key column.

➤ You cannot have derived data.

You already know that you're in the second normal form, so let's look at the other two rules.

First, do you have any columns that have dependencies other than the primary key? Yes! Actually, there are a couple of columns that are dependent on the PartNo as much as, if not more than, the primary key of this table. Weight and Description are both entirely dependent on the PartNo column — you again need to split into another table.

> **NOTE** *Your first tendency here might be to also lump* UnitPrice *into this category, and you would be partially right. The* Products *table that you create here can and should have a* UnitPrice *column in it — but it is of a slightly different nature. Indeed, perhaps it would be better named* ListPrice *because it is the cost you have set in general for that product. The difference for the* UnitPrice *in the* OrderDetails *table is twofold. First, you may offer discounts that would change the price at time of sale. This means that the price in the* OrderDetails *record may be different from the planned price that you will keep in the* Products *table. Second, the price you plan to charge will change over time with factors such as inflation, but changes in future prices do not change what you have charged on your actual orders of the past. In other words, price is one of those odd circumstances where there are really two flavors of it — one dependent on the* PartNo, *and one dependent on the primary key for the* OrderDetails *table (in other words* OrderID *and* LineItem).*

First, you need to create a new table (call it `Products` — it's shown in Table 8-6) to hold your part information. This new table will hold the information that you had in `OrderDetails` that was more dependent on `PartNo` than on `OrderID` or `LineItem`:

TABLE 8-6: The Products Table

PARTNO (PK)	DESCRIPTION	WT
1A4536	Flange	6
OR2400	Injector	.5
OR2403	Injector	.5
4I5436	Head	3
3X9567	Pump	5
8G9200	Fan	3
8G5437	Fan	3
3H6250	Control	5
8G9200	Fan	3
2P5523	Housing	1
3X9567	Pump	5

You can then chop all but the foreign key out of the `OrderDetails` table (as shown in Table 8-7):

TABLE 8-7: Removing Products from the OrderDetails Table

ORDERNO (PK)	LINEITEM (PK)	PARTNO	QTY	UNIT PRICE	TOTAL PRICE
100	1	1A4536	5	15	75
100	2	OR2400	4	27	108
100	3	OR2403	4	29	116
100	4	4I5436	1	750	750
101	1	3X9567	1	62.50	62.50
102	1	8G9200	7	12	84
102	2	8G5437	1	15	15

ORDERNO (PK)	LINEITEM (PK)	PARTNO	QTY	UNIT PRICE	TOTAL PRICE
102	3	3H6250	1	32	32
103	1	8G9200	40	12	480
103	2	2P5523	1	165	165
103	3	3X9567	1	42	42

That takes care of the first problem (cross-column dependency), but it doesn't deal with derived data. You have a column called `TotalPrice` that contains data that can actually be derived from multiplying `Qty` by `UnitPrice`. This is a no-no in normalization.

NOTE *Derived data is one of the places that you'll see me "denormalize" data most often. Why? Speed! A query that reads* WHERE `TotalPrice` > $100 *runs faster than one that reads* WHERE `Qty` * `UnitPrice` > 50 — *particularly if you are able to index your computed* `TotalPrice`.

On the other side of this, however, I do sometimes take more of a hybrid approach by utilizing a computed column and letting SQL Server keep a sum of the other two columns for me (you may recall my using this idea for the `PreviousSalary` *example in the* `Employees` *table of the Accounting database in Chapter 5). If this is a very important column from a performance perspective (you're running lots of columns that filter based on the values in this column), you may want to add an index to your new computed column. The significance of this is that the index "materializes" the computed data. What does that mean? Well, it means that even SQL Server doesn't have to calculate the computed column on the fly — instead, it calculates it once when the row is stored in the index, and, thereafter, uses the precalculated column. It can be very fast indeed, and you'll examine it further in Chapter 9. That said, there is a trade-off (if there wasn't, everyone would do it this way all the time, right?) — space. You're storing data that doesn't need to be stored, and if you do that to every possible piece of derived data, it can really add up. More space means more data to read, and that can mean things actually get* slower. *The point here is to weigh your options and make a balanced choice.*

So, to reach the third normal form, you just need to drop off the `TotalPrice` column and compute it when needed. That dependency having been excised, you have finally achieved the normalization goal: the key, the whole key, and nothing but the key.

Other Normal Forms

There are a few other forms out there that are considered, at least by academics, to be part of the normalization model. These include:

➤ **Boyce-Codd Normal Form** (considered really just to be a variation on third normal form): This one tries to address situations in which you have multiple overlapping candidate keys. This can happen only if:

   a. All the candidate keys are composite keys (that is, it takes more than one column to make up the key).

   b. There is more than one candidate key.

   c. The candidate keys each have at least one column that is in common with another candidate key.

   This is typically a situation whereby any number of solutions works. It is almost never logically thought of outside the academic community.

➤ **Fourth Normal Form:** This one tries to deal with issues surrounding multi-valued dependence. This is the situation whereby, for an individual row, no column depends on a column other than the primary key and depends on the whole primary key (meeting third normal form). However, there can be rather odd situations where one column in the primary key can depend separately on other columns in the primary key. These are rare, and don't usually cause any real problem. As such, they are largely ignored in the database world, and I will not address them here.

➤ **Fifth Normal Form:** This deals with non-loss and loss decompositions. Essentially, there are certain situations where you can decompose a relationship such that you cannot logically recompose it into its original form. Again, these are rare, largely academic, and I won't deal with them any further here.

This is, of course, just a really quick look at these — and that's deliberate on my part. The main reason you need to know these in the real world is either to impress your friends (or prove to them you're a "know it all") and to not sound like an idiot when some database guru comes to town and starts talking about them. However you choose to use it, I do recommend against attempting to use this knowledge to get dates. . . .

UNDERSTANDING RELATIONSHIPS

Well, I've always heard from women that men immediately leave the room if you even mention the word "relationship." With that in mind, I hope that I didn't just lose about half my readers.

I am, of course, kidding — but not by as much as you might think. Experts say the key to successful relationships is that you know the role of both parties and that everyone understands the boundaries and rules of the relationship that they are in. I can be talking about database relationships with that statement every bit as much as people relationships.

There are three kinds of major relationships:

➤ One-to-one

➤ One-to-many

➤ Many-to-many

Each of these has some variation, depending on whether one side of the relationship is nullable. For example, instead of a one-to-one relationship, you might have a zero or one-to-one relationship.

One-to-One

This is exactly what it says it is. A one-to-one relationship is one where the fact that you have a record in one table means that you have exactly one matching record in another table.

To illustrate a one-to-one relationship, let's look at a slight variation of a piece of the earlier example. Imagine that you have customers — just as you did in an earlier example. This time, however, imagine that you are a subsidiary of a much larger company. Your parent company wants to be able to track all of its customers, and to be able to tell the collective total of each customer's purchases — regardless of which subsidiary(s) the customer made purchases with.

Even if all the subsidiaries run out of one server at the main headquarters, there's a very good chance that the various subsidiaries would be running their own databases. One way to track all customer information, which would facilitate combining it later, would be to create a master customer database owned by the parent company. The subsidiaries would then maintain their own customer tables, but do so with a one-to-one relationship to the parent company's customer table. Any customer record created in the parent company would imply that you needed to have one in the subsidiaries also. Any creation of a customer record in a subsidiary would require that one also be created in the parent company's copy.

A second example — one that used to apply frequently to SQL Server prior to version 7.0 — is when you have too much information to fit in one row. Remember that the maximum row size for SQL Server is 8,060 bytes of non-BLOB data. That's a lot harder to fill than version 6.5's 1,962 bytes, but you can still have situations that require you to store a very large number of columns or even fewer very wide columns. One way to get around this problem was to actually create two different tables and split the rows between the tables. You could then impose a one-to-one relationship. The combination of the matching rows in the two tables then meets the larger row size requirement.

 NOTE *SQL Server has no inherent method of enforcing a true one-to-one relationship. You can say that table A requires a matching record in table B, but when you then add that table B must have a matching record in table A, you create a paradox — which table gets the record first? If you need to enforce this kind of relationship in SQL Server, the best you can do is force all inserts to be done via a stored procedure. The stored procedure can have the logic to insert into both tables or neither table. Neither foreign key constraints nor triggers can handle this circular relationship.*

Zero or One-to-One

SQL Server can handle the instance of zero or one-to-one relationships. This is essentially the same as a one-to-one, with the difference that one side of the relationship has the option of either having a record or not having one.

Going back to the parent company versus subsidiary example, you might prefer to create a relationship where the parent company needs to have a matching record for each subsidiary's records, but the subsidiary doesn't need the information from the parent. You could, for example, have subsidiaries that have very different customers (such as a railroad and a construction company). The parent company wants to know about *all* the customers regardless of which business they came from, but your construction company probably doesn't care about your railroad customers. In such a case, you would have *zero or one* construction customers to *one* parent company customer record.

Zero or one-to-one relationships can be enforced in SQL Server through:

➤ **A combination of a unique or primary key with a foreign key constraint.** A foreign key constraint can enforce that *at least* one record must exist in the "one" (or parent company in our example) table, but it can't ensure that *only* one exists (there could be more than one). Using a primary key or unique constraint would ensure that one was indeed the limit.

➤ **Triggers.** Note that triggers would be required in both tables.

 NOTE *The reason SQL Server can handle a zero or one-to-one, but not a one-to-one relationship is due to the "which goes first" problem. In a true one-to-one relationship, you can't insert into either table because the record in the other table isn't there yet — it's a paradox. However, with a zero or one-to-one, you can insert into the required table first (the "one"), and the optional table (the "zero or one"), if desired, second. This same problem holds true for the "one-to-one or many" and the "one to zero, one, or many" relationships.*

One-to-One or Many

This is one form of your run-of-the-mill, average, everyday foreign key kind of relationship. Usually, this is found in some form of header/detail relationship. A great example of this is the `Orders` table, as shown in Figure 8-3. `OrderDetails` (the "one or many" side of the relationship) doesn't make much sense without an `Orders` header to belong to (does it do you much good to have an order for a part if you don't know who the order is for?). Likewise, it doesn't make much sense to have an order if there wasn't anything actually ordered (for example, "Gee, look, ACME company ordered absolutely nothing yesterday.").

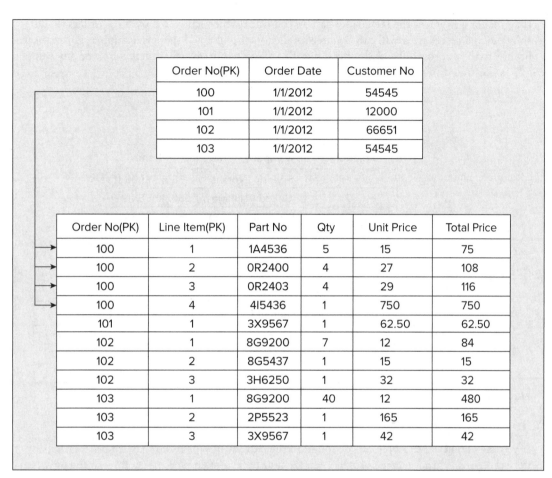

Order No(PK)	Order Date	Customer No
100	1/1/2012	54545
101	1/1/2012	12000
102	1/1/2012	66651
103	1/1/2012	54545

Order No(PK)	Line Item(PK)	Part No	Qty	Unit Price	Total Price
100	1	1A4536	5	15	75
100	2	0R2400	4	27	108
100	3	0R2403	4	29	116
100	4	4I5436	1	750	750
101	1	3X9567	1	62.50	62.50
102	1	8G9200	7	12	84
102	2	8G5437	1	15	15
102	3	3H6250	1	32	32
103	1	8G9200	40	12	480
103	2	2P5523	1	165	165
103	3	3X9567	1	42	42

FIGURE 8-3

This one, however, gives you the same basic problem that you had with one-to-one relationships. It's still that chicken or egg thing — which came first? Again, in SQL Server, the only way to implement this fully is by restricting all data to be inserted or deleted via stored procedures.

One-to-Zero, One, or Many

This is the other, and perhaps even more common, form of the run-of-the-mill, average, everyday, foreign key relationship. The only real difference in implementation here is that the referencing field (the one in the table that has the foreign key constraint) is allowed to be null; that is, the fact that you have a record in the "one" table doesn't necessarily mean that you have any instances of matching records in the referencing table.

Imagine for a moment the scenario whereby you track which shipper is used for orders that are shipped, and also have a will call counter for customer pickup. If there is a shipper, you want to limit it to the approved list of shippers, but it's still quite possible that there won't be any shipper at all, as illustrated in Figure 8-4.

Shipper ID	Company Name	Phone
1	Speedy Express	(503) 5559831
2	United Package	(503) 5553199
3	Federal Shipping	(503) 5559931

Order ID	Order Date	Customer ID	Shipper ID	Ship To Address
10500	2012-04-09	LAMAI	1	1 rue Alsace-Lorraine
10501	2012-04-09	BLAUS	3	Forsterstr 57
10502	2012-04-09	PERIC	1	Calle Dr. Jorge...

FIGURE 8-4

A virtually identical example can be found in the AdventureWorks database in the relationship between `Purchasing.PurchaseOrderHeader` and `Purchasing.ShipMethod`, with the only real difference being that this is a list of companies shipping *to* you rather than *from* you.

> **NOTE** *This kind of relationship usually sets up what is called a domain relationship. A domain is a limited list of values that the dependent table must choose from — nothing outside the domain list is considered a valid option. The table that holds the rows that make up the domain list is commonly referred to as a domain or lookup table. Nearly all databases you create are going to have at least one, and probably many, domain tables in them. The* `Shippers` *table is a domain table — the purpose of having it isn't just to store the information on the name and phone number of the shipper, but also to limit the list of possible shippers in the* `Orders` *table.*

In SQL Server, you can enforce this kind of relationship through two methods:

> **FOREIGN KEY constraint:** You simply declare a FOREIGN KEY constraint on the table that serves as the "many" side of the relationship, and reference the table and column that is to be the "one" side of the relationship (you'll be guaranteed only one in the referenced table because you must have a PRIMARY KEY or UNIQUE constraint on the column(s) referenced by a foreign key).

> **Triggers:** Actually, for all the early versions of SQL Server, this was the only option for true referential integrity. You actually need to add two triggers — one for each side of the relationship. Add a trigger to the table that is the "many" side of the relationship and check that any row inserted or changed in that table has a match in the table it depends on (the "one" side of the relationship). Then, you add a delete trigger and an update trigger to the other table — this trigger checks records that are being deleted (or changed) from the referenced table to make sure that it isn't going to *orphan* (make it so it doesn't have a reference).

You've previously read about the performance ramifications of the choices between the two in Chapter 6. Using a FOREIGN KEY constraint is generally faster — particularly when there is a violation. That being said, triggers may still be the better option in situations where you're going to have a trigger executing anyway (or some other special constraint need).

Many-to-Many

In this type of relationship, both sides of the relationship may have several records — not just one — that match. An example of this is the relationship of products to orders. A given order may have many products. Likewise, any given product may be ordered many times. You still may, however, want to relate the tables in question — for example, to ensure that an order is for a product that you know about (it's in your Products table).

SQL Server has no way of physically establishing a direct many-to-many relationship, so you have to cheat by having an intermediate table to organize the relationship. Some tables create your many-to-many relationships almost by accident as a normal part of the normalization process — others are created entirely from scratch for the sole purpose of establishing this kind of relationship. This latter "middleman" kind of table is often called either a *linking table*, an *associate table*, or sometimes a *merge table*.

First, let's look at a many-to-many relationship that is created in the normal course of normalization. An example of this can be found in the Accounting database's OrderDetails table (you created the Accounting database in Chapters 5 and 6), which creates a many-to-many relationship between your Orders and Products tables, as shown in Figure 8-5.

Order No (PK)	Order Date	Customer No
100	1/1/2012	54545
101	1/1/2012	12000
102	1/1/2012	66651
103	1/1/2012	54545

Order No (PK)	Line Item (PK)	Part No	Qty	Unit Price	Total Price
100	1	1A4536	5	15	75
100	2	0R2400	4	27	108
100	3	0R2403	4	29	116
100	4	4I5436	1	750	750
101	1	3X9567	1	62.50	62.50
102	1	8G9200	7	12	84
102	2	8G5437	1	15	15
102	3	3H6250	1	32	32
103	1	8G9200	40	12	480
103	2	2P5523	1	165	165
103	3	3X9567	1	42	42

Part No (PK)	Description	Wt.
1A4536	Flange	6
0R2400	Injector	.5
0R2403	Injector	.5
4I5436	Head	3
3X9567	Pump	5
8G9200	Fan	3
8G5437	Fan	3
3H6250	Control	5
2P5523	Housing	1

FIGURE 8-5

By using the join syntax that you learned back in Chapter 4, you can relate one product to the many orders that it's been part of, or you can go the other way and relate an order to all the products on that order.

Let's move on now to the second example — one where you create an associate table from scratch just so you can have a many-to-many relationship. I'll take the example of a user and a group of rights that a user can have on the system.

You might start with a Permissions table that looks something like this:

PermissionID	Description
1	Read
2	Insert
3	Update
4	Delete

Then you add a Users table:

UserID	Full Name	Password	Active
JohnD	John Doe	Jfz9..nm3	1
SamS	Sam Spade	klk93)md	1

Now comes the problem — how do you define which users have which permissions? Your first inclination might be to just add a column called Permissions to the Users table:

UserID	Full Name	Password	Permissions	Active
JohnD	John Doe	Jfz9..nm3	1	1
SamS	Sam Spade	klk93)md	3	1

This seems fine for only a split second, and then a question begs to be answered — what about when your users have permission to do more than one thing?

In the older, flat file days, you might have just combined all the permissions into the one cell, like so:

UserID	Full Name	Password	Permissions	Active
JohnD	John Doe	Jfz9..nm3	1,2,3	1
SamS	Sam Spade	klk93)md	1,2,3,43	1

This violates the first normal form, which said that the values in any column must be atomic. In addition, this would be very slow because you would have to procedurally parse out each individual value within the cell.

What you really have between these two tables, Users and Permissions, is a many-to-many relationship — you just need a way to establish that relationship within the database. You do this by adding an associate table, as shown in Figure 8-6. Again, this is a table that, in most cases, doesn't add any new data to the database other than establishing the association between rows in two other tables.

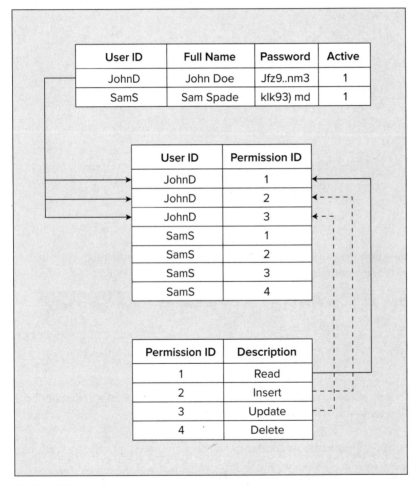

FIGURE 8-6

With the addition of the new table (a good name might be UserPermissions), you can now mix and match permissions to your users.

Note that, for either example, the implementation of referential integrity is the same — each of the base tables (the tables that hold the underlying data and have the many-to-many relationship) has a one-to-many relationship with the associate table. This can be done via either a trigger or a FOREIGN KEY constraint.

DIAGRAMMING DATABASES

Entity-relationship diagrams (ERDs) are an important tool in good database design. Small databases can usually be easily created from a few scripts and implemented directly without drawing things out at all. The larger your database gets, however, the faster it becomes very problematic to just do things "in your head." ERDs solve a ton of problems because they allow you to quickly visualize and understand both the entities and their relationships.

Fortunately, SQL Server includes a *very* basic diagramming tool that you can use as a starting point for building rudimentary ERDs.

 NOTE *Serious ER diagramming is usually done with an application that is specifically designed to be an ER diagramming tool. These tools almost always support at least one of a couple of industry standard diagramming methods. Even some of the more mass-market diagramming tools — such as Visio — support a couple of ERD methodologies. SQL Server has an ERD tool built in, and therein lies the problem. The tools that are included with SQL Server 2012 are a variation on a toolset and diagramming methodology that Microsoft has used in a number of tools for many years now. The problem is that they do not compete with any ERD standard that I've seen anywhere else. Despite their shortcomings, I've decided to stick with what I know you have — the built-in tools that ship with SQL Server. I do, however, encourage you to examine the commercially available ERD tools out there to see the rich things that they offer to simplify your database-design efforts.*

You can open SQL Server's built-in tools by navigating to the Diagrams node of the database you want to build a diagram for (expand your server first, and then the database). Some of what you are going to see you'll find familiar — some of the dialog boxes are the same as you saw in Chapter 5 when you were creating tables.

The SQL Server diagramming tools don't give you all that many options, so you'll find that you'll get to know them fairly quickly. Indeed, if you're familiar with the relationship editor in Access, much of the SQL Server tools will seem very familiar.

TRY IT OUT Diagramming

Let's start by creating a diagram. You can create a new diagram by following these steps:

1. Right-clicking the Database Diagrams node underneath the AdventureWorks database and choosing the New Database Diagram option.

 NOTE *As you saw back in Chapter 5, you may (if it's the first time you've tried to create a diagram) see a dialog box come up warning you that some of the objects needed to support diagramming aren't in the database and asking if you want to create them — choose Yes. It is worth noting also that those objects can't be created in a database without an owner. If your AdventureWorks database doesn't have one, you'll be prompted here to assign an owner in the Files page of the database properties. Right-click on the AdventureWorks database, choose properties, go to the Files page, and select yourself as the database owner.*

SQL Server starts out with the same Add Table dialog box you saw in Chapter 5 — the only thing different is the listing of tables (see Figure 8-7).

2. Select all the tables (remember to hold down the Ctrl key to select more than one table), as shown in Figure 8-8.

FIGURE 8-7   **FIGURE 8-8**

3. Click Add and, after a brief pause while SQL Server draws all the tables you selected, click the Close button. SQL Server adds the tables to the diagram, but, depending on your screen resolution, they are probably very difficult to see because of the zoom on the diagram.

4. To pull more of the tables into view, change the zoom setting in the toolbar. Finding the right balance between being able to see many tables at once and making them so small you can't read them is a bit of a hassle, but you should be able to adjust to something that meets your particular taste — for now, I've set mine at 75 percent so I can squeeze in more of the tables at once (fitting all tables in is not that realistic with a database of any real size table-count-wise), as shown in Figure 8-9.

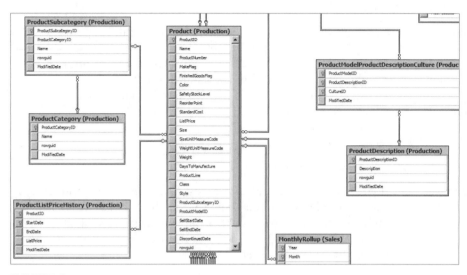

FIGURE 8-9

How It Works

You'll notice right away that there is a lot more than what you saw with your first look at the diagram tools back in Chapter 5. SQL Server enumerates through each table you have said you want added and analyzed to determine what other objects are associated with those tables. The various other items you see beyond the table itself are some of the many other objects that tie into tables — primary keys and foreign keys.

So, having gotten a start, you can use this diagram as a launching point for learning how the diagramming tool works and building a few tables here and there.

NOTE *Although you're going to create just a single diagram for this database, you can have as many as you'd like. For a diagram to be useful, you have to be able to see enough of it to have context; in a very large or complex database, this could get ugly if you try to put all the tables into a single diagram. Be aware that each table can participate in any number of diagrams (including zero!) and create diagrams that work for you.*

Tables

Each table has its own window you can move around. The primary key is shown with the little symbol of a key in the column to the left of the name like the one next to the `CustomerID` in Figure 8-10.

FIGURE 8-10

Just like in Chapter 5, this is the default view for the table — you can select from several others that allow you to edit the very makeup of the table. To check out your options for views of a table, just right-click the table that you're interested in. The default is column names only, but you should also take an interest in the choice of Custom as you did in Chapter 5; this or Standard is what you would use when you want to edit the table from right within the diagram (very nice!).

Adding and Deleting Tables

You can add a new table to the diagram in one of two ways.

➤ **For an existing table:** If you have a table that already exists in the database (but not in the diagram), but now you want to add it to your diagram, you simply click the Add Table button on the diagramming window's toolbar. You'll be presented with a list of all the tables in the database — just choose the one that you want to add, and it will appear along with any relationships it has to other tables in the diagram.

➤ **For a new table:** If you want to add a completely new table, click on New Table on the diagramming window's toolbar or right-click in the diagram and choose New Table; you'll be asked for a name for the new table, and the table will be added to the diagram in Column Properties view. Simply edit the properties to have the column names, data types, and so on that you want, and you have a new table in the database.

NOTE *Let me take a moment to point out a couple of gotchas in this process.*

First, don't forget to add a primary key to your table. SQL Server does not automatically do this, nor does it even prompt you (as Access does). This is a somewhat less than intuitive process. To add a primary key, you must select the columns that you want to have in the key. Then right-click and choose Set Primary Key.

Next, be aware that your new table is not actually added to the database until you choose to save — this is also true of any edits that you make along the way.

TRY IT OUT   **Adding Tables from Within the Diagram**

Let's go ahead and add a table to the database just to learn how it works.

1. Start by clicking the New Table button on the left side of the diagramming window's toolbar. When prompted for a name, choose a name of `CustomerNotes` (see Figure 8-11). You should then get a new window table using the Standard view.

2. Notice that I've added several columns to my table, along with a primary key (remember, select the columns you want to be the primary key, and then right-click and choose Set Primary Key).

3. Before you click to save this, try something out — open up the Management Studio, and try to run a query against your new table:

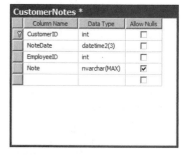

CustomerNotes *		
Column Name	Data Type	Allow Nulls
🔑 CustomerID	int	☐
NoteDate	datetime2(3)	☐
EmployeeID	int	☐
Note	nvarchar(MAX)	☑
		☐

FIGURE 8-11

```
USE AdventureWorks;

SELECT * FROM CustomerNotes;
```

Code snippet Chap08.sql

Back comes an error message:

```
Msg 208, Level 16, State 1, Line 1
Invalid object name 'CustomerNotes'.
```

That's because your table exists only as an edited item on the diagram — it won't be added until you actually save the changes you've just made.

> **NOTE** *If you look at the* CustomerNotes *table in the diagram window at this point, you should see an * to the right of the name — that's there to tell you that there are unsaved changes in that table.*

4. Now, switch back to the Management Studio. There are two save options:

➤ **Save:** This saves the changes to both the diagram and to the database (this is the little disk icon on the toolbar).

➤ **Generate Change Script:** This saves the changes to a script so it can be run at a later time. (This is found in the Table Designer menu or as an icon on the Table Designer toolbar.)

> **NOTE** *The Table Designer toolbar contains several smart icons that provide quick access to many frequently used table design features. If it does not come up by default in the designer, you can add it by right-clicking any open space in the toolbar and selecting the Table Designer toolbar.*

5. Go ahead and choose Save, and you'll be prompted for the name of your diagram and confirmation (after all, you're about to alter your database — there's no "undo" for this).

6. Confirm the changes, and try running that query again against your `CustomerNotes` table. You should not receive an error this time because the table has now been created. (You won't get any rows back, but the query should still run.)

How It Works

When you create a diagram, SQL Server creates a script behind the scenes that looks basically just as the scripts did back in Chapter 6 when you were scripting your own changes. However, these scripts are not actually generated and run until you choose to save the diagram.

Okay, you've got your `CustomerNotes` table into the database, but now you notice a problem — the way your primary key is declared, you can have only one note per customer. More than likely, you are going to keep taking more and more notes on the customer over time. That means that you need to change your primary key. This leaves you with a couple of options depending on your requirements:

> **Make the date part of the primary key:** This is problematic from two standpoints. First, you're tracking which employee took the note — what if two different employees wanted to add notes at the same time? You could, of course, potentially address this by also adding `EmployeeID` to the primary key. Second, what's to say that even the same employee wouldn't want to enter two completely separate notes on the same day (okay, so, because this is a `datetime` field, he could do it as long as he didn't get two rows inserted at the same millisecond — but just play along with me here...there's a principle at stake)? Oops, now even having the `EmployeeID` in the key doesn't help you.

> **Add another column to help with the key structure:** You could do this by adding a counter column for each note per customer. As yet another alternative, you could just add an identity column to ensure uniqueness — it means that your primary key doesn't really relate to anything, but that isn't always a big deal (although it does mean that you have one more index that has to be maintained) and it does allow you to have a relatively unlimited number of notes per customer.

TRY IT OUT **Editing Tables from Within a Diagram**

I'm going to take the approach of adding a column I'll call "Sequence" to the table. By convention (it's not a requirement and not everyone does it this way), primary keys are normally the first columns in your table. If you were going to be doing this by script yourself, you'd probably just issue an `ALTER TABLE` statement and `ADD` the column — this would stick your new column down at the end of the column list. If you wanted to fix that, you'd have to copy all the data to a holding table, drop any relationships to or from the old table, drop the old table, CREATE a new table that has the columns and column order you want, and then re-establish the relationships and copy the data back in (a long and tedious process). With the diagramming tools, however, SQL Server takes care of all that for you.

To insert a new row in the middle of everything, just follow these steps:

1. Right-click the row that is to immediately follow the row you want to insert and select Insert Column. The tool is nice enough to bump everything down for you to create space just like in Figure 8-12.

2. You can then add your new column and reset the Primary Key, as shown in Figure 8-13 (select both rows, right-click, and choose Set Primary Key).

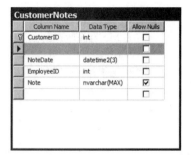

FIGURE 8-12

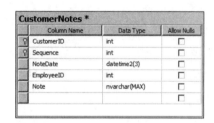

FIGURE 8-13

3. Now just save, and you have a table with the desired column order. Just to verify this, try using sp_help:

```
EXEC sp_help CustomerNv otes;
```

Code snippet Chap08.sql

You'll see that you have the column order you expect:

```
. . . .
CustomerID
Sequence
NoteDate
EmployeeID
Note
. . . .
```

NOTE *Depending on your specific option settings, you may run into an error here when you save the* `CustomerNotes` *table. At issue is a safety feature that is meant to prevent you from accidentally overwriting tables while in the Designer. If you get an error referencing an option called "Prevent saving changes that require table re-creation," you can find that in the Options dialog box under the Tools menu — you'll need to navigate to the Designers ➪ Table and Database Designers item in this dialog box, and then deselect the "Prevent saving changes that require table re-creation" option. Your table should then save without further difficulty.*

NOTE *Making things like column order changes happens to be one area where the built-in tools positively excel. I've used a couple of other ERD tools, and they all offered the promise of synchronizing a change in column order between the database and the diagram — the success has been pretty hit and miss. (In other words, be very careful about doing it around live data.)*

Also, under the heading of one more thing — use the scripting option rather than the live connection to the database to make changes like this if you're operating against live data. That way you can fully test the script against test databases before risking your real data. Be sure to also fully back up your database before making this kind of change.

Editing Table Properties and Objects That Belong to the Table

Beyond the basic attributes that you've looked at thus far, you can also edit many other facets of your tables. You can edit or add to tables in two different ways:

➤ **Properties:** These are edited in a window that pops up and docks, by default, on the right side of the Management Studio inside the diagramming window. To bring up the properties window, click the Properties Window icon on the toolbar in the Management Studio.

➤ **Objects that belong to the table, such as indexes, constraints, and relationships:** These are edited in their own dialog boxes, which you can access by right-clicking the table in the diagram and choosing the item that you want to set.

These are important facets of diagram-based editing, so let's look at some of the major players.

Properties Window

Figure 8-14 shows the Properties window for the `CustomerNotes` table.

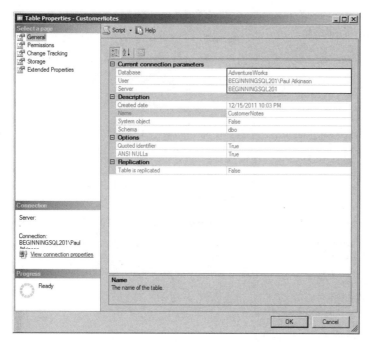

FIGURE 8-14

You can use this Properties window to set several key table properties — most notably what schema the table belongs to and whether the table has an `Identity` column.

Relationships

You get to this dialog box by right-clicking the table heading and choosing Relationships or by selecting the Relationships icon on the Table Designer toolbar. Much like it sounds, this dialog box allows you to edit the nature of the relationships between tables. As you can see from Figure 8-15, the relationships for the `CustomerNotes` table doesn't yet have anything in it.

For now, just realize that you can edit just about anything to do with relationships here.

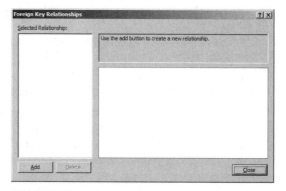

FIGURE 8-15

You could, for example, create a relationship to another table just by clicking Add and filling out the various boxes. Again, you'll look into this further in a page or two.

Indexes/Keys

A lot of this dialog box may be something of a mystery to you at this point — you haven't gotten to the chapter on indexing yet, so some of the terms may seem a bit strange. Still, take a look at what you get in Figure 8-16 (again, either right-click the table heading and choose Indexes/Keys . . ., or choose the Manage Indexes and Keys icon from the Table Designer toolbar).

From here, you can create, edit, and delete indexes. You can also establish which filegroup you want the index to be stored on (in most instances, you'll just want to leave this alone). You'll look further into indexes in the next chapter.

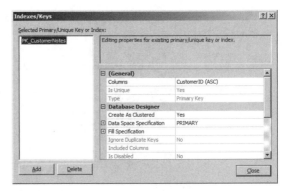

Check Constraints

Moving on to the next menu option (or icon if you're using the toolbar to get to these dialog boxes that you'll examine here), you can manage check constraints, as shown in Figure 8-17.

Again, this one is pretty much grayed out. Why? Well, there aren't any constraints of any kind other than a primary key defined for the `CustomerNotes` table, and that primary key is dealt with on the Index/Keys tab. This particular dialog box is for check constraints only — if you want to see this tab in full action, you need to click Add and add a constraint.

FIGURE 8-16

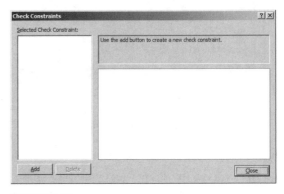

FIGURE 8-17

Creating Relationships in Diagrams

Well, you've seen what the diagramming tool offers you relative to tables, so, as promised, next up on the list is the relationship line (and the underlying details of that relationship).

Looking at a relationship line, the side with the key is the side that is the "one" side of a relationship. The side that has the infinity symbol represents your "many" side. The tools have no relationship line available to specifically represent relationships where zero is possible (it still uses the same line). In addition, the only relationships that actually show in the diagram are ones that are declared using foreign key constraints. Any relationship that is enforced via triggers — regardless of the type of relationship — will not cause a relationship line to appear.

Looking at the AdventureWorks diagram again, try right-clicking the `SalesOrderHeader` table and selecting Relationships. This brings up a more populated version of the Relationship dialog box you looked at in the previous section — the Relationships dialog box for the `SalesOrderHeader` table is shown in Figure 8-18.

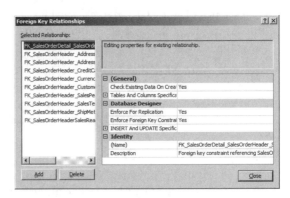

FIGURE 8-18

From here, you can edit the nature of the relationship. You can set such things as cascading actions, whether the foreign key is enabled or disabled (for example, if you want to deliberately add data in that violates the relationship), and even change the name of the relationship.

Database designers seem to vary widely in their opinions regarding names for relationships. Some don't care what they are named, but I prefer to use a verb phrase to describe my relationships — for example, in the Customers/Orders relationship, I would probably name it CustomerHasOrders or something of that ilk. It's nothing critical — most of the time you won't even use it — but I find that it can be really helpful when I'm looking at a long object list or a particularly complex ER diagram where the lines may run across the page past several unrelated entities. Whether you use that naming convention or one of your own devising, I do recommend making one and sticking with it.

Adding Relationships in the Diagramming Tool

Just drag and drop — it's that easy. The only trick is making sure that you start and end your drag in the places you meant to. If in doubt, select the column(s) you're interested in before starting your drag.

TRY IT OUT   Adding a Relationship

Let's add a relationship between the new CustomerNotes table (you created it in the last section) and the Customers table — after all, if it's a customer note you probably want to make sure that you are taking notes on a valid customer. To do this, follow these steps:

1. Click and hold in the gray area to the left of the CustomerID column in the Customers table, and then drag your mouse until it is pointing at the CustomerID column in the CustomerNotes table. A dialog box should pop up to confirm the column mapping between the related tables (see Figure 8-19).

2. If you did your drag-and-drop right, the names of the columns on both sides of the relationship should come up right to start with, but if they came up with something other than you expected, don't worry too much about — just click the combo box for the table you want to change columns for and select the new column, changing the name of the relationship from the default of FK_CustomerNotes_Customers to FKCustomerHasNotes.

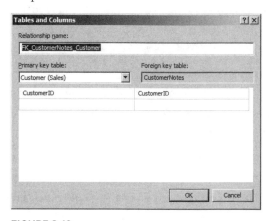

FIGURE 8-19

3. Click OK. You are taken to the more standard relationship dialog box so you can set any other settings you may want to adjust before you save the new relationship to the table.

4. Change the DELETE RULE and UPDATE RULE actions to CASCADE — ensuring that if the related customer record ever gets updated or deleted, the notes for that customer also get updated or deleted as necessary. You can see what this looks like in Figure 8-20.

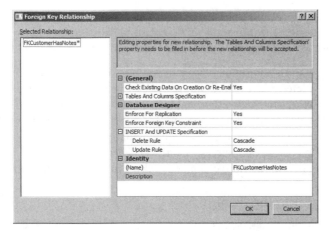

FIGURE 8-20

5. With this done, you can click ⊙K and see the new relationship line in your diagram.

How It Works

Much like when you added the table in the previous section, SQL Server is constructing SQL behind the scenes to make the changes you need. So far, it has added the relationship to the diagram only — if you hover over that relationship, you even see a tooltip with the relationship's name and nature, as shown in Figure 8-21.

FIGURE 8-21

 NOTE *Notice the asterisk on both tables!!! The changes you have made have been added only to the change list that you've made to the diagram — they will not be added to the physical database until you choose to save the diagram!*

There is an instance when the way the line is displayed will change — when you "disable" the foreign key. You saw how to disable constraints in the last chapter, and you can do it in the Relationship dialog box by changing the Enforce Foreign Key Constraint dropdown setting to No. Doing so changes your line to let you know that the constraint has been disabled. It will look something like Figure 8-22.

FIGURE 8-22

If you see one of these, your first question should be "Why is that disabled?" Maybe it was intentional, but you'll want to be sure.

DENORMALIZATION

I'm going to keep this relatively short because this topic tends to get fairly advanced, but remember not to get carried away with the normalization of your data.

As I stated early in this chapter, normalization is one of those things that database designers sometimes wear like a cross. It's somehow turned into a religion for them, and they begin normalizing data for the sake of normalization rather than for the good things it does to their databases. Here are a couple of things to think about in this regard:

➤ **If declaring a computed column or storing some derived data allows you to run a report more effectively, by all means put it in.** Just remember to take into account the benefit versus the risk. (For example, what if your "summary" data gets out of synch with the data it can be derived from? How will you determine that it happened, and how will you fix it if it does happen?)

➤ **Sometimes, by including just one (or more) denormalized column in a table, you can eliminate or significantly cut the number of joins necessary to retrieve information.** Watch for these scenarios — they actually come up reasonably frequently. I've dealt with situations where adding one column to one commonly used base table cut a nine-table join down to just three, and cut the query time by about 90 percent in the process.

➤ **If you're keeping historical data — data that largely goes unchanged and is just used for reporting — the integrity issue becomes a much smaller consideration.** Once the data is written to a read-only area and verified, you can be reasonably certain that you won't have "out of sync" problems, which are one of the major problems that data normalization addresses. At that point, it may be much nicer (and faster) to just "flatten" (denormalize) the data out into a few tables and speed things up.

➤ **The fewer tables that have to be joined, the happier the users who do their own reports are going to be.** The user base out there continues to get more and more savvy with the tools they are using. Increasingly, users are coming to their DBA and asking for direct access to the database to do their own custom reporting. For these users, a highly normalized database can look like a maze and become virtually useless. Denormalizing your data can make life much easier for these users.

All that said, if in doubt, normalize things. There is a reason why that is the way relational systems are typically designed. When you err on the side of normalizing, you are erring on the side of better data integrity, and on the side of better performance in a transactional environment.

BEYOND NORMALIZATION

Normalization isn't the same as design, but it's a good first step. In this section, you'll see a basic set of "beyond normalization" rules of the road in design. Very few of these are hard and fast kinds of rules — they are just things to think about. The most important thing to understand here is that, while normalization is a big thing in database design, it is not the only thing.

Keep It Simple

I run into people on a regular basis who have some really slick and different ways to do things. Some of the time, I wind up seeing some ideas that are incredibly cool and incredibly useful. Other times I see ideas that are incredibly cool, but not very useful. As often as not though, I see ideas that are neither — they may be new, but that doesn't make them good.

Before I step too hard on your creative juices here, let me clarify what I'm trying to get across — don't accept the "because we've always done it that way" approach to things, but also recognize that the tried and true probably continues to be true for a reason — it usually works.

SQL Server 2012 continues to bring all new ways to overdo it in terms of making things too complex. Complex data rules and even complex data types are available through powerful and flexible new additions to the product (code-driven functions and data types). Try to avoid instilling more complexity in your database than you really need to. A minimalist approach usually (but not always) yields something that is not only easier to edit, but also runs a lot faster.

Choosing Data Types

In keeping with the minimalist idea, choose what you need, but only what you need.

For example, if you're trying to store months (as the number, 1–12) — those can be done in a single byte by using a `tinyint`. Why then do I regularly come across databases where a field that's only going to store a month is declared as an `int` (which is four bytes)? Don't use an `nchar` or `nvarchar` if you're never going to do anything that requires Unicode — these data types take up two bytes for every one as compared to their non-Unicode cousins.

> ### WASTED SPACE IS WASTED SPEED
>
> There is a tendency to think about data type choice as being a space issue. When I bring this up in person, I sometimes hear the argument, "Ah, disk space is cheap these days!" Well, beyond the notion that a name-brand solid-state hard drive still costs more than I care to throw away on laziness, there's also a network bandwidth issue. If you're passing an extra 100 bytes down the wire for every row, and you pass a 100 record result, that's about 10KB worth of extra data you just clogged your network with. Still not convinced? Now, say that you have just 100 users performing 50 transactions per hour — that's over 50MB of wasted network bandwidth per hour.
>
> Furthermore, one of your jobs as a SQL developer is to produce something that performs well. You can dance around it all you want, but as the database grows, you'll find that space matters if only because the hard disk is the slowest part of your server. Minimizing disk reads is a fantastic way to speed up your queries, and doubling the number of records per page (by halving the number of bytes per record) is a great step toward that.
>
> The bottom line is, most things that happen with your database will happen repetitively — that means that small mistakes snowball and can become rather large.

Err on the Side of Storing Things

There was an old movie called *The Man Who Knew Too Much* — Hitchcock, I believe. That man wasn't keeping data.

Every time that you're building a database, you're going to come across the question of, "Are we going to need that information later?" Here's my two-bit advice on that — when in doubt, keep it. You see, most of the time you can't get back the data that has already come and gone.

I guarantee that at least once (and probably many, many more times than that), a customer (remember, customers are basically anyone who needs something from you — there is such a thing as an internal customer, not just the ones in Accounts Receivable) will come to you and say something like, "Can you give me a report on how much we paid each non-incorporated company last year?"

Okay, so are you storing information on whether or not your vendor is a corporation? You had better be if you are subject to U.S. tax law (1099 reporting). So you turn around and say that you can handle that, and the customer replies, "Great! Can you print that out along with their address as of the end of the year?"

Oops — I'm betting that you don't have past addresses, or, at the very least, aren't storing the date that the address changed. In short, you never know what a user of your system is going to ask for — try to make sure you have it. Just keep in mind that you don't want to be moving unnecessary amounts of data up and down your network wire (see my comments on choosing a data type). If you're storing the data just for posterity, make sure you don't put it in any of your application's SELECT statements if it isn't needed (actually, this should be your policy regardless of why you're storing the data).

 NOTE *If you think that there may be legal ramifications either way (both in keeping it and in getting rid of it), consult your attorney. Sometimes you're legally obligated to keep data a certain amount of time; other times it's best to get rid of information as soon as legally possible.*

DRAWING UP A QUICK EXAMPLE

In this section, you'll walk quickly through a process of designing the invoicing database that you already started in the section on normalization. For the most part, you're going to just be applying the diagramming tools to what you've already designed, but I'll also toss in a few new issues to show how they affect your design.

Creating the Database

Unlike a lot of the third-party diagramming tools out there, the SQL Server diagramming tools will not create the database for you — you have to already have it created in order to get as far as having the diagram available to work with.

You're not going to be playing with any data to speak of, so just create a small database called `Invoice`. I'll go ahead and use the dialog box in the Management Studio for the sake of this example.

After right-clicking the Databases node of my server and selecting New Database, I enter information for a database called `Invoice` that is set up as 3MB in size.

Because you already read a chapter on creating databases (and for the sake of brevity), I'm just going to accept the defaults on all the other options, as shown in Figure 8-23.

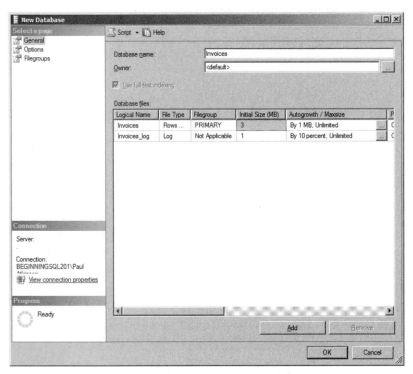

FIGURE 8-23

Adding the Diagram and the Initial Tables

As you did when creating your AdventureWorks diagram, you want to follow these steps to add tables:

1. Expand the node for your database (it should have been added underneath the Databases node, but you may need to right-click the databases node and choose Refresh) and accept the dialog box asking if you want to add the objects needed to support diagramming.

2. Right-click the Diagrams node and select New Database Diagram. The Add Table dialog box pops up, but because there are no user tables in your database, you'll just want to click Close so you wind up with a clean sheet.

3. Now you're ready to start adding new tables. You can either click the New Table icon on the toolbar, or right-click anywhere in the diagram and select New Table. Start off by adding in the `Orders` table, as shown in Figure 8-24.

Orders *				
Column Name	Condensed Type	Nullable	Default Value	Identity
OrderID	int	No		☑
OrderDate	date	No	SYSDATETIME()	☐
CustomerNo	int	No		☐
				☐

FIGURE 8-24

 NOTE *Note that I've changed from the default view — which doesn't have the Default Value and Identity columns as part of it — over to the custom view. I also had to choose Modify Custom and select the Default Value and Identity columns to be added to the custom view.*

Let's stop long enough to look at a couple of the decisions that you made here. While you have addressed the issue of normalization, you haven't addressed any of the other basics yet. First up of those is the question of data types.

Because `OrderID` is the primary key for the table, you need to be sure that you allow enough room for your values to be unique as you insert more and more data. If this were a table into which you weren't going to be making very many inserts, you might choose a smaller data type, but because it is your `Orders` table (and you probably hope to be entering lots of orders), you'll push the size up a bit. In addition, numeric order numbers seem suitable (make sure you ask your customers about issues like this) and facilitate the use of an automatic numbering mechanism in the form of an identity column. If you need more than 2 billion or so order numbers (in which case, I may want some stock in your company), you can take a look at the larger `BigInt` data type. (Suffice to say that I'm certain you won't have too many orders for that data type to hold — just keep in mind the extra space used, although that's often trivial in the larger schema of how much space the database as a whole is using.)

`OrderDate` uses the `Date` data type. You may want to utilize one of the `DateTime` data types instead if you want the time of day on your order in addition to just the date. Date is more compact and meets the need for the simple invoicing database. Be careful in your `DateTime` data type choices though; you'll find that some of them work easier in some languages than others do. For example, Visual Basic prior to .NET threw fits when you played around with `smalldatetime` fields, and could even be temperamental with the then standard `DateTime`. You could get around the problems, but it was a pain. Even with .NET, you're generally going to want to use the newer `DateTime2` data type instead of `DateTime`, as it has a more direct crossover to the `DateTime` data type in .NET.

Your customer has told you (and you've seen in the earlier sample data) that `CustomerNo` is five digits, all numeric. This is one of those areas where you start saying to your customer, "Are you sure you're never going to be using alpha characters in there?" The next question may be, "Do leading zeroes matter?" Assuming the answers are yes and no, respectively, you can go with an integer because it is:

➤ Faster on lookups.

➤ Smaller in size — four bytes will cover a five-digit number easily, but it takes five bytes minimum (six if you're using variable-length fields) to handle five characters.

> **NOTE** *Note that you're kind of cheating on this one — realistically, the customer number for this table is really being defined by the relationship you're going to be building with the* Customers *table. Because that's the last table you'll see in this example, you're going ahead and filling in the blanks for this field now.*
>
> *Really, though, there's something else to focus on here. Storing this as a number is done for performance and efficiency — not for any business rule. In fact, this can be dangerous. Consider a ZIP code. Now I'm going to date myself and not pay any attention to those newfangled ZIP+4 numbers, and I'm also going to get provincial and stick with American ZIP codes only: five numeric characters. Should you store a ZIP code as a number?*
>
> *Well, a number is smaller and faster to deal with, as I mentioned previously. However, what happens when you encounter someone with a PO box in Boston, MA? 02112, stored as an integer, becomes 2112 (which is a great album but a lousy ZIP code). If the data were something other than a ZIP code, you may have no idea how many leading zeroes you missed. In general, try to choose a data type that's not just efficient, but accurate as well.*

After data types, you also had to decide on the size of the column — this was a no-brainer for this particular table because all the data types have fixed sizes.

Next on the hit list is whether or not the rows can be null. In this case, you can be sure that you want all this information and that it should be available at the time you enter the order, so you won't allow nulls.

> **NOTE** *I've touched on this before, but you just about have to drag me kicking and screaming in order to get me to allow nulls in my databases. There are situations where you just can't avoid it — "undefined" values are legitimate. I'll still often fill text fields with actual text saying "Value Unknown" or something like that.*
>
> *The reason I do this is because nullable fields promote errors in much the same way that undeclared variables do. Whenever you run across null values in the table, you wind up asking yourself, "Gee, did I mean for that to be there, or did I forget to write a value into the table for that row?" — that is, do I have a bug in my program?*

The next issue you faced was default values. You couldn't have a default for OrderID because you were making it an identity column (the two are mutually exclusive). For OrderDate, however, a default made some level of sense. If an OrderDate isn't provided, in this case you can assume that the order date is today. Last, but not least, is the CustomerNo — which customer would you default to? Nope — can't do that here.

Next up was the issue of an identity column. OrderID is an ideal candidate for an identity column — the value has no meaning other than keeping the rows unique. Using a counter such as an identity field gives you a nice, presentable, and orderly way to maintain that unique value. You don't have any reason to change the identity seed and increment, so don't. Leave it starting at one and incrementing by one.

Now you're ready to move on to the next table — the OrderDetails table, as defined in Figure 8-25.

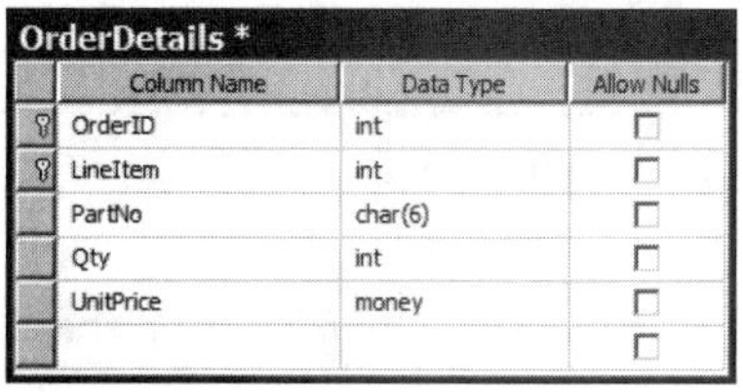

FIGURE 8-25

For this table, note the following columns:

➤ **OrderID:** This will have a foreign key to it, so your data type is decided for you — it must be of the same type and size as the field it's referencing, so it's going to be an int.

➤ **LineItem:** Start over again with each row, so you probably could have gotten as little as a tinyint here. You should probably go with an int on this one just for safety's sake. (I've had people exceed limits that have been set on this sort of thing before.)

➤ **PartNo:** For this table this is actually defined by the fact that it needs to match up with the PartNo in the Products table. It's using a char(6) in that table (you'll come to it shortly), so that's what you'll make it here.

➤ **Qty:** This is guesswork. The question is, what's the largest order you can take as far as quantity for one line item goes? Because you don't know what you're selling, you can't really make a guess on a maximum quantity (for example, if you were selling barrels of oil, you might literally be buying millions of barrels at a time). You're also using an int here, but you would have needed a data type that accepted decimals if you were selling things like gallons of fuel or things by weight, so be sure to consider your needs carefully.

➤ **UnitPrice:** This is relatively easy. Because this field will hold a monetary value, its data type hints at money. Be careful with this though. How many decimal places do you really need? U.S. developers will tend toward thinking they only need two (several currencies often trade in more decimal places), but what about commodity items? For example, gasoline is generally sold in fractions of a cent. The money data type handles four decimal places, which meets most currency needs.

Moving along, you're again (no surprise here) considering all data fields to be required. No, you're not allowing nulls anywhere.

No defaults seem to make sense for this table, so you can skip that part also.

Identity? The temptation might be to mark OrderID as an identity column again. Don't do that! Remember that OrderID is a value that you're going to match to a column in another table. That table already has a value (as it happens, set by identity, but it didn't necessarily have to be that way), so setting your column to identity would cause a collision. You would be told that you can't do your insert because you're trying to set an identity value. All the other columns either get their data from another table or require user input of the data. `IsRowGuid` does not apply again.

That takes you to the `Products` and `Customers` tables, as shown in Figures 8-26 and 8-27, respectively.

Products *		
Column Name	Data Type	Allow Nulls
🔑 PartNo	char(6)	☐
Description	varchar(15)	☐
Weight	tinyint	☐
		☐

FIGURE 8-26

Customers *		
Column Name	Data Type	Allow Nulls
🔑 CustomerNo	int	☐
CustomerName	varchar(50)	☐
CustomerAddress	varchar(50)	☐
		☐

FIGURE 8-27

Let's hit the highlights on the choices here and move on.

➤ **PartNo:** This has been defined by the data that you saw when you were looking at normalization. It's a numeric, followed by an alpha, followed by four numerics. That's six characters, and it seems to be fixed. You would want to have a serious discussion with the customer — under oath if you can manage it -- about the notion that the size of the part number can't get any larger but, assuming that's okay, you can go with a `char(6)` here. That's because a `char` takes up slightly less overhead than a `varchar`, and you know that the length is going to always remain the same (this means that there's no benefit from the variable size).

> **NOTE** Let me reiterate the importance of being sure that your customers are really considering their future needs. The `PartNo` column using a simple six-character field is an example of where you might want to be very suspicious. Part numbers are one of those things that people develop new philosophies on almost as often as my teenage daughter develops new taste in clothes. Today's inventory manager will swear that's all he ever intends to use and will be sincere in it, but tomorrow there's a new inventory manager or perhaps your organization merges with another organization that uses a 10-digit numeric part number. Expanding the field isn't that bad of a conversion, but any kind of conversion carries risks, so you want to get it right the first time.

➤ **Description:** This is one of those guessing games. Sometimes a field like this is driven by your user interface requirements (don't make it wider than can be displayed on the screen), other times you're truly guessing at what is "enough" space. Here you use a variable-length `char` over a regular `char` for two reasons:

➤ To save a little space

➤ So you don't have to deal with trailing spaces (look at the `char` versus `varchar` data types back in Chapter 1 if you have questions on this)

You haven't used an nchar or nvarchar because this is a simple invoicing system for a U.S. business, and you're not concerned about localization issues. If you're dealing with a multi-lingual scenario, you'll want to pay much more attention to the Unicode data types. You'll also want to consider them if you're storing inherently international information such as URLs, which can easily have kanji and similar characters in them.

➤ **Weight:** This is similar to Description in that it is somewhat of a guess. You've used a tinyint here because your products will not be over 255 pounds. Note that you are also preventing yourself from keeping decimal places in your weight (integers only). As discussed back under PartNo, make sure you consider your needs carefully — conservative can be great, but being over-conservative can cause a great deal of work later.

➤ **CustomerNo:** I described this field back when you were doing the Orders table.

➤ **CustomerName and CustomerAddress:** These are pretty much the same situation as Description — the question is, how much is enough? But you need to be sure that you don't give too much.

As before, all fields are required (there will be no nulls in either table) and no defaults are called for. Identity columns also do not seem to fit the bill here, as both the customer number and part number have special formats that do not lend themselves to the automatic numbering system that an identity provides.

Adding the Relationships

Okay, to make the diagram less complicated, I've gone through all four of the tables and changed the view on them down to just Column Names. You can do this, too, by simply right-clicking the table and selecting the Column Names menu choice.

You should get a diagram that looks similar to Figure 8-28.

You may not have the exact same positions for your table, but the contents should be the same. You're now ready to start adding relationships, but you probably ought to stop and think about what kind of relationships you need.

FIGURE 8-28

All the relationships that you'll draw with the relationship lines in the SQL Server diagram tool are going to be one-to-zero, one, or many relationships. SQL Server doesn't really know how to do any other kind of relationship implicitly. As discussed earlier in the chapter, you can add things such as unique constraints and triggers to augment what SQL Server will do naturally with relations, but, assuming you don't do any of that, you're going to wind up with a one-to-zero, one, or many relationship.

NOTE *The bright side is that this is by far the most common kind of relationship out there. In short, don't sweat it that SQL Server doesn't cover every base here. The standard foreign key constraint (which is essentially what your reference line represents) fits the bill for most things that you need to do, and the rest can usually be simulated via some other means.*

I'm going to start with the central table in your system — the `Orders` table. First, look at any relationships that it may need. In this case, you have one — it needs to reference the `Customers` table. This is going to be a one-to-many relationship with `Customers` as the parent (the one) and `Orders` as the child (the many) table.

To build the relationship (and a foreign key constraint to serve as the foundation for that relationship), do the following:

1. Click and hold in the leftmost column of the `Customers` table (in the gray area), right where the `CustomerNo` column is.

2. Drag to the same position (the gray area) next to the `CustomerNo` column in the `Orders` table and let go of the mouse button. SQL Server promptly pops up with the first of two dialog boxes to confirm the configuration of this relationship. The first, shown in Figure 8-29, confirms which columns actually relate.

 NOTE *As I pointed out earlier in the chapter, don't sweat it if the names that come up don't match with what you intended — just use the combo boxes to change them back so both sides have* `CustomerNo` *in them. Note also that the names don't have to be the same — keeping them the same just helps ease confusion in situations when they really are the same.*

3. Click OK for this dialog box, and then also click OK to accept the defaults of the Foreign Key Relationship dialog box. As soon as you click OK in the second dialog box, you have your first relationship in your new database, as shown in Figure 8-30.

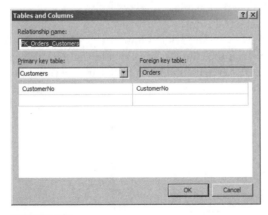

FIGURE 8-29   **FIGURE 8-30**

4. Now you can just do the same thing for your other two relationships. You need to establish a one-to-many relationship from `Orders` to `OrderDetails` (there will be one order header for one or more order details) based on `OrderID`. Also, you need a similar relationship going from `Products` to `OrderDetails` (there will be one `Products` record for many `OrderDetails` records) based on `ProductID`, as shown in Figure 8-31.

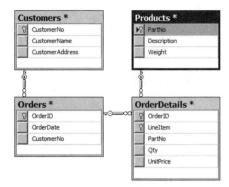

FIGURE 8-31

Adding Some Constraints

As you were going through the building of your tables and relationships, I mentioned a requirement that you still haven't addressed. This requirement needs a constraint to enforce it: the part number is formatted as `9A9999` where `9` indicates a numeric digit `0–9` and `A` indicates an alpha (non-numeric) character.

You can add that requirement now by right-clicking the `Products` table and selecting Check Constraints to bring up the dialog box shown in Figure 8-32.

It is at this point that you are ready to click Add and define the constraint. To restrict part numbers entered to the format you've established, you're going to need the `LIKE` operator:

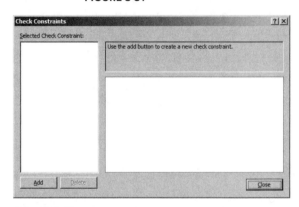

FIGURE 8-32

```
(PartNo LIKE '[0-9][A-Z][0-9][0-9][0-9][0-9]')
```

This essentially evaluates each character that the user is trying to enter in the `PartNo` column of your table. The first character will have to be 0 through 9, the second A through Z (an alpha), and the next four will again have to be numeric digits (the 0 through 9 thing again). You can just enter this into the text box labeled Expression. In addition, you're going to change the default name for your constraint from `CK_Products` to `CKPartNo`, as shown in Figure 8-33.

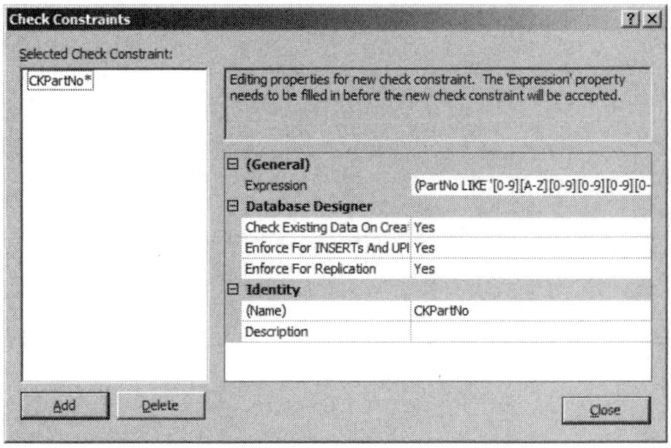

That didn't take you too long — and you now have your first database that you designed!!!

FIGURE 8-33

This was, of course, a relatively simple model — but you've now done the things that make up perhaps 90 percent or more of the actual data architecture.

SUMMARY

Database design is a huge concept, and it's one that has many excellent books dedicated to it. It is essentially impossible to get across every database design notion in just a chapter or two.

In this chapter, I have, however, gotten you off to a solid start. You've seen that data is considered normalized when you take it out to the third normal form. At that level, repetitive information has been eliminated and the data is entirely dependent on the key — in short, the data is dependent on: "The key, the whole key, and nothing but the key." You've seen that normalization is, however, not always the right answer — strategic denormalization of your data can simplify the database for users and speed reporting performance. Finally, you've looked at some non-normalization-related concepts in your database design, plus how to make use of the built-in diagramming tools to design your database.

In the next chapter, you will be taking a very close look at how SQL Server stores information and how to make the best use of indexes.

EXERCISES

1.   Normalize the following data into the third normal form:

PATIENT	SSN	PHYSICIAN	HOSPITAL	TREATMENT	ADMITDATE	RELEASEDATE
Sam Spade	55-55-5555	Albert Schweitzer	Mayo Clinic	Lobotomy	10/01/2011	11/07/2011
Sally Nally	333-33-3333	Albert Schweitzer	NULL	Cortisone Injection	10/10/2011	10/10/2011
Peter Piper	222-22-2222	Mo Betta	Mustard Clinic	Pickle Extraction	11/07/2011	1107/2011
Nicki Doohickey	123-45-6789	Sheila Sheeze	Mustard Clinic	Cortisone Injection	1107/2011	11/07/2011

▶ WHAT YOU LEARNED IN THIS CHAPTER

TOPIC	CONCEPT
Normalizing Data	There are six normal forms, but you'll most commonly use the third normal form. 3NF can be remembered as keeping all your data dependent on the key, the whole key, and nothing but the key.
Creating Relationships	Your data can require relationships from one-to-one, one-to-many, or many-to-many, plus optional (zero-to-one, and so on) forms. Enforcing these in SQL Server may use constraints, triggers, or other mechanisms.
Diagramming	You can create one or more diagrams per database to help visualize your data model. The modeling tools also provide an easy way to alter your table structure and relationships.
Denormalization	Sometimes speed dictates that you violate 3NF. When you do so, you may bring about significant performance improvements, but at the cost of additional overhead needed to enforce database consistency.
Beyond Normalization	Normalization is a good start to design, but it's not the whole story. Choosing appropriate data types and storing the right columns are both critical elements in a well-designed database.

SQL Server Storage and Index Structures

WHAT YOU WILL LEARN IN THIS CHAPTER:

➤ The value of indexing for data retrieval

➤ The cost of indexing

➤ How indexes are structured

➤ Types of indexes

➤ Some guidelines for choosing indexes

➤ How to tell when you've chosen good indexes

➤ Ways to get SQL Server to tell you what indexes to use

Indexes are a critical part of your database planning and system maintenance. They provide SQL Server (and any other database system for that matter) with additional ways to look up data and take shortcuts to that data's physical location. Adding the right index can cut huge percentages of time off your query executions. Unfortunately, too many poorly planned indexes can be ineffective or actually increase the time it takes for your query to run. Indeed, indexes tend to be one of the most misunderstood objects that SQL Server offers, and therefore, they also tend to be one of the most mismanaged.

You will be considering indexes rather closely in this chapter from both a developer's and an administrator's point of view, but in order to understand indexes, you also need to understand how data is stored in SQL Server. For that reason, you will start by taking a look at SQL Server's data-storage mechanism. Once you understand what the indexes are actually trying to organize, seeing how they do so will hopefully make more sense to you.

SQL SERVER STORAGE

Data in SQL Server can be thought of as existing in something of a hierarchy of structures. The hierarchy is pretty simple. Some of the objects within the hierarchy are things that you will deal with directly, and will therefore understand easily. A few others exist under the covers, and while they can be directly addressed in some cases, they usually are not. Let's take a look at them one by one.

The Database

Okay — this one is easy. I can just hear people out there saying, "Duh! I knew that." Yes, you probably did, but I point it out as a unique entity here because it is the highest level of storage (for a given server). This is also the highest level at which a *lock* can be established, although you cannot explicitly create a database-level lock.

 NOTE *A lock is something of a hold and a place marker that is used by the system. As you do development using SQL Server — or any other database for that matter — you will find that understanding and managing locks is absolutely critical to your system.*

 NOTE *You will read a lot more extensively about locking in Chapter 14, but you will see the lockability of objects within SQL Server discussed in passing as you look at storage.*

The Extent

An *extent* is the basic unit of storage used to allocate space for tables and indexes. It is made up of eight contiguous 8KB data *pages*, for a total size of 64KB.

The concept of allocating space based on extents, rather than actual space used, can be somewhat difficult to understand for people used to operating system storage principles. The important points about an extent include:

➤ Once an extent is full, the next record takes up not just the size of the record, but the size of a whole new extent. Many people who are new to SQL Server get tripped up in their space estimations in part because of the allocation of an extent at a time rather than a record at a time.

➤ By pre-allocating this space, SQL Server saves the time of allocating new space with each record.

It may seem like a waste that a whole extent is taken up just because one too many rows were added to fit on the currently allocated extent(s), but the amount of space wasted this way is typically not that much. Still, it can add up — particularly in a highly fragmented environment — so it's definitely something you should keep in mind.

The good news in taking up all this space is that SQL Server skips some of the allocation-time overhead. Instead of worrying about allocation issues every time it writes a row, SQL Server deals with additional space allocation only when a new extent is needed.

> **NOTE** *Don't confuse the space that an extent is taking up with the space that a database takes up. Whatever space is allocated to the database is what you'll see disappear from your disk drive's available-space number. An extent is merely how things are, in turn, allocated within the total space reserved by the database.*

The Page

Much like an extent is a unit of allocation within the database, a *page* is the unit of allocation within a specific extent. There are eight pages to every extent.

A page is the last level you reach before you are at the actual data row. Whereas the number of pages per extent is fixed, the number of rows per page is not — that depends entirely on the size of the row, which can vary. You can think of a page as being something of a container for both table- and index-row data. A row is, in general, not allowed to be split between pages.

Page Types

There are a number of different *page types*. For the purposes of this book, the types you care about are:

➤ **Data:** *Data pages* are pretty self-explanatory. They are the actual data in your table, with the exception of any BLOB data that is not defined with the text-in-row option, `varchar(max)` or `varbinary(max)`.

➤ **Index:** *Index pages* are also pretty straightforward. They hold both the non-leaf and the leaf level pages (you'll examine what these are later in the chapter) of a non-clustered index, as well as the non-leaf level pages of a clustered index. These index types will become much clearer as you continue through this chapter.

Page Splits

When a page becomes full, it splits. This means more than just a new page being allocated — it also means that approximately half the data from the existing page is moved to the new page.

The exception to this process is when a clustered index is in use. If there is a clustered index and the next inserted row would be physically located as the last record in the table, a new page is created, and the new row is added to the new page without relocating any of the existing data. You will see much more on page splits as you investigate indexes.

Rows

You have heard much about "row level locking," so it shouldn't be a surprise to hear this term. Rows can be up to 8KB.

In addition to the limit of 8,060 characters, there is also a maximum of 1,024 standard (non-sparse) columns. In practice, you'll rarely run out of columns before you run into the 8,060 character limit.

The max of 1,024 columns gives you an average column width of just under 8 bytes. For most uses, you'll easily exceed that average (and therefore exceed the 8,060 characters before the 1,024 columns). The exception to this tends to be in measurement and statistical information — where you have a large number of different things that you are storing numeric samples of. Still, even those applications will find it a rare day when they bump into the 1,024-column-count limit. When you do, you can explore the notion of sparse columns, so let's look at that.

Sparse Columns

Sparse columns, in terms of a special data structure, were introduced with SQL Server 2008. These are meant to deal with the recurring scenario where you have columns that you essentially just need "sometimes." That is, they are going to be null a high percentage of the time. There are many scenarios where, if you bump into a few of these kinds of columns, you tend to bump into a ton of them. Using sparse columns, you can increase the total number of allowed columns in a single table to 30,000.

Internally, the data from columns marked as being sparsely populated is embedded within a single column — allowing a way to break the former limitation of 1,024 columns without major architectural changes.

`Image`, `text`, `ntext`, `geography`, `geometry`, `timestamp`, and all user-defined data types are prohibited from being marked as a sparse column.

> **NOTE** *While sparse columns are handled natively by newer versions of the SQL Native Client, other forms of data access will have varying behavior when accessing sparse columns. The* `sparse` *property of a column will be transparent when selecting a column by name, but when selecting it using an "*" in the select list, different client access methods will vary between supplying the sparse columns as a unified XML column and not showing those columns at all. If you have that issue, you'll want to try upgrading your client libraries as soon as reasonably possible.*

> **NOTE** *Sparse columns largely fall under the heading of "advanced topic," but I do want you to know they are there and can be a viable solution for particular scenarios.*

UNDERSTANDING INDEXES

Webster's dictionary defines an index as:

> **NOTE** *A list (as of bibliographical information or citations to a body of literature) arranged usually in alphabetical order of some specified datum (as author, subject, or keyword).*

I'll take a simpler approach in the context of databases and say that indexes are a way of potentially getting to data a heck of a lot quicker. Still, the Webster's definition isn't too bad — even for the specific purposes here.

Perhaps the key thing to point out in the Webster's definition is the word "usually." The definition of "alphabetical order" changes depending on a number of rules. For example, in SQL Server, you have a number of different collation options available to you. Among these options are:

➤ **Binary:** Sorts by the numeric representation of the character (for example, in ASCII, a space is represented by the number 32, the letter "D" is 68, and the letter "d" is 100). Because everything is numeric, this is the fastest option. Unfortunately, it's not at all the way in which people think, and can also really wreak havoc with comparisons in your WHERE clause.

➤ **Dictionary order:** This sorts things just as you would expect to see in a dictionary, with a twist. You can set a number of additional options to determine sensitivity to case, accent, and character set.

It's fairly easy to understand that if you tell SQL Server to pay attention to case, "A" is not going to be equal to "a." Likewise, if you tell it to be case insensitive, "A" will be equal to "a." Things get a bit more confusing when you add accent sensitivity. SQL Server pays attention to diacritical marks, and therefore "a" is different from "á," which is different from "à." Where many people get even more confused is in how collation order affects not only the equality of data, but also the sort order (and, therefore, the way it is stored in indexes).

By way of example, let's look at the equality of a couple of collation options in the following table, and what they do to the sort order and equality information:

COLLATION ORDER	COMPARISON VALUES	INDEX STORAGE ORDER
Dictionary order, case insensitive, accent insensitive (the default)	A = a = à = á = â = Ä = ä = Å = å	a, A, à, â, á, Ä, ä, Å, å
Dictionary order, case insensitive, accent insensitive, uppercase preference	A = a = à = á = â = Ä = ä = Å = å	A, a, à, â, á, Ä, ä, Å, å
Dictionary order, case sensitive, accent sensitive	A ≠ a, Ä ≠ ä, Å ≠ å, a ≠ à ≠ á ≠ â ≠ ä ≠ å, A ≠ Ä ≠ Å	A, a, à, á, â, Ä, ä, Å, å

The point here is that what happens in your indexes depends on the collation information you have established for your data. Collation can be set at the database and column level, so you have a fairly fine granularity in your level of control. If you're going to assume that your server is case insensitive, you need to be sure that the documentation for your system deals with this, or you had better plan on a lot of tech support calls — particularly if you're selling outside of the United States. Imagine you're an independent software vendor (ISV) and you sell your product to a customer who installs it on an existing server (which is going to seem like an entirely reasonable thing to the customer), but that existing server happens to be an older server that's set up as case sensitive. You're going to get a support call from one very unhappy customer.

NOTE *Once the collation order has been set, changing it is very difficult (but possible), so be certain of the collation order you want before you set it.*

B-Trees

The concept of a *balanced tree*, or *B-Tree*, is certainly not one that was created with SQL Server. Indeed, B-Trees are used in a very large number of indexing systems, both in and out of the database world.

A B-Tree simply attempts to provide a consistent and relatively low-cost method of finding your way to a particular piece of information. The *balanced* in the name is pretty much self-descriptive. A B-Tree is, with the odd exception, self-balancing, meaning that every time the tree branches, approximately half the data is on one side and half is on the other side. The *tree* in the name is also probably pretty obvious at this point (hint: tree, branch — see a trend here?). It's there because, when you draw the structure and turn it upside down, it has the general form of a tree.

Searching B-Trees

A B-Tree starts at the *root node* (another stab at the tree analogy there, but not the last). This root node can, if there is a small amount of data, point directly to the actual location of the data. In such a case, you would end up with a structure that looked something like Figure 9-1.

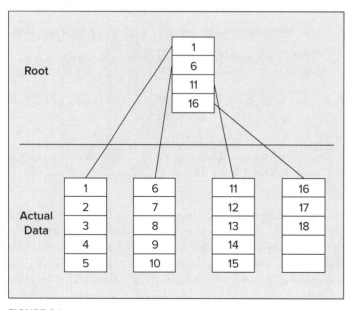

FIGURE 9-1

So, you start at the root and look through the records until you find the last page that starts with a value less than what you're looking for. You then obtain a pointer to that node and look through it until you find the row that you want.

In most situations though, there is too much data to reference from the root node, so the root node points at intermediate nodes — or what are called *non-leaf level nodes*. Non-leaf level nodes are nodes that are somewhere in between the root and the node that tells you where the data is physically stored. Non-leaf level nodes can then point to other non-leaf level nodes, or to *leaf level nodes* (last tree analogy reference — I promise). Leaf level nodes are the nodes where you obtain the real reference to the actual physical data. Much like the leaf is the end of the line for navigating the tree, the node you get to at the leaf level is the end of the line for your index. From there, you can go straight to the actual data node that has your data on it.

As you can see in Figure 9-2, you start with the root node just as before, and then move to the node that starts with the highest value that is equal to or less than what you're looking for and is also in the next level down. You then repeat the process: Look for the node that has the highest starting value at or below the value for which you're looking. You keep doing this, level by level down the tree, until you get to the leaf level — from there you know the physical location of the data and can quickly navigate to it.

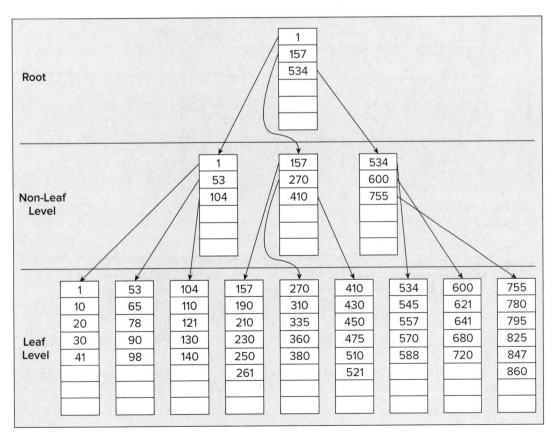

FIGURE 9-2

Updating B-Trees: A First Look at Page Splits

All of this works quite nicely on the read side of the equation — it's the insert that gets a little tricky. Recall that the *B* in B-Tree stands for *balanced*. You may also recall that I mentioned that a B-Tree is balanced because about half the data is on either side every time you run into a branch in the tree. B-Trees are sometimes referred to as *self-balancing* because the way new data is added to the tree generally prevents them from becoming lopsided.

When you add data to the tree, a node eventually becomes full and you need to split it. Because in SQL Server, a node equates to a page, this is called a *page split*, illustrated in Figure 9-3.

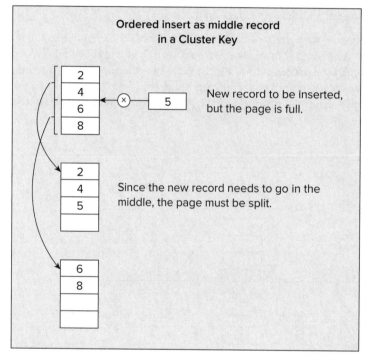

Ordered insert as middle record in a Cluster Key

| 2 |
| 4 |
| 6 |
| 8 |

New record to be inserted, but the page is full.

5

| 2 |
| 4 |
| 5 |
| |

Since the new record needs to go in the middle, the page must be split.

| 6 |
| 8 |
| |
| |

FIGURE 9-3

> **NOTE** *When a page split occurs, data is automatically moved around to keep things balanced. The first half of the data is left on the old page, and the rest of the data is added to a new page — thus you have about a 50-50 split, and your tree remains balanced.*

If you think about this splitting process a bit, you'll realize that it adds a substantial amount of overhead at the time of the split. Instead of inserting just one page, you are:

➤ Creating a new page

➤ Migrating rows from the existing page to the new page

> ➤ Adding your new row to one of the pages

> ➤ Adding another entry in the parent node

But the overhead doesn't stop there. Because you're in a tree arrangement, you have the possibility for something of a cascading action. When you create the new page (because of the split), you need to make another entry in the parent node. This entry in the parent node also has the potential to cause a page split at that level, and the process starts all over again. Indeed, this possibility extends all the way up to and can even affect the root node.

If the root node splits, you actually end up creating two additional pages. Because there can be only one root node, the page that was formerly the root node is split into two pages and becomes a new intermediate level of the tree. An entirely new root node is then created, and will have two entries (one to the old root node, one to the split page).

Needless to say, page splits can have a very negative impact on system performance and are characterized by behavior where your process on the server seems to just pause for a few seconds (while the pages are being split and rewritten).

You will learn about page-split prevention before you're done with this chapter.

> **NOTE** *While page splits at the leaf level are a common fact of life, page splits at intermediate nodes happen far less frequently. As your table grows, every layer of the index experiences page splits, but because the intermediate nodes have only one entry for several entries on the next lower node, the number of page splits gets less and less frequent as you move further up the tree. Still, for a split to occur above the leaf level, there must have already been a split at the next lowest level — this means that page splits up the tree are cumulative (and expensive performance-wise) in nature.*

SQL Server has several types of indexes (which you will read more about shortly), but they all make use of this B-Tree approach in some way or another. Indeed, they are all very similar in structure, thanks to the flexible nature of a B-Tree. Still, you'll see that there are indeed some significant differences, and these can have an impact on the performance of your system.

> **NOTE** *For an SQL Server index, the nodes of the tree come in the form of pages, but you can actually apply this concept of a root node, the non-leaf level, the leaf level, and the tree structure to more than just SQL Server or even just databases.*

How Data Is Accessed in SQL Server

In the broadest sense, there are only two ways in which SQL Server retrieves the data you request:

> ➤ Using a table scan

> ➤ Using an index

Which method SQL Server uses to run your particular query will depend on what indexes are available, what columns you are asking about, the kind of joins you are doing, and the size of your tables.

Use of Table Scans

A *table scan* is a pretty straightforward process. When a table scan is performed, SQL Server starts at the physical beginning of the table, looking through every row in the table. As it finds rows that match the criteria of your query, it includes them in the result set.

You may hear lots of bad things about table scans, and in general, they will be true. However, table scans can actually be the fastest method of access in some instances. Typically, this is the case when retrieving data from rather small tables. The exact size where this becomes the case varies widely according to the width of your table and the specific nature of the query.

 NOTE *See if you can spot why the use of* EXISTS *in the* WHERE *clause of your queries has so much to offer performance-wise when it fits the problem. When you use the* EXISTS *operator, SQL Server stops as soon as it finds one record that matches the criteria. If you had a million-record table and it found a matching record on the third record, use of the* EXISTS *option would have saved you the reading of 999,997 records!* NOT EXISTS *works in much the same way.*

Use of Indexes

When SQL Server decides to use an index, the process actually works somewhat similarly to a table scan, but with a few shortcuts.

During the query optimization process, the optimizer takes a look at all the available indexes and chooses the best one (this is primarily based on the information you specify in your joins and WHERE clause, combined with statistical information SQL Server keeps on index makeup). Once that index is chosen, SQL Server navigates the tree structure to the point of data that matches your criteria and again extracts only the records it needs. The difference is that because the data is sorted, the query engine knows when it has reached the end of the current range it is looking for. It can then end the query, or move on to the next range of data as necessary.

If you ponder the query topics studied thus far (Chapter 7 specifically), you may notice some striking resemblances to how the EXISTS option works. The EXISTS keyword allowed a query to quit running the instant that it found a match. The performance gains using an index are similar or better than EXISTS since the process of searching for data can work in a similar fashion; that is, the server can use the sort of the index to know when there is nothing left that's relevant and can stop things right there. Even better, however, is that by using an index, you don't have to limit yourself to Boolean situations (does the piece of data I was after exist — yes or no?). You can apply this same notion to the beginning and end of a range. You can gather ranges of data with essentially the same benefits that an index gives to finding data. What's more, you can do a very fast lookup (called a SEEK) of your data rather than hunt through the entire table.

> **NOTE** *Although I'm comparing index versus* EXISTS *operator function, don't get the impression that indexes replace the* EXISTS *operator altogether (or vice versa). The two are not mutually exclusive; they can be used together, and often are. I mention them here together only because they have the similarity of being able to tell when their work is done, and quit before getting to the physical end of the table.*

Index Types and Index Navigation

Although there are nominally two types of base index structures in SQL Server (*clustered* and *non-clustered*), there are actually, internally speaking, three different types:

➤   Clustered indexes

➤   Non-clustered indexes, which comprise:

   ➤   Non-clustered indexes on a heap

   ➤   Non-clustered indexes on a clustered index

The way the physical data is stored varies between clustered and non-clustered indexes. The way SQL Server traverses the B-Tree to get to the end data varies between all three index types.

All SQL Server indexes have leaf level and non-leaf level pages. As mentioned during the B-Trees discussion, the leaf level is the level that holds the "key" to identifying the record and the non-leaf level pages are guides to the leaf level.

The indexes are built over either a clustered table (if the table has a clustered index) or what is called a *heap* (what's used for a table without a clustered index).

➤   **Clustered tables:** Any table that has a clustered index on it. Clustered indexes are discussed in detail shortly, but what they mean to the table is that the data is physically stored in a designated order. Individual rows are uniquely identified through the use of the *cluster key* — the columns that define the clustered index.

> **NOTE** *This should bring to mind the question, "What if the clustered index is not unique?" That is, how can you use a clustered index to uniquely identify a row if the index is not a unique index? The answer lies under the covers: SQL Server forces any clustered indexes to be unique — even if you don't define them that way. Fortunately, it does this in a way that doesn't change how you use the index. You can still insert duplicate rows if you want, but SQL Server adds a suffix to the key internally to ensure that the row has a unique identifier.*

➤   **Heaps:** Any table that does not have a clustered index on it. In this case, a unique identifier, or *row ID (RID)*, is created based on a combination of the extent, pages, and row offset (places from the top of the page) for that row. A RID is necessary only if there is no cluster key available (no clustered index).

Clustered Indexes

A *clustered index* is unique for any given table — you can only have one per table. You don't have to have a clustered index, but you'll find it to be one of the most commonly chosen types for a variety of reasons that will become apparent as you look at index types.

What makes a clustered index special is that the leaf level of a clustered index is the actual data — that is, the data is re-sorted to be stored in the same physical order of the index sort criteria state. This means that once you get to the leaf level of the index, you're done; you're at the data. Any new record is inserted according to its correct physical order in the clustered index. How new pages are created changes depending on where the record needs to be inserted.

In the case of a new record that needs to be inserted into the middle of the index structure, a normal page split occurs. The last half of the records from the old page are moved to the new page, and the new record is inserted into the new or old page as appropriate.

In the case of a new record that is logically at the end of the index structure, a new page is created, but only the new record is added to the new page, as shown in Figure 9-4.

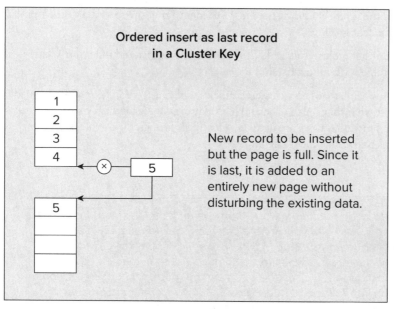

FIGURE 9-4

Navigating the Tree

As indicated previously, even the indexes in SQL Server are stored in a B-Tree. Theoretically, a B-Tree always has half of the remaining information in each possible direction as the tree branches. Let's take a look at a visualization of what a B-Tree looks like for a clustered index (see Figure 9-5).

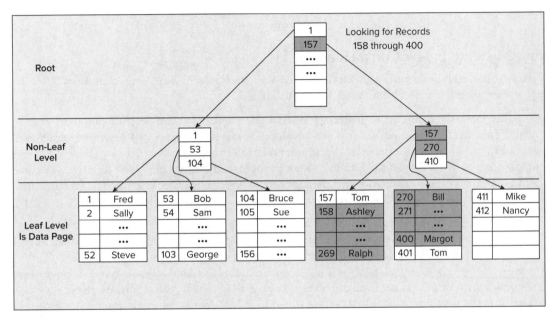

FIGURE 9-5

As you can see, it looks essentially identical to the more generic B-Trees discussed earlier in the chapter. Figure 9-5 shows a range search (something clustered indexes are particularly good at) for numbers 158–400. All SQL has to do is navigate to the first record and include all remaining records on that page. SQL knows it needs the rest of that page because the information from the node one level up notifies it that it'll also need data from a few other pages. Because this is an ordered list, it can be sure it's continuous — that means if the next page has records that should be included, the rest of this page must be included. It can just start spewing out data from those pages without having to do any verification.

Because all searches begin at the root, there must be an easy way to navigate to the root node. SQL Server can locate the root node based on an entry that you can see in the system metadata view called sys.indexes.

By looking through the page that serves as the root node, it can determine the next page it needs to examine (the second page on the second level as I have it drawn here). It then continues the process. With each step it takes down the tree, it is getting to smaller and smaller subsets of data. Eventually, it will get to the leaf level of the index. In the case of a clustered index, getting to the leaf level of the index means that SQL Server has also reached your desired row(s) and your desired data.

> **NOTE** *I can't stress enough the importance of this distinction: With a clustered index, when you've fully navigated the index you've fully navigated to your data. How much of a performance difference this can make really shows its head as you look at non-clustered indexes — particularly when the non-clustered index is built over a clustered index.*

Non-Clustered Indexes on a Heap

Non-clustered indexes on a heap work very similarly to clustered indexes in most ways. They do, however, have a few notable differences, discussed here.

The leaf level is not the data — instead, it is the level at which you can obtain a pointer to that data. This pointer comes in the form of a row identifier or RID, which, as I described earlier in the chapter, is made up of the extent, page, and row offset for the particular row that the index is pointing to. Even though the leaf level is not the actual data (instead, it has the RID), you can find the data with only one more step than with a clustered index. Because the RID has the full information on the location of the row, you can go directly to the data from the RID.

Don't, however, misunderstand this "one more step" to mean that there's only a small amount of overhead difference and that non-clustered indexes on a heap run nearly as fast as a clustered index. With a clustered index, the data is physically in the order of the index. That means, for a range of data, when you find the row that has the beginning of your data on it, there's a good chance that the other rows are on that page with it (that is, you're already physically almost to the next record because they are stored together). With a heap, the data is not linked together in any way other than through the index. From a physical standpoint, there is absolutely no sorting of any kind. This means that from a physical read standpoint, your system may have to retrieve records from all over the file. Indeed, it's quite possible (possibly even probable) that you'll wind up fetching data from the same page several separate times. SQL Server has no way of knowing it has to come back to that physical location because there is no link between the data. With the clustered index, it knows that's the physical sort, and can therefore grab it all in just one visit to the page.

> **NOTE** *Just to be fair to the non-clustered index on a heap: When compared to the clustered index, the odds are extremely high that any page that has already been read once will still be in the memory cache and, as such, will be retrieved extremely quickly. Still, it does add some additional logical operations to retrieve the data.*

Figure 9-6 shows the same search that performed on the clustered index, only with a non-clustered index on a heap this time.

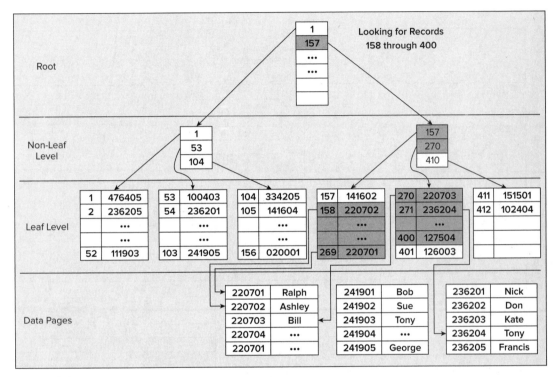

FIGURE 9-6

Through most of the index navigation, things work exactly as they did before. The server starts out at the same root node, and it traverses the tree, dealing with more and more focused pages, until it gets to the leaf level of the index. This is where you can see the difference. With a clustered index, it could have stopped right here, but with a non-clustered index, it still has more work to do. If the non-clustered index is on a heap, there is just one more level to go. It takes the row ID from the leaf level page and navigates to it. It is not until this point that it is at your actual data.

Non-Clustered Indexes on a Clustered Table

With *non-clustered indexes on a clustered table*, the similarities continue — but so do the differences. Just as with non-clustered indexes on a heap, the non-leaf level of the index looks pretty much as it did for a clustered index. The difference does not come until you get to the leaf level.

At the leaf level, there is a rather sharp difference from what you've seen with the other two index structures: You have yet another index to look over. With clustered indexes, when the server got to the leaf level, it found the actual data. With non-clustered indexes on a heap, it didn't find the actual data, but it did find an identifier that let it go right to the data (it was just one step away). With non-clustered indexes on a clustered table, it finds the cluster key. That is, it finds enough information to make use of the clustered index.

You end up with something that looks like Figure 9-7.

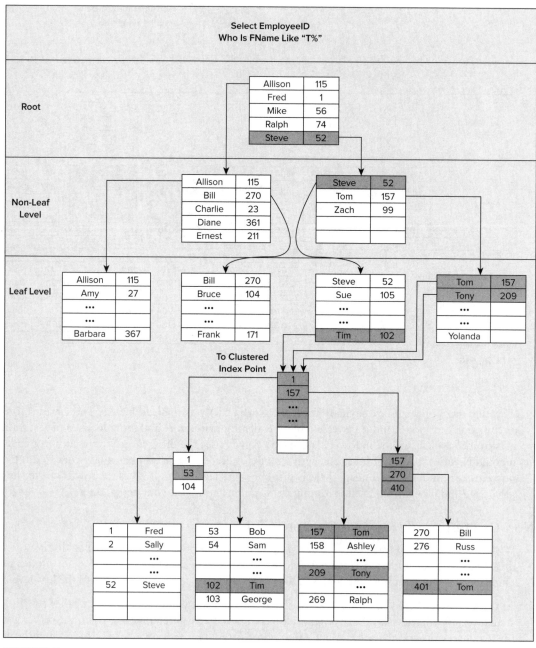

FIGURE 9-7

What you end up with is two entirely different kinds of lookups.

Why does the server require this additional step? Remember that the clustered index defines the actual physical ordering of the data rows on the disk. If a row is updated such that its cluster key changes, that row has to move to a page where it's sorted correctly. Were you to store a RID in the non-clustered index (like you do on a heap), the RID for this row would change, and every single non-clustered index would have to be updated. Storing the cluster key ensures that wherever the row may wander off to, it's still locatable by the index.

In the example from the diagram (Figure 9-7), SQL Server starts off with a ranged search, the same as before. It does one single lookup in your index and can look through the non-clustered index to find a continuous range of data that meets the criterion (LIKE 'T%'). This kind of lookup is called a *seek*.

> **NOTE** *I need to repeat this to get you in the right frame of mind. When your search criteria match an index well enough that the index can navigate directly to a particular spot in your data, that's called a seek. Let that word become associated with puppies, kittens, apple pie, or whatever brings you warm feelings. Index seeks are a great sign that your indexes are being properly used.*

The second kind of lookup then starts — the lookup using the clustered index. This second lookup is very fast; the problem lies in the fact that it must happen multiple times. You see, SQL Server retrieved a list from the first index lookup (a list of all the names that start with "T"), but that list doesn't logically match up with the cluster key in any continuous fashion. Each record needs to be looked up individually, as shown in Figure 9-8.

Needless to say, this multiple-lookup situation introduces more overhead than if you had just used the clustered index from the beginning. The first index search — the one through your non-clustered index — requires very few logical reads.

For example, if I have a table with 1,000 bytes per row and I do a lookup similar to the one in Figure 9-8 (say, something that returns five or six rows), it only takes something to the order of 8–10 logical reads to get the information from the non-clustered index. However, that only gets me as far as being ready to look up the rows in the clustered index. Those lookups cost approximately 3–4 logical reads *each*, or 15–24 additional reads. That probably doesn't seem like that big a deal at first, but look at it this way.

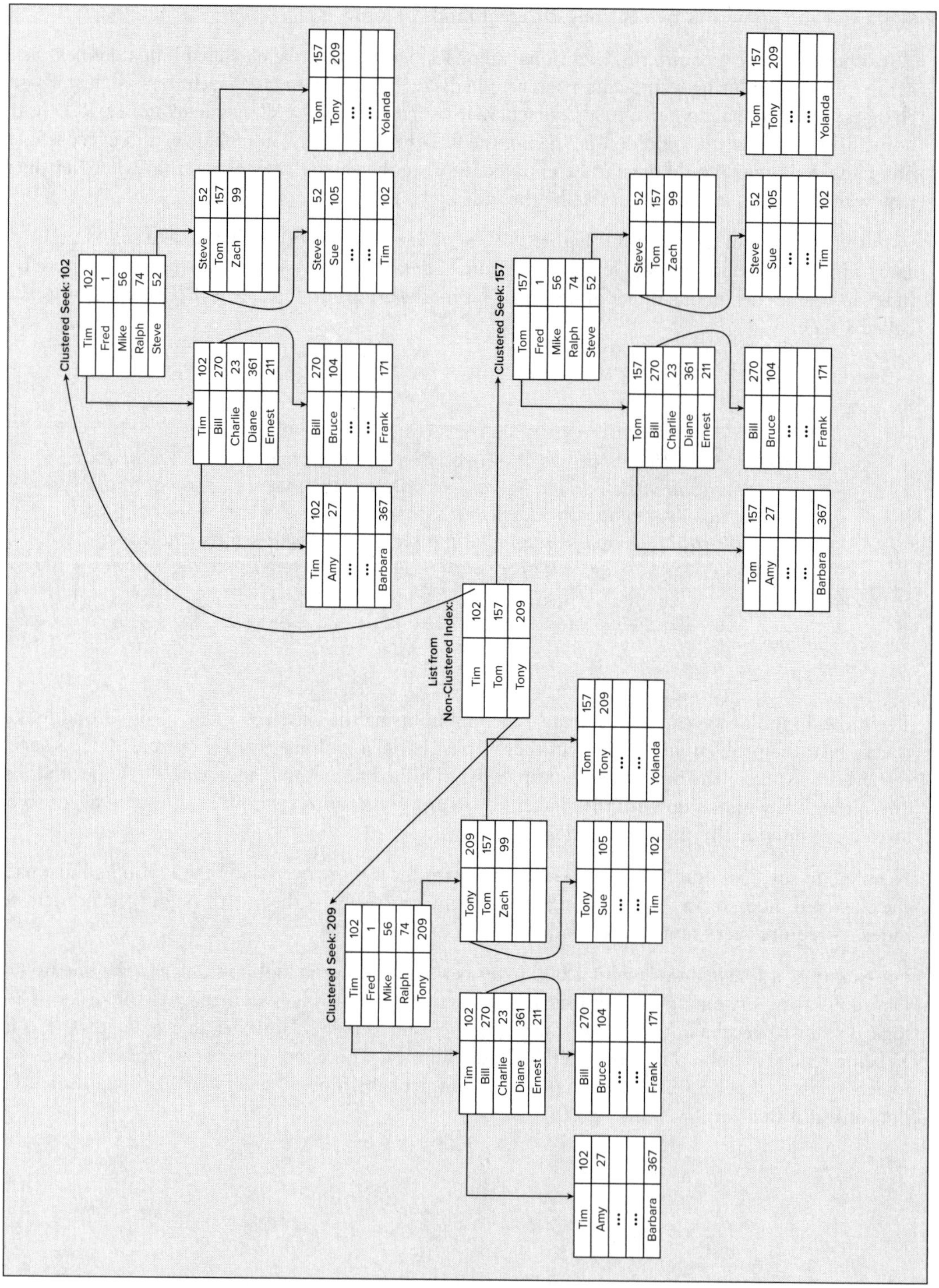

FIGURE 9-8

Logical reads went from 3 minimum to 24 maximum — that's an 800 percent increase in the amount of work that had to be done.

Now expand this thought out to something where the range of values from the non-clustered index wasn't just five or six rows, but five or six thousand, or five or six *hundred* thousand rows — that's going to be a huge impact.

 NOTE *Don't let the extra overhead versus a clustered index scare you — the point isn't meant to scare you away from using indexes, but rather to point out that a non-clustered index is most often not going to be as efficient as a clustered index from a read perspective (it can, in some instances, actually be a better choice at insertion time). An index of any kind is usually (there are exceptions) the fastest way to do a lookup. I'll explain what index to use and why later in the chapter.*

CREATING, ALTERING, AND DROPPING INDEXES

The DDL around indexes works much as it does on other objects such as tables. Let's take a look at each DDL statement, starting with the CREATE.

Indexes can be created in two ways:

➤ Through an explicit CREATE INDEX command

➤ As an implied object when a constraint is created

Each of these has its own quirks about what it can and can't do, so let's look at each of them individually.

The CREATE INDEX Statement

The CREATE INDEX statement does exactly what it sounds like — it creates an index on the specified table or view based on the stated columns.

The syntax to create an index is somewhat drawn out and introduces several items that I haven't really talked about up to this point:

```
CREATE [UNIQUE] [CLUSTERED|NONCLUSTERED]
INDEX <index name> ON <table or view name>(<column name> [ASC|DESC] [,...n])
INCLUDE (<column name> [, ...n]
[WHERE <condition>])
[WITH
[PAD_INDEX = { ON | OFF }]
```

```
[[,] FILLFACTOR = <fillfactor>]
[[,] IGNORE_DUP_KEY = { ON | OFF }]
[[,] DROP_EXISTING = { ON | OFF }]
[[,] STATISTICS_NORECOMPUTE = { ON | OFF }]
[[,] SORT_IN_TEMPDB = { ON | OFF }]
[[,] ONLINE = { ON | OFF }
[[,] ALLOW_ROW_LOCKS = { ON | OFF }
[[,] ALLOW_PAGE_LOCKS = { ON | OFF }
[[,] MAXDOP = <maximum degree of parallelism>
[[,] DATA_COMPRESSION = { NONE | ROW | PAGE}
]
[ON {<filegroup> | <partition scheme name> | DEFAULT }]
```

 NOTE There is legacy syntax available for many of these options, and so you may see that syntax put into use to support prior versions of SQL Server. That syntax is, however, considered deprecated and will be removed at some point. I highly recommend that you stay with the newer syntax when possible.

 NOTE There is a similar but sufficiently different syntax for creating XML indexes. That will be handled separately at the end of this section.

Loosely speaking, this statement follows the same CREATE <object type> <object name> syntax that you've seen plenty of already (and will see even more of). The primary hitch in things is that there are a few intervening parameters that you haven't seen elsewhere.

Just as you'll see with triggers in Chapter 15, you do have to add an extra clause onto your CREATE statement to deal with the fact that an index isn't really a standalone kind of object. It has to go together with a table or view, and you need to state the table that the column(s) are ON.

After the ON <table or view name>(<column name>) clause, everything is optional. You can mix and match these options. Many of them are seldom used, but some (such as FILLFACTOR) can have a significant impact on system performance and behavior, so let's look at them one by one.

ASC/DESC

These two options allow you to choose between an ascending and a descending sort order for your index. The default is ASC, which is, as you might guess, ascending order.

A question that might come to mind is why ascending versus descending matters — SQL Server can just look at an index backward if it needs the reverse sort order. Life is not, however, always quite so simple. Looking at the index in reverse order works just fine if you're dealing with only one column, or if your sort is always the same for all columns, but what if you need to mix sort orders within an index? That is, what if you need one column sorted ascending, but the other descending? Because the indexed columns are stored together, reversing the way you look at the index for one column also reverses the order for the additional columns. If you explicitly state that one column is ascending and the other is descending, you invert the second column right within the physical data — there is suddenly no reason to change the way that you access your data.

As a quick example, imagine a reporting scenario where you want to order your employee list by the hire date, beginning with the most recent (a descending order), but you also want to order by their last name (an ascending order). Before indexes were available, SQL Server had to perform operations — one for the first column and one for the second. Having control over the physical sort order of your data provides flexibility in the way you can combine columns.

INCLUDE

This one is supported with SQL Server 2005 and later. Its purpose is to provide better support for what are called *covering indexes*.

When you INCLUDE columns as opposed to placing them in the ON list, SQL Server only adds them at the leaf level of the index. Because each row at the leaf level of an index corresponds to a data row, what you're doing is essentially including more of the raw *data* in the leaf level of your index. If you think about this, you can probably make the guess that INCLUDE really applies only to non-clustered indexes (clustered indexes already *are* the data at the leaf level, so there would be no point).

Why does this matter? Well, as you'll read further as the book goes on, SQL Server stops working as soon as it has what it actually needs. So if while traversing the index it can find all the data that it needs without continuing to the actual data row, it won't bother going to the data row (what would be the point?). By including a particular column in the index, you may "cover" a query that utilizes that particular index at the leaf level and save the I/O associated with using that index pointer to go to the data page.

 NOTE *Careful not to abuse this one! When you include columns, you are enlarging the size of the leaf level of your index pages. That means fewer rows fit per page, and therefore, more I/O may be required to see the same number of rows. The result is that your effort to speed up one query may slow down others. To quote an old film from the '80s, "Balance, Daniel-san — balance!" Think about the effects on all parts of your system, not just the particular query you're working on that moment.*

WHERE

WHERE, an optional clause added with SQL Server 2008, allows you to place conditions on which rows are included in your index. The syntax is the same as the WHERE clause you're familiar with from the SELECT statement, but with a few restrictions. I'll go into more detail when I talk about filtered indexes later in this chapter.

WITH

WITH is an easy one; it just tells SQL Server that you'll indeed supply one or more of the options that follow.

PAD_INDEX

In the syntax list, this one comes first — but that seems odd when you understand what PAD_INDEX does. In short, it determines just how full the non-leaf level pages of your index will be (as a percentage) when the index is first created. You don't state a percentage on PAD_INDEX because it uses whatever percentage you specify in the FILLFACTOR option that follows. Setting PAD_INDEX = ON is meaningless without a FILLFACTOR (which is why it seems odd that it comes first).

FILLFACTOR

When SQL Server first creates an index, the pages are, by default, filled as full as they can be, minus two records. You can set the FILLFACTOR to be any value between 1 and 100. This number determines how full your pages are as a percentage, once index construction is completed. Keep in mind, however, that as your pages split, your data is still distributed 50-50 between the two pages — you cannot control the fill percentage on an ongoing basis other than regularly rebuilding the indexes (something you should do).

You want to use a FILLFACTOR when you need to adjust the page densities. Think about things this way:

➤ If it's an OLTP system, you want a low FILLFACTOR to allow for more updates without page splits.

➤ If it's an OLAP or other very stable (in terms of changes — very few additions and deletions) system, you want as high a FILLFACTOR as possible to reduce the number of pages that must be read from disk.

➤ If you have something that has a medium transaction rate and a lot of report-type queries against it, you probably want something in the middle (not too low, not too high).

If you don't provide a value, SQL Server fills your pages to two rows short of full, with a minimum of one row per page (for example, if your row is 8,000 characters wide, you can fit only one row per page, so leaving things two rows short wouldn't work).

IGNORE_DUP_KEY

The IGNORE_DUP_KEY option is a way of doing little more than circumventing the system. In short, it causes a unique constraint to have a slightly different action from that which it would otherwise have.

Normally, a unique constraint, or unique index, does not allow any duplicates of any kind — if a transaction tried to create a duplicate based on a column that is defined as unique, that transaction is rolled back and rejected. After you set the IGNORE_DUP_KEY option, however, you'll get mixed behavior. You still receive an error message, but the error is only of a warning level. The record is still not inserted.

This last line — the record is still not inserted — is a critical concept from an IGNORE_DUP_KEY standpoint. A rollback isn't issued for the transaction (the error is a warning error rather than a critical error), but the duplicate row is rejected.

Why would you do this? Well, it's a way of storing unique values without disturbing a transaction that tries to insert a duplicate. For whatever process is inserting the would-be duplicate, it may not matter at all that it's a duplicate row (no logical error from it). Instead, that process may have an attitude that's more along the lines of, "Well, as long as I know there's one row like that in there, I'm happy — I don't care whether it's the specific row that I tried to insert or not."

DROP_EXISTING

If you specify the DROP_EXISTING option, any existing index with the name in question is dropped prior to construction of the new index. This option is much more efficient than simply dropping and re-creating an existing index when you use it with a clustered index. If you rebuild an exact match of the existing index, SQL Server knows that it need not touch the non-clustered indexes, while an explicit drop and create involves rebuilding all non-clustered indexes twice in order to accommodate the different row locations. If you change the structure of the index using DROP_EXISTING, the NCIs are rebuilt only once instead of twice. Furthermore, you cannot simply drop and re-create an index created by a constraint, for example, to implement a certain FILLFACTOR. DROP_EXISTING is a workaround to this.

STATISTICS_NORECOMPUTE

By default, SQL Server attempts to automate the process of updating the statistics on your tables and indexes. By selecting the STATISTICS_NORECOMPUTE option, you are saying that you take responsibility for the updating of the statistics. In order to turn this option off, you need to run the UPDATE STATISTICS command, but not use the NORECOMPUTE option.

I strongly recommend against using this option. Why? Well, the statistics on your index are what the query optimizer uses to determine just how helpful your index is for a given query. The statistics on an index are changing constantly as the data in your table goes up and down in volume and as the specific values in a column change. When you combine these two facts, you should see that not updating your statistics means that the query optimizer will run your queries based on out-of-date information. Leaving the automatic statistics feature on means that the statistics update regularly (just how often depends on the nature and frequency of your updates to the table). Conversely, turning automatic statistics off means that either you will be out of date or you will need to set up a schedule to manually run the UPDATE STATISTICS command.

SORT_IN_TEMPDB

Using this option makes sense only when tempdb is stored on a physically separate drive from the database that is to contain the new index. This is largely an administrative function, so I'm not going to linger on this topic for more than a brief overview of what it is and why it makes sense only when tempdb is on a separate physical device.

When SQL Server builds an index, it has to perform multiple reads to take care of the various index construction steps:

1. **Read through all the data.** The Server constructs a leaf row corresponding to each row of actual data. Just like the actual data and final index, these go into pages for interim storage. These intermediate pages are not the final index pages, but rather a holding place to temporarily store things every time the sort buffers fill up.

2. **Make a separate run through these intermediate pages.** This merges them into the final leaf pages of the index.

3. **Build non-leaf pages.** These are built as the leaf pages are populated.

If the SORT_IN_TEMPDB option is not used, the intermediate pages are written out to the same physical files that the database is stored in. This means that the reads of the actual data have to compete with the writes of the build process. The two cause the disk heads to move to different places (read vs. write). The result is that the disk heads are constantly moving back and forth — this takes time.

If, on the other hand, SORT_IN_TEMPDB is used, the intermediate pages are written to tempdb rather than the database's own file. If they are on separate physical drives, this means that there is no competition between the read and write operations of the index build. Keep in mind, however, that this works only if tempdb is on a separate physical drive from your database file; otherwise, the change is only in name, and the competition for I/O is still a factor.

> **NOTE** *If you're going to use* SORT_IN_TEMPDB, *make sure that there is enough space in* tempdb *for large files.*

ONLINE

Setting this to ON forces the table to remain available for general access, and does not create any locks that block users from the index and/or table. By default, the full index operation grabs the locks (eventually a table lock) needed for full and efficient access to the table. The side effect, however, is that your users are blocked out. (Yeah, there's a small irony there; you're likely building an index to make the database more usable, but you essentially make the table unusable while you do it.)

Now, you're probably thinking something like: "Oh, that sounds like a good idea — I'll do that every time so my users are unaffected." Poor thinking. Keep in mind that any index construction like that is probably a very I/O-intensive operation, so it is affecting your users one way or the other. Now, add that there is a lot of additional overhead required in the index build for it to make sure that it doesn't step on the toes of any of your users. If you let SQL Server have free rein over the table while it's building the index, the index is built much faster, and the overall time that the build is affecting your system is much smaller.

> **NOTE** ONLINE *index operations are supported only in the Enterprise Edition of SQL Server. You can execute the* index *command with the* ONLINE *directive in other editions, but it will be ignored, so don't be surprised if you use* ONLINE *and find your users still blocked out by the* index *operation if you're using a lesser edition of SQL Server.*

ALLOW ROW/PAGE LOCKS

This is a longer term directive than ONLINE and is a very, very advanced topic. For purposes of this book and taking into consideration how much I've introduced so far on locking, let's stick with a pretty simple explanation.

Through much of the book thus far, I have repeatedly used the term "lock." As I explained early on, this is something of a placeholder to avoid conflicts in data integrity. The ALLOW settings you're looking at here determine whether this index will allow row or page locks. This falls under the heading of *extreme* performance tweak.

MAXDOP

This is overriding the system setting for the maximum degree of parallelism for purposes of building this index. Parallelism is not something I talk about elsewhere in this book, so I'll give you a mini-dose of it here.

In short, the degree of parallelism is how many processes are put to use for one database operation (in this case, the construction of an index). There is a system setting called the max degree of parallelism that allows you to limit how many processors there are per operation. The MAXDOP option in the index creation options allows you to set the degree of parallelism to be either higher or lower than the base system setting, as you deem appropriate.

DATA COMPRESSION

Starting in 2008, SQL Server supports compressing the data in your tables or indexes. While the compression details are hidden, the effect is to store your data in much less space on disk, at the cost of some CPU cycles to compress and decompress it. As disk access is the database performance boogeyman, this can often be a good idea.

Despite that, the default is NONE, and there's a good reason for that: data compression is only supported in SQL Server Enterprise Edition. If you're using Standard or Express Edition, there's no data compression for you.

The other two options are whether to compress by ROW or by PAGE. The choice is based on the percentage of updates versus scans, and it isn't trivial. Making this choice is beyond the scope of this book; if you find this is something you want to pursue (and your implementation will be using SQL Enterprise Edition), you'll want to research this online or in a more advanced text such as *Professional Microsoft SQL Server 2012 Administration* by Adam Jorgensen.

ON

SQL Server gives you the option of storing your indexes separately from the data by using the ON option. This can be nice from a couple of perspectives:

- ➤ The space that is required for the indexes can be spread across other drives.
- ➤ The I/O for index operations does not burden the physical data retrieval.

There's more to this, but this is hitting the area of *highly* advanced stuff. It is very data and use dependent, and it's out of the scope of this book.

Creating XML Indexes

XML indexes were first added in SQL Server 2005. The indexing of something as unstructured as XML has been a problem that many have tried to solve, but few have done with any real success, so count your lucky stars that you have this fine tool available if you're storing XML data. Let's get to what XML indexes are about.

This is another of those "chicken or egg?" things, in that you haven't really looked at XML at all in this book thus far. Still, I consider this more of an index topic than an XML topic. Indeed, the XML index-creation syntax supports all the same options you saw in the previous look at the CREATE statement, with the exception of WHERE, IGNORE_DUP_KEY, and ONLINE. So, here is a bit of hyperfast background.

Unlike the relational data that you've been looking at thus far, XML tends to be relatively unstructured. It utilizes tags to identify data, and can be associated with what's called a schema to provide type and validation information to that XML-based data. The unstructured nature of XML requires the notion of "navigating" or "path" information to find a data "node" in an XML document. Now indexes, on the other hand, try to provide very specific structure and order to data — this poses something of a conflict.

You can create indexes on columns in SQL Server that are of XML type. The primary requirements of doing this are:

➤ The table containing the XML you want to index *must* have a clustered index on it.

➤ A "primary" XML index must exist on the XML data column before you can create "secondary" indexes (more on this in a moment).

➤ XML indexes can be created only on columns of XML type (and an XML index is the only kind of index you can create on columns of that type).

➤ The XML column must be part of a base table — you cannot create the index on a view.

The Primary XML Index

The first index you create on an XML index must be declared as a "primary" index. When you create a primary index, SQL Server creates a new clustered index that combines the clustered index of the base table together with data from whatever XML node you specify.

Secondary XML Indexes

Nothing special here — much as non-clustered indexes point to the cluster key of the clustered index, secondary XML indexes point at primary XML indexes. Once you create a primary XML index, you can create up to 248 more XML indexes on that XML column.

Implied Indexes Created with Constraints

I guess I call this one "index by accident." It's not that the index shouldn't be there — it has to be there if you want the constraint that created the index. It's just that I've seen an awful lot of situations where the only indexes on the system were those created in this fashion. Usually, this implies that the administrators and/or designers of the system are virtually oblivious to the concept of indexes.

However, you'll also find yet another bizarre twist on this one — the situation where the administrator or designer knows how to create indexes, but doesn't really know how to tell what indexes are already on the system and what they are doing. This kind of situation is typified by duplicate indexes. As long as they have different names, SQL Server is more than happy to create them for you.

Implied indexes are created when one of two constraints is added to a table:

➤   A PRIMARY KEY

➤   A UNIQUE constraint (aka, an *alternate key*)

You've seen plenty of the CREATE syntax up to this point, so I won't belabor it; however, note that all the options except for {CLUSTERED|NONCLUSTERED} and FILLFACTOR are not allowed when creating an index as an implied index to a constraint.

Creating Indexes on Sparse and Geospatial Columns

These are definitely beyond the scope of a beginning book, but sparse columns and data with a geospatial data type can both have special indexes created on them. Again, keep this in mind if you have application for these special-needs types of columns.

CHOOSING WISELY: DECIDING WHICH INDEX GOES WHERE AND WHEN

By now, you're probably thinking to yourself, "Gee, I'm always going to create clustered indexes!" There are plenty of good reasons to think that way. Just keep in mind that there are also some reasons not to.

Choosing which indexes to include and which not to is a tough process, and in case that wasn't enough, you have to make some decisions about what type you want them to be. The latter decision is made simultaneously easier and harder by the fact that you can have only one clustered index. It means that you have to choose wisely to get the most out of it.

Selectivity

Indexes, particularly non-clustered indexes, are primarily beneficial in situations where there is a reasonably high level of *selectivity* within the index. By selectivity, I'm referring to the percentage of values in the column that are unique. The higher the percentage of unique values within a column, the higher the selectivity is said to be, and the greater the benefit of indexing.

If you think back to what you just read about non-clustered indexes — particularly the section on non-clustered indexes versus a clustered index — you'll recall that the lookup in the non-clustered index is really only the beginning. You still need to make another loop through the clustered index in order to find the real data. Even with the non-clustered index on a heap, you still end up with multiple physically separate reads to perform.

If one lookup in your non-clustered index will generate multiple additional lookups in a clustered index, you are quite possibly better off with the table scan. The exponential effect that's possible here is actually quite amazing. Consider that the looping process created by the non-clustered index is not worth it if you don't have somewhere in the area of 90–95 percent uniqueness in the indexed column.

Clustered indexes are substantially less affected by this because, once you're at the start of your range of data — unique or not — you're there. There are no additional index pages to read. Still, more than likely, your clustered index has other things for which it could be put to greater use.

> **NOTE** *One other exception to the rule of selectivity has to do with foreign keys. If your table has a column that is a* `foreign key`, *in all likelihood, you're going to benefit from having an index on that column. Why* `foreign keys` *and not other columns? Well, foreign keys are frequently the target of joins with the table they reference. Indexes, regardless of selectivity, can be very instrumental in join performance because they allow what is called a merge join. A merge join obtains a row from each table and compares them to see if they match the join criteria (what you're joining on). Because there are indexes on the related columns in both tables, the* `seek` *for both rows is very fast.*
>
> *The point here is that selectivity is not everything, but it is a big issue to consider. If the column in question is not in a foreign key situation, it is almost certainly the second only to the, "How often will this be used?" question in terms of issues you need to consider.*

TRY IT OUT **See Which Index Is Used**

In this exercise, you'll pick one of the larger tables out of the AdventureWorks database and learn how you might choose one or more indexes to place on it. To choose, one critical step is to examine whether SQL Server actually uses the index you're creating. Hopefully this chapter leaves you with the beginning of an instinct for creating useful indexes, but even after years of doing this I never rely on my assumptions. There's simply no substitute for checking.

The `Production.TransactionHistory` table has something a little north of 113K rows, which is big enough that index seeks are certainly a desirable result for any query, so that's the target you'll use. You're going to look for an ID range within this table, chosen across two columns: `ReferenceOrderID` and `ReferenceOrderLineID`. The table, as it exists already, has an index across those two columns.

Here are two queries that represent different ways you need to retrieve data from this table. One is for a range of `ReferenceOrderIDs` and a specific `ReferenceOrderLineID`, and the other is the opposite.

```
SELECT *
FROM [Production].[TransactionHistory]
WHERE ReferenceOrderLineID = 0
    AND ReferenceOrderID BETWEEN 41500 AND 42000;

SELECT *
```

```
FROM [Production].[TransactionHistory]
WHERE ReferenceOrderLineID BETWEEN 0 AND 2
    AND ReferenceOrderID = 41599;
```

Code snippet Chap09.sql

Using SSMS pointed to AdventureWorks, look at the estimated execution plan for each of these queries by selecting Display Estimated Query Plan from the Query menu. The plans should look more or less like what's shown in Figure 9-9.

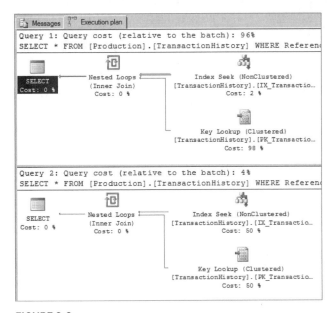

FIGURE 9-9

There are some slight differences between the two, but both use an index seek of the existing index called IX_TransactionHistory_ReferenceOrderID_ReferenceOrderLineID. As its name implies, this non-clustered index is on ReferenceOrderID and ReferenceOrderLineID, in that order.

What you'll do next is disable this index and create a new one in the opposite order, and then check your query plans again. First, then, you can disable the existing index like so:

```
ALTER INDEX [IX_TransactionHistory_ReferenceOrderID_ReferenceOrderLineID]
ON [Production].[TransactionHistory] DISABLE;
```

Having done that, create the new, test index. Start its name with IX2 so that you can more easily see whether it's used in the query plan window, even though that's not a good naming convention. I won't have anyone thinking I told you to start numbering your indexes.

```
CREATE NONCLUSTERED INDEX
    [IX2_TransactionHistory_ReferenceOrderLineID_ReferenceOrderID]
ON [Production].[TransactionHistory]
(

    [ReferenceOrderLineID] ASC,
    [ReferenceOrderID] ASC

);
```

Code snippet Chap09.sql

As you can see, the column order is reversed both in the index name and in its definition. Now re-check the query plan on the query samples and see whether they'll use this new index. Figure 9-10 shows the new query plan, which looks much like the old one.

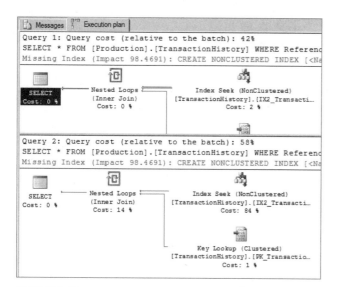

FIGURE 9-10

Clearly, the new index is being used for a seek. That's the good news, but look what else is in the query plan (in green, near the top):

```
Missing Index (Impact 98.4691):
CREATE NONCLUSTERED INDEX [<Name of Missing Index, sysname,>]
ON [Production].[TransactionHistory] ([ReferenceOrderID],[ReferenceOrderLineID])
```

That's right, SQL Server wants you — is begging you — to create an index for better performance, and it looks exactly like the one you just disabled. It believes it can run at least one of these queries over 98 percent faster with this index in place. So while your new IX2 index does get used, it's hardly optimal. Re-enable the original index with an ALTER INDEX...REBUILD and run the query plans one last time with both indexes in place.

```
ALTER INDEX [IX_TransactionHistory_ReferenceOrderID_ReferenceOrderLineID]
ON [Production].[TransactionHistory] REBUILD;
```

Code snippet Chap09.sql

Did you catch what happened? The first query continues to use your new IX2 index, while the second uses the original, now rebuilt, index.

Before you move on, remove the test index (reverting AdventureWorks to its original state) with a DROP INDEX.

How It Works

There are a couple things to take note of in this example.

➤ **The original index was acceptable to both queries.** This was because one query was in exactly the right order. It was acceptable to the other query because of the selectivity of ReferenceOrderID making the order less critical.

➤ **The reversed index was used for both queries.** This was because it worked better than a table scan, but it was far enough from optimal to spawn a missing index hint for one query.

➤ **The missing index hint, although repeated for both query plans, applies to only one.** Only one index at a time is suggested, and it is repeated for each query. That's just a feature.

➤ **The performance doesn't change.** For the query that uses your reversed index by choice, the difference between its performance with that index and the original is so minor that the index maintenance (cost of updates) is certainly not worth the miniscule improvement in performance.

SQL Server makes use of your indexes when it can, but you need to be wise about choosing them. The right choice here is almost certainly to keep only the original index, because it serves both queries well. More than anything, though, the takeaway lesson here is to be thorough about testing index usage across your expected workload.

Watching Costs: When Less Is More

Remember that while indexes speed up performance when they're reading data, they are actually very costly when modifying data. Indexes are not maintained by magic. Every time that you make a modification to your data, any indexes related to that data also need to be updated. Think of the time you're putting in during the updates as money invested. Every time you read from an index, you're getting paid back in time saved, but for each index that's not used, your investment is lost.

When you insert a new row, a new entry must be made into every index on your table. Remember, too, that when you update a row, it is handled as a delete and insert — again, your indexes must be updated. But wait! There's more! (Feeling like a late-night infomercial here.) When you delete records, again, you must update all the indexes, too — not just the data. For every index that you create, you are creating one more block of entries that has to be updated.

Notice, by the way, that I said entries plural — not just one. Remember that a B-Tree has multiple levels to it. Every time that you make a modification to the leaf level, there is a chance that a page split will occur, and that one or more non-leaf level pages must also be modified to have the reference to the proper leaf page.

Sometimes — quite often actually — not creating that extra index is the thing to do. Sometimes, the best thing to do is choose your indexes based on the transactions that are critical to your system and use the table in question. Does the code for the transaction have a WHERE clause in it? What column(s) does it use? Is there a sorting required?

Choosing That Clustered Index

Remember that you can have only one clustered index, so you need to choose it wisely.

By default, your primary key is created with a clustered index. This is often the best place to have it, but not always (indeed, it can seriously hurt you in some situations), and if you leave things this way, you won't be able to use a clustered index anywhere else. The point here is that you shouldn't just unthinkingly accept the default. Think about it when you are defining your primary key — do you really want it to be a clustered index?

If you decide that you indeed want to change things, that is, you don't want to declare things as being clustered, just add the NONCLUSTERED keyword when you create your table. For example:

```
CREATE TABLE MyTableKeyExample
(
    Column1    int IDENTITY
      PRIMARY KEY NONCLUSTERED,
    Column2    int
)
```

Code snippet Chap09.sql

Once the index is created, the only way to change it is to drop and rebuild it, so you want to get it set correctly up front.

Keep in mind that if you change which column(s) your clustered index is on, SQL Server needs to do a complete resorting of your entire table (remember, for a clustered index, the table sort order and the index order are the same). Now, consider a table you have that is 5,000 characters wide and has several million rows in it — that is an awful lot of data that must be reordered. Several questions should come to mind from this:

➤ **How long will it take?** It could be a long time, and there really isn't a good way to estimate that time.

➤ **Do I have enough space?** Figure that in order to do a resort on a clustered index, you will, on average, need an *additional* 1.2 times (the working space plus the new index) the amount of space your table is already taking up. This can turn out to be a very significant amount of space if you're dealing with a large table — make sure you have the room to do it in. All this activity, by the way, happens in the database itself, so this is also affected by how you have your maximum size and growth options set for your database.

➤ **Should I use the SORT_IN_TEMPDB option?** If tempdb is on a separate physical array from your main database and it has enough room, the answer is probably yes.

The Pros

Clustered indexes are best for queries when the column(s) in question is frequently the subject of a ranged query. This kind of query is typified by use of the BETWEEN statement or the < or > symbol. Queries that use a GROUP BY and make use of the MAX, MIN, and COUNT aggregators are also great examples of queries that use ranges and love clustered indexes. Clustering works well here because the search can go straight to a particular point in the physical data, keep reading until it gets to the end of the range, and then stop. It is extremely efficient.

Clusters can also be excellent when you want your data sorted (using ORDER BY) based on the cluster key.

The Cons

There are two situations in which you don't want to create that clustered index. The first is fairly obvious — when there's a better place to use it. I know I'm sounding repetitive here, but don't use a clustered index on a column just because it seems like the thing to do (primary keys are the common culprit here). Be sure that you don't have another column that it's better suited to first.

Perhaps the much bigger no-no use for clustered indexes, however, is when you're doing a lot of inserts in a non-sequential order. Remember that concept of page splits? Well, here's where it can come back and haunt you big time.

Imagine this scenario: You are creating an accounting system. You want to make use of the concept of a transaction number for your primary key in your transaction files, but you also want those transaction numbers to be somewhat indicative of what kind of transaction it is (it really helps troubleshooting for your accountants). So you come up with something of a scheme — you'll place a prefix on all the transactions indicating what sub-system they come out of. They will look something like this:

```
ARXXXXXX              Accounts Receivable Transactions
GLXXXXXX              General Ledger Transactions
APXXXXXX              Accounts Payable Transactions
```

where XXXXXX is a sequential numeric value.

This seems like a great idea, so you implement it, leaving the default of the clustered index going on the primary key.

At first glance, everything about this setup looks fine. You're going to have unique values, and the accountants will love the fact that they can infer where something came from based on the transaction number. The clustered index seems to make sense because they are often querying for ranges of transaction IDs.

Ah, if only it were that simple. Think about your inserts for a bit. With a clustered index, you originally had a nice mechanism to avoid much of the overhead of page splits. When a new record was inserted that was to go after the last record in the table, even if there was a page split, only that record would go to the new page — SQL Server wouldn't try to move around any of the old data. Now you've messed things up though.

New records inserted from the General Ledger wind up going on the end of the file just fine (GL is last alphabetically, and the numbers are sequential). The AR and AP transactions have a major problem though — they are going to be doing non-sequential inserts. When AP000025 gets inserted and there isn't room on the page, SQL Server will see AR000001 in the table and know that it's not a sequential insert. Half the records from the old page will be copied to a new page before AP000025 is inserted.

The overhead of this can be staggering. Remember that you're dealing with a clustered index, and that the clustered index is the data. The data is in index order. This means that when you move the index to a new page, you are also moving the data. Now imagine that you're running this accounting system in a typical OLTP environment (you don't get much more OLTP-like than an accounting system) with a bunch of data-entry people keying in vendor invoices or customer orders as fast as they can. You'll have page splits occurring constantly, and every time you do, you're going to see a brief hesitation for users of that table while the system moves data around.

Fortunately, there are a couple of ways to avoid this scenario:

➤ **Choose a cluster key that is sequential in its inserting.** You can either create an identity column for this or have another column that logically is sequential to any transaction entered regardless of the system.

➤ **Choose not to use a clustered index on this table.** This is often the best option in a situation like this because an insert into a non-clustered index on a heap is usually faster than one on a cluster key.

 NOTE *Even as I've told you to lean toward sequential cluster keys to avoid page splits, you also have to realize that there's a cost there. Among the downsides of sequential cluster keys is concurrency (two or more people trying to get to the same object at the same time). It's all about balancing out what you want, what you're doing, and what it's going to cost you elsewhere.*

This is perhaps one of the best examples of why I have gone into so much depth about how things work. You need to think through how things are actually going to get done before you have a good feel for what the right index to use (or not to use) is.

Column Order Matters

Just because an index has two columns, it doesn't mean that the index is useful for any query that refers to either column.

An index is only considered for use if the first column listed in the index is used in the query. The bright side is that there doesn't have to be an exact one-for-one match to every column — just the first. Naturally, the more columns that match (in order), the better, but only the first creates a definite do-not-use situation.

Think about things this way. Imagine that you are using a phone book. Everything is indexed by last name and then first name — does this sorting do you any real good if all you know is that the person you want to call is named Fred? On the other hand, if all you know is that his last name is Blake, the index still serves to narrow the field for you.

One of the occasional mistakes that I see in index construction is the belief that one index that includes all the columns will be helpful for all situations. Indeed, what you're really doing is storing all the data a second time. The index is totally ignored if the first column of the index isn't mentioned in the JOIN, ORDER BY, or WHERE clauses of the query.

Covering Indexes

By now you might be getting just a little down on the concept of non-clustered indexes. Sure, they're better than table scans, and yes, you can have only one cluster, but darn, that extra overhead of a cluster lookup (or RID lookup, if there's no cluster on your table) is really a drag. Fortunately, you have options, but as always, there's a cost.

Simply put, a covering index contains all the data your query needs. Once SQL Server finds what it needs, it stops looking, as I've said before. That applies to the final lookup on an index as much as anywhere else. If all that's required to resolve your query is in one of the index keys, or is included on the leaf, there's no reason to do the lookup.

The most basic and obvious covering index is the clustered index. All the data in your table is on the leaf, so the cluster covers any query.

The next layer of covering indexes comes from those that can resolve a query using only their key values. Think of an index on a foreign key column and a query using EXISTS for a foreign key ID value on that table. SQL can simply seek within the index for the ID value, stop once the ID is found (or not), and return the EXISTS Boolean without ever looking up any other detail about the table.

Finally, you can INCLUDE non-key columns in the leaf of your index. Although this may appear to be a panacea for cluster key lookups, it's not free. Your index keys stay the same size, so seeking is still quite fast, but the leaves must grow to accommodate the additional data. Furthermore, every time that data is inserted, updated, or deleted, the amount of bits that have to be slung around to compensate has grown. Still, for common queries that really must be fast, this can be a wonderful tool.

 NOTE *Some of the best SQL Server minds I work with are a bit warped, which seems to be almost a requirement. Some of you with that sort of mind are probably already dreaming up scenarios where you include all the columns your table has in one or more non-clustered indexes, effectively creating multiple clustered indexes on the same table. Back away from the precipice. The amount of overhead involved in inserts, updates, deletes, and even reads from your new indexes can overwhelm your system if you're not careful. Be sparing.*

Filtered Indexes

All the indexes you've seen so far have one thing in common: each has an entry in the leaf for every single row in the table. As it happens, that's not strictly a requirement, and there are times when you'll want to sharply limit which rows appear in your index.

Creating a filtered index is as simple as including the WHERE clause described earlier in the chapter. The syntax is so simple, but the usage is something else entirely. Why would you want to create such an index?

Let's take a quick look at the makeup of the data in the Sales.SalesOrderDetail table in AdventureWorks. Specifically, let's see what the order counts for the special offers look like.

```
SELECT SpecialOfferID, COUNT(*) OrderCount
FROM Sales.SalesOrderDetail
GROUP BY SpecialOfferID
ORDER BY COUNT(*) DESC
```

As you can see, offer 1 is by far the most popular. Offer 1, of course, is the "there was no special offer" special offer — not really what you're after when you're searching for information about special offers applied. If you want to run queries to check on special offer usage by product, you could create a filtered index including only those rows that actually have a genuine offer applied.

```
CREATE INDEX ix_SalesOrderDetail_ProductID_filt_SpecialOffers
ON Sales.SalesOrderDetail (ProductID)
WHERE SpecialOfferID > 1;
```

Code snippet Chap09.sql

You can use this index whenever a query is run that includes a compatible WHERE expression. What's notable about the filtered index is this:

➤ **The index depth is much, much less than one on the full table.** You're only indexing a few thousand rows rather than over a hundred thousand, so traversing the index is much faster.

➤ **Because the index only contains special offer rows, maintaining it on INSERT/UPDATE/DELETE operations is much cheaper.** Changes to rows with a SpecialOfferID of 1, which represent the vast majority, do not impact this index at all.

> **NOTE** One relatively common use for filtered indexes is to effectively allow a unique constraint on a NULLable column. By creating a unique index with a WHERE <column> IS NOT NULL clause, you can prevent duplicates in the real data and still permit as many NULL values as exist.

ALTER INDEX

The ALTER INDEX command is somewhat deceptive in what it does. Up until now, ALTER commands have always been about changing the definition of your object. You ALTER tables to add or disable constraints and columns, for example. ALTER INDEX is different — it is all about maintenance and zero about structure. If you need to change the makeup of your index, you still need either to DROP and CREATE it or to CREATE and use the index with the DROP_EXISTING=ON option.

As you saw earlier in the chapter, SQL Server gives you an option for controlling just how full your leaf level pages are and, if you choose, another option to deal with non-leaf level pages. Unfortunately, these are proactive options. They are applied once, and then you need to reapply them as necessary by rebuilding your indexes and reapplying the options.

In the upcoming section on maintenance, you'll look more at the wheres and whys of utilizing this command, but for now, take it on faith that you'll use maintenance commands like ALTER INDEX as part of your regular maintenance routine.

The ALTER INDEX syntax looks like this:

```
ALTER INDEX { <name of index> | ALL }
    ON <table or view name>
    { REBUILD
        [ [ WITH (
          [ PAD_INDEX  = { ON | OFF } ]
        | [[,] FILLFACTOR = <fillfactor>
        | [[,] SORT_IN_TEMPDB = { ON | OFF } ]
        | [[,] IGNORE_DUP_KEY = { ON | OFF } ]
        | [[,] STATISTICS_NORECOMPUTE = { ON | OFF } ]
        | [[,] ONLINE = { ON | OFF } ]
        | [[,] ALLOW_ROW_LOCKS = { ON | OFF } ]
        | [[,] ALLOW_PAGE_LOCKS = { ON | OFF } ]
        | [[,] MAXDOP = <max degree of parallelism>
                ) ]
          | [ PARTITION = <partition number>
              [ WITH ( <partition rebuild index option>
                   [ ,...n ] ) ] ] ]
    | DISABLE
    | REORGANIZE
        [ PARTITION = <partition number> ]
        [ WITH ( LOB_COMPACTION = { ON | OFF } ) ]
    | SET ([ ALLOW_ROW_LOCKS= { ON | OFF } ]
          | [[,] ALLOW_PAGE_LOCKS = { ON | OFF } ]
          | [[,] IGNORE_DUP_KEY = { ON | OFF } ]
          | [[,] STATISTICS_NORECOMPUTE = { ON | OFF } ]
          )
    } [ ; ]
```

Several of the options are common to the CREATE INDEX command, so I'll skip redefining those particular ones here. Beyond that, a fair amount of the ALTER-specific options are fairly detailed and relate to dealing with things like fragmentation (you'll get to fragmentation and maintenance shortly) or are more administrator oriented and usually used on an ad hoc basis to deal with very specific problems. The core elements here should, however, be part of your regular maintenance planning.

You'll start by looking at a couple of top parameters and then look at the options that are part of your larger maintenance-planning needs.

Index Name

You can name a specific index if you want to maintain one specific index, or use ALL to indicate that you want to perform this maintenance on every index associated with the named table.

Table or View Name

Pretty much just what it sounds like — the name of the specific object (table or view) that you want to perform the maintenance on. Note that it needs to be one specific table (you can feed it a list and say, "Do all of these please!").

REBUILD

This is the "industrial-strength" approach to fixing an index. If you run ALTER INDEX with this option, the old index is completely thrown away and a new one reconstructed from scratch. The result is a truly optimized index, where every page in both the leaf and the non-leaf levels of the index has been reconstructed as you have defined it (either with defaults or using switches to change things like the fillfactor). If the index in question is clustered, the physical data is also reorganized.

By default, the pages are reconstituted to be full, minus two records. Just as with the CREATE TABLE syntax, you can set the FILLFACTOR to be any value between 0 and 100. This number is the percent that your pages are full once the database reorganization is complete. Remember, though, that as your pages split, your data is still distributed 50-50 between the two pages — you cannot control the fill percentage on an ongoing basis unless you regularly rebuild the indexes.

 NOTE *Careful with this one. As soon as you kick off a* rebuild*, the index you are working on is essentially gone until the* rebuild *is complete. Any queries that rely on that index may become exceptionally slow (potentially by orders of magnitude). This is the sort of thing you want to test on an offline system first to have an idea how long it's going to take, and then schedule to run in off hours (preferably with someone monitoring it to be sure it's back online when peak hours come along).*

This one can have major side effects while it runs, and thus it falls squarely in the domain of the database administrator in my not-so-humble opinion.

DISABLE

This one does what it says, only in somewhat drastic fashion. It would be nice if all this command did was take your index offline until you decided further what you wanted to do, but instead, it essentially marks the index as unusable. Once an index is disabled, it must be rebuilt (not reorganized, but rebuilt) before it is active again. The opposite of an ALTER INDEX … DISABLE isn't ENABLE; that doesn't even exist. You must perform an ALTER INDEX … REBUILD.

This is one you're very, very rarely going to do yourself (you would more likely just drop the index). It is far more likely to happen during an SQL Server upgrade or some other oddball situation. That said, you may remember doing this earlier in the chapter. The usefulness there was that, during testing, DISABLE and REBUILD preserved the index definition so you didn't have to use the whole original create script again.

 NOTE *Yet another BE CAREFUL warning on this one. If you disable the clustered index for your table, it has the effect of disabling the table. The data remains, but is inaccessible to all indexes (because they all depend on the clustered index) until you rebuild the clustered index.*

REORGANIZE

BINGO! from the developer perspective. With REORGANIZE, you hit much more of a happy medium in life. When you reorganize your index, you get a slightly less complete optimization than you get with a full rebuild, but one that occurs online (users can still utilize the index).

This should, if you're paying attention, bring about the question, "What exactly do you mean by '*slightly* less complete'?" Well, REORGANIZE works only on the leaf level of your index — non-leaf levels of the index go untouched. This means that you're not quite getting a full optimization, but for the lion's share of indexes, that is not where your real cost of fragmentation is (though it can happen, and your mileage may vary).

Given its much lower impact on users, this is typically the tool you'll want to use as part of your regular maintenance plan. You'll look into this a bit more later when talking fragmentation.

Dropping Indexes

If you're constantly reanalyzing the situation and adding indexes, don't forget to drop indexes, too. Remember the overhead on inserts. It doesn't make much sense to look at the indexes that you need and not also think about which indexes you do not need. Always ask yourself: "Can I get rid of any of these?"

The syntax to drop an index is pretty much the same as that used to drop a table. The only hitch is that you need to qualify the index name with the table or view it is attached to:

```
DROP INDEX <table or view name>.<index name>
```

or alternatively

```
DROP INDEX <index name> ON <table or view name>
```

And it's gone.

Taking a Hint from the Query Plan

SQL Server 2008 brought a great new feature that you've already seen if you read the chapter in order: an indexing hint right within the query-plan information. Such a hint will tell you about one index (at a time) that the query optimizer thought would have helped, but that didn't exist. Realistically, after creating a suggested index, you don't need to strictly check whether this query will use it; it will be used for this query, even if it won't ever be used by any other again. If you get this hint with an important query, in most cases you'll want to take it.

 NOTE *SQL Server will not suggest filtered indexes, even when one presents an optimal solution. It will, however, suggest covering indexes. There's a danger there: if you have an index on the same key that would cover but for one or two included columns, the hint will effectively suggest a new index when a replacement may work. As always, pay attention to dropping indexes as well as creating them.*

Why Isn't Your Index Being Used?

This is one area where a lot fewer questions get asked than should. What I mean is that I've seen many times when queries are written that result in table scans — and ridiculously poor performance because of that — yet developers simply ignore the problem because "there's already an index on that column." Because there's an index on "that column," there's nothing more they can do (they think), and so the performance problems must be unavoidable.

I'm going to repeat it one last time: test, test, test! Check whether your indexes are in use. If they're not in use, start looking for the reason — out of order WHERE clauses, lack of selectivity, suggested indexes, or unindexable conditions — and repair the problem.

Most of this you've just read about in this chapter, so I'd like to spend a moment now on unindexable conditions and what you might want to do about them.

Let's say you need to locate those products in the AdventureWorks database that you still sell — that is, there's a SellEndDate that's either NULL or it's after today. For "after today," I'll use a date that's far in the future (12/31/9999), despite the Y10K problem that might invoke later.

```
SELECT ProductID, Name
FROM Production.Product
WHERE ISNULL(SellEndDate, '99991231') >= GETDATE()
```

Code snippet Chap09.sql

To make this perform better, you may think it's obvious (can you sense a trap?) that you want to put an index on SellEndDate. What you'll find if you check, though, is that no matter how selective that is, no matter how few rows might actually be returned from that query, that index will never be used. To learn why, look at the query and note which column is used to limit the output.

What's being used isn't SellEndDate, but ISNULL(SellEndDate, '99991231'), which (not surprisingly) doesn't have an index on it at all. When you filter on a function, rather than a column, you won't have an index that works.

There are really only a couple solutions when you get there. Either you can create that function as a persisted computed column and put an index on it — ouch, your whole cluster will have to be rewritten to accommodate the new column — or else you can try to find a way to rewrite the query such that the column is compared without a function wrapper.

Use the Database Engine Tuning Advisor

It is my hope that you'll learn enough about indexes not to need the Database Engine Tuning Advisor all that much, but it can still be quite handy. It works by taking a workload file, which you generate using the SQL Server Profiler (not a beginner topic, I'm afraid, so not included in this book), and looking over that information for what indexes and/or partitions work best on your system.

The Database Engine Tuning Advisor is found on the Tools menu of the SQL Server Management Studio. It can also be reached as a separate program item from the Windows Start menu. As with most any tuning tool, I don't recommend using this tool as the sole way to decide what indexes to build, but it can be quite handy at making some suggestions that you may not have thought of.

MAINTAINING YOUR INDEXES

As developers, we often tend to forget about our product after it goes out the door. For many kinds of software, that's something you can get away with just fine — you ship it and move on to the next product or next release. However, with database-driven projects, it's virtually impossible to get away with this approach. You need to take responsibility for the product well beyond the delivery date. That's life in the persistence layer.

Please don't take me to mean that you have to go serve a stint in the tech support department — I'm actually talking about something even more important: *maintenance planning.*

There are really two issues to be dealt with in terms of the maintenance of indexes:

➤   Page splits

➤   Fragmentation

Both are related to page density, and while the symptoms are substantially different, the troubleshooting tool is the same, as is the cure.

Fragmentation

I've already talked about page splits quite a bit, but I haven't really touched on *fragmentation*. I'm not talking about the fragmentation that you may have heard of with your O/S files and the defrag tool you use, because that won't help with database fragmentation.

Fragmentation happens when your database grows, pages split, and then data is eventually deleted. While the B-Tree mechanism is really not that bad at keeping things balanced from a growth point of view, it doesn't really have a whole lot to offer as you delete data. Eventually, you may get down to a situation where you have one record on this page, a few records on that page — a situation where many of your data pages are holding only a small fraction of the amount of data that they could hold.

The first problem with this is probably the first you would think about — wasted space. Remember that SQL Server allocates an extent of space at a time. If only one page has one record on it, that extent is still allocated.

The second problem is the one that is more likely to cause you grief: Records that are spread out all over the place cause additional overhead in data retrieval. Instead of just loading one page and grabbing the 10 rows it requires, SQL Server may have to load 10 separate pages to get that same information. It isn't just reading the row that causes effort — SQL Server has to read that page in first. More pages means more work on reads.

That being said, database fragmentation does have its good side — OLTP systems positively love fragmentation. Any guesses as to why? Page splits. Pages that don't have much data in them can have data inserted with little or no risk of page splits.

So, high fragmentation equates to poor read performance, but it also equates to excellent insert performance. As you might expect, this also means that OLAP systems really don't like fragmentation.

Identifying Fragmentation versus Likelihood of Page Splits

SQL Server provides a special metadata function called `sys.dm_db_index_physical_stats` that is particularly useful in helping you identify just how full the pages and extents in your database are. You can then use that information to make some decisions about what you want to do to maintain your database.

`sys.dm_db_index_physical_stats` is what is called a *table valued function* (you'll learn more about these in Chapter 13). In short, this means that while it's a function, you can use it much as you would a table, which means that you can actually stick WHERE conditions on it and other similar constructs. The syntax for the function itself is pretty simple:

```
sys.dm_db_index_physical_stats (
    { <database id> | NULL | 0 | DEFAULT }
    , { <object id> | NULL | 0 | DEFAULT }
    , { <index id> | NULL | 0 | -1 | DEFAULT }
    , { <partition no> | NULL | 0 | DEFAULT }
    , { <mode> | NULL | DEFAULT }
)
```

Note that it is demanding the rather non-intuitive `ids` as input values rather than the logical names that you might be more used to. Fortunately, SQL Server gives you a number of functions that work on returning the proper ID for a given object on the server or in the database.

To see an example of how to use this, let's get all the index information from the `Sales` `.SalesOrderDetail` table. Since I've said you should get all the indexes in the table, you just need the ID for the table — not any individual indexes. Since the function is table valued, you need to write a query to return the results from the function. For example:

```
DECLARE @db_id SMALLINT;
DECLARE @object_id INT;
SET @db_id = DB_ID(N'AdventureWorks');
SET @object_id = OBJECT_ID(N'AdventureWorks.Sales.SalesOrderDetail');
```

```
SELECT database_id, object_id, index_id, index_depth, avg_fragmentation_in_percent,
page_count
FROM sys.dm_db_index_physical_stats(@db_id,@object_id,NULL,NULL,NULL);
```

Code snippet Chap09.sql

The output is far more self-describing that the previous tools were in this area:

```
database_id object_id    index_id    index_depth avg_fragmentation_in_percent page_
count
----------- ----------- ----------- ----------- ---------------------------- ----------
8           610101214   1           3           0.565885206143896            1237
8           610101214   2           3           1.70731707317073             410
8           610101214   3           2           6.14035087719298             228

(3 row(s) affected)
```

The function also has a veritable sea of other information available, so feel free to explore further, but let's walk through the columns, shown in Table 9-1, that are most interesting in terms of fragmentation.

> **NOTE** *A number of fields tell you things like what kind of index structure it is (clustered versus non-clustered), number of fragmented pages, and other things of interest. There are also several columns that reside firmly at the advanced level of advanced SQL Server, so don't be too stressed if you don't understand every column this function offers.*

TABLE 9-1: dm_db_index_physical_stats Output

STAT	WHAT IT MEANS
database id	The SQL Server internal identifier for the database you want to run the function against. NULL results in information being returned on all databases. Keep in mind that when you choose the NULL option, you must also set all subsequent parameters to NULL. 0 and DEFAULT all are functionally equivalent to NULL for this parameter.
object id	The SQL Server internal identifier for the table you want to run the function against. NULL results in information being returned on all tables. Keep in mind that when you choose the NULL option, you must also set all subsequent parameters to NULL. 0 and DEFAULT all are functionally equivalent to NULL for this parameter.

continues

TABLE 9-1 *(continued)*

STAT	WHAT IT MEANS
index id	The internal identifier for the index you want to run the function against. NULL results in information being returned on all indexes. Note that if the table is clustered, the clustered index is always numbered 1, and if the table is a heap, the heap is index 0. Non-clustered indexes will be numbers 2 or higher. When you choose the NULL option, you must also set partition_no to NULL. -1 and DEFAULT all are functionally equivalent to NULL for this parameter.
partition no	This is a bit beyond the scope of this book, but tables and indexes can be partitioned into separate physical storage units. Use this parameter to identify a specific partition you want fragmentation information on. NULL results in information being returned on all partitions. 1 and DEFAULT all are functionally equivalent to NULL for this parameter.
Mode	Mode defines the level of scan used to generate the statistics returned. Choices include DEFAULT, NULL, LIMITED, SAMPLED, or DETAILED. DEFAULT and NULL are functionally equivalent to LIMITED.
Logical Scan Fragmentation	The percentage of pages that are out of order as checked by scanning the leaf pages of an index. Only relevant to scans related to a clustered table. An out-of-order page is one for which the next page indicated in the index allocation map (IAM) is different from that pointed to by the next page pointer in the leaf page.
Extent Scan Fragmentation	This one is telling whether an extent is not physically located next to the extent that it should be logically located next to. This just means that the leaf pages of your index are not physically in order (though they still can be logically), and it shows what percentage of the extents this problem pertains to.

Now, the question is how do you use this information once you have it? The answer is, of course, that it depends.

Using the output from your fragmentation query, you have a decent idea of whether your database is full, fragmented, or somewhere in between (the latter is, most likely, what you want to see). If you're running an OLAP system, having full pages would be great — fragmentation would bring on depression. For an OLTP system, you would want much the opposite (although only to a point).

So, how do you take care of the problem? To answer that, you need to look into the concept of index rebuilding and FILLFACTORs.

Rebuilding an Index with ALTER INDEX

As you saw earlier in the chapter, SQL Server gives you an option for controlling just how full your leaf level pages are and, if you choose, another option to deal with non-leaf level pages. Unfortunately, these are proactive options. They are applied once, and then you need to reapply them as necessary by rebuilding or reorganizing your indexes to reapply the options.

To rebuild indexes, you can either drop them and create them again (if you do, using the DROP_EXISTING option usually is a good idea), or make use of the ALTER INDEX command with the REBUILD option. Keep in mind, however, what was said previously about rebuilding indexes — unless you have the ONLINE option available, rebuilding indexes takes the index (and possibly the entire table) totally offline until the rebuild is complete. In general, reorganizing is going to be a better option.

A reorg affects only the leaf level of the index (where most of the issue is likely to be anyway) and keeps the index online while the reorg is taking place. Reorganizing your indexes restructures all the leaf level information in those indexes, and reestablishes a base percentage that your pages are full. If the index in question is a clustered index, the physical data is also reorganized. Unfortunately, REORGANIZE does not allow for the change of several index settings, such as FILLFACTOR.

Using FILLFACTOR

If the index has not had a specific FILLFACTOR specified, the pages will be reconstituted to be full, minus two records. Just as with the CREATE TABLE syntax, you can set the FILLFACTOR to be any value between 1 and 100 as long as you are doing a full rebuild (as opposed to just a reorg). This number is the percent that your pages are full once the database reorganization is complete. Remember, though, that as your pages split, your data is still distributed 50-50 between the two pages — you cannot control the fill percentage on an ongoing basis other than by regularly rebuilding the indexes.

You use a FILLFACTOR when you need to adjust the page densities. As already discussed, lower page densities (and therefore lower FILLFACTORS) are ideal for OLTP systems where there are a lot of insertions; this helps prevent page splits. Higher page densities are desirable with OLAP systems (fewer pages to read, but no real risk of page splitting due to few to no inserts).

If you wanted to rebuild the index that serves as the primary key for the Sales.SalesOrderDetail you were looking at earlier with a fill factor of 65, you would issue an ALTER INDEX command as follows:

```
ALTER INDEX PK_SalesOrderDetail_SalesOrderID_SalesOrderDetailID
    ON Sales.SalesOrderDetail
    REBUILD WITH (FILLFACTOR = 100)
```

Code snippet Chap09.sql

 NOTE *This is a good time to digress and revisit the idea of your object names. Notice how long this name is. The more characters, the more chance for typos. Balance that against the need for the name to be meaningful. For this particular query, my own naming conventions would probably have dropped the inclusion of the table name (when referring to an index, you usually already know what table you're talking about) and eliminated the underscores to wind up with something like* PKSalesOrderIDSalesOrderDetailID. *The name implies the nature of the index (it's supporting a primary key) and the columns involved. Be careful, however, with using the column name idea. On the rare occasion you wind up with several columns in your index, it can make for an unruly index name.*

You can then rerun the `sys.dm_db_index_physical_stats` to see the effect:

```
database_id object_id    index_id    index_depth avg_fragmentation_in_percent
page_count
----------- ----------- ----------- ----------- ---------------------------- -----------
8           610101214   1           3           0.0810372771474878           1234
8           610101214   2           3           1.70731707317073             410
8           610101214   3           2           6.14035087719298             228

(3 row(s) affected)
```

The big one to notice here is the change in `avg_fragmentation_in_percent`. Assuming you're looking for high page densities (higher read performance), you want the number as low as possible. The number didn't quite reach 0 percent because SQL Server has to deal with page and row sizing, but it gets as close as it can.

Several things to note about `ALTER TABLE REINDEX/REORG` and `FILLFACTOR`:

➤ **If a FILLFACTOR isn't provided:** The `ALTER TABLE` uses whatever setting was used to build the index previously. If one was never specified, the `FILLFACTOR` makes the page full (which is too full for most situations).

➤ **If a FILLFACTOR is provided:** The `FILLFACTOR` value becomes the default `FILLFACTOR` for that index.

➤ **While a REORGANIZE is done live and a REBUILD can be (if you have the licensing required to enable that feature), it's not recommended:** I strongly recommend against it because it locks resources and can cause a host of problems. At the very least, look at doing it at non-peak hours.

SUMMARY

Indexes are sort of a cornerstone topic in SQL Server or any other database environment, and are not something to be taken lightly. They can drive your performance successes, but they can also drive your performance failures.

The following are top-level principles to think about with indexes:

➤ Clustered indexes are usually faster than non-clustered indexes (one could come very close to saying always, but there are exceptions).

➤ Only place non-clustered indexes on columns where you are going to get a high level of selectivity (that is, 95 percent or more of the rows are unique).

➤ All Data Manipulation Language (DML: INSERT, UPDATE, DELETE, SELECT) statements can benefit from indexes, but inserts, deletes, and updates (remember, they use a delete and insert approach) are slowed by indexes. The lookup part of a query is helped by the index, but anything that modifies data will have extra work to do (to maintain the index in addition to the actual data).

➤ Indexes take up space.

➤ Indexes are used only when the first column in the index is relevant to your query.

➤ Indexes can hurt as much as they help — know why you're building the index, and don't build indexes you don't need.

➤ Indexes can provide structured data performance to your unstructured XML data, but keep in mind that like other indexes, there is overhead involved.

When you're thinking about indexes, ask yourself these questions:

QUESTION	RESPONSE
Are there a lot of inserts or modifications to this table?	If yes, keep indexes to a minimum. This kind of table usually has modifications done through single-record lookups of the primary key, and usually, this is the only index you want on the table. If the inserts are non-sequential, think about using something other than a clustered index.
Is this a reporting table? That is, not many inserts, but reports run lots of different ways?	More indexes are fine. Target the clustered index to frequently used information that is likely to be extracted in ranges. OLAP installations will often have many times the number of indexes seen in an OLTP environment.
Is there a high level of selectivity on the data?	If yes, and it is frequently the target of a WHERE clause, add that index.
Have you dropped the indexes you no longer need?	If not, why not?
Do you have a maintenance strategy established?	If not, why not?

EXERCISES

1. Name at least two ways of determining which indexes can be found on the HumanResources .Employee table in the AdventureWorks database.

2. Create a non-clustered index on the ModifiedDate column of the Production.ProductModel table in the AdventureWorks database.

3. Delete the index you created in Exercise 2.

▶ WHAT YOU LEARNED IN THIS CHAPTER

TOPIC	CONCEPT
Databases, files, extents, and pages	SQL Server organizes its file in a hierarchical structure. The root of the structure is the database, which contains files. Each file is allocated in extents, each of which is eight 8KB pages.
Page splits	When new data is written to a page, it is sometimes necessary for SQL Server to split a page in half, writing half the data onto a new page. If the new page requires new allocation space, a whole new extent must be allocated, making page splits potentially expensive.
Indexes	An index is a fast way to look up a particular row or range of rows based on the index key. Searching the index's B-Tree is almost always vastly faster than scanning the whole table and testing each row.
Clustered/non-clustered indexes	In a clustered index, the complete data row is written at the leaf level of the B-Tree, effectively ordering the entire table in the order dictated by the cluster key. Thus, only one clustered index is possible per table. In a non-clustered index, only columns specified in the INCLUDE clause are written to the row. If additional columns are needed by the query, they'll be looked up via either a row identifier or a cluster key stored at the index leaf.
CREATE INDEX	Creating and dropping indexes is similar to creating and dropping other database objects. ALTER is used in a slightly different context, more for index maintenance than for changing the structure.
Indexing strategy	Because there is a cost to maintaining indexes that is paid at insert, update, and delete time, it is important in a busy environment to choose indexes carefully. By carefully selecting your clustered index (if any) and creating a useful set of non-clustered indexes, you can vastly improve the performance of your queries. Too many or badly chosen indexes, however, can be a hindrance to transactional activity without offering significant performance benefits.
Index maintenance	The choices you make for your index-maintenance options depend on the purpose of your database. Think carefully before adjusting things like FILLFACTOR, and be sure to create jobs to regularly maintain your indexes for best performance.

10

Views

- ➤ The nature of views, and how they can be used
- ➤ How to create, alter, and drop views using T-SQL
- ➤ View management using SSMS
- ➤ How to use views for abstraction and security
- ➤ An introduction to indexed (or materialized) views

Up to this point, you've been dealing with base objects — objects that have some level of substance of their own. In this chapter, you're going to go virtual (well, mostly anyway), and take a look at views.

Views have a tendency to be used either too much or not enough — rarely just right. When you're done with this chapter, you should be able to use views to:

- ➤ Reduce apparent database complexity for end users
- ➤ Prevent sensitive columns from being selected, while still affording access to other important data
- ➤ Add additional indexing to your database to speed query performance — even when you're not using the view the index is based on

A view is, at its core, nothing more than a stored query. What's great is that you can mix and match your data from base tables (or other views) to create what will, in most respects, function just like an ordinary base table. You can create a simple query that selects from only one table and leaves some rows or columns out, or you can create a complex query that joins several tables and makes them appear as one.

CREATING SIMPLE VIEWS

The syntax for a view, in its most basic form, is a combination of a couple of things you've already seen in the book — the basic CREATE statement that you saw back in Chapter 5, plus a SELECT statement like you've used over and over again:

```
CREATE VIEW <view name>
AS
<SELECT statement>
```

The preceding syntax just represents the minimum, of course, but it's still all you need in a large percentage of the situations. The more extended syntax looks like this:

```
CREATE VIEW [<schema name>].<view name> [(<column name list>)]
[WITH [ENCRYPTION] [[,] SCHEMABINDING] [[,] VIEW_METADATA]]
AS
<SELECT statement>
[WITH CHECK OPTION][;]
```

You'll be looking at each piece of this individually, but, for now, let's go ahead and dive right in with an extremely simple view.

TRY IT OUT   Creating a Simple View

You can call this one your customer phone list, and create it as CustomerPhoneList_vw in the Accounting database that you created back in Chapter 5:

Available for download on Wrox.com

```
USE Accounting;
GO

CREATE VIEW CustomerPhoneList_vw
AS
    SELECT CustomerName, Contact, Phone
    FROM Customers;
```

Notice that when you execute the CREATE statement in the Management Studio, it works just like all the other CREATE statements you've done — it doesn't return any rows. It just lets you know that the view has been created:

```
Command(s) completed successfully.
```

Now switch to using the grid view (if you're not already there) to make it easy to see more than one result set. Then run a SELECT statement against your view — using it just as you would for a table — and another against the Customers table directly:

```
SELECT * FROM CustomerPhoneList_vw;

SELECT * FROM Customers;
```

Code snippet Chap10.sql

How It Works

What you get back looks almost identical to the previous result set — indeed, in the columns that they have in common, the two result sets *are* identical. To clarify how SQL Server is looking at your query on the view, let's break it down logically a bit. The SELECT statement in your view is defined as:

```
SELECT CustomerName, Contact, Phone
FROM Customers;
```

So when you run:

```
SELECT * FROM CustomerPhoneList_vw;
```

you are essentially saying to SQL Server: "Give me all of the rows and columns you get when you run the statement SELECT CustomerName, Contact, Phone FROM Customers."

You've created something of a pass-through situation — that is, your view hasn't really changed anything, but rather just "passed through" a filtered version of the data it was accessing. What's nice about that is that you have reduced the complexity for the end user. In this day and age, where you have so many tools to make life easier for the user, this may not seem like all that big of a deal — but to the user, it is.

 NOTE *Be aware that, by default, there is nothing special done for a view. The view runs just as if it were a query run from the command line — there is no pre-optimization of any kind. This means that you are adding one more layer of overhead between the request for data and the data being delivered, and thus, that a view is never going to run quite as fast as if you had just run the underlying* SELECT *statement directly. That said, views exist for a reason — be it security or simplification for the user — so balance your need against the overhead to fit your particular situation.*

Let's go with another view that illustrates what you can do in terms of hiding sensitive data. For this example, let's go back to the Employees *table in the Accounting database (you'll create a special version of the now familiar Accounting database a little later in the chapter). Take a look at the table layout:*

EMPLOYEES
EmployeeID
FirstName
MiddleInitial
LastName
Title
SSN
Salary

continues

(continued)

EMPLOYEES
HireDate
TerminationDate
ManagerEmpID
Department

Federal law in the United States protects some of this information — you must limit access to a "need to know" basis. Other columns, however, are free for anyone to see. What if you want to expose the unrestricted columns to a group of people, but don't want them to be able to see the general table structure or data? One solution is to keep a separate table that includes only the columns that you need:

EMPLOYEES
EmployeeID
FirstName
MiddleInitial
LastName
Title
HireDate
TerminationDate
ManagerEmpID
Department

While on the surface this would meet your needs, it is extremely problematic:

➤ You use disk space twice.

➤ You have a synchronization problem if one table gets updated and the other doesn't.

➤ You have double I/O operations (you have to read and write the data in two places instead of one) whenever you need to insert, update, or delete rows.

Views provide an easy and relatively elegant solution to this problem. When you use a view, the data is stored only once (in the underlying table or tables) — eliminating all of the problems just described. Instead of building a completely separate table, you can just build a view that will function in a nearly identical fashion.

Available for download on Wrox.com

To make sure you know the state of your Accounting database, you should create a special version of it for use in the next example or two. To do this, load the `Chapter10AccountingDBCreate.sql` file (supplied with the source code) into the Management Studio and run it. Then add the following view to the AccountingChapter10 database:

Chapter10AccountingDBCreate.sql

```
USE AccountingChapter10;
GO

CREATE VIEW Employees_vw
AS
SELECT    EmployeeID,
          FirstName,
          MiddleInitial,
          LastName,
          Title,
          HireDate,
          TerminationDate,
          ManagerEmpID,
          Department
FROM Employees;
```

You are now ready to let everyone have access — directly or indirectly — to the data in the `Employees` table. Users who have the "need to know" can now be directed to the `Employees` table, but you continue to deny access to other users. Instead, the users who do not have that "need to know" can have access to the `Employees_vw` view. If they want to make use of it, they do it just the same as they would against a table:

```
SELECT *
FROM Employees_vw;
```

Chap10.sql

> **NOTE** *This actually gets into one of the sticky areas of naming conventions. Because I've been using the _vw suffix, it's pretty easy to see that this is a view and not a table. Sometimes, you'll want to make the names a little more secure than that, so you might want to deliberately leave the _vw off. Doing so means that you have to use a different name (`Employees` is already the name of the base table), but you'd be surprised how many users won't know that there's a difference between a view and a table if you do it this way.*

Views as Filters

This will probably be one of the shortest sections in the book. Why? Well, it doesn't get much simpler than this.

You've already seen how to create a simple view — you just use an easy SELECT statement. How do you filter the results of your queries? With a WHERE clause. Views use a WHERE in exactly the same way.

Let's take the `Employees_vw` view from the last section, and beef it up a bit by making it a list of only current employees. To do this, you need to make only two changes.

First, you have to filter out employees who no longer work for the company. Would a current employee have a termination date? Probably not, so, if you limit the results to rows with a NULL TerminationDate, you've got what you're after.

The second change illustrates another simple point about views working just like queries — the column(s) contained in the WHERE clause does not need to be included in the SELECT list. In this case, it doesn't make any sense to include the termination date in the result set, as you're talking about current employees.

  Using a View to Filter Data

With these two points in mind, let's create a new view by changing the old view around just a little bit:

Available for
download on
Wrox.com

```
CREATE VIEW CurrentEmployees_vw
AS
SELECT     EmployeeID,
           FirstName,
           MiddleInitial,
           LastName,
           Title,
           HireDate,
           ManagerEmpID,
           Department
FROM Employees
WHERE TerminationDate IS NULL;
```

Chap10.sql

In addition to the new name change and the WHERE clause, note that this example also eliminates the TerminationDate column from the SELECT list.

Let's test how this works a little bit by running a straight SELECT statement against the Employees table and limiting the SELECT list to the things that you care about:

Available for
download on
Wrox.com

```
SELECT     EmployeeID,
           FirstName,
           LastName,
           TerminationDate
FROM Employees;
```

Chap10.sql

This returns a few columns from all the rows in the entire table:

EmployeeID	FirstName	LastName	TerminationDate
1	Peter	Principle	NULL
2	Billy Bob	Boson	NULL
3	Joe	Dokey	NULL
4	Steve	Smith	2007-01-31
5	Howard	Kilroy	NULL

```
6            Mary                  Contrary              2008-01-01

(6 row(s) affected)
```

Now let's check out the view:

```
SELECT    EmployeeID,
          FirstName,
          LastName
FROM CurrentEmployees_vw;
```

Chap10.sql

The result set has become a bit smaller:

```
EmployeeID  FirstName                LastName
----------- ------------------------ ------------------------
1           Peter                    Principle
2           Billy Bob                Boson
3           Joe                      Dokey
5           Howard                   Kilroy

(4 row(s) affected)
```

A few people are missing compared to first SELECT — just the way you wanted it.

How It Works

As discussed before, the view really is just a SELECT statement that's been hidden from the users so that they can ignore what the SELECT statement says, and instead just consider the results it produces as if it were a table — you can liken this to the derived tables discussed back in Chapter 7. Because the data was filtered down before you referenced the view by name, the query doesn't even need to consider that data (the view has done that for you).

More Complex Views

Even though I use the term "complex" here, don't let that scare you. The toughest thing in views is still, for the most part, simpler than most other things in SQL.

What you're doing with more complex views is really just adding joins, summarization, and perhaps some column renaming.

Perhaps one of the most common uses of views is to flatten data — that is, the removal of the complexity discussed at the beginning of the chapter. Imagine that you are providing a view for management to make it easier to check on sales information. No offense to managers who are reading this book, but managers who write their own complex queries are still a rather rare breed — even in the information age.

For an example, let's briefly go back to using the AdventureWorks database. Your manager wants to be able to do simple queries that will tell him or her which orders have been placed for which parts and which account number was used to place the order. So, you create a view that your manager can use to perform very simple queries on — remember that you are creating this one in AdventureWorks:

```
USE AdventureWorks
GO

CREATE VIEW CustomerOrders_vw
AS
SELECT sc.AccountNumber,
       soh.SalesOrderID,
       soh.OrderDate,
       sod.ProductID,
       pp.Name,
       sod.OrderQty,
       sod.UnitPrice,
       sod.UnitPriceDiscount * sod.UnitPrice * sod.OrderQty AS TotalDiscount,
       sod.LineTotal
FROM   Sales.Customer AS sc
INNER JOIN Sales.SalesOrderHeader AS soh
       ON sc.CustomerID = soh.CustomerID
INNER JOIN Sales.SalesOrderDetail AS sod
       ON soh.SalesOrderID = sod.SalesOrderID
INNER JOIN Production.Product AS pp
       ON sod.ProductID = pp.ProductID;
```

Now do a SELECT:

```
SELECT *
FROM CustomerOrders_vw;
```

Chap10.sql

You wind up with a bunch of rows — over 121,000 — but you also wind up with information that is far simpler for the average manager to comprehend and sort out. What's more, with not that much training, the manager (or whoever the user might be) can get right to the heart of what he or she is looking for:

```
SELECT AccountNumber, LineTotal
FROM CustomerOrders_vw
WHERE OrderDate = '01/07/2006';
```

Chap10.sql

The user doesn't need to know how to do a four-table join — it is hidden in the view. Instead, he or she needs only limited skills (and limited imagination for that matter) in order to get the job done.

```
AccountNumber LineTotal
------------- --------------------------------------
AW00014937    3578.270000
```

```
AW00018710    3578.270000
AW00025713     699.098200
AW00020558     699.098200

(4 row(s) affected)
```

> **NOTE** Have you ever heard that "a little knowledge is a dangerous thing"? I'd like to warn you about handing a set of complex views to a manager or anyone else with little SQL knowledge. As I said, when you SELECT from a view the view's underlying SQL is what's executed. Also, a view can be used like a table. So what happens if you join two views, each of which contains a complex query? SQL Server will attempt to find an efficient execution plan for the now doubly complex SQL, and although it's pretty good at optimizing, it can be confused by a sufficiently large number of tables. Join a few of the wrong views together and you can bring the server to its knees. Danger aside, it's still a good idea sometimes to hand a view like the one you just created over to a user.

That's a useful view, but you could make your query even more targeted. Let's say that you want your view to return yesterday's sales. You'll need to make only slight changes to the query:

Available for download on Wrox.com

```
USE AdventureWorks
GO

CREATE VIEW YesterdaysOrders_vw
AS
SELECT sc.AccountNumber,
       soh.SalesOrderID,
       soh.OrderDate,
       sod.ProductID,
       pp.Name,
       sod.OrderQty,
       sod.UnitPrice,
       sod.UnitPriceDiscount * sod.UnitPrice * sod.OrderQty AS TotalDiscount,
       sod.LineTotal
FROM   Sales.Customer AS sc
INNER JOIN   Sales.SalesOrderHeader AS soh
       ON sc.CustomerID = soh.CustomerID
INNER JOIN   Sales.SalesOrderDetail AS sod
       ON soh.SalesOrderID = sod.SalesOrderID
INNER JOIN Production.Product AS pp
       ON sod.ProductID = pp.ProductID
WHERE CAST(soh.OrderDate AS Date) =
       CAST(DATEADD(day,-1,GETDATE()) AS Date);
```

All the dates in the AdventureWorks database are old enough that this view wouldn't return any data, so let's modify a few existing rows to test it:

```
USE AdventureWorks
```

```
UPDATE Sales.SalesOrderHeader
SET OrderDate = CAST(DATEADD(day,-1,GETDATE()) AS Date),
    DueDate = CAST(DATEADD(day,11,GETDATE()) AS Date),
    ShipDate = CAST(DATEADD(day,6,GETDATE()) AS Date)
WHERE Sales.SalesOrderHeader.SalesOrderID BETWEEN 43659 AND 43662;
```

Chap10.sql

The core of this is a relatively simple UPDATE statement that resets the dates on a few orders to be relative to yesterday (the day before whatever day you run that UPDATE statement). The GETDATE() function is, just as you would expect, getting your current date. I'll discuss some of the other pieces in a bit. For now, I'll ask that you take this one largely on faith, and trust that you'll need to run this to have a value in AdventureWorks that will come up for your view. You should see a result from the Management Studio that looks something like this:

```
(4 row(s) affected)
```

> **NOTE** *Be aware that the message will appear on the Messages tab only if you are using the Management Studio's Results In Grid mode. It should show up in your Results table if you're in text mode.*

The OrderID might vary, but the rest should hold pretty true.

Now let's run a query against your view and see what you get:

```
SELECT AccountNumber, SalesOrderID, OrderDate FROM YesterdaysOrders_vw;
```

Chap10.sql

You can see that the four orders do show up. Indeed, because each has several line items, you should wind up with a total of 51 rows:

```
AccountNumber  SalesOrderID  OrderDate
-------------  ------------  ------------------------
AW00000676     43659         2007-09-30 00:00:00.000
AW00000676     43659         2007-09-30 00:00:00.000
AW00000676     43659         2007-09-30 00:00:00.000
AW00000676     43659         2007-09-30 00:00:00.000
...
...
AW00000227     43662         2007-09-30 00:00:00.000
AW00000227     43662         2007-09-30 00:00:00.000

(51 row(s) affected)
```

Using the DATEADD and CAST Functions

The join, while larger than most of the ones you've created thus far, is still pretty straightforward. You keep adding tables, joining a column in each new table to a matching column in the tables that you've already named. As always, note that the columns do not have to have the same name — they just have to have data that relates to one another.

Because this was a relatively complex join, take a look at what's going on in the query that supports this view.

The WHERE clause is where things get interesting:

```
WHERE CAST(soh.OrderDate AS Date) =
      CAST(DATEADD(day,-1,GETDATE()) AS Date)
```

It's a single comparison, but you use several functions to come up with the result.

It's very tempting to simply compare the OrderDate in the SalesOrderHeader table to GETDATE() (today's date) minus one day — the subtraction operation is what the DATEADD function is all about. DATEADD can add (you subtract by using negative numbers) any amount of time you want to deal with. You just tell it what date you want to operate on, and what unit of time you want to add to it (days, weeks, years, minutes, and so on). On the surface, you should just be able to grab today's date with GETDATE() and then use DATEADD to subtract one day. The problem is that GETDATE() returns the datetime data type and therefore includes the current time of day, so you get back only rows from the previous day that happened at the same time of day down to 3.3333 milliseconds (the level of precision for a datetime field) — not a likely match. This example takes things one more step and uses the CAST function to cast the dates on both sides of the equation to a data type that does not support time-of-day-less-before comparison. Therefore, the view shows any sale that happened any time on the previous date.

 NOTE *Note that this code would not have worked on SQL Server 2005 and earlier installations, as the* Date *data type was introduced with SQL Server 2008. In older versions of SQL Server, you must use the* CONVERT *function to change the date to a* varchar *formatted without the time, and then perform the comparison.*

Using a View to Change Data — Before INSTEAD OF Triggers

As I've said before, a view works *mostly* like a table does from an in-use perspective (obviously, creating them works quite a bit differently). Now you're going to come across some differences, however.

It's surprising to many, but you can run INSERT, UPDATE, and DELETE statements against a view successfully. There are several points, however, that you need to keep in mind when changing data through a view:

➤ **If the view contains a join:** You won't, in most cases, be able to INSERT or DELETE data unless you make use of an INSTEAD OF trigger. An UPDATE can, in some cases (as long as you are only updating columns that are sourced from a single table), work without INSTEAD OF triggers, but it requires some planning, or you'll bump into problems very quickly.

➤ **If your view references only a single table:** You can INSERT data using a view without the use of an INSTEAD OF trigger provided all the required fields in the table are exposed in the view or have defaults. Even for single table views, if there is a column not represented in the view that does not have a default value, you must use an INSTEAD OF trigger if you want to allow an INSERT.

➤ **You can, to a limited extent, restrict what is and isn't inserted or updated in a view.**

Now, I've already mentioned INSTEAD OF triggers several times. The problem here is the complexity of INSTEAD OF triggers and that I haven't discussed triggers with you to any significant extent yet. As is often the case in SQL Server items, there is something of the old chicken versus egg thing going on ("Which came first?"). I need to discuss INSTEAD OF triggers because of their relevance to views, but I'm also not ready to talk about INSTEAD OF triggers unless you understand both of the objects (tables and views) that they can be created against.

The way I am going to handle things for this chapter is to address views the way they used to be — before there was such a thing as INSTEAD OF triggers. Although I won't deal with the specifics of INSTEAD OF triggers in this chapter, I'll make sure you understand when they must be used. I'll then come back and address these issues more fully when you look briefly at INSTEAD OF triggers in Chapter 15.

> **NOTE** *Having said that, I will provide this bit of context — an* INSTEAD OF *trigger is a special kind of trigger that essentially runs "instead" of whatever statement caused the trigger to fire. The result is that it can see what your statement would have done, and then make decisions right in the trigger about how to resolve any conflicts or other issues that might have come up. It's very powerful, but also fairly complex stuff, which is why I'm going to defer it for now.*

➤ **Dealing with changes in views with joined data:** If the view has more than one table, using a view to modify data is, in many cases, out — sort of anyway — unless you use an INSTEAD OF trigger (more on this in a moment). Because using multiple tables creates some ambiguities in the key arrangements, Microsoft locks you out by default when you do this. To resolve that problem, you can use an INSTEAD OF trigger to examine the altered data and explicitly tell SQL Server what you want to do with it.

➤ **Required fields must appear in the view or have default value:** By default, if you are using a view to insert data (there must be a single table SELECT in the underlying query or at least you must limit the insert to affect just one table and have all required columns represented), you must be able to supply some value for all required fields (fields that don't allow NULLs). Note that by "supply some value," I don't mean that it has to be in the SELECT list — a default covers the bill rather nicely. Just be aware that any columns that do not have defaults and do not accept NULL values will need to appear in the view in order for INSERTs to be allowed through the view. The only way to get around this is — you guessed it — with an INSTEAD OF trigger.

Limit What's Inserted into Views — WITH CHECK OPTION

The WITH CHECK OPTION is one of those obscure features in SQL Server. The rules are simple — in order for you to update or insert data using the view, the resulting row must qualify to appear in the view results. Restated, the inserted or updated row must meet any WHERE criterion that's used in the SELECT statement that underlies your view.

TRY IT OUT   **WITH CHECK OPTION**

To illustrate the WITH CHECK OPTION, let's continue working with the AdventureWorks database, and create a view to show only Portland, Oregon, area addresses. You have only limited fields to work with in your Address table, so you're going to have to make use of the PostalCode in order to determine where the area address is. You've been provided enough information to allow you to filter based on PostalCodes that start with 970, 971, and 972 for the Portland side of the border, and 98660 to 98699 for the Vancouver, Washington, side, so you can apply it in a view:

Available for download on Wrox.com

```
CREATE VIEW PortlandAreaAddresses_vw
AS
SELECT AddressID,
        AddressLine1,
        City,
        StateProvinceID,
        PostalCode,
        ModifiedDate
FROM Person.Address
WHERE PostalCode LIKE '970%'
    OR PostalCode LIKE '971%'
    OR PostalCode LIKE '972%'
    OR PostalCode LIKE '986[6-9]%'
WITH CHECK OPTION;
```

Chap10.sql

Run a SELECT * against this view, and about 792 rows are returned:

```
AddressID  AddressLine1         City         StProvID  PostalCode  ModifiedDate
---------- -------------------- ------------ --------- ----------- ------------
22         636 Vine Hill Way    Portland     58        97205       2005-06-24
312        1286 Cincerto Circle Lake Oswego  58        97034       2006-01-23
322        1 Mt. Dell Drive     Portland     58        97205       2006-01-24
...
...
29792      5186 Oeffler Ln.     Beaverton    58        97005       2007-03-20
29822      2613 West I St.      Beaverton    58        97005       2007-12-25
29856      1132 Plymouth Dr.    Lake Oswego  58        97034       2008-04-07

(792 row(s) affected)
```

Now try to update one of the rows using the view — set the `PostalCode` to anything other than a value starting with 97 or 98:

```
UPDATE PortlandAreaAddresses_vw
SET PostalCode = '33333'  -- it was 97205
WHERE AddressID = 22;
```

Chap10.sql

SQL Server promptly tells you that you are a scoundrel and that you should be burned at the stake for your actions — well, not really, but it does make its point:

```
Msg 550, Level 16, State 1, Line 1
The attempted insert or update failed because the target view either specifies
    WITH CHECK OPTION or spans a view that specifies WITH CHECK OPTION and one or
    more rows resulting from the operation did not qualify under the CHECK OPTION
    constraint.
The statement has been terminated.
```

How It Works

The `WHERE` clause filters things in the view to show only postal codes that start with 970, 971, 972, or 9866-9869, and the `WITH CHECK OPTION` says any `INSERT` or `UPDATE` statements must meet that `WHERE` clause criteria (which a `33333` postal code does not).

Because your update wouldn't meet the `WHERE` clause criteria, it is thrown out; however, if you were to update the row right in the base table:

```
UPDATE Person.Address
SET PostalCode = '33333'  -- it was 97205
WHERE AddressID = 22;
```

Chap10.sql

SQL Server's reply is a lot friendlier:

```
(1 row(s) affected)
```

The restriction applies only to the view — not to the underlying table. This can actually be quite handy in a rare circumstance or two. Imagine a situation in which you want to allow some users to insert or update data in a table, but only when the updated or inserted data meets certain criteria. You could easily deal with this restriction by adding a `CHECK` constraint to your underlying table — but this might not always be an ideal solution.

Imagine now that you've added a second requirement — we still want other users to be able to insert data into the table without meeting these criteria. Uh oh, the `CHECK` constraint will not discriminate between users. By using a view together with a `WITH CHECK OPTION`, you can point the restricted users to the view, and let the unrestricted users make use of the base table or a view that has no such restriction.

Note that this works on an INSERT, too. Run an INSERT that violates the WHERE clause and you'll see your old friend, the "terminator" error, exactly as you did with the UPDATE.

EDITING VIEWS WITH T-SQL

The main point to remember when you edit views with T-SQL is that you are completely replacing the existing view. The only differences between using the ALTER VIEW statement and using the CREATE VIEW statement are:

➤   ALTER VIEW expects to find an existing view, whereas CREATE doesn't.

➤   ALTER VIEW retains any permissions that have been established for the view.

➤   ALTER VIEW retains any dependency information.

The second of these is the biggie. If you perform a DROP, and then use a CREATE, you have *almost* the same effect as using an ALTER VIEW statement. The problem is that you need to entirely re-establish your permissions about who can and can't use the view.

DROPPING VIEWS

It doesn't get much easier than this:

```
DROP VIEW <view name>, [<view name>,[ ...n]]
```

And it's gone.

> **NOTE** *Nothing in SQL is ever that easy. Dropping a view is as simple as it gets, and that means there's at least one exception. If you have any objects created* WITH SCHEMABINDING *that depend on your view, you'll get an error when you try to do this. There's more on* SCHEMABINDING *at the end of this chapter.*

CREATING AND EDITING VIEWS IN THE MANAGEMENT STUDIO

Creating and modifying objects in SQL Server is always done, at some level, through T-SQL statements like those you've been working with. Even when working through the GUI, such as when you were using database diagrams in Chapter 8, your actions were put in place by T-SQL generated in accordance with the options you selected in Management Studio. Here you'll see much the same thing: you can create and modify views from a simple drag-and-drop interface, and the T-SQL to implement your changes will be automatically generated and run.

Creating Views in Management Studio

For people who really don't know what they are doing, this has to be a rather cool feature in the Management Studio. Building views is a snap, and you really don't have to know all that much about queries in order to get it done.

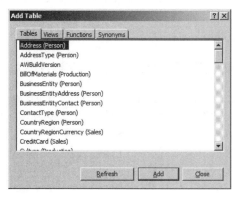

FIGURE 10-1

To take a look at this, fire up the Management Studio, open up the AdventureWorks database sub-node of the Databases node, and right-click Views. Select New View, and up comes the dialog box shown in Figure 10-1.

This dialog box makes it easy for you to choose which tables you're going to be including data from. The `Address` table is selected in Figure 10-1, but you're going to be working with not only a different table, but *four* other tables.

This should prompt the question: "How do I select more than one table?" Easy — just hold down your Ctrl key while selecting all the tables you want. For now, start by clicking the `Customer` table, and then pressing and holding your Ctrl key while you also select the `SalesOrderHeader`, `SalesOrderDetail`, and `Product` tables. You should wind up with all of them highlighted. Now click Add, and SQL Server adds several tables to your view (indeed, on most systems, you should be able to see them being added to the view editor that you're about to take a look at).

Before you close the Add Table dialog box, take a moment to notice the Views, Functions, and Synonyms tabs along the top of this dialog box. Because views can reference these objects directly, the dialog box gives you a way of adding them directly.

For now, however, just click Add and check out the view editor that appears, as in Figure 10-2.

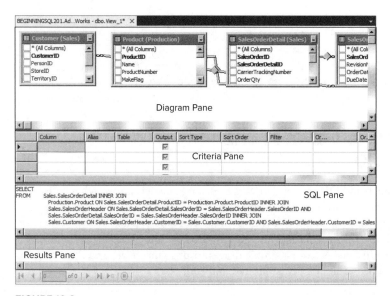

FIGURE 10-2

There are four panes to the View Builder — each of which can be independently turned on or off:

➤ The Diagram pane

➤ The Criteria pane

➤ The SQL pane

➤ The Results pane

For those of you who have worked with Access, the Diagram pane works much as it does in Access queries. You can add and remove tables, and even define relationships. Each of those added tables, checked columns, and defined relationships automatically reflected in the SQL pane in the form of the SQL required to match the diagram. To identify each of the icons on the toolbar, just hover your mouse pointer over them for a moment or two, and you get a tooltip that indicates the purpose of each button.

NOTE *You can add tables either by right-clicking in the Diagram pane (the top one in Figure 10-2) and choosing Add Table or by clicking the Add Table toolbar button (the one with an arrow pointing right in the very top left of the icon).*

Now select the following columns, so that your Diagram pane looks like the one shown in Figure 10-3.

➤ **Customer:** AccountNumber

➤ **SalesOrderHeader:** SalesOrderID and OrderDate

➤ **SalesOrderDetail:** OrderQty, ProductID, UnitPrice, and LineTotal

➤ **Product:** Name

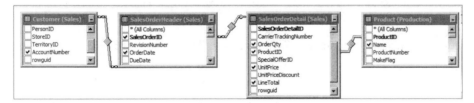

FIGURE 10-3

Note that I am just showing the diagram pane here to save space (and also that I've rearranged the tables a bit to straighten the relationship lines). If you have the Grid pane up while you select the columns, you would see each column appear in the Grid pane as you select it. With the SQL pane up, you will also see the columns appear in the SQL code.

In case you haven't recognized it yet, you're building the same view that you built as your first complex view (CustomerOrders_vw). The only thing that's tricky is the computed column (TotalDiscount). To create that one, you have to manually type the equation (Sales .SalesOrderDetail.UnitPriceDiscount * Sales.SalesOrderDetail.UnitPrice * Sales .SalesOrderDetail.OrderQty) into the SQL pane or type it into the Column column in the Grid pane along with its alias (see Figure 10-4).

Figure 10-4 shows the following grid and SQL panes:

Column	Alias	Table	Output	Sort Type	Sort Order
SalesOrderID		SalesOrde...	☑		
OrderDate		SalesOrde...	☑		
Sales.SalesOrderDetail.UnitPriceDiscount * Sales.SalesOrderDetail.UnitPrice * Sales.SalesOrder...	TotalDiscount		☑		

```
SELECT   Sales.Customer.AccountNumber, Production.Product.Name, Sales.SalesOrderDetail.OrderQty, Sales.SalesOrderDetail.ProductID, Sales.SalesOrderDetail.UnitPrice,
         Sales.SalesOrderDetail.LineTotal, Sales.SalesOrderHeader.SalesOrderID, Sales.SalesOrderHeader.OrderDate,
         Sales.SalesOrderDetail.UnitPriceDiscount * Sales.SalesOrderDetail.UnitPrice * Sales.SalesOrderDetail.OrderQty AS TotalDiscount
FROM     Sales.SalesOrderDetail INNER JOIN
         Production.Product ON Sales.SalesOrderDetail.ProductID = Production.Product.ProductID INNER JOIN
         Sales.SalesOrderHeader ON Sales.SalesOrderDetail.SalesOrderID = Sales.SalesOrderHeader.SalesOrderID AND
         Sales.SalesOrderDetail.SalesOrderID = Sales.SalesOrderHeader.SalesOrderID INNER JOIN
         Sales.Customer ON Sales.SalesOrderHeader.CustomerID = Sales.Customer.CustomerID AND Sales.SalesOrderHeader.CustomerID = Sales.Customer.CustomerID
```

FIGURE 10-4

When all is said and done, the View Builder gives you the following SQL code:

```
SELECT   Sales.Customer.AccountNumber,
         Sales.SalesOrderHeader.SalesOrderID,
         Sales.SalesOrderHeader.OrderDate,
         Sales.SalesOrderDetail.ProductID,
         Production.Product.Name,
         Sales.SalesOrderDetail.OrderQty,
         Sales.SalesOrderDetail.UnitPrice,
         Sales.SalesOrderDetail.UnitPriceDiscount *
            Sales.SalesOrderDetail.UnitPrice *
            Sales.SalesOrderDetail.OrderQty AS TotalDiscount,
         Sales.SalesOrderDetail.LineTotal
FROM     Sales.SalesOrderDetail
INNER JOIN Production.Product
 ON Sales.SalesOrderDetail.ProductID = Production.Product.ProductID
INNER JOIN Sales.SalesOrderHeader
 ON Sales.SalesOrderDetail.SalesOrderID = Sales.SalesOrderHeader.SalesOrderID
 AND Sales.SalesOrderDetail.SalesOrderID = Sales.SalesOrderHeader.SalesOrderID
INNER JOIN Sales.Customer
 ON Sales.SalesOrderHeader.CustomerID = Sales.Customer.CustomerID
 AND Sales.SalesOrderHeader.CustomerID = Sales.Customer.CustomerID
```

Although it's not formatted the same, if you look it over, you'll find that it's basically the same code you wrote by hand!

> **NOTE** If you've been struggling with learning your T-SQL query syntax, you can use this tool to play around with the syntax of a query. Just drag and drop some tables into the Diagram pane and select the column you want from each table. For the most part, SQL Server will build you a query. You can then use the syntax from the View Builder to learn how to build it yourself next time.

Now go ahead and save it (the disk icon in the toolbar is how I do it) as `CustomerOrders2_vw` and close the View Builder.

Editing Views in the Management Studio

Modifying your view in the Management Studio is as easy as creating it was. The only real difference is that you need to navigate to your specific view and right-click it. Choose Modify and you'll be greeted with the same friendly query designer that you used with your query when it was created.

AUDITING: DISPLAYING EXISTING CODE

What do you do when you have a view, but you're not sure what it does? The first option should be easy at this point — just go into the Management Studio as if you're going to edit the view. Go to the Views sub-node, select the view you want to edit, right-click, and choose Modify View. You'll see the code behind the view, complete with color-coding.

Unfortunately, you won't always have the Management Studio around to hold your hand through this stuff (you might be using a lighter weight tool of some sort). The bright side is that you have two reliable ways of getting at the actual view definition:

➤ `sp_helptext`

➤ The `sys.modules metadata` function

Using `sp_helptext` is highly preferable because when new releases come out, it automatically updates changes to the system tables.

 NOTE *There is, arguably, a third option: directly accessing the* `syscomments` *system table. Microsoft has been warning for a couple of releases now about not using system tables directly. As of this writing,* `syscomments` *is still there, but the results that come out of it when you run a query have some bogus information in them. They may work fine for you, but, given that Microsoft has been recommending against using* `syscomments` *for a while now, it probably makes sense to move on to the more "approved" methods.*

Let's run `sp_helptext` against one of the views you created in the AdventureWorks database earlier in the chapter — `YesterdaysOrders_vw`:

```
EXEC sp_helptext YesterdaysOrders_vw;
```

Available for download on Wrox.com

Chap10.sql

SQL Server obliges you with the code for the view:

```
Text
---------------------------------------------------------------------
CREATE VIEW YesterdaysOrders_vw
AS
```

```
SELECT    sc.AccountNumber,
          soh.SalesOrderID,
          soh.OrderDate,
          sod.ProductID,
          pp.Name,
          sod.OrderQty,
          sod.UnitPrice,
          sod.UnitPriceDiscount * sod.UnitPrice * sod.OrderQty AS TotalDiscount,
          sod.LineTotal
FROM      Sales.Customer AS sc
INNER JOIN   Sales.SalesOrderHeader AS soh
     ON sc.CustomerID = soh.CustomerID
INNER JOIN   Sales.SalesOrderDetail AS sod
     ON soh.SalesOrderID = sod.SalesOrderID
INNER JOIN Production.Product AS pp
     ON sod.ProductID = pp.ProductID
WHERE CAST(soh.OrderDate AS Date) =
      CAST(DATEADD(day,-1,GETDATE()) AS Date)
```

Now let's try it the other way — using the `sys.sql_modules` metadata function. The only major hassle with using this function is that all the objects are coded in object IDs.

> **NOTE** *Object IDs are SQL Server's internal way of keeping track of things. They are integer values rather than the names that you've used for your objects. In general, they are outside the scope of this book, but it is good to realize they are there, as you will find them used by scripts you copy from other people or you might just bump into them later in your SQL endeavors.*

Fortunately, you can get around this by using the `OBJECT_ID()` function:

```
SELECT *
FROM sys.sql_modules
WHERE object_id = OBJECT_ID('dbo.YesterdaysOrders_vw');
```

Chap10.sql

Again, you get the same block of code (indeed, all `sp_helptext` does is run what amounts to this same query).

> **NOTE** *Note that, by default, the Results in Text option in the Query window limits the results from any individual column to just 256 characters, so running the previous `sys.sql_modules` query may get you a truncated version of the text for the view. If you look at it in grid mode, the limit is 64KB, so everything comes through. You can change the maximum number of characters per column by going to Tools ⇨ Options ⇨ Query Results ⇨ SQL Server ⇨ Results to Text and changing the appropriate setting.*

PROTECTING CODE: ENCRYPTING VIEWS

If you're building any kind of commercial software product, odds are that you're interested in protecting your source code. Views are the first place you see the opportunity to do just that.

All you have to do to encrypt your view is use the WITH ENCRYPTION option. This one has a couple of tricks to it if you're used to the WITH CHECK OPTION clause:

➤   WITH ENCRYPTION goes after the name of the view, but *before* the AS keyword.

➤   WITH ENCRYPTION does not use the OPTION keyword.

In addition, remember that if you use an ALTER VIEW statement, you are replacing the existing view except for access rights. This means that the encryption is also replaced. If you want the altered view to be encrypted, you must use the WITH ENCRYPTION clause in the ALTER VIEW statement.

Let's do an ALTER VIEW on your CustomerOrders_vw view that you created in AdventureWorks. If you haven't yet created the CustomerOrders_vw view, just change the ALTER to CREATE:

Available for download on Wrox.com

```
ALTER VIEW CustomerOrders_vw
WITH ENCRYPTION
AS
SELECT     sc.AccountNumber,
           soh.SalesOrderID,
           soh.OrderDate,
           sod.ProductID,
           pp.Name,
           sod.OrderQty,
           sod.UnitPrice,
           sod.UnitPriceDiscount * sod.UnitPrice *
                 sod.OrderQty AS TotalDiscount,
           sod.LineTotal
FROM       Sales.Customer AS sc
INNER JOIN   Sales.SalesOrderHeader AS soh
           ON sc.CustomerID = soh.CustomerID
INNER JOIN   Sales.SalesOrderDetail AS sod
           ON soh.SalesOrderID = sod.SalesOrderID
INNER JOIN Production.Product AS pp
           ON sod.ProductID = pp.ProductID;
```

Now run an sp_helptext on your CustomerOrders_vw:

```
EXEC sp_helptext CustomerOrders_vw
```

Chap10.sql

SQL Server promptly tells you that it can't do what you're asking:

```
The text for object 'CustomerOrders_vw' is encrypted.
```

The heck you say, and promptly go to the `sys.sql_modules` metadata function:

```
SELECT *

FROM sys.sql_modules
WHERE object_id = OBJECT_ID('dbo.CustomerOrders_vw');
```

Chap10.sql

But that doesn't get you very far either — SQL Server recognizes that the table was encrypted and gives you a NULL result.

In short, your code is safe and sound. Even if you pull it up in other viewers (such as the Management Studio, which actually won't even give you the Modify option on an encrypted table), you'll find it useless.

> **NOTE** *Make sure you store your source code somewhere before using the* WITH ENCRYPTION *option. Once it's been encrypted, there is no way to get it back. If you haven't stored your code away somewhere and you need to change it, you may find yourself re-writing it from scratch.*

ABOUT SCHEMA BINDING

Schema binding essentially takes the things that your view is dependent upon (tables or other views), and "binds" them to that view. The significance of this is that no one can make alterations to those objects (CREATE, ALTER) unless he or she drops the schema-bound view first.

Why would you want to do this? Well, there are a few reasons why this can come in handy:

➤ **It prevents your view from becoming "orphaned" by alterations in underlying objects:** Imagine, for a moment, that someone performs a DROP or makes some other change (even deleting a column could cause your view grief), but doesn't pay attention to your view. Oops. If the view is schema bound, this is prevented from happening.

➤ **To allow indexed views:** If you want an index on your view, you *must* create it using the SCHEMABINDING option. (You'll look at indexed views just a few paragraphs from now.)

➤ **To allow for dependent schema-bound objects:** If you are going to create a schema-bound user-defined function (and there are instances where your function *must* be schema bound) that references your view, your view must also be schema bound.

Keep these in mind as you are building your views.

MAKING YOUR VIEW LOOK LIKE A TABLE WITH VIEW_METADATA

This option has the effect of making your view look very much like an actual table to DB-LIB, ODBC, and OLE DB clients. Without this option, the metadata passed back to the client API is that of the base table(s) that your view relies on.

Providing this metadata information is required to allow for any client-side cursors (cursors your client application manages) to be updatable. Note that, if you want to support such cursors, you're also going to need to use an INSTEAD OF trigger.

INDEXED (MATERIALIZED) VIEWS

When a view is referred to, the logic in the query that makes up the view is essentially incorporated into the calling query. Unfortunately, this means that the calling query just gets that much more complex. The extra overhead of determining the impact of the view (and what data it represents) on the fly can actually get very high. What's more, you're often including additional joins into your query in the form of the tables that are joined in the view. Indexed views give you a way of taking care of some of this impact before the query is run.

An indexed view is essentially a view that has a set of unique values "materialized" into the form of a clustered index. The advantage of this is that it provides a very quick lookup in terms of pulling the information behind a view together. After the first index (which must be a clustered index against a unique set of values), SQL Server can also build additional indexes on the view using the cluster key from the first index as a reference point. That said, nothing comes for free — there are some restrictions about when you can and can't build indexes on views (I hope you're ready for this one — it's an awfully long list!):

➤ The view must use the SCHEMABINDING option.

➤ If it references any user-defined functions (more on these later), these must also be schema bound.

➤ The view must not reference any other views — just tables and UDFs.

➤ The view cannot contain any OUTER JOINS, nor can it contain the same table more than once.

➤ All tables and UDFs referenced in the view must utilize a two-part naming convention (not even three-part and four-part names are allowed). For example, dbo.Customers and MySchema.SomeUDF. They also must also have the same owner as the view.

➤ The view can contain some aggregates (for example, COUNT, SUM) but not others (for example, AVG, MIN).

➤ The view must be in the same database as all objects referenced by the view.

➤ The ANSI_NULLS and QUOTED_IDENTIFIER options must have been turned on (using the SET command) at the time the view *and all underlying tables* were created.

➤ Any functions referenced by the view must be deterministic.

At this point, you might be looking at the number of restrictions and wondering whether it wouldn't be less trouble to just give the whole topic a miss. In fact, I hesitated before deciding to proceed with this topic in a book intended for beginners; it feels a bit like handing the keys to the sports car to my teenager. This is a very powerful feature, so I want you to learn to use it safely.

TRY IT OUT   Your First Indexed View

This simple example demonstrates the happy path before you move on to some of the gotchas. To create an example indexed view, start by making a few alterations to the `CustomerOrders_vw` object that you created earlier in the chapter:

Available for download on Wrox.com

```
ALTER VIEW CustomerOrders_vw
WITH SCHEMABINDING
AS
SELECT     sc.AccountNumber,
           soh.SalesOrderID,
           soh.OrderDate,
           sod.ProductID,
           pp.Name,
           sod.OrderQty,
           sod.UnitPrice,
           sod.UnitPriceDiscount * sod.UnitPrice *
               sod.OrderQty AS TotalDiscount,
           sod.LineTotal
FROM       Sales.Customer AS sc
INNER JOIN   Sales.SalesOrderHeader AS soh
       ON sc.CustomerID = soh.CustomerID
INNER JOIN   Sales.SalesOrderDetail AS sod
       ON soh.SalesOrderID = sod.SalesOrderID
INNER JOIN Production.Product AS pp
       ON sod.ProductID = pp.ProductID;
```

Chap10.sql

The big point to notice here is that you have to make your view use the SCHEMABINDING option. This is really just the beginning though — you don't have an indexed view as yet. Instead, what you have is a view that *can* be indexed. Before you actually build the index, let's get a baseline of how queries against your view would currently be executed. Take a simple SELECT against the view:

Available for download on Wrox.com

```
SELECT * FROM CustomerOrders_vw;
```

Chap10.sql

Seems simple enough, but remember that there are four tables underlying this view. If you choose to display the estimated execution plan (one of the icons on the toolbar), as shown in Figure 10-5, you see a somewhat complex set of steps to execute your query.

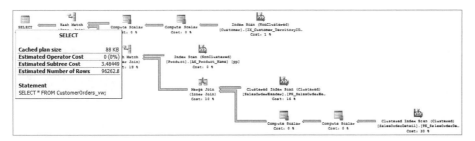

FIGURE 10-5

You can get the yellow popup by hovering your mouse over the top-left node of the execution plan. This is the top node of the execution plan, and looking at the Estimated Subtree Cost on this node shows you the estimated cost for the entire query (for me, it is 3.48449). Now that you've seen how complex the query is and seen the estimated cost, you're ready to move on to creating the index.

When you create the index, the first index created on the view must be clustered and unique:

Available for download on Wrox.com

```
CREATE UNIQUE CLUSTERED INDEX ivCustomerOrders
ON CustomerOrders_vw(AccountNumber, SalesOrderID, ProductID);
```

Chap10.sql

This can take a few seconds as SQL Server executes the view and writes the entire output onto the disk. Once this command has executed, you have a clustered index on your view (see Figure 10-6), and you're ready to again check out the Estimated Execution Plan for your basic SELECT.

Notice that this is a substantially more simplistic query. The estimated cost of execution has also dropped by over 50 percent. Does this mean your

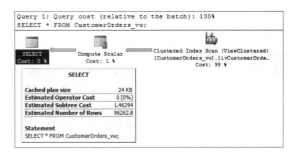

FIGURE 10-6

index is a good idea? Well, simply put — no. It means it *might* be. Much like any index, you need to keep in mind the maintenance cost of the index. How much is maintaining this index going to slow down the INSERT, UPDATE, and DELETE statements against the underlying tables?

Because this view joins several tables together, performing any kind of data modification can require significantly more work than without the index. Let's take a look at AccountNumber AW00029722 in your new view:

Available for download on Wrox.com

```
SELECT COUNT(*) as RowsPerAccount
FROM CustomerOrders_vw
WHERE AccountNumber = 'AW00029722'
```

Chap10.sql

```
RowsPerAccount
--------------
530

(1 row(s) affected)
```

How It Works

That account is one row in the Accounts table, but over five hundred rows in the view depend on it. If you were to update a field in the `Sales.Customers` table that's in the view (in this case you're safe because the `AccountNumber` field is a computed column), you might think you're updating only one row in `Sales.Customers`, but you're actually updating every row in the clustered index for that customer as well. When you start talking about increasing SQL Server's workload by two orders of magnitude (or more) on simple operations, that should give you pause.

INDEXING AN AGGREGATE VIEW

Now let's take that sports car and open her up a bit. Another use for indexed views is to provide surprisingly quick access to aggregate data that might take whole seconds — or minutes — to compute in real time. Let's say your manager wants to see up-to-the-moment sales figures by day, and does so by running the following query:

```
SELECT    soh.OrderDate,
    SUM(sod.OrderQty) TotalOrderQty,
    AVG(sod.UnitPrice) AveragePrice,
    AVG(sod.UnitPriceDiscount * sod.UnitPrice * sod.OrderQty)
        AS AverageDiscount,
    SUM(sod.LineTotal) TotalSale
FROM Sales.Customer AS sc
INNER JOIN Sales.SalesOrderHeader AS soh
    ON sc.CustomerID = soh.CustomerID
INNER JOIN    Sales.SalesOrderDetail AS sod
    ON soh.SalesOrderID = sod.SalesOrderID
GROUP BY soh.OrderDate;
```

Chap10.sql

The result shows total sales quantity and price information for each customer for each day. That's great, but you're justifiably concerned that this will be too slow as the database grows. Using an indexed view, you can pre-compute aggregate values. You begin by creating a schema-bound version of this query as a view:

```
CREATE VIEW CustomerTotalOrdersByDay_vw
WITH SCHEMABINDING
AS
SELECT    soh.OrderDate,
    SUM(sod.OrderQty) TotalOrderQty,
    AVG(sod.UnitPrice) AveragePrice,
    AVG(sod.UnitPriceDiscount * sod.UnitPrice * sod.OrderQty)
```

```
            AS AverageDiscount,
           SUM(sod.LineTotal) TotalSale
FROM Sales.Customer AS sc
INNER JOIN Sales.SalesOrderHeader AS soh
    ON sc.CustomerID = soh.CustomerID
INNER JOIN  Sales.SalesOrderDetail AS sod
    ON soh.SalesOrderID = sod.SalesOrderID
GROUP BY soh.OrderDate;
```

Then you create your clustered index:

```
CREATE UNIQUE CLUSTERED INDEX ivCustomerOrdersAggregate
ON CustomerTotalOrdersByDay_vw(OrderDate);
```

Chap10.sql

And SQL Server politely responds by rebuffing your efforts.

```
Msg 10125, Level 16, State 1, Line 1
Cannot create index on view "AdventureWorks.dbo.CustomerTotalOrdersByDay_vw" because it
uses aggregate "AVG". Consider eliminating the aggregate, not indexing the view, or
using alternate aggregates. For example, for AVG substitute SUM and COUNT_BIG, or for
COUNT, substitute COUNT_BIG.
```

Here you've run into the first hurdle. Indexed views can contain only a limited set of aggregates: those for which the aggregate value can be recomputed by looking only at the altered source row(s). If you have a COUNT, and you INSERT a row, you know the new value of the COUNT without going back through and counting all the rows; you just add one. An average, though, isn't so easy. MIN and MAX are out as well; if you delete the current MIN or MAX, you have to look through all the rows to find the new value. Fortunately, SQL has helpfully offered an out, and you should take it.

Available for download on Wrox.com

```
ALTER VIEW CustomerTotalOrdersByDay_vw
WITH SCHEMABINDING
AS
SELECT   soh.OrderDate,
     SUM(sod.OrderQty) TotalOrderQty,
     SUM(sod.UnitPrice) TotalUnitPrice,
     SUM(sod.UnitPriceDiscount * sod.UnitPrice * sod.OrderQty)
         AS TotalDiscount,
     SUM(sod.LineTotal) TotalSale
FROM     Sales.Customer AS sc
INNER JOIN  Sales.SalesOrderHeader AS soh
    ON sc.CustomerID = soh.CustomerID
INNER JOIN  Sales.SalesOrderDetail AS sod
    ON soh.SalesOrderID = sod.SalesOrderID
GROUP BY soh.OrderDate;
```

Then try again to create your clustered index:

```
CREATE UNIQUE CLUSTERED INDEX ivCustomerOrdersAggregate
ON CustomerTotalOrdersByDay_vw(OrderDate);
```

Chap10.sql

That sports car is really difficult to handle. This time, SQL Server comes up with a new complaint.

```
Msg 10138, Level 16, State 1, Line 2
Cannot create index on view 'AdventureWorks.dbo.CustomerTotalOrdersByDay_vw' because its
select list does not include a proper use of COUNT_BIG. Consider adding
COUNT_BIG(*) to select list.
```

This is a little obscure, but if you're going to use indexed views at all you have to know that you can't compute any aggregates unless you include a count of the rows used to compute them. If you don't have any aggregates, you're fine, but if you do, you also have to include COUNT_BIG(). COUNT_BIG() is simply a count of rows like COUNT(), but it's a BIGINT instead of INT (and an indexed view will accept no substitutes). Well, you need that anyway if computing that average is important. Add it to your view:

```
ALTER VIEW CustomerTotalOrdersByDay_vw
WITH SCHEMABINDING
AS
SELECT    soh.OrderDate,
    SUM(sod.OrderQty) TotalOrderQty,
    SUM(sod.UnitPrice) TotalUnitPrice,
    SUM(sod.UnitPriceDiscount * sod.UnitPrice * sod.OrderQty)
        AS TotalDiscount,
    SUM(sod.LineTotal) TotalSale,
    COUNT_BIG(*) TotalRows
FROM      Sales.Customer AS sc
INNER JOIN    Sales.SalesOrderHeader AS soh
    ON sc.CustomerID = soh.CustomerID
INNER JOIN    Sales.SalesOrderDetail AS sod
    ON soh.SalesOrderID = sod.SalesOrderID
GROUP BY soh.OrderDate;
```

And now you can successfully create the index.

```
CREATE UNIQUE CLUSTERED INDEX ivCustomerOrdersAggregate
ON CustomerTotalOrdersByDay_vw(OrderDate);
```

Chap10.sql

The index contains only one row per day (about 1,125 rows to the non-aggregate's 121,000) and is kept up to date almost instantaneously.

Like that sports car, indexed views are very expensive to maintain, but they can provide certain types of operation an enormous performance boost (besides being pretty flashy). However, if you use too many you can run into serious trouble in a lot of areas; update performance, locking issues, and code maintenance can get problematic in a hurry. Basically, it's a balancing act, and each database and each index requires a separate decision. That said, indexed views are definitely something you want to be able to bring out of the garage when nothing else will do.

SUMMARY

Views tend to be the most overused or most underused tools in most of the databases I've seen — there seems to be no middle ground. Some people like to use them to abstract seemingly everything (often forgetting that they are adding another layer to the process when they do this). Others just seem to forget that views are even an option. Personally, like most things, I think you should use a view when it's the right tool to use — not before, not after. Things to remember with views include:

➤ Stay away from building views based on views — instead, adapt the appropriate query information from the first view into your new view.

➤ Remember that a view using the WITH CHECK OPTION provides some flexibility that can't be duplicated with a normal CHECK constraint.

➤ Encrypt views when you don't want others to be able to see your source code (,) for either commercial products or general security reasons, but also remember to keep a copy of your unencrypted code; it can't be retrieved after you've encrypted it.

➤ Using an ALTER VIEW completely replaces the existing view other than permissions. This means you must include the WITH ENCRYPTION and WITH CHECK OPTION clauses in the ALTER statement if you want encryption and restrictions to be in effect in the altered view.

➤ Use sp_helptext to display the supporting code for a view — avoid using the system tables.

➤ Minimize the use of views for production queries — they add additional overhead and hurt performance.

Common uses for views include:

➤ Filtering rows

➤ Protecting sensitive data

➤ Reducing visible database complexity

➤ Abstracting multiple physical databases into one logical database

In the next chapter, you'll take a look at batches and scripting. Batches and scripting will lead you right into stored procedures — the closest thing that SQL Server has to its own programs.

EXERCISES

1. Add a view called `Sales.PersonSales` in the AdventureWorks database that shows each person's `CustomerID`, name in `LastName`, `Firstname` format, and the total of his or her sales.

2. Change the view you just created to be encrypted.

3. Build an index against your new view based on the `CustomerID` column.

► WHAT YOU LEARNED IN THIS CHAPTER

TOPIC	CONCEPT
The view object	Views (at least unindexed views) have only a logical, not a physical, existence in the database. They are usable as tables, but present a view of the data that can include joins, aggregates, and filters.
Editing views in T-SQL	Views are ordinary T-SQL queries written in a single statement, managed as objects using `CREATE VIEW`, `ALTER VIEW`, and `DROP VIEW`.
Working with views in SSMS	SQL Server Management Studio provides graphical tools to manage views, allowing you to use drag-and-drop rather than T-SQL statements.
Examining view code	The T-SQL that makes up your views can be seen through the use of `sp_helptext` (and, less safely, `syscomments`), unless your views are encrypted using the `WITH ENCRYPTION` option.
Advanced view options	`WITH SCHEMABINDING` is needed to prevent your views from being orphaned, to permit materialization, and to allow dependent objects to be schema bound for similar reasons. `VIEW_METADATA` exists to make your view appear to be a table to external clients.
Indexed views	Indexing a view materializes the view's data on disk for a vast improvement in read performance. View indexes are managed by the SQL Server engine, so the data is kept current almost instantaneously when the source tables are updated. Not every view can be indexed; indexing a view requires that the base view meet many sometimes very restrictive criteria.

11

Writing Scripts and Batches

WHAT YOU WILL LEARN IN THIS CHAPTER:

➤ How to combine T-SQL statements into scripts and batches

➤ Scope of variables and IDENTITY values

➤ Error handling in scripts

➤ How to run a batch from the command line

➤ How to build and run dynamic SQL statements

➤ T-SQL control of flow statements

Whether you've realized it or not, you've already been writing SQL *scripts*. Every CREATE statement that you write, every ALTER, every SELECT is all (if you're running a single statement) or part (multiple statements) of a script. It's hard to get excited, however, over a script with one line in it — could you imagine Hamlet's "To be, or not to be . . ." if it had never had the lines that follow — you wouldn't have any context for what he was talking about.

SQL scripts are much the same way. Things get quite a bit more interesting when you string several commands together into a longer script — a full play or at least an act to finish the Shakespeare analogy. Now imagine adding a richer set of language elements from .NET to the equation — now you're ready to write an epic!

Scripts generally have a unified goal. That is, all the commands that are in a script are usually building up to one overall purpose. Examples include scripts to build a database (these might be used for a system installation), scripts for system maintenance (backups, Database Consistency Checker utilities [DBCCs], index defragmentation, and more) — scripts for anything where several commands are usually run together.

In this chapter, you'll look at scripts and learn about the notion of *batches* — which control how SQL Server groups your commands. In addition, you will learn how *sqlcmd* — the command-line utility — relates to scripts.

> **NOTE** *sqlcmd was first added in SQL Server 2005. For backward compatibility only, SQL Server continues to support osql.exe (the previous tool that did command-line work). You may also see references to isql.exe (do not confuse this with isqlw.exe), which served this same function in earlier releases. isql.exe is no longer supported.*

UNDERSTANDING SCRIPT BASICS

A script technically isn't a script until you store it in a file where it can be pulled up and reused. SQL scripts are stored as text files. The SQL Server Management Studio provides many tools to help you with your script writing. The basic query window is color coded to help you not only recognize keywords, but also understand their nature. In addition, you have IntelliSense, a step debugger, code templates, the object browser, and more.

Scripts are usually treated as a unit. That is, you are normally executing the entire script or nothing at all. They can make use of both system functions and local variables. As an example, let's look at a script that would insert order records in the Accounting database that you created back in Chapter 5:

```
USE Accounting;
DECLARE @Ident int;

INSERT INTO Orders
(CustomerNo,OrderDate, EmployeeID)
VALUES
(1, GETDATE(), 1);
SELECT @Ident = SCOPE_IDENTITY();
INSERT INTO OrderDetails
(OrderID, PartNo, Description, UnitPrice, Qty)
VALUES
(@Ident, '2R2416', 'Cylinder Head', 1300, 2);
SELECT 'The OrderID of the INSERTed row is ' + CONVERT(varchar(8),@Ident);
```

Code snippet Chap11.sql.

> **NOTE** *If you didn't keep your populated version of the Accounting database, a script to re-create it in a state usable for this chapter can be downloaded from the Wrox support website (*wrox.com*).*

There are six distinct commands working here, covering a range of different things that you might do in a script. This script uses both system functions and local variables, the USE statement, INSERT statements, and both assignment and regular versions of the SELECT statement. They are all working in unison to accomplish one task — to insert complete orders into the database.

Selecting a Database Context with the USE Statement

The USE statement sets the current database. This affects any place where you are making use of default values for the database portion of a fully qualified object name. This particular example does not indicate what database the tables in the INSERT or SELECT statements are from, but, because it includes a USE statement prior to the INSERT and SELECT statements, they use that database (in this case, Accounting). Without the USE statement, you are at the mercy of whoever executes the script to make certain that the correct database was current when the script was executed.

> **NOTE** *Usually, if you are naming database-specific tables in your script (that is, non-system tables), you want to use the USE command. I also find it very helpful if the script is meant to modify a specific database — as I've said in prior chapters, I can't tell you how many times I've accidentally created a large number of tables in the master database that were intended for a user database.*
>
> *Don't take this as meaning that you should always include a USE statement in your script — it depends on the purpose of the script. If your intent is to have a general-purpose script, leaving out the USE statement might actually be helpful.*

Next, the script has a DECLARE statement to declare a variable. You've seen DECLARE statements used in a few scripts used earlier in the book, but let's visit them a bit more formally.

Declaring Variables

The most common form of the DECLARE statement has a pretty simple syntax:

```
DECLARE @<variable name> <variable type>[= <value>][,
   @<variable name> <variable type>[= <value>][,
   @<variable name> <variable type>[= <value>]]]
```

You can declare just one variable at a time, or several. It's common to see people reuse the DECLARE statement with each variable they declare, rather than use the comma-separated method. It's up to you, but no matter which method you choose, you must initialize the variable (using the = syntax) or the value of your variable will be NULL until you explicitly set it to some other value.

In this case, you've declared a local variable called @ident as an integer. I've chosen not to initialize it, as the whole purpose of this variable is to accept a value from another source. Technically, you could have gotten away without declaring this variable — instead, you could have chosen to just use SCOPE_IDENTITY() directly. SCOPE_IDENTITY() is a system function. It is always available, and it supplies the last identity value that was assigned in the current connection within the current scope. As with most system functions, you should make a habit of explicitly moving the value in SCOPE_IDENTITY() to a local variable. That way, you're sure that it won't get changed accidentally. There was no danger of that in this case, but, as always, be consistent.

> **NOTE** *I like to move a value I'm taking from a system function into my own variable. That way I can safely use the value and know that it's being changed only when I change it. With the system function, you sometimes can't be certain when it's going to change because most system functions are not set by you, but by the system. That creates a situation whereby it would be very easy to have the system change a value at a time you weren't expecting it, and wind up with the most dreaded of all computer terms: unpredictable results.*

Now you know how to declare *scalar variables*. A scalar variable is one that holds a single, atomic value, like an integer or a string. SQL Server also allows you to declare *table variables*. A table variable is declared similarly to a scalar variable, and has the same scope, but it can hold any number of, well, rows. You'll look at table variables in more depth later, but for now here's a primer.

```
DECLARE @<variable name> TABLE (
    <column spec> [, . . .]
)
```

The syntax begins with a DECLARE, but continues as if one were creating a table, for example:

```
DECLARE @InterestingRows TABLE (
    RowID int NOT NULL IDENTITY PRIMARY KEY,
    Descriptor VARCHAR(255) NOT NULL
)
```

What's interesting is that the table variable can have key constraints, identity columns, and many other features of a full-fledged table. You've already been exposed to temporary tables in Chapter 7 (if you're reading the book in order, anyway), and table variables are useful in similar situations. You'll read later about some criteria to help you choose between the two.

Setting the Value in Your Variables

Well, you now know how to declare variables, but the question that follows is, "How do you change their values?" There are three ways to set the value in a variable. You can initialize it in the DECLARE statement, use a SELECT statement, or use a SET statement. Functionally, SET and SELECT work almost the same, except that a SELECT statement can do a couple more things:

> ➤ SELECT can assign a value from a column in the SELECT statement

> ➤ SELECT can assign values to many variables in the same statement

So why have two ways of doing this? SELECT predates SET back in SQL Server history, so why go to the trouble to implement SET at all? Suffice to say that SET is now part of the ANSI/ISO standard, and that's why it's been put in there. However, I can't find anything wrong with the same functionality in SELECT — even ANSI/ISO seems to think that it's okay. I'm sure there's a purpose in the redundancy, but what it is I can't tell you. That said, there are some differences in the way they are used in practice.

Setting Variables Using SET

SET is typically used for setting variables in the fashion that you see in more procedural languages. Examples of typical uses are:

```
SET @TotalCost = 10
SET @TotalCost = @UnitCost * 1.1
```

Notice that these are all straight assignments that use either explicit values or another variable. With a SET, you cannot assign a value to a variable from a query — you have to separate the query from the SET. For example:

```
USE AdventureWorks;

DECLARE @Test money;
SET @Test = MAX(UnitPrice) FROM [Order Details];
SELECT @Test;
```

causes an error, but:

```
USE AdventureWorks;

DECLARE @Test money;
SET @Test = (SELECT MAX(UnitPrice) FROM Sales.SalesOrderDetail);
SELECT @Test;
```

Code snippet Chap11.sql

works just fine.

> **NOTE** *Although this latter syntax works, by convention, code is never implemented this way. Again, I don't know for sure why it's "just not done that way," but I suspect that it has to do with readability — you want a* SELECT *statement to be related to retrieving table data, and a* SET *to be about simple variable assignments.*

Initializing Variables

When you first declare a variable, its value by default is NULL. If you'd prefer a value be assigned right away, you can simply finish your DECLARE statement with an = <value> clause and you'll have a value right from the start.

```
DECLARE @Counter INT = 0;

DECLARE @@MaxPrice MONEY = (SELECT MAX(UnitPrice) FROM Sales.SalesOrderDetail);
```

Code snippet Chap11.sql

The syntax and rules for initializing variables follow exactly the same pattern as using SET.

Setting Variables Using SELECT

SELECT is typically used to assign variable values when the source of the information you're storing in the variable is from a query. For example, the last illustration would be typically done using a SELECT:

```
USE AdventureWorks;

DECLARE @Test money;
SELECT @Test = MAX(UnitPrice) FROM Sales.SalesOrderDetail;
SELECT @Test;
```

Code snippet Chap11.sql

Notice that this is a little cleaner (it takes less verbiage to do the same thing).

So again, the convention on when to use which goes like this:

➤ Use SET when you are performing a simple assignment of a variable — where your value is already known in the form of an explicit value or some other variable.

➤ Use SELECT when you are basing the assignment of your variable on a query.

> **NOTE** *I'm not going to pick any bones about the fact that you'll see me violate this last convention in many places in this book. Using SET for variable assignment first appeared in version 7.0, and I must admit that nearly a decade after that release, I still haven't completely adapted yet. Nonetheless, this seems to be something that's really being pushed by Microsoft and the SQL Server community, so I strongly recommend that you start out on the right foot and adhere to the convention.*

Reviewing System Functions

There are over 30 parameterless system functions available. The older ones in the mix start with an @@ sign — a throwback to when they were commonly referred to as "global variables." Thankfully that name has gone away in favor of the more accurate "system functions," and the majority of all system functions now come without the @@ prefix. Some of the ones you should be most concerned with are in Table 11-1:

TABLE 11-1: Common System Functions

VARIABLE	PURPOSE	COMMENTS
`@@DATEFIRST`	Returns what is currently set as the first day of the week (say, Sunday versus Monday).	Is a system-wide setting — if someone changes the setting, you may not get the result you expect.
`@@ERROR`	Returns the error number of the last T-SQL statement executed on the current connection. Returns 0 if no error.	Is reset with each new statement. If you need the value preserved, move it to a local variable immediately after the execution of the statement for which you want to preserve the error code.
`@@IDENTITY`	Returns the last identity value inserted as a result of the last `INSERT` or `SELECT INTO` statement in the current connection.	Is set to `NULL` if no identity value was generated. This is true even if the lack of an identity value was due to a failure of the statement to run. If multiple inserts are performed by just one statement, only the last identity value is returned.
`IDENT_CURRENT ('table_name')`	Returns the last identity value inserted for a specified table regardless of session or scope.	Nice in the sense that it doesn't get overwritten if you're inserting into multiple tables, but can give you a value other than what you were expecting if other connections are inserting into the specific table.
`@@OPTIONS`	Returns information about options that have been set using the `SET` command.	Because you get only one value back, but can have many options set, SQL Server uses binary flags to indicate what values are set. To test whether the option you are interested is set, you must use the option value together with a bitwise operator.
`@@REMSERVER`	Used only in stored procedures. Returns the value of the server that called the stored procedure.	Handy when you want the sproc to behave differently depending on the remote server (often a geographic location) from which it was called. Still, in this era of .NET, I would question whether anything needing this variable might have been better written using other functionality found in .NET.
`@@ROWCOUNT`	One of the most used system functions. Returns the number of rows affected by the last statement.	Commonly used in non-runtime error checking. For example, if you try to `DELETE` a row using a `WHERE` clause, and no rows are affected, that implies that something unexpected happened. You can then raise an error manually.

continues

TABLE 11-1 *(continued)*

VARIABLE	PURPOSE	COMMENTS
SCOPE_IDENTITY()	Similar to @@IDENTITY, but returns the last identity inserted within the current session and scope.	Very useful for avoiding issues where a trigger or nested stored procedure has performed additional inserts that have overwritten your expected identity value. If you are trying to retrieve an identity value for an insert you've just performed, this is the way to go.
@@SERVERNAME	Returns the name of the local server that the script is running from.	Can be changed by using sp_addserver and then restarting SQL Server, but rarely required.
@@TRANCOUNT	Returns the number of active transactions — essentially the transaction nesting level — for the current connection.	A ROLLBACK TRAN statement decrements @@TRANCOUNT to 0 unless you are using save points. BEGIN TRAN increments @@ TRANCOUNT by 1. COMMIT TRAN decrements @@TRANCOUNT by 1.
@@VERSION	Returns the current version of SQL Server, as well as the date, processor, and O/S architecture.	Unfortunately, this doesn't return the information into any kind of structured field arrangement, so you have to parse it if you want to use it to test for specific information. Also be sure to check out the xp_msver extended stored procedure.

Don't worry if you don't recognize some of the terms in a few of these. They will become clear in due time, and you will have this table or Bonus Appendix 1 to look back on for reference at a later date. The thing to remember is that there are sources you can go to in order to find out a whole host of information about the current state of your system and your activities.

Retrieving IDENTITY Values

SCOPE_IDENTITY is one of the most important of all the system functions. An identity column is one where you don't supply a value, and SQL Server inserts a numbered value automatically.

In the example case, you obtain the value of SCOPE_IDENTITY() right after performing an insert into the Orders table. The issue is that you don't supply the key value for that table — it's automatically created as you do the insert. Now you want to insert a record into the OrderDetails table, but you need to know the value of the primary key in the associated record in the Orders table (remember, there is a foreign key constraint on the OrderDetails table that references the Orders table). Because SQL Server generated that value instead of you supplying it, you need to have a way to retrieve that value for use in your dependent inserts later on in the script. SCOPE_IDENTITY() gives you that automatically generated value because it was the last statement run.

In this example, you could have easily gotten away with not moving SCOPE_IDENTITY() to a local variable — you could have just referenced it explicitly in your next INSERT query. I make a habit of always moving it to a local variable, however, to avoid errors on the occasions when I do need to keep a copy. An example of this kind of situation is if you had yet another INSERT that was dependent on the identity value from the INSERT into the Orders table. If I hadn't moved it into a local variable, it would be lost when I did the next INSERT, because it would have been overwritten with the value from the OrderDetails table, which, because OrderDetails has no identity column, means that SCOPE_IDENTITY() would have been set to NULL. Moving the value of SCOPE_IDENTITY() to a local variable also lets me keep the value around for the statement where I printed the value for later reference.

Let's create a couple of tables to try this out:

Available for
download on
Wrox.com

```
CREATE TABLE TestIdent
(
    IDCol   int     IDENTITY
    PRIMARY KEY
);

CREATE TABLE TestChild1
(
    IDcol   int
    PRIMARY KEY
    FOREIGN KEY
    REFERENCES TestIdent(IDCol)
);

CREATE TABLE TestChild2
(
    IDcol   int
    PRIMARY KEY
    FOREIGN KEY
    REFERENCES TestIdent(IDCol)
);
```

Code snippet Chap11.sql

What you have here is a parent table — it has an identity column for a primary key (as it happens, that's the only column it has). You also have two child tables. They each are the subject of an identifying relationship — that is, they each take at least part (in this case all) of their primary key by placing a foreign key on another table (the parent). So what you have is a situation where the two child tables need to get their key from the parent. Therefore, you need to insert a record into the parent first, and then retrieve the identity value generated so you can make use of it in the other tables.

TRY IT OUT Using SCOPE_IDENTITY()

Now that you have some tables to work with, you can try a little test script:

```
/******************************************
** This script illustrates how the identity
** value gets lost as soon as another INSERT
** happens
****************************************** */

DECLARE @Ident INT;   -- This will be a holding variable
/* We'll use it to show how you can
** move values from system functions
** into a safe place.
*/
INSERT INTO TestIdent
  DEFAULT VALUES;
SET @Ident = SCOPE_IDENTITY();
PRINT 'The value we you got originally from SCOPE_IDENTITY() was ' +
CONVERT(varchar(2),@Ident);
PRINT 'The value currently in SCOPE_IDENTITY() is '
    + CONVERT(varchar(2),SCOPE_IDENTITY());

/* On this first INSERT using SCOPE_IDENTITY(), you're going to get lucky.
** You'll get a proper value because there is nothing between the
** original INSERT and this one. You'll see that on the INSERT that
** will follow after this one, you won't be so lucky anymore. */
INSERT INTO TestChild1
VALUES
  (SCOPE_IDENTITY());

PRINT 'The value you got originally from SCOPE_IDENTITY() was ' +
CONVERT(varchar(2),@Ident);
IF (SELECT SCOPE_IDENTITY()) IS NULL
  PRINT 'The value currently in SCOPE_IDENTITY() is NULL';
ELSE
  PRINT 'The value currently in SCOPE_IDENTITY() is '
    + CONVERT(varchar(2),SCOPE_IDENTITY());
-- The next line is just a spacer for your print out
PRINT '';
/* The next line is going to blow up because the one column in
** the table is the primary key, and primary keys can't be set
** to NULL. SCOPE_IDENTITY() will be NULL because you just issued an
** INSERT statement a few lines ago, and the table you did the
** INSERT into doesn't have an identity field. Perhaps the biggest
** thing to note here is when SCOPE_IDENTITY() changed - right after
** the next INSERT statement. */
INSERT INTO TestChild2
VALUES
    (SCOPE_IDENTITY());
```

Code snippet Chap11.sql

How It Works

What you're doing in this script is seeing what happens if you depend on SCOPE_IDENTITY() directly rather than move the value to a safe place. When you execute the preceding script, everything's going to work just fine until the final INSERT. That final statement is trying to make use of SCOPE_IDENTITY() directly, but the preceding INSERT statement has already changed the value in SCOPE_IDENTITY(). Because that statement is on a table with no identity column, the value in SCOPE_IDENTITY() is set to NULL. Because you can't have a NULL value in your primary key, the last INSERT fails:

```
(1 row(s) affected)
The value you got originally from SCOPE_IDENTITY() was 1
The value currently in SCOPE_IDENTITY() is 1

(1 row(s) affected)
The value you got originally from SCOPE_IDENTITY() was 1
The value currently in SCOPE_IDENTITY() is NULL

Msg 515, Level 16, State 2, Line 41
Cannot insert the value NULL into column 'IDcol', table
    'Accounting.dbo.TestChild2'; column does not allow nulls. INSERT fails.
The statement has been terminated.
```

If you make just one little change (to save the original SCOPE_IDENTITY() value):

```
/******************************************
** This script illustrates how the identity
** value gets lost as soon as another INSERT
** happens
****************************************** */

DECLARE @Ident   int;  -- This will be a holding variable

/* You'll use it to show how you can
** move values from system functions
** into a safe place.
*/
INSERT INTO TestIdent
  DEFAULT VALUES;
SET @Ident = SCOPE_IDENTITY();
PRINT 'The value you got originally from SCOPE_IDENTITY() was ' +
CONVERT(varchar(2),@Ident);
PRINT 'The value currently in SCOPE_IDENTITY() is '
    + CONVERT(varchar(2),SCOPE_IDENTITY());

/* On this first INSERT using SCOPE_IDENTITY(), you're going to get lucky.
** You'll get a proper value because there is nothing between your
** original INSERT and this one. You'll see that on the INSERT that
** will follow after this one, you won't be so lucky anymore. */
INSERT INTO TestChild1
VALUES
  (SCOPE_IDENTITY());

PRINT 'The value you got originally from SCOPE_IDENTITY() was ' +
```

```
CONVERT(varchar(2),@Ident);
IF (SELECT SCOPE_IDENTITY()) IS NULL
   PRINT 'The value currently in SCOPE_IDENTITY() is NULL';
ELSE
   PRINT 'The value currently in SCOPE_IDENTITY() is '
      + CONVERT(varchar(2),SCOPE_IDENTITY());
-- The next line is just a spacer for your print out
PRINT '';
/* This time all will go fine because you are using the value that
** you have placed in safekeeping instead of SCOPE_IDENTITY() directly.*/
INSERT INTO TestChild2
VALUES
   (@Ident);
```

Code snippet Chap11.sql

This time everything runs just fine:

```
(1 row(s) affected)
The value you got originally from SCOPE_IDENTITY() was 1
The value currently in SCOPE_IDENTITY() is 1
(1 row(s) affected)
The value you got originally from SCOPE_IDENTITY() was 1
The value currently in SCOPE_IDENTITY() is NULL
(1 row(s) affected)
```

> **NOTE** *In this example, it was fairly easy to tell that there was a problem because of the attempt at inserting a* NULL *into the primary key. Now, imagine a far less pretty scenario — one where the second table did have an identity column. You could easily wind up inserting bogus data into your table and not even knowing about it — at least not until you already had a very serious data integrity problem on your hands!*

> **NOTE** *Up to this point, this entire example could have been written using* @@ IDENTITY *rather than* SCOPE_IDENTITY(), *and indeed in the prior edition of this book that's exactly how it was. The reason I prefer* SCOPE_IDENTITY() *for this general case is that the two functions behave differently in one important way. If an insert causes a trigger to fire and that trigger causes an insert into a different table containing another identity column,* @@IDENTITY *will pick up that value — it was created during the current connection.* SCOPE_IDENTITY() *will pick up only the insert done in the current batch scope. For most cases where the two differ,* SCOPE_IDENTITY() *is what's needed, and otherwise they're the same.*

Generating SEQUENCES

Sometimes an identity column is just too limiting when it comes to retrieving a sequence of values. Identities exist only within a single table. They never cycle or repeat numbers and their increments occur whenever anyone accesses the table — if you want to reserve a range of numbers from an identity column, forget it. What's more, to alter an identity (or the values within an identity column) is deliberately difficult. For the more general case of providing a number sequence, SQL Server 2012 now contains the SEQUENCE object.

A sequence returns the next value(s) requested, incremented by the value defined at creation. By virtue of its existence as an independent object, the next value from a sequence can be retrieved before an insert is performed (take that, identity!), be applied across multiple tables, be ordered by an arbitrary column list, and even cycle through to its minimum value once the maximum is reached, if desired.

Creating SEQUENCES

Before I talk about how mind-bogglingly useful a sequence can be, first let's look at how to create a sequence. The syntax for building a sequence object is:

```
CREATE SEQUENCE [schema_name.]sequence_name
        [ <sequence_property_assignment> [ ,...n ] ]
    [ ; ]

<sequence_property_assignment>::=
{
    [ AS { built_in_integer_type | user-defined_integer_type } ]
    | START WITH <constant>
        | INCREMENT BY <constant>
        | { MINVALUE <constant> | NO MINVALUE }
        | { MAXVALUE <constant> | NO MAXVALUE }
        | { CYCLE | NO CYCLE }
        | { CACHE [<constant> ] | NO CACHE }
}
```

Each of these elements, shown in Table 11-2, is pretty straightforward.

TABLE 11-2: SEQUENCE Syntax Elements

ELEMENT	DESCRIPTION
sequence_name	The sequence_name is the unique name of the sequence you're creating.
AS {type}	Sequences are always some kind of integer. The AS clause is optional; by default, any sequence you create are of type int. Other permitted types are tinyint, smallint, bigint (see a pattern?), decimal or numeric types with a scale of 0 — again, integers — and any user-defined type based on one of those integer types.

continues

TABLE 11-2 *(continued)*

ELEMENT	DESCRIPTION
START WITH <constant>	This constant is what you get the very first time you retrieve a number from the sequence. Because the sequence can only return values between its MINVALUE and MAXVALUE, this is required to be in that range. By default, the sequence starts with MINVALUE for an ascending sequence, and MAXVALUE for a descending sequence So if you want something else, this is the place to specify that.
INCREMENT BY <constant>	The sequence is incremented by this constant each time a number is retrieved from a sequence using the NEXT VALUE FOR function. If the constant provided is positive, the sequence is *ascending*; otherwise, it is *descending*. The INCREMENT BY cannot be 0 (thus enforcing the distinction between a sequence and a constant).
MINVALUE | NO MINVALUE	MINVALUE is the lowest value the sequence can hold. If you don't specify a MINVALUE, this is the lowest value the data type you're using can hold — even if it's negative. If you want to start counting at 1, this is a perfect place to say so (provided you've accepted the default for START WITH).
MAXVALUE | NO MAXVALUE	Like MINVALUE, MAXVALUE looks to the data type for its default. If your sequence doesn't cycle, attempts to read beyond MAXVALUE will produce an error.
CYCLE | NO CYCLE	Although NO CYCLE behaves like an identity (and is the default for sequences) — incrementing up to MAXVALUE and then throwing an error — a sequence set to CYCLE restarts from the minimum (for an ascending sequence) or maximum (for descending) once its limit is reached. Because this can repeat values, it's not that useful for an identity-replacement primary key, but it's great for partitioning data into a series of buckets.
CACHE [<constant>] | NO CACHE	If you're a performance wonk like I am, you know that going to disk when you don't really need to is a crime. Specifying a value for CACHE means the sequence won't return to the disk until that number of entries is retrieved from the sequence. It doesn't even eat up a lot of memory; instead of storing all the next values in cache, it just holds in memory the current value and how many more to deliver before hitting this disk. This is as safe as your server is stable; an unexpected shutdown may result in losing the rest of the cache.

Using Sequences

Sequences are the proactive solution to the problem that's solved reactively by SCOPE_IDENTITY().
The whole purpose of the identity value retrieval functions is to figure out, after the fact, what value
was assigned. Using a SEQUENCE object permits you to start with the value and save it to as many
places as you need. Let's look at how that can work.

First you'll create a similar set of tables to those you used before, this time adding a SEQUENCE
object.

```
CREATE TABLE TestSequence
(
  SeqCol    int    NOT NULL
  PRIMARY KEY
);

CREATE TABLE TestSeqChild1
(
  SeqCol    int
  PRIMARY KEY
  FOREIGN KEY
  REFERENCES TestSequence(SeqCol)
);

CREATE TABLE TestSeqChild2
(
  SeqCol    int
  PRIMARY KEY
  FOREIGN KEY
  REFERENCES TestSequence(SeqCol)
);

CREATE SEQUENCE SeqColSequence AS int
    START WITH 1
INCREMENT BY 1
MINVALUE 0;
```

Code snippet Chap11.sql

Remember the dance you had to perform using the identity to perform the insert into the parent
table, and then figure out exactly how to get the correct value into the child? Let's do that with the
Sequence tables.

```
DECLARE @Seq   int;  -- This variable will hold your Sequence value

-- Retrieve the next value in the sequence
SELECT @Seq = NEXT VALUE FOR SeqColSequence;

PRINT 'The value you got from SeqColSequence was ' +
CONVERT(varchar(2),@Seq);

/* Now you have the value of the next ID you're going to work with.
```

```
** Inserting that value into the parent and child tables becomes
** a simple matter of performing the inserts using the variable.  */

INSERT INTO TestSequence (SeqCol) VALUES (@Seq);

INSERT INTO TestSeqChild1 VALUES (@Seq);

INSERT INTO TestSeqChild2 VALUES (@Seq);
```

Code snippet Chap11.sql

When you used an identity column, the code had to

1. Declare a variable.
2. Insert the parent value.
3. Populate the variable with SCOPE_IDENTITY().
4. Insert the child values.

Using a sequence, the code changes to

1. Declare a variable.
2. Grab the next value in the sequence.
3. Insert the parent and child values.

Sequences are, for this situation, a little less error-prone and in my view a bit more intuitive than using identities. That said, this is a new object in SQL Server 2012, so despite its usefulness you should be prepared for the existence of a lot of identity columns out there. Code written before 2012 will certainly not use sequences, and old SQL developers take time to adopt new conventions.

Using @@ROWCOUNT

In the many queries that you ran up to this point, it's always been pretty easy to tell how many rows a statement affected — the Query window tells you. For example, if you run:

Available for
download on
Wrox.com

```
USE AdventureWorks
SELECT * FROM Person.Person;
```

Code snippet Chap11.sql

you see all the rows in Person, but you also see a count on the number of rows affected by your query (in this case, it's all the rows in the table):

```
(19972 row(s) affected)
```

But what if you need to programmatically know how many rows were affected? Much like SCOPE_IDENTITY(), @@ROWCOUNT is an invaluable tool in the fight to know what's going on as your script runs — but this time the value is how many rows were affected rather than your identity value.

Let's examine this just a bit further with an example:

```
USE AdventureWorks;
GO

DECLARE @PersonCount int;  --Notice the single @ sign
SELECT * FROM Person.Person;
SELECT @PersonCount = @@ROWCOUNT;
PRINT 'The value of @@ROWCOUNT was ' +
CONVERT(varchar(6),@RowCount);
```

Code snippet Chap11.sql

This again shows you all the rows, but notice the new line that you get on the Messages tab:

```
The value of @@ROWCOUNT was 19972
```

You'll take a look at ways this might be useful when you look at stored procedures later in the book. For now, just realize that this provides you with a way to learn something about what a statement did, and it's not limited to use SELECT statements — UPDATE, INSERT, and DELETE also set this value.

> **NOTE** *If you look through the example, you might notice that, much as I did with* SCOPE_IDENTITY(), *I chose to move the value off to a holding variable.* @@ROWCOUNT *is reset with a new value the very next statement, so, if you're doing multiple activities with the* @@ROWCOUNT *value, you should move it into a safe-keeping area.*

GROUPING STATEMENTS INTO BATCHES

A *batch* is a grouping of T-SQL statements into one logical unit. All of the statements within a batch are combined into one execution plan, so all statements are parsed together and must pass a validation of the syntax or none of the statements will execute. Note, however, that this does not prevent runtime errors from happening. In the event of a runtime error, any statement that has been executed prior to the runtime error will still be in effect. To summarize, if a statement fails at parse-time, nothing runs. If a statement fails at runtime, all statements until the statement that generated the error have already run.

All the scripts you have run up to this point are made up of one batch each. Even the script you've been analyzing so far in this chapter makes up just one batch. To separate a script into multiple batches, you make use of the GO statement. The GO statement:

> ➤ Must be on its own line (nothing other than a comment can be on the same line); there is an exception to this discussed shortly, but think of a GO as needing to be on a line to itself.

> ➤ Causes all statements since the beginning of the script or the last GO statement (whichever is closer) to be compiled into one execution plan and sent to the server independently of any other batches.

➤ Is not a T-SQL command, but, rather, a command recognized by the various SQL Server command utilities (sqlcmd and the Query window in the Management Studio).

A Line to Itself

The GO command should stand alone on its own line. Technically, you can start a new batch on the same line after the GO command, but you'll find this puts a serious damper on readability. T-SQL statements cannot precede the GO statement, or the GO statement will often be misinterpreted and cause either a parsing error or some other unexpected result. For example, if you use a GO statement after a WHERE clause:

Available for
download on
Wrox.com

```sql
SELECT * FROM Person.Person WHERE BusinessEntityID = 1; GO
```

Code snippet Chap11.sql

the parser becomes somewhat confused:

```
Msg 102, Level 15, State 1, Line 1
Incorrect syntax near 'GO'.
```

Each Batch Is Sent to the Server Separately

Because each batch is processed independently, an error in one batch does not prevent another batch from running. To illustrate, take a look at some code:

Available for
download on
Wrox.com

```sql
USE AdventureWorks;

DECLARE @MyVarchar varchar(50);   --This DECLARE only lasts for this batch!

SELECT @MyVarchar = 'Honey, I''m home...';

PRINT 'Done with first Batch...';

GO

PRINT @MyVarchar;   --This generates an error since @MyVarchar
                    --isn't declared in this batch
PRINT 'Done with second Batch';

GO

PRINT 'Done with third batch';   -- Notice that this still gets executed
                                 -- even after the error

GO
```

Code snippet Chap11.sql

If there were any dependencies between these batches, either everything would fail or, at the very least, everything after the point of error would fail — but it doesn't. Look at the results if you run the previous script:

```
Done with first Batch...
Msg 137, Level 15, State 2, Line 2
Must declare the scalar variable "@MyVarchar".
Done with third batch
```

Again, each batch is completely autonomous in terms of runtime issues. Keep in mind, however, that you can build in dependencies in the sense that one batch may try to perform work that depends on the first batch being complete — we'll see some of this in the next section when I talk about what can and can't span batches.

GO Is Not a T-SQL Command

Thinking that GO is a T-SQL command is a common mistake. GO is a command that is recognized only by the editing tools (Management Studio, sqlcmd). If you use a third-party tool, it might not support the GO command, but most that claim SQL Server support will.

When the editing tool encounters a GO statement, it sees it as a flag to terminate that batch, package it up, and send it as a single unit to the server — *without* including the GO. That's right, the server itself has absolutely no idea what GO is supposed to mean.

If you try to execute a GO command in a pass-through query using ODBC, OLE DB, ADO, ADO .NET, SqlNativeClient, or any other access method, you'll get an error message back from the server. The GO is merely an indicator to the tool that it is time to end the current batch, and time, if appropriate, to start a new one.

Errors in Batches

Errors in batches fall into two categories:

➤ Syntax errors

➤ Runtime errors

If the query parser finds a *syntax error*, processing of that batch is cancelled immediately. Because syntax checking happens before the batch is compiled or executed, a failure during the syntax check means none of the batch will be executed — regardless of the position of the syntax error within the batch.

Runtime errors work quite a bit differently. Any statement that has executed before the runtime error was encountered is already done, so anything that statement did will remain intact unless it is part of an uncommitted transaction. (Transactions are covered in Chapter 14, but the relevance here is that they imply an all or nothing situation.) What happens beyond the point of the runtime error depends on the nature of the error. Generally speaking, runtime errors terminate execution of the batch from the point where the error occurred to the end of the batch. Some runtime errors, such as a referential-integrity violation, will only prevent the offending statement from executing — all other statements in the batch are still be executed. This later scenario is why error checking is so important — I cover error checking in full in the chapter on stored procedures (Chapter 12).

When to Use Batches

Batches have several purposes, but they all have one thing in common — they are used when something has to happen either before or separately from everything else in your script.

Statements That Require Their Own Batch

There are several commands that absolutely must be part of their own batch. These include:

➤ CREATE DEFAULT

➤ CREATE PROCEDURE

➤ CREATE RULE

➤ CREATE TRIGGER

➤ CREATE VIEW

If you want to combine any of these statements with other statements in a single script, you need to break them up into their own batches by using a GO statement.

> **NOTE** Note that, if you DROP an object, you may want to place the DROP in its own batch or at least with a batch of other DROP statements. Why? Well, if you're going to later create an object with the same name, the CREATE will fail during the parsing of your batch unless the DROP has already happened. That means you need to run the DROP in a separate and prior batch so it will be complete when the batch with the CREATE statement executes.

Using Batches to Establish Precedence

Perhaps the most likely scenario for using batches is when precedence is required — that is, you need one task to be completely done before the next task starts. Most of the time, SQL Server deals with this kind of situation just fine — the first statement in the script is the first executed, and the second statement in the script can rely on the server being in the proper state when the second statement runs. There are times, however, when SQL Server can't resolve this kind of issue.

Let's take the example of creating a database together with some tables:

```
USE master;

CREATE DATABASE Test;

CREATE TABLE TestTable
(
    col1    int,
    col2    int
);
```

Code snippet Chap11.sql

Execute this and, at first, it appears that everything has gone well:

```
Command(s) completed successfully.
```

However, things are not as they seem — check out the INFORMATION_SCHEMA in the Test database:

```
USE Test;

SELECT TABLE_CATALOG
FROM INFORMATION_SCHEMA.TABLES
WHERE TABLE_NAME = 'TestTable';
```

Code snippet Chap11.sql

And you'll notice something is missing:

```
(0 row(s) affected)
```

Hey! Why was the table created in the wrong database? The answer lies in what database was current when you ran the CREATE TABLE statement. In this case, it happened to be the master database, so that's where the table was created.

 NOTE *Note that you may have been somewhere other than the master database when you ran this, so you may get a different result. That's kind of the point though — you could be in pretty much any database. That's why utilizing the* USE *statement is so important.*

When you think about it, this seems like an easy thing to fix — just make use of the USE statement, but before you test your new theory, you have to get rid of the old (okay, not that old) database:

```
USE MASTER;
DROP DATABASE Test;
DROP TABLE TestTable;
```

You can then run your newly modified script:

```
CREATE DATABASE Test;

USE Test;

CREATE TABLE TestTable
(
    col1    int,
    col2    int
);
```

Code snippet Chap11.sql

Unfortunately, this has its own problems:

```
Msg 911, Level 16, State 1, Line 3
Database 'Test' does not exist. Make sure that the name is entered correctly.
```

The parser tries to validate your code and finds that you are referencing a database with your USE command that doesn't exist. Ahh, now you see the need for batches. You need the CREATE DATABASE statement to be completed before you try to use the new database:

```
CREATE DATABASE Test;
GO

USE Test;
CREATE TABLE TestTable
(
    col1    int,
    col2    int
);
```

Code snippet Chap11.sql

Now things work a lot better. Your immediate results look the same:

```
Command(s) completed successfully.
```

But when you run your INFORMATION_SCHEMA query, things are confirmed:

```
TABLE_CATALOG
--------------------
Test
(1 row(s) affected)
```

Let's move on to another example that shows an even more explicit need for precedence.

When you use an ALTER TABLE statement that significantly changes the type of a column or adds columns, you cannot make use of those changes until the batch that makes the changes has completed.

If you add a column to your TestTable table in your Test database and then try to reference that column without ending the first batch, like so:

```
USE Test;

ALTER TABLE TestTable
  ADD col3 int;
INSERT INTO TestTable
  (col1, col2, col3)
VALUES
  (1,1,1);
```

Code snippet Chap11.sql

you get an error message — SQL Server cannot resolve the new column name, and therefore complains:

```
Msg 207, Level 16, State 1, Line 6
Invalid column name 'col3'.
```

Add one simple GO statement after the ADD col3 int, however, and everything is working fine:

```
(1 row(s) affected)
```

RUNNING FROM THE COMMAND PROMPT: SQLCMD

sqlcmd is a utility that allows you to run scripts from a command prompt in a Windows command box. This can be very nice for executing conversion or maintenance scripts, as well as a quick and dirty way to capture a text file.

sqlcmd replaces the older osql. osql is still included with SQL Server for backward compatibility only. An even older command-line utility — isql — is no longer supported, and you should be prepared for osql to follow it into oblivion.

The syntax for running sqlcmd from the command line includes a large number of switches, and looks like this:

```
sqlcmd
[{ { -U <login_id> [ -P <password> ] } | -E trusted connection }]

[ -N encrypt connection ][ -C trust the server certificate ]
[ -z <new password> ] [ -Z <new password> and exit]
[ -S <server name> [ \<instance name> ] ] [ -H <workstation name> ]
[ -d <database name> ]
[ -l <login timeout> ] [ -A dedicated admin connection]
[ -i <input file> ] [ -o <output file> ]
[ -f <codepage> | i: <codepage> [ < , o: <codepage> ] ]
[ -u unicode output] [ -r [ 0 | 1 ] msgs to stderr ]
[ -R use client regional settings]
[ -q "<query>" ] [ -Q "<query>" and exit]
[ -e echo input ] [ -t <query timeout> ]
[ -I enable Quoted Identifiers ]
[ -v var = "<value>"...] [ -x disable variable substitution ]
[ -h <headers> ][ -s <column separator> ] [ -w <column width> ]
[ -W remove trailing spaces ]
[ -k [ 1 | 2 ] remove [replace] control characters ]
[ -y <display width> ] [-Y <display width> ]
[ -b on error batch abort] [ -V <severity level> ] [ -m <error level> ]
[ -a <packet size> ][ -c <cmd end> ]
[ -L [ c ] list servers [clean output] ]
[ -p [ 1 ] print statistics [colon format]]
[ -X [ 1 ] ] disable commands, startup script,
              environment variables [and exit]
  [ -? show syntax summary]
```

The single biggest thing to keep in mind with these flags is that many of them (but, oddly enough, not all of them) are case sensitive. For example, both -Q and -q execute queries, but the first exits sqlcmd when the query is complete, and the second won't.

So, let's try a quick query direct from the command line. Again, remember that this is meant to be run from the Windows command prompt (don't use the Management Console):

```
SQLCMD -Usa -Pmypass -Q "SELECT * FROM AdventureWorks.Production.Location"
```

> **NOTE** The -P is the flag that indicates the password. If your server is configured with something other than a blank password (and it should be!), you'll need to provide that password immediately following the -P with no space in between. If you are using Windows authentication instead of SQL Server authentication, substitute an -E and nothing else in the place of both the -U and -P parameters (remove both, but replace with just one -E).

If you run this from a command prompt, you should get something like:

```
C:\>SQLCMD -E -Q "SELECT * FROM AdventureWorks.Production.Location"
LocationID Name                 CostRate      Availability ModifiedDate
---------- -------------------------- ------------ -----
         1 Tool Crib                               0.0000
    .00 1998-06-01 00:00:00.000
         2 Sheet Metal Racks                       0.0000
    .00 1998-06-01 00:00:00.000
         3 Paint Shop                              0.0000
    .00 1998-06-01 00:00:00.000
         4 Paint Storage                           0.0000
    .00 1998-06-01 00:00:00.000
         5 Metal Storage                           0.0000
    .00 1998-06-01 00:00:00.000
         6 Miscellaneous Storage                   0.0000
    .00 1998-06-01 00:00:00.000
         7 Finished Goods Storage                  0.0000
    .00 1998-06-01 00:00:00.000
        10 Frame Forming                          22.5000
  96.00 1998-06-01 00:00:00.000
        20 Frame Welding                          25.0000
 108.00 1998-06-01 00:00:00.000
        30 Debur and Polish                       14.5000
 120.00 1998-06-01 00:00:00.000
        40 Paint                                  15.7500
 120.00 1998-06-01 00:00:00.000
        45 Specialized Paint                      18.0000
  80.00 1998-06-01 00:00:00.000
        50 Subassembly                            12.2500
 120.00 1998-06-01 00:00:00.000
```

```
        60 Final Assembly                                    12.2500
120.00 1998-06-01 00:00:00.000
```

```
(14 rows affected)
```

```
C:\>
```

Now, let's create a quick text file to see how it works when including a file. At the command prompt, type the following:

```
C:\>copy con testsql.sql
```

This should take you down to a blank line (with no prompt of any kind), where you can enter in this:

```
SELECT * FROM AdventureWorks.Production.Location
```

Then press F6 and Return (this ends the creation of your text file). You should get back a message like:

```
1 file(s) copied.
```

Now retry your earlier query using a script file this time. The command line at the prompt has only a slight change to it:

```
C:\>sqlcmd -Usa -Pmypass -i testsql.sql
```

This should get you exactly the same results as you had when you ran the query using -Q. The major difference is, of course, that you took the command from a file. The file could have had hundreds — if not thousands — of commands in it.

TRY IT OUT   **Generating a Text File with sqlcmd**

As a final example of sqlcmd, let's utilize it to generate a text file that you might import into another application for analysis (Excel for example).

Back in Chapter 10, you created a view that listed yesterday's orders for you. First, you're going to take the core query of that view, and stick it into a text file:

```
C:\copy con YesterdaysOrders.sql
```

This should again take you down to a blank line (with no prompt of any kind), where you can enter this:

```
USE AdventureWorks

SELECT   sc.AccountNumber,
         soh.SalesOrderID,
         soh.OrderDate,
         sod.ProductID,
         pp.Name,
         sod.OrderQty,
         sod.UnitPrice,
         sod.UnitPriceDiscount * sod.UnitPrice * sod.OrderQty AS TotalDiscount,
```

```
                sod.LineTotal
FROM        Sales.Customer AS sc
INNER JOIN    Sales.SalesOrderHeader AS soh
        ON sc.CustomerID = soh.CustomerID
INNER JOIN    Sales.SalesOrderDetail AS sod
        ON soh.SalesOrderID = sod.SalesOrderID
INNER JOIN Production.Product AS pp
        ON sod.ProductID = pp.ProductID
WHERE CAST(soh.OrderDate AS Date) =
        CAST(DATEADD(day,-1,GETDATE()) AS Date)
```

Again press F6 and press Enter to tell Windows to save the file for you.

You now have a text file source for your query, and are nearly ready to have `sqlcmd` help you generate your output. First, however, you need there to be some data from yesterday. Note that none of the sample data is going to have data from yesterday unless you just ran the UPDATE statement you used in Chapter 10. This statement changes a block of orders to yesterday's date. Let's run that statement one more time (you can do this through the Query window if you like):

```
USE AdventureWorks

UPDATE Sales.SalesOrderHeader
SET OrderDate = CAST(DATEADD(day,-1,GETDATE()) AS Date),
    DueDate = CAST(DATEADD(day,11,GETDATE()) AS Date),
    ShipDate = CAST(DATEADD(day,6,GETDATE()) AS Date)
WHERE SalesOrderID < 43663;
```

Okay, now you have at least one row that is an order with yesterday's date. So you're most of the way ready to go; however, to get the results into a text file, you need to add some extra parameters to the sqlcmd command line — this time to tell SQL Server where to put the output:

```
C:\>sqlcmd -UMyLogin -PMyPass -iYesterdaysOrders.sql -oYesterdaysOrders.txt
```

There won't be anything special or any fanfare when sqlcmd is done running this — you'll simply get your Windows drive prompt again (C:\ most likely), but check out what is in the `YesterdaysOrders` `.txt` file now:

```
C:\>TYPE YesterdaysOrders.txt
```

This gives you just one row:

```
C:\>TYPE YesterdaysOrders.txt
AccountNumber SalesOrderID OrderDate                ProductID   Name
                                  OrderQty UnitPrice        TotalDiscount
      LineTotal
------------- ------------ ---------------------- ----------- -----------------
----------------------------------- -------- ---------------------- ----------------
------ ------------------------------------
AW00029825           43659 2011-12-31 00:00:00.000        776 Mountain-100 Blac
k, 42                              1         2024.9940
0.0000                    2024.994000
AW00029825           43659 2011-12-31 00:00:00.000        777 Mountain-100 Blac
```

```
k, 44                                    3                   2024.9940
0.0000                         6074.982000
AW00029825            43659 2011-12-31 00:00:00.000          778 Mountain-100 Blac
k, 48                                    1                   2024.9940
0.0000                         2024.994000
...
AW00029994            43662 2011-12-31 00:00:00.000          738 LL Road Frame - B
lack, 52                                 1                   178.5808
0.0000                          178.580800
AW00029994            43662 2011-12-31 00:00:00.000          766 Road-650 Black, 6
0                                        3                   419.4589
0.0000                         1258.376700
AW00029994            43662 2011-12-31 00:00:00.000          755 Road-450 Red, 60
                                         1                   874.7940
0.0000                          874.794000

(51 rows affected) C:\>
```

How It Works

You started out by bundling the SQL commands you would need into a single script — first, the USE command, and then the actual SELECT statement.

You then executed your statement using sqlcmd. The –U and –P commands provided the login username and password information just as they did earlier in the chapter. The –i parameter told sqlcmd that you had an input file, and you included that filename *immediately* following the –i parameter. Finally, you included the –o parameter to tell sqlcmd that you wanted the output written to a file (you, of course, and then provided a filename — YesterdaysOrders.txt). Don't get confused by the two files both named YesterdaysOrders — they are separate files with the .sql and .txt files separating what their particular use is for.

There is a wide variety of parameters for sqlcmd, but the most important are the login, the password, and the one that says what you want to do (straight query or input file). You can mix and match many of these parameters to obtain fairly complex behavior from this seemingly simple command-line tool.

DYNAMIC SQL: USING THE EXEC COMMAND

Okay, so all this saving stuff away in scripts is all fine and dandy, but what if you don't know what code you need to execute until runtime?

 NOTE As a side note, notice that you are done with sqlcmd for now — the following examples should be run utilizing the Management Console.

Generating Your Code on the Fly

SQL Server allows you, with a few gotchas, to build your SQL statement on the fly using string manipulation. The need to do this usually stems from not being able to know the details about something until runtime. The syntax looks like this:

```
EXEC ({<string variable>|'<literal command string>'})
```

Or:

```
EXECUTE ({<string variable>|'<literal command string>'})
```

As with executing a stored proc, whether you use the EXEC or EXECUTE makes no difference.

Let's build an example in the AdventureWorks database by creating a dummy table to grab dynamic information out of:

```sql
USE AdventureWorks;
GO

--Create The Table. You'll pull info from here for your dynamic SQL
CREATE TABLE DynamicSQLExample
(
    TableID     int   IDENTITY   NOT NULL
        CONSTRAINT PKDynamicSQLExample
                PRIMARY KEY,
    SchemaName  varchar(128)    NOT NULL,
    TableName   varchar(128)    NOT NULL
);
GO

/* Populate the table. In this case, you're grabbing every user
** table object in this database                              */
INSERT INTO DynamicSQLExample
SELECT s.name AS SchemaName, t.name AS TableName
    FROM sys.schemas s
    JOIN sys.tables t
      ON s.schema_id = t.schema_id;
```

Code snippet Chap11.sql

This should return a response something like:

```
(73 row(s) affected)
```

> **NOTE** To quote the old advertising disclaimer: "Actual results may vary." It's going to depend on which examples you've already followed along with in the book, which ones you haven't, and which ones you took the initiative and did a DROP on once you were done with them. In any case, don't sweat it too much.

Okay, so what you now have is a list of all the tables in your current database. Now let's say that you wanted to select some data from one of the tables, but you wanted to identify the table only at runtime by using its ID. For example, pull out all the data for the table with an ID of 25:

Available for download on Wrox.com

```
DECLARE @SchemaName    varchar(128);
DECLARE @TableName     varchar(128);

-- Grab the table name that goes with your ID
SELECT @SchemaName = SchemaName, @TableName = TableName
    FROM DynamicSQLExample
    WHERE TableID = 25;

-- Finally, pass that value into the EXEC statement
EXEC ('SELECT * FROM ' + @SchemaName + '.' + @TableName);
```

Code snippet Chap11.sql

If your table names went into the `DynamicSQLExample` table the way they did here (and bear in mind, they may not have), a `TableID` of 25 should equate to the `Production.UnitMeasure` table. If so, you should wind up with something like this (the rightmost columns have been snipped for brevity):

```
UnitMeasureCode Name                    ModifiedDate
--------------- --------------------    -----------------------
BOX             Boxes                   1998-06-01 00:00:00.000
BTL             Bottle                  1998-06-01 00:00:00.000
C               Celsius                 1998-06-01 00:00:00.000
...
...
PC              Piece                   1998-06-01 00:00:00.000
PCT             Percentage              1998-06-01 00:00:00.000
PT              Pint, US liquid         1998-06-01 00:00:00.000

(38 row(s) affected)
```

Understanding the Dangers of Dynamic SQL

Like most things that are of interest, using EXEC is not without its little trials and tribulations. Among the gotchas of EXEC are:

➤   It runs under a separate scope than the code that calls it — that is, the calling code can't reference variables inside the EXEC statement, and the EXEC can't reference variables in the calling code after they are resolved into the string for the EXEC statement. If you need to pass values between your dynamic SQL and the routine that calls it, consider using sp_executesql.

➤   By default, it runs under the same security context as the current user — not that of the calling object (an object generally runs under the context of the object's owner, not the current user).

➤   It runs under the same connection and transaction context as the calling object (I'll discuss this further in Chapter 14).

➤   Concatenation that requires a function call must be performed on the EXEC string prior to actually calling the EXEC statement — you can't do the concatenation of function in the same statement as the EXEC call.

➤ EXEC cannot be used inside a user-defined function.

➤ If you're not careful, EXEC can provide an attack vector for hackers.

Each of these can be a little difficult to grasp, so let's look at each individually.

The Scope of EXEC

Determining variable scope with the EXEC statement is something less than intuitive. The actual statement line that calls the EXEC statement has the same scope as the rest of the batch or procedure that the EXEC statement is running in, but the code that is performed as a result of the EXEC statement is considered to be in its own batch. As is so often the case, this is best shown with an example:

Available for
download on
Wrox.com

```
USE AdventureWorks;
/* First, you'll declare to variables. One for stuff you're putting into
** the EXEC, and one that you think will get something back out (it won't)
*/
DECLARE @InVar   varchar(50);
DECLARE @OutVar  varchar(50);

-- Set up your string to feed into the EXEC command
SET @InVar = '
SELECT @OutVar = FirstName FROM Person.Person WHERE BusinessEntityID = 1
';
-- Now run it
EXEC (@Invar);
-- Now, just to show there's no difference,
-- run the select without using a in variable
EXEC ('
SELECT @OutVar = FirstName FROM Person.Person WHERE BusinessEntityID = 1
');
-- @OutVar will still be NULL because you haven't been able to put anything in it
SELECT @OutVar;
```

Code snippet Chap11.sql

Now, look at the output from this:

```
Msg 137, Level 15, State 1, Line 1
Must declare the scalar variable "@OutVar".
Msg 137, Level 15, State 1, Line 1
Must declare the scalar variable "@OutVar".


-------------------------------------------------
NULL

(1 row(s) affected)
```

SQL Server wastes no time in telling you that you're a scoundrel and clearly don't know what you're doing. Why do you get a Must Declare error message when you have already declared @OutVar? Because you've declared it in the outer scope — not within the EXEC itself.

Let's look at what happens if you run things a little differently:

```
USE AdventureWorks;
-- This time, you only need one variable. It does need to be longer though.
DECLARE @InVar varchar(200);
/* Set up your string to feed into the EXEC command. This time you're going
** to feed it several statements at a time. They will all execute as one
** batch.
*/
SET @InVar = 'DECLARE @OutVar varchar(50);
SELECT @OutVar = FirstName FROM Person.Person WHERE BusinessEntityID  = 1;
SELECT ''The Value Is '' + @OutVar';
-- Now run it
EXEC (@Invar);
```

This time you get back results closer to what you expect:

```
-------------------------------------------------------------
The Value Is Ken
```

> **NOTE** *Notice the way that I'm using two quote marks right next to each other to indicate that I really want a quote mark rather than to terminate the string.*

So, what you've seen here is that you have two different scopes operating, and never the twain shall meet. There is, unfortunately, no way to pass information between the inside and outside scopes without using an external mechanism such as a temporary table or a special stored procedure called sp_executesql. If you decide to use a temp table to communicate between scopes, just remember that any temporary table created within the scope of your EXEC statement will only live for the life of that EXEC statement.

> **NOTE** *This behavior of a temp table only lasting the life of your EXEC procedure will show up again when you are dealing with triggers and sprocs.*

A Small Exception to the Rule

There is one thing that happens inside the scope of the EXEC that can be seen after the EXEC is done — system functions — so, things like @@ROWCOUNT can still be used. Again, let's look at a quick example:

```
USE AdventureWorks;

EXEC('SELECT * FROM Production.UnitMeasure');

SELECT 'The Rowcount is ' + CAST(@@ROWCOUNT as varchar);
```

This yields (after the result set):

```
The Rowcount is 38
```

Security Contexts and EXEC

This is a tough one to cover at this point because I haven't covered the issues yet with stored procedures and security. Still, the discussion of the EXEC command belonged here rather than in the sprocs chapter, so here you are (this is the only part of this discussion that gets wrapped up in sprocs, so bear with me).

When you give people the right to run a stored procedure, you imply that they also gain the right to perform the actions called for within the sproc. For example, let's say you had a stored procedure that lists all the employees hired within the last year. People who has rights to execute the sproc can do so (and get results back) even if they do not have rights to the Employees table directly. This is really handy for reasons you will explore later in the sprocs chapter.

Developers usually assume that this same implied right is valid for an EXEC statement also — it isn't. Any reference made inside an EXEC statement will, by default, be run under the security context of the current user. So, let's say I have the right to run a procedure called spNewEmployees, but I do not have rights to the Employees table. If spNewEmployees gets the values by running a simple SELECT statement, everything is fine. If, however, spNewEmployees uses an EXEC statement to execute that SELECT statement, the EXEC statement will fail because I don't have the rights to perform a SELECT on the Employees table.

Because you don't have that much information on sprocs yet, I'm going to bypass further discussion of this for now, but you will come back to it when I discuss sprocs later on.

Use of Functions in Concatenation and EXEC

This one is actually more of a nuisance than anything else because there is a reasonably easy workaround. Simply put, you can't run a function against your EXEC string in the argument for an EXEC. For example:

```
USE AdventureWorks;

-- This won't work
DECLARE @NumberOfLetters int = 15;
EXEC('SELECT LEFT(Name,' + CAST(@NumberOfLetters AS varchar)
        + ') AS ShortName
FROM Production.Product');
GO
-- But this does
DECLARE @NumberOfLetters AS int = 15;
DECLARE @str AS varchar(255);
SET @str = 'SELECT LEFT(Name,' + CAST(@NumberOfLetters AS varchar) + ')
    AS ShortName
FROM Production.Product';
EXEC(@str);
```

Code snippet Chap11.sql

The first instance gets an error message because the CAST function needs to be fully resolved prior to the EXEC line:

```
Msg 102, Level 15, State 1, Line 9
Incorrect syntax near 'CAST'.
```

But the second line works just fine because it is already a complete string:

```
ShortName
---------------
Adjustable Race
All-Purpose Bik
AWC Logo Cap
...
...
Women's Tights,
Women's Tights,
Women's Tights,
```

EXEC and UDFs

This is a tough one to touch on because I haven't gotten to user-defined functions as yet (that's coming in Chapter 13), but suffice to say that you are not allowed to use EXEC to run dynamic SQL within a UDF — period. (Using EXEC to run a sproc is, however, legal in a few cases.)

SQL Injection and EXEC

As a beginning programmer, many security-related issues aren't really yours to bother with just yet. Other people — such as your DBA — will be working hard to ensure your application architecture is secure, so that's largely not been a topic for this book. In this case, however, the danger is so clear that I'll make an exception.

When you use dynamic SQL, make sure you know that what's getting concatenated and run is code you'd approve of. To do that, make sure that user-supplied values are either scrubbed, or (by preference) not used at all in the SQL strings you're building. If you're executing code containing a user-entered string, well . . . you're running whatever a clever user wants you to run. That's one form of what's called a SQL Injection attack, and you can avoid it by making sure that whatever goes into your SQL strings is carefully controlled.

USING CONTROL-OF-FLOW STATEMENTS

Control-of-flow statements are a veritable must for any programming language these days. I can't imagine having to write my code where I couldn't change which commands to run depending on a condition. T-SQL offers most of the classic choices for control-of-flow situations, including:

➤ IF ... ELSE

➤ GOTO

➤   WHILE

➤   WAITFOR

➤   TRY/CATCH

There is also the CASE statement (aka SELECT CASE, DO CASE, and SWITCH/BREAK in other languages), but it doesn't have quite the level of control-of-flow capabilities that you've probably come to expect from other languages.

The IF . . . ELSE Statement

IF . . . ELSE statements work much as they do in any language, although I equate them closest to C in the way they are implemented. The basic syntax is:

```
IF <Boolean Expression>
    <SQL statement> | BEGIN <code series> END
[ELSE
    <SQL statement> | BEGIN <code series> END]
```

The expression can be pretty much any expression that evaluates to a Boolean.

> **NOTE** *This brings up one of the most common traps that I see SQL programmers fall into — improper user of* NULLs*. I can't tell you how often I have debugged stored procedures only to find a statement like:*
>
> ```
> IF @myvar = NULL
> ```
>
> *This will, of course, never be true on most systems (see below), and will wind up bypassing all their* NULL *values. Instead, it needs to read:*
>
> ```
> IF @myvar IS NULL
> ```
>
> *The exception to this is dependent on whether you have set the* ANSI_NULLS *option to* ON *or* OFF*. The default is that this is* ON*, in which case you'll see the behavior just described. Although you can change this behavior by setting* ANSI_NULLS *to* OFF*, I strongly recommend against this because it violates the ANSI standard. (It's also just plain wrong.)*

Note that only the very next statement after the IF is considered to be conditional (as per the IF). You can include multiple statements as part of your control-of-flow block using BEGIN . . . END, but I'll discuss that one a little later in the chapter.

To show off a simple version of this, let's run an example that's very common to build scripts. Imagine for a moment that you want to CREATE a table if it's not there, but to leave it alone if it already exists. You could make use of the EXISTS operator. (You may recall my complaint that the Books Online calls EXISTS a keyword when I consider it an operator.)

```
-- You'll run a SELECT looking for the table to start with to
-- prove it's not there
SELECT 'Found Table ' + s.name + '.' + t.name
    FROM sys.schemas s
    JOIN sys.tables t
        ON s.schema_id = t.schema_id
    WHERE s.name = 'dbo'
      AND t.name = 'MyIFTest';


-- Now you can run your conditional CREATE statement
IF NOT EXISTS (
    SELECT s.name AS SchemaName, t.name AS TableName
        FROM sys.schemas s
        JOIN sys.tables t
            ON s.schema_id = t.schema_id
        WHERE s.name = 'dbo'
          AND t.name = 'MyIFTest'
            )
    CREATE TABLE MyIFTest(
        Col1    int         PRIMARY KEY
        );

-- And now look again to prove that it's been created.
SELECT 'Found Table ' + s.name + '.' + t.name
    FROM sys.schemas s
    JOIN sys.tables t
        ON s.schema_id = t.schema_id
    WHERE s.name = 'dbo'
      AND t.name = 'MyIFTest';
```

Code snippet Chap11.sql

The meat of this is in the middle — notice that your CREATE TABLE statement runs only if no
matching table already exists. The first check you did on it (right at the beginning of the script)
found the table didn't exist, so you know that the IF is going to be true and your CREATE TABLE will
execute.

```
------------------------------------------------------------------

(0 row(s) affected)


------------------------------------------------------------------

Found Table dbo.MyIFTest

(1 row(s) affected)
```

The ELSE Clause

Now this thing about being able to run statements conditionally is just great, but it doesn't really deal
with all the scenarios you might want to deal with. Quite often — indeed, most of the time — when

you deal with an IF condition, you have specific statements you want to execute not just for the true condition, but also a separate set of statements that you want to run if the condition is false — or the ELSE condition.

> **NOTE** *You will run into situations where a Boolean cannot be evaluated — that is, the result is unknown (for example, if you are comparing to a NULL). Any expression that returns a result that would be considered as an unknown result will be treated as FALSE.*

The ELSE statement works pretty much as it does in any other language. The exact syntax may vary slightly, but the nuts and bolts are still the same; the statements in the ELSE clause are executed if the statements in the IF clause are not.

To expand the earlier example just a bit, let's actually print a warning message when you do not create a table:

```
-- Now you can run your conditional CREATE statement
IF NOT EXISTS (
    SELECT s.name AS SchemaName, t.name AS TableName
        FROM sys.schemas s
        JOIN sys.tables t
            ON s.schema_id = t.schema_id
        WHERE s.name = 'dbo'
          AND t.name = 'MyIFTest'
                )
    CREATE TABLE MyIFTest(
        Col1    int         PRIMARY KEY
        );
ELSE
    PRINT 'WARNING: Skipping CREATE as table already exists';
```

Code snippet Chap11.sql

If you have already run the preceding example, the table already exists, and running this second example should get you the warning message:

```
WARNING: Skipping CREATE as table already exists
```

Grouping Code into Blocks

Sometimes you need to treat a group of statements as though they were all one statement (if you execute one, you execute them all — otherwise, you don't execute any of them). For instance, the IF statement, by default, considers only the very next statement after the IF to be part of the conditional code. What if you want the condition to require several statements to run? Life would be pretty miserable if you had to create a separate IF statement for each line of code you wanted to run if the condition holds.

Thankfully, like most any language with an IF statement, SQL Server gives you a way to group code into blocks that are considered to all belong together. The block is started when you issue a BEGIN statement and continues until you issue an END statement. It works like this:

```
IF <Expression>
BEGIN   --First block of code starts here -- executes only if
        --expression is TRUE
   Statement that executes if expression is TRUE
   Additional statements
   ...
   ...
   Still going with statements from TRUE expression
   IF <Expression>   --Only executes if this block is active
      BEGIN
         Statement that executes if both outside and inside
            expressions are TRUE
         Additional statements
         ...
         ...
         Still statements from both TRUE expressions
      END
   Out of the condition from inner condition, but still
      part of first block
END   --First block of code ends here
ELSE
BEGIN
   Statement that executes if expression is FALSE
   Additional statements
   ...
   ...
   Still going with statements from FALSE expression
END
```

Notice your ability to nest blocks of code. In each case, the inner blocks are considered to be part of the outer block of code. I have never heard of there being a limit to how many levels deep you can nest your BEGIN...END blocks, but I would suggest that you minimize them. There are definitely practical limits to how deep you can keep them readable — even if you are particularly careful about the formatting of your code.

Just to put this notion into play, let's make yet another modification to table creation. This time, you're going to provide an informational message regardless of whether the table was created.

```
-- This time you're adding a check to see if the table DOES already exist
-- You can remove it if it does so that the rest of your example
-- can test the IF condition. Just remove this first IF EXISTS
-- block if you want to test the ELSE condition below again.

IF EXISTS (
     SELECT s.name AS SchemaName, t.name AS TableName
        FROM sys.schemas s
        JOIN sys.tables t
            ON s.schema_id = t.schema_id
        WHERE s.name = 'dbo'
```

```
            AND t.name = 'MyIFTest'
                )
        DROP TABLE MyIFTest;

-- Now you can run your conditional CREATE statement
IF NOT EXISTS (
    SELECT s.name AS SchemaName, t.name AS TableName
        FROM sys.schemas s
        JOIN sys.tables t
            ON s.schema_id = t.schema_id
        WHERE s.name = 'dbo'
            AND t.name = 'MyIFTest'
                )
    BEGIN
        PRINT 'Table dbo.MyIFTest not found.';
        PRINT 'CREATING: Table dbo.MyIFTest';
        CREATE TABLE MyIFTest(
            Col1    int    PRIMARY KEY
            );
    END
ELSE
        PRINT 'WARNING: Skipping CREATE as table already exists';
```

Code snippet Chap11.sql

Now, I've mixed all sorts of uses of the IF statement there. I have the most basic IF statement — with no BEGIN...END or ELSE. In the other IF statement, the IF portion uses a BEGIN...END block, but the ELSE does not.

 NOTE *I did this one this way just to illustrate how you can mix them. That said, I recommend you go back to my old axiom of "be consistent." It can be really hard to deal with what statement is being controlled by what IF...ELSE condition if you are mixing the way you group things. In practice, if I'm using BEGIN...END on any statement within a given IF, I use them for every block of code in that IF statement even if there is only one statement for that particular condition.*

The CASE Statement

The CASE statement is, in some ways, the equivalent of one of several different statements depending on the language from which you're coming. Statements in procedural programming languages that work in a similar way to CASE include:

➤ Switch: C, C#, C++, Java, php, Perl, Delphi

➤ Select Case: Visual Basic

➤ Do Case: Xbase

➤ Evaluate: COBOL

I'm sure there are others — these are just from the languages that I've worked with in some form or another over the years. The big drawback in using a CASE statement in T-SQL is that it is, in many ways, more of a substitution operator than a control-of-flow statement.

There is more than one way to write a CASE statement — with an input expression or a Boolean expression. The first option is to use an input expression that will be compared with the value used in each WHEN clause. The SQL Server documentation refers to this as a *simple CASE*:

```
CASE <input expression>
WHEN <when expression> THEN <result expression>
[...n]
[ELSE <result expression>]
END
```

Option number two is to provide an expression with each WHEN clause that will evaluate to TRUE/FALSE. The docs refer to this as a *searched CASE*:

```
CASE
WHEN <Boolean expression> THEN <result expression>
[...n]
[ELSE <result expression>]
END
```

Perhaps what's nicest about CASE is that you can use it "inline" with (that is, as an integral part of) a SELECT statement. This approach can actually be quite powerful.

A Simple CASE

A simple CASE takes an expression that equates to a Boolean result. Let's get right to an example:

Available for download on Wrox.com

```
USE AdventureWorks;
GO

SELECT TOP 10 SalesOrderID,
                SalesOrderID % 10 AS 'Last Digit',
                Position = CASE SalesOrderID % 10
                                WHEN 1 THEN 'First'
                                WHEN 2 THEN 'Second'
                                WHEN 3 THEN 'Third'
                                WHEN 4 THEN 'Fourth'
                                ELSE 'Something Else'
                            END
    FROM Sales.SalesOrderHeader;
```

Code snippet Chap11.sql

For those of you who aren't familiar with it, the % operator is for a *modulus*. A modulus works in a similar manner to the divide by (/), but it gives you only the remainder — therefore, 16 % 4 = 0 (4 goes into 16 evenly), but 16 % 5 = 1 (16 divided by 5 has a remainder of 1). In the example, because you're dividing by 10, the modulus gives you the last digit of the number you're evaluating.

Let's see what you get with this:

```
SalesOrderID Last Digit  Position
------------ -----------  --------------
43697        7            Something Else
43698        8            Something Else
43699        9            Something Else
43700        0            Something Else
43701        1            First
43702        2            Second
43703        3            Third
43704        4            Fourth
43705        5            Something Else
43706        6            Something Else

(10 row(s) affected)
```

Notice that whenever there is a matching value in the list, the THEN clause is invoked. Because you have an ELSE clause, any value that doesn't match one of the previous values is assigned whatever you've put in your ELSE. If you leave the ELSE out, any such value is given a NULL.

Let's go with one more example that expands on what you can use as an expression. This time, you'll use another column from your query:

```
USE AdventureWorks;
GO

SELECT TOP 10 SalesOrderID % 10 AS 'OrderLastDigit',
    ProductID % 10 AS 'ProductLastDigit',
    "How Close?" = CASE SalesOrderID % 10
        WHEN ProductID % 1 THEN 'Exact Match!'
        WHEN ProductID % 1 - 1 THEN 'Within 1'
        WHEN ProductID % 1 + 1 THEN 'Within 1'
        ELSE 'More Than One Apart'
    END
FROM Sales.SalesOrderDetail
ORDER BY SalesOrderID DESC;
```

Code snippet Chap11.sql

Notice that this one uses equations every step of the way, yet it still works:

```
OrderLastDigit ProductLastDigit How Close?
-------------- ---------------- --------------------
3              2                More Than One Apart
3              9                More Than One Apart
3              8                More Than One Apart
2              2                More Than One Apart
2              8                More Than One Apart
1              7                Within 1
1              0                Within 1
```

```
1               1               Within 1
0               2               Exact Match!
0               4               Exact Match!
(10 row(s) affected)
```

As long as the expression evaluates to a specific value type that is compatible with the input expression, it can be analyzed, and the proper THEN clause applied.

A Searched CASE

This one works pretty much the same as a simple CASE, with only two slight twists:

➤   There is no input expression (remember that's the part between the CASE and the first WHEN).

➤   The WHEN expression must evaluate to a Boolean value (whereas in the simple CASE examples you've just looked at, you used values such as 1, 3, and ProductID + 1).

Perhaps what I find the coolest about this kind of CASE is that you can completely change around what is forming the basis of your expression — you can mix and match column expressions, depending on your different possible situations.

As usual, I find the best way to get across how this works is via an example:

Available for
download on
Wrox.com

```
SELECT TOP 10 SalesOrderID % 10 AS 'OrderLastDigit',
    ProductID % 10 AS 'ProductLastDigit',
    "How Close?" = CASE
        WHEN (SalesOrderID % 10) < 3 THEN 'Ends With Less Than Three'
        WHEN ProductID = 6 THEN 'ProductID is 6'
        WHEN ABS(SalesOrderID % 10 - ProductID) <= 1 THEN 'Within 1'
        ELSE 'More Than One Apart'
    END
FROM Sales.SalesOrderDetail
ORDER BY SalesOrderID DESC;
```

Code snippet Chap11.sql

This is substantially different from those simple CASE examples, but it still works:

```
OrderLastDigit ProductLastDigit How Close?
-------------- ---------------- ------------------------
3               2               More Than One Apart
3               9               More Than One Apart
3               8               More Than One Apart
2               2               Ends With Less Than Three
2               8               Ends With Less Than Three
1               7               Ends With Less Than Three
1               0               Ends With Less Than Three
1               1               Ends With Less Than Three
0               2               Ends With Less Than Three
0               4               Ends With Less Than Three
(10 row(s) affected)
```

There are a few of things to pay particular attention to in how SQL Server evaluates things:

➤ Even when two conditions evaluate to TRUE, only the first condition is used. For example, the second-to-last row meets both the first (the last digit is smaller than 3) and third (the last digit is within 1 of the ProductID) conditions. For many languages, including Visual Basic, this kind of statement always works this way. If you're from the C world (or one of many similar languages), however, you'll need to remember this when you are coding; no "break" statement is required — it always terminates after one condition is met.

➤ You can mix and match what fields you're using in your condition expressions. In this case, you used SalesOrderID, ProductID, and both together.

➤ You can perform pretty much any expression as long as, in the end, it evaluates to a Boolean result.

Let's try this out with a slightly more complex example. In this example, you're not going to do the mix-and-match thing — instead, you'll stick with just the one column you're looking at (you could change columns being tested — but, most of the time, you won't need to). Instead, you're going to deal with a more real-life scenario that was part of a solution for a rather large e-commerce site.

The scenario is this: Marketing people really like nice, clean prices. They hate it when you apply a 10 percent markup over cost, and start putting out prices like $10.13, or $23.19. Instead, they like slick prices that end in numbers like 49, 75, 95, or 99. In this scenario, you're supposed to create a possible new price list for analysis, and they want it to meet certain criteria.

If the new price ends with less than 50 cents (such as the previous $10.13 example), marketing would like the price to be bumped up to the same dollar amount but ending in 49 cents ($10.49 for that example). Prices ending with 50 cents to 75 cents should be changed to end in 75 cents, and prices ending with more than 75 cents should be changed to end with 95 cents. Let's take a look at some examples of what they want:

IF THE NEW PRICE IS	THEN IT SHOULD BECOME
$10.13	$10.49
$17.57	$17.75
$27.75	$27.75
$79.99	$79.95

Technically speaking, you could do this with nested IF...ELSE statements, but:

➤ It would be much harder to read — especially if the rules were more complex.

➤ You would have to implement the code using a cursor (*bad!*) and examine each row one at a time.

In short — *yuck!*

A CASE statement is going to make this process relatively easy. What's more, you're going to be able to place your condition inline to your query and use it as part of a set operation — this almost always means that you'll get much better performance than you would with a cursor.

The marketing department has decided it would like to see what things would look like if you increased prices by 10 percent, so you'll plug a 10 percent markup into a CASE statement, and, together with a little extra analysis, you'll get the numbers you're looking for:

```
USE AdventureWorks;
GO

/* I'm setting up some holding variables here. This way, if you get asked
** to run the query again with a slightly different value, you'll have
** to change it in only one place.
*/
DECLARE @Markup     money;
DECLARE @Multiplier money;

SELECT @Markup = .10;                -- Change the markup here
SELECT @Multiplier = @Markup + 1;    -- You want the end price, not the
                                     -- amount of the increase, so add 1




/* Now execute things for your results. Note that you're limiting things
** to the top 10 items for brevity -- in reality, you either wouldn't do
** this at all, or you would have a more complex WHERE clause to
** limit the increase to a particular set of products
*/
SELECT TOP 10 ProductID, Name, ListPrice,
    ListPrice * @Multiplier AS "Marked Up Price", "New Price" =
    CASE WHEN FLOOR(ListPrice * @Multiplier + .24)
                > FLOOR(ListPrice * @Multiplier)
                    THEN FLOOR(ListPrice * @Multiplier) + .95
         WHEN FLOOR(ListPrice * @Multiplier + .5) >
                FLOOR(ListPrice * @Multiplier)
                    THEN FLOOR(ListPrice * @Multiplier) + .75
         ELSE FLOOR(ListPrice * @Multiplier) + .49
    END
FROM Production.Product
WHERE ProductID % 10 = 0  -- this is to reduce the number of rows affected
ORDER BY ProductID DESC;
```

Code snippet Chap11.sql

The FLOOR function you see here is a pretty simple one — it takes the value supplied and rounds down to the nearest integer.

Now, I don't know about you, but I get very suspicious when I hear the word "analysis" come out of someone's lips — particularly if that person is in a marketing or sales role. Don't get me wrong — those people are doing their jobs just like I am. The thing is, once they ask a question one way, they usually want to ask the same question another way. That being the case, I went ahead and set this up as a script — now all you need to do when they decide they want to try it with 15 percent is make a change to the initialization value of @Markup. Let's see what you got this time with that 10 percent markup though:

PRODUCTID	NAME	LISTPRICE	MARKED UP PRICE	NEW PRICE
990	Mountain-500 Black, 42	539.99	593.989	593.95
980	Mountain-400-W Silver, 38	769.49	846.439	846.49
970	Touring-2000 Blue, 46	1214.85	1336.335	1336.49
960	Touring-3000 Blue, 62	742.35	816.585	816.75
950	ML Crankset	256.49	282.139	282.49
940	HL Road Pedal	80.99	89.089	89.49
930	HL Mountain Tire	35	38.5	38.75
920	LL Mountain Frame – Silver, 52	264.05	290.455	290.49
910	HL Mountain Seat/Saddle	52.64	57.904	57.95
900	LL Touring Frame – Yellow, 50	333.42	366.762	366.95

Look these over for a bit, and you'll see that the results match what you were expecting. What's more, you didn't have to build a cursor to do it.

Looping with the WHILE Statement

The WHILE statement works much as it does in other languages to which you have probably been exposed. Essentially, a condition is tested each time you come to the top of the loop. If the condition is still TRUE, the loop executes again — if not, you exit.

The syntax looks like this:

```
WHILE <Boolean expression>
      <sql statement> |
[BEGIN
      <statement block>
      [BREAK]
      <sql statement> | <statement block>
      [CONTINUE]
END]
```

While you can just execute one statement (much as you do with an IF statement), you'll almost never see a WHILE that isn't followed by a BEGIN...END with a full statement block.

The BREAK statement is a way of exiting the loop without waiting for the bottom of the loop to come and the expression to be re-evaluated.

TO BREAK OR NOT TO BREAK?

I'm sure I won't be the last to tell you this, but using a BREAK is generally thought of as something of bad form in the classical sense. I tend to sit on the fence on this one. I avoid using them if reasonably possible. Most of the time, I can indeed avoid them just by moving a statement or two around while still coming up with the same results. The advantage of this is usually more readable code. It is simply easier to handle a looping structure (or any structure for that matter) if you have a single point of entry and a single exit. Using a BREAK violates this notion.

All that being said, sometimes you can actually make things worse by reformatting the code to avoid a BREAK. In addition, I've seen people write much slower code for the sake of not using a BREAK statement — bad idea.

The CONTINUE statement is something of the complete opposite of a BREAK statement. In short, it tells the WHILE loop to go back to the beginning. Regardless of where you are in the loop, you immediately go back to the top and re-evaluate the expression (exiting if the expression is no longer TRUE).

You can now try a short example here just to get your feet wet. As I mentioned, WHILE loops tend to be rare in non-cursor situations, so forgive me if this example seems lame.

What you're going to do is create a monitoring process using your WHILE loop and a WAITFOR command (you'll look at the specifics of WAITFOR in the next section). You're going to be automatically updating your statistics once per day:

Available for
download on
Wrox.com

```
WHILE 1 = 1
BEGIN
    WAITFOR TIME '01:00';
    EXEC sp_updatestats;
    RAISERROR('Statistics Updated for Database', 1, 1) WITH LOG;
END
```

Code snippet Chap11.sql

This would update the statistics for every table in your database every night at 1 AM and write a log entry of that fact to both the SQL Server log and the Windows application log. If you want check to see if this works, leave this running all night and then check your logs in the morning.

 NOTE *An infinite loop like this isn't the way that you would normally want to schedule a task. If you want something to run every day, set up a SQL Agent job using the Management Studio. In addition to not keeping a connection open all the time (which the preceding example would do), you also get the capability to make follow-up actions dependent on the success or failure of your script. Also, you can e-mail or net-send messages regarding the completion status.*

The WAITFOR Statement

There are often things that you either don't want to happen or simply can't have happen right this moment, but you also don't want to have to hang around waiting for the right time to execute something.

No problem — use the WAITFOR statement and have SQL Server wait for you. The syntax is incredibly simple:

```
WAITFOR
    DELAY <'time'> | TIME <'time'>
```

The WAITFOR statement does exactly what it says it does — that is, it waits for whatever you specify as the argument to occur. You can specify either an explicit time of day for something to happen, or you can specify an amount of time to wait before doing something.

The DELAY Parameter

The DELAY parameter specifies an amount of time to wait. You cannot specify a number of days — just time in hours, minutes, and seconds. The maximum allowed delay is 24 hours. So, for example:

```
WAITFOR DELAY '01:00';
```

runs any code prior to the WAITFOR, and then reaches the WAITFOR statement, and stops for one hour, after which execution of the code continues with whatever the next statement was.

The TIME Parameter

The TIME parameter specifies to wait until a specific time of day. Again, you cannot specify any kind of date — just the time of day using a 24-hour clock. Once more, this gives you a one-day time limit for the maximum amount of delay. For example:

```
WAITFOR TIME '01:00';
```

runs any code prior to the WAITFOR, reaches the WAITFOR statement, and then stops until 1 AM. After that point, execution of the code continues with whatever the next statement was after the WAITFOR.

Dealing with Errors with TRY/CATCH Blocks

In days of yore (meaning anything before SQL Server 2005), your error-handling options were pretty limited. You could check for error conditions, but you had to do so proactively. Indeed, in some cases you could have errors that would cause you to leave your procedure or script without an opportunity to trap it at all (this can still happen, but you have options that really cut down the instances where it does). I'm going to save a more full discussion of error handling for the stored procedures discussion in Chapter 12, but I'll touch on the fundamentals of the new TRY/CATCH blocks here.

A TRY/CATCH block in SQL Server works remarkably similarly to those used in any C-derived language (C, C++, C#, Delphi, and a host of others). The syntax looks like this:

```
BEGIN TRY
    { <sql statement(s)> }
END TRY
BEGIN CATCH
    { <sql statement(s)> }
END CATCH [ ; ]
```

In short, SQL Server will "try" to run anything within the BEGIN...END that goes with your TRY block. If, and only if, an error condition occurs that has an error level of 11–19, SQL Server exits the TRY block immediately and begins with the first line in your CATCH block. Because there are more possible error levels than just 11–19, Table 11-3 shows what you have there:

TABLE 11-3: SQL Error Levels

ERROR LEVEL	NATURE	DESCRIPTION
1–10	Informational only.	This includes things like context changes such as settings being adjusted or NULL values found while calculating aggregates. These will not trigger a CATCH block, so if you need to test for this level of error, you'll need to do so manually by checking @@ERROR.
11–19	Relatively severe errors.	These are errors that can be handled by your code (foreign key violations, as an example). Some of these can be severe enough that you are unlikely to want to continue processing (such as a memory exceeded error), but at least you can trap them and exit gracefully.
20–25	Very severe.	These are generally system-level errors. Your server-side code will never know this kind of error happened, as the script and connection will be terminated immediately.

Keep these in mind — if you need to handle errors outside the 11–19 level range, you'll need to make other plans.

Now, to test this out, you'll make some alterations to your CREATE script that you built back when you were looking at IF...ELSE statements. You may recall that part of the reason for your original test to see whether the table already existed was to avoid creating an error condition that might have caused your script to fail. That kind of test is the way things have been done historically (and there really wasn't much in the way of other options). With the advent of TRY/CATCH blocks, you could just try the CREATE and then handle the error if one were given:

Available for download on Wrox.com

```
BEGIN TRY
    -- Try and create your table
    CREATE TABLE MyIFTest(
        Col1    int        PRIMARY KEY
    );
END TRY
BEGIN CATCH
```

```
    -- Uh oh, something went wrong, see if it's something
    -- you know what to do with
    DECLARE @ErrorNo     int,
            @Severity    tinyint,
            @State       smallint,
            @LineNo      int,
            @Message     nvarchar(4000);
    SELECT
        @ErrorNo = ERROR_NUMBER(),
        @Severity = ERROR_SEVERITY(),
        @State = ERROR_STATE(),
        @LineNo = ERROR_LINE (),
        @Message = ERROR_MESSAGE();

    IF @ErrorNo = 2714 -- Object exists error, you knew this might happen
        PRINT 'WARNING: Skipping CREATE as table already exists';
    ELSE -- hmm, you don't recognize it, so report it and bail
    BEGIN
        PRINT @Message+' ErrorNo: '+CONVERT(NVARCHAR(5),@ErrorNo)
            + ' Severity: '+CONVERT(NVARCHAR(5),@Severity);
        RAISERROR(@Message, 16, 1 );
    END
END CATCH
```

Code snippet Chap11.sql

Notice I used some special functions to retrieve the error condition, so let's take a look at those in Table 11-4.

 NOTE *Also note that I moved them into variables that were controlled by me so they would not be lost.*

TABLE 11-4: System Functions to Retrieve the Error Condition

FUNCTION	RETURNS
ERROR_NUMBER()	The actual error number. If this is a system error, there will be an entry in the `sysmessages` table (use `sys.messages` to look it up) that matches to that error and contains some of the information you'll get from the other error-related functions.
ERROR_SEVERITY()	This equates to what is sometimes called "error level" in other parts of this book and Books Online. My apologies for the inconsistency — I'm guilty of perpetuating something that Microsoft started doing a few versions ago.

FUNCTION	RETURNS
ERROR_STATE()	I use this as something of a place mark. This is always 1 for system errors. When I discuss error handling in more depth in the next chapter, you'll see how to raise your own errors. At that point, you can use state to indicate things like at what point in your stored procedure, function, or trigger the error occurred (this helps with situations where a given error can be handled in any one of many places).
ERROR_PROCEDURE()	We did not use this in the preceding example because it is only relevant to stored procedures, functions, and triggers. This supplies the name of the procedure that caused the error — very handy if your procedures are nested at all — because the procedure that causes the error may not be the one to actually handle that error.
ERROR_LINE()	Just what it says — the line number of the error.
ERROR_MESSAGE()	The text that goes with the message. For system messages, this is the same as what you'll see if you select the message from the sys .messages function. For user-defined errors, it's the text supplied to the RAISERROR function.

In this example, I utilized a known error ID that SQL Server raises if you attempt to create an object that already exists. You can see all system error messages by selecting them from the sys.messages table function.

 NOTE *Beginning with SQL Server 2005, the* sys.messages *output got so lengthy that it's hard to find what you're looking for by just scanning it. My solution is less than elegant but is rather effective — I just artificially create the error I'm looking for and see what error number it gives me (simple solutions for simple minds like mine!).*

I simply execute the code I want to execute (in this case, the CREATE statement) and handle the error if there is one — there really isn't much more to it than that.

You will look at error handling in a far more thorough fashion in the next chapter. In the meantime, you can use TRY/CATCH to give basic error handling to your scripts.

SUMMARY

Understanding scripts and batches is the cornerstone to an understanding of programming with SQL Server. The concepts of scripts and batches lay the foundation for a variety of functions, from scripting complete database builds to programming stored procedures and triggers.

Local variables have scope for only one batch. Even if you have declared the variable within the same overall script, you will still get an error message if you don't re-declare it (and start over with assigning values) before referencing it in a new batch.

There are many system functions available. I provided a listing of some of the most useful system functions, but there are many more. Try checking out the Books Online or Bonus Appendix 1 at the back of this book for some of the more obscure ones. System functions do not need to be declared, and are always available. Some are scoped to the entire server, while others return values specific to the current connection.

You can use batches to create precedence between different parts of your scripts. The first batch starts at the beginning of the script, and ends at the end of the script or the first GO statement — whichever comes first. The next batch (if there is another) starts on the line after the first one ends and continues to the end of the script or the next GO statement — again, whichever comes first. The process continues to the end of the script. The first batch from the top of the script is executed first, the second is executed second, and so on. All commands within each batch must pass validation in the query parser, or none of that batch will be executed; however, any other batches will be parsed separately and will still be executed (if they pass the parser).

You saw how you can create and execute SQL dynamically. This can afford you the opportunity to deal with scenarios that aren't always 100 percent predictable or situations where something you need to construct your statement is actually itself a piece of data.

Finally, you took a look at the control-of-flow constructs that SQL Server offers. By mixing these constructs, you can conditionally execute code, create loops, or provide for a form of string substitution.

In the next couple of chapters, you will take the notions of scripting and batches to the next level, and apply them to stored procedures, user-defined functions, and triggers — the closest things that SQL Server has to actual programs.

EXERCISES

1. Write a simple script that creates two integer variables (one called `Var1` and one called `Var2`), places the values 2 and 4 in them, respectively, and then outputs the value of the two variables added together.

2. Create a variable called `MinOrder` and populate it with the smallest line item amount after discount for AdventureWorks `CustomerID` 1. (Careful: You're dealing with currency here, so don't just assume you're going to use an `int`.) Output the final value of `MinOrder`.

3. Use `sqlcmd` to output the results of the query `SELECT COUNT(*) FROM Sales.Customers` to the console window.

▶ **WHAT YOU LEARNED IN THIS CHAPTER**

TOPIC	CONCEPT
Scripts and batches	A script is a stored file full of T-SQL statements. A batch is a series of T-SQL commands that is run as a unit. A single script can contain one or more batches.
The USE statement	Used at the beginning of a batch to select the database context for the following statements.
Variables	Named with an @ sign and declared using DECLARE @variable_name followed by a data type, variables are scoped within a block of T-SQL code. You can set their values using SET or SELECT.
Retrieving IDENTITY values	When you insert a row that gets an identity value, you can retrieve that value using SCOPE_IDENTITY().
Sequences	Sequences return an ever-incrementing or cycling sequence of numbers, and are useful to replace identity columns among other things.
GO	The GO statement, which is not a part of T-SQL, is recognized by SSMS as a batch delimiter.
EXEC	Using the EXEC command, you can assemble T-SQL statements in plain text and cause the system to execute them. This is very dangerous, and should be done with great care.
IF...ELSE and WHILE	T-SQL has similar looping structures to other programming languages.
CASE	Chooses the first matching path from many options. Can be used inline within a single T-SQL statement.
TRY...CATCH	TRY will detect errors within a certain severity range and, instead of throwing the error back to the caller, will transfer control to the CATCH block, allowing you to perform error handling.

12

Stored Procedures

WHAT YOU WILL LEARN IN THIS CHAPTER:

➤ What a stored procedure is, and when you'll want to use one

➤ How to create, alter, and drop stored procedures

➤ Ways to pass input and output parameters

➤ Error handling

➤ Performance considerations

➤ How to use the debugger

Ah, the good stuff. If you're a programmer coming from a procedural language, this is probably the part you've been waiting for. It's time to get down to the main variety of code of SQL Server, but before you get going too far down that road, I need to prepare you for what lies ahead. There's probably a lot less than you're expecting and, at the very same time, a whole lot more. You've got the venerable T-SQL stored procedure capabilities, plus since SQL Server 2008, you've had .NET support — giving you a veritable "ooh la la!" of possibilities.

You see, a *stored procedure*, sometimes referred to as a *sproc* (which I usually say as one word, but I've sometimes heard pronounced as "ess-proc"), is really just something of a script — or more correctly speaking, a *batch* — that is stored in the database rather than in a separate file. Now this comparison is not an exact one by any means — sprocs have things, such as input parameters, output parameters, and return values, that a script doesn't really have, but the comparison is not that far off either.

For now, SQL Server's only "programming" language continues to be T-SQL, and that leaves you miles short of the kind of procedural horsepower that you expect when you think of a procedural or object-oriented programming language. However, T-SQL blows C, C++, Visual Basic, Java, Delphi, or whatever away when it comes to what T-SQL is supposed to do — work on data definition, manipulation, and access. But T-SQL's horsepower stops right about there — at data access and management. In short, it has an adequate amount of power to get most simple things done, but it's not always the place to do it.

This chapter doesn't focus too much on T-SQL's shortcomings — instead, it focuses on how to get the most out of T-SQL, and even includes a smattering of what .NET can add to the picture. I'll give you a look at parameters, return values, control of flow, looping structures, both basic and advanced error trapping, and more. In short, this is a big chapter that deals with many subjects. All of the major subject areas are broken into their own sections, so you can take them one step at a time, but let's start right out with the basics of creating a sproc.

CREATING THE SPROC: BASIC SYNTAX

You create a sproc pretty much the same way as you create any other object in a database, except that you use the AS keyword that you first saw when you took a look at views. The basic syntax looks like this:

```
CREATE PROCEDURE|PROC <sproc name>
    [<parameter name> [schema.]<data type> [VARYING] [= <default value>] [OUT [PUT]]
        [READONLY]
    [,<parameter name> [schema.]<data type> [VARYING] [= <default value>] [OUT[PUT]]
        [READONLY]
[,  ...
    ...
        ]]
[WITH
    RECOMPILE| ENCRYPTION | [EXECUTE AS { CALLER|SELF|OWNER|<'user name'>}]
[FOR REPLICATION]
AS
    <code> | EXTERNAL NAME <assembly name>.<assembly class>.<method>
```

As you can see, you still have the same basic CREATE <Object Type> <Object Name> syntax that is the backbone of every CREATE statement. The only oddity here is the choice between PROCEDURE and PROC. Either option works just fine, but as always, I recommend that you be consistent regarding which one you choose (personally, I like the saved keystrokes of PROC, but I do understand about the readability of PROCEDURE). The name of your sproc must follow the rules for naming as outlined in Chapter 1.

After the name comes a list of parameters. Parameterization is optional, and I'll defer that discussion until a little later in the chapter.

Last, but not least, comes your actual code following the AS keyword.

An Example of a Basic Sproc

Perhaps the best example of basic sproc syntax is to get down to the most basic of sprocs — a sproc that returns all the columns in all the rows on a table — in short, everything to do with a table's data.

TRY IT OUT | Creating a Basic Sproc

I would hope that by now you have the query that would return all the contents of a table down cold (Hint: SELECT * FROM...). If not, I suggest you return to the chapter on basic query syntax. In order to create a sproc that performs this basic query — go ahead and do this one against the Employee table (in the HumanResources schema) — you just add the query in the code area of the sproc syntax:

```
USE AdventureWorks
GO
CREATE PROC spEmployee
    AS
        SELECT * FROM HumanResources.Employee;
```

Code snippet Chap12.sql

How It Works

Not too rough, eh? If you're wondering why I put the GO keyword in before the CREATE syntax (if you were just running a simple SELECT statement, you wouldn't need it), it's because most non-table CREATE statements cannot share a batch with any other code. Indeed, even with a CREATE TABLE statement, leaving out the GO can become rather dicey. In this case, having the USE command together with your CREATE PROC statement would have been a no-no and would have generated an error.

Now that you have your sproc created, execute it to see what you get:

```
EXEC spEmployee;
```

You get exactly what you would have gotten if you had run the SELECT statement that's embedded in the sproc:

```
BusinessEntityID NationalIDNumber LoginID
---------------- ---------------- -------------------------------------------
1                295847284        adventure-works\ken0                     ---
2                245797967        adventure-works\terri0                   ---
3                509647174        adventure-works\roberto0                 ---
...
288              954276278        adventure-works\rachel0                  ---
289              668991357        adventure-works\jae0                     ---
290              134219713        adventure-works\ranjit0                  ---
  (290 row(s) affected)
```

> **NOTE** *Note that I've trimmed several columns from the right side of the result set (we can only fit so much in the width of a book!) — you'll get additional columns for things like* JobTitle*,* BirthDate*, and so on.*

You've just written your first sproc. It was easy, of course, and frankly, for most situations, sproc writing isn't nearly as difficult as most database people would like to have you think (job preservation), but there are lots of possibilities, and you've only seen the beginning.

CHANGING STORED PROCEDURES WITH ALTER

I'm going to admit something here — a great deal of the text you're about to read in this and the next section ("Dropping Sprocs") has simply been cut and pasted from the chapter on views. What I'm pointing out by telling you this is that they work almost identically from the standpoint of what an ALTER statement does.

The main thing to remember when you edit sprocs with T-SQL is that you are completely replacing the existing sproc. The only differences between using the ALTER PROC statement and using the CREATE PROC statement are:

➤ **ALTER PROC:** Expects to find an existing sproc, where CREATE doesn't.

➤ **ALTER PROC:** Retains any permissions (also often referred to as *rights*) that have been established for the sproc. It keeps the same object ID within system objects and allows the dependencies to be kept. For example, if procedure A calls procedure B and you drop and re-create procedure B, you no longer see the dependency between the two. If you use ALTER, it is all still there.

➤ **ALTER PROC:** Retains any dependency information on other objects that may call the sproc being altered.

The last of these three is the biggie.

> **NOTE** *If you perform a DROP and then use a CREATE, you have almost the same effect as using an ALTER PROC statement with one rather big difference — if you DROP and CREATE, you will need to entirely reestablish your permissions on who can and can't use the sproc.*

DROPPING SPROCS

It doesn't get much easier than this:

```
DROP PROC|PROCEDURE <sproc name>[;]
```

And it's gone.

PARAMETERIZING SPROCS

A stored procedure gives you some (or in the case of .NET, a *lot* of) procedural capability and also gives you a performance boost (more on that later), but it wouldn't be much help in most circumstances if it couldn't accept some data to tell it what to do. For example, it doesn't do much good to have a `spDeleteVendor` stored procedure if you can't tell it what vendor you want to delete, so you use an *input parameter*. Likewise, you often want to get information back out of the sproc — not just one or more recordsets of table data, but also information that is more direct. An example here might be where you update several records in a table and you'd like to know just how many you updated. Often, this isn't easily handed back in recordset form, so you make use of an *output parameter*.

From outside the sproc, parameters can be passed in either by position or by reference. From the inside, it doesn't matter which way they come in — they are declared the same either way.

Declaring Parameters

Declaring a parameter requires two to four of these pieces of information:

➤ The name

➤ The data type

➤ The default value

➤ The direction

The syntax is:

```
@parameter_name [AS] datatype [= default|NULL] [VARYING] [OUTPUT|OUT]
```

The name has a pretty simple set of rules to it. First, it must start with the @ sign (just like variables do). Other than that, the rules for naming are pretty much the same as the rules for naming described in Chapter 1, except that parameter names cannot have embedded spaces.

The data type, much like the name, must be declared just as you would for a variable — with a valid SQL Server built-in or user-defined data type.

 NOTE *One special thing in declaring the data type is to remember that, when declaring a parameter of type* CURSOR, *you must also use the* VARYING *and* OUTPUT *options. The use of this type of parameter is pretty unusual and well outside the scope of this book, but keep it in mind in case you see it in Books Online or other documentation and wonder what that's all about.*

Note also that OUTPUT *can be abbreviated to* OUT.

The default is another way parameters work (almost) just like variables. With variables, you can supply a default or not, and if you don't they're always initialized to a NULL value. Parameters, similarly, can have a default value or not. However, if you don't supply a default value, the parameter is assumed to be required, and a beginning value must be supplied when the sproc is called.

So, for example, let's try a slightly different version of the previous sproc. This time, you'll be supplying name information from the `Person.Person` table and accepting a filter for the last name:

```
USE AdventureWorks;

GO

CREATE PROC spEmployeeByName
    @LastName   nvarchar(50)
AS

SELECT p.LastName, p.FirstName, e.JobTitle, e.HireDate
FROM Person.Person p
JOIN HumanResources.Employee e
    ON p. BusinessEntityID = e.BusinessEntityID
WHERE p.LastName LIKE @LastName + '%';
```

Try this sproc supplying the required parameter:

```
EXEC spEmployeeByName 'Dobney';
```

Code snippet Chap12.sql

You get a very short list back (indeed, just one employee):

```
LastName      FirstName     JobTitle                       HireDate
------------  ------------  -----------------------------  ----------
Dobney        JoLynn        Production Supervisor - WC60   1998-01-26
```

 NOTE *Be careful using wildcard matches, such as the* `LIKE` *statement used in the preceding code. This particular example would likely perform okay because the wildcard is at the end. Keep in mind that wildcards used at the beginning of a search effectively eliminate the opportunity for SQL Server to use an index because any starting character is potentially a match.*

Now check what happens if you don't supply the default:

```
EXEC spEmployeeByName;
```

SQL Server wastes no time in informing you of the error of your ways:

```
Msg 201, Level 16, State 4, Procedure spEmployeeByName, Line 0
Procedure or Function 'spEmployeeByName' expects parameter '@LastName',
which was not supplied.
```

Because no default was provided, the parameter is assumed to be required.

Supplying Default Values

To make a parameter optional, you have to supply a default value. This looks just like you're initializing a variable: you just add an = together with the value you want to use for a default after the data type, but before the comma. Once you've done this, the users of your sproc can decide to supply no value for that parameter, or they can provide their own values.

So, for example, if you wanted to allow the parameter in the previous example to be optional, you just modify the parameter declaration to include a default:

```
USE AdventureWorks;

DROP PROC spEmployeeByName; -- Get rid of the previous version
GO
CREATE PROC spEmployeeByName
@LastName nvarchar(50) = NULL
AS
IF @LastName IS NOT NULL
    SELECT p.LastName, p.FirstName, e.JobTitle, e.HireDate
    FROM Person.Person p
    JOIN HumanResources.Employee e
        ON p.BusinessEntityID = e.BusinessEntityID
    WHERE p.LastName LIKE @LastName + '%';
ELSE
    SELECT p.LastName, p.FirstName, e.JobTitle, e.HireDate
    FROM Person.Person p
    JOIN HumanResources.Employee e
        ON p.BusinessEntityID = e.BusinessEntityID;
```

Notice how I used the control of flow constructs you learned in the previous chapter on scripting to decide which is the better query to run. The differences are subtle, with only the addition of a WHERE clause really differentiating the choices.

Given your new default, you can now run the sproc without a parameter:

```
EXEC spEmployeeByName;
```

Code snippet Chap12.sql

And, as expected, you get a more full result set:

```
LastName      FirstName     JobTitle                      HireDate
------------  ------------  ----------------------------  ----------
Sánchez       Ken           Chief Executive Officer       2003-02-15
Duffy         Terri         Vice President of Engineering  2002-03-03
Tamburello    Roberto       Engineering Manager           2001-12-12
...

...
Valdez        Rachel        Sales Representative          2007-07-01
Pak           Jae           Sales Representative          2006-07-01
Vakey Chudu   Ranjit        Sales Representative          2006-07-01

(290 row(s) affected)
```

If you were to run this with the same parameter (Dobney) as before, you would still wind up with the same results as you did before — the only change is that you've now allowed the parameter to be optional and handled the situation where the parameter was not supplied.

Creating Output Parameters

Sometimes you want to pass non-recordset information out to whatever called your sproc, perhaps to create a modified version of the last two sprocs, for example.

Perhaps one of the most common uses for this is with sprocs that do inserts into tables with identity values. Often the code calling the sproc wants to know what the identity value was when the process is complete.

To show this off, you'll utilize a stored procedure that is already in the AdventureWorks database — uspLogError. It looks like this:

```
-- uspLogError logs error information in the ErrorLog table about the
-- error that caused execution to jump to the CATCH block of a
-- TRY...CATCH construct. This should be executed from within the scope
-- of a CATCH block otherwise it will return without inserting error
-- information.
CREATE PROCEDURE [dbo].[uspLogError]
    @ErrorLogID [int] = 0 OUTPUT -- contains the ErrorLogID of the row
inserted
AS                                      -- by uspLogError in the ErrorLog table
BEGIN
    SET NOCOUNT ON;

    -- Output parameter value of 0 indicates that error
    -- information was not logged
    SET @ErrorLogID = 0;

    BEGIN TRY
        -- Return if there is no error information to log
        IF ERROR_NUMBER() IS NULL
            RETURN;

        -- Return if inside an uncommittable transaction.
        -- Data insertion/modification is not allowed when
        -- a transaction is in an uncommittable state.
        IF XACT_STATE() = -1
        BEGIN
            PRINT 'Cannot log error since the current transaction is in an
uncommittable state. '
                + 'Rollback the transaction before executing uspLogError in order
to successfully log error information.';
            RETURN;
        END

        INSERT [dbo].[ErrorLog]
            (
            [UserName],
            [ErrorNumber],
```

```
                    [ErrorSeverity],
                    [ErrorState],
                    [ErrorProcedure],
                    [ErrorLine],
                    [ErrorMessage]
                    )
            VALUES
                    (
                    CONVERT(sysname, CURRENT_USER),
                    ERROR_NUMBER(),
                    ERROR_SEVERITY(),
                    ERROR_STATE(),
                    ERROR_PROCEDURE(),
                    ERROR_LINE(),
                    ERROR_MESSAGE()
                    );

            -- Pass back the ErrorLogID of the row inserted
            SET @ErrorLogID = @@IDENTITY;
    END TRY
    BEGIN CATCH
        PRINT 'An error occurred in stored procedure uspLogError: ';
        EXECUTE [dbo].[uspPrintError];
        RETURN -1;
    END CATCH
END;
```

Note the sections that I've highlighted here — these are the core to your output parameter. The first declares the parameter as being an output parameter. The second makes the insert that utilizes the identity value, and, finally, the SET statement captures the identity value. When the procedure exists, the value in @ErrorLogID is passed to the calling script.

Let's utilize the TRY/CATCH example from the tail end of the last chapter, but this time you'll make the call to uspLogError:

```
USE AdventureWorks;

BEGIN TRY
-- Try to create your table
CREATE TABLE OurIFTest(
    Col1    int     PRIMARY KEY
    )
END TRY
BEGIN CATCH
    -- Uh oh, something went wrong, see if it's something
    -- we know what to do with
    DECLARE @MyOutputParameter int;

    IF ERROR_NUMBER() = 2714 -- Object exists error; we knew this might
happen
    BEGIN
        PRINT 'WARNING: Skipping CREATE as table already exists';
        EXEC dbo.uspLogError @ErrorLogID = @MyOutputParameter OUTPUT;
```

```
            PRINT 'An error was logged. The Log ID for your error was '
                    + CAST(@MyOutputParameter AS varchar);
    END
    ELSE    -- hmm, we don't recognize it, so report it and bail
        RAISERROR('something not good happened this time around', 16, 1 );
END CATCH
```

Code snippet Chap12.sql

If you run this in a database that does not already have the OurIFTest table, you will get a simple:

```
Command(s) completed successfully.
```

But run it where the OurIFTest table already exists (for example, run it twice if you haven't run the CREATE code before) and you get something to indicate the error:

```
WARNING: Skipping CREATE as table already exists
An error was logged. The Log ID for your error was 1
```

 NOTE *Note that the actual error log ID number you see will depend on whether the* ErrorLog *table has already had other errors inserted in it before you ran this test.*

Now run a little SELECT against the error log table:

```
SELECT *
FROM ErrorLog
WHERE ErrorLogID = 1; -- change this value to whatever your
                      -- results said it was logged as
```

And you can see that the error was indeed properly logged:

```
ErrorLogID  UserName    ErrorMessage
----------- ----------- ------------------------------------------------
1           dbo         There is already an object named 'OurIFTest' ...

(1 row(s) affected)
```

There are several things that you should take note of between the sproc itself and the usage of it by the calling script:

➤ **The OUTPUT keyword was required for the output parameter in the sproc declaration.**

➤ **You must use the OUTPUT keyword when you call the sproc, much as you did when you declared the sproc.** This gives SQL Server advance warning about the special handling that parameter will require. Be aware, however, that forgetting to include the OUTPUT keyword won't create a runtime error (you won't get any messages about it), but the value for the output parameter won't be moved into your variable (you'll just wind up with what was already there — most likely a NULL value). This means that you'll have what I consider to be the most dreaded of all computer problems — unpredictable results.

➤ **The variable you assign the output result to does *not* have to have the same name as the internal parameter in the sproc.** For example, in the previous sproc, the internal parameter in the error logging sproc was called @ErrorLogID, but the variable the value was passed to was called @MyOutputParameter.

➤ **The EXEC (or EXECUTE) keyword was required because the call to the sproc wasn't the first thing in the batch.** You can leave off the EXEC if the sproc call is the first thing in a batch. Personally, I recommend that you train yourself to use it regardless.

Confirming Success or Failure with Return Values

You'll see return values used in a couple of ways. The first is to actually return data, such as an identity value or the number of rows that the sproc affected. Consider this an evil practice from the dark ages. Instead, move on to the way that return values should be used and what they are really there for — determining the execution status of your sproc.

> **NOTE** *If it sounds like I have an opinion on how return values should be used, it's because I most definitely do. I was actually originally taught to use return values as a "trick" to get around having to use output parameters — in effect, as a shortcut. Happily, I overcame this training. The problem is that, like most shortcuts, you're cutting something out and, in this case, what you're cutting out is rather important.*
>
> *Using return values as a means of returning data back to your calling routine clouds the meaning of the return code when you need to send back honest-to-goodness error codes. In short — don't go there!*

Return values are all about indicating success or failure of the sproc, and even the extent or nature of that success or failure. For the C-style programmers among you, this should be a fairly easy strategy to relate to — it is a common practice to use a function's return value as a success code, with any non-zero value indicating some sort of problem. If you stick with the default return codes in SQL Server, you'll find that the same rules hold true.

How to Use RETURN

Actually, your program will receive a return value whether you supply one or not. By default, SQL Server automatically returns a value of zero when your procedure is complete.

To pass a return value back from the sproc to the calling code, simply use the RETURN statement:

```
RETURN [<integer value to return>]
```

> **NOTE** *Note that the return value must be an integer.*

Perhaps the biggest thing to understand about the RETURN statement is that it unconditionally exits from your sproc. That is, no matter where you are in your sproc, not one more line of code will execute after you have issued a RETURN statement.

By unconditionally, I don't mean that a RETURN statement is executed regardless of where it is in code. On the contrary, you can have many RETURN statements in your sproc, and they only execute when the normal conditional structure of your code issues the command. Once that happens, however, there is no turning back.

Let's illustrate this idea of how a RETURN statement affects things by writing a very simple test sproc:

Available for download on Wrox.com

```
USE AdventureWorks;
GO

CREATE PROC spTestReturns
AS
      DECLARE @MyMessage          varchar(50);
      DECLARE @MyOtherMessage     varchar(50);

      SELECT @MyMessage = 'Hi, it''s that line before the RETURN';
      PRINT @MyMessage;
      RETURN;
      SELECT @MyOtherMessage = 'Sorry, but you won''t get this far';
      PRINT @MyOtherMessage;
RETURN;
```

Code snippet Chap12.sql

> **NOTE** *Note that I didn't choose to initialize the two message variables in the declaration this time. Why? Well, in this case, I believe it makes for substantially more readable code if I keep the initialization on its own line — this is going to be true with most any string variable where the initial value is more than a few characters long.*

Okay, now you have a sproc, but you need a small script to test a couple of things. What you want to see is:

➤ What gets printed

➤ What value the RETURN statement returns

To capture the value of a `RETURN` statement, you need to assign it to a variable during your `EXEC` statement. For example, the following code assigns whatever the return value is to `@ReturnVal`:

```
EXEC @ReturnVal = spMySproc;
```

Now let's put this into a more useful script to test your sproc:

```
DECLARE @Return int;

EXEC @Return = spTestReturns;
SELECT @Return;
```

Code snippet Chap12.sql

Short but sweet — when you run it, you see that the `RETURN` statement did indeed terminate the code before anything else could run:

```
Hi, it's that line before the RETURN

-----------
0
(1 row(s) affected)
```

You also got back the return value for the sproc, which was zero. Notice that the value was zero even though you didn't specify a specific return value. That's because the default is always zero.

> **NOTE** *Think about this for a minute — if the return value is zero by default, that means that the default return is also, in effect, "No Errors." This has some serious dangers to it. The key point here is to make sure that you always explicitly define your return values — that way, you are reasonably certain to be returning a value you intended, rather than something by accident.*

Now, just for grins, let's alter that sproc to verify that you can send whatever integer value you want back as the return value:

```
USE AdventureWorks;
GO

ALTER PROC spTestReturns
AS
    DECLARE @MyMessage         varchar(50);
    DECLARE @MyOtherMessage    varchar(50);

    SELECT @MyMessage = 'Hi, it''s that line before the RETURN';
    PRINT @MyMessage
    RETURN 100;
```

```
    SELECT @MyOtherMessage = 'Sorry, but we won''t get this far';
    PRINT @MyOtherMessage;
RETURN;
```

Code snippet Chap12.sql

Now rerun your test script and you'll get the same result save for that change in return value:

```
Hi, it's that line before the RETURN

-----------
100
(1 row(s) affected)
```

MORE ON DEALING WITH ERRORS

Okay, so you got a taste of error handling at the end of the previous chapter when you looked at TRY/CATCH blocks. Indeed, those are the way to perform traditional error handling when you only need to support SQL Server 2005 and newer. There is, however, a lot more to think about in SQL Server errors and error handling than just TRY/CATCH. So let's take a bit deeper look at things. . . .

> **NOTE** *Sure. We don't need this section. I mean, my code never has errors, and your code never has errors, and we never run into problems, right? Okay, well, now that we've had our moment of fantasy for today, let's get down to reality. Things go wrong — it's just the way that life works in the wonderful world of software engineering. Fortunately, you can do something about it. Unfortunately, you're probably not going to be happy with the tools you have. Fortunately again, there are ways to make the most out of what you have, and ways to hide many of the inadequacies of error handling in the SQL world.*

Three common error types can happen in SQL Server:

➤ Errors that create runtime errors and stop your code from proceeding.

➤ Errors that SQL Server knows about, but that don't create runtime errors such that your code stops running (these can also be referred to as *inline* errors).

➤ Errors that are more logical in nature and to which SQL Server is essentially oblivious.

Now, here things get a bit sticky and versions become important, so hang with me as we go down a very much winding road. . . .

NOTE *As I write this, most SQL Server texts for 2012 are not out, but I'll go ahead and venture the same guess that was made for the 2008 version of this book under similar circumstances — that is, most beginning books will not discuss much in the way of prior versions. Indeed, I've generally avoided detailed discussion of how things were done in prior versions because it just adds more complexity. That said, I'm going to touch on prior versions in this section. Why? Well, there are still a lot of legacy installations out there, so many database developers will work with code that predates SQL Server 2005 (when* TRY/CATCH *was first introduced). Well, there was no formal error handler in SQL Server 2000 and earlier.*

With this is mind, I'm going to give you a slimmed-down version of how error handling used to be — if for no other reason than to help you grasp the "why they did it that way" in older code you may come across. If you're certain that you're going to be a "SQL Server 2005 code or newer only" kind of DBA — and, really, the odds are decent — by all means, feel free to skip this.

One thing remains common between the old and new error handling models — higher-level runtime errors.

It is possible to generate errors that cause SQL Server to terminate the script immediately. This was true prior to TRY/CATCH, and it remains true even in the TRY/CATCH era. Errors that have enough severity to generate a runtime error are problematic from the SQL Server side of the equation. TRY/CATCH logic is a bit more flexible for some errors than what you had prior to SQL Server 2005, but there are still times when your sproc doesn't even know that something bad happened because the sproc in question terminated immediately and without notice (at least not to the sproc itself) on the error. On the bright side, all the current data access object models pass through the message on such errors, so you know about them in your client application and can do something about them there.

> **THE WAY WE WERE . . .**
>
> In SQL Server 2000 and earlier, there was no formal error handler. You did not have an option that said, "If any error happens, go run this code over in this other spot." Instead, you had to monitor for error conditions within your code and then decide what to do at the point you detected the error (possibly well after the actual error occurred).

Handling Inline Errors

Inline errors are those pesky little things where SQL Server keeps running as such, but hasn't, for some reason, succeeded in doing what you wanted it to do. For example, try to insert a record into the `Person.BusinessEntityContact` table that doesn't have a corresponding record in the `BusinessEntity` or `Person` table:

```
USE AdventureWorks;
GO

INSERT INTO Person.BusinessEntityContact
            (BusinessEntityID
            ,PersonID
            ,ContactTypeID)
    VALUES
            (0,0,1);
```

Code snippet Chap12.sql

SQL Server won't perform this insert for you because there is a FOREIGN KEY constraint on both `BusinessEntityID` and `PersonID` that references other tables. Because there is not a matching record in both tables, the record you are trying to insert into `Person.BusinessEntityContact` violates both of those foreign key constraints and is rejected:

```
Msg 547, Level 16, State 0, Line 1
The INSERT statement conflicted with the FOREIGN KEY constraint
"FK_BusinessEntityContact_Person_PersonID". The conflict occurred in database
"AdventureWorks", table "Person.Person", column 'BusinessEntityID'.
The statement has been terminated.
```

Pay attention to that error 547 up there — that's something you can use.

> **NOTE** It's worth noting that just the first foreign-key violation shows up in the error SQL Server provided. This is because SQL Server got to that error, saw it, and knew there was no point in going further. If you fixed the first error, the second would be detected and you would again error out.

Making Use of @@ERROR

You already read some about this bad boy when you were looking at scripting, but it's time to get a lot friendlier with this particular system function.

To review, `@@ERROR` contains the error number of the last T-SQL statement executed. If the value is zero, no error occurred. This is somewhat similar to the `ERROR_NUMBER()` function you saw in the last chapter when you first discussed TRY/CATCH blocks. Whereas `ERROR_NUMBER()` is only valid within a CATCH block (and remains the same regardless of where you are within that CATCH block), `@@ERROR` receives a new value with each statement you execute.

> **NOTE** *The caveat with* @@ERROR *is that it is reset with each new statement. This means that if you want to defer analyzing the value, or you want to use it more than once, you need to move the value into some other holding bin — a local variable that you have declared for this purpose.*

Play with this just a bit using the INSERT example from before:

```
USE AdventureWorks;
GO

DECLARE    @Error    int;

-- Bogus INSERT - there is no PersonID or BusinessEntityID of 0. Either of
-- these could cause the error we see when running this statement.
INSERT INTO Person.BusinessEntityContact
            (BusinessEntityID
            ,PersonID
            ,ContactTypeID)
        VALUES
            (0,0,1);

-- Move our error code into safekeeping. Note that, after this statement,
-- @@Error will be reset to whatever error number applies to this statement
SELECT @Error = @@ERROR;

-- Print out a blank separator line
PRINT '';

-- The value of our holding variable is just what we would expect
PRINT 'The Value of @Error is ' + CONVERT(varchar, @Error);

-- The value of @@ERROR has been reset - it's back to zero
-- since our last statement (the PRINT) didn't have an error.
PRINT 'The Value of @@ERROR is ' + CONVERT(varchar, @@ERROR);
```

Code snippet Chap12.sql

Now execute your script and you can examine how @@ERROR is affected:

```
Msg 547, Level 16, State 0, Line 4
The INSERT statement conflicted with the FOREIGN KEY constraint
"FK_BusinessEntityContact_Person_PersonID". The conflict occurred in database
"AdventureWorks", table "Person.Person", column 'BusinessEntityID'.
The statement has been terminated.

The Value of @Error is 547
The Value of @@ERROR is 0
```

This illustrates pretty quickly the issue of saving the value from @@ERROR. The first error statement is only informational in nature. SQL Server has thrown that error, but hasn't stopped the code from executing. Indeed, the only part of that message that your sproc has access to is the error number. That error number resides in @@ERROR for just that next T-SQL statement; after that, it's gone.

> **NOTE** *Notice that* @Error *and* @@ERROR *are two separate and distinct variables and can be referred to separately. This isn't just because of the case difference. (Depending on how you have your server configured, case sensitivity can affect your variable names.) It's because of the difference in scope. The* @ *or* @@ *is part of the name, so the number of* @ *symbols on the front makes each one separate and distinct from the other.*

Using @@ERROR in a Sproc

Okay, so let's start with an assumption here: If you're using @@ERROR, the likelihood is that you are not using TRY/CATCH blocks. If you have not made this choice for backward compatibility reasons, I'm going to bop you upside the head and suggest you reconsider — TRY/CATCH is the much cleaner and all-around better way.

> **NOTE** TRY/CATCH *handles varieties of errors that in previous versions would have ended your script execution.*

That said, TRY/CATCH is out of the equation if backward compatibility with SQL Server 2000 or prior is what you need, so let's take a (very) quick look.

What I'm going to do is have you look at two short procedures. Both are based on things you have already done in scripting or in earlier stored-procedure examples, but now I want to show you how inline error checking works when it works, and how it doesn't when it doesn't (in particular, when inline does not work, but TRY/CATCH would).

Let's start with the referential integrity example you did earlier in this chapter:

Available for
download on
Wrox.com

```
USE AdventureWorks;
GO

INSERT INTO Person.BusinessEntityContact
            (BusinessEntityID
            ,PersonID
            ,ContactTypeID)
        VALUES(0,0,1);
```

Code snippet Chap12.sql

You may recall this got you a simple 547 error. This error is trappable. You could trap this in a simple script, but let's do it as a sproc since procedural stuff is supposedly what you're working on here.

```
USE AdventureWorks
GO

CREATE PROC spInsertValidatedBusinessEntityContact
    @BusinessEntityID int,
    @PersonID int,
    @ContactTypeID int
AS
BEGIN

    DECLARE @Error int;

    INSERT INTO Person.BusinessEntityContact
        (BusinessEntityID
        ,PersonID
        ,ContactTypeID)
    VALUES
        (@BusinessEntityID, @PersonID, @ContactTypeID);

    SET @Error = @@ERROR;

    IF @Error = 0
        PRINT 'New Record Inserted';
    ELSE
    BEGIN
        IF @Error = 547 -- Foreign Key violation. Tell them about it.
            PRINT 'At least one provided parameter was not found. Correct and retry';
        ELSE -- something unknown
            PRINT 'Unknown error occurred. Please contact your system admin';
    END
END
```

Now try executing this with values that work:

```
EXEC spInsertValidatedBusinessEntityContact 1, 1, 11;
```

Your insert happens correctly, so no error condition is detected (because there isn't one).

```
(1 row(s) affected)
New Record Inserted
```

Now, try something that should blow up:

```
EXEC spInsertValidatedBusinessEntityContact 0, 1, 11;
```

Code snippet Chap12.sql

And you see not only the actual SQL Server message but the message from your error trap. Note that there is no way, by using inline error checking, to squelch the SQL Server message; doing that requires TRY/CATCH.

```
Msg 547, Level 16, State 0, Procedure spInsertValidatedBusinessEntityContact, Line
11
The INSERT statement conflicted with the FOREIGN KEY constraint
"FK_BusinessEntityContact_Person_PersonID". The conflict occurred in database
"AdventureWorks", table "Person.Person", column 'BusinessEntityID'.
The statement has been terminated.
At least one provided parameter was not found. Correct and retry
```

As you can see, you could detect the error without a TRY/CATCH block.

Now, let's move on to an example of why TRY/CATCH is better — a situation where a TRY/CATCH works fine, but where inline error checking fails. To show this one off, all you need to do is use the same example for TRY/CATCH that you saw in the scripting chapter. It looked like this:

```
BEGIN TRY
    -- Try and create our table
    CREATE TABLE OurIFTest(
        Col1    int         PRIMARY KEY
        )
END TRY
BEGIN CATCH
    -- Uh oh, something went wrong, see if it's something
    -- we know what to do with
    DECLARE @ErrorNo    int,
            @Severity   tinyint,
            @State      smallint,
            @LineNo     int,
            @Message    nvarchar(4000);
    SELECT
        @ErrorNo = ERROR_NUMBER(),
        @Severity = ERROR_SEVERITY(),
        @State = ERROR_STATE(),
        @LineNo = ERROR_LINE (),
        @Message = ERROR_MESSAGE();

    IF @ErrorNo = 2714 -- Object exists error, we knew this might happen
        PRINT 'WARNING: Skipping CREATE as table already exists';
    ELSE -- hmm, we don't recognize it, so report it and bail
        RAISERROR(@Message, 16, 1 );
END CATCH
```

It worked just fine. But if you try to do this using inline error checking, you'll have a problem:

```
CREATE TABLE OurIFTest(
    Col1    int         PRIMARY KEY
    );
IF @@ERROR != 0
    PRINT 'Problems!';
ELSE
    PRINT 'Everything went OK!';
```

Code snippet Chap12.sql

Run this (you'll need to run it twice to generate the error if the table isn't already there) and you'll quickly find out that, without the TRY block, SQL Server aborts the script entirely on the particular error you're generating here:

```
Msg 2714, Level 16, State 6, Line 2
There is already an object named 'OurIFTest' in the database.
```

Notice that your PRINT statements never got a chance to execute — SQL Server had already terminated processing. With TRY/CATCH you could trap and handle this error, but using inline error checking, your attempts to trap an error like this will fail.

Handling Errors Before They Happen

Sometimes you have errors that SQL Server doesn't really have an effective way to even know about, let alone tell you about. Other times you want to prevent the errors before they happen. These you need to check for and handle yourself.

To try this out, let's make a new version of an existing sproc in AdventureWorks called HumanResources .uspUpdateEmployeeHireInfo — you can call yours HumanResources.uspUpdateEmployeeHireInfo2. In this, you'll address some business rules that are logical in nature, but not necessarily implemented in the database (or, in this case, even possible to handle with constraints). Let's start by taking a look at the existing sproc:

Available for download on Wrox.com

```
USE AdventureWorks;
GO

CREATE PROCEDURE HumanResources.uspUpdateEmployeeHireInfo2
    @BusinessEntityID int,
    @JobTitle nvarchar(50),
    @HireDate datetime,
    @RateChangeDate datetime,
    @Rate money,
    @PayFrequency tinyint,
    @CurrentFlag dbo.Flag
WITH EXECUTE AS CALLER
AS
BEGIN
    SET NOCOUNT ON;

    BEGIN TRY
        BEGIN TRANSACTION;

        UPDATE HumanResources.Employee
        SET JobTitle = @JobTitle,
            HireDate = @HireDate,
            CurrentFlag = @CurrentFlag
        WHERE BusinessEntityID = @BusinessEntityID;

        INSERT INTO HumanResources.EmployeePayHistory
            (BusinessEntityID,
             RateChangeDate,
```

```
            Rate,
            PayFrequency)
        VALUES (@BusinessEntityID, @RateChangeDate, @Rate, @PayFrequency);

        COMMIT TRANSACTION;
    END TRY
    BEGIN CATCH
        -- Rollback any active or uncommittable transactions before
        -- inserting information in the ErrorLog
        IF @@TRANCOUNT > 0
        BEGIN
            ROLLBACK TRANSACTION;
        END

        EXECUTE dbo.uspLogError;
    END CATCH;
END;
```

Code snippet Chap12.sql

What's going on in this sproc is pretty straightforward: There are two statements (one to update the existing employee record and one to handle the additional history record) plus a very generic error handler. What you get to do is add some new code to this sproc to recognize some specific errors that might occur and provide return values that will notify the client with context-sensitive error information. I won't ask you to take the time to trap every potential error here, but you can quickly catch some basics just to see how things might work. (Feel free to explore further on your own.)

The error handler in this sproc is very generic and doesn't really do anything that is specific to this particular sproc, so let's start by considering some of the errors that might occur in this sproc, for example:

➤ **An employee whose** `BusinessEntityID` **doesn't already exist:** The `UPDATE` statement in the sproc actually runs just fine (no errors) without a valid `BusinessEntityID`. It just fails to find a match and winds up affecting zero rows; the error here is logical in nature, and SQL Server sees no problem with it at all. You should detect this condition yourself and trap it at this point before the sproc continues (because there is a foreign key between `EmployeePayHistory` and `Employee`, SQL Server winds up raising an error on the `INSERT` statement when it can't find a matching `BusinessEntityID`).

➤ **Two updates affecting the same** `BusinessEntityID` **at the same** `RateChangeDate`: Again, the `UPDATE` statement has no issues with such an update, but the `INSERT` statement does (the primary key for `EmployeePayHistory` is the composite of `BusinessEntityID` and `RateChangeDate`).

Let's address each of these in a new version of the sproc.

First, there's some groundwork to lay. While SQL Server doesn't really have the concept of a constant, I'm going to use some variables as though they are constants. By doing so, I'll get away from just returning numbers and, instead, return a variable name that makes my code more readable by indicating the nature of the error I'm returning.

```
...
...
SET NOCOUNT ON;

-- Set up "constants" for error codes
DECLARE @BUSINESS_ENTITY_ID_NOT_FOUND int = -1000,
        @DUPLICATE_RATE_CHANGE int = -2000;

BEGIN TRY
...
...
```

> **NOTE** *You may be curious as to why I'm using negative values here for my errors. Although there is no real standard on such things, I tend to use positive values for return codes that are informational in nature (perhaps there are multiple possible successful outcomes and I want to indicate which successful outcome occurred) and negative values for errors. You can find your own path on such things; just make sure you follow the cardinal rule — be consistent! Also, I am deliberately using the initialization syntax that became available in SQL Server 2008. If you're working with older versions, you'll need other syntax (you would change the declare to* `DECLARE @BUSINESS_ENTITY_ID_NOT_FOUND int;` `SET @BUSINESS_ENTITY_ID_NOT_FOUND = -1000;`*). That is purely for backward compatibility reasons, so adjust accordingly.*

Next, you can test how many rows were affected by the UPDATE to HumanResources.Employee and utilize that to detect a BusinessEntityID Not Found error:

```
...
...
UPDATE HumanResources.Employee
SET JobTitle = @JobTitle,
    HireDate = @HireDate,
    CurrentFlag = @CurrentFlag
WHERE BusinessEntityID = @BusinessEntityID;

IF @@ROWCOUNT > 0
-- things happened as expected
  INSERT INTO HumanResources.EmployeePayHistory
      (BusinessEntityID,
       RateChangeDate,
       Rate,
       PayFrequency)
  VALUES (@BusinessEntityID, @RateChangeDate, @Rate, @PayFrequency);
ELSE
```

```
-- ruh roh, the update didn't happen, so skip the insert,
-- set the return value and exit
BEGIN
    PRINT 'BusinessEntityID Not Found';
    ROLLBACK TRAN;
    RETURN @BUSINESS_ENTITY_ID_NOT_FOUND;
END
   . . .
   . . .
```

NOTE Note the removal of the `HireDate` column from the `UPDATE`.

As I mentioned earlier, the `RETURN` immediately exits the sproc supplying the return value provided (in this case, `-1000` — the amount matching your variable). Your client application can now test the return value and match it against a known list of possible errors.

NOTE If you plan to use constant error codes, do something to enforce the link between your values and the ones in your client application. SQL Server still doesn't have a genuine "constant" type, so you're left to your own devices on this, but at the very least draw your values from a common spreadsheet. Another possible solution might be a lookup table of error values that is used by both the sprocs and the application code.

Now you can move on to the second potential error. You have a couple of ways you can handle this. You could pre-query the `EmployeePayHistory` table to see if it already has a matching row, and then avoid the `INSERT` entirely. Alternatively, you can just allow SQL Server to detect the error and just beef up the error handler to address that known possibility. In this case, I'm going to opt for the latter. As I've suggested before, it is almost always better to treat the rule and handle the exception. I'd like to think that this particular error will occur very infrequently, so you can largely assume it isn't going to happen and address it when it does. With this in mind, you only need to make some alterations to your error handler:

```
   . . .
   . . .
BEGIN CATCH
    -- Rollback any active or uncommittable transactions before
    -- inserting information in the ErrorLog
    IF @@TRANCOUNT > 0
    BEGIN
        ROLLBACK TRANSACTION;
    END

    EXECUTE dbo.uspLogError;

    IF ERROR_NUMBER() = 2627    -- Primary Key violation
```

```
      BEGIN
            PRINT 'Duplicate Rate Change Found';
            RETURN @DUPLICATE_RATE_CHANGE;
      END
   END CATCH;
   ...
   ...
```

Okay, so with all these changes in place, let's take a look at your new overall sproc. While this is a new sproc, I'm highlighting only those lines that change versus the original you cloned it from:

Available for
download on
Wrox.com

```
CREATE PROCEDURE HumanResources.uspEmployeeHireInfo2</codeScreen>
      @BusinessEntityID [int],
      @JobTitle [nvarchar](50),
      @HireDate [datetime],
      @RateChangeDate [datetime],
      @Rate [money],
      @PayFrequency [tinyint],
      @CurrentFlag [dbo].[Flag]
WITH EXECUTE AS CALLER
AS
BEGIN
      SET NOCOUNT ON;

      -- Set up "constants" for error codes
      DECLARE @BUSINESS_ENTITY_ID_NOT_FOUND int = -1000,
            @DUPLICATE_RATE_CHANGE          int = -2000;

   BEGIN TRY
      BEGIN TRANSACTION;

      UPDATE HumanResources.Employee
      SET JobTitle = @JobTitle,
         HireDate = @HireDate,
         CurrentFlag = @CurrentFlag
      WHERE BusinessEntityID = @BusinessEntityID;

      IF @@ROWCOUNT > 0
      -- things happened as expected
        INSERT INTO HumanResources.EmployeePayHistory
           (BusinessEntityID,
            RateChangeDate,
            Rate,
            PayFrequency)
        VALUES
           (@BusinessEntityID,
            @RateChangeDate,
            @Rate,
            @PayFrequency);
      ELSE
      -- ruh roh, the update didn't happen, so skip the insert,
      -- set the return value and exit
      BEGIN
        PRINT 'BusinessEntityID Not Found';
```

```
            ROLLBACK TRAN;
            RETURN @BUSINESS_ENTITY_ID_NOT_FOUND;
        END

            COMMIT TRANSACTION;
    END TRY
    BEGIN CATCH
        -- Rollback any active or uncommittable transactions before
        -- inserting information in the ErrorLog
        IF @@TRANCOUNT > 0
        BEGIN
            ROLLBACK TRANSACTION;
        END

        EXECUTE dbo.uspLogError;

        IF ERROR_NUMBER() = 2627    -- Primary Key violation
        BEGIN
            PRINT 'Duplicate Rate Change Found';
            RETURN @DUPLICATE_RATE_CHANGE;
        END
    END CATCH;
END;
```

Code snippet Chap12.sql

Go ahead and run this once:

```
DECLARE @Return int;

EXEC @Return = HumanResources.uspEmployeeHireInfo2
    @BusinessEntityID = 1,
    @JobTitle = 'His New Title',
    @HireDate = '1996-07-01',
    @RateChangeDate = '2008-07-31',
    @Rate = 15,
    @PayFrequency = 1,
    @CurrentFlag = 1;

SELECT @Return;
```

Code snippet Chap12.sql

Everything seems to run fine. Execute it a second time, however, and you get some different results:

```
Duplicate Rate Change Found

-----------
-2000

(1 row(s) affected)
```

You tried to insert a second row with the same pay history, but SQL Server wouldn't allow that. The sproc uses PRINT to supply informative output in case the statement is executed without the Query window, and it's outputting a specific return value that the client can match against a value in a resource list.

Now, let's try the same basic test, but use an invalid BusinessEntityID:

```
DECLARE @Return int;

EXEC @Return = HumanResources.uspEmployeeHireInfo2
    @BusinessEntityID = 99999,
    @JobTitle = 'My Invalid Employee',
    @HireDate = '2008-07-31',
    @RateChangeDate = '2008-07-31',
    @Rate = 15,
    @PayFrequency = 1,
    @CurrentFlag = 1;

SELECT @Return;
```

Code snippet Chap12.sql

You get a similar error message and return code, but each is slightly different to allow for the specific error detected:

```
BusinessEntityID Not Found

-----------
-1000

(1 row(s) affected)
```

Note that this wasn't a SQL Server error — as far as SQL Server's concerned, everything about life is just fine. What's nice, though, is that, were you using a client program (say one you wrote in C#, VB.NET, C++, or some other language), you could, as with your duplicate insert pay history item, track the -1000 against a known constant and send a very specific message to the end user.

Manually Raising Errors

Sometimes you have errors that SQL Server doesn't really know about, but you wish it did. For example, perhaps in the previous example you don't want to return -1000. Instead, you'd like to create a runtime error at the client end that the client would then use to invoke an error handler and act accordingly. To do this, you use the RAISERROR command in T-SQL. The syntax is pretty straightforward:

```
RAISERROR (<message ID | message string | variable>, <severity>, <state>
[, <argument>
[,<...n>]] )
[WITH option[,...n]]
```

Let's take a look at what these mean.

Message ID/Message String

The message ID or message string you provide determines which message is sent to the client.

Using a message ID creates a manually raised error with the ID that you specified and the message that is associated with that ID as found in the `sys.messages` system view in the master database.

> **NOTE** *If you want to see what your SQL Server has as predefined messages, you can always perform a* `SELECT * FROM master.sys.messages`. *This includes any messages you've manually added to your system using the* `sp_addmessage` *stored procedure or through the SQL Server Management Studio.*

You can also just supply a message string in the form of ad hoc text without creating a more permanent message in the system:

```
RAISERROR ('Hi there, I''m an error', 1, 1);
```

Code snippet Chap12.sql

This raises a rather simple error message:

```
Hi there, I'm an error
Msg 50000, Level 1, State 1
```

Notice that the assigned message number, even though you didn't supply one, is `50000`. This is the default error value for any ad hoc error. It can be overridden using the `WITH SETERROR` option.

Severity

You got a quick overview of this when looking at `TRY/CATCH` in the chapter on scripting. For those of you already familiar with Windows servers, severity should be an old friend. *Severity* is an indication of just how bad things really are based on this error. For SQL Server, however, what severity codes mean can get a little bizarre. They can range from informational (severities 1–18), to system level (19–25), and even to catastrophic (20–25). If you raise an error of severity 19 or higher (system level), the `WITH LOG` option must also be specified; 20 and higher automatically terminates the users' connections. (Kind of fun if you're feeling particularly ornery, but they *hate* that!)

So, let's get back to what I meant by bizarre. SQL Server actually varies its behavior into more ranges than Windows does, or even than the Books Online tells you about. Errors fall into six major groupings, as shown in Table 12-1.

TABLE 12-1: SQL Server Error Severity Levels

GROUP	DESCRIPTION
1–10	Purely informational, but returns the specific error code in the message information.
11–16	If you do not have a TRY/CATCH block set up, these terminate execution of the procedure and raise an error at the client. The state is shown to be whatever value you set it to. If you have a TRY/CATCH block defined, that handler is called rather than raising an error at the client.
17	Usually, only SQL Server should use this severity. Basically, it indicates that SQL Server has run out of resources — for example, tempdb is full — and can't complete the request. Again, a TRY/CATCH block gets this before the client does.
18–19	Both of these are severe errors and imply that the underlying cause requires system administrator attention. With 19, the WITH LOG option is required, and the event show up in the Windows Event Log. These are the final levels at which you can trap the error with a TRY/CATCH block — after this, it goes straight to the client.
20–25	Your world has just caved in, as has the user's connection. Essentially, this is a fatal error. The connection is terminated. As with 19, you must use the WITH LOG option and a message, if applicable, shows up in the Event Log.

State

State is an ad hoc value. It's something that recognizes that exactly the same error may occur at multiple places within your code. The notion is that this gives you an opportunity to send something of a place marker for where exactly the error occurred.

State values can be between 1 and 127. If you are troubleshooting an error with Microsoft tech support, they apparently have some arcane knowledge that hasn't been shared with you about what some of these mean. I'm told that if you make a tech-support call to Microsoft, they are likely to ask about and make use of this state information, and having spent the early part of my career on the other end of those phones, I expect I'm told right.

Error Arguments

Some predefined errors accept arguments. These allow you to make the error somewhat more dynamic by changing to the specific nature of the error. You can also format your error messages to accept arguments.

When you want to use dynamic information in what is otherwise a static error message, you need to format the fixed portion of your message so that it leaves room for the parameterized section of the message. You do so by using placeholders. If you're coming from the C or C++ world, you'll recognize the parameter placeholders immediately; they are similar to the printf command arguments. If you're not from the C world, these may seem a little odd to you. All the placeholders start with the % sign and are then coded for the kind of information (think data type) you'll be passing to them, as shown in Table 12-2.

TABLE 12-2: Parameter Placeholders

PLACEHOLDER TYPE INDICATOR	TYPE OF VALUE
`D`	Signed integer; Books Online indicates that `it` is an acceptable choice, but I've had problems getting it to work as expected
`O`	Unsigned octal
`P`	Pointer
`S`	String
`U`	Unsigned integer
`X` or `x`	Unsigned hexadecimal

In addition, you have the option to prefix any of these placeholder indicators with some additional flag and width information, as shown in Table 12-3.

TABLE 12-3: Placeholder Options

FLAG	WHAT IT DOES
- (dash or minus sign)	Left-justify; only makes a difference when you supply a fixed width
+ (plus sign)	Indicates the positive or negative nature if the parameter is a signed numeric type
`0`	Tells SQL Server to pad the left side of a numeric value with zeros until it reaches the width specified in the width option
# (pound sign)	Applies only to octal and hex values; tells SQL Server to use the appropriate prefix (`0` or `0x`) depending on whether it is octal or hex
`' '`	Pads the left of a numeric value with spaces if positive

Last, but not least, you can also set the width, precision, and long/short status of a parameter:

- **Width**: Set by simply supplying an integer value for the amount of space you want to hold for the parameterized value. You can also specify a `*`, in which case SQL Server automatically determines the width according to the value you've set for precision.
- **Precision:** Determines the maximum number of digits output for numeric data.
- **Long/Short:** Set by using an `h` (short) or `I` (long) when the type of the parameter is an integer, octal, or hex value.

Let's use this in a simple example:

Available for download on Wrox.com

```
RAISERROR ('This is a sample parameterized %s, along with a zero
padding and a sign%+010d',1,1, 'string', 12121);
```

Code snippet Chap12.sql

If you execute this, you get back something that looks a little different from what's in the quotation marks:

```
This is a sample parameterized string, along with a zero
padding and a sign+000012121
Msg 50000, Level 1, State 1
```

The extra values supplied were inserted, in order, into your placeholders, with the final value being reformatted as specified.

WITH <option>

Currently, you can mix and match three options when you raise an error:

➤ **LOG:** This tells SQL Server to log the error to the SQL Server error log and the Windows Application Log. This option is required with severity levels that are 19 or higher.

➤ **SETERROR:** By default, a RAISERROR command doesn't set @@ERROR with the value of the error you generated. Instead, @@ERROR reflects the success or failure of your actual RAISERROR command. SETERROR overrides this and sets the value of @@ERROR to be equal to your error ID.

➤ **NOWAIT:** Immediately notifies the client of the error.

Re-throwing Errors

A good rule of thumb used by developers well beyond just the narrow confines of the T-SQL world is only to catch an error you can handle. Any error you don't know what to do with should simply be passed on up to the caller, who may (or may not) know what to do with it, but at least you're not in the way.

Up until SQL Server 2012, T-SQL developers have had little recourse with regard to this rule. CATCH doesn't let you specify only specific errors to catch, and once you're in there all you've ever been able to do (with respect to passing an error up the chain) is to call RAISERROR. That's something, but it's not everything. RAISERROR can send an error upstream, but the original context (such as a line number) is lost. You're not really throwing the same error up to the caller, but rather throwing an imperfect copy.

Well, no more. With SQL Server 2012, you can finally THROW an error back up the chain if you're not ready to deal with it. THROW is in some ways very similar to RAISERROR, but with a few important distinctions. To begin with, here's the syntax for THROW:

```
THROW [ error_number, message, state] [ ; ]
```

The first thing you might notice is that all the parameters for THROW are optional. If you're within a CATCH block, THROW can be called with no parameters. In that case, it simply re-throws exactly the error that dropped you into the CATCH block in the first place. That way, you can handle all the known or expected errors yourself, but leave unknown or unexpected errors to be handled upstream if you want.

The next thing to notice is that the parameters you do have look very similar to the parameters for RAISERROR — but there is no parameter for severity. That's because THROW, when it is called with parameter values specified, always uses a severity of 16. Remember that 16 means no Windows log is written by default, but current code will stop (and, if you're in a TRY block, control will move to the CATCH block).

Other differences between THROW and RAISERROR:

➤ With THROW, the error_number parameter need not already exist in sys.messages. Don't be lazy about that, though — make sure your errors are defined somewhere.

➤ RAISERROR message strings use printf-style syntax for dynamic messaging, whereas THROW does not. If you want to customize the message you THROW, you'll have to concatenate it yourself ahead of time.

➤ The statement before a THROW must be terminated with a semicolon (;).

Try out this adaptation of an earlier example to see how THROW works. Here you'll try to add values to a column with a primary key defined.

Available for
download on
Wrox.com

```
BEGIN TRY
        INSERT OurIFTest(Col1) VALUES (1);
END TRY
BEGIN CATCH
        -- Uh oh, something went wrong, see if it's something
        -- we know what to do with
        PRINT  'Arrived in the CATCH block.';

        DECLARE @ErrorNo    int,
                @Severity   tinyint,
                @State      smallint,
                @LineNo     int,
                @Message    nvarchar(4000);
        SELECT
            @ErrorNo = ERROR_NUMBER(),
            @Severity = ERROR_SEVERITY(),
            @State = ERROR_STATE(),
            @LineNo = ERROR_LINE (),
            @Message = ERROR_MESSAGE();

        IF @ErrorNo = 2714 -- Object exists error, not likely this time
            PRINT 'WARNING: object already exists';
        ELSE -- hmm, we don't recognize it, so report it and bail
            THROW;
END CATCH
```

Code snippet Chap12.sql

The first time you run this, it should come off without a hitch, but the second run will produce an error. While the error does transfer control to the CATCH block, it's re-thrown in all its original glory for the caller (in this case, you) to handle as you like.

```
(0 row(s) affected)
Msg 2627, Level 14, State 1, Line 3
Violation of PRIMARY KEY constraint 'PK__OurIFTes__A259EE54ABA6728E'.
Cannot insert duplicate key in object 'dbo.OurIFTest'. The duplicate key value is (1).
```

Adding Your Own Custom Error Messages

You can make use of a special system stored procedure to add your own messages to the system. The sproc is called `sp_addmessage`, and the syntax looks like this:

```
sp_addmessage [@msgnum =] <msg id>,
[@severity =] <severity>,
[@msgtext =] <'msg'>
[, [@lang =] <'language'>]
[, [@with_log =] [TRUE|FALSE]]
[, [@replace =] 'replace']
```

All the parameters mean pretty much the same thing that they did with RAISERROR, except for the addition of the language and replace parameters and a slight difference with the WITH LOG option.

@lang

This specifies the language to which this message applies. What's cool here is that you can specify a separate version of your message for any language supported in `syslanguages`.

@with_log

This works just the same as it does in RAISERROR in that, if set to TRUE, the message automatically logs to both the SQL Server error log and the NT application log when raised (the latter only when running under NT). The only trick here is that you indicate that you want this message to be logged by setting this parameter to TRUE rather than using the WITH LOG option.

@replace

If you are editing an existing message rather than creating a new one, you must set the `@replace` parameter to `'REPLACE'`. If you leave this off, you'll get an error if the message already exists.

> **NOTE** *Creating a set list of additional messages for use by your applications can greatly enhance reuse, but more important, it can significantly improve readability of your application. Imagine if every one of your database applications made use of a constant list of custom error codes. You could then easily establish a constants file (a resource or include library, for example) that had a listing of the appropriate errors; you could even create an include library that had a generic handling of some or all of the errors. In short, if you're going to be building multiple SQL Server apps in the same environment, consider using a set list of errors that is common to all your applications. Keep in mind, however, that many system administrators do not like application-specific changes to affect the master database (which is where your custom error message is written), so if you are not in control of your own server, make sure that the use of custom error messages is allowed on the server before writing code that depends on them.*

Using sp_addmessage

As has already been indicated, `sp_addmessage` creates messages in much the same way as you create ad hoc messages using `RAISERROR`.

As an example, let's assume that AdventureWorks is implementing a rule that says that orders can't be entered if the orders are more than seven days old. Knowing this rule, you can add your own custom message that tells the users about issues with their order date:

```
sp_addmessage
    @msgnum = 60000,
    @severity = 10,
    @msgtext = '%s is not a valid Order date.
Order date must be within 7 days of current date.';
```

Code snippet Chap12.sql

Execute the sproc and it confirms the addition of the new message: `Command(s) completed successfully.`

 NOTE *No matter what database you're working with when you run* `sp_addmessage`, *the actual message is added to the master database and can be viewed at any time by looking at the* `sys.messages` *system view. The significance of this is that, if you migrate your database to a new server, the messages need to be added to that new server (the old ones are still in the master database of the old server). As such, I strongly recommend keeping all your custom messages stored in a script somewhere so they can easily be added into a new system.*

Removing an Existing Custom Message

To get rid of the custom message, use the following:

```
sp_dropmessage <message number>
```

WHAT A SPROC OFFERS

Now that you've spent some time looking at how to build a sproc, you might be wondering why you should use them. Some of the reasons are pretty basic; others may not come to mind right away if you're new to the RDBMS world. The primary benefits of sprocs include:

➤ Making processes that require procedural action callable

➤ Security

➤ Performance

Creating Callable Processes

As I've already indicated, a sproc is something of a script that is stored in the database. The nice thing is that, because it is a database object, you can call to it — you don't have to manually load it from a file before executing it.

Sprocs can call to other sprocs (called *nesting*). For SQL Server 2012, you can nest up to 32 levels deep. This gives you the capability of reusing separate sprocs much as you would make use of a subroutine in a classic procedural language. The syntax for calling one sproc from another sproc is exactly the same as it is calling the sproc from a script.

Using Sprocs for Security

Many people don't realize the full use of sprocs as a tool for security. Much like views, you can create a sproc that returns a recordset without having to give the user authority to the underlying table. Granting users the right to execute a sproc implies that they can perform any action within the sproc, provided that the action is taken within the context of the sproc. That is, if you grant users authority to execute a sproc that returns all the records in the Customers table, but not access to the actual Customers table, the users can still get data out of the Customers table, provided they do it by using the sproc (trying to access the table directly won't work).

What can be really handy here is that you can give users access to modify data through the sproc, but then only give them read access to the underlying table. They can modify data in the table provided that they do it through your sproc (which will likely be enforcing some business rules). They can then hook directly up to your SQL Server using Excel, Access, or whatever to build their own custom reports with no risk of "accidentally" modifying the data.

 NOTE *Setting users up to directly link to a production database via Access or Excel has to be one of the most incredibly powerful and yet stupid things you can do to your system. While you are empowering your users, you are also digging your own grave in terms of the resources they will use and long-running queries they will execute (naturally, they will be oblivious to the havoc this causes your system).*

If you really must give users direct access, consider using mirroring, replication, or backups and restores to create a completely separate copy of the database (or just the tables they need access to) for them to use. This helps ensure you against record locks, queries that bog down the system, and a whole host of other problems.

Sprocs and Performance

Generally speaking, sprocs can do a lot to help the performance of your system. Keep in mind, however, that like most things in life, there are no guarantees — indeed, you can create some processes in sprocs that substantially slow the process if the sproc hasn't been designed intelligently.

Where does that performance come from? Well, when you create a sproc, the process works something like what you see in Figure 12-1.

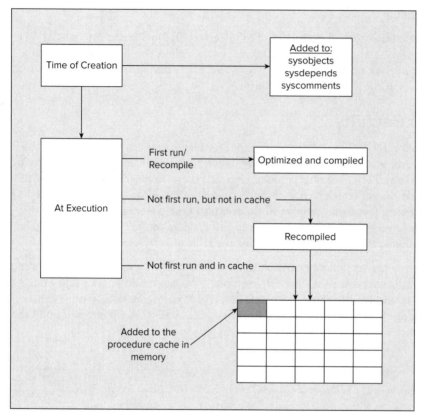

FIGURE 12-1

You start by running the CREATE PROC procedure. This parses the query to make sure that the code should actually run. The one difference versus running the script directly is that the CREATE PROC command can make use of what's called *deferred name resolution*. Deferred name resolution ignores the fact that you may have some objects that don't exist yet. This gives you the chance to create these objects later.

After the sproc has been created, it sits in wait for the first time that it is executed. At that time, the sproc is optimized and a query plan is compiled and cached on the system. Subsequent times that you run your sproc will, unless you specify otherwise using the WITH RECOMPILE option, generally use that cached query plan rather than create a new one. (There are situations in which the sproc will be recompiled, but that is beyond the scope of this book.) This means that whenever the sproc is used it can skip much of the optimization and compilation process. Exactly how much time this saves varies depending on the complexity of the batch, the size of the tables involved in the batch, and the number of indexes on each table. Usually, the amount of time saved is seemingly small — say, perhaps 1 second or less for most scenarios — yet that difference can really add up in terms of percentage

(1 second is still 100 percent faster than 2 seconds). The difference can become even more extreme when you need to make several calls or when you are in a looping situation.

When a Good Sproc Goes Bad

Perhaps one of the most important things to recognize on the downside of sprocs is that, unless you manually interfere (using the WITH RECOMPILE option), they are optimized based on either the first time that they run or when the statistics have been updated on the table(s) involved in any queries.

That "optimize once, use many times" strategy is what saves the sproc time, but it's a double-edged sword. If your query is dynamic in nature (the query is built up as it goes using the EXEC command), the sproc may be optimized for the way things ran the first time, only to find that things never run that way again — in short, it may be using the wrong plan!

It's not just dynamic queries in sprocs that can cause this scenario either. Imagine a web page that lets you mix and match several criteria for a search. For example, let's say that you wanted to add a sproc to the AdventureWorks database that would support a web page that allows users to search for an order based on:

➤ Customer name

➤ Sales Order ID

➤ Product ID

➤ Order date

The user is allowed to supply any mix of the information, with each new piece of information supplied making the search a little more restricted and theoretically faster.

The approach you probably want to take is to have more than one query and to select the right query to run depending on what was supplied by the user. The first time that you execute your sproc, it runs through a few IF...ELSE statements and picks the right query to run. Unfortunately, it's just the right query for that particular time you ran the sproc (and an unknown percentage of the other times). Any time after that first time that the sproc selects a different query to run, it will still use the query plan based on the first time the sproc ran. In short, the query performance is really going to suffer.

Using the WITH RECOMPILE Option

You can choose to use the security and compartmentalization of code benefits of a sproc, but still ignore the precompiled code side of things. This lets you get around this issue of not using the right query plan, because you're certain that a new plan was created just for this run. To do this, you make use of the WITH RECOMPILE option, which you can include in two different ways.

➤ You can include the WITH RECOMPILE at runtime. You simply include it with the execution script:

```
EXEC spMySproc '1/1/2012'
    WITH RECOMPILE
```

Code snippet Chap12.sql

This tells SQL Server to throw away the existing execution plan and create a new one — but just this once — that is, just for this time that you've executed the sproc using the WITH RECOMPILE option. Without further action, SQL will continue to use the new plan forevermore.

➤ You can choose to make things more permanent by including the WITH RECOMPILE option right within the sproc. If you do things this way, you add the WITH RECOMPILE option immediately before the AS statement in your CREATE PROC or ALTER PROC statements.

If you create your sproc with this option, the sproc will recompile each time that it runs, regardless of other options chosen at runtime.

EXTENDED STORED PROCEDURES (XPS)

The advent of .NET in SQL Server has really changed the area of Extended Stored Procedures. These used to be the bread and butter of the hard-core code scenarios — when you hit those times where basic T-SQL and the other features of SQL Server just wouldn't give you what you needed.

With the availability of .NET to deal with things like O/S file access and other external communication or complex formulas, the day of the XP would seem to be waning. XPs still have their place in the world for few reasons:

➤ **Performance:** For times where performance is so critical that you want the code running genuinely in process to SQL Server (this is truly a *radical* approach in the .NET era).

➤ **Security:** For situations where your administrators do not allow .NET code to execute for security reasons (though allowing XPs, but not .NET, is somewhat silly if you ask me . . .).

For purposes of this book, I'll merely say that SQL Server does allow for the idea of externally written code that runs as a .DLL in process with SQL Server. XPs are created using C or C++.

A BRIEF LOOK AT RECURSION

Recursion is one of those things that isn't used very often in programming. Still, it's also one of those things for which, when you need it, there never seems to be anything else that quite does the trick. As a "just in case," a brief review of what recursion is seems in order.

The brief version is that *recursion* is the situation where a piece of code calls itself. The dangers here should be fairly self-evident — if it calls itself once, what's to keep it from calling itself over and over again? The answer to that is *you*. That is, *you* need to make sure that if your code is going to be called recursively, you provide a *recursion check* to make sure you bail out when it's appropriate.

I'd love to say that the example I'm going to use is all neat and original — but it isn't. Indeed, for an example, I'm going to use the classic recursion example that's used with about every textbook recursion discussion I've ever seen — please accept my apologies now. It's just that it's an example that can be understood by just about anyone, so here we go.

So what is that classic example? Factorials. For those who have had a while since math class (or their last recursion discussion), a factorial is the value you get when you take a number and multiply it successively by that number less one, the next value less one, and so on, until you get to one. For example, the factorial of 5 (mathematically expressed as "5!") is 120 — that's 5*4*3*2*1.

So, let's look at an implementation of such a recursive sproc:

```
CREATE PROC spFactorial
@ValueIn int,
@ValueOut int OUTPUT
AS
DECLARE @InWorking int;
DECLARE @OutWorking int;
IF @ValueIn <= 1
BEGIN
    SELECT @InWorking = @ValueIn - 1;

    EXEC spFactorial @InWorking, @OutWorking OUTPUT;

    SELECT @ValueOut = @ValueIn * @OutWorking;
END
ELSE
BEGIN
    SELECT @ValueOut = 1;
END
RETURN;
GO
```

Code snippet Chap12.sql

So, what you're doing is accepting a value in (that's the value you want a factorial of) and providing a value back out (the factorial value you've computed). The surprising part is that the sproc does not, in one step, do everything it needs to calculate the factorial. Instead, it just takes one number's worth of the factorial and then turns around and calls itself. The second call deals with just one number's worth and then again calls itself. This can go on and on up to a limit of 32 levels of recursion. Once SQL Server gets 32 levels deep, it raises an error and ends processing.

> **NOTE** Note that any calls into .NET assemblies count as an extra level in your recursion count, but anything you do within those assemblies does not count against the recursion limit. While .NET functionality in SQL Server is beyond the scope of this book, keep in mind that it is a potential way around nesting level issues.

Let's try out this recursive sproc with a little script:

```
DECLARE @WorkingOut int;
DECLARE @WorkingIn int;
SELECT @WorkingIn = 5;
EXEC spFactorial @WorkingIn, @WorkingOut OUTPUT;

PRINT CAST(@WorkingIn AS varchar) + ' factorial is '
+ CAST(@WorkingOut AS varchar);
```

Code snippet Chap12.sql

This gets you the expected result of 120:

```
5 factorial is 120
```

You can try different values for @WorkingIn and things should work just fine with two rather significant hitches:

➤ Arithmetic overflow when the factorial grows too large for the int (or even bigint) data type

➤ The 32-level recursion limit

You can test the arithmetic overflow easily by putting any large number in — anything bigger than about 13 works for this int example.

Testing the 32-level recursion limit takes a little bit more modification to your sproc. This time, you'll determine the *triangular* of the number. This is very similar to finding the factorial, except that you use addition rather than multiplication. Therefore, 5 triangular is just 15 (5+4+3+2+1). Let's create a new sproc to test this one out — it looks just like the factorial sproc with only a few small changes:

```
CREATE PROC spTriangular
@ValueIn int,
@ValueOut int OUTPUT
AS
DECLARE @InWorking int;
DECLARE @OutWorking int;
IF @ValueIn != 1
BEGIN
        SELECT @InWorking = @ValueIn - 1;

        EXEC spTriangular @InWorking, @OutWorking OUTPUT;

        SELECT @ValueOut = @ValueIn + @OutWorking;
END
ELSE
BEGIN
        SELECT @ValueOut = 1;
END
RETURN;
GO
```

As you can see, there weren't that many changes to be made. Similarly, you only need to change your sproc call and the PRINT text for your test script:

```
DECLARE @WorkingOut int;
DECLARE @WorkingIn int;
SELECT @WorkingIn = 5;
EXEC spTriangular @WorkingIn, @WorkingOut OUTPUT;

PRINT CAST(@WorkingIn AS varchar) + ' Triangular is '
+ CAST(@WorkingOut AS varchar);
```

Code snippet Chap12.sql

Running this with a `@ValueIn` of 5 gets your expected 15:

```
5 Triangular is 15
```

However, if you try to run it with an `@ValueIn` of more than 32, you get an error:

```
Msg 217, Level 16, State 1, Procedure spTriangular, Line 10
Maximum stored procedure, function, trigger, or view nesting level exceeded
(limit 32).
```

I'd love to say there's some great workaround to this, but, unless you can somehow segment your recursive calls (run it 32 levels deep, come all the way back out of the call stack, and then run down it again), you're pretty much out of luck. Just keep in mind that most recursive functions can be rewritten to be a more standard looping construct — which doesn't have any hard limit. Be sure you can't use a loop before you force yourself into recursion.

DEBUGGING

Long ago and far away (SQL Server 2000), the Management Studio had real live debugging tools. They were a little clunky, in the sense that they really only worked around stored procedures (there wasn't a way to debug just a script, and debugging triggers required you to create a sproc that would fire the trigger), but, with some workarounds here and there, you had the long-sought-after debugger. SQL Server 2005 came along and removed all debugging functionality from the Management Studio (it was in the product, but you had to use the Visual Studio installation that is part of the SQL Server Data Tools in order to get at it — not very handy in any case, but nonexistent if you didn't install SSDT for some reason). I'm happy to say that debugging returned to the Management Studio in 2008, and it's better than ever!

Starting the Debugger

The debugger in SQL Server 2012 is pretty easy to find. Much of using the debugger works as it does in VB or C# — probably like most modern debuggers, for that matter. Simply choose the Debug menu (available when a query window is active). You can then choose from options to get things started: Start Debugging (Alt+F5) or Step Into (F11).

Let's do a little bit of setup to show the debugger in action, both in a standard script and in a stored procedure scenario. To do this, you can use the script you were just working with in the previous section (to exercise the `spTriangular` stored procedure you created earlier in the chapter). The script looked like this:

```
DECLARE @WorkingOut int;
DECLARE @WorkingIn int = 5;

EXEC spTriangular @WorkingIn, @WorkingOut OUTPUT;

PRINT CAST(@WorkingIn AS varchar) + ' Triangular is '
    + CAST(@WorkingOut AS varchar);
```

With this script as the active query window, let's start a debugging run with the Step Into option (choose it from the Debug menu or simply press F11).

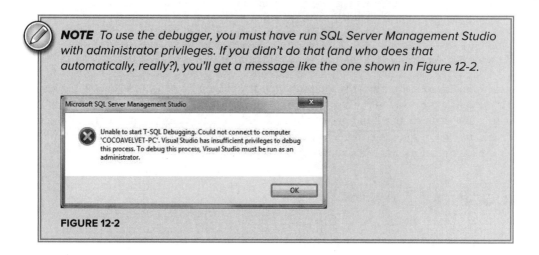

NOTE *To use the debugger, you must have run SQL Server Management Studio with administrator privileges. If you didn't do that (and who does that automatically, really?), you'll get a message like the one shown in Figure 12-2.*

FIGURE 12-2

Parts of the Debugger

Several things are worth noticing when the Debugger window first comes up:

FIGURE 12-3

➤   The arrow on the left (shown in Figure 12-3) indicates the *current execution line* — this is the next line of code that will be executed if you do a "go" or you start stepping through the code.

FIGURE 12-4

➤   There are icons at the top (see Figure 12-4) to indicate some different options, including:

➤   **Continue:** This runs to the end of the sproc or the next breakpoint (including a watch condition).

➤   **Break All:** This pauses all processing in the current debugging context and shows you the next line of executable code.

➤   **Stop Debugging:** Again, this does what it says — it stops execution immediately. The debugging window does remain open, however.

➤   **Show Next Statement:** This moves the cursor to the next statement that will be executed.

➤   **Step Into:** This executes the next line of code and stops prior to running the following line of code, regardless of which procedure or function that code is in. If the line of code being executed is calling a sproc or function, Step Into has the effect of calling that sproc or function, adding it to the call stack, changing the Locals window to represent the newly nested sproc rather than the parent, and then stopping at the first line of executable code in the nested sproc.

➤ **Step Over:** This executes every line of code required to take you to the next statement that is at the same level in the call stack. If you are not calling another sproc or a UDF, this command acts just like a Step Into. If, however, you are calling another sproc or a UDF, a Step Over takes you to the statement immediately following where that sproc or UDF returned its value.

➤ **Step Out:** This executes every line of code up to the next line of code at the next highest point in the call stack. You can think of this as "finish the current function or procedure," because once you return to the caller the debugger will again break and wait.

➤ **Toggle Breakpoints and Remove All Breakpoints:** In addition, you can set breakpoints by clicking in the left margin of the code window. Breakpoints are points that you set to tell SQL Server to "stop here!" when the code is running in debug mode. This is handy in big sprocs or functions where you don't want to have to deal with every line — you just want it to run up to a point and stop every time it gets there. You'll read more about breakpoints later in this chapter.

In addition, there is a choice that brings up the Breakpoints window, which is a list of all breakpoints that are currently set (again, handy in larger blocks of code). There are also a few of what I'll call "status" windows; let's go through a few of the more important of these.

The Locals Window

As I indicated back at the beginning of the book, I'm pretty much assuming that you have experience with some procedural language out there. As such, the Locals window (shown in Figure 12-5 as it matches with the current statement shown in Figure 12-4) probably isn't all that new of a concept to you. Simply put, it shows you the current value of all the variables that are currently in scope. The list of variables in the Locals window may change (as may their values) as you step into nested sprocs and back out again. Remember — these are only the variables that are in scope as of the next statement to run.

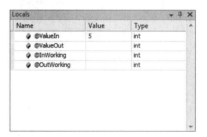

FIGURE 12-5

In Figure 12-5, you're at the start of your first run through this sproc, so the value for the @ValueIn parameter has been set, but all other variables and parameters are not yet set and thus are effectively null.

Three pieces of information are provided for each variable or parameter:

➤ The name

➤ The current value

➤ The data type

However, perhaps the best part to the Locals window is that you can edit the values in each variable. That means it's a lot easier to change things on the fly to test certain behaviors in your sproc.

The Watch Window

Here you can set up variables that you want to keep track of regardless of where you currently are in the call stack. You can either manually type in the name of the variable you want to watch, or you can select that variable in code, right click, and then select Add Watch. In Figure 12-6, I've added a watch for @ValueOut, but, because you haven't addressed that variable in code, you can see that no value has been set for it as yet.

One thing you can do in SQL Server 2012 that you couldn't before is include expressions in the Watch window. You can include most kinds of operation, including T-SQL queries so long as they return only a single value. In Figure 12-6, look at the watch value counting all the rows in the Sales.SalesOrderHeader table that have a territory matching @WorkingIn.

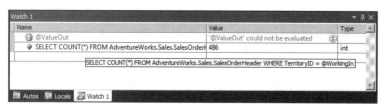

FIGURE 12-6

The Call Stack Window

The Call Stack window provides a listing of all the sprocs and functions that are currently active in the process that you are running. The handy thing here is that you can see how far in you are when you are running in a nested situation, and you can change between the nesting levels to verify what current variable values are at each level.

In Figure 12-7, I've stepped into the code for spTriangular such that the current working value is 3. If you're following along, you can just watch the @ValueIn variable in your Locals window and see how it changes as you step in. Your call stack now has several instances of spTriangular running as you've stepped into it (one for 5, one for 4, and now one for 3), as well as providing information on what statement is next in the current scope.

```
Call Stack
  Name                                                                              Lang
  spTriangular(BEGINNINGSQL2012.AdventureWorks)(int @ValueIn, int @ValueOut) Line 8    Tran
  spTriangular(BEGINNINGSQL2012.AdventureWorks)(int @ValueIn, int @ValueOut) Line 13   Tran
  spTriangular(BEGINNINGSQL2012.AdventureWorks)(int @ValueIn, int @ValueOut) Line 13   Tran
  SQLQuery1.sql() Line 5                                                               Tran

  Call Stack   Breakpoints   Command Window   Immediate Window   Output
```

FIGURE 12-7

The Output Window

Much as it sounds, the Output window is the spot where SQL Server prints any output. This includes result sets, as well as the return value when your sproc has completed running, but also provides debug information from the process you're debugging. Some example output from the middle of a debug run is shown in Figure 12-8.

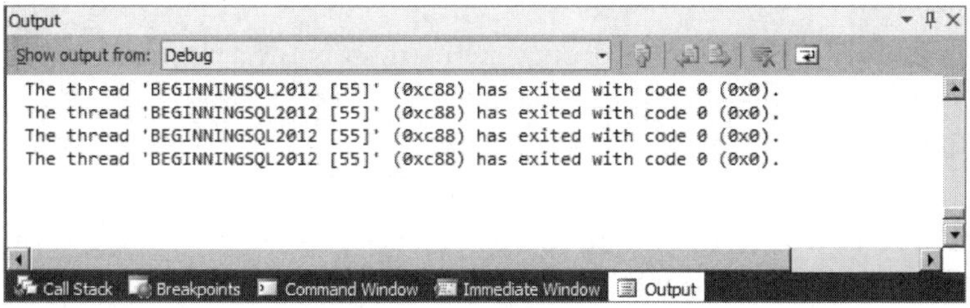

FIGURE 12-8

The Command Window

The Command window is probably going to be beyond common use as it has been since SQL Server 2008. In short, it allows you something of a command line mode to access debugger commands and other objects. It is, however, cryptic at best. Examples of commands you could issue would be something like:

```
>Debug.StepInto
```

There are a whole host of commands available to IntelliSense, but you'll find that many of these are not actually available when debugging. If you're familiar with the Visual Studio debugger command window, that's what this is modeled on, and you can use it similarly.

Taking a Break: Breakpoints

When I start debugging, quite often I'll remember the voice of Private Hicks in *Aliens*, when he first hears about the mission — "It's a bug hunt," he says with a sigh, obviously (and inaccurately) anticipating tedium. He may have been wildly wrong about the character of his task, but it's not so far off in this context. Breakpoints are a tool you have to reduce the tedium a bit.

Often you'll find yourself making more than just one pass through a sproc (or a series of nested sprocs) hunting for the cause of some bug. Usually what happens is you figure out where the bug *isn't* first — that is, there are swaths of code where everything's going just fine, and if there's a problem it's contained in other areas. For efficiency's sake you don't want to step through all that known-good code time and again to get to the bad stuff. This is what breakpoints are for.

As I said earlier, breakpoints are a way of saying "stop here" to the debugger. Instead of stepping into, over, or out, you can just use Continue to run the code right up until the next breakpoint. That way, you can skip over all that stuff you've already tested and get right to the good . . . er, bad stuff.

How to Set and Use Breakpoints

The most common way to set a breakpoint is to click the line you want to stop on and press F9. What's fun is that you can set breakpoints even before you start the debugger, and they'll persist when you get in there. You can set as many breakpoints as you like.

On the Debug menu, you can see more ways to manipulate breakpoints. You can delete them all, disable them all, or (if they're already disabled) enable them all from this menu. Disabling is a good way to preserve breakpoint locations while you step through code you'd otherwise have skipped.

Stopping at breakpoints is automatic. If you're in the debugger, you're stopping at all (enabled) breakpoints.

Breakpoint Conditions

Because breakpoints are all about narrowing the search space, it makes sense that you may want breakpoints that you only stop at sometimes. In SQL Server 2012, you can now place conditions on breakpoints.

Let's say, for example, that you know something in a larger procedure is calling your factorial function with a number that's too large. While there are a lot of very easy and straightforward ways to go about solving a problem like that, it does help to locate the offending code.

You can set a breakpoint in spFactorial that stops only when @ValueIn is more than a given value, say 12. When the code breaks there, you can step out and discover what the conditions were that caused the procedure to be thus abused.

To add a condition to a breakpoint, right-click the breakpoint (either from within the Breakpoint window, from the breakpoint glyph in the left column, or on the actual row of code under the Breakpoint context menu item) and select Condition. Set up an expression (in this case, @ValueIn > 12) and a condition (Is True), and you're all set. Figure 12-9 gives you an idea what that will look like in the Breakpoint window when you're done.

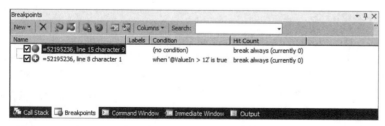

FIGURE 12-9

Using Hit Counts

Hit counts offer a different kind of condition for a breakpoint. A hit count is exactly what it sounds like: a value that increments each time the breakpoint is reached. Hit counts are all zero when you start a debugging session, and they increment throughout the session. You can set conditions on a hit count based on reaching a specific hit count ("break when this is hit for the fifth time"), a multiple of a count ("break every third time"), or greater than or equal to a count ("once this reaches 10, break every time"). Using hit counts is another way to reduce the space you're searching for a bug.

Setting a hit count test is a lot like setting a breakpoint condition, except rather than selecting Condition, you select Hit Count.

Breakpoint Filters

Filters let you limit a breakpoint to stop execution only when called from certain processes or threads. Using it is pretty straightforward mechanically; when you select Filters from the Breakpoint menu, you even get a little syntax primer right there to help you through it.

Breakpoint Locations

From the Breakpoint menu, you can set a breakpoint location based on line and character position; you'll rarely want to, though. This is useful when, for example, multiple statements exist on a single line and you want to stop on one that's not the first. In general, my solution to that is to fix the code so there's only one statement on a line, but if that's not your speed then you've got this option.

Using the Debugger Once It's Started

Now that you have the preliminaries out of the way and the debugger window up, you should be ready to start walking through the code. If you were walking through some of the descriptions before, stop the debugger and restart it so we're in the same place.

The first executable line of your sproc is a bit deceptive — it is the DECLARE statement for @WorkingIn. Normally variable declarations are not considered executable, but, in this case, you are initializing the variable as part of the declaration, so the initialization code is seen by the debugger. You should notice that none of your variables has yet been set (the initialization code is next to run, but has not actually executed yet). You should then follow these steps:

1. Step forward using the menu choice, the tooltip, or simply press F11. You should see (via the Locals window) @WorkingIn get initialized to your value of 5 — @WorkingOut is not initialized as part of the declaration (refer to Figure 12-10 for what this should look like).

2. Use the Step Into key one more time. You enter into your first execution of the spTriangular stored procedure and land at the first executable line in the sproc — an IF statement. It will look something like Figure 12-11.

```
BEGINNINGSQL2012.[A...dbo].[spTriangular]  ×  SQLQuery1.sql - BEGI..n (53)) Debugging...*

CREATE PROC spTriangular
    @ValueIn int,
    @ValueOut int OUTPUT
AS
DECLARE @InWorking int;
DECLARE @OutWorking int;
IF @ValueIn != 1
BEGIN
        SELECT @InWorking = @ValueIn - 1;

        EXEC spTriangular @InWorking, @OutWorking OUTPUT;

        SELECT @ValueOut = @ValueIn + @OutWorking;
END
ELSE
```

Locals			
Name	Value		Type
@WorkingOut			int
@WorkingIn	5		int

Autos Locals

FIGURE 12-10

FIGURE 12-11

3. Because the value of @ValueIn is indeed not equal to 1, you step into the BEGIN...END block specified by your IF statement. Specifically, you move to the SELECT statement that initializes the @InWorking parameter for this particular execution of the procedure. As you'll see later, if the value of @ValueIn had indeed been 1, execution would have immediately dropped down to the ELSE statement.

4. Again, step forward one line by pressing F11, or using the Step Into icon or menu choice, until just *before* you enter the next instance of spTriangular, as you see in Figure 12-12.

FIGURE 12-12

 NOTE *Pay particular attention to the value of* @InWorking *in the Locals window. Notice that it changed to the correct value (*@ValueIn *is currently* 5, *so* 5–1 *is* 4*) as set by your* SELECT *statement. Also notice that the Call Stack window has only the current instance of your sproc in it (plus the current statement) — because you haven't stepped down into the nested versions of the sproc yet, you see only one instance.*

5. Step into the next statement. Because this is the execution of a sproc, you're going to see a number of different things change in the debugger (see Figure 12-13). Notice that it *appears* that your arrow that indicates the current statement jumped back up to the IF statement. Why? Well, this is a new instance of what is otherwise the same sproc. You can tell this based on the Call Stack window — notice that it now has two instances of your sproc listed. The one at the top (with the yellow arrow) is the current instance, and the one with the red breakpoint dot is a parent instance that is now waiting for something further up in the call stack. Notice also that the @ValueIn parameter has the value of 4 — that is the value you passed in from the outer instance of the sproc.

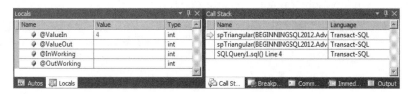

FIGURE 12-13

6. If you want to see the value of variables in the scope of the outer instance of the sproc, just double-click that instance's line in the Call Stack window (the one with the green arrow) and you'll see several things changed in your debugging windows, as shown in Figure 12-14.

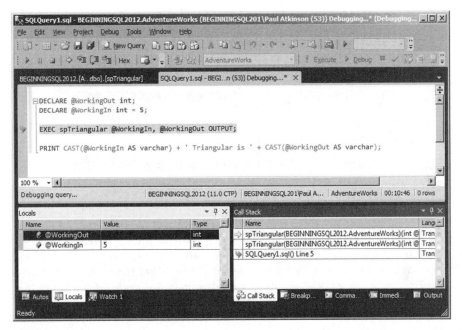

FIGURE 12-14

There are two things to notice here.

> The values of your variables have changed back to those in the scope of the outer (and currently selected) instance of the sproc.

> The icon for your current execution line is different. This new green arrow is meant to show that this is the current line in this instance of the sproc, but it is not the current line in the overall call stack.

7. Go back to the current instance by double-clicking the top item in the Call Stack window. Then step in three more times. This should bring you to the top line (the IF statement) in the third instance of the sproc. Notice that the call stack has become three deep and that the values of the variables and parameters in the Locals window have changed again. Last, but not least, notice that this time the @ValueIn parameter has a value of 3. Repeat this process until the @ValueIn parameter has a value of 1.

8. Step into the code one more time and you'll see a slight change in behavior. This time, because the value in @ValueIn is equal to 1, execution moves into the BEGIN...END block defined with your ELSE statement.

9. Because you've reached the bottom (or anchor), you're ready to start going back up the call stack. Use Step Into through the last line of your procedure and you'll find that the call stack is back to only four levels. Also, notice that the output parameter (@OutWorking) has been appropriately set.

10.   This time, let's do something different and do a Step Out (Shift+F11). If you're not paying attention, it will look like absolutely nothing has changed (Figure 12-15 shows the Local and Call Stack windows).

FIGURE 12-15

 NOTE *In this case, to use the old cliché, looks are deceiving. Again, notice the change in the Call Stack window and in the values in the Locals window — you stepped out of what was then the current instance of the sproc and moved up a level in the Call Stack. If you now keep stepping into the code (F11), your sproc has finished running and you'll see the final version of your status windows and their respective finishing values. A big word of caution here! If you want to see the final values (such as an output parameter being set), make sure that you use the Step Into option to execute the last line of code.*

 NOTE *If you use an option that executes several lines at once, such as a Go or Step Out, all you will get is the Output window without any final variable information.*

 NOTE *A workaround is to place a break point on the last point at which you expect to perform a* RETURN *in the outermost instance of your sproc. That way, you can run in whatever debug mode you want, but still have execution halt in the end so you can inspect your final variables.*

So, you should now understand how the Debugger can be very handy indeed.

UNDERSTANDING .NET ASSEMBLIES

Because of just how wide open a topic assemblies are, as well as their potential to add exceptional complexity to your database, these are largely considered out of scope for this title, save for one thing — letting you know they are there.

.NET assemblies can be associated with your system and utilized to provide the power behind truly complex operations. You could, just as an example, use a .NET assembly in a user-defined function to provide data from an external data source (perhaps one that has to be called on the fly, such as a new feed or stock quote), even though the structure and complex communications required would have ruled out such a function in prior versions.

Without going into too much detail on them for now, let's look at the syntax for adding an assembly to your database:

```
CREATE ASSEMBLY  <assembly name> AUTHORIZATION <owner name> FROM <path to assembly>
WITH PERMISSION_SET = [SAFE | EXTERNAL_ACCESS | UNSAFE]
```

The CREATE ASSEMBLY part of things works as pretty much all the CREATE statements have — it indicates the type of object being created and the object name.

Then comes the AUTHORIZATION — this allows you to set a context that the assembly is always to run under. That is, if it has tables it needs to access, how you set the user or role name in AUTHORIZATION determines whether it can access those tables or not.

After that, you go to the FROM clause. This is essentially the path to your assembly, along with the manifest for that assembly.

Finally, you have WITH PERMISSION_SET. This has three options:

➤ **SAFE:** This one is, at the risk of sounding obvious, well . . . safe. It restricts the assembly from accessing anything that is external to SQL Server. Things like files or the network are not available to the assembly.

➤ **EXTERNAL_ACCESS:** This allows external access, such as to files or the network, but requires that the assembly still run as managed code.

➤ **UNSAFE:** This one is, at the risk of again sounding obvious, unsafe. It allows your assembly not only to access external system objects, but also to run unmanaged code.

 NOTE *I cannot stress enough the risks you are taking when running .NET assemblies in anything other than* SAFE *mode. Even in* EXTERNAL_ACCESS *mode you are allowing the users of your system to access your network, files, or other external resources in what is essentially an aliased mode — that is, they may have access to things that you would rather they not, and they will be aliased on your network to whatever your SQL Server login is while they are making those accesses. Be very, very careful with this stuff.*

WHEN TO USE STORED PROCEDURES

Sprocs are the backbone of code in SQL Server. You can create reusable code and get improved performance and flexibility at the same time. You can use a variety of programming constructs that you might be familiar with from other languages, but sprocs aren't meant for everything.

Pros to sprocs include:

➤ Usually better performance

➤ Possible use as a security insulation layer (control how a database is accessed and updated)

➤ Reusable code

➤ Compartmentalization of code (can encapsulate business logic)

➤ Flexible execution depending on dynamics established at runtime

Cons to sprocs include:

➤ Not portable across platforms (Oracle, for example, has a completely different kind of implementation of sprocs)

➤ May get locked into the wrong execution plan in some circumstances (actually hurting performance)

The pros of using sprocs are commonly much more relevant than the cons. If you're not worried about porting your database code to another RDBMS (like Oracle or MySQL), and you have a chunk of code that needs to be run repeatedly, write a stored procedure.

SUMMARY

Wow! That's a lot to have to take in for one chapter. Still, this is among the most important chapters in the book in terms of functioning as a developer in SQL Server.

Stored procedures are written as a parameterized batch of TSQL. Once created, permissions can be managed on the procedure independently from permissions on the underlying objects, allowing you to carefully limit access to objects in your database. What's more, there is powerful error handling available to prevent ugly system errors from appearing.

The first time a stored procedure is run, it generates a query plan based on the parameters used that time. You can force this to change using RECOMPILE, but if it doesn't need to change then you gain performance by allowing this plan to be stored and reused.

SQL Server Management Studio has a powerful debugger available to help you step through your procedures and find bugs. The debugger has undergone significant enhancement in SQL Server 2012, including the addition of conditional breakpoints and hit counts.

Sprocs are not the solution to everything, but they are still the cornerstones of SQL Server programming. In the next chapter, you'll take a look at the sprocs' very closely related cousin — the user-defined function (UDF).

EXERCISES

1. Change the spTriangular procedure to throw a sensible error to the caller when it is called with an input that's going to overflow the max recursion (32).

2. Debug your spTriangular procedure, setting a breakpoint that will stop execution only on the anchor instance call (that is, when @ValueIn = 1). This breakpoint should be outside the BEGIN/ END block.

▶ WHAT YOU LEARNED IN THIS CHAPTER

TOPIC	CONCEPT
Stored procedures	Named batches of code that are callable by other SQL batches. Creating, altering, and dropping sprocs is similar to other SQL objects.
Parameters	Sprocs can have both input and output parameters. Parameters are declared with a name beginning with @, a data type, and optionally a default value. Any parameter without a default is required.
Return values	Sprocs return an integer value with RETURN, or 0 by default. While they can be put to any use, the accepted purpose of the return value is a result code, with 0 indicating success.
Error handling	In current versions of SQL Server, error handling is done through TRY/CATCH blocks. Any error with a severity over 17 is a system error and will not be handled by TRY/CATCH, but other errors can be either gracefully dealt with or thrown back to the client. You can use @@ERROR or the ERROR_NUMBER() and related functions to extract error details in the CATCH block.
Purpose of sprocs	Programmers use sprocs for three main reasons: performance, encapsulation, and security. Performance, because sproc performance is often better than ad hoc querying due to eliminated compile time. Encapsulation, because having a named, callable procedure to encapsulate business logic encourages code reuse and prevents errors. Security, because you can restrict user rights to running sprocs, rather than addressing tables directly.
Debugger	SSMS has a script debugger that can step through individual batches, sprocs, triggers, or any running T-SQL code. You can view local variable values in the Locals window or flexibly set up watch values in the Watch window. Breakpoints with a variety of stop conditions can be created to let known-good code run while stopping where errors are suspected.
.NET assemblies	It's possible to attach .NET code to SQL such that it can be called like a sproc. This allows the full power and speed of .NET code to be available within T-SQL once the code is attached with CREATE ASSEMBLY. Allowing external access with your callable .NET code is dangerous, and should be done only in coordination with appropriate administrative resources.

13

User-Defined Functions

WHAT YOU WILL LEARN IN THIS CHAPTER:

➤ What a user-defined function (UDF) is, and how it differs from stored procedures or views

➤ How to create UDFs that return either scalar values or tables

➤ The importance of .NET UDFs within SQL Server

Well, here you are already at one of my favorite topics. Long after their introduction, *user-defined functions* — or UDFs — remain one of the more underutilized and misunderstood objects in SQL Server. In short, these were awesome when Microsoft first introduced them in SQL Server 2000, and the addition of .NET functionality back in SQL Server 2005 just added all that much more to them. One of the best things about UDFs from your point of view is, provided you've done the book in order, you already know most of what you need to write them. They are actually very, very similar to stored procedures — they just have certain behaviors and capabilities about them that set them apart and make them *the* answer in many situations.

In this chapter, not only am I going to introduce you to UDFs, but I'm also going to give you a look at the different types of UDFs, how they vary from stored procedures (often called sprocs), and, of course, what kinds of situations you might want to use them in. Finally, you'll take a quick look at how you can use .NET to expand on their power.

WHAT A UDF IS

A user-defined function is, much like a sproc, an ordered set of T-SQL statements that are pre-optimized and compiled and can be called to work as a single unit. The primary difference between them is how results are returned. Because of things that need to happen in order to support these different kinds of returned values, UDFs have a few more limitations to them than sprocs do.

NOTE *Sprocs were covered in Chapter 12, so if you'd like a refresher just turn to the previous chapter. If you're not familiar with stored procedures and you skipped straight here, I'd recommend working through that chapter before starting this one.*

NOTE *Okay, so I've said what a UDF is, so I suspect I ought to take a moment to say what it is not. A UDF is definitely NOT a generic replacement for any arbitrary sproc — it is just a different option that offers you yet one more form of code flexibility.*

With a sproc, you can pass parameters in and also get values in parameters passed back out. You can return a value, but that value is really intended to indicate success or failure rather than return data. You can also return result sets, but you can't really use those result sets in a query without first inserting them into some kind of table (usually a temporary table) to work with them further.

With a UDF, however, you can pass parameters *in*, but not out. Instead, the concept of output parameters has been replaced with a much more robust return value. As with system functions, you can return a scalar value — what's particularly nice, however, is that this value is not limited to just the integer data type as it would be for a sproc. Instead, you can return almost any SQL Server data type (more on this in the next section).

As they like to say in late-night television commercials: "But wait! There's more!" The "more" is that you are actually not just limited to returning scalar values — you can also return tables. This is wildly powerful, and you'll look into this fully later in the chapter.

So, to summarize, there are two types of UDFs:

➤ Those that return a scalar value

➤ Those that return a table

Let's take a look at the general syntax for creating a UDF:

```
CREATE FUNCTION [<schema name>.]<function name>
    ( [ <@parameter name> [AS] [<schema name>.]<data type>
        [ = <default value> [READONLY]]
        [ ,...n ] ] )
RETURNS {<scalar type>|TABLE [(<table definition>)]}
    [ WITH [ENCRYPTION]|[SCHEMABINDING]|
[ RETURNS NULL ON NULL INPUT | CALLED ON NULL INPUT ] |
    [EXECUTE AS { CALLER|SELF|OWNER|<'user name'>} ]
]
[AS] { EXTERNAL NAME <external method> |
BEGIN
    [<function statements>]
    {RETURN <type as defined in RETURNS clause>|RETURN (<SELECT statement>)}
END }[;]
```

This is kind of a tough one to explain because parts of the optional syntax are dependent on the choices you make elsewhere in your CREATE statement. The big issues here are whether you are returning a scalar data type or a table and whether you're doing a T-SQL-based function or doing something utilizing the CLR and .NET. Let's look at each type individually.

UDFS RETURNING A SCALAR VALUE

This type of UDF is probably the most like what you might expect a function to be. Much like most of SQL Server's own built-in functions, they return a scalar value to the calling script or procedure; functions such as GETDATE() or USER() return scalar values.

As I indicated earlier, one of the truly great things about a UDF is that you are not limited to an integer for a return value — instead, it can be of any valid SQL Server data type (including user-defined data types!), except for BLOBs, cursors, and timestamps. Even if you wanted to return an integer, a UDF should look very attractive to you for two reasons:

➤ **Unlike sprocs, the whole purpose of the return value is to serve as a meaningful piece of data.** For sprocs, a return value is meant as an indication of success or failure and, in the event of failure, to provide some specific information about the nature of that failure.

➤ **You can perform functions inline to your queries.** For instance, you can include it as part of your SELECT statement. You can't do that with a sproc.

So, that said, you'll now create a simple UDF to get your feet wet on the whole idea of how you might utilize them differently from a sproc. I'm not kidding when I say this is a simple one from a code point of view, but I think you'll see how it illustrates the sprocs versus UDFs point.

One of the most common function-like requirements I see is a desire to determine whether an entry in a datetime field occurred on a specific day. The usual problem here is that your datetime field has specific time-of-day information that prevents it from easily being compared with just the date. Indeed, you've already seen this problem in some of the comparisons in previous chapters.

Let's go back to the Accounting database that you created in Chapter 5. Imagine for a moment that you want to know all the orders that came in during a particular fiscal year. Let's make it a little more interesting, though, by stipulating that the folks in Accounting can be a little arbitrary about exactly when a fiscal year starts and ends; they'd like to be able to choose when it does.

To begin, let's add a few orders in with a year's worth of dates. You'll just pick customer and employee IDs you know already exist in their respective tables (if you don't have any records there, you'll need to insert a couple of dummy rows to reference). I'm also going to create a small loop to add several rows:

Available for
download on
Wrox.com

```
USE Accounting;

DECLARE @Counter  int = 1;

WHILE @Counter <= 24
BEGIN
```

```
INSERT INTO Orders
    VALUES (1, DATEADD(mm, @Counter, SYSDATETIME()), 1);
    SET @Counter = @Counter + 1;
END
```

So, this gets you 24 rows inserted, with each row being inserted one month apart starting next month. That's enough to test the function. Now you're ready to run a simple query to see what orders came in during the year ending, say, in three months' time. You might try something like:

```
SELECT *
FROM Orders
WHERE OrderDate BETWEEN DATEADD(mm, 3, SYSDATETIME())
AND DATEADD(mm, 15, SYSDATETIME())
```

Unfortunately, this query will not get you back exactly what you want. The fiscal year ending in 15 months doesn't include the order placed three months from now; that's the last day of the prior fiscal year.

> *NOTE If you're working on this late at night (as I often do), you might have populated the data before midnight and queried it thereafter. That would skip the row three months in the future, and might fool you into thinking you got the right results back. To continue following along, you can always substitute a literal date (such as* `'1/1/2011'`*) for the* `SYSDATETIME()` *function. The important thing is to keep your wits about you despite the hour.*

Time for a little more advanced date logic. You need to go from the end of the fiscal year back one year then forward one day. To do that, I'll nest a little date logic.

```
DECLARE @YearEnding DATE = DATEADD(MONTH, 15, SYSDATETIME());
-- Create a date variable storing the end of the fiscal year

SELECT *
FROM Orders
WHERE OrderDate
BETWEEN /* Between is inclusive, so the start and end are part of the range */
    DATEADD(day, 1, DATEADD(year, -1, @YearEnding))  /* Start of date range */
    AND @YearEnding /* End of date range (the fiscal year end you want) */
```

> **NOTE** As complicated as this is, it's far simpler than in versions of SQL Server prior to 2008. Back then you didn't have the DATE data type; you only had DATETIME. Thus the orders you created would have a time of day attached, and the end date above — at midnight — wouldn't include orders after midnight on the last day.
>
> Furthermore, trimming the time from a date was more complicated. If you're using SQL Server 2005 or earlier, you don't have access to the DATE data type used here. Instead of the relatively simple and intelligible syntax of today — CAST (OrderDate AS DATE) — you'll be likely to see something genuinely ugly, which would look more like WHERE CONVERT(varchar(12), OrderDate, 101) = CONVERT(varchar(12), GETDATE(), 101).
>
> This time, you will get back every row within the fiscal year ending in 15 months. Unfortunately, this isn't exactly the most readable code. Imagine you had a large series of dates you needed to perform such comparisons against — it can get very ugly indeed.

TRY IT OUT   Create a Scalar UDF

So now let's look at doing the same thing with a simple user-defined function. First, you'll need to create the actual function. This is done with the new CREATE FUNCTION command, and it's formatted much like a sproc. For example, you might code this function like this:

Available for download on Wrox.com

```
CREATE FUNCTION IsInFiscalYear (@YearEnding DATE, @CompareDate DATE)
RETURNS BIT
AS
BEGIN
        DECLARE @out BIT = 0; --Assume FALSE

        IF @CompareDate BETWEEN DATEADD(day, 1, DATEADD(year, -1, @YearEnding))
    AND @YearEnding
        SET @out = 1;  --Conditionally set to TRUE

        RETURN @out;
END;
```

Code snippet Chap13.sql

where the fiscal year end date and the order date are passed in as the parameters, and the task of comparing the dates is included in the function body. The function returns 1 (true) if the order date is in the range, and 0 otherwise.

How It Works

Note that the preceding function is a SQL Server 2008 (or later) compatible version, relying on the DATE data type, as well as assigning a default value to the @out variable. If you wanted to do a comparison function like this in SQL Server 2005 (as you did with the query-based example), you would need to use DATETIME variables and the CONVERT function to truncate dates. For example:

```
CREATE FUNCTION IsInFiscalYear2005 (@YearEnding DATETIME, @CompareDate DATETIME)
RETURNS BIT
AS
BEGIN
        DECLARE @out BIT,
        @YearEndingTruncated DATETIME,
        @CompareDateTruncated DATETIME;

        SET @out = 0;

        SELECT
        @YearEndingTruncated =
            CAST(CONVERT(varchar(12), @YearEnding, 101) AS DATETIME),
        @CompareDateTruncated =
            CAST(CONVERT(varchar(12), @CompareDate, 101) AS DATETIME);

        IF @CompareDateTruncated BETWEEN
            (day, 1, DATEADD(year, -1, @YearEndingTruncated))
            AND @YearEndingTruncated
        SET @out = 1;

        RETURN @out;
END
```

Code snippet Chap13.sql

This does such a simple function, yet accomplishing it takes a great deal of, well, text. Imagine embedding that in your query...you'd need a wall of comments to help users later to understand what you'd done! Having placed it in a function, however, your query now looks a lot less verbose:

```
DECLARE @YearEnding DATE = DATEADD(MONTH, 15, SYSDATETIME());

SELECT *
FROM Orders
    WHERE dbo.IsInFiscalYear(@YearEnding, OrderDate) = 1;
```

Code snippet Chap13.sql

You get back the same set as with the standalone query. Even for a simple query like this one, the new code is quite a bit more readable. The call works pretty much as it would from most languages that support functions. There is, however, one hitch — the schema (dbo. in this case) is required. SQL Server will, for some reason, not resolve scalar value functions the way it does with other objects.

As you might expect, there is a lot more to UDFs than just readability. You can embed queries in them and use them as an encapsulation method for subqueries. Almost anything you can do procedurally that returns a discrete value could also be encapsulated in a UDF and used inline with your queries.

Let's take a look at a very simple subquery example. The subquery version looks like this:

```sql
USE AdventureWorks;

SELECT Name,
       ListPrice,
       (SELECT AVG(ListPrice) FROM Production.Product) AS Average,
        ListPrice - (SELECT AVG(ListPrice) FROM Production.Product)
         AS Difference
FROM Production.Product
WHERE ProductSubcategoryID = 1; -- The Mountain Bikes Sub-cat
```

Code snippet Chap13.sql

This returns a pretty simple set of data:

```
Name                           ListPrice   Average          Difference
-----------------------------  ----------- ---------------  --------------
Mountain-100 Silver, 38        3399.99     438.6662         2961.3238
Mountain-100 Silver, 42        3399.99     438.6662         2961.3238
Mountain-100 Silver, 44        3399.99     438.6662         2961.3238
Mountain-100 Silver, 48        3399.99     438.6662         2961.3238
Mountain-100 Black, 38         3374.99     438.6662         2936.3238
Mountain-100 Black, 42         3374.99     438.6662         2936.3238
...
...
Mountain-500 Silver, 52        564.99      438.6662         126.3238
Mountain-500 Black, 40         539.99      438.6662         101.3238
Mountain-500 Black, 42         539.99      438.6662         101.3238
Mountain-500 Black, 44         539.99      438.6662         101.3238
Mountain-500 Black, 48         539.99      438.6662         101.3238
Mountain-500 Black, 52         539.99      438.6662         101.3238

(32 row(s) affected)
```

Let's try it again, only this time you'll encapsulate both the average and the difference into two functions. The first encapsulates the task of calculating the average and the second does the subtraction.

```sql
CREATE FUNCTION dbo.AveragePrice()
RETURNS money
WITH SCHEMABINDING
AS
BEGIN
    RETURN (SELECT AVG(ListPrice) FROM Production.Product);
END
GO

CREATE FUNCTION dbo.PriceDifference(@Price money)
RETURNS money
AS
BEGIN
    RETURN @Price - dbo.AveragePrice();
END
```

Code snippet Chap13.sql

Notice that it's completely legal to embed one UDF in another one.

> **NOTE** Note that the WITH SCHEMABINDING option works for functions just the way that it did for views — if a function is built using schema-binding, any object that function depends on cannot be altered or dropped without first removing the schema-bound function. In this case, schema-binding wasn't really necessary, but I wanted to point out its usage and also prepare this example for something you're going to do with it a little later in the chapter.

Now let's run the query using the new functions instead of the old subquery model:

```
USE AdventureWorks

SELECT Name,
    ListPrice,
    dbo.AveragePrice() AS Average,
    dbo.PriceDifference(ListPrice) AS Difference
FROM Production.Product
WHERE ProductSubcategoryID = 1; -- The Mountain Bikes Sub-cat
```

Code snippet Chap13.sql

This yields the same results you had with your subquery.

Note that, beyond the readability issue, you also get the added benefit of reuse out of this. For a little example like this, it probably doesn't seem like a big deal, but as your functions become more complex, it can be quite a time saver.

UDFS THAT RETURN A TABLE

User-defined functions in SQL Server are not limited to just returning scalar values. They can return something far more interesting — tables. Now, while the possible impacts of this are sinking in on you, I'll go ahead and add that the table that is returned is, for the most part, usable much as any other table is. You can perform a JOIN against it and even apply WHERE conditions against the results. It's *very* cool stuff indeed.

Inline UDFs

To make the change to using a table as a return value is not hard at all — a table is just like any other SQL Server data type as far as a UDF is concerned. To illustrate this, you'll build a relatively simple one to start:

```
USE AdventureWorks
GO

CREATE FUNCTION dbo.fnContactList()
RETURNS TABLE
AS
RETURN (SELECT BusinessEntityID,
               LastName + ',' + FirstName AS Name
          FROM Person.Person);
GO
```

This function returns a table of selected records and does a little formatting — joining the last and first names, and separating them with a comma.

At this point, you're ready to use your function just as you would use a table:

```
SELECT *
FROM dbo.fnContactList();
```

Code snippet Chap13.sql

Now, let's add a bit more fun into things. What you did with this table up to this point could have been done just as easily — more easily, in fact — with a view. But what if you wanted to parameterize a view? What if, for example, you wanted to accept last names to filter the results (without having to manually put in your own WHERE clause)? It might look something like this:

```
--CREATE your view
CREATE VIEW vFullContactName
AS
SELECT p.BusinessEntityID,
           LastName + ',' + FirstName AS Name,
           ea.EmailAddress
      FROM Person.Person as p
      LEFT OUTER JOIN Person.EmailAddress ea
        ON ea.BusinessEntityID = p.BusinessEntityID;
GO
```

This would yield what was asked for, with a twist. You can't parameterize things right in the view itself, so you have to include a WHERE clause in the query:

```
SELECT *
FROM vFullContactName
WHERE Name LIKE 'Ad%';
```

Code snippet Chap13.sql

This should return results that look something like this:

```
BusinessEntityID Name                                    EmailAddress
---------------- --------------------------------------- ---------------------------
67               Adams, Jay                              jay0@adventure-works.com
```

301	Adams, Frances	frances0@adventure-works.com
305	Adams, Carla	carla0@adventure-works.com
...		
...		
16901	Adams, Adam	adam46@adventure-works.com
16902	Adams, Eric	eric57@adventure-works.com
16910	Adams, Jackson	jackson47@adventure-works.com

```
(87 row(s) affected)
```

To simplify things a bit, you can encapsulate everything in a function instead:

Available for
download on
Wrox.com

```
USE AdventureWorks;
GO

CREATE FUNCTION dbo.fnContactSearch(@LastName nvarchar(50))
RETURNS TABLE
AS
RETURN (SELECT p.BusinessEntityID,
            LastName + ', ' + FirstName AS Name,
            ea.EmailAddress
        FROM Person.Person as p
        LEFT OUTER JOIN Person.EmailAddress ea
          ON ea.BusinessEntityID = p.BusinessEntityID
        WHERE LastName Like @LastName + '%');
GO
```

Now you're set up pretty well — to execute it, you just call the function and provide the parameter:

```
SELECT *
FROM fnContactSearch('Ad');
```

Code snippet Chap13.sql

And you get back the same result set — no WHERE clause, no filtering the SELECT list, and, as our friends down under would say, no worries. You can use this over and over again without having to use the old cut-and-paste trick. Note, also, that while you could have achieved similar results with a sproc and an EXEC command, you couldn't directly join the results of the sproc to another table.

Well, all this would probably be exciting enough, but sometimes you need more than just a single SELECT statement. Sometimes, you want more than just a parameterized view. Indeed, much as you saw with some of the scalar functions, you may need to execute multiple statements in order to achieve the results that you want. User-defined functions support this notion just fine. Indeed, they can return tables that are created using multiple statements — the only big difference when using multiple statements is that you must both name and define the metadata (much as you would for a table variable) for what you'll be returning.

To illustrate this example, I'll discuss a very common problem in the relational database world — hierarchical data.

Imagine for a moment that you are working in the human resources department. You have an Employee table, and it has a unary relationship (a foreign key that relates to another column in the same table) that relates employees to their bosses through the ManagerID column — that is, the way you know who is someone's boss is by relating the ManagerID column back to another EmployeeID. A very common need in a scenario like this is to be able to create a reporting tree — that is, a list of all of the people who exist below a given manager in an organizational chart.

Historically, relational databases had a major weakness in dealing with hierarchical data. Numerous articles, white papers, and books have been written on this subject. Fortunately, SQL Server 2008 introduced a new methodology for dealing with hierarchical data. Since 2008, the hierarchyID data type and a collection of built-in functions can help you deal with tree type data structures in your relational database. These features are somewhat advanced and take quite a bit of effort to master, so I'm just going to skim them in this edition.

 NOTE *If you would like to see examples of the* hierarchyID *data type functionality, check out the* OrganizationNode *and* OrganizationLevel *columns of the* HumanResources.Employee *table in AdventureWorks.*

For purposes of illustrating the capabilities of the UDF, you are going to handle hierarchies the way you've been forced to for ages — call it the "old school method." Since AdventureWorks doesn't have a good example of this older (and still far more prevalent) way of storing hierarchical data, you'll create your own version of the Employee table (call it Employee2) that implements this "old school method" of addressing hierarchies. If you ran the BuildAndPopulateEmployee2.sql file back in Chapter 3, you already have this new version of Employee. If you didn't, go ahead and execute it now.

Available for
download on
Wrox.com

Code snippet BuildAndPopulateEmployee2.sql.

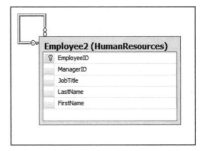

FIGURE 13-1

The table created by this script is represented in Figure 13-1.

Assuming you've executed the script and have the Employee2 table, let's see if you can retrieve a list of reports for Karla Huntington.

At first glance, this seems pretty easy. If you wanted to know all the people who report to Karla, you might write a query that would join the Employee table back to itself — something like:

Available for
download on
Wrox.com

```
USE AdventureWorks;

SELECT
        TheReport.EmployeeID,
        TheReport.JobTitle,
        TheReport.LastName,
        TheReport.FirstName
```

```
FROM
        HumanResources.Employee2 as TheBoss
JOIN HumanResources.Employee2 AS TheReport
        ON TheBoss.EmployeeID = TheReport.ManagerID
WHERE TheBoss.LastName = 'Huntington' AND TheBoss.FirstName = 'Karla';
```

Code snippet Chap13.sql

Again, at first glance, this might appear to give you what you want:

```
EmployeeID  JobTitle                        LastName             FirstName
----------- ------------------------------- -------------------- -----------
5           VP of Engineering               Olsen                Ken
6           VP of Professional Services     Cross                Gary
7           VP of Security                  Lebowski             Jeff
(3 row(s) affected)
```

But, in reality, you have a bit of a problem here. At issue is that you want all of the people in Karla's reporting chain — not just those who report to Karla directly, but those who report to people who report to Karla, and so on. You see that if you look at all the records in your newly created Employee2 table, you'll find a number of employees who report to Ken Olsen, but they don't appear in the results of this query.

> **NOTE** *Okay, so some of the quicker or more experienced among you may now be saying something like, "Hey, no problem! I'll just join back to the* Employee2 *table one more time and get the next level of reports!" You could probably make this work for such a small dataset, or for any situation where the number of levels of your hierarchy is fixed — but what if the number of hierarchy levels isn't fixed? What if people are reporting to Robert Cheechov, and still others report to people under Robert Cheechov — it could go on virtually forever. Now what? Glad you asked. . . .*

What you really need is a function that returns all the levels of the hierarchy below whatever EmployeeID (and, therefore, ManagerID) you provide — you need a tree. To do this, you have a classic example of the need for *recursion*. A block of code is said to recurse any time it calls itself. You saw an example of this in the previous chapter with the spTriangular stored procedure. Think about this scenario for a moment:

1. You need to figure out all the people who report to the manager that you want.

2. For each person in Step 1, you need to know who reports to him or her.

3. Repeat Step 2 until there are no more subordinates.

This is recursion all the way. What this means is that you're going to need several statements to make your function work: some statements to figure out the current level and at least one more to call the same function again to get the next lowest level.

Let's put it together. Notice the couple of changes in the declaration of your function. This time, you need to associate a name with the return value (in this case, `@Reports`) — this is required any time you're using multiple statements to generate your result. Also, you have to define the table that you will be returning — this allows SQL Server to validate whatever you try to insert into that table before it is returned to the calling routine.

```
CREATE FUNCTION dbo.fnGetReports
        (@EmployeeID AS int)
        RETURNS @Reports TABLE
        (
        EmployeeID    int        NOT NULL,
        ManagerID    int        NULL
        )
AS
BEGIN

    /* Since you'll need to call this function recursively - that is
    ** once for each reporting employee (to make sure that they don't have
    ** reports of their own), you need a holding variable to keep track
    ** of which employee you're currently working on. */
    DECLARE @Employee AS int;

    /* This inserts the current employee into the working table. The
    ** significance here is that you need the first record as something
    ** of a primer due to the recursive nature of the function - this is how
    ** you get it. */
    INSERT INTO @Reports
        SELECT EmployeeID, ManagerID
        FROM HumanResources.Employee2
        WHERE EmployeeID = @EmployeeID;

    /* Now you also need a primer for the recursive calls you're getting
    ** ready to start making to this function. This would probably be better
    ** done with a cursor, but you haven't gotten to that chapter yet,
    ** so.... */
    SELECT @Employee = MIN(EmployeeID)
    FROM HumanResources.Employee2
    WHERE ManagerID = @EmployeeID;

    /* This next part would probably be better done with a cursor but you
    ** haven't gotten to that chapter yet, so you'll fake it. Notice the
    ** recursive call to the function! */
    WHILE @Employee IS NOT NULL
        BEGIN
            INSERT INTO @Reports
                SELECT *
```

```
                 FROM fnGetReports(@Employee);

                 SELECT @Employee = MIN(EmployeeID)
                 FROM HumanResources.Employee2
                 WHERE EmployeeID > @Employee
                     AND ManagerID = @EmployeeID;
        END

    RETURN;

    END
    GO
```

Code snippet Chap13.sql

I've written this one to provide just minimal information about the employee and his or her manager — I can join back to the `Employee2` table, if need be, to fetch additional information. I also took a little bit of liberty with the requirements on this one and added in the selected manager to the results. This was done primarily to support the recursion scenario and also to provide something of a base result for your result set. Speaking of which, let's look at your results — Karla is `EmployeeID` 4; to do this, you'll feed that into your function:

```
SELECT * FROM fnGetReports(4);
```

This gets you not only the original one person who reported to Karla Huntington, but also those who report to Ken Olsen (who reports to Ms. Huntington) and Ms. Huntington herself (remember, I added her as something of a starting point).

```
EmployeeID  ManagerID
----------- -----------
4           1
5           4
8           5
9           5
10          5
11          5
6           4
7           4

(8 row(s) affected)
```

Now, let's go the final step here and join this back to actual data. You'll use it much as you did your original query looking for the reports of Karla Huntington:

```
DECLARE @EmployeeID int;

SELECT @EmployeeID = EmployeeID
FROM HumanResources.Employee2 e
WHERE LastName = 'Huntington'
AND FirstName = 'Karla';

SELECT e.EmployeeID, e.LastName, e.FirstName, m.LastName AS ReportsTo
```

```
FROM HumanResources.Employee2 AS e
JOIN dbo.fnGetReports(@EmployeeID) AS r
  ON e.EmployeeID = r.EmployeeID
JOIN HumanResources.Employee2 AS m
  ON m.EmployeeID = r.ManagerID;
```

Code snippet Chap13.sql

This returns all seven employees who are under Ms. Huntington:

```
EmployeeID  LastName        FirstName       ReportsTo
----------- --------------- --------------- ---------------
4           Huntington      Karla           Smith
5           Olsen           Ken             Huntington
8           Gutierrez       Ron             Olsen
9           Bray            Marky           Olsen
10          Cheechov        Robert          Olsen
11          Gale            Sue             Olsen
6           Cross           Gary            Huntington
7           Lebowski        Jeff            Huntington

(8 row(s) affected)
```

So, as you can see, you can actually have very complex code build your table results for you, but the output is still a table and, as such, it can be used just like any other table.

Understanding Determinism

Any coverage of UDFs would be incomplete without discussing *determinism*. If SQL Server is going to build an index over something, it must be able to deterministically define (define with certainty) the item being indexed. Why does this matter to functions? Well, because you can have functions that feed data to things that will be indexed (such as computed columns or indexed views).

User-defined functions are either *deterministic* or *non-deterministic*. The determinism is defined not by any kind of parameter, but rather by what SQL Server can tell about what the function is doing. If, given a specific set of valid inputs, the function returns exactly the same value every time, the function is said to be deterministic. An example of a built-in function that is deterministic is SUM(). The sum of 3, 5, and 10 is always going to be 18 — *every* time the function is called with those values as inputs. The value of GETDATE(), however, is non-deterministic — it changes pretty much every time you call it.

NOTE *Non-determinism shows up where you least expect it sometimes. To illustrate, try to imagine why a function like* DATEPART(<interval type>, <date value>), *which can (for example) return the current day of the week, is non-deterministic. You might think that because a given date is always the same day of the week, the same input guarantees the same output: the very definition of determinism. However, different system values for* DATEFIRST *can shift the value for any given day. Because the output is dependent on this external variable, the function is non-deterministic.*

To be considered deterministic, a function has to meet four criteria:

➤ **The function must be schema-bound.** This means that any objects on which the function depends has a dependency recorded and no changes to those objects are allowed without first dropping the dependent function.

➤ **All other functions referred to in your function must also be deterministic.** It doesn't matter whether they are user- or system-defined functions.

➤ **The function cannot use an extended stored procedure.**

The importance of determinism shows up if you want to build an index on a view or computed column. Indexes on views or computed columns are allowed only if the result of the view or computed column can be reliably determined. This means that, if the view or computed column refers to a non-deterministic function, no index is allowed on that view or column. This situation isn't necessarily the end of the world, but you'll want to think about whether a function is deterministic or not before creating indexes against views or columns that use that function.

So, this should beget the question: "How do I figure out whether my function is deterministic?" Well, beyond checking the rules I've already described, you can also have SQL Server tell you whether your function is deterministic — it's stored in the `IsDeterministic` property of the object. To check this out, you can make use of the `OBJECTPROPERTY` function. For example, you could check out the determinism of your `IsInFiscalYear` function that you used earlier in the chapter:

```
USE Accounting;

SELECT OBJECTPROPERTY(OBJECT_ID('IsInFiscalYear'), 'IsDeterministic');
```

Code snippet Chap13.sql

It may come as a surprise to you (or maybe not) that this function is *not* deterministic:

```
-----------
0
(1 row(s) affected)
```

Look back through the list of requirements for a deterministic function and see if you can figure out why this one doesn't meet the grade.

 NOTE *When I was working on this example, I got one of those not-so-nice little reminders about how it's the little things that get you. You see, I was certain this function should be deterministic, and, of course, it wasn't. After too many nights writing until the morning hours, I completely missed the obvious —* SCHEMABINDING.

Fortunately, you can fix the only problem this one has. All you need to do is add the WITH SCHEMABINDING option to your function, and you'll see better results:

```
ALTER FUNCTION IsInFiscalYear (@YearEnding DATE, @CompareDate DATE)
RETURNS bit
WITH SCHEMABINDING
AS
BEGIN
    DECLARE @out BIT = 0;

    IF @CompareDate BETWEEN
DATEADD(day, 1, DATEADD(year, -1, @YearEnding)) AND @YearEnding
        SET @out = 1;

    RETURN @out;
END
```

Code snippet Chap13.sql

Now, you just rerun your OBJECTPROPERTY query:

```
-----------
1
(1 row(s) affected)
```

And voilà — a deterministic function!

Here are a couple examples that explore the boundaries a bit. Hopefully these will help you see how you can create determinism when you need it. First, take a look at this function, which returns the order date from a given SalesOrderID:

```
USE AdventureWorks;
GO

CREATE FUNCTION dbo.SalesOrderDate(@SalesOrderID INT)
RETURNS DATE
WITH SCHEMABINDING
AS
BEGIN
    DECLARE @SODate DATE;

    SELECT @SODate = OrderDate
    FROM Sales.SalesOrderHeader
    WHERE SalesOrderID = @SalesOrderID;

    RETURN @SODate;
END
```

Code snippet Chap13.sql

This function is deterministic (you can check by using OBJECTPROPERTY, as you did above) even though it reaches into a table for its return value. Remember that determinism means for a given set of inputs, the output is always the same; you can see from this example that the state of the database (the information currently stored) is an implicit input to a SQL Server function.

Now create a function, dependent on the last one, that computes the age (in days) of a sales order. It's easy to do, but this function is non-deterministic.

```
CREATE FUNCTION dbo.SalesOrderAge(@SalesOrderID INT)
RETURNS INT
WITH SCHEMABINDING
AS
BEGIN
    DECLARE @SODate DATE, @SOAge INT;
    SET @SODate = dbo.SalesOrderDate(@SalesOrderID);
    SET @SOAge = DATEDIFF(Day, @SODate, SYSDATETIME());
    RETURN @SOAge;
END
```

Code snippet Chap13.sql

Because it uses SYSDATETIME(), which is non-deterministic, this function cannot possibly be deterministic. If you need a deterministic version of this age function, one way is to move the non-deterministic portion out (to the caller, in this case):

```
ALTER FUNCTION dbo.SalesOrderAge(@SalesOrderID INT, @CurrentDate DATE)
RETURNS INT
WITH SCHEMABINDING
AS
BEGIN
    DECLARE @SODate DATE, @SOAge INT;
    SET @SODate = dbo.SalesOrderDate(@SalesOrderID);
    SET @SOAge = DATEDIFF(Day, @SODate, @CurrentDate);
    RETURN @SOAge;
END
```

You can see that this function uses a date parameter instead of a non-deterministic function within the UDF, so it should be deterministic. Go ahead and check it with OBJECTPROPERTY:

```
USE AdventureWorks;

SELECT OBJECTPROPERTY(OBJECT_ID('SalesOrderAge'), 'IsDeterministic');
```

Code snippet Chap13.sql

DEBUGGING USER-DEFINED FUNCTIONS

This actually works just the same as the sproc example you saw in Chapter 12.

Simply set up a script that calls your function, and begin stepping through the script (using the toolbar icon, or pressing F11). You can then step right into your UDF.

USING .NET IN A DATABASE WORLD

As discussed in Chapter 12, the ability to use .NET assemblies in your stored procedures and functions was added to SQL Server back in SQL Server 2005. Much as it does with sprocs, this has enormous implications for functions.

Considering that most who read this title are beginners, it's hard to fully relate the impact that .NET has in your database world. The reality is that you won't use it all that often, and yet, when you do, the effects can be profound. Need to implement a complex formula for a special function? No problem. Need to access external data sources such as credit card authorization companies and such things? No problem. Need to access other complex data sources? No problem. In short, things you used to have to either skip or perform extremely complex development to achieve (in some cases, it was all smoke and mirrors before) suddenly became relatively straightforward.

What does this mean in terms of functions? Well, I already gave the example of implementing a complex formula in a function. But now imagine something like external tabular data — let's say representing a `.csv` or some other data in a tabular fashion — very doable with a .NET assembly created as a function in SQL Server.

.NET assemblies in SQL Server remain, however, something of an advanced concept, and one I'll defer to a book that doesn't have *Beginner* in the title. That said, it's important to understand that the option is available and consider it as something worth researching in that "Wow, I have no idea how we're going to do this!" situation.

SUMMARY

What you learned in this chapter was, in many ways, not new at all. Indeed, much of what goes into user-defined functions is the same set of statements, variables, and general coding practices that you have already seen in scripting and stored procedures. However, UDFs still provide you a wonderful new area of functionality that was not previously available in SQL Server. You can now encapsulate a wider range of code, and even use this encapsulated functionality inline with your queries. What's more, you can now also provide parameterized views and dynamically created tables.

User-defined functions are, in many ways, the most exciting of all the new functionality added to SQL Server. In pondering their uses, I have already come to realize that I'm only scratching the surface of their potential. Over the life of this next release, I suspect that developers will implement UDFs in ways I have yet to dream of — let's hope you'll be one of those developers!

EXERCISES

1. Reimplement the `spTriangular` function from Chapter 12 as a function instead of as a stored procedure.

2. Create a function that takes as inputs a `SalesOrderID`, a `CurrencyCode`, and a date, and returns a table of all the `SalesOrderDetail` rows for that Sales Order including `Quantity`, `ProductID`, `UnitPrice`, and the unit price converted to the target currency based on the end of day rate for the date provided. Exchange rates can be found in the `Sales.CurrencyRate` table.

▶ WHAT YOU LEARNED IN THIS CHAPTER

TOPIC	CONCEPT
`CREATE FUNCTION`	User-defined functions allow you to encapsulate complex business logic for use in your queries. They can return scalar values or tables.
Scalar UDFs	UDFs that return an atomic value in virtually any SQL Server data type. Scalar UDFs can be used inline within almost any part of your queries.
Table-values UDFs	UDFs that return a table of values. These can be included in the `FROM` clause of a SQL statement.
Deterministic functions	Functions that, for the same set of inputs, must always return the same output. SQL Server evaluates whether your functions are deterministic and keeps an indicator in the system tables, accessible using the `OBJECTPROPERTY` function.

14

Transactions and Locks

WHAT YOU WILL LEARN IN THIS CHAPTER:

➤ What a transaction is, and how and when to use one

➤ How SQL Server uses the log to manage database concurrency

➤ When SQL will lock resources, and what types of locks exist

➤ How to manage locking

➤ The difference between ordinary lock waits and deadlocks

This is one of those chapters that, when you go back to work, makes you sound like you've had your Wheaties today. Nothing you're going to learn about in this chapter is wildly difficult, yet transactions and locks tend to be two of the most misunderstood areas in the database world. As such, this beginning (or at least I think it's a basic) concept is going to make you start to look like a real pro.

In this chapter, my goals are to:

➤ Demystify transactions

➤ Examine how the SQL Server log and checkpoints work

➤ Unlock your understanding of locks

You'll learn why these topics are so closely tied to each other and how to minimize problems with each.

UNDERSTANDING TRANSACTIONS

Transactions are all about atomicity. Atomicity is the concept that something should act as a unit. From a database standpoint, it's about the smallest grouping of one or more statements that should be considered to be *all or nothing*.

Often, when dealing with data, you want to make sure that if one thing happens, another thing happens, or that neither of them does. Indeed, this can be carried out to the degree where 20 things (or more) all have to happen together or nothing happens. Let's look at a classic example.

Imagine that you are a banker. Sally comes in and wants to transfer $1,000 from checking to savings. You are, of course, happy to oblige, so you process her request.

Behind the scenes, something like this is happening:

```
UPDATE checking
   SET Balance = Balance - 1000
   WHERE Account = 'Sally'
UPDATE savings
   SET Balance = Balance + 1000
   WHERE Account = 'Sally'
```

This is a hyper-simplification of what's going on, but it captures the main thrust of things: You need to issue two statements — one for each account.

Now what if the first statement executes and the second one doesn't? Sally would be out a thousand dollars! That might, for a short time, seem okay from your perspective (heck, you just made a thousand bucks!), but not for long. By that afternoon you'd have a steady stream of customers leaving your bank — it's hard to stay in the bank business with no depositors.

ACID Transactions

This situation doesn't come up if your system is designed to use ACID transactions. By applying what you find in this chapter, you can ensure that your transactions pass the ACID test:

➤ **Atomicity:** The transaction is all or nothing.

➤ **Consistency:** All constraints and other data integrity rules have been adhered to, and all related objects (data pages and index pages) have been updated completely.

➤ **Isolation:** Each transaction is completely isolated from any other transaction. The actions of one transaction cannot be interfered with by the actions of a separate transaction.

➤ **Durability:** After a transaction is completed, its effects are permanently in place in the system. The data is *safe*, in the sense that things such as a power outage or other non-disk system failure does not lead to data that is only half written.

Throughout this chapter, virtually everything you read comes back to support the ACID transaction principles.

Introducing Transaction Operations

What you need is a way to be certain that if the first statement executes, the second statement executes. There really isn't a way that you can be certain of that — all sorts of things can go wrong, from hardware failures to simple things, such as violations of data integrity rules. Fortunately, however, there is a way to do something that serves the same overall purpose — you can essentially forget that the first statement ever happened. You can enforce at least the notion that if one thing didn't happen, nothing did — at least within the scope of your transaction.

In order to capture this notion of a transaction, however, you must define very definite boundaries. A transaction must have very definitive beginning and end points. Actually, every SELECT, INSERT, UPDATE, and DELETE statement you issue in SQL Server is part of an implicit transaction. Even if you issue only one statement, that one statement is considered to be a transaction — everything about the statement is executed, or none of it is. Indeed, by default, that is the length of a transaction — one statement.

But what if you need to have more than one statement be all or nothing, as in the preceding bank example? In such a case, you need a way of marking the beginning and end of a transaction, as well as the success or failure of that transaction. To that end, there are several T-SQL statements that you can use to mark these points in a transaction. You can:

➤ **BEGIN** a transaction: Set the starting point.

➤ **COMMIT** a transaction: Make the transaction a permanent, irreversible part of the database.

➤ **ROLLBACK** a transaction: Disregard all changes, essentially forgetting that the transaction ever happened.

➤ **SAVE** a transaction: Establish a specific marker to allow you to do only a partial rollback.

You'll look over all of these individually before you put them together into your first transaction.

Using BEGIN TRAN

The beginning of the transaction is probably one of the easiest concepts to understand in the transaction process. Its sole purpose in life is to denote the point that is the beginning of a unit. If, for some reason, you are unable or do not want to commit the transaction, this is the point to which all database activity will be rolled back. That is, everything beyond this point that is not eventually committed will effectively be forgotten, as far as the database is concerned.

The syntax is:

```
BEGIN TRAN[SACTION] [<transaction name>|<@transaction variable>]
  [ WITH MARK [ <'description'> ]]
```

I won't dwell on the WITH MARK option here because it is a topic having to do with very advanced point in time transaction work, which tends to be more administrator oriented and is well outside of the scope of this book.

Using COMMIT TRAN

The committing of a transaction is the end of a completed transaction. At the point that you issue the COMMIT TRAN, the transaction is considered *durable*. That is, the effect of the transaction is now permanent and will last even if you have a system failure (as long as you have a backup or the database files haven't been physically destroyed). The only way to undo whatever the transaction accomplished is to issue a new transaction that, functionally speaking, is a reverse of your first transaction.

The syntax for a COMMIT looks pretty similar to a BEGIN:

```
COMMIT TRAN[SACTION] [<transaction name>|<@transaction variable>]
```

Using ROLLBACK TRAN

Whenever I think of a ROLLBACK, I think of the old movie *The Princess Bride*. If you've ever seen the film (if you haven't, I highly recommend it), you'll know that the character Vizzini (considered a genius in the film) has a rule: When a job goes wrong, you go back to the beginning.

That is some mighty good advice. A ROLLBACK does just what Vizzini suggests — it goes back to the beginning. In this case, it's your transaction that goes back to the beginning. Anything that happened since the associated BEGIN statement is effectively forgotten. The only exception to going back to the beginning is through the use of what are called *save points,* which I'll describe shortly.

The syntax for a ROLLBACK again looks pretty much the same as a BEGIN or COMMIT, with the exception of allowance for a save point.

```
ROLLBACK TRAN[SACTION] [<transaction name>|<save point name>|
    <@transaction variable>|<@savepoint variable>]
```

Using SAVE TRAN

To save a transaction is essentially to create something of a bookmark. You establish a name for your bookmark (you can have more than one). After this bookmark is established, you can reference it in a rollback. What's nice about this is that you can roll back to the exact spot in the code that you want to just by naming a save point to which you want to roll back.

The syntax is simple enough:

```
SAVE TRAN[SACTION] [<save point name>| <@savepoint variable>]
```

The point to remember about save points is that they are cleared on ROLLBACK — that is, even if you save five save points, once you perform one ROLLBACK they are all gone. You can start setting new save points again and rolling back to those, but whatever save points you had when the ROLLBACK was issued are gone.

SAVE TRAN can get extremely confusing and I can't recommend it for the beginning user, but keep it in mind as being there.

TRY IT OUT **Working with Transactions**

Several years ago, I had a co-worker — a talented software architect — come up to me and ask, "How do you undo an update statement?" He'd done an update without a where clause…on a live server. My first reply was to ask whether he was in a transaction; because he wasn't, we had to restore from a backup.

Besides enforcing business rules (such as the account example at the beginning of this chapter), one common use for transactions in SQL Server is testing. My co-worker knew immediately upon executing his update that it was wrong based on the number of rows affected; this and other hints can tell you whether it's time to commit your work, or use rollback.

In SQL Server Management Studio, open a query window and use the AdventureWorks database. You're going to give a person called Steve Ma a new middle name. Within that context, run the following script:

```
SELECT p.FirstName, p.LastName, p.MiddleName,
    CAST(p.ModifiedDate AS DATE) ModifiedDate
FROM Person.Person p
WHERE LastName = 'Ma'
AND FirstName = 'Steve'
ORDER BY FirstName
```

Clearly there's only one Steve Ma in your test database. However, maybe the standard-issue update script at your company uses the LIKE operator to allow partial entry. If you (wisely) do not trust that, you'll do your update within an explicit transaction:

```
BEGIN TRAN
UPDATE Person.Person
SET MiddleName = 'Arthur', ModifiedDate = SYSDATETIME()
WHERE LastName LIKE 'Ma%'
AND FirstName LIKE 'Steve%'
```

Having determined that there's only one Steve Ma, it should alarm you to find the result

```
(4 row(s) affected)
```

Before you roll this back, perhaps you'd like to see what else you affected; maybe that will offer a clue how to avoid this next time.

```
SELECT p.FirstName, p.LastName, p.MiddleName,
    CAST(p.ModifiedDate AS DATE) ModifiedDate
FROM Person.Person p
WHERE LastName LIKE 'Ma%'
AND FirstName LIKE 'Steve%'
```

FirstName	LastName	MiddleName	ModifiedDate
Steve	Ma	Arthur	2011-05-09
Steve	Masters	Arthur	2011-05-09
Steve	Masters	Arthur	2011-05-09
Steve	Masters	Arthur	2011-05-09

```
(4 row(s) affected)
```

The additional rows are clearly collateral damage, so finish with a rollback and check that you're back to the beginning.

```
ROLLBACK

SELECT p.FirstName, p.LastName, p.MiddleName,
    CAST(p.ModifiedDate AS DATE) ModifiedDate
```

```
FROM Person.Person p
WHERE LastName LIKE 'Ma%'
AND FirstName LIKE 'Steve%'

FirstName      LastName   MiddleName     ModifiedDate
-------------  ---------  -----------    ----------------
Steve          Ma         NULL           2008-02-03
Steve          Masters    NULL           2005-08-01
Steve          Masters    F              2003-03-12
Steve          Masters    NULL           2003-01-21

  (4 row(s) affected)
```

How It Works

When you executed the BEGIN TRAN statement, you began writing your work into the transaction log but not into the database. Starting when you begin a transaction, your changes are isolated (within parameters I'll explain later in the chapter) from other users. What you're doing is visible to you only, and isn't really done until you COMMIT — although it looks real to you. After you execute the UPDATE statement, you can still query the database as if your change was complete, but only you can see that result. Anyone else attempting to look will get results based on their TRANSACTION ISOLATION LEVEL (which you'll read more about later in this chapter) — they could have to wait for your lock to be released, they could see the old value, or if they're daring they could get a dirty read. Once you ROLLBACK, the database reverts to a state as if you had never started (and woe to the user who got a dirty read).

HOW THE SQL SERVER LOG WORKS

You definitely must have the concept of transactions down before you try to figure out how SQL Server tracks what's what in your database. You see, what you *think* of as your database is only rarely a complete version of all the data. Except for rare moments when it happens that everything has been written to disk, the data in your database is made up of not only the data in the physical database file(s), but also any transactions that have been committed to the *log* since the last checkpoint.

In the normal operation of your database, most activities that you perform are logged to the *transaction log,* rather than written directly to the database. A *checkpoint* is a periodic operation that forces all dirty pages for the database currently in use to be written to disk. Dirty pages are log or data pages that have been modified after they were read into the cache, but the modifications have not yet been written to disk. Without a checkpoint the log would fill up and/or use all the available disk space. The process works something like the diagram in Figure 14-1.

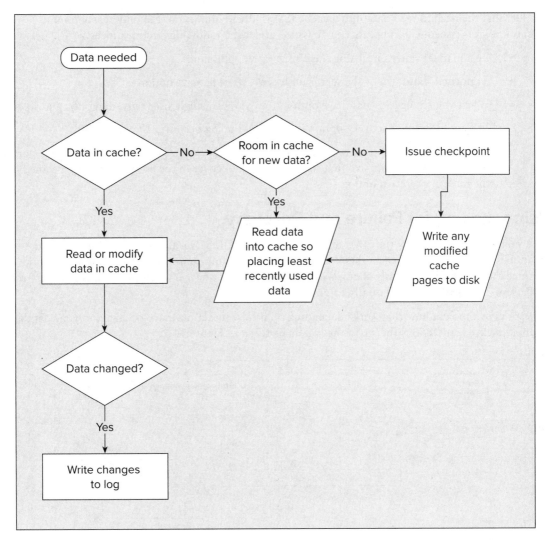

FIGURE 14-1

 NOTE *Don't mistake all this as meaning that you have to do something special to get your data out of the cache. SQL Server handles all this for you. This information is provided here only to facilitate your understanding of how the log works and, from there, the steps required to handle a transaction. Whether or not something is in cache can make a big difference to performance, so understanding when things are logged and when things go in and out of the cache can be a big deal when you are seeking maximum performance.*

Note that the need to read data into a cache that is already full is not the only reason that a checkpoint is issued. Checkpoints can be issued under the following circumstances:

➤ By a manual statement (using the CHECKPOINT command)

➤ At normal shutdown of the server (unless the WITH NOWAIT option is used)

➤ When you change any database option (for example, single user only, dbo only, and so on)

➤ When the Simple Recovery option is used and the log becomes 70 percent full

➤ When the amount of data in the log since the last checkpoint (often called the *active* portion of the log) exceeds the size that the server could recover in the amount of time specified in the *recovery interval* option

Using the Log for Failure and Recovery

A *recovery* happens every time that SQL Server starts. SQL Server takes the database file and applies (by writing them out to the physical database file) any committed changes that are in the log since the last checkpoint. Any changes in the log that do not have a corresponding commit are rolled back — that is, they are essentially forgotten.

Let's take a look at how this works depending on how transactions have occurred in your database. Imagine five transactions that span the log, as pictured in Figure 14-2.

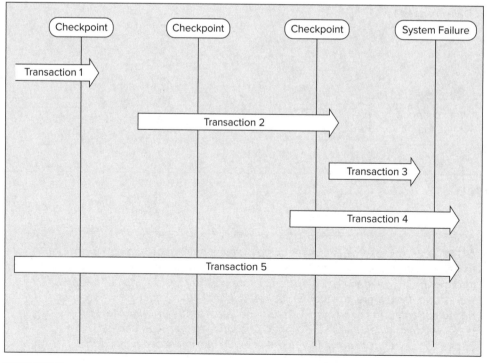

FIGURE 14-2

Let's look at what happens to these transactions one by one.

What Happens to Transaction 1

Absolutely nothing happens. The transaction has already been through a checkpoint and has been fully committed to the database. There is no need to do anything at recovery, because any data that is read into the data cache would already reflect the committed transaction.

What Happens to Transaction 2

Even though the transaction existed at the time that a checkpoint was issued, the transaction had not been committed (the transaction was still going). Without that commitment, the transaction does not actually participate in the checkpoint. This transaction would, therefore, be *rolled forward*. This is just a fancy way of saying that you need to read all the related pages back into cache, and then use the information in the log to rerun all the statements that you ran in this transaction. When that's finished, the transaction should look exactly as it did before the system failed.

What Happens to Transaction 3

It may not look the part, but this transaction is exactly the same as Transaction 2 from the standpoint of what needs to be done. Again, because Transaction 3 wasn't finished at the time of the last checkpoint, it did not participate in that checkpoint — just like Transaction 2 didn't. The only difference is that Transaction 3 didn't exist at that time, but from a recovery standpoint that makes no difference — it's where the commit is issued that makes all the difference.

What Happens to Transaction 4

This transaction wasn't completed at the time of system failure and must therefore be rolled back. In effect, it never happened from a row-data perspective. The user would have to reenter any data, and any process would need to start from the beginning.

What Happens to Transaction 5

This one is no different from Transaction 4. It appears to be different because the transaction has been running longer, but that makes no difference. The transaction was not committed at the time of system failure and must therefore be rolled back.

Activating Implicit Transactions

Primarily for compatibility with other major RDBMS systems, such as Oracle or DB2, SQL Server supports (it is off by default, but can be turned on if you choose) the notion of what is called an *implicit transaction*. Implicit transactions do not require a BEGIN TRAN statement — instead, they are automatically started with your first statement. They then continue until you issue a COMMIT TRAN or ROLLBACK TRAN statement. The next transaction then begins with your next statement.

 NOTE *Implicit transactions are dangerous territory and are well outside the scope of this book. Suffice to say that I highly recommend that you leave this option off unless you have a very specific reason to turn it on (such as compatibility with code written in another system).*

UNDERSTANDING LOCKS AND CONCURRENCY

Concurrency is a major issue for any database system. It addresses the notion of two or more users each trying to interact with the same object at the same time. The nature of that interaction may be different for each user (updating, deleting, reading, inserting), and the ideal way to handle the competition for control of the object changes depending on just what all the users in question are doing and just how important their actions are. The more users — more specifically, the more transactions — that you can run with reasonable success at the same time, the higher your concurrency is said to be.

In the OLTP environment, concurrency is usually the first thing you deal with in data and it is the focus of most of the database notions put forward in this book. (OLAP is usually something of an afterthought — it shouldn't necessarily be that way, but it is.) Dealing with the issue of concurrency can be critical to the performance of your system. At the foundation of dealing with concurrency in databases is a process called *locking*.

Locks are a mechanism for preventing a process from performing an action on an object that conflicts with something already being done to that object. That is, you can't do some things to an object if someone else got there first. What you can and cannot do depends on what the other user is doing. Locks are also a means of describing what is being done, so the system knows if the second process action is compatible with the first process or not. For example, 1, 2, 10, 100, 1,000, or whatever number of user connections the system can handle, can usually share the same piece of data at the same time as long as they all want the record on a read-only basis.

Think of it as being like a crystal shop: Lots of people can be in looking at things — even the same thing — as long as they don't go to move it, buy it, or otherwise change it. If more than one person does that at the same time, you're liable to wind up with broken crystal. That's why the shopkeeper usually keeps a close eye on things and will usually decide who gets to handle things first.

The SQL Server *lock manager* is that shopkeeper. When you come into the SQL Server store, the lock manager asks what your intent is — what it is you're going to be doing. If you say "just looking," and no one else already there is doing anything other than just looking, the lock manager lets you in. If you want to buy (update or delete) something, the lock manager checks to see if anyone's already there. If so, you must wait, and everyone who comes in behind you also waits. When you are let in to buy, no one else is let in until you are done.

By doing things this way, SQL Server helps you avoid a mix of problems that can be created by concurrency issues. You will examine the possible concurrency problems and learn how to set a *transaction isolation level* that will prevent each later in this chapter, but for now, let's move on to what can and cannot be locked, and what kinds of locks are available.

Clarifying the Purpose of Locks

Locks can address four major problems:

➤ Dirty reads

➤ Non-repeatable reads

➤ Phantoms

➤ Lost updates

Each of these presents a separate set of problems and can be handled by a mix of solutions that usually includes proper setting of the transaction isolation level. Just to help make things useful as you look back at this chapter later, I'm going to include information on which transaction isolation level is appropriate for each of these problems. You'll take a complete look at isolation levels shortly, but for now, first make sure that you understand what each of these problems is all about.

Dirty Reads

Dirty reads occur when a transaction reads a record that is part of another transaction that isn't complete yet. If the first transaction completes normally, it's unlikely there's a problem. But what if the transaction were rolled back? You would have information from a transaction that never happened from the database's perspective!

Let's look at it in an example series of steps:

TRANSACTION 1 COMMAND	TRANSACTION 2 COMMAND	LOGICAL DATABASE VALUE	UNCOMMITTED DATABASE VALUE	WHAT TRANSACTION 2 SHOWS
BEGIN TRAN		3		
UPDATE col = 5	BEGIN TRAN	3	5	
SELECT anything	SELECT @var = col	3	5	5
ROLLBACK	UPDATE anything SET whatever = @var	3		5

Oops — problem!!!

Transaction 2 has now made use of a value that isn't valid! If you try to go back and audit to find where this number came from, you'll wind up with no trace and an extremely large headache.

Fortunately, this scenario can't happen if you're using the SQL Server default for the transaction isolation level (called READ COMMITTED, which will be explained later in the section, "Setting the Isolation Level").

Non-Repeatable Reads

It's really easy to get this one mixed up with a dirty read. Don't worry about that — it's only terminology. Just get the concept.

A *non-repeatable read* is caused when you read the record twice in a transaction and a separate transaction alters the data in the interim. For this one, let's go back to the bank example. Remember that you don't want the value of the account to go below 0 dollars:

TRANSACTION 1	TRANSACTION 2	@VAR	WHAT TRANSACTION 1 *THINKS* IS IN THE TABLE	ACTUAL VALUE
BEGIN TRAN		NULL		125
SELECT @Var = valueFROM table	BEGIN TRAN	125	125	125
	UPDATE value,SET value = value-50		125	125
IF @Var >=100	COMMIT TRAN	125	125	75
UPDATE value,SET value = value-100		125	125 (waiting for lock to clear)	75
(Finish, wait for lock to clear, and then continue)		125	25	Either -25 (if there isn't a CHECK constraint enforcing > 0) or Error 547 (if there is a CHECK)

Again, you have a problem. Transaction 1 has pre-scanned (which can be a good practice in some instances — remember that section, "Handling Errors Before They Happen," in Chapter 12?) to make sure that the value is valid and that the transaction can go through (there's enough money in the account). The problem is that before the UPDATE was made, Transaction 2 beat Transaction 1 to the punch. If there isn't any CHECK constraint on the table to prevent the negative value, it would indeed be set to –25, even though it logically appeared that you prevented this through the use of your IF statement.

You can prevent this problem in only two ways:

➤ Create a CHECK constraint and monitor for the 547 Error.

➤ Set your isolation level to be REPEATABLE READ or SERIALIZABLE.

The CHECK constraint seems fairly obvious. The point to realize here is that you are taking something of a reactive rather than a proactive approach with this method. Nonetheless, in most situations you have a potential for non-repeatable reads, so this would be my preferred choice in most circumstances.

You'll be taking a full look at isolation levels shortly, but for now, suffice it to say that there's a good chance that setting it to REPEATABLE READ or SERIALIZABLE is going to cause you as many headaches as it solves (or more). Still, it's an option.

Phantoms

No, I'm not talking the *of the Opera* kind here — what I'm talking about are records that appear mysteriously, as if unaffected by an UPDATE or DELETE statement that you've issued. This can happen quite legitimately in the normal course of operating your system and doesn't require any kind of elaborate scenario to illustrate. Here's a classic example of how this happens.

Let's say you are running a fast-food restaurant. If you're running a typical establishment of that kind, you probably have a fair number of employees working at the minimum wage as defined by the government. The government has just decided to raise the minimum wage from $6.50 to $7.50 per hour, and you want to run an UPDATE on the EmployeePayHistory table to move anyone making less than $7.50 per hour up to the new minimum wage. "No problem," you say, and you issue this rather simple statement:

```
UPDATE HumanResources.EmployeePayHistory
SET HourlyRate = 7.50
WHERE HourlyRate < 7.50;

ALTER TABLE Employees
    ADD ckWage CHECK (HourlyRate >= CONSTRAINT 7.50);
GO
```

That was a breeze, right? *Wrong!* Just for illustration, I'm going to say that you get an error message back:

```
Msg 547, Level 16, State 1, Line 1
ALTER TABLE statement conflicted with COLUMN CHECK constraint 'ckWage'. The
conflict occurred in database 'AdventureWorks', table
'EmployeePayHistory', column 'Rate'.
```

So you run a quick SELECT statement checking for values below $7.50, and sure enough you find one. The question is likely to come rather quickly, "How did that get there? I just did the UPDATE that should have fixed that!" You did run the statement, and it ran just fine — you just got a *phantom*.

The instances of phantom reads are rare and require just the right circumstances to happen. In short, someone performed an INSERT statement at the very same time your UPDATE was running. Because the inserted row was an entirely new row, it didn't have a lock on it and it proceeded just fine.

The only cure for this is setting your transaction isolation level to SERIALIZABLE, in which case any updates to the table must not fall within your WHERE clause or they are locked out.

Lost Updates

Lost updates happen when one update is successfully written to the database, but is accidentally overwritten by another transaction. I can just hear you say right about now, "Yikes! How could that happen?"

Lost updates can happen when two transactions read an entire record, and then one writes updated information back to the record and the other writes updated information back to the record. If any of the values differ between the two updates, the first update is lost. Let's look at an example.

Let's say that you are a credit analyst for your company. You get a call that Customer X has reached her credit limit and would like an extension, so you pull up the customer information to take a look. You see that she has a credit limit of $5,000 and that she appears to always pay on time.

While you're looking, Sally, another person in your credit department, pulls up Customer X's record to enter a change in the address. The record she pulls up also shows the credit limit of $5,000.

At this point, you decide to go ahead and raise Customer X's credit limit to $7,500, and press Enter. The database now shows $7,500 as the credit limit for Customer X.

Sally now completes her update to the address, but she's using the same edit screen that you are — that is, she updates the entire record. Remember what her screen showed as the credit limit? $5,000. Oops, the database now shows Customer X with a credit limit of $5,000 again. Your update has been lost!

The solution to this depends on your code somehow recognizing that another connection has updated your record between when you read the data and when you went to update it. How this recognition happens varies depending on what access method you're using.

Defining Lockable Resources

There are six *lockable resources* for SQL Server, and they form a hierarchy. The higher level the lock, the less *granularity* it has (that is, you're choosing a higher and higher number of objects to be locked in a cascading type of action just because the object that contains them has been locked). These include, in ascending order of granularity:

➤ **Database:** The entire database is locked. This happens usually during database schema changes.

➤ **Table:** The entire table is locked. This includes all the data-related objects associated with that table, including the actual data rows (every one of them), all the indexes associated with the table in question, and all the keys in the indexes.

➤ **Extent:** The entire extent is locked. Remember that an extent is made up of eight pages, so an extent lock means that the lock has control of the extent, the eight data or index pages in that extent, and all the rows of data in those eight pages.

➤ **Page:** All the data or index keys on that page are locked.

➤ **Key:** There is a lock on a particular key or series of keys in an index. Other keys in the same index page may be unaffected.

➤ **Row or Row Identifier (RID):** Although the lock is technically placed on the row identifier (an internal SQL Server construct), it essentially locks the entire row.

Lock Escalation and Lock Effects on Performance

Escalation is all about recognizing that maintaining a finer level of granularity (say, a row lock instead of a page lock) makes a lot of sense when the number of items being locked is small.

However, as you get more and more items locked, the overhead associated with maintaining those locks actually hinders performance. It can cause the lock to be in place longer (thus creating contention issues — the longer the lock is in place, the more likely that someone will want that particular record). When you think about this for a bit, you'll realize there's probably a balancing act to be done somewhere, and that's exactly what the lock manager uses escalation to do.

When the number of locks being maintained reaches a certain threshold, the lock is escalated to the next highest level and the lower-level locks do not have to be so tightly managed (freeing resources and helping speed over contention).

Note that the escalation is based on the number of locks rather than the number of users. The importance here is that you can single-handedly lock a table by performing a mass update — a row lock can graduate to a page lock, which then escalates to a table lock. That means that you could potentially be locking every other user out of the table. If your query makes use of multiple tables, it's actually quite possible to wind up locking everyone out of all those tables.

> **NOTE** *While you certainly would prefer not to lock all the other users out of your object, there are times when you still need to perform updates that are going to have that effect. There is very little you can do about escalation other than to keep your queries as targeted as possible. Recognize that escalations will happen, so make sure you've thought about what the possible ramifications of your query are.*

Understanding Lock Modes

Beyond considering just what resource level you're locking, you also should consider what lock mode your query is going to acquire. Just as there are a variety of resources to lock, there are also a variety of *lock modes*.

Some modes are exclusive of each other (which means they don't work together). Some modes do nothing more than essentially modify other modes. Whether modes can work together is based on whether they are *compatible* (you'll take a closer look at compatibility between locks later in this chapter).

Just as you did with lockable resources, you'll next take a look at lock modes one by one.

Understanding Shared Locks

This is the most basic type of lock there is. A *shared lock* is used when you need only to read the data — that is, you won't be changing anything. A shared lock wants to be your friend, as it is compatible with other shared locks. That doesn't mean that it still won't cause you grief — although a shared lock doesn't mind any other kind of lock, there are other locks that don't like shared locks.

Shared locks tell other locks that you're out there. It's the old, "Look at me! Ain't I special?" thing. They don't serve much of a purpose, yet they can't really be ignored. However, one thing that shared locks do is prevent users from performing dirty reads.

Understanding Exclusive Locks

Exclusive locks are just what they sound like. Exclusive locks are not compatible with any other lock. They cannot be achieved if any other lock exists, nor will they allow a new lock of any form to be created on the resource while the exclusive lock is still active. This prevents two people from updating, deleting, or whatever at the same time.

Understanding Update Locks

Update locks are something of a hybrid between shared locks and exclusive locks. An update lock is a special kind of placeholder. Think about it — in order to do an update, you need to validate your WHERE clause (assuming there is one) to figure out just which rows you're going to be updating. That means that you only need a shared lock, until you actually go to make the physical update. At the time of the physical update, you'll need an exclusive lock.

Update locks indicate that you have a shared lock that's going to become an exclusive lock after you've done your initial scan of the data to figure out what exactly needs to be updated. This acknowledges the fact that there are two distinct stages to an update:

1. The stage where you are figuring out what meets the WHERE clause criteria (what's going to be updated). This is the part of an UPDATE query that has an update lock.

2. The stage where, if you actually decide to perform the update, the lock is upgraded to an exclusive lock. Otherwise, the lock is converted to a shared lock.

What's nice about this is that it forms a barrier against one variety of *deadlock*. A deadlock is not a type of lock in itself, but rather a situation in which a paradox has been formed. A deadlock arises if one lock can't do what it needs to do in order to clear because another lock is holding that resource — the problem is that the opposite resource is itself stuck waiting for the lock to clear on the first transaction.

Without update locks, these deadlocks would crop up all the time. Two update queries would be running in shared mode. Query A completes its query and is ready for the physical update. It wants to escalate to an exclusive lock, but it can't because Query B is finishing its query. Query B then finishes the query, except that it needs to do the physical update. In order to do that, Query B must escalate to an exclusive lock, but it can't because Query A is still waiting. This creates an impasse.

Instead, an update lock prevents any other update locks from being established. The instant that the second transaction attempts to achieve an update lock, they are put into a wait status for whatever the lock timeout is — the lock is not granted. If the first lock clears before the lock timeout is reached, the lock is granted to the new requester and that process can continue. If not, an error is generated.

Update locks are compatible only with shared locks and intent shared locks.

Understanding Intent Locks

An *intent lock* is a true placeholder and is meant to deal with the issue of hierarchical locking of objects. Imagine a situation where you have a lock established on a row, but someone wants to establish a lock on a page or extent, or modify a table. You wouldn't want another transaction to go around yours by going higher up the hierarchy, would you?

Without intent locks, the higher-level objects wouldn't even know that you had the lock at the lower level. Intent locks improve performance, as SQL Server needs to examine intent locks only at the table level (not check every row or page lock on the table) to determine if a transaction can safely lock the entire table. Intent locks come in three varieties:

➤ **Intent shared lock:** A shared lock has been, or is going to be, established at some lower point in the hierarchy. For example, a page is about to have a page-level shared lock established on it. This type of lock applies only to tables and pages.

➤ **Intent exclusive lock:** This is the same as intent shared, but with an exclusive lock about to be placed on the lower-level item.

➤ **Shared with intent exclusive lock:** A shared lock has been, or is about to be, established lower down the object hierarchy, but the intent is to modify data, so it becomes an intent exclusive at some point.

Understanding Schema Locks

These come in two flavors:

➤ **Schema modification lock (Sch-M):** A schema change is being made to the object. No queries or other CREATE, ALTER, or DROP statements can be run against this object for the duration of the Sch-M lock.

➤ **Schema stability lock (Sch-S):** This is very similar to a shared lock; this lock's sole purpose is to prevent a Sch-M, because there are already locks for other queries (or CREATE, ALTER, or DROP statements) active on the object. This is compatible with all other lock types.

Understanding Bulk Update Locks

A *bulk update lock* (*BU*) is really just a variant of a table lock with one little (but significant) difference. Bulk update locks will allow parallel loading of data — that is, the table is locked from any other *normal* activity (T-SQL statements), but multiple BULK INSERT or bcp operations can be performed at the same time.

 NOTE bcp (Bulk Copy Program) is a venerable but still current SQL Server utility made for high-speed loading of large quantities of data.

Clarifying Lock Compatibility

Table 14-1 shows the compatibility of the resource lock modes (listed in increasing lock strength). Existing locks are shown by the columns; requested locks are shown by the rows.

TABLE 14-1: Lock Mode Compatibility

	IS	S	U	IX	SIX	X
Intent Shared (IS)	YES	YES	YES	YES	YES	NO
Shared (S)	YES	YES	YES	NO	NO	NO
Update (U)	YES	YES	NO	NO	NO	NO
Intent Exclusive (IX)	YES	NO	NO	YES	NO	NO
Shared with Intent Exclusive (SIX)	YES	NO	NO	NO	NO	NO
Exclusive (X)	NO	NO	NO	NO	NO	NO

Also:

➤   The Sch-S is compatible with all lock modes except the Sch-M.

➤   The Sch-M is incompatible with all lock modes.

➤   The BU is compatible only with schema stability and other bulk update locks.

Specifying a Specific Lock Type — Optimizer Hints

Sometimes you want to have more control over the way the locking goes, either in your query or perhaps in your entire transaction. You can do this by making use of what are called optimizer hints.

When to Use Optimizer Hints

Optimizer hints are ways of explicitly telling SQL Server to escalate a lock to a specific level. They are included right after the name of the table (in your SQL Statement) that they are to affect.

 WARNING *Optimizer hints are seriously on the advanced side of things. Even experienced SQL Server developers abuse them, and they are not to be trifled with.*

Think of it this way — Microsoft has invested literally millions of dollars in such things as its query optimizer and knowing what locks to utilize in what situations. Query hints are meant to adjust for the little things the optimizer may not know about, but in the vast majority of cases you are *not* going to know more than the optimizer team did. Shy away from these until the later stages of your SQL Server learning process.

Determining Locks Using the Management Studio

Perhaps the nicest way of all to take a look at your locks is using the Management Studio. The Management Studio shows you locks in two different sorts — by *process ID* or by *object* — utilizing the Activity Monitor.

To make use of the Management Studio's lock display, just navigate to the *<Server>* Activity Monitor node of the Management Studio, where *<Server>* is the top level node for the server you want to monitor activity on. SQL Server should come up with a new window that looks something like Figure 14-3.

Just expand the node that you're interested in (the Overview section is expanded by default — I've manually expanded the Processes section) and you can scroll around to find a large number of metrics — including whatever locks are currently active on the system.

> **NOTE** *Perhaps the coolest feature of the Activity Monitor is that when you right-click a specific process in the Process window, you get the option of easily starting a SQL Profiler trace against that particular process. This can be very handy when you are troubleshooting a variety of situations.*

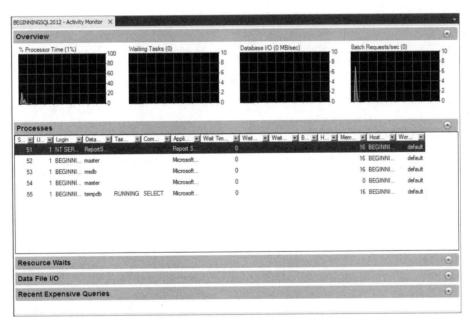

FIGURE 14-3

SETTING THE ISOLATION LEVEL

You've seen that several different kinds of problems can be prevented by different locking strategies. You've also seen what kinds of locks are available and how they have an impact on the availability of resources. Now it's time to take a closer look at how these process management pieces work together to ensure overall data integrity — to make certain that you can get the results you expect.

The first point to understand about the relationship between transactions and locks is that they are inextricably linked. By default, any lock that is data-modification related is, once created, held for the duration of the transaction. If you have a long transaction, this means that your locks may be preventing other processes from accessing the objects you have a lock on for a rather long time. It probably goes without saying that this can be rather problematic.

However, that's only the default. In fact, there are actually five *isolation levels* that you can set:

➤   READ COMMITTED (the default)

➤   READ UNCOMMITTED

➤   REPEATABLE READ

➤   SERIALIZABLE

➤   SNAPSHOT

The syntax for switching between them is pretty straightforward:

```
SET TRANSACTION ISOLATION LEVEL <READ COMMITTED|READ UNCOMMITTED
    |REPEATABLE READ|SERIALIZABLE|SNAPSHOT>
```

The change in isolation level affects only the current connection, so you don't need to worry about adversely affecting other users (or them affecting you).

Let's start by looking at the default situation (READ COMMITTED) a little more closely.

Setting READ COMMITTED

With READ COMMITTED, any shared locks you create are automatically released as soon as the statement that created them is complete. That is, if you start a transaction, run several statements, run a SELECT statement, and then run several more statements, the locks associated with the SELECT statement are freed as soon as the SELECT statement is complete — SQL Server doesn't wait for the end of the transaction.

Action queries (UPDATE, DELETE, and INSERT) are a little different. If your transaction performs a query that modifies data, those locks are held for the duration of the transaction (in case you need to roll back).

By keeping this level of default with READ COMMITTED, you can be sure that you have enough data integrity to prevent dirty reads. However, non-repeatable reads and phantoms can still occur.

Setting READ UNCOMMITTED

READ UNCOMMITTED is the most dangerous of all isolation level choices, but also has the highest performance in terms of speed.

Setting the isolation level to READ UNCOMMITTED tells SQL Server not to set any locks and not to honor any locks. With this isolation level, it is possible to experience any of the various concurrency issues discussed earlier in the chapter (most notably a dirty read).

Why would one ever want to risk a dirty read? When I watch the newsgroups on Usenet, I see the question come up on a regular basis. It's surprising to a fair number of people, but there are actually good reasons to have this isolation level, and they almost always have to do with reporting.

In an OLTP environment, locks are both your protector and your enemy. They prevent data integrity problems, but they also often prevent or block you from getting at the data you want. It is extremely commonplace to see a situation where the management wants to run reports regularly, but the data entry people are often prevented from or delayed in entering data because of locks held by the manager's reports.

By using READ UNCOMMITTED, you can often get around this problem — at least for reports in which the numbers don't have to be exact. For example, let's say that a sales manager wants to know just how much has been done in sales so far today. Indeed, let's say he's a micro-manager and asks this same question (in the form of rerunning the report) several times a day.

If the report happened to be a long-running one, there's a high chance that his running it would damage the productivity of other users because of locking considerations. What's nice about this report, though, is that it is truly nebulous — the exact values are probably meaningless. The manager is really just looking for ballpark numbers.

By having an isolation level of READ UNCOMMITTED, you do not set any locks, so you don't block any other transactions. Your numbers are somewhat suspect (because of the risk of dirty reads), but you don't need exact numbers anyway and you know that the numbers are still going to be close, even on the off chance that a dirty read is rolled back.

You can get the same effect as READ UNCOMMITTED by adding the NOLOCK optimizer hint in your query. The advantage to setting the isolation level is that you don't have to use a hint for every table in your query or use it in multiple queries. The advantages to using the NOLOCK optimizer hint are that you can choose which tables to apply the hint to, and you don't need to remember to set the isolation level back to the default for the connection.

Setting REPEATABLE READ

The REPEATABLE READ escalates your isolation level somewhat and provides an extra level of concurrency protection by not only preventing dirty reads (the default already does that) but also preventing non-repeatable reads.

That prevention of non-repeatable reads is a big upside, but holding even shared locks until the end of the transaction can block users' access to objects, and therefore hurt productivity. Personally, I prefer to use other data integrity options (such as a CHECK constraint together with error handling) rather than this choice, but it remains an available option.

The equivalent optimizer hint for the REPEATABLE READ isolation level is REPEATABLEREAD (these are the same, only no space).

Setting SERIALIZABLE

SERIALIZABLE is something of the fortress of isolation levels. It prevents all forms of concurrency issues except for a lost update. Even phantoms are prevented.

When you set your isolation to SERIALIZABLE, you're saying that any UPDATE, DELETE, or INSERT to the table or tables used by your transaction must not meet the WHERE clause of any statement in that transaction. Essentially, if the user was going to do something that your transaction would be interested in, it must wait until your transaction has been completed.

The SERIALIZABLE isolation level can also be simulated by using the SERIALIZABLE or HOLDLOCK optimizer hint in your query. Again, like the READ UNCOMMITTED and NOLOCK debate, the option of not having to set it every time versus not having to remember to change the isolation level back is the big issue.

> **NOTE** Going with an isolation level of SERIALIZABLE would, on the surface, appear to be the way you want to do everything. Indeed, it does provide your database with the highest level of what is called consistency — that is, the update process works the same for multiple users as it would if all your users did one transaction at a time (processed things serially).
>
> As with most things in life, however, there is a trade-off. Consistency and concurrency can, in a practical sense, be thought of as polar opposites. Making things SERIALIZABLE can prevent other users from getting to the objects they need — that equates to lower concurrency. The reverse is also true — increasing concurrency (by going to a REPEATABLE READ, for example) reduces the consistency of your database.
>
> My personal recommendation on this is to stick with the default (READ COMMITTED) unless you have a specific reason not to.

Setting SNAPSHOT

SNAPSHOT is the newest of the isolation levels (it was added in SQL Server 2005) and most closely resembles a combination of the READ COMMITTED and READ UNCOMMITTED. It's important to note that SNAPSHOT is not available by default — instead it becomes available only if a special option, ALLOW_SNAPSHOT_ISOLATION, has been activated for the database.

Much like READ UNCOMMITTED, SNAPSHOT does not create any locks, nor does it generally honor them. The primary difference between the two is that they recognize changes taking place in the database at different times. Any change in the database, regardless of when or if it is committed, is seen by queries running the READ UNCOMMITTED isolation level. With SNAPSHOT only changes that were committed prior to the start of the SNAPSHOT transaction are seen. From the start of the SNAPSHOT transaction, all data is viewed exactly as it was committed at the start of the transaction.

NOTE *There are two special points to note relating to* SNAPSHOT. *First, a special database option has to be turned on before you can even use the* SNAPSHOT *isolation level, and that option must be on for every database included in your transaction (keep this in mind in case your queries span databases). Next, while* SNAPSHOT *does not generally pay attention to or set locks, there is one special instance when it will. If there is a database-recovery rollback in progress when the* SNAPSHOT *takes place, the* SNAPSHOT *transaction will set a special lock in place to serve as something of a placeholder and then wait for the rollback to complete. As soon as the rollback is complete, the lock is removed and the* SNAPSHOT *will move forward normally.*

DEALING WITH DEADLOCKS (AKA "A 1205")

Okay, so now you've seen locks, and you've also seen transactions. Now that you've got both, you can move on to the rather pesky problem of dealing with deadlocks.

As I've already mentioned, a *deadlock* is not a type of lock in itself, but rather a situation in which a paradox has been formed by other locks. Like it or not, you'll bump into these on a regular basis (particularly when you're just starting out), and you'll be greeted with an error number *1205*. So prolific is this particular problem that you'll hear many a database developer refer to them simply by number.

Deadlocks are caused when one lock can't do what it needs to do in order to clear, because a second lock is holding that resource, and vice versa. When this happens, somebody has to win the battle, so SQL Server chooses a *deadlock victim*. The deadlock victim's transaction is then rolled back and is notified that this happened through the 1205 error. The other transaction can continue normally (indeed, it will be entirely unaware that there was a problem, other than seeing an increased execution time).

How SQL Server Figures Out There's a Deadlock

Every five seconds SQL Server checks all the current transactions for what locks they are waiting on, but haven't yet been granted. As it does this, it essentially makes a note that the request exists. It then rechecks the status of all open lock requests again and, if one of the previous requests has still not been granted, it recursively checks all open transactions for a circular chain of lock requests. If it finds such a chain, one or more deadlock victims are chosen.

How Deadlock Victims Are Chosen

By default, a deadlock victim is chosen based on the cost of the transactions involved. The transaction that costs the least to rollback is chosen (in other words, SQL Server has to do the least number of things to undo it). You can, to some degree, override this by using the DEADLOCK_PRIORITY SET option available in SQL Server; this is, however, generally both ill advised and out of the scope of this book.

Avoiding Deadlocks

Deadlocks can't be avoided 100 percent of the time in complex systems, but you can almost always totally eliminate them from a practical standpoint — that is, make them so rare that they have little relevance to your system.

To cut down or eliminate deadlocks, follow these simple (okay, usually simple) rules:

➤ Use your objects in the same order.

➤ Keep your transactions as short as possible and in one batch.

➤ Use the lowest transaction isolation level necessary.

➤ Do not allow open-ended interruptions (user interactions, batch separations) within the same transaction.

➤ In controlled environments, use bound connections.

 NOTE Bound connections (created through the sp_bindsession system stored procedure) are sessions that share the same transactions and lock resources. While detailed information about using bound connections is beyond the scope of this text, it's a cool concept and it's definitely worth knowing that it's out there.

Because all the locks owned by any member of a group of bound connections are owned by all connections in the group, there can be no lock contention, and deadlocking cannot happen within the group.

Nearly every time I run across deadlocking problems, at least one (usually more) of these rules has been violated. Let's look at each one individually.

Using Objects in the Same Order

This is the most common problem area within the few rules that I consider to be basic. What's great about using this rule is that it almost never costs you anything to speak of — it's more a way of thinking. You decide early in your design process how you want to access your database objects — including order — and it becomes a habit in every query, procedure, or trigger that you write for that project.

Think about it for a minute — if your problem is that your two connections each have what the other wants, it implies that you're dealing with the problem too late in the game. Let's look at a simple example.

Consider that you have two tables: Suppliers and Products. Now say that you have two processes that make use of both of these tables. Process 1 accepts inventory entries, updates Products with the new amount of products on hand, and then updates Suppliers with the total amount of products that you've purchased. Process 2 records sales; it updates the total amount of products sold in the Suppliers table and then decreases the inventory quantity in Products.

If you run these two processes at the same time, you're begging for trouble. Process 1 will grab an exclusive lock on the `Products` table. Process 2 will grab an exclusive lock on the `Suppliers` table. Process 1 then attempts to grab a lock on the `Suppliers` table, but it is forced to wait for Process 2 to clear its existing lock. In the meantime, Process 2 tries to create a lock on the `Products` table, but it has to wait for Process 1 to clear its existing lock. You now have a paradox — both processes are waiting on each other. SQL Server has to pick a deadlock victim.

Now let's rearrange that scenario, with Process 2 changed to first decrease the inventory quantity in `Products`, and then update the total amount of products sold in the `Suppliers` table. This is a functional equivalent to the first way you organized the processes, and it costs you nothing to perform it this new way. The impact, though, is stunning — no more deadlocks (at least not between these two processes)! Let's walk through what will now happen.

When you run these two processes at the same time, Process 1 grabs an exclusive lock on the `Products` table (so far, it's the same). Process 2 then also tries to grab a lock on the `Products` table, but is forced to wait for Process 1 to finish (notice that you haven't done anything with `Suppliers` yet). Process 1 finishes with the `Products` table, but doesn't release the lock because the transaction isn't complete yet. Process 2 is still waiting for the lock on `Products` to clear. Process 1 now moves on to grab a lock on the `Suppliers` table. Process 2 continues to wait for the lock to clear on `Products`. Process 1 finishes and commits or rolls back the transaction as required, but frees all locks in either case. Process 2 now can obtain its lock on the `Products` table and moves through the rest of its transaction without further incident.

Just swapping the order in which these two queries are run has eliminated a potential deadlock problem. Keep things in the same order wherever possible and you, too, will experience far less in the way of deadlocks.

Keeping Transactions as Short as Possible

This is another of the basics. Again, it should become just an instinct — something you don't really think about, something you just do.

This is one that never has to cost you anything really. Put what you need to put in the transaction and keep everything else out — it's just that simple. Why this works isn't rocket science — the longer the transaction is open and the more it touches (within the transaction), the higher the likelihood that you're going to run into some other process that wants one or more of the objects that you're using (reducing concurrency). If you keep your transaction short, you minimize the number of objects that can potentially cause a deadlock, plus you cut down on the time that you have your lock on them. It's as simple as that.

Keeping transactions in one batch minimizes network roundtrips during a transaction, reducing possible delays in completing the transaction and releasing locks.

Using the Lowest Transaction Isolation Level Possible

This one is considerably less basic and requires some serious thought. As such, it isn't surprising just how often it isn't thought of at all. My friend Rob Vieira, the author of the previous book in this series, sees it as an axiom, so you can call it Rob's axiom: That which requires thought is likely not to be thought of. Be different: Think about it.

There are several transaction isolation levels available. The default is READ COMMITTED. Using a lower isolation level holds shared locks for a shorter duration than using a higher isolation level does, thereby reducing locking contention.

No Open-Ended Transactions

This is probably the most commonsense of all the recommendations here, but it's one that's often violated because of past practices.

One of the ways developers used to prevent lost updates (mainframe days here, folks!) was just to grab the lock and hold it until they were done with it. I can't tell you how problematic this was (can you say *yuck?*).

Imagine this scenario (it's a real-life example): Someone in your service department likes to use update screens (exclusive locks) instead of display screens (shared locks) to look at data. He goes on to look at a work order. Now his buddy calls and asks if he's ready for lunch. "Sure!" comes the reply, and the service clerk heads off to a rather long lunch (one to two hours). Everyone who is interested in this record is now locked out of it for the duration of this clerk's lunch.

Wait — it gets worse. In the days of the mainframe, you used to see the concept of queuing far more often (it actually can be quite efficient). Now someone submits a print job (which is queued) for this work order. It sits in the queue waiting for the record lock to clear. Because it's a queue environment, every print job piles up behind that first print job (which is going to wait for that person's lunch before clearing).

This is a rather extreme example, but I'm hoping that it clearly illustrates the point. Don't ever create locks that will still be open when you begin some form of open-ended process. Usually I'm talking user interaction (like the employee out to lunch earlier), but it could be any process that has an open-ended wait to it.

SUMMARY

Transactions and locks are both cornerstones of how SQL Server works and, therefore, help you maximize your development of solutions in SQL Server.

By using transactions, you can make sure that everything you need to have happen as a unit happens, or none of it does. SQL Server's use of locks ensures that you avoid the pitfalls of concurrency to the maximum extent possible (you'll never avoid them entirely, but it's amazing how close you can come with a little — okay, a lot — of planning). By using the two together, you can pass what the database industry calls the *ACID test*. If a transaction is ACID, it has all four ACID characteristics:

- ➤ Atomicity
- ➤ Consistency
- ➤ Isolation
- ➤ Durability

In short, by using transactions and locks, you can minimize deadlocks, ensure data integrity, and improve the overall efficiency of your system.

In the next chapter, you'll be looking at triggers. Indeed, you'll see that, for many of the likely uses of triggers, the concepts of transactions and rollbacks will be at the very center of the trigger.

EXERCISE

1. Cause a deadlock using updates on `Person.Person` and `HumanResources.Employee`. You will have to run different queries in sequence within two transactions using at least two query windows within Management Studio to do this. Hint: If you `BEGIN TRANSACTION` within a query window, the transaction stays open until you `COMMIT`, `ROLLBACK`, or kill the connection.

▶ WHAT YOU LEARNED IN THIS CHAPTER

TOPIC	CONCEPT
`BEGIN TRANSACTION,` `COMMIT, ROLLBACK`	You can make SQL Server treat a series of SQL statements as a single, atomic operation by putting the statements into a transaction. After a `BEGIN TRANSACTION` statement, all the statements can be kept or made to have "never happened" by either a `COMMIT` or a `ROLLBACK`, respectively.
The transaction log	Activity against the database is performed against both the transaction log and the actual database. The two are synchronized during `CHECKPOINT` operations that occur periodically but can be called manually.
Concurrency	When more than one user can access the database, it is necessary to lock certain resources from time to time in order to enforce ACID (atomic, consistent, isolated, durable) transactions.
Locks and lockable resources	Locks come in many varieties, most commonly shared and exclusive. Locks can be against data, schema, or system resources. Data locking can occur at a row, page, or table level.
Transaction isolation level	Setting a transaction isolation level of `SERIALIZABLE` ensures perfect ACID transactions but impedes concurrency. Lower levels such as `REPEATABLE READ`, `READ COMMITTED`, or `SNAPSHOT` permit greater concurrency while creating limited data consistency risks.
Deadlocks (1205 errors)	Two or more processes are waiting for each other, such that they can never finish. SQL Server will detect this deadlock condition and kill one of the processes. The killed process can be retried, or else the code can be refactored to prevent deadlocks.

15

Triggers

WHAT YOU WILL LEARN IN THIS CHAPTER:

➤ What is a trigger?

➤ Using triggers for more flexible referential integrity

➤ Using triggers to create flexible data integrity rules

➤ Using `INSTEAD OF` triggers to create more flexible updatable views

➤ Other common uses for triggers

➤ Controlling the firing order of triggers

➤ Performance considerations

Ah, triggers. Triggers are cool, triggers are neat, and triggers are our friends. At the very same time, triggers are evil, triggers are ugly, and triggers are our enemy. In short, I am often asked, "Should I use triggers?" The answer is, like most things in SQL, it depends. There's little that's black and white in the wonderful world of SQL Server — triggers are definitely a very plain shade of gray.

From a beginner's point of view (and by this chapter in this book, I hope you're a lot less of a beginner — but still . . .), you really want to be *certain* you know what you're doing before you go the triggers route, so sit back, listen, learn, and decide for yourself whether they are right for you.

In this chapter, I'll try to give you a complete look at triggers in all of their colors — from black all the way to white and a whole lot in between. By the time you're done, you should have an idea of just how complex the decision about when and where not to use triggers is. You'll also have an inkling of just how powerful and flexible they can be.

Most of all, if I've done my job well, you won't be a trigger extremist (which *so* many SQL Server people I meet are) with the distorted notion that triggers are evil and should never be used. Neither will you side with at the other end of the spectrum, who think that triggers are the solution to all the world's problems. The right answer in this respect is that triggers can do a lot for you, but they can also cause a lot of problems. The trick is to use them when they are the right things to use, and not to use them when they aren't.

Some common uses of triggers include:

> **Enforcing referential integrity:** Although I recommend using *Declarative Referential Integrity (DRI)* whenever possible, there are many things that DRI won't do (for example, referential integrity across databases or even servers, many complex types of relationships, and so on).

> **Creating audit trails:** This means writing out records that keep track of not just the most current data, but also the actual change history for each record. This may eventually become less popular with the change-data tracking that SQL Server 2008 added, but triggers are still a pretty popular choice.

> **Creating functionality similar to a CHECK constraint:** Unlike CHECK constraints, this can work across tables, databases, or even servers.

> **Substituting your own statements in the place of a user's action statement:** This is typically used to enable inserts in complex views.

In addition, you have the new, but rarer case of the Data Definition Language (DDL) trigger, which is about monitoring changes in the structure of your table.

And these are just a few. So, with no further ado, it's time to look at exactly what a trigger is.

WHAT IS A TRIGGER?

A trigger is a special kind of stored procedure that fires in response to specific events. There are two kinds of triggers: Data Definition Language (DDL) triggers and Data Manipulation Language (DML) triggers.

DDL triggers fire in response to someone changing the structure of your database in some way (CREATE, ALTER, DROP, and similar statements). These are critical to some installations (particularly high-security installations), but are pretty narrow in use. In general, you only need to look into using these where you need extreme auditing of changes/history of your database structure. Their use is a fairly advanced concept and, as such, I'm covering them here as mostly a "be aware these exist" thing, and you'll move on to the meatier version of triggers.

DML triggers are pieces of code that you attach to a particular table or view. Unlike sprocs, where you need to explicitly invoke the code, the code in triggers is automatically run whenever the event(s) you attached the trigger to occur in the table. Indeed, you *can't* explicitly invoke triggers — the only way to do this is by performing the required action in the table that they are assigned to.

NOTE *Beyond not being able to explicitly invoke a trigger, you'll find two other things that exist for sprocs but are missing from triggers:*

➤ **Parameters:** *While triggers take no parameters, they do have a mechanism for figuring out what records they are supposed to act on (you'll investigate this further later in the chapter).*

➤ **Return codes:** *While you can use the* RETURN *keyword, you cannot return a specific return code (because you didn't explicitly call the trigger, what would you return a return code to?).*

What events can you attach triggers to? There are only three action query types you can use in SQL: You can insert rows into a table (or view), update rows, or delete them. So, there are three types of triggers, plus hybrids that come from mixing and matching the events and timing that fire them:

➤ INSERT triggers

➤ DELETE triggers

➤ UPDATE triggers

➤ A mix and match of any of the above

NOTE *It's worth noting that there are times when a trigger will not fire, even though it seems that the action you are performing falls into one of the preceding categories. At issue is whether the operation you are doing is in a logged activity or not. For example, a* DELETE *statement is a normal, logged activity that would fire any delete trigger, but a* TRUNCATE TABLE, *which has the effect of deleting rows, just deallocates the space used by the table — there is no individual deletion of rows logged, and no trigger is fired. Bulk operations will not, by default, fire triggers (you can explicitly tell the bulk operation to fire the triggers).*

The syntax for creating triggers looks an awful lot like all the other CREATE syntax examples, except, as with a table, it has to be attached to a table — a trigger can't stand on its own.

Let's take a look:

```
CREATE TRIGGER <trigger name>
   ON [<schema name>.]<table or view name>
   [WITH ENCRYPTION | EXECUTE AS <CALLER | SELF | <user> >]
   {{{FOR|AFTER} <[DELETE] [,] [INSERT] [,] [UPDATE]>} |INSTEAD OF}
   [NOT FOR REPLICATION]
AS
   < <sql statements> | EXTERNAL NAME <assembly method specifier> >
```

As you can see, the all-too-familiar CREATE <object type> <object name> is still there, as well as the execution stuff you've seen in many other objects — this syntax includes the ON clause to indicate the table to which this trigger is going to be attached, as well as when and under what conditions it fires.

ON

This part just names the object you are creating the trigger against. Keep in mind that, if the type of the trigger is an AFTER trigger (if it uses FOR or AFTER to declare the trigger), the target of the ON clause must be a table — AFTER triggers are not supported for views.

WITH ENCRYPTION

This works just as it does for views and sprocs. If you add this option, you can be certain that no one can view your code (not even you!). This is particularly useful if you are going to build software for commercial distribution, or if you are concerned about security and don't want your users to see what data you're modifying or accessing. Obviously, you should keep a copy of the code required to create the trigger somewhere else, in case you want to re-create it sometime later.

As with views and sprocs, the thing to remember when using the WITH ENCRYPTION option is that you must reapply it every time you use ALTER on your trigger. If you make use of an ALTER TRIGGER statement and do not include the WITH ENCRYPTION option, the trigger is no longer encrypted.

FOR|AFTER

The FOR (or, alternatively, you can use AFTER; they mean the same thing) clause indicates under what type of action(s) you want this trigger to fire. You can have the trigger fire whenever there is an INSERT, UPDATE, or DELETE, or any mix of the three. So, for example, your FOR clause could look something like:

```
FOR INSERT, DELETE
```

. . . or:

```
FOR UPDATE, INSERT
```

. . . or:

```
FOR DELETE
```

As stated in the section about the ON clause, triggers declared using the FOR or AFTER clause can be attached only to tables — no views are allowed (see INSTEAD OF triggers for those).

INSERT Trigger

The code for any trigger that you mark as FOR INSERT is executed anytime that someone inserts a new row into your table. For each row that is inserted, SQL Server creates a copy of that new row and inserts it in a special table that exists only within the scope of your trigger. That table is called Inserted, and you'll see much more of it over the course of this chapter. The big thing to understand is that the `Inserted` table lives only as long as your trigger does. Think of it as not existing before your trigger starts or after your trigger completes.

DELETE Trigger

This works much the same as an `INSERT` trigger does, save that the `Inserted` table is empty (after all, you deleted rather than inserted, so there are no records for the `Inserted` table). Instead, a copy of each record that was deleted is inserted into another table called `Deleted`. That table, like the `Inserted` table, is limited in scope to just the life of your trigger.

UPDATE Trigger

More of the same, save for a twist. The code in a trigger declared as FOR UPDATE is fired whenever an existing record in your table changes. The twist is that there's no such table as UPDATED. Instead, SQL Server treats each row as if the existing record has been deleted and a totally new record was inserted. As you can probably guess from that, a trigger declared as FOR UPDATE contains not one but two special tables called `Inserted` and `Deleted`. The two tables have exactly the same number of rows, of course.

> **NOTE** When I say "an existing record has changed," there's something you should be aware of — the record doesn't have to actually change to a new value. Imagine you perform an UPDATE that sets the inventory quantity to 0 for a thousand products, half of which already had a quantity of 0. Your INSERTED and DELETED tables will contain the full thousand rows, including the five hundred that were included in the UPDATE but whose new value matches the old.

The FOR|AFTER versus the INSTEAD OF Clause

In addition to deciding which kinds of queries will fire your trigger (INSERT, UPDATE, and/or DELETE), you also have some choice as to when the trigger fires. While the FOR (or AFTER) trigger has been around a long time and is what most people think of as a trigger, you can also run what is called an INSTEAD OF trigger. Which of these two you use affects whether your SQL code runs before you enter the trigger (FOR|AFTER) or does not (INSTEAD OF). In either case, you will be in your trigger before any changes are truly committed to the database.

Confusing? Probably. You can try it a different way with a diagram that shows where each choice fires (see Figure 15-1).

The thing to note here is that, regardless of which choice you make, SQL Server puts together two working tables — one holding a copy of the records that were inserted (and, incidentally, called `Inserted`) and one holding a copy of any records that were deleted (called `Deleted`). You'll look into the uses of these working tables a little later. For now realize that, with INSTEAD OF triggers, the creation of these working tables happens *before* any constraints are checked. With FOR triggers, on the other hand, these tables are created after constraints are checked. The key to INSTEAD OF triggers is that you can actually run your own code in the place of whatever the user requested. This means you can clean up ambiguous INSERT problems in views. It also means that you can take action to clean up constraint violations before the constraint is checked.

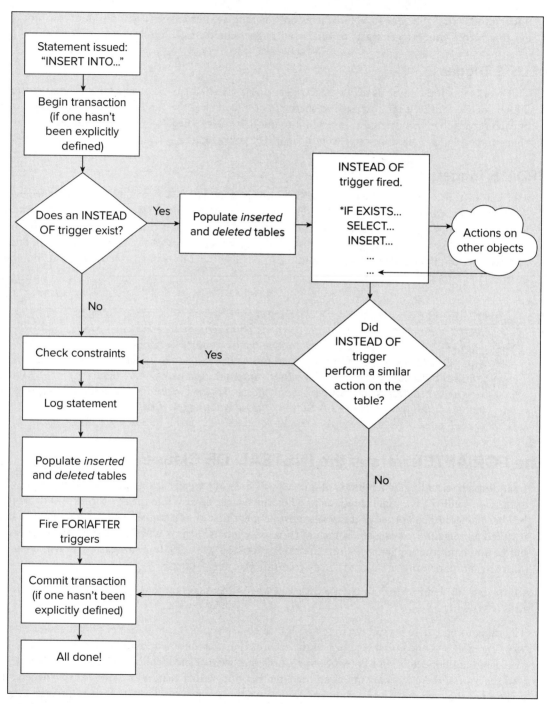

FIGURE 15-1

NOTE *As positively glorious as this sounds, this is actually pretty complex stuff. It means that you need to anticipate every possibility. In addition, it means that you are effectively adding a* preprocess *(a process that runs before the main code) to every query that changes data in any way for this table (this is not a good thing performance-wise). Cool as they sound,* INSTEAD OF *triggers fall in the category of fairly advanced stuff and are well outside the scope of this book.*

Triggers using the FOR and AFTER declaration behave identically. The big difference between them and INSTEAD OF triggers is that they build their working tables *after* any constraints have been checked.

NOT FOR REPLICATION

Adding this option slightly alters the rules for when the trigger fires. With this option in place, the trigger does not fire whenever a replication-related task modifies your table. Usually a trigger fires (to do the housekeeping, cascading, and so on) when the original table is modified and there is often no point in doing it again.

AS

Exactly as it was with sprocs, this is the meat of the matter. The AS keyword tells SQL Server that your code is about to start. From this point forward, you're into the scripted portion of your trigger.

USING TRIGGERS FOR DATA INTEGRITY RULES

Although they shouldn't be your first option, triggers can also perform the same functionality as a CHECK constraint or even a DEFAULT. The answer to the question "Should I use triggers versus CHECK constraints?" is the rather definitive: "It depends." If a CHECK can do the job, it's probably the preferable choice. There are times, however, when a CHECK constraint just won't do the job, or when something inherent in the CHECK process makes it less desirable than a trigger. Examples of where you would want to use a trigger over a CHECK include:

➤ Your business rule needs to reference data in a separate table.

➤ Your business rule needs to check the *delta* (difference between before and after) of an UPDATE.

➤ You require a customized error message.

A summary table of when to use which type of data integrity mechanism is provided at the end of Chapter 6.

This really just scratches the surface of things. Because triggers are highly flexible, deciding when to use them really just comes down to balancing your need to get something special done with the overhead triggers incur and other approaches you might take to address your need.

Dealing with Requirements Sourced from Other Tables

CHECK constraints are great — fast and efficient — but they don't do everything you'd like them to. Perhaps the biggest shortcoming shows up when you need to verify data across tables.

To illustrate this, let's take a look at the `Sales.SalesOrderDetail` and `Sales.SpecialOfferProduct` tables in the AdventureWorks database. The relationship looks like Figure 15-2.

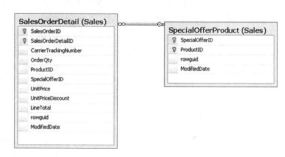

FIGURE 15-2

So under normal DRI, you can be certain that no `SalesOrderDetail` item can be entered into the `SalesOrderDetail` table unless there is a matching `ProductID` in the `SpecialOfferProduct` table (even if the special offer record is "no discount"). In this case, however, maybe you're looking for something more than just the norm.

The Inventory Department has been complaining that the Customer Support people keep placing orders for products that are marked discontinued. They would like to have such orders rejected before they get into the system.

You can't deal with this using a CHECK constraint, because the place where you know about the discontinued status (the `Product` table) is a separate table from where you are placing the restriction (the `SalesOrderDetail` table). Don't sweat it though — you can tell the Inventory department, "No problem!" You just need to use a trigger:

```
CREATE TRIGGER Sales.SalesOrderDetailNotDiscontinued
   ON Sales.SalesOrderDetail
   FOR INSERT, UPDATE
AS

   IF EXISTS
      (
       SELECT 'True'
       FROM Inserted i
       JOIN Production.Product p
          ON i.ProductID = p.ProductID
       WHERE p.DiscontinuedDate IS NOT NULL
      )
   BEGIN
      RAISERROR('Order Item is discontinued. Transaction Failed.',16,1)
      ROLLBACK TRAN
   END
```

Code snippet Chap15.sql

Let's go ahead and test out the handiwork. First, you need a record or two that fails when it hits the trigger. Unfortunately, AdventureWorks has apparently never discontinued a product before — you'll just have to change that . . .

```
UPDATE Production.Product
SET DiscontinuedDate = '01-01-2008'
WHERE ProductID = 680
```

Now, knowing that you have a discontinued product, go ahead and add an order detail item that violates the constraint. Note that I've chosen an existing order (43659) for you to tack this item onto:

```
INSERT INTO Sales.SalesOrderDetail
VALUES
(43659, '4911-403C-98', 1, 680, 1, 1431.50,0.00, NEWID(), GETDATE())
```

Code snippet Chap15.sql

This gets the rejection that you expect:

```
Msg 50000, Level 16, State 1, Procedure SalesOrderDetailNotDiscontinued, Line 14
Order Item is discontinued. Transaction Failed.
Msg 3609, Level 16, State 1, Line 1
The transaction ended in the trigger. The batch has been aborted.
```

Remember that you could, if desired, also create a custom error message to raise, instead of the ad hoc message that you used with the RAISERROR command.

> **NOTE** *If you're working along with these, but trying to keep your AdventureWorks database close to its original state, don't forget to return ProductID 680 back to its null discontinued date.*

Using Triggers to Check the Delta of an Update

Sometimes, you're not interested as much in what the value was or is, as you are in how much it changes. While there isn't any one column or table that gives you that information, you can calculate it by making use of the Inserted and Deleted tables in your trigger.

TRY IT OUT **Validating Data with a Trigger**

To check this out, take a look at the Production.ProductInventory table. ProductInventory has a column called Quantity. Recently, there has been a rush on several products, and AdventureWorks has been selling out of several items. Because AdventureWorks needs more than just a few customers to stay in business in the long run, it has decided to institute a rationing system on its products. The Inventory department has requested that you prevent orders from being placed that try to sell more than half of the units in stock for any particular product.

To implement this, you'll need to make use of both the `Inserted` and `Deleted` tables:

```
CREATE TRIGGER Production.ProductIsRationed
   ON Production.ProductInventory
   FOR UPDATE
AS

   IF EXISTS
      (
      SELECT 'True'
      FROM Inserted i
      JOIN Deleted d
         ON i.ProductID = d.ProductID
        AND i.LocationID = d.LocationID
      WHERE (d.Quantity - i.Quantity) > d.Quantity / 2
        AND d.Quantity - i.Quantity > 0
      )
   BEGIN
      RAISERROR('Cannot reduce stock by more than 50%% at once.',16,1)
      ROLLBACK TRAN
   END
```

Code snippet Chap15.sql

How It Works

Before you test this, let's analyze what exactly this code is going to do.

➤ You're making use of an `IF EXISTS` just as you have throughout this chapter. You want to do the rollback only if something exists that meets the evil, mean, and nasty criteria that you'll be testing for.

➤ You join the `Inserted` and `Deleted` tables together — this is what gives you the chance to compare the two.

➤ The `WHERE` clause is the point where things might become a bit confusing. The first line of it is pretty straightforward. It implements the business requirement as discussed — updates to the `Quantity` column that are more than half the units you previously had on hand will meet the `EXISTS` criterion and cause the conditional code to run (thus rejecting the transaction).

➤ The next line, though, is not quite so straightforward. As with all things in programming, you need to go beyond the nominal statement of the problem, and think about other ramifications. The requirement really applies only to reductions in orders — you certainly don't want to restrict how many units are put *in* stock — so you need to make sure that the trigger worries only about updates where the number in stock after the update is less than before the update. The `> 0` requirement also addresses the scenario where there was only one item in stock. In such a scenario, you want to go ahead and sell that last one, but 1-1 is greater than ½, and the trigger would have rejected it without that `> 0` addition.

➤ If both of these conditions have been met (over 50 percent and a reduction, rather than addition, to the inventory), you raise the error. Notice the use of two `%` signs, rather than one, in RAISERROR. Remember that a % works as a placeholder for a parameter, so one % by itself won't show up when your error message comes out (in fact, it will produce a different error). By putting two in a row (%%), you let SQL Server know that you really do want to print a percent sign.

Okay — let's check how it works. You can just pick a record and try to do an update that reduces the stock by more than 50 percent:

```
UPDATE Production.ProductInventory
SET Quantity = 1  -- Was 408 if you want to set it back
WHERE ProductID = 1
    AND LocationID = 1
```

Available for download on Wrox.com

Code snippet Chap15.sql

I just picked "Adjustable Race" as the victim, but you could have chosen any ProductID, as long as you set the value to less than 50 percent of its previous value. If you do, you'll get the expected error:

```
Msg 50000, Level 16, State 1, Procedure ProductIsRationed, Line 16
Cannot reduce stock by more than 50% at once.
Msg 3609, Level 16, State 1, Line 1
The transaction ended in the trigger. The batch has been aborted.
```

Like in any other part of SQL Server, there are lots of ways you could have approached this, but each has its own strengths and pitfalls. You could, for example, have implemented this in the SalesOrderDetail table by referencing the actual order quantity against the current Quantity amount, but you would have had to deal with several problems:

➤ **Updates that change:** Is the process that's creating the SalesOrderDetail record updating ProductInventory before or after the SalesOrderDetail record? That makes a difference in how you make use of the Quantity value in the ProductInventory table to calculate the effect of the transaction.

➤ **The inventory external to the SalesOrderDetails table updates would not be affected:** They could still reduce the inventory by more than half (this may actually be a good thing in many circumstances, but it's something that has to be thought about).

Using Triggers for Custom Error Messages

I've already touched on this in some of the earlier examples, but remember that triggers can be handy for when you want control over the error message or number that gets passed back to your user or client application.

With a CHECK constraint for example, you're just going to get the standard 547 error along with its rather nondescript explanation. As often as not, this is less than helpful in terms of the user really figuring out what went wrong — indeed, your client application often doesn't have enough information to make an intelligent and helpful response on behalf of the user.

In short, sometimes you create triggers when there is already something that would give you the data integrity that you want, but won't give you enough information to handle it.

 NOTE *It's worth noting that the need for custom error messages in SQL Server should be relatively rare, although passing custom error codes is often useful. Why not pass the custom error message? Well, one would think that you probably have an application layer on top of it, and it is likely going to want to put more context on the error anyway, so the SQL-Server-specific text may not be all that useful. Using a special error code may, however, be very useful to your application in terms of determining what exactly happened and applying the correct client-side error handling code.*

OTHER COMMON USES FOR TRIGGERS

In addition to the straight data integrity uses, triggers have a number of other uses. Indeed, the possibilities are fairly limitless, but here are a few common examples:

➤ Updating summary information

➤ Feeding de-normalized tables for reporting

➤ Setting condition flags

As you can see, the possibilities are pretty far-reaching — it's really all about your particular situation and the needs of your particular system.

OTHER TRIGGER ISSUES

You have most of it now but if you're thinking you are finished with triggers, think again. As I indicated early in the chapter, triggers create an awful lot to think about. The sections that follow attempt to point out some of the biggest issues you need to consider, plus provide some information on additional trigger features and possibilities.

Triggers Can Be Nested

A nested trigger is one that did not fire directly as a result of a statement that you issued, but rather because of a statement that was issued by another trigger.

This can actually set off quite a chain of events, with one trigger causing another trigger to fire, which, in turn, causes yet another trigger to fire, and so on. Just how deep the triggers can fire depends on:

➤ **Whether nested triggers are turned on for your system.** This is a system-wide, not database-level option; it is set using the Management Studio or `sp_configure`, and defaults to on. Note that `INSTEAD OF` queries can be nested regardless of this setting.

➤ **Whether there is a limit of nesting to 32 levels deep.**

➤ **Whether a trigger has already been fired.** A trigger can, by default, be fired only once per trigger transaction. Once fired, it ignores any other calls as a result of activity that is part of the same trigger action. Once you move on to an entirely new statement (even within the same overall transaction), the process can start all over again.

In most circumstances, you actually want your triggers to nest (thus the default), but you need to think about what's going to happen if you get into a circle of triggers firing triggers. If it comes back around to the same table twice, the trigger does not fire the second time, and something you think is important may not happen; for example, a data integrity violation may get through. It's also worth noting that, if you do a `ROLLBACK` anywhere in the nesting chain, the entire chain is rolled back. In other words, the entire nested trigger chain behaves as a transaction.

Triggers Can Be Recursive

What is a recursive trigger? A trigger is said to be *recursive* when something the trigger does eventually causes that same trigger to be fired. It may be directly (by an action query done to the table on which the trigger is set) or indirectly (through the nesting process).

Recursive triggers are rare. Indeed, by default, recursive triggers are turned off. This is, however, a way of dealing with the situation just described where you are nesting triggers and you want the update to happen the second time around. Recursion, unlike nesting, is a database-level option and can be set using the `sp_dboption` system sproc.

The danger in recursive triggers is that you'll get into some form of unintended loop. As such, you'll need to make sure that you get some form of recursion check in place to stop the process if necessary.

Triggers Don't Prevent Architectural Changes

This is a classic good news/bad news story.

Using triggers is positively great in terms of making it easy to create architecture changes. Indeed, I often use triggers for referential integrity early in the development cycle (when I'm more likely to be making lots of changes to the design of the database), and then change to DRI late in the cycle when I'm close to production.

When you want to drop a table and re-create it using DRI, you must first drop all the constraints before dropping the table. This can create quite a maze in terms of dropping multiple constraints, making your changes, and then adding the constraints again. It can be quite a wild ride trying to make sure that everything drops that is supposed to so that your changed scripts run. Then it's just as wild a ride to make sure that you've got everything back on that needs to be. Triggers take care of all this because they don't care that anything has changed until they actually run. There's the rub, though — when they run. You see, it means that you may change architecture and break several triggers without even realizing that you've done it. It won't be until the first time that those triggers try to address the object(s) in question that you find the error of your ways. By that time, you may find together exactly what you did and why.

Both sides have their hassles — just keep the hassles in mind no matter which method you're employing.

Triggers Can Be Turned Off without Being Removed

Sometimes, just like with CHECK constraints, you want to turn off the integrity feature so you can perform some valid action that violates the constraint. (Importation of data is probably the most common such action.)

Another common reason for doing this is when you are performing some sort of bulk insert (importation again), but you are already 100 percent certain the data is valid. In this case, you may want to turn off the triggers to eliminate their overhead and speed up the insert process.

You can turn a trigger off and on by using an ALTER TABLE statement. The syntax looks like this:

```
ALTER TABLE <table name>
    <ENABLE|DISABLE> TRIGGER <ALL|<trigger name>>
```

As you might expect, my biggest words of caution in this area are, don't forget to re-enable your triggers!

One last thing. If you're turning them off to do some form of mass importation of data, I highly recommend that you kick out all your users and go to either single-user mode, dbo-only mode, or both. This ensures that no one sneaks in behind you while you have the triggers turned off.

Trigger Firing Order

In long ago releases of SQL Server (7.0 and prior), developers had no control over firing order. Indeed, you may recall me discussing how there was only one of any particular kind of trigger (INSERT, UPDATE, and DELETE) prior to 7.0, so firing order was something of a moot point. Later releases of SQL Server provide a limited amount of control over which triggers go in what order. For any given table (not views because firing order can be specified only for AFTER triggers and views accept only INSTEAD OF triggers), you can elect to have one (and only one) trigger fired first. Likewise, you can elect to have one (and only one) trigger fired last. All other triggers are considered to have no preference on firing order — that is, there is no guarantee what order triggers with a firing order of NONE will fire in, other than that they will fire after the FIRST trigger (if there is one) is complete and before the LAST trigger (again, if there is one) begins (see Figure 15-3).

The creation of a trigger that is to be FIRST or LAST works just the same as any other trigger. You state the firing order preference after the trigger has already been created using a special system stored procedure, sp_settriggerorder.

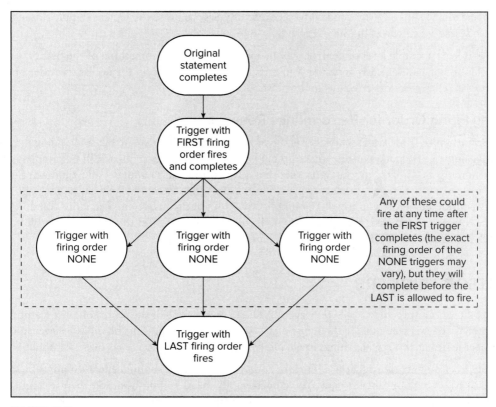

FIGURE 15-3

The syntax of `sp_settriggerorder` looks like this:

```
sp_settriggerorder[@triggername =] '<trigger name>',
    [@order =] '{FIRST|LAST|NONE}',
    [@stmttype =] '{INSERT|UPDATE|DELETE}'
    [, [@namespace =] {'DATABASE' | 'SERVER' | NULL} ]
```

There can be only one trigger that is considered to be FIRST for any particular action (INSERT, UPDATE, or DELETE). Likewise, there can be only one LAST trigger for any particular action. Any number of triggers can be considered to be NONE — that is, the number of triggers that don't have a particular firing order is unlimited.

So, the question should be, why do I care what order they fire in? Well, often you won't care at all. At other times, it can be important logic-wise or just a good performance idea. Let's consider what that means in a bit more detail.

Controlling Firing Order for Logic Reasons

Why would you *need* to have one trigger fire before another? The most common reason is that the first trigger lays some sort of foundation for, or otherwise validates, what comes afterwards. Separate triggers also allow one part of the code to be disabled (remember that NO CHECK thing you did a few sections ago?) while other parts of the code continue to function. The downside is that, if you go ahead and separate your code into separate triggers, you lose the logical stepping order that the code had when it was in one trigger.

By having at least a simple level of control over firing order, you have something of the best of both worlds — you can logically separate your triggers, but still maintain the necessary order of precedence on what piece of code runs first or last.

Controlling Firing Order for Performance Reasons

On the performance front, a FIRST trigger is the only one that really has any big thing going for it. If you have multiple triggers, but only one of them is likely to generate a rollback (for example, it may be enforcing a complex data integrity rule that a constraint can't handle), you would want to consider making such a trigger a FIRST trigger. This ensures that the most likely cause of a rollback is already considered before you invest any more activity in your transaction. The more you do before the rollback is detected, the more that you'll have to roll back. Get the highest probability of a rollback happening resolved before performing less risky activities.

INSTEAD OF TRIGGERS

INSTEAD OF triggers were added in SQL Server 2000 and remain one of the more complex features of SQL Server. While it is well outside the scope of a "beginning" concept, I'm still a big believer in even the beginner learning about what things are *available*, and so I'll touch on what these are about here.

Essentially, an INSTEAD OF trigger is a block of code you can use as an interceptor for anything that anyone tries to do to your table or view. You can either go ahead and do whatever the user requests or, if you choose, go so far as doing something that is entirely different.

Like regular triggers, INSTEAD OF triggers come in three flavors: INSERT, UPDATE, and DELETE. In each case, the most common use is the same — resolving ambiguity about which table(s) is to receive the actual changes when you're dealing with a view based on multiple tables.

PERFORMANCE CONSIDERATIONS

I've seen what appear almost like holy wars happen over the pros and cons, evil and good, and light and dark of triggers. The worst of it tends to come from purists — people who love the theory, and that's all they want to deal with, or people that have figured out how flexible triggers are and want to use them for seemingly everything.

My two-bits worth on this is, as I stated early in the chapter, use them when they are the right things to use. If that sounds sort of noncommittal and ambiguous — good! Programming is rarely black and white, and databases are almost never that way. I will, however, point out some facts for you to think about.

Triggers Are Reactive Rather Than Proactive

What I mean here is that triggers happen after the fact. By the time that your trigger fires, the entire query has run and your transaction has been logged (but not committed and only to the point of the statement that fired your trigger). This means that if the trigger needs to roll things back, it has to undo what is potentially a ton of work that's already been done. *Slow!* Keep this knowledge in balance though. How big an impact this adds up to depends strongly on how big your query is.

So what, you say. Well, compare this to the notion of constraints, which are proactive — that is, they happen before your statement is really executed. That means they detect things that will fail and prevent them from happening earlier in the process. This usually means that they run at least slightly faster — much faster on more complex queries. Note that this extra speed really shows itself to any significant extent only when a rollback occurs.

What's the end analysis here? Well, if you're dealing with very few rollbacks, and/or the complexity and execution time of the statements affected are low, there probably isn't much of a difference between triggers and constraints. There's some, but probably not much. If, however, the number of rollbacks is unpredictable or you know it's going to be high, you'll want to stick with constraints if you can (and frankly, I suggest sticking with constraints unless you have a very specific reason not to).

Triggers Don't Have Concurrency Issues with the Process That Fires Them

You may have noticed throughout this chapter that the examples often make use of the ROLLBACK statement, even though they don't issue a BEGIN TRAN. That's because a trigger is always implicitly part of the same transaction as the statement that caused the trigger to fire.

If the firing statement was not part of an explicit transaction (one where there was a BEGIN TRAN), it would still be part of its own one-statement transaction. In either case, a ROLLBACK TRAN issued inside the trigger will still roll back the entire transaction.

Another upshot of this part-of-the-same-transaction business is that triggers inherit the locks already open on the transaction they are part of. This means that you don't have to do anything special to make sure that you don't bump into the locks created by the other statements in the transaction. You have free access within the scope of the transaction, and you see the database based on the modifications already placed by previous statements within the transaction.

Using IF UPDATE() and COLUMNS_UPDATED

In an UPDATE trigger, you can often limit the amount of code that actually executes within the trigger by checking to see whether the column(s) you're interested in are the ones that have been changed. To do this, you make use of the UPDATE() or COLUMNS_UPDATED() functions. Let's look at each.

The UPDATE() Function

The UPDATE() function has relevance only within the scope of a trigger. Its sole purpose in life is to provide a Boolean response (true/false) to whether a particular column has been updated. You can use this function to decide whether a particular block of code needs to run — for example, if that code is relevant only when a particular column is updated.

Let's run a quick example of this by modifying one of the earlier triggers.

```
ALTER TRIGGER Production.ProductIsRationed
    ON Production.ProductInventory
    FOR UPDATE
AS
```

```
IF UPDATE(Quantity)
BEGIN
  IF EXISTS
    (
     SELECT 'True'
     FROM Inserted i
     JOIN Deleted d
       ON i.ProductID = d.ProductID
      AND i.LocationID = d.LocationID
      WHERE (d.Quantity - i.Quantity) > d.Quantity / 2
       AND d.Quantity > 0
    )
  BEGIN
    RAISERROR('Cannot reduce stock by more than 50%% at once.',16,1)
    ROLLBACK TRAN
  END
END
```

Code snippet Chap15.sql

With this change, you'll now limit the rest of the code to run only when the `Quantity` column (the one you care about) has been changed. The user can change the value of any other column and you don't care. This means that you'll execute fewer lines of code and, therefore, this trigger performs slightly better than the previous version.

The COLUMNS_UPDATED() Function

This one works somewhat differently from `UPDATE()`, but has the same general purpose. What `COLUMNS_UPDATED()` gives you is the ability to check multiple columns at one time. In order to do this, the function uses a bitmask that relates individual bits in one or more bytes of `varbinary` data to individual columns in the table. It ends up looking something like Figure 15-4.

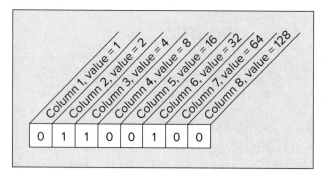

FIGURE 15-4

In this case, the single byte of data is telling you that the second, third, and sixth columns were updated — the rest were not.

In the event that there are more than eight columns, SQL Server just adds another byte on the right side and keeps counting (see Figure 15-5).

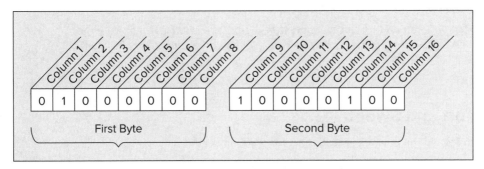

FIGURE 15-5

This time the second, ninth, and fourteenth columns were updated.

I can hear you out there: "Gee, that's nice — but how do I make any use of this?" Well, to answer that, you have to get into the world of Boolean algebra.

Making use of this information means that you need to add the binary value of all the bytes, considering the leftmost digit to be the least significant. So, if you want your comparison to take into account 2, 5, and 7, you need to add the binary value of each bit: 2 + 16 + 64. Then you need to compare the sum of the binary values of your columns to the bitmask by using bitwise operators, as shown in Table 15-1.

TABLE 15-1: Bitwise Operators

OPERATOR	DESCRIPTION
|	Represents bitwise OR
&	Represents bitwise AND
^	Represents bitwise Exclusive OR

As I read back over what I've just written, I realize that it is correct, but about as clear as mud, so let's look a little closer at what I mean with a couple of examples.

Imagine that you updated a table that contained five columns. If you updated the first, third, and fifth columns, the bitmask used by COLUMNS_UPDATED would contain 10101000, from 1 + 4 + 16 = 21. You could then use COLUMNS_UPDATED() > 0 to find out if any column was updated.

➤ COLUMNS_UPDATED() ^ 21 = 0 to find out if *all* of the columns specified (in this case 1, 3, and 5) were updated and nothing else was.

➤ COLUMNS_UPDATED() & 21 = 21 to find out if all of the columns specified were updated, but the state of other columns doesn't matter.

➤ COLUMNS_UPDATED | 21 != 21 to find out if any column *other* than those we're interested in was updated.

NOTE *Understand that this is tough stuff — Boolean math is not exactly the easiest of concepts to grasp for most people, so check things carefully and TEST, TEST, TEST!*

Keep It Short and Sweet

I feel like I'm stating the obvious here, but it's for a good reason.

I can't tell you how often I see bloated, stupid code in sprocs and triggers. I don't know whether it's that people get in a hurry, or if they just think that the medium they are using is fast anyway, so it won't matter.

Remember that a trigger is part of the same transaction as the statement in which it is called. This means the statement is not complete until your trigger is complete. Think about it — if you write long-running code in your trigger, this means that every piece of code that you create that causes that trigger to fire will, in turn, be long running. This can really cause heartache when you are trying to figure out why your code is taking so long to run. You write what appears to be a very efficient sproc, but it performs terribly. You may spend weeks and yet never figure out that your sproc is fine — it just fires a trigger that is too long-winded.

Don't Forget Triggers When Choosing Indexes

Another common mistake. You look through all your sprocs and views figuring out what the best mix of indexes is — and totally forget that you have significant code running in your triggers.

This is the same notion as the "short and sweet" notion — long-running queries make for long-running statements, which, in turn, lead to long-running everything. Don't forget your triggers when you optimize!

Try Not to Roll Back within Triggers

This one's hard because rollbacks are so often a major part of what you want to accomplish with your triggers.

Just remember that AFTER triggers (which are far and away the most common type of trigger) happen after most of the work is already done — that means a rollback is expensive. This is where DRI picks up almost all of its performance advantage. If you are using many ROLLBACK TRAN statements in your triggers, make sure that you look for errors before you execute the statement that fires the trigger. Because SQL Server can't be proactive in this situation, you need to be proactive for it. Test for errors beforehand rather than wait for the rollback.

DROPPING TRIGGERS

The process of dropping triggers works only slightly differently than it has worked for almost everything else thus far. The only real trick is that, like tables, trigger names are scoped at the schema level. This means that you can have two objects with a trigger of the same name, as long as the object

the trigger is placed against it in a different schema than the trigger of the same name. Restated, the trigger is named in terms of the schema it's in, rather than the object it is associated with — odd when you realize it is subsidiary to the table or view it is attached to. The syntax looks like:

```
DROP TRIGGER [<schema>.]<trigger name>
```

Other than the schema issue, dropping triggers is pretty much the same as any other drop.

DEBUGGING TRIGGERS

Most everything to do with the debugger works the same for triggers as it does for anything else. The only real trick is a result of the fact that you can't directly call triggers in the way you can scripts or stored procedures.

Fortunately, most developer types are reasonably intelligent people, so, if you think about it, you probably can anticipate how you can get around starting the debugger for triggers — you just need to debug a statement that causes a trigger to fire.

> **NOTE** *In releases prior to SQL Server 2008, direct debugging of scripts wasn't available. This meant you needed to create a stored procedure that would cause a trigger to be debugged if you wanted to debug that trigger — happily, this is no longer the case.*

Because Chapter 12 reviewed the basics of debugging fairly thoroughly, I'm going to cut right to the proverbial chase and show you debugging triggers in action. All you need to do to show this off is run a bit of code that exercises the trigger you most recently worked with in this chapter. You can then step into that script, so you can watch the debugger run through it line by line:

Available for download on Wrox.com

```
BEGIN TRAN
   -- This one should work
   UPDATE Production.ProductInventory
   SET Quantity = 400  -- Was 408 if you want to set it back
   WHERE ProductID = 1
     AND LocationID = 1

   -- This one shouldn't
   UPDATE Production.ProductInventory
   SET Quantity = 1  -- Was 408 if you want to set it back
   WHERE ProductID = 1
     AND LocationID = 1
IF @@TRANCOUNT > 0
   ROLLBACK TRAN
```

Code snippet Chap15.sql

With this script up in the Query Window in Management Studio, you can just press F11 to step into the script (or set a breakpoint and then use any of the several options that start the debugger). You'll start, of course, at the BEGIN TRAN statement. Continue to step into the script (F11) until you execute the first UPDATE statement, and note that you wind up in the trigger. Figure 15-6 shows the call stack as you enter the trigger for the first time.

FIGURE 15-6

Now, go ahead and step out of the first UPDATE, and into the second UPDATE. Because the first UPDATE statement didn't match the violation test in the trigger, you exited almost immediately, but this second time you should see, as you step through, that the code that aborts the transaction fires.

In short, you can utilize a single script that, in this case, has two statements meant to test the two possible code paths in your trigger. Obviously, you need more complex scripting to handle the possible code paths for more complex triggers, but, beyond that, the debugging needs are pretty much as they are for testing any other code in T-SQL.

SUMMARY

Triggers are an extremely powerful tool that can add tremendous flexibility to both your data integrity and the overall operation of your system. That being said, they are not something to take lightly. Triggers can greatly enhance the performance of your system if you use them for proper summarization of data, but they can also be the bane of your existence. They can be very difficult to debug (even now that SQL has a proper debugger), and a poorly written trigger affects not only the trigger itself, but also any statement that causes that trigger to fire.

Before you get too frustrated with triggers — or before you get too bored with the couple of trigger templates that fill about 90 percent of your trigger needs — keep in mind that there are a large number of tools out there that will auto-generate triggers for you that meet certain requirements.

EXERCISES

1. Write a trigger for the Product table to ensure the list price can never be raised more than 15 percent in a single change.

2. Modify the trigger from Exercise 1 to execute its check code only if the ListPrice column is updated.

▶ **WHAT YOU LEARNED IN THIS CHAPTER**

TOPIC	CONCEPT
`CREATE TRIGGER`	Similar to other `CREATE`, `ALTER`, and `DROP` syntax, `CREATE TRIGGER` builds a trigger object. Uniquely, it attaches the trigger to a specific table and a selection of specific DML actions. Each time one of the selected actions is performed, the trigger code will run as part of the same transaction.
Common uses for triggers	Using triggers for referential integrity is still occasionally done, because it was at one time the only way. More commonly, triggers are used for complex data integrity resolution, of the kind not possible with constraints (which are more efficient when they can be used). Triggers can check multiple tables, check deltas with the `INSERTED` and `DELETED` tables, or deliver custom error messages, among other things.
Architectural considerations	Triggers can be nested, although nesting can be disabled. Triggers can also call themselves recursively, again as an option. Be careful how much code you require to be executed for each update!
`INSTEAD OF` triggers	Views that otherwise would not be updateable can be made so through the use of `INSTEAD OF` triggers. This type of trigger intercepts DML commands addressed to the view and, rather than trying to interpret those commands as individual table operations, runs the trigger code instead, thus providing the `INSERTED` and `DELETED` tables as inputs.
Trigger performance	Remember that triggers fire for every applicable DML operation on a table. If a trigger costs much time, it will dramatically slow your operations. In addition, triggers that reach into other tables can create locking issues.

16

A Brief XML Primer

WHAT YOU WILL LEARN IN THIS CHAPTER:

➤ The nature of XML

➤ How an XML document is structured

➤ Well formed and valid XML

➤ How SQL Server deals with XML

➤ Methods used to retrieve and modify data within XML documents in SQL Server

➤ How to retrieve relational data in XML format

So, here you are — most of the structural stuff is done at this point, so you're ready to start moving on to the peripheral stuff. That is, you're ready to start looking at things that are outside of what one usually actively thinks of when working with relational database systems. It's not that some of the items you still have to cover aren't things that you would normally expect out of a relational database system — it's just that you don't really *need* these in order to have a functional SQL Server. Indeed, there are so many things included in SQL Server now, that it's difficult to squeeze everything into one book.

This chapter starts by presenting some background for what has become an increasingly integral part of SQL Server — XML. It then moves on to looking at some of the many features SQL Server has to support XML. The catch here is that XML is entirely its own animal — it's a completely different kind of thing than the relational system you've been working with up to this point. Why then does SQL Server include so much functionality to support it? The short answer is that XML is probably the most important thing to happen to data since the advent of data warehousing.

XML has actually been around for years now but, while the talk was big, its actual usage was not what it could have been. Since the late '90s, XML has gone into wider and wider use as a generic way to make data feeds and reasonable-sized data documents available. XML provides a means to make data self-describing — that is, you can define type and validation information that can go along with the XML document so that no matter whom the consumers are (even if they don't know anything about how to connect to SQL Server), they can understand what the rules for that data are.

XML is often not a very good place to *store* data, but it is a positively spectacular way of making data *useful* — as such, the ways of utilizing XML will likely continue to grow, and grow, and grow.

So, with all that said, this chapter looks at:

➤   What XML is

➤   What other technologies are closely tied to XML

> **NOTE** *I mentioned a bit ago that XML is usually not a good way to store data, but there are exceptions. One way that XML is being utilized for data storage is for archival purposes. XML compresses very well, and it is in a very open kind of format that will be well understood for many years to come — if not forever. Compare that to, say, just taking a SQL Server 2008 backup. A decade from now when you need to restore some old data to review archival information, you may very well not have a SQL Server installation that can handle such an old backup file, but odds are very strong indeed that you'll have something around that can both decompress (assuming you used a mainstream compression library such as ZIP) and read your data. Very handy for such "deep" archives.*

XML BASICS

There are tons and tons of books out there on XML (for example, Wrox's *Professional XML*, by Evjen et al.). Given how full this book already is, my first inclination was to shy away from adding too much information about XML itself, and assume that you already knew something about XML. I have, however, come to realize that even all these years after XML hit the mainstream, I continue to know an awful lot of database people who think that XML "is just some web technology," and, therefore, have spent zero time on it — they couldn't be more wrong.

XML is first and foremost an *information* technology. It is *not* a web-specific technology at all. Instead, it just tends to be thought of that way (usually by people who don't understand XML) for several reasons — such as:

➤   XML is a *markup* language, and looks a heck of a lot like HTML to the untrained eye.

➤   XML is often easily *transformed* into HTML. As such, it has become a popular way to keep the information part of a page, with a final transformation into HTML only on request — a separate transformation can take place based on criteria (such as what browser is asking for the information).

➤   One of the first widely used products to support XML was Microsoft's Internet Explorer.

➤   The Internet is quite often used as a way to exchange information, and that's something that XML is ideally suited for.

Like HTML, XML is a text-based markup language. Indeed, they are both derived from the same original language, called SGML. SGML has been around for much longer than the Internet (at least what we think of as the Internet today), and is most often used in the printing industry or in government-related documentation. Simply put, the "S" in SGML doesn't stand for simple (for the curious, SGML stands for "standard generalized markup language") — SGML is anything but intuitive and is actually a downright pain to learn. (I did some reading on SGML while doing research for this book, and found it needlessly obtuse.) XML, on the other hand, tends to be reasonably easy to decipher.

So, this might have you asking the question: "Great — where can I get a listing of XML tags?" Well, you can't — at least, not in the sense that you're thinking when you ask the question. XML has very few tags that are actually part of the language. Instead, it provides ways of defining your own tags and utilizing tags defined by others (such as the industry groups I mentioned earlier in the chapter). XML is largely about flexibility — which includes the ability for you to set your own rules for your XML through the use of either an XML schema document (XSD) or the older Document Type Definition (DTD).

An XML document has very few rules placed on it just because it happens to be XML. The biggie is that it must be what is called *well formed*. You'll look into what well formed means shortly. Now, just because an XML document meets the criteria of being well formed doesn't mean that it would be classified as being valid. Valid XML must not only be well formed, but must also live up to any restrictions placed on the XML document by XSDs or DTDs that document references. I will briefly examine DTDs and XSDs later on in this chapter.

XML can also be transformed. In short, this means that it is relatively easy for you to turn XML into a completely different XML representation or even a non-XML format. One of the most common uses for this is to transform XML into HTML for rendering on the web. The need for this transformation presents you with your first mini-opportunity to compare and contrast HTML with XML. In the simplest terms, XML is about information, and HTML is about presentation. Thus, a common usage is to retrieve page *information* in XML, and then render the HTML differently depending on (say) whether the browser is running on a desktop or mobile device.

The information stored in XML is denoted through the use of what are called elements and attributes. *Elements* are usually created through the use of an opening and a closing tag (there's an exception, but you'll see that later) and are identified with a case-sensitive name (no spaces allowed). *Attributes* are items that further describe elements and are embedded in the element's start tag. Attribute values must be in matched single or double quotes.

Parts of an XML Document

Well, a few of the names have already flown by, but it makes sense, before you get too deep into things, to stop and create something of a glossary of terms that you're going to be utilizing while talking about XML documents.

What I am really going to be doing here is providing a listing of all the major parts of an XML document that you will run into, as shown in Figure 16-1. Many of the parts of the document are optional, though a few are not. In some cases, having one thing means that you must have another. In other cases, the parts of the document are relatively independent of each other.

I will take things in something of a hierarchical approach (things that belong "inside" of something will be listed after whatever they belong inside of) and, where it makes sense, in the order you'll come across them in a given XML document.

The Document

The document encompasses everything from the very first character to the last. When I refer to an XML document, I am referring to both the structure and the content of that particular XML document. Not every bit of XML is a document, however. An XML document has a hierarchy of tags leading to a single *root node* (more on that in a minute). If your XML has more than one root node, it's not a document, but an XML *fragment*. Figure 16-1 shows the structure of a document.

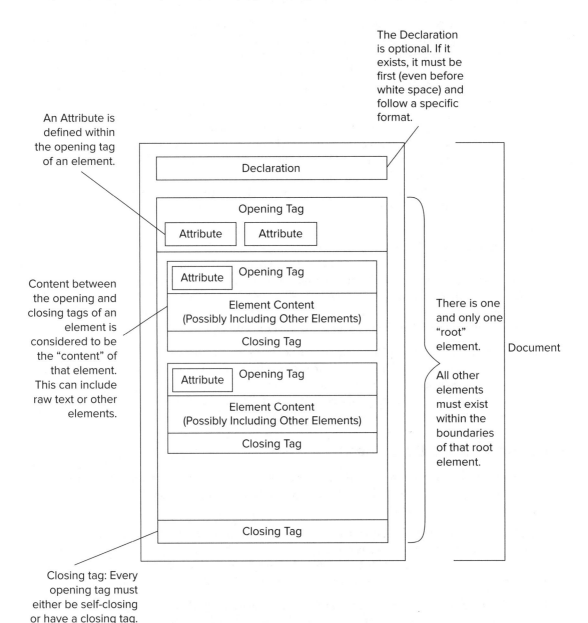

FIGURE 16-1

Declaration

The *declaration* is technically optional, but, as a practical matter, should always be included. If it exists, it must be the very first thing in the document. *Nothing* can be before the declaration, not even white space (spaces, carriage returns, tabs, whatever) — nothing.

The declaration is made with a special tag that begins with a question mark (which indicates that this tag is a preprocessor directive) and the xml moniker:

```
<?xml version="1.0"?>
```

The declaration has one required attribute (something that further describes the element) — the *version*. In the preceding example, I've declared that this is an XML document and also that it is to comply with version 1.0 of the XML specification (as of this writing, there is also a version 1.1, though you'll want to stick with 1.0 wherever possible for the broadest compatibility).

The declaration can optionally have one additional attribute — this one is called encoding, and it describes the nature of the character set this XML document utilizes. XML can handle a few different character sets, most notably UTF-16 and UTF-8. UTF-16 is essentially the Unicode specification, which is a 16-bit encoding specification that allows for most characters in use in the world today. The default encoding method is UTF-8, which is backward compatible to the older ASCII specification. A full declaration would look like this:

```
<?xml version='1.0' encoding='UTF-8'?>
```

 NOTE *Elements that start with the letters* xml *are strictly forbidden by the specification — instead, they are reserved for future expansion of the language.*

Elements

Elements serve as a piece of glue to hold together descriptive information about something — it honestly could be anything. Elements define a clear start and end point for your descriptive information. Usually, elements exist in matched pairs of tags known as an opening tag and a closing tag. Optionally, however, the opening tag can be *self-closing* — essentially defining what is known as an *empty element*.

The structure for an XML element looks pretty much as HTML tags do. An opening tag will begin with an opening angle bracket (<), contain a name and possibly some attributes, and then end with a closing angle bracket (>):

```
<ATagForANormalElement>
```

The exception to the rule is if the element is self-closing, in which case the closing angle bracket of the opening tag is preceded with a forward slash (/):

```
<SelfClosingElement/>
```

Closing tags will look exactly like the opening tag (case sensitive), but each will start with a slash (/) before the name of the element it's closing:

```
<ATagForANormalElement >     <== Opening Tag
Some data or whatever can go in here.
We're still going strong with our data.
</ATagForANormalElement >    <== Closing Tag
```

Elements can also contain attributes (which you'll look at shortly) as part of the opening (but not the closing) tag for the element. Finally, elements can contain other elements, but, if they do, the inner element must be closed before closing the outer element:

```
<OuterElement>
    <InnerElement>
    </InnerElement>
</OuterElement>
```

You will come back to elements shortly when you look at what it means to be well formed.

Nodes

When you map out the hierarchies that naturally form in an XML document, they wind up taking on the familiar tree model that you see in just about any hierarchical relationship, illustrated in Figure 16-2. Each intersection point in the tree is referred to as a *node*.

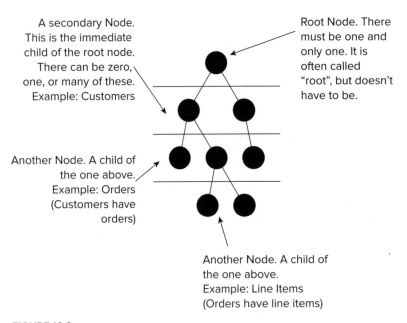

A secondary Node. This is the immediate child of the root node. There can be zero, one, or many of these. Example: Customers

Root Node. There must be one and only one. It is often called "root", but doesn't have to be.

Another Node. A child of the one above. Example: Orders (Customers have orders)

Another Node. A child of the one above. Example: Line Items (Orders have line items)

FIGURE 16-2

An XML document can have many different kinds of nodes. The most common is an element, which is a very generic kind of container; you can create and name all the element nodes you want. There are also comment nodes (which, predictably, serve the same role as comments in your T-SQL code, but are still nodes), processing instruction nodes, and text nodes. In this chapter, as in real-life XML, you'll deal almost exclusively with elements.

The contents of an XML document can be navigated based on node levels and the values in each node (or its attributes).

The "Root" Node

Perhaps one of the most common points of confusion in XML documents is over what is called the *root node*. Every XML document must have exactly one (no more, no less) root node. The root node is an element that contains any other elements in the document (if there are any). You can think of the root node as being the unification point that ties all the nodes below it together and gives them structure within the scope of any particular XML document. So, what's all the confusion about? Well, it usually falls into two camps: those who don't know they need to have a singular root node (which you now know), and those who don't understand how root nodes are named (which you will understand in a moment).

Because the general statement is usually "You must have a root node," people often interpret that to mean that they must have a node that is called root. Indeed, you'll occasionally find XML documents that do have a root node named Root (or root or ROOT — remember, XML tags are case sensitive). The reality, however, is that root nodes follow the exact same naming scheme as any other element with only one exception — the name must be unique throughout the document. That is, no other element in the entire document can have the same name as the root.

 NOTE *The existence of a root node is a key difference between an XML document and an XML fragment. Often, when extracting things from SQL Server, you'll be extracting little pieces of XML that belong to a large whole. These are referred to as XML fragments. Because an XML fragment is not supposed to be the whole document, it doesn't have a root node.*

Attributes

Attributes exist only within the context of an element. They are implemented as a way of further describing an element, and are placed within the boundaries of the opening tag for the element:

```
<SomeElement MyFirstAttribute="Hi There" MySecondAttribute="25">
    Optionally, some other XML
</SomeElement>
```

Regardless of the data type of the information in the value for the attribute, the value must be enclosed in either single or double quotes.

> **NOTE** *By default, XML documents have no concept of data type. You will read about the ways of describing the rules of individual document applications later in this chapter. At that time, you'll see that there are some ways of compelling data type — it's just that you set the rules for it; XML does not do that by itself.*

No Defects — Being Well Formed

The part of the rules that define how XML must look — that is, what elements are okay, how they are defined, what parts they have — is about whether an XML document is well formed.

Actually, all SGML-based languages have something of the concept of being well formed. Heck, even HTML has something of the concept of being well formed — it's just that it has been largely lost in the fact that HTML is naturally more forgiving and that browsers ignore many errors.

If you're used to HTML at all, you've seen some pretty sloppy stuff as far as a tag-based language goes. XML has much stricter rules about what is and isn't okay. The short rendition looks like this:

➤ Every XML document *must* have a unique root node.

➤ Every tag must have a matching (case-sensitive) closing tag unless the opening tag is self-closing.

➤ Tags cannot straddle other tags (you must close all inner tags before closing outer tags).

➤ You can't use restricted characters for anything other than what they indicate to the XML parser. If you need to represent any of these special characters, you need to use an escape sequence (which will be translated back to the character you requested).

> **NOTE** *It's worth noting that HTML documents are more consistently "well formed" than in years past. Around the time that XML came out, a specification for XHTML was also developed — that is, HTML that is also valid XML. Many developers today try to make their HTML meet XHTML standards with the result being, at the least, much more well formed HTML.*

The following is an example of a document that is well formed:

```
<?xml version="1.0" encoding="UTF-8"?>

<ThisCouldBeCalledAnything>
 <AnElement>
  <AnotherElement AnAttribute="Some Value">
   <AselfClosingElement AttributeThatNeedsASpecialCharacter="Fred&quot;s
flicks"/>
  </AnotherElement>
 </AnElement>
</ThisCouldBeCalledAnything>
```

> **NOTE** *Notice that I didn't need to have a closing tag at all for the declaration. That's because the declaration is a preprocessor directive — not an element. Essentially, it is telling the XML parser some things it needs to know before the parser can get down to the real business of dealing with the XML.*

But this document is not well formed. Do you see why not?

```xml
<?xml version="1.0" encoding="UTF-8"?>

<ThisCouldBeCalledAnything>
 <AnElement>
  <AnotherElement AnAttribute="Some Value">
   <AselfClosingElement AttributeThatNeedsASpecialCharacter="Fred&quot;s
flicks"/>
   </AnElement>
   </AnotherElement>
</ThisCouldBeCalledAnything>
```

I opened the tag `AnElement` before I opened `AnotherElement`. You must close inner tags before closing their outer tags, so this document is not well formed.

So, this has been an extremely abbreviated version of what's required for your XML document to be considered to be well formed, but it pretty much covers the basics for the limited scope of XML coverage in this book.

> **NOTE** *Understanding these concepts is going to be absolutely vital to your survival (well, comprehension at least) in the rest of the chapter. The example that is covered next should reinforce things for you, but, if after looking at the XML example, you find you're still confused, read the preceding text again or check out* Professional XML *by Bill Evjen et al. or some other XML book. Your sanity depends on knowing this stuff before you move on to the styling and schema issues at the end of the chapter.*

An XML Example

Okay — if there's one continuing theme throughout this book, it's got to be that I don't like explaining things without tossing out an example or two. As I've said earlier, this isn't an XML book, so I'm not going to get carried away with my examples here, but there must be some. If you're like me or any developer I've ever worked with, you'll want to get your hands dirty as a way to really learn...well, anything, but certainly this stuff.

Throughout the remainder of this chapter, you're going to find that life is an awful lot easier if you have some sort of XML editing tool (Microsoft offers a free one called XML Notepad). Because XML is text based, you can easily open and edit XML documents in Notepad — the problem is that you're not going to get any error checking. How are you going to know that your document is well formed? Sure, you can look it over if it's just a few lines, but get to a complete document or a style sheet document (I will discuss transformations later in the chapter), and life will quickly become very difficult.

One tool you certainly have handy is SSDT: the SQL Server Data Tools, which you'll make use of a great deal in the coming chapters. For the purposes here, SSDT is a bit much — it's a complete integrated development suite, capable of handling complex development projects — but it has a great built-in XML editor. Rather than opening or creating a project in SSDT, just go into the environment and create a new file of type XML. SSDT will then give you visual cues (such as the classic red squiggly line) when your document isn't well formed.

 NOTE *As a side note, you can also perform a rather quick and dirty check to see whether your XML is well formed by opening the document in Microsoft's Internet Explorer — it will complain to you if the document is not well formed.*

For this example, you're going to look at an XML representation of what some of the AdventureWorks data might look like. In this case, I'm going to have you build out some order information. You're going to start with just a few things and grow from there.

First, you know that you need a root node for any XML document that you're going to have. The root node can be called anything you want, as long as it is unique within your document. A common way of dealing with this is to call the root `root`. Another common example would be to call it something representative of what the particular XML document is all about.

For these purposes, you can start off with something very simple, and just use `root`:

Available for download on Wrox.com

```
<?xml version="1.0" encoding="UTF-8"?>
<root>
</root>
```

Code snippet Chap16XML1.xml

INTELLISENSE AND XML

If you're working within SSDT (or Visual Studio in general), you'll notice that IntelliSense will pop up with suggestions for possible tags while you type. Feel free to use those shortcuts while you go through the examples in this chapter. Just highlight the one you want and press Tab to have IntelliSense complete your typing for you.

You also might have noticed that SSDT provides the XML declaration for you when you create the document...very handy, this development environment.

Just that quickly you've created your first well formed XML document. Notice that it includes the `<?xml>` tag that you saw in the earlier illustration. While Visual Studio put that in for you, it didn't have to; it's actually an optional item. The only restriction related to it is that, if you include it, it must be first. For best practice reasons as well as clearness, you should leave it in.

Actually, by the rules of XML, any tag starting with `<?xml>` is considered to be a reserved tag — that is, you shouldn't name your tags that, as they are reserved for current or future use of the W3C as XML goes into future versions.

So, moving on, you have your first well formed XML document. Unfortunately, this document is about as plain as it can get — it doesn't really contain anything useful. Well, for this example, you'll be working on describing order information, so you might want to start putting in some information that is descriptive of an order. Let's start with a `SalesOrderHeader` tag:

```xml
<?xml version="1.0" encoding="UTF-8"?>
<root>
    <SalesOrderHeader/>
</root>
```

Code snippet Chap16XML2.xml

Okay — so this is getting monotonous — isn't it? You now know that you have one order in your XML document, but you still don't know anything about it. Let's expand on it some by adding a few *attributes*:

```xml
<?xml version="1.0" encoding="UTF-8"?>
<root>
   <SalesOrderHeader CustomerID="510" SalesOrderID="43663"
OrderDate="2011-07-01T00:00:00" />
</root>
```

Code snippet Chap16XML3.xml

Well, it doesn't really take a rocket scientist to be able to discern the basics about the order at this point:

➤   The customer's ID number is 510.

➤   The order ID number was 43663.

➤   The order was placed on July 1, 2011.

Basically, as you have things, it equates to a row in the `SalesOrderHeader` table in AdventureWorks in SQL Server. If the customer had several orders, it might look something like:

```xml
<?xml version="1.0" encoding="UTF-8"?>
<root>
   <SalesOrderHeader CustomerID="510" SalesOrderID="43663"
OrderDate="2009-07-01T00:00:00"/>
   <SalesOrderHeader CustomerID="510" SalesOrderID="44281"
OrderDate="2009-10-01T00:00:00"/>
   <SalesOrderHeader CustomerID="510" SalesOrderID="45040"
```

```
OrderDate="2010-01-01T00:00:00"/>
 <SalesOrderHeader CustomerID="510" SalesOrderID="46606"
OrderDate="2010-07-01T00:00:00"/>
 <SalesOrderHeader CustomerID="510" SalesOrderID="47661"
OrderDate="2010-10-01T00:00:00"/>
 <SalesOrderHeader CustomerID="510" SalesOrderID="49824"
OrderDate="2011-04-01T00:00:00"/>
 <SalesOrderHeader CustomerID="510" SalesOrderID="55285"
OrderDate="2011-10-01T00:00:00"/>
 <SalesOrderHeader CustomerID="510" SalesOrderID="61178"
OrderDate="2012-01-01T00:00:00"/>
 </root>
```

Code snippet Chap16XML4.xml

While this is a perfectly legal — and even well formed — example of XML, it doesn't really represent the hierarchy of the data as you might want. You might, for example, want to build your XML a little differently, and represent the notion that customers are usually considered to be higher in the hierarchical chain (they are the "parent" to orders if you will). You could represent this by changing the way you express customers. Instead of an attribute, you could make it an element in its own right — including having its own attributes — and nest that particular customer's orders inside the customer element:

```
<?xml version="1.0" encoding="UTF-8"?>
<root>
<Customer CustomerID="510" AccountNumber="AW00000510">
 <SalesOrderHeader SalesOrderID="43663" OrderDate="2009-07-01T00:00:00"/>
 <SalesOrderHeader SalesOrderID="44281" OrderDate="2009-10-01T00:00:00"/>
 <SalesOrderHeader SalesOrderID="45040" OrderDate="2010-01-01T00:00:00"/>
 <SalesOrderHeader SalesOrderID="46606" OrderDate="2010-07-01T00:00:00"/>
 <SalesOrderHeader SalesOrderID="47661" OrderDate="2010-10-01T00:00:00"/>
 <SalesOrderHeader SalesOrderID="49824" OrderDate="2011-04-01T00:00:00"/>
 <SalesOrderHeader SalesOrderID="55285" OrderDate="2011-10-01T00:00:00"/>
 <SalesOrderHeader SalesOrderID="61178" OrderDate="2012-01-01T00:00:00"/>
</Customer>
</root>
```

Code snippet Chap16XML5.xml

If you have more than one customer, that's not a problem — you just add another customer node:

```
<?xml version="1.0" encoding="UTF-8"?>
<root>
<Customer CustomerID="510" AccountNumber="AW00000510">
 <SalesOrderHeader SalesOrderID="43663" OrderDate="2009-07-01T00:00:00"/>
 <SalesOrderHeader SalesOrderID="44281" OrderDate="2009-10-01T00:00:00"/>
 <SalesOrderHeader SalesOrderID="45040" OrderDate="2010-01-01T00:00:00"/>
 <SalesOrderHeader SalesOrderID="46606" OrderDate="2010-07-01T00:00:00"/>
 <SalesOrderHeader SalesOrderID="47661" OrderDate="2010-10-01T00:00:00"/>
 <SalesOrderHeader SalesOrderID="49824" OrderDate="2011-04-01T00:00:00"/>
 <SalesOrderHeader SalesOrderID="55285" OrderDate="2011-10-01T00:00:00"/>
```

```
    <SalesOrderHeader SalesOrderID="61178" OrderDate="2012-01-01T00:00:00"/>
  </Customer>
  <Customer CustomerID="512" AccountNumber="AW00000512">
    <SalesOrderHeader SalesOrderID="46996" OrderDate="2010-08-01T00:00:00"/>
    <SalesOrderHeader SalesOrderID="48018" OrderDate="2010-11-01T00:00:00"/>
    <SalesOrderHeader SalesOrderID="49090" OrderDate="2011-02-01T00:00:00"/>
    <SalesOrderHeader SalesOrderID="50231" OrderDate="2011-05-01T00:00:00"/>
  </Customer>
  </root>
```

Code snippet Chap16XML6.xml

Indeed, this can go to unlimited levels of hierarchy (subject, of course, to whatever your parser can handle). You could, for example, add a level for individual line items in the order.

Determining Elements versus Attributes

The first point to understand here is that there is no hard and fast rule for determining what should be an element versus an attribute. An attribute describes the properties of the element that it is an attribute of. Child elements of an element do much the same thing. So how, then, do you decide which should be which? Why are attributes even necessary? Well, like most things in life, it's something of a balancing act.

Attributes make a lot of sense in situations where the value is a one-to-one relationship with, and is inherently part of, the element. In AdventureWorks, for example, you have only one customer number per customer ID — this is ideal for an attribute. As you are transforming the relational data to XML, the columns of a table will often make good attributes to an element directly related to individual rows of a table.

Elements tend to make more sense if there is more of a one-to-many relationship between the element and what's describing it. In the example earlier in the chapter, there are many sales orders for each customer. Technically speaking, you could have had each order be an attribute of a customer element, but then you would have needed to repeat much of the customer element information over and over again. Similarly, if your AdventureWorks database allowed for the notion of customers having aliases (multiple account numbers — similar to how they have multiple contacts), you may have wanted to have an `AccountNumber` element under the customer and have its attribute describe individual instances of names.

 NOTE *Whichever way you go here, stick to one rule I've emphasized many times throughout the book — be consistent. Once something of a given nature is defined as being an attribute in one place, lean toward keeping it an attribute in other places unless its nature is somehow different in the new place you're using it. One more time: Be consistent.*

Namespaces

With all this freedom to create your own tags, to mix and match data from other sources, and to just otherwise do your own thing, there are bound to be a few collisions here and there about what things are going to use what names in which places. For example, an element with a name of "letter" might have entirely different structure, rules, and meaning to an application built for libraries (for whom a letter is probably a document written from one person to another person) than it would to another application, say one describing fonts (which might describe the association between a character set and a series of glyphs).

To take this example a little further, the nature of XML is such that industry organizations around the world are slowly agreeing on naming and structure conventions to describe various types of information in their industries. Library organizations may have agreed on element formats describing books, plays, movies, letters, essays, and so on. At the same time, the operating systems and/or graphics industries may have agreed on element formats describing pictures, fonts, and document layouts.

Now, imagine that we, the poor hapless developers that we are, have been asked to write an application that needs to render library content. Obviously, library content makes frequent use of things like fonts — so, when you refer to something called "letter" in your XML, are you referring to something to do with the font or is it a letter from a person to another person (say, from Thomas Jefferson to George Washington)? There is clearly a conflict, and you need a way to resolve it.

That's where namespaces come in. *Namespaces* describe a domain of elements and attributes and their structure. The structure that supports letters in libraries would be described in a libraries namespace. Likewise, the graphics industry would likely have its own namespaces that would describe letters as they relate to that industry. The information for a namespace is stored in a reference document, and can be found using a *Uniform Resource Identifier (URI)* — a special name, not dissimilar from a URL — that will eventually resolve to a reference document.

NAMESPACE URIS

It is traditional to the point of a near law that namespaces are identified by URIs that look an awful lot like the kind of URL you might enter into a web browser's address bar. Don't be fooled: This is just a way of making a unique name, and there's no reason to think you can browse to anything at that "address." That said, some namespaces are based on standards you can find at those locations, but there's no requirement that a namespace URI be a valid web URL.

If you're using someone else's namespace (such as Microsoft's SQL namespace), you can probably find the URI with a little research (in this case, `schemas-microsoft-com:xml-sql`). You can also create your own namespace URIs, so long as you don't collide with someone else's...hence the usefulness of the URI format.

When you build XML documents that refer to both library and graphics constructs, you simply reference the namespaces for those industries. In addition, you qualify elements and attributes whose nature you want the namespace to describe. By qualifying your names using namespaces, you make sure that, even if a document has elements that are structurally different but have the same name, you can refer to the parts of your document with complete confidence that you are not referring to the wrong kind of element or attribute.

To reference a namespace to the entire document, you simply add the reference as a special attribute (called xmlns) to your root. The reference will provide both a local name (like the alias you give to a table in T-SQL; this is how you want to refer to the namespace locally) and the URI that will eventually resolve to your reference document. You can also add namespace references (again, using xmlns) to other nodes in the document if you want to apply that namespace only within the particular scope of the node you assign the namespace to.

What follows is an example of an XML document (specifically, this is an XML schema document, or XSD, but it's still XML) that you will be making use of later in the chapter. Notice several things about it as relates to namespaces:

The document references three namespaces as attributes in the root element (called Schema) — one each for XDR (with no alias, meaning this is the default schema for this document), a Microsoft data type namespace (aliased as dt, this one builds a list about the number and nature of different data types), and, last, but not least, a special SQL namespace (aliased as sql) used for working with SQL Server XML integration. Note that namespaces, like everything else in XML, are case sensitive.

Some attributes, including one in the root, are qualified with namespace information (see the sql: relation attribute, for example).

```xml
<?xml version="1.0" encoding="UTF-8"?>
<Schema xmlns="urn:schemas-microsoft-com:xml-data"
                xmlns:dt="urn:schemas-microsoft-com:data types"
                xmlns:sql="urn:schemas-microsoft-com:xml-sql"
                sql:xsl="../Customers.xsl">
    <ElementType name="Root" content="empty"  />
    <ElementType name="Customers" sql:relation="Customers">
        <AttributeType name="CustomerID"/>
        <AttributeType name="CompanyName"/>
        <AttributeType name="Address"/>
        <AttributeType name="City"/>
        <AttributeType name="Region"/>
        <AttributeType name="PostalCode"/>
        <attribute type="CustomerID" sql:field="CustomerID"/>
        <attribute type="CompanyName" sql:field="CompanyName"/>
        <attribute type="Address" sql:field="Address"/>
        <attribute type="City" sql:field="City"/>
        <attribute type="Region" sql:field="Region"/>
        <attribute type="PostalCode" sql:field="PostalCode"/>
    </ElementType>
</Schema>
```

Code snippet Chap16XML7.xml

The `sql` data type references a couple of special attributes. You do not have to worry about whether the Microsoft data types namespace also has a field or relation data type because you are fully qualifying your attribute names. Even if the data types namespace does have an attribute called `field`, your XML parser will still know to treat this element by the rules of the `sql` namespace.

Element Content

Another notion of XML and elements that deserves mention (which is close to all it will get here) is the concept of *element content.*

Elements can contain data beyond the attribute level and nested elements. Although nested elements are certainly one form of element content (one element contains the other), XML also allows for row text information to be contained in an element. For example, you can have an XML document that looks something like the following:

Available for download on Wrox.com

```
<?xml version="1.0" encoding="UTF-8"?>
<root>
   <Customer CustomerID="ALFKI" CompanyName="Alfreds Futterkiste">
    <Note Date="2009-08-25T00:00:00">
    The customer called in today and placed another order. Says they really like our
work and would like it if we would consider establishing a location closer to their
base of operations.
    </Note>
    <Note Date="2009-08-26T00:00:00">
    Followed up with the customer on new location. Customer agrees to guarantee us
$5,000 per month in business to help support a new office.
    </Note>
    </Customer>
</root>
```

Code snippet Chap16XML8.xml

The contents of the `Note` elements, such as "`The customer called …` " are neither an element nor an attribute, yet they are valid XML data: a text node.

Be aware that such data exists in XML, but SQL Server will not output data in this format using any of the automatic styling methods. The row/column approach of RDBMS systems lends itself far better to elements and attributes. To output data such as the notes in the previous example, you would need to use some of the methods that allow for more explicit output formats of your XML (and these can be non-intuitive at best) or perform a transformation on the output after you select it. I will cover transformations as the last item in this chapter.

Being Valid versus Being Well Formed — Schemas and DTDs

Just because an XML document is well formed does not mean that it is *valid XML.* Now, while that is sinking in on you I'll tell you that *no* XML is considered "valid" unless it has been validated against some form of specification document. Currently, there are only two recognized types of specification documents — a Document Type Definition, or DTD, and an XML Schema Document, or XSD.

The basic premise behind both varieties of validation documents is much the same. While XML as a language defines the most basic rules that a XML document must comply with, DTDs and XSDs seek to define what the rules are for a particular *class* of XML document. The two approaches are implemented somewhat differently and each offers distinct advantages over the other:

➤ **DTDs:** This is the old tried and true. DTDs are utilized in SGML (XML is an SGML application — you can think of SGML being a superset of XML, but incredibly painful to learn), and have the advantage of being a very well known and accepted way of doing things. There are tons of DTDs already out there that are just waiting for you to utilize them.

The downside (you knew there had to be one — right?) is that the "old" is operative in my "old tried and true" statement. Not that being old is a bad thing, but in this case, DTDs are definitely not up to speed with what else has happened in document technology. DTDs do not really allow for such seemingly rudimentary things as restricting data types. You'll find that DTDs — at least in terms of being used with XML — are largely being treated as deprecated at this point in favor of XSDs.

➤ **XML schema documents:** XSDs have the distinct advantage of being strongly typed. What's cool about them is that you can effectively establish your own complex data types — types that are made up based on combinations of one or more other data types (including other complex data types) or require specialized pattern matching (for example, a Social Security number is just a number, but it has special formatting that you could easily enforce via an XML schema). XML schemas also have the advantage, as their name suggests, of being an XML document themselves. This means that a lot of the skills in writing your XML documents also apply to writing schemas (though there's still plenty to learn) and that schemas can, themselves, be self-describing — right down to validating themselves against yet another schema.

WELL FORMED XML VERSUS VALID XML

Well formed XML adheres to the structural definition of the general XML document specification; this is pretty static, and has nothing to do with your application. Valid XML requires a schema (either an XSD or a DTD) to validate against, and is almost certainly specific to the data you're trying to store.

WHAT SQL SERVER BRINGS TO THE PARTY

So, now you have all the basics of what XML *is* down. What you need is to understand the relevance in SQL Server.

XML functionality was a relatively late addition to SQL Server. Indeed, it first appeared as a downloadable add-on to SQL Server 7.0. What's more, a significant part of the functionality was originally more an addition to Internet Information Server (IIS) than to SQL Server.

With SQL Server 2000, the XML side of things moved to what Microsoft called a "Web Release" model, and was updated several times. With SQL Server 2005, XML finished moving into the core product. While most of the old functionality remains supported, SQL Server continues to add more core features that makes XML an integral part of things rather than the afterthought that XML sometimes seemed to be in early releases.

What functionality? Well, in SQL Server 2012 XML comes to the forefront in several places:

➤ Support for multiple methods of selecting data out of normal columns and receiving them in XML format

➤ Support for storing XML data natively within SQL Server using the XML data type

➤ Support for querying data that is stored in its original XML format using XQuery (a special query language for XML) and other methods

➤ Support for enforcing data integrity in the data being stored in XML format using XML schemas

➤ Support for indexing XML data

➤ Support for hierarchical data — granting special support for the tree-like structures that are so common in XML data

And this is just the mainstream stuff.

The support for each of these often makes use of several functional areas of XML support, so next you'll look at XML support one piece at a time.

Defining a Column as Being of XML Type

You've already seen the most basic definition of an XML column. For example, if you examine a simplified definition of the `Production.ProductModel` table in the AdventureWorks database, it might look something like this:

```
CREATE TABLE Production.ProductModel
(
    ProductModelID      int             IDENTITY(1,1) PRIMARY KEY NOT NULL,
    Name                dbo.Name        NOT NULL,
    CatalogDescription  xml             NULL,
    Instructions        xml             NULL,
    rowguid             uniqueidentifier ROWGUIDCOL NOT NULL,
    ModifiedDate        datetime        NOT NULL
        CONSTRAINT DF_ProductModel_ModifiedDate  DEFAULT (GETDATE()),
);
```

So, let's consider what you have here in terms of these two XML columns.

➤ They are defined with a data type of XML, so you will have XML data type methods available to you (more on those coming up soon).

➤ They have allowed NULLs but could have just as easily chosen NOT NULL as a constraint. Note, however, that the NOT NULL would be enforced on whether the row had any data for that column, not whether that data was valid.

➤ In this case the XML is considered "non-typed XML." That is, since the definition has not associated any schema with it, SQL Server doesn't really know anything about how this XML is supposed to behave to be considered "valid." The actual `Production` `.ProductModel` table uses typed XML, which you'll see shortly.

The first of these is implied in any column that is defined with the data type XML rather than just plain text. You will see much more about this in the next XML data type section.

The second goes with any data type in SQL Server — you can specify whether you allow NULL data for that column.

So, the real meat in terms of changes you can make at definition time has to do with whether you specify your XML column as being typed or non-typed XML. The non-typed definition that you saw in the preceding example means that SQL Server knows very little about any XML stored in the column and, therefore, can do little to police its validity. If you set the column up as being typed XML, you are providing much more definition about what is considered "valid" for any XML that goes in our column.

The AdventureWorks database already has *schema collections* that match the validation you want to place on these two XML columns, so let's look at how you would change your CREATE statement to adjust to typed XML. As I said previously, validation requires a schema, and the schemas needed for these columns already exist (more on creating those in a minute), so all that's needed is to specify the schema for each column. SQL Server will handle the validation once a schema is identified.

```
CREATE TABLE Production.ProductModel
(
    ProductModelID      int IDENTITY(1,1) PRIMARY KEY NOT NULL,
    Name                dbo.Name NOT NULL,
    CatalogDescription  xml
        (CONTENT [Production].[ProductDescriptionSchemaCollection]) NULL,
    Instructions        xml
        (CONTENT [Production].[ManuInstructionsSchemaCollection]) NULL,
    rowguid             uniqueidentifier ROWGUIDCOL NOT NULL,
    ModifiedDate        datetime NOT NULL,
    CONSTRAINT [PK_ProductModel_ProductModelID] PRIMARY KEY CLUSTERED

);
```

This represents the way it is defined in the actual AdventureWorks sample (note that CONTENT is an optional keyword here). In order to insert a record into the `Production.ProductModel` table, you must either leave the `CatalogDescription` and `Instructions` fields blank or supply XML that is valid when tested against their respective schemas.

XML Schema Collections

XML schema collections are really nothing more than named persistence of one or more schema documents into the database. The name amounts to a handle to your set of schemas. By referring to that collection, you are indicating that the XML typed column or variable must be valid when matched against all of the schemas in that collection.

You can view existing schema collections. To do this, you use the built-in XML_SCHEMA_ NAMESPACE() function. The syntax looks like this:

```
XML_SCHEMA_NAMESPACE( <SQL Server schema> , <xml schema collection> ,
[<namespace>] )
```

This is just a little confusing, so let's touch on these parameters, which are shown in Table 16-1.

TABLE 16-1: XML_SCHEMA_NAMESPACE Parameters

PARAMETER	DESCRIPTION
SQL Server schema	This is your relational database schema (not to be confused with the XML schema). For example, for the table Production.ProductModel, Production is the relational schema. For Sales.SalesOrderHeader, Sales is the relational schema.
xml schema collection	The name used when the XML schema collection was created. In your CREATE table example previously, you referred to the ProductDescriptionSchemaCollection and ManuInstructionsSchemaCollection XML schema collections.
Namespace	Optional name for a specific namespace within the XML schema collection. Remember that XML schema collections can contain multiple schema documents — this would return anything that fell within the specified namespace.

So, to use this for the Production.ManuInstructionsSchemaCollection schema collection, you would make a query like this:

```
SELECT XML_SCHEMA_NAMESPACE('Production','ManuInstructionsSchemaCollection');
```

This spews forth a ton of unformatted XML:

```
<xsd:schema xmlns:xsd="http://www.w3.org/2001/XMLSchema"
xmlns:t="http://schemas.microsoft.com/sqlserver/2004/07/adventure-works/
ProductModelManuInstructions"
targetNamespace="http://schemas.microsoft.com/sqlserver/2004/07/adventure-works/Pro
ductModelManuInstructions" elementFormDefault="qualified"><xsd:element
name="root"><xsd:complexType mixed="true"><xsd:complexContent
mixed="true"><xsd:restriction base="xsd:anyType"><xsd:sequence><xsd:element
name="Location" maxOccurs="unbounded"><xsd:complexType
mixed="true"><xsd:complexContent mixed="true"><xsd:restriction
base="xsd:anyType"><xsd:sequence><xsd:element name="step" type="t:StepType"
maxOccurs="unbounded" /></xsd:sequence><xsd:attribute name="LocationID"
type="xsd:integer" use="required" /><xsd:attribute name="SetupHours"
type="xsd:decimal" /><xsd:attribute name="MachineHours" type="xsd:decimal"
/><xsd:attribute name="LaborHours" type="xsd:decimal" /><xsd:attribute
name="LotSize" type="xsd:decimal"
```

```
/></xsd:restriction></xsd:complexContent></xsd:complexType></xsd:element></xsd:
sequence></xsd:restriction></xsd:complexContent></xsd:complexType></xsd:
element><xsd:complexType name="StepType" mixed="true"><xsd:complexContent
mixed="true"><xsd:restriction base="xsd:anyType"><xsd:choice minOccurs="0"
maxOccurs="unbounded"><xsd:element name="tool" type="xsd:string"
/><xsd:element name="material" type="xsd:string" /><xsd:element
name="blueprint" type="xsd:string" /><xsd:element name="specs"
type="xsd:string"
/><xsd:element name="diag" type="xsd:string" /></xsd:choice>
</xsd:restriction></xsd:complexContent>
</xsd:complexType></xsd:schema>
```

SQL Server strips out any whitespace between tags, so if you create a schema collection with all sorts of pretty indentations for readability, SQL Server will remove them for the sake of efficient storage. If you copy and paste that into your development area, SSDT will reformat that much more neatly for you.

> **NOTE** *Again, note that the default number of characters returned for text results in Management Studio is only 256 characters. If you're using text view, you will want to go Tools ⇨ Options ⇨ Query Results ⇨ SQL Server ⇨ Results to Text and change the maximum number of characters displayed.*

Creating, Altering, and Dropping XML Schema Collections

The CREATE, ALTER, and DROP notions for XML schema collections work in a manner that is *mostly* consistent with how other such statements have worked thus far in SQL Server. I'll run through them here, but pay particular attention to the ALTER statement, as it is the one that has a few quirks you haven't seen in other ALTER statements you've worked with.

CREATE XML SCHEMA COLLECTION

Again, the CREATE is the typical CREATE <object type> <object name> syntax that you've seen throughout the book, and uses the AS keyword you've seen with stored procedures, views, and other less structured objects:

```
CREATE XML SCHEMA COLLECTION [<SQL Server schema>.] <collection name>
    AS { <schema text> | <variable containing the schema text> }
```

So if, for example, you wanted to create an XML schema collection that is similar to the Production.ManuInstructionsSchemaCollection collection in AdventureWorks, you might execute something like the following:

```
CREATE XML SCHEMA COLLECTION ProductDescriptionSchemaCollectionSummaryRequired
    AS
    '<xsd:schema targetNamespace="http://schemas.microsoft.com/sqlserver/2004/07/
adventure-works/ProductModelWarrAndMain"
        xmlns="http://schemas.microsoft.com/sqlserver/2004/07/adventure-
works/ProductModelWarrAndMain"
        elementFormDefault="qualified"
```

```
        xmlns:xsd="http://www.w3.org/2001/XMLSchema" >
        <xsd:element name="Warranty"  >
            <xsd:complexType>
                <xsd:sequence>
                    <xsd:element name="WarrantyPeriod" type="xsd:string"  />
                    <xsd:element name="Description" type="xsd:string"  />
                </xsd:sequence>
            </xsd:complexType>
        </xsd:element>
    </xsd:schema>
    <xs:schema targetNamespace="http://schemas.microsoft.com/sqlserver/2004/07/
adventure-works/ProductModelDescription"
        xmlns="http://schemas.microsoft.com/sqlserver/2004/07/adventure-works/
ProductModelDescription"
        elementFormDefault="qualified"
        xmlns:mstns="http://tempuri.org/XMLSchema.xsd"
        xmlns:xs="http://www.w3.org/2001/XMLSchema"
        xmlns:wm="http://schemas.microsoft.com/sqlserver/2004/07/adventure-works/
ProductModelWarrAndMain" >
        <xs:import namespace="http://schemas.microsoft.com/sqlserver/2004/07/
adventure-works/ProductModelWarrAndMain" />
        <xs:element name="ProductDescription" type="ProductDescription" />
            <xs:complexType name="ProductDescription">
                <xs:sequence>
                    <xs:element name="Summary" type="Summary" minOccurs="1" />
                </xs:sequence>
                <xs:attribute name="ProductModelID" type="xs:string" />
                <xs:attribute name="ProductModelName" type="xs:string" />
            </xs:complexType>
            <xs:complexType name="Summary" mixed="true" >
                <xs:sequence>
                    <xs:any processContents="skip" namespace="http://www.w3.org/
1999/xhtml" minOccurs="0" maxOccurs="unbounded" />
                </xs:sequence>
            </xs:complexType>
    </xs:schema>';
```

Code snippet Chap16.sql

 NOTE *Note that the URI portion of the namespace declaration must be entered on a single line. It is shown here word wrapped onto multiple lines because there is a limit to the number of characters we can show per line in print. Make sure you include the entire URI on a single line.*

This one happens to be just like the `Production.ManuInstructionsSchemaCollection` schema collection, but I've altered the schema to require the summary element rather than having it optional. Since the basic structure is the same, I utilized the same namespaces.

ALTER XML SCHEMA COLLECTION

This one is just slightly different from other ALTER statements in the sense that it is limited to just adding new pieces to the collection rather than changing existing schemas. The syntax looks like this:

```
ALTER XML SCHEMA COLLECTION [<SQL Server schema>.] <collection name>
    ADD { <schema text> | <variable containing the schema text> }
```

> **NOTE** *I'm surprised that this functionality hasn't been expanded since the last release of SQL Server, but, in the meantime, let me stress that this is a tool for adding to your schema collection rather than changing or removing what's there. To change an existing schema, you must drop the schema collection and add it back in, which you can't do while there are typed XML columns that refer to it. If you're starting to wonder how you get around this, I'll stop you now: You don't. It's trouble to alter a schema collection if it's heavily used.*

DROP XML SCHEMA COLLECTION

This is one of those classic "does what it says" things and works just like any other DROP:

```
DROP XML SCHEMA COLLECTION  [<SQL Server schema>.] <collection name>
```

So, to get rid of the ProductDescriptionSchemaCollectionSummaryRequired schema collection you created earlier, you could execute:

Available for download on Wrox.com

```
DROP XML SCHEMA COLLECTION ProductDescriptionSchemaCollectionSummaryRequired;
```

Code snippet Chap16.sql

And it's gone.

XML Data Type Methods

The XML data type carries several intrinsic methods with it. These methods are unique to the XML data type, and no other current data type has anything that is at all similar (well, some other data types have methods, but just not these ones). The syntax within these methods varies a bit because they are based on different, but mostly industry-standard, XML access methods. The basic syntax for calling the method is standardized though:

```
<instance of xml data type>.<method>
```

There are a total of five methods available:

> ➤ **.query**: An implementation of the industry-standard XQuery language. This allows you to access data within your XML by running XQuery-formatted queries. XQuery allows for the

prospect that you may be returning multiple pieces of data rather than a discrete value, and thus the return type of an XQuery statement is always XML.

➤ **.value**: This one allows you to access a discrete value within a specific element or attribute. Using `.value`, you can compel your return to a specific data type, but you'll get an error if the data found by your statement can't be cast to that type.

➤ **.modify**: This is Microsoft's own extension to XQuery. Whereas XQuery is limited to requesting data (no modification language), the `modify` method extends XQuery to allow for data modification.

➤ **.nodes**: Used to break up XML data into individual, more relational-style rows.

➤ **.exist**: Much like the IF EXISTS clause you can use in standard SQL, the `exist()` XML data type method tests to see whether a specific kind of data exists. In the case of `exist()`, the test is to see whether a particular node or attribute has an entry in the instance of XML you're testing.

.query (SQL Server's Implementation of XQuery)

`.query` is an implementation of the industry-standard XQuery language. The result works much like a SQL query, except that the results are for matching XML data nodes rather than relational rows and columns.

`.query` requires a parameter that is a valid XQuery to be run against your instance of XML data. For example, if you wanted the steps out of the product documentation for Product ID 66, you could run the following:

```
SELECT ProductModelID, Instructions.query('declare namespace PI="http://
schemas.microsoft.com/sqlserver/2004/07/adventure-works/ProductModelManuInstructions";
    /PI:root/PI:Location/PI:step') AS Steps
FROM Production.ProductModel
WHERE ProductModelID = 66;
```

 NOTE *Note that the URI portion of the namespace declaration must be entered on a single line. They are shown here word wrapped onto multiple lines because there is a limit to the number of characters we can show per line in print. Make sure you include the entire URI on a single line.*

The result is rather verbose, so I've truncated the right side of it, but you can see that I've trimmed things down such that you're getting only those nodes at the step level or lower in the XML hierarchy:

```
ProductModelID Steps
-------------- --------------------------------------------------------
66                     <PI:step xmlns:PI="http://schemas.microsoft.com/sqlser...
                            Put the <PI:material>Seat post Lug (Product N...
```

```
                        </PI:step><PI:step xmlns:PI="http://schemas.micro...
                            Insert the <PI:material>Pinch Bolt (Product N...
                        </PI:step><PI:step xmlns:PI="http://schemas.micro...
                            Attach the <PI:material>LL Seat (Product Numb...
                        </PI:step><PI:step xmlns:PI="http://schemas.micro...
                            Inspect per specification <PI:specs>FI-620</P...
                        </PI:step>

(1 row(s) affected)
```

It's also worth pointing out that all the XML still came in one column in one row per data row in the database. Even if the XQuery string had asked only for a single data point (that looks like a scalar), it would still be of type XML; the XML returned by XQuery will be whatever you query out, and doesn't need to be valid or even well formed.

What XQuery really returns is a sequence. This isn't a T-SQL sequence like you read about earlier — rather, it's an ordered set of results from the XML document, returned as XML. If your XQuery returns more than one node (or text element, or whatever you query out), you get all of it unless you specify that you only want one. Even then the one element you do request is just a single-element sequence.

 NOTE *It bears repeating that* `.query` *cannot modify data; it is a read-only operation.*

Notice, by the way, my need to declare the namespace in this. Since a namespace is declared as part of the referenced schema collection, you can see how it really expands and virtually destroys the readability of the query. You can fix that by using the WITH XMLNAMESPACES() declaration:

Available for
download on
Wrox.com

```
WITH XMLNAMESPACES ('http://schemas.microsoft.com/sqlserver/2004/07/
adventure-works/ProductModelManuInstructions' AS PI)

SELECT ProductModelID, Instructions.query('/PI:root/PI:Location/PI:step') AS Steps
FROM Production.ProductModel
WHERE ProductModelID = 66;
```

Code snippet Chap16.sql

 NOTE *Note that the URI portion of the namespace declaration must be entered on a single line. They are shown here word wrapped onto multiple lines because there is a limit to the number of characters we can show per line in print. Make sure you include the entire URI on a single line.*

This gives you a somewhat more readable query, but yields the same result set.

It might seem tempting very soon when you look at XQuery to replace that string literal with a variable, building XQuery syntax dynamically by assembling a query string and passing it to `.query`. In short, you can't — `.query` expects a string literal containing the XQuery statement to be executed. That statement can be quite long, but it can't be contained within a variable.

 NOTE *You may find it interesting to navigate to the actual URI of the* `ProductManualInstructions`. *After a brief introductory HTML page, it will point you at the actual schema document used by the query. Again, there's no requirement that this be possible, but for many standards a page does exist at the address used as the namespace URI.*

XQuery is a whole separate language from T-SQL, and I'm not going to go any further here in trying to teach it to you, but I will give you some idea what it can do so, like so many topics I have to just gloss over here, you can decide whether it looks like a topic you want to research more. Far from being simply a set of XML navigation tools, which is more or less what XPath is, XQuery has calculations, aggregates, logic tools, control-of-flow syntax, and very powerful ways to return something that can be either exactly like or entirely unlike the original XML content. If you need to do powerful XML analysis, dig further into XQuery.

.value

The `.value` method is all about querying discrete data. It uses a special XML navigation syntax called XPath to locate a specific node and extract a scalar value. The syntax looks like this:

```
<instance of xml data type>.value (<XPath location>, <non-xml SQL Server Type>)
```

The trick here is to make certain that the XPath specified really will return a discrete value of the type you're requesting.

If, for example, you wanted to know the value of the `LaborHours` attribute in the first `Location` element for `ProductModelID` 66, you might write something like:

```
WITH XMLNAMESPACES ('http://schemas.microsoft.com/sqlserver/2004/07/
adventure-works/ProductModelManuInstructions' AS PI)

SELECT ProductModelID,
    Instructions.value('(/PI:root/PI:Location/@LaborHours)[1]',
                        'decimal (5,2)') AS Location
FROM Production.ProductModel
WHERE ProductModelID = 66;
```

Code snippet Chap16.sql

 NOTE *As before, the URI has been split to fit on the page. Make sure you include the entire URI on a single line.*

Check the results:

```
ProductModelID Location
-------------- -------------------------------------
66             1.50

(1 row(s) affected)
```

Note that SQL Server has extracted just the specified attribute value (in this case, the `LaborHours` attribute of the `Location` node) as a discrete piece of data. The data type of the returned values must be castable into a non-XML type in SQL Server, and must return a scalar value — that is, you cannot have multiple rows.

.modify

Ah, here things get just a little interesting.

XQuery, left in its standard W3C form, is a read-only kind of thing — that is, it is great for selecting data but offers no equivalents to `INSERT`, `UPDATE`, or `DELETE`. Bummer deal! Well, Microsoft is apparently having none of that and has done its own extension to XQuery to provide data manipulation for XML data using something like the XQuery language. This extension to XQuery is called XML Data Manipulation Language, or XML DML. XML DML adds three new commands to XQuery:

➤   insert

➤   delete

➤   replace value of

 NOTE *Note that these new commands, like all XML keywords, are case sensitive.*

Each of these does what it implies, with `replace value of` taking the place of SQL's `UPDATE` statement.

If, for example, you wanted to increase the original 1.5 labor hours in your `.value` example, you might write something like:

Available for
download on
Wrox.com

```
WITH XMLNAMESPACES ('http://schemas.microsoft.com/sqlserver/2004/07/
adventure-works/ProductModelManuInstructions' AS PI)

UPDATE Production.ProductModel
SET Instructions.modify('replace value of (/PI:root/PI:Location/@LaborHours)[1]
with 1.75')
WHERE ProductModelID = 66;
```

Code snippet Chap16.sql

> **NOTE** As before, the URI has been split to fit on the page. Make sure you include the entire URI on a single line.

Now if you rerun your `.value` command:

```
WITH XMLNAMESPACES ('http://schemas.microsoft.com/sqlserver/2004/07/
adventure-works/ProductModelManuInstructions' AS PI)

SELECT ProductModelID,
    Instructions.value('(/PI:root/PI:Location/@LaborHours)[1]',
    'decimal (5,2)') AS Location
FROM Production.ProductModel
WHERE ProductModelID = 66;
```

Code snippet Chap16.sql

> **NOTE** As before, the URI has been split to fit on the page. Make sure you include the entire URI on a single line.

You get the new value:

```
ProductModelID Location
-------------- ---------------------------------------
66              1.75

(1 row(s) affected)
```

> **NOTE** Note the way that this is essentially an UPDATE *within an* UPDATE. *You are modifying the SQL Server row, so you must use an* UPDATE *statement to tell SQL Server that your row of relational data (which just happens to have XML within it) is to be updated. You must also use the* replace value of *keyword to specify the XML portion of the update. You can just run a simple* UPDATE *to replace the whole XML document with a new one, but to change one piece of data in place requires* .modify.

.nodes

`.nodes` is used to take blocks of XML and separate what would have, were it stored in a relational form, been multiple rows of data. Taking one XML document and breaking it into individual parts in this way is referred to as *shredding* the document.

What `.nodes` is doing is essentially breaking the instances of XML data into their own tables (with as many rows as there are instances of data meeting that XQuery criteria). As you might expect, this means you need to treat `.nodes` results as a table rather than as a column. The primary difference between `.nodes` and a typical table is that you must *cross apply* your `.nodes` results back to the specific table that you are sourcing your XML data from (because `.nodes` is actually a function, not a table). So, `.nodes` really involves more syntax than just ".nodes" — think of it somewhat like a join, but using the special CROSS APPLY keyword in the place of the JOIN and `.nodes` instead of the ON clause. It looks like this:

```
SELECT <column list>
FROM <source table>
CROSS APPLY <column name>.nodes(<XQuery>) AS <table alias for your .nodes results>
```

This is fairly confusing stuff, so let's look back at the `.value` example earlier for clarification. You see a query that looked for a specific entry and, therefore, got back exactly one result:

Available for
download on
Wrox.com

```
WITH XMLNAMESPACES ('http://schemas.microsoft.com/sqlserver/2004/07/
adventure-works/ProductModelManuInstructions' AS PI)

SELECT ProductModelID,
    Instructions.value('(/PI:root/PI:Location/@LaborHours)[1]',
                        'decimal (5,2)') AS Location
FROM Production.ProductModel
WHERE ProductModelID = 66;
```

Code snippet Chap16.sql

 NOTE *As before, the URI has been split to fit on the page. Make sure you include the entire URI on a single line.*

`.value` expects a scalar result, so you needed to make certain your XQuery would return just that single value per individual row of XML. `.nodes` tells SQL Server to use XQuery to map to a specific location and treat each entry found in that XQuery as an individual row instead of a discrete value.

Available for
download on
Wrox.com

```
WITH XMLNAMESPACES ('http://schemas.microsoft.com/sqlserver/2004/07/
adventure-works/ProductModelManuInstructions' AS PI)

SELECT pm.ProductModelID,
    pmi.Location.value('./@LocationID', 'int') AS LocationID,
    pmi.Location.value('./@LaborHours', 'decimal(5,2)') AS LaborHours
FROM Production.ProductModel pm
CROSS APPLY pm.Instructions.nodes('/PI:root/PI:Location') AS pmi(Location);
```

Code snippet Chap16.sql

 NOTE *As before, the URI has been split to fit on the page. Make sure you include the entire URI on a single line.*

Notice that through your use of the `.nodes` method, you are essentially turning one table (`ProductModel`) into two tables (the source table and the `.nodes` results from the `Instructions` column within the `ProductModel` table). Take a look at the results:

```
ProductModelID LocationID  LaborHours
-------------- ----------- ------------------------------------------
7              10          2.50
7              20          1.75
7              30          1.00
7              45          0.50
7              50          3.00
7              60          4.00
10             10          2.00
10             20          1.50
10             30          1.00
10             4           1.50
10             50          3.00
10             60          4.00
43             50          3.00
44             50          3.00
47             10          1.00
47             20          1.00
47             50          3.50
48             10          1.00
48             20          1.00
48             50          3.50
53             50          0.50
66             50          1.75
67             50          1.00

(23 row(s) affected)
```

Code snippet Chap16.sql

As you can see, you are getting back multiple rows for many of what were originally single rows in the `ProductModel` table. For example, `ProductModelID` 7 had six different instances of the `Location` element, so you received six rows instead of just the single row that existed in the `ProductModel` table.

While this is, perhaps, the most complex of the various XML data type methods (with respect to SQL syntax anyway...XQuery is a whole language, after all), the power that it gives you to transform XML data for relational use is virtually limitless.

.exist

`.exist` works something like the `EXISTS` statement in SQL. It accepts an expression (in this case, an XQuery expression rather than a SQL expression) and will return a Boolean indication of whether the expression was true. (`NULL` is also a possible outcome.)

If, in the `.modify` example, you had wanted to show rows that contain steps that had spec elements, you could have used `.exist`:

```
WITH XMLNAMESPACES ('http://schemas.microsoft.com/sqlserver/2004/07/
adventure-works/ProductModelManuInstructions' AS PI)

SELECT ProductModelID, Instructions
FROM Production.ProductModel
WHERE Instructions.exist('/PI:root/PI:Location/PI:step/PI:specs') = 1
```

Code snippet Chap16.sql

 NOTE *Pay particular attention to the point at which the test condition is being applied!*

 NOTE *For example, the code would show you rows where at least one step had a spec element in it — it does not necessarily require that every step have the spec element. If you wanted every element to be tested, you would need to either pull the elements out as individual rows (using* .nodes*) or place the test condition in the XQuery.*

 NOTE *Note that the URI portion of the namespace declaration must be entered on a single line. They are shown here word wrapped onto multiple lines because there is a limit to the number of characters we can show per line in print. Make sure you include the entire URI on a single line.*

Enforcing Constraints Beyond the Schema Collection

You are, I sincerely hope, used to the concept of constraints by now. You've dealt with them extensively in this book. Well, if your relational database needs constraints, it follows that your XML data does too. Indeed, you've already implemented much of the idea of constraints in XML through the use of schema collections. But what if you want to enforce requirements that go beyond the base schema?

Surprisingly, you cannot apply XML data type methods within a constraint declaration. How do you get around this problem? Well, wrap the tests up in a user-defined function (UDF), and then utilize that function in your constraint.

 NOTE *I have to admit I'm somewhat surprised that the methods are not usable within the* CONSTRAINT *declaration, but things like functions are. All I can say is "go figure. . . ." I'll just quietly hope they fix this in some future release, as it seems a significant oversight on something that shouldn't have been all that difficult (yeah, I know — easy for me to say since they have to write that code, not me!).*

Retrieving Relational Data in XML Format

Retrieving relational data is the area that SQL Server already had largely figured out even in the older releases. You had a couple of different options, and you had still more options within those options — between them all, things have been pretty flexible for quite some time. Let's take a look . . . .

The FOR XML Clause

This clause is at the root of many of the different integration models available. It is essentially just an option added onto the end of the existing T-SQL SELECT statement, but serves as the primary method for taking data stored in normal relational format and outputting it as XML.

Let's look at the SELECT statement syntax from Chapter 3:

```
SELECT [TOP (<expression>) [PERCENT] [WITH TIES]] <column list>
[FROM <source table(s)/view(s)>]
[WHERE <restrictive condition>]
[GROUP BY <column name or expression using a column in the SELECT list>]
[HAVING <restrictive condition based on the GROUP BY results>]
[ORDER BY <column list>]
[[FOR XML {RAW|AUTO|EXPLICIT|PATH [(<element>)]}
  [, XMLDATA | XMLSCHEMA [(<target namespace>)]]
  [, ELEMENTS [XSINIL | ABSENT]][, BINARY base 64][ROOT('<root definition>')]]
[OPTION (<query hint>, [, ...n])]
```

Most of this should seem pretty trivial by now — after all, you've been using this syntax throughout a lot of hard chapters by this time — but it's time to focus in on that FOR XML line . . . .

FOR XML provides four different initial options for how you want your XML formatted in the results:

➤ **RAW:** This sends each row of data in your result set back as a single data element, with the element name of "row" and with each column listed as an attribute of the "row" element. Even if you join multiple tables, RAW outputs the results with the same number of elements as you would have rows in a standard SQL query.

➤ **AUTO:** This option labels each element with the table name or alias that represents the source of the data. If there is data output from more than one table in the query, the data from each table is split into separate, nested elements. If AUTO is used, an additional option, ELEMENTS, is also supported if you would like column data presented as elements rather than as attributes.

➤ **EXPLICIT:** This one is certainly the most complex to format your query with, but the end result is that you have a high degree of control of what the XML looks like in the end. With this option, you impose something of a hierarchy for the data that's being returned, and then format your query such that each piece of data belongs to a specific hierarchy level (and gets assigned a tag accordingly) as desired. This choice has largely been supplanted by the PATH option, and is here primarily for backward compatibility.

➤ **PATH:** This was added to try to provide the level of flexibility of EXPLICIT in a more usable format — this is generally going to be what you want to use when you need a high degree of control of the format of the output.

NOTE *Note that none of these options provide the required root element. If you want the XML document to be well formed, you will need to wrap the results with proper opening and closing tags for your root element or have SQL Server do it for you (using the* ROOT *option described later). While this is in some ways a hassle, it is also a benefit — it means that you can build more complex XML by stringing multiple XML queries together and wrapping the different results into one XML file.*

In addition to the four major formatting options, there are other optional parameters that further modify the output that SQL Server provides in an XML query:

➤ **XMLDATA/XMLSCHEMA:** These tell SQL Server that you would like to prepend one of two forms of an XML schema to the results. XMLDATA works under the older XDR format, which was common before the W3C finalized the spec for XML schema documents. You'll want to use XMLSCHEMA here unless you have a very specific reason for using the older XDR format, as the XMLDATA option is provided only for backward compatibility and does not support newer data types added since SQL Server 2005.

➤ **ELEMENTS:** This option is available only when you are using the AUTO formatting option. It tells SQL Server that you want the columns in your data returned as nested elements rather than as attributes.

➤ **BINARY BASE64:** This tells SQL Server to encode any binary columns (binary, varbinary, image) in base64 format. This option is implied (SQL Server will use it even if you don't state it) if you are also using the AUTO option. It is required when using EXPLICIT and RAW queries.

➤ **TYPE:** Tells SQL Server to return the results reporting the XML data type instead of the default Unicode character type.

➤ **ROOT:** This option will have SQL Server add the root node for you so you don't have to. You can either supply a name for your root or use the default (root).

Next, you'll explore all these options in a little more detail.

RAW

This is something of the "no fuss, no muss" option. The idea here is to just get it done — no fanfare, no special formatting at all — just the absolute minimum to translate a row of relational data into an element of XML data. The element is named "row" (creative, huh?), and each column in the Select list is added as an attribute using whatever name the column would have appeared with, if you had been running a more traditional SELECT statement.

 NOTE *One downside to the way in which attributes are named is that you need to make certain that every column has a name. Normally, SQL Server will just show no column heading if you perform an aggregation or other calculated column and don't provide an alias — when doing XML queries, everything must have a name, so don't forget to alias calculated columns.*

So, start things out with something relatively simple. Imagine that your manager has asked you to provide a query that lists a few customers' orders — say Customer IDs 1 and 2. After cruising through just the first five or so chapters of the book, you would probably say, "No problem!" and supply something like:

```
USE AdventureWorks;

SELECT Sales.Customer.CustomerID,
    Sales.Customer.AccountNumber,
    Sales.SalesOrderHeader.SalesOrderID,
    CAST(Sales.SalesOrderHeader.OrderDate AS date) AS OrderDate
FROM Sales.Customer
JOIN Sales.SalesOrderHeader
    ON Sales.Customer.CustomerID = Sales.SalesOrderHeader.CustomerID
WHERE Sales.Customer.CustomerID = 29890 OR Sales.Customer.CustomerID = 30067;
```

Code snippet Chap16.sql

So, you go hand your boss the results:

```
CustomerID   AccountNumber  SalesOrderID  OrderDate
-----------  -------------  ------------  ----------
29890        AW00029890     43671         2005-07-01
29890        AW00029890     45049         2006-01-01
29890        AW00029890     45790         2006-04-01
29890        AW00029890     46619         2006-07-01
29890        AW00029890     47672         2006-10-01
29890        AW00029890     48732         2007-01-01
29890        AW00029890     49866         2007-04-01
29890        AW00029890     61187         2008-01-01
30067        AW00030067     43672         2005-07-01
30067        AW00030067     44294         2005-10-01
30067        AW00030067     45052         2006-01-01
30067        AW00030067     45792         2006-04-01
30067        AW00030067     46622         2006-07-01
30067        AW00030067     47673         2006-10-01
30067        AW00030067     48768         2007-01-01
30067        AW00030067     49860         2007-04-01
30067        AW00030067     51100         2007-07-01
30067        AW00030067     55287         2007-10-01
30067        AW00030067     61222         2008-01-01
30067        AW00030067     67272         2008-04-01

(20 row(s) affected)
```

Easy, right? Well, now the boss comes back and says, "Great — now I'll just have Billy Bob write something to turn this into XML — too bad that will probably take a day or two." This is your cue to step in and say, "Oh, why didn't you say so?" and simply add three keywords:

```
USE AdventureWorks;

SELECT Sales.Customer.CustomerID,
    Sales.Customer.AccountNumber,
```

```
    Sales.SalesOrderHeader.SalesOrderID,
    CAST(Sales.SalesOrderHeader.OrderDate AS date) AS OrderDate
FROM Sales.Customer
JOIN Sales.SalesOrderHeader
  ON Sales.Customer.CustomerID = Sales.SalesOrderHeader.CustomerID
WHERE Sales.Customer.CustomerID = 29890 OR Sales.Customer.CustomerID = 30067
FOR XML RAW;
```

Code snippet Chap16.sql

You have just made the boss very happy. The output is a one-to-one match versus what you would have seen in the result set had you run just a standard SQL query:

```
<row CustomerID="29890" AccountNumber="AW00029890" SalesOrderID="43671"
OrderDate="2005-07-01" />
<row CustomerID="29890" AccountNumber="AW00029890" SalesOrderID="45049"
OrderDate="2006-01-01" />
<row CustomerID="29890" AccountNumber="AW00029890" SalesOrderID="45790"
OrderDate="2006-04-01" />
<row CustomerID="29890" AccountNumber="AW00029890" SalesOrderID="46619"
OrderDate="2006-07-01" />
<row CustomerID="29890" AccountNumber="AW00029890" SalesOrderID="47672"
OrderDate="2006-10-01" />
<row CustomerID="29890" AccountNumber="AW00029890" SalesOrderID="48732"
OrderDate="2007-01-01" />
<row CustomerID="29890" AccountNumber="AW00029890" SalesOrderID="49866"
OrderDate="2007-04-01" />
<row CustomerID="29890" AccountNumber="AW00029890" SalesOrderID="61187"
OrderDate="2008-01-01" />
<row CustomerID="30067" AccountNumber="AW00030067" SalesOrderID="43672"
OrderDate="2005-07-01" />
<row CustomerID="30067" AccountNumber="AW00030067" SalesOrderID="44294"
OrderDate="2005-10-01" />
<row CustomerID="30067" AccountNumber="AW00030067" SalesOrderID="45052"
OrderDate="2006-01-01" />
<row CustomerID="30067" AccountNumber="AW00030067" SalesOrderID="45792"
OrderDate="2006-04-01" />
<row CustomerID="30067" AccountNumber="AW00030067" SalesOrderID="46622"
OrderDate="2006-07-01" />
<row CustomerID="30067" AccountNumber="AW00030067" SalesOrderID="47673"
OrderDate="2006-10-01" />
<row CustomerID="30067" AccountNumber="AW00030067" SalesOrderID="48768"
OrderDate="2007-01-01" />
<row CustomerID="30067" AccountNumber="AW00030067" SalesOrderID="49860"
OrderDate="2007-04-01" />
<row CustomerID="30067" AccountNumber="AW00030067" SalesOrderID="51100"
OrderDate="2007-07-01" />
<row CustomerID="30067" AccountNumber="AW00030067" SalesOrderID="55287"
OrderDate="2007-10-01" />
<row CustomerID="30067" AccountNumber="AW00030067" SalesOrderID="61222"
OrderDate="2008-01-01" />
<row CustomerID="30067" AccountNumber="AW00030067" SalesOrderID="67272"
OrderDate="2008-04-01" />
```

> **NOTE** *Be aware that Management Studio will truncate any column where the length exceeds the number set in the Options menu in the Results to Text tab (the maximum is 8192). This issue exists in the results window (grid or text) and if you output directly to a file. This is an issue with the tool — not SQL Server itself. If you use another method to retrieve results (ADO for example), you shouldn't encounter an issue with this.*

You have one element in XML for each row of data your query produced. All column information, regardless of what table was the source of the data, is represented as an attribute of the "row" element. The downside of this is that you haven't represented the true hierarchical nature of your data — orders are only placed by customers. The upside, however, is that the XML DOM — if that's the model you're using — is going to be much less deep and, hence, will have a slightly smaller footprint in memory and perform better, depending on what you're doing.

AUTO

AUTO takes a somewhat different approach to your data than RAW does. AUTO tries to format things a little better for you — naming elements based on the table (or the table alias if you use one). In addition, AUTO recognizes the notion that your data probably has some underlying hierarchical notion to it that is supposed to be represented in the XML.

Let's go back to the customer orders example from the last section. This time, you'll use the AUTO option, so you can see the difference versus the rather plain output you got with RAW. You'll also use aliasing extensively to make your elements have more realistic names:

Available for
download on
Wrox.com

```
USE AdventureWorks;

SELECT Customer.CustomerID,
    Customer.AccountNumber,
    [Order].SalesOrderID,
    CAST([Order].OrderDate AS date) AS OrderDate
FROM Sales.Customer Customer
JOIN Sales.SalesOrderHeader [Order]
    ON Customer.CustomerID = [Order].CustomerID
WHERE Customer.CustomerID = 29890 OR Customer.CustomerID = 30067
FOR XML AUTO;
```

Code snippet Chap16.sql

The first apparent difference is that the element name has changed to the name or alias of the table that is the source of the data. Notice also that I was able to output XML that included the SQL Server keyword Order by delimiting it in square brackets. Another even more significant difference appears when you look at the XML more thoroughly (I have again cleaned up the output a bit for clarity):

```
<Customer CustomerID="29890" AccountNumber="AW00029890">
  <Order SalesOrderID="43671" OrderDate="2005-07-01" />
  <Order SalesOrderID="45049" OrderDate="2006-01-01" />
  <Order SalesOrderID="45790" OrderDate="2006-04-01" />
  <Order SalesOrderID="46619" OrderDate="2006-07-01" />
  <Order SalesOrderID="47672" OrderDate="2006-10-01" />
  <Order SalesOrderID="48732" OrderDate="2007-01-01" />
  <Order SalesOrderID="49866" OrderDate="2007-04-01" />
  <Order SalesOrderID="61187" OrderDate="2008-01-01" />
</Customer>
<Customer CustomerID="30067" AccountNumber="AW00030067">
  <Order SalesOrderID="43672" OrderDate="2005-07-01" />
  <Order SalesOrderID="44294" OrderDate="2005-10-01" />
  <Order SalesOrderID="45052" OrderDate="2006-01-01" />
  <Order SalesOrderID="45792" OrderDate="2006-04-01" />
  <Order SalesOrderID="46622" OrderDate="2006-07-01" />
  <Order SalesOrderID="47673" OrderDate="2006-10-01" />
  <Order SalesOrderID="48768" OrderDate="2007-01-01" />
  <Order SalesOrderID="49860" OrderDate="2007-04-01" />
  <Order SalesOrderID="51100" OrderDate="2007-07-01" />
  <Order SalesOrderID="55287" OrderDate="2007-10-01" />
  <Order SalesOrderID="61222" OrderDate="2008-01-01" />
  <Order SalesOrderID="67272" OrderDate="2008-04-01" />
</Customer>
```

Data that is sourced from the second table (as determined by the SELECT list) is nested inside the data sourced from the first table. In this case, your Order elements are nested inside your Customer elements. If a column from the Order table were listed first in your select list, Customer would be nested inside Order.

 NOTE *Pay attention to this business of the ordering of your* SELECT *list. Think about the primary question your XML query is meant to solve. Arrange your* SELECT *list such that the style that it produces fits the goal of your XML. Sure, you could always re-style it into the different form — but why do that if SQL Server could have just produced it for you that way in the first place?*

The downside to using AUTO is that the resulting XML data model ends up being slightly more complex. The upside is that the data is more explicitly broken up into a hierarchical model. This makes life easier when the elements are more significant breaking points — such as where you have a doubly sorted report (for example, Order sorted within Customer).

EXPLICIT

The word "explicit" is an interesting choice for this option — it loosely describes the kind of language you're likely to use while trying to create your query. The EXPLICIT option takes much more effort to prepare, but it also rewards that effort with very fine granularity of control over what's an element and what's an attribute, as well as what elements are nested in what other elements. EXPLICIT enables you to define each level of the hierarchy and how each level is going to look. In order to define the hierarchy, you create what is internally called the *universal table*. The universal table is, in many respects, just like any other result set you might produce in SQL Server. It is usually produced by making use of UNION statements to piece it together one level at a time, but you could, for example, build much of the data in a UDF and then make a SELECT against that to produce the final XML. The big difference between the universal table and a more traditional result set is that you must provide sufficient metadata right within your result set such that SQL Server can then transform that result set into an XML document in the schema you desire.

What do I mean by "sufficient metadata"? Well, to give you an idea of just how complex this can be, look at Table 16-2, which shows a real universal table.

TABLE 16-2: Example of a Universal Table

TAG	PARENT	CUSTOMER!1! CUSTOMERID	CUSTOMER!1! COMPANYNAME	ORDER!2! ORDERID	ORDER!2!ORDERDATE
1	NULL	ALFKI	Alfreds Futterkiste	NULL	NULL
2	1	ALFKI	Alfreds Futterkiste	10643	2007-08-25 00:00:00.000
2	1	ALFKI	Alfreds Futterkiste	10692	2007-10-03 00:00:00.000
2	1	ALFKI	Alfreds Futterkiste	10702	2007-10-13 00:00:00.000
2	1	ALFKI	Alfreds Futterkiste	10835	2008-01-15 00:00:00.000
2	1	ALFKI	Alfreds Futterkiste	10952	2008-03-16 00:00:00.000
2	1	ALFKI	Alfreds Futterkiste	11011	2008-04-09 00:00:00.000
2	1	ALFKI	Alfreds Futterkiste	11078	2009-05-01 00:00:00.000
2	1	ALFKI	Alfreds Futterkiste	11079	NULL
2	1	ALFKI	Alfreds Futterkiste	11080	2010-07-22 16:48:00.000
2	1	ALFKI	Alfreds Futterkiste	11081	2010-07-22 00:00:00.000
2	1	ALFKI	Alfreds Futterkiste	11087	2010-08-05 17:37:52.520
1	NULL	ANTON	Antonio Moreno Taquería	NULL	NULL

TAG	PARENT	CUSTOMER!1! CUSTOMERID	CUSTOMER!1! COMPANYNAME	ORDER!2! ORDERID	ORDER!2!ORDERDATE
2	1	ANTON	Antonio Moreno Taquería	10365	2006-11-27 00:00:00.000
2	1	ANTON	Antonio Moreno Taquería	10507	2007-04-15 00:00:00.000
2	1	ANTON	Antonio Moreno Taquería	10535	2007-05-13 00:00:00.000
2	1	ANTON	Antonio Moreno Taquería	10573	2007-06-19 00:00:00.000
2	1	ANTON	Antonio Moreno Taquería	10677	2007-09-22 00:00:00.000
2	1	ANTON	Antonio Moreno Taquería	10682	2007-09-25 00:00:00.000
2	1	ANTON	Antonio Moreno Taquería	10856	2008-01-28 00:00:00.000

EXPLICIT is used only for extremely detailed situations. Many of the things you might want to do with EXPLICIT can now be more easily performed using the PATH option. In general, you'll want to look at all other options first, and consider EXPLICIT an option of last resort — it's very advanced in nature and difficult to understand, and, as such, I consider further discussion of EXPLICIT to be beyond the scope of this book.

> **NOTE** I don't have to use EXPLICIT very often, but I'll tell you about the last time I did in case it helps you to realize when you might want to use it. I was writing a Windows service that needed to retrieve data from a table in a SQL Server database and send it to a vendor for processing. The vendor had a very specific format for the XML documents they would accept; they even had an XSD that I had to validate against. The schema, naturally, wasn't going to be satisfied with the output from a simple RAW or AUTO format. I might have been able to use PATH, but I'm a bit old-school sometimes and EXPLICIT worked out just fine — the XML I generated matched their XSD perfectly. The point is that EXPLICIT and PATH are there for when your output format has to be tightly controlled.

PATH

Now let's switch gears just a little bit and get down to a more "real" XML approach to getting data.

While EXPLICIT has not been deprecated as yet, make no mistake — PATH is really *meant* to be a better way of doing what EXPLICIT originally was the only way of doing. PATH makes a lot of sense in a lot of ways, and it is how I recommend that you do complex XML output in most cases.

> **NOTE** *This is a more complex recommendation than it might seem. The Microsoft party line on this is that* PATH *is easier. Well,* PATH *is easier in many ways, but, as you're going to see, it has its own set of "Except for this, and except for that, and except for this other thing" that can twist your brain into knots trying to understand exactly what to do. In short, in some cases,* EXPLICIT *is actually easier if you don't know XPath. The thing is, if you're dealing with XML, XPath should be on your learn list anyway, so, if you're going to know it, you should find the XPath-based approach more usable.*
>
> *Note, however, that if you need backward compatibility to SQL Server 2000, you're going to need to stick with* EXPLICIT.

In its most straightforward sense, the PATH option isn't that bad at all. So, you'll start getting your feet wet by focusing on just the basics of using PATH. From there, you'll get to things that are a bit more complex and learn some of what PATH has to offer.

PATH 101

With PATH, you have a model that molds an existing standard to get at your data — XPath. XPath has an accepted standard, and provides a way of pointing at specific points in your XML schema. For PATH, you're just utilizing a lot of the same rules and ideas in order to say how data should be treated in a native XML sort of way.

How PATH treats the data you refer to depends on a number of rules including whether the column is named or unnamed (like EXPLICIT, the alias is the name if you use an alias). If the column does have a name, a number of additional rules are applied as appropriate.

Let's look at some of the possibilities.

> **NOTE** *XPath is its own thing, and there are entire books dedicated to just that topic.* PATH *utilizes a wide variety of what's available in XPath, and so there really is too much to cover here for a single chapter in a beginning book. That said, I'm going to touch on the basics here, and give you a taste of the more advanced stuff in the next section. From there, it's really up to you whether you want to learn XPath more fully, and from there, what pieces of it are understood by* PATH.

Unnamed Columns

Data from a column that is not named will be treated as raw text within the row's element. To demonstrate this, let's take a somewhat modified version of the example used for XML RAW. What you're going to do here is list the two customers you're interested in and the number of orders they have placed:

```
SELECT CustomerID, COUNT(*)
FROM Sales.SalesOrderHeader Orders
WHERE CustomerID = 29890 OR CustomerID = 30067
GROUP BY CustomerID
FOR XML PATH;
```

Code snippet Chap16.sql

Check the output from this:

```
<row><CustomerID>29890</CustomerID>8</row>
<row><CustomerID>30067</CustomerID>12</row>
```

A row element for each row in the query is created — much as you saw with RAW — but notice the difference in how it treated your column data.

Since the CustomerID column was named, it was placed in its own element (you'll explore this more in the next section) — notice, however, the number 8 in the results. This is just loose embedded text for the row element — it isn't even associated directly with the CustomerID since it is outside the CustomerID element.

> **NOTE** *I feel like I'm repeating myself for the five thousandth time by saying this, but, again, remember that the exact counts (4 and 8 in my case) that come back may vary on your system depending on how much you have been playing with the data in the* SalesOrderHeader *table. The key thing is to see how the counts are not associated with the* CustomerID, *but instead just raw text associated with the row.*

My personal slant on this is that the situations where loose text at the level of the top element is a valid way of doing things is pretty limited. The rules do say you can do it, but I believe it makes for data that is not very clear. Still, this is how it works — use it as it seems to fit the needs of your particular system.

Named Columns

This is where things get considerably more complex rather quickly. In their most simple form, named columns are just as easy as unnamed ones were — indeed, you saw one of them in the previous example. If a column is a simple named column using PATH, it is merely added as an additional element to the row.

```
<CustomerID>30067</CustomerID>12</row>
```

The CustomerID column was a simple named column.

You can, however, add special characters into your column name to indicate that you want special behaviors for this column. Let's look at a few of the most important.

@

No, that's not a typo — the @ symbol is really the heading to this section. If you add an @ sign to your column name, SQL Server will treat that column as an attribute of the previous column. Note that you also have to delimit the alias in brackets to hide the @ sign (which is usually an indicator of a variable). Let's move the `CustomerID` to be an attribute of the top element for the row:

```sql
SELECT CustomerID AS [@CustomerID], COUNT(*)
FROM Sales.SalesOrderHeader Orders
WHERE CustomerID = 29890 OR CustomerID = 30067
GROUP BY CustomerID
FOR XML PATH;
```

Code snippet Chap16.sql

This yields:

```xml
<row CustomerID="29890">8</row>
<row CustomerID="30067">12</row>
```

Notice that your order count remained a text element of the row — only the column that you identified as an attribute moved in. You could take this to the next step by naming your count and prefixing it to make it an attribute also:

```sql
SELECT CustomerID AS [@CustomerID],
       COUNT(*) AS [@OrderCount]
FROM Sales.SalesOrderHeader Orders
WHERE CustomerID = 29890 OR CustomerID = 30067
GROUP BY CustomerID
FOR XML PATH;
```

Code snippet Chap16.sql

With this, you no longer have your loose text for the element:

```xml
<row CustomerID="29890" OrderCount="8"/>
<row CustomerID="30067" OrderCount="12"/>
```

Also notice that SQL Server was smart enough to realize that everything was contained in attributes — with no lower-level elements or simple text, it chose to make it a self-closing tag (see the `/` at the end of the element).

So, why did I indicate that this stuff was tricky? Well, there are a lot of different "it only works if . . ." kind of rules here. To demonstrate this, let's make a simple modification to the original query. This one seems like it should work, but SQL Server will throw a hissy fit if you try to run it:

```sql
SELECT CustomerID,
       COUNT(*) AS [@OrderCount]
FROM Sales.SalesOrderHeader Orders
WHERE CustomerID = 29890 OR CustomerID = 30067
```

```
GROUP BY CustomerID
FOR XML PATH;
```

What I've done here is to go back to `CustomerID` as its own element. What, at first glance, you would expect to happen is to get a `CustomerID` element with `OrderCount` as an attribute, but it doesn't quite work that way:

```
Msg 6852, Level 16, State 1, Line 1
Attribute-centric column '@OrderCount' must not come after a non-attribute-centric
sibling in XML hierarchy in FOR XML PATH.
```

The short rendition of the "What's wrong?" answer is that it doesn't really know what it's supposed to be an attribute of. Is it an attribute of the row, or an attribute of the `CustomerID`?

/

Yes, a forward slash.

Much like @, this special character indicates special things you want done. Essentially, you use it to define something of a path — a hierarchy that relates an element to those things that belong to it. It can exist anywhere in the column name except as the first character. To demonstrate this, you're going to utilize your last (failed) sample query, and build into it what you were looking for when you got the error.

First, you need to alter the `OrderID` to have information on what element it belongs to:

```
SELECT CustomerID,
       COUNT(*) AS 'CustomerID/OrderCount'
  FROM Sales.SalesOrderHeader Orders
 WHERE CustomerID = 29890 OR CustomerID = 30067
 GROUP BY CustomerID
 FOR XML PATH;
```

By adding the /, and then placing `CustomerID` before the slash, you are telling SQL Server that `OrderCount` is below `CustomerID` in a hierarchy. Now, there are many ways an XML hierarchy can be structured, so let's see what SQL Server does with this:

```
<row><CustomerID>29890<OrderCount>8</OrderCount></CustomerID></row>
<row><CustomerID>30067<OrderCount>12</OrderCount></CustomerID></row>
```

Now, if you recall, you wanted to make `OrderCount` an attribute of `CustomerID`, so, while you have `OrderCount` below `CustomerID` in the hierarchy, it's still not quite in the place you wanted it. To do that, you can combine / and @, but you need to fully define all the hierarchy. Now, since I suspect this is a bit confusing, let's take it in two steps — first, the way you might be tempted to do it, but that will yield a similar error to the earlier example:

```
SELECT CustomerID,
       COUNT(*) AS 'CustomerID/@OrderCount'
FROM Sales.SalesOrderHeader Orders
WHERE CustomerID = 29890 OR CustomerID = 30067
GROUP BY CustomerID
FOR XML PATH;
```

Code snippet Chap16.sql

Error time:

```
Msg 6852, Level 16, State 1, Line 1
Attribute-centric column 'CustomerID/@OrderCount' must not come after a
non-attribute-centric sibling in XML hierarchy in FOR XML PATH.
```

To fix this, you need to understand a bit about how things are constructed when building the XML tags. The key is that the tags are essentially built in the order you list them. So, if you want to add attributes to an element, you need to keep in mind that they are part of the element tag — that means you need to define any attributes before you define any other content of that element (sub elements or raw text).

In this case, you are presenting the CustomerID as being raw text, but the OrderCount as being an attribute (okay, backwards of what would be likely in real life, but hang with me here). This means you are telling SQL Server things backwards. By the time it sees the OrderCount information it is already done with attributes for CustomerID and can't go back.

So, to fix things, you simply need to tell it about the attributes before you tell it about any more elements or raw text:

```
SELECT COUNT(*) AS [CustomerID/@OrderCount],
       CustomerID
FROM Sales.SalesOrderHeader Orders
WHERE CustomerID = 29890 OR CustomerID = 30067
GROUP BY CustomerID
FOR XML PATH;
```

Code snippet Chap16.sql

This probably seems counterintuitive, but, again, think of the order in which things are being written. The attributes are written first, and then, and only then, can you write the lower-level information for the CustomerID element. Run it, and you'll get what you were after:

```
<row><CustomerID OrderCount="8">29890</CustomerID></row>
<row><CustomerID OrderCount="12">30067</CustomerID></row>
```

OrderCount has now been moved into the attribute position just as you desired, and the actual CustomerID is still raw text embedded in the element.

NOTE *Follow the logic of the ordering of what you ask for a bit, because it works for most everything. So, if you wanted* CustomerID *to also be an attribute rather than raw text, but wanted it to be after* OrderCount, *you can do that — you just need to make sure that it comes after the* OrderCount *definition.*

But Wait, There's More . . .

As I said earlier, XPath has its own complexity and is a book's worth to itself, but I don't want to leave you with just the preceding text and say that's all there is.

@ and / will give you a great deal of flexibility in building the XML output just the way you want it, and probably meet the need well for most beginning applications. If, however, you need something more, there is still more out there waiting for you. For example, you can:

➤   "Wildcard" data such that it's all run together as text data without being treated as separate columns.

➤   Embed native XML data from XML data type columns.

➤   Use XPath node tests — these are special XPath directives that change the behavior of your data.

➤   Use the data() directive to allow multiple values to be run together as one data point in the XML.

➤   Utilize namespaces.

OPENXML

Many of the concepts you've learned in this chapter up to this point stray toward what I would call advanced SQL Server topics. OPENXML strays even farther, and thus I will not delve too deep into it here. I do, however, want to make sure you understand what it does and some of the situations it can be useful for. Keep in mind that many of the things OPENXML was created for are now handled in a more native way by simply placing your XML into a native XML data type and using the XML type methods discussed earlier in the chapter.

When the original XML feature set was first introduced back in SQL Server 2000, the native XML data type did not yet exist. Developers had FOR XML, and thus significant power for turning relational data into XML, but we needed something to make XML addressable in a relational formal — that something was OPENXML.

OPENXML is a rowset function that opens your string much as other rowset functions (such as OPENQUERY and OPENROWSET) work. This means that you can join to an XML document, or even use it as the source of input data by using an INSERT..SELECT or a SELECT INTO. The major difference is that it requires you to use a couple of system stored procedures to prepare your document and clear the memory after you're done using it.

To set up your document, you use sp_xml_preparedocument. This moves the string into memory and pre-parses it for optimal query performance. The XML document will stay in memory until you explicitly say to remove it or you terminate the connection that `sp_xml_preparedocument` was called on. The syntax is pretty simple:

```
sp_xml_preparedocument @hdoc = <integer variable> OUTPUT,
[, @xmltext = <character data>]
[, @xpath_namespaces = <uri to a namespace>]
```

> **NOTE** *Note that, if you are going to provide a namespace URI, you need to wrap it in the < and > symbols at both ends (for example, `<root xmlns:sql ="run: schemas-microsoft-com:xml-sql>`).*

The parameters of this sproc are fairly self-describing:

> ➤ **@hdoc:** If you've ever programmed to the Windows API (and to tons of other things, but this is a common one), you've seen the h before — it's Hungarian notation for a handle. A handle is effectively a pointer to a block of memory where something (could be about anything) resides. In this case, this is the handle to the XML document that you've asked SQL Server to parse and hold on to for you. This is an output variable — the variable you reference here will, after the sproc returns, contain the handle to your XML. Be sure to store it away, as you will need it when you make use of OPENXML.

> ➤ **@xmltext:** Is what it says it is — the actual XML that you want to parse and work with.

> ➤ **@xpath_namespaces:** Any namespace reference(s) your XML needs to operate correctly.

After calling this sproc and saving away the handle to your document, you're ready to make use of OPENXML. The syntax for it is slightly more complex:

```
OPENXML(<document handle>,<XPath to base node>[, <mapping flags>])
[WITH (<Schema Declaration>|<Table Name>)]
```

You have pretty much already read about the handle — this is going to be an integer value that you received as an output parameter for your `sp_xml_preparedocument` call.

> **NOTE** *Microsoft is inconsistent when documenting this call; some pages, such as the `sp_xml_preparedocument` page, use the old handle naming convention (`@hdoc`) while others, such as the OPENXML page, use a name more indicative of the data type (`@idoc`). In documentation examples I'll follow their lead in the name of consistency, but in code I'm going to standardize on `@idocs`.*

When you make your call to OPENXML, you must supply a path to a node that will serve as a starting point for all your queries. The schema declaration can refer to all parts of the XML document by navigating relative to the base node you set here.

Next up are the mapping flags. These assist you in deciding whether you want to favor elements or attributes in your OPENXML results. The options are shown in Table 16-3.

TABLE 16-3: Mapping Flag Options

BYTE VALUE	DESCRIPTION
0	Same as 1 except that you can't combine it with 2 or 8 (2 + 0 is still 2). This is the default.
1	Unless combined with 2, only attributes will be used. If there is no attribute with the name specified, a NULL is returned. This can also be added to either 2 or 8 (or both) to combine behavior, but this option takes precedence over option 2. If XPath finds both an attribute and an element with the same name, the attribute wins.
2	Unless combined with 1, only elements will be used. If there is no element with the name specified, a NULL is returned. This can also be added to either 1 or 8 (or both) to combine behavior. If combined with 1, the attribute will be mapped if it exists. If no attribute exists, the element will be used. If no element exists, a NULL is returned.
8	Can be combined with 1 or 2. Consumed data should not be copied to the overflow property @mp:xmltext (you would have to use the MetaProperty schema item to retrieve this). If you're not going to use the MetaProperties — and most of the time you won't be — I recommend this option. It cuts a small (okay, *very* small) amount of overhead out of the operation.

Finally comes the schema or table. If you're defining a schema and are not familiar with XPath, this part can be a bit tricky. Fortunately, this particular XPath use isn't very complex and should become second nature fairly quickly (it works a lot like directories do in Windows).

The schema can vary somewhat in the way you declare it. The definition is declared as:

```
WITH (
<Column Name> <data type> [{<Column XPath>|<MetaProperty>}]
[,<Column Name> <data type> [{<Column XPath>|<MetaProperty>}]
  ...
```

➤ The column name is just that — the name of the attribute or element you are retrieving. This will also serve as the name you refer to when you build your SELECT list, perform JOINs, and so on.

➤ The data type is any valid SQL Server data type. Because XML can have data types that are not equivalents of those in SQL Server, an automatic coercion will take place if necessary, but this is usually predictable.

➤ The column XPath is the XPath pattern (relative to the node you established as the starting point for your OPENXML function) that gets you to the node you want for your column — whether an element or attribute gets used is dependent on the flags parameter as described earlier. If this is left off, SQL Server assumes you want the current node as defined as the starting point for your OPENXML statement.

➤ MetaProperties are a set of special variables that you can refer to in your OPENXML queries. They describe various aspects of whatever part of the XML DOM you're interested in. To use them, just enclose them in single quotes and put them in the place of the column XPath. Available MetaProperties include:

➤ **@mp:id**: Don't confuse this with the XML id that you looked at with EXPLICIT. While this property serves a similar function, it is a unique identifier (within the scope of the document) of the DOM node. The difference is that this value is system generated — as such, you can be sure it is there. It is guaranteed to refer to the same XML node as long as the document remains in memory. If the id is zero, it is the root node (its @mp:parentid property, as referred to next, will be NULL).

➤ **@mp:parentid**: This is the same as @mp:id, only for the parent.

➤ **@mp:localname**: Provides the non-fully qualified name of the node. It is used with prefix and namespace URI (Uniform Resource Identifier — you'll usually see it starting with URN) to name element or attribute nodes.

➤ **@mp:parentlocalname**: This is the same as @mp:localname, only for the parent.

➤ **@mp:namespaceuri**: Provides the namespace URI of the current element. If the value of this attribute is NULL, no namespace is present.

➤ **@mp:parentnamespaceuri**: This is the same as @mp:namespaceuri, only for the parent.

➤ **@mp:prefix**: Stores the namespace prefix of the current element name.

➤ **@mp:prev**: Stores the mp:id of the previous sibling relative to a node. Using this, you can tell something about the ordering of the elements at the current level of the hierarchy. For example, if the value of @mp:prev is NULL, you are at the first node for this level of the tree.

➤ **@mp:xmltext**: This MetaProperty is used for processing purposes, and contains the actual XML for the current element.

Of course, you can always save yourself a ton of work by bypassing all these parameters. You get to do this if you have a table that directly relates (names and data types) to the XPath starting point that you've specified in your XML. If you do have such a table, you can just name it and SQL Server will make the translation for you!

Okay, that's a lot to handle, but you're not quite finished yet. You see, when you're all done with your XML, you need to call sp_xml_removedocument to clean up the memory where your XML document was stored. Thankfully, the syntax is incredibly easy:

```
sp_xml_removedocument [hdoc = ]<handle of XML doc>
```

> **NOTE** *I can't stress enough how important it is to get in the habit of always cleaning up after yourself. I know that, in saying that, I probably sound like your mother. Well, like your mother, SQL Server will clean up after you some, but, like your mother, SQL Server won't clean up after you every time. SQL Server will clean things up when you terminate the connection, but what if you are using connection pooling? Some connections may never go away if your system is under load. It's an easy sproc to implement, so do it — every time!*

Okay, I'm sure you've been bored waiting for me to get to how you really make use of this — so now it's time for the all-important example.

Imagine that you are merging with another company and need to import some of its data into your system. For this example, imagine that you're working on importing a few `shippers` that this company has and your company doesn't. For this example, you're going to import the rows into the Accounting database that you created back in Chapter 5 (you can find the create syntax for the table with the Chapter 5 code — only the `Shippers` table should be required for this to work). A sample of what your script might look like to import these from an XML document might be:

```
USE Accounting;

DECLARE @idoc      int;
DECLARE @xmldoc    nvarchar(4000);

-- define the XML document
SET @xmldoc = '
<ROOT>
<Shipper ShipperID="100" CompanyName="Billy Bob&apos;s Great Shipping"/>
<Shipper ShipperID="101" CompanyName="Fred&apos;s Freight"/>
</ROOT>
';

--Load and parse the XML document in memory
EXEC sp_xml_preparedocument @idoc OUTPUT, @xmldoc;

--List out what our shippers table looks like before the insert
SELECT * FROM Shippers;

-- ShipperID is an IDENTITY column, so we need to allow direct updates
SET IDENTITY_INSERT Shippers ON

--See our XML data in a tabular format
SELECT * FROM OPENXML (@idoc, '/ROOT/Shipper', 0) WITH (
    ShipperID          int,
    CompanyName        nvarchar(40));

--Perform and insert based on that data
INSERT INTO Shippers
(ShipperID, ShipperName)
SELECT * FROM OPENXML (@idoc, '/ROOT/Shipper', 0) WITH (
```

```
        ShipperID              int,
        CompanyName            nvarchar(40));

--Set things back to normal
SET IDENTITY_INSERT Shippers OFF;

--Now look at the Shippers table after our insert
SELECT * FROM Shippers;

--Now clear the XML document from memory
EXEC sp_xml_removedocument @idoc;
```

Code snippet Chap16.sql

The final result set from this looks just like what you wanted:

```
ShipperID    ShipperName
-----------  -----------------------------  -----------------------
1            United Parcel Service          2008-11-05 18:51:42.673

(1 row(s) affected)

ShipperID    CompanyName
-----------  ---------------------------------------
100          Billy Bob's Great Shipping
101          Fred's Freight

(2 row(s) affected)

(2 row(s) affected)

ShipperID    ShipperName
-----------  -----------------------------  -----------------------
1            United Parcel Service          2008-11-05 18:51:42.673
100          Billy Bob's Great Shipping     2008-11-09 20:56:29.177
101          Fred's Freight                 2008-11-09 20:56:29.177

(3 row(s) affected)
```

Code snippet Chap16.sql

You now have one more way to get XML query results, and a way to get XML turned into relational data. Keep in mind that OPENXML has other parameters and features for you to explore as you continue on your SQL Server journey.

A BRIEF WORD ON XSLT

Well now, this takes you to the last, but far and away the most complex, of the things you'll be dealing with in this chapter. The Extensible Stylesheet Language Transformations side of things is something of a little extra toss into the XML world that increases the power of XML multifold. You see, using XSLT, you can transform your XML document into other forms.

To get you going on a quick start here, take a look at an XML document (for you old-schoolers out there, this was produced from Microsoft's old Northwind database example):

```xml
<?xml version="1.0" encoding="UTF-8"?>
<root>
  <Customer CustomerID="ALFKI" CompanyName="Alfreds Futterkiste">
      <Products ProductID="28" ProductName="Rössle Sauerkraut"/>
      <Products ProductID="39" ProductName="Chartreuse verte"/>
      <Products ProductID="46" ProductName="Spegesild"/>
  </Customer>
  <Customer CustomerID="BLONP" CompanyName="Blondesddsl père et fils">
      <Products ProductID="28" ProductName="Rössle Sauerkraut"/>
      <Products ProductID="29" ProductName="Thüringer Rostbratwurst"/>
      <Products ProductID="31" ProductName="Gorgonzola Telino"/>
      <Products ProductID="38" ProductName="Côte de Blaye"/>
      <Products ProductID="39" ProductName="Chartreuse verte"/>
      <Products ProductID="41" ProductName="Jack&apos;s New England Clam Chowder"/>
      <Products ProductID="46" ProductName="Spegesild"/>
      <Products ProductID="49" ProductName="Maxilaku"/>
  </Customer>
</root>
```

What you have here is something XML does very well — hierarchies. In this case, you have a situation where customers have ordered different products. What your XML document is laid out to tell you is what products your customers have purchased. It seems like a reasonable question — doesn't it?

> **NOTE** Note that this is a purely visual example — you do not need to load the Northwind samples here as this was purely an "in book" example.

Now, time for me to twist things on you a bit — what if I change the question to be more along the lines of "Which customers have ordered each product?" Now your perspective has changed dramatically. At this point, a much better hierarchy would be one that had the products on the outside and the customers on the inside. In that scenario, it would be your customers (rather than your products) that were repeated multiple times (once for each product), but it would get more to the root of the question.

With XML coupled with XSL transformations, this is no big deal. You see, I don't want to change the data that I'm looking at at all — I just need to *transform* my XML document so that I can *look* at it differently.

> **NOTE** Don't confuse my saying, "The way I look at the data" to mean how I visually look at it — what I'm talking about is more of how the data is perceived. Part of that is just how ready the data is to be used in a particular fashion. With customers at the top of the hierarchy, the data doesn't seem very ready for use to answer questions that are product focused. What you need is to change the data to be product-focused — just like my questions.

So let's look back at the same exact data, but transformed into another look:

```xml
<?xml version="1.0" encoding="UTF-8"?>
<root>
 <Products ProductID="28" ProductName="Rössle Sauerkraut">
        <Customer CustomerID="ALFKI" CompanyName="Alfreds Futterkiste"/>
        <Customer CustomerID="BLONP" CompanyName="Blondesddsl père et fils"/>
 </Products>
 <Products ProductID="29" ProductName="Thüringer Rostbratwurst">
        <Customer CustomerID="BLONP" CompanyName="Blondesddsl père et fils"/>
 </Products>
 <Products ProductID="31" ProductName="Gorgonzola Telino">
        <Customer CustomerID="BLONP" CompanyName="Blondesddsl père et fils"/>
 </Products>
 <Products ProductID="38" ProductName="Côte de Blaye">
        <Customer CustomerID="BLONP" CompanyName="Blondesddsl père et fils"/>
 </Products>
 <Products ProductID="39" ProductName="Chartreuse verte">
        <Customer CustomerID="ALFKI" CompanyName="Alfreds Futterkiste"/>
        <Customer CustomerID="BLONP" CompanyName="Blondesddsl père et fils"/>
 </Products>
 <Products ProductID="41" ProductName="Jack&apos;s New England Clam Chowder">
        <Customer CustomerID="BLONP" CompanyName="Blondesddsl père et fils"/>
 </Products>
 <Products ProductID="46" ProductName="Spegesild">
        <Customer CustomerID="ALFKI" CompanyName="Alfreds Futterkiste"/>
        <Customer CustomerID="BLONP" CompanyName="Blondesddsl père et fils"/>
 </Products>
 <Products ProductID="49" ProductName="Maxilaku">
        <Customer CustomerID="BLONP" CompanyName="Blondesddsl père et fils"/>
 </Products>
</root>
```

Again, this is the same data — just a different perspective.

But hang on a sec — why limit yourself to just XML? While going over every type of transformation you could do is well outside the scope of this book, it is important to understand that XSL transforms are possible to and from a wide variety of formats. You can transform to other XML layouts, but you can also transform to other formats entirely such as CSV files or even a Word document (the newest versions of Office conveniently store virtually all saved data as XML).

 NOTE *Note that I've presented XSLT here just as a concept. SQL Server does very little with XSLT — focusing on the data rather than how the data is presented. The key thing to take from this is the understanding that what is fundamentally the same data may be formatted in XML many different ways, and that XSLT provides a means for transforming XML into alternative layouts within XML, as well as to non-XML formats.*

SUMMARY

Well, there you have an extreme whirlwind tour of XML, DTDs, schemas, and a bit of XQuery and XPath to boot. It is impossible in one chapter to address a topic as broad as XML and its related technologies; however, I hope this chapter has at least provided insight into what XML is all about and what is involved in making use of it at the most basic level.

XML is one of the most important technologies to hit the industry in the last 10 or more years. It provides a flexible, very transportable way of describing data. This ease of description will help to facilitate not only the website development that you hear so much about, but also the kind of behind-the-scenes information exchange that businesses have wanted for a very long time indeed.

EXERCISES

1. Assume you have an XML Schema Collection called `dbo.SalesOrderXML`. Declare a SQL Server variable called `SalesOrder` whose contents will be validated against this schema collection.

2. The following XML will be rejected by SQL Server as not well formed. Why?

```
<note>
    <to>TSQLWonk</to>
    <from>Bob</From>
    <subject>Reminder</subject>
</note>
```

▶ WHAT YOU LEARNED IN THIS CHAPTER

TOPIC	CONCEPT
XML	XML, or eXtensible Markup Language, is a tag-based document format based off the SGML standard. While XML doesn't actually do anything, it is a very flexible information storage format that has become the de facto standard for a huge number of data exchange transactions.
Node	XML tags are hierarchically nested, and each point in the hierarchy is a node. The most common node type is an Element, but there are also Comment nodes, Processing Instruction nodes, and Text nodes.
Namespaces	Because XML allows anyone to define tags, tag names can easily intersect across domains. To eliminate ambiguity, namespaces identified by URIs can specify which meaning for each tag is desired.
Well formed XML	XML is well formed when it complies with the general XML document standard. This has nothing to do with content and everything to do with structure: The tags must be properly closed and nested, each document requires a single root node, attribute values must be quoted, and reserved characters cannot be misused.
XML Schema Document	XSDs and their older cousins DTDs (Document Type Definitions) define a set of rules that the content of an XML document must follow.
Valid XML	XML that has been validated against an XSD or DTD.
XML Schema Collection	How SQL Server internally stores an XML schema to perform validation.
XML Methods	SQL Server has five methods it can run against XML data: `.query` runs XQuery syntax and returns and XML-formatted sequence; `.value` returns a scalar value from an XPath-identified location in the document; `.modify`, not allowed in ordinary XQuery, lets you change the content of the XML; `.nodes` returns a table of node contents; `.exist` checks an XML document for the existence of a node or data point.
FOR XML	Part of the common T-SQL `SELECT` statement, `FOR XML` changes the return format of the query to XML. Using the modifiers `RAW`, `AUTO`, `EXPLICIT`, and `PATH`, you can take varying degrees of control over the exact output format.
OPENXML	An older way of parsing and querying XML within SQL Server, this is still around but not needed when the other access methods are available.

17

Business Intelligence Fundamentals

WHAT YOU WILL LEARN IN THIS CHAPTER:

➤ The nature of BI and the problems it's intended to solve

➤ How a data warehouse differs from a transactional database

➤ Different ways to develop a data warehouse

➤ Understanding dimensional data modeling

➤ Types of facts and dimensions used in data warehouses

➤ How to design an ETL process that's appropriate for BI

➤ Common patterns in BI reporting

SQL Server 2012 includes a whole suite of tools and technologies centered around the idea of business intelligence, and the next chapter (Chapter 18) is going to be the first to describe those tools and the techniques for using them. As a beginner with SQL Server, though, the phrase *business intelligence* may not be entirely familiar to you. This chapter gives you an introduction to BI that will serve as a reference point as you learn about the tools you're going to work with. Once you know what BI is all about, you'll have a foundation to work from in the next chapter; Microsoft has added significantly to an already large BI feature set for SQL Server 2012.

You should know that this chapter is going to be a bit of a departure, in that it is likely to exist almost entirely without code. For some of you, that's going to be kind of a "whew!" moment, as you heave a sigh of relief. Others — probably the larger portion — are going to look very skeptical right now. For you, I'd like to first apologize, but I do think this is necessary background. However, second I can reassure you that the next chapter will be all about the code and the methods of implementing the ideas presented in this chapter.

WHAT IS BUSINESS INTELLIGENCE?

Ever since the first entrepreneur bravely hung out a shingle, businesses have required leaders to make intelligent decisions. Obviously, this requirement has gone unmet countless times, but behind every company that can truly call itself a success is a series of decisions that enabled that success.

In the high and far-off days of yore, the leaders who created successful businesses made their decisions by talking to the people involved and making gut calls about the direction of the company. Some had systems, or strategies, or perhaps just an ineffable instinct that led them toward the right product, the perfect acquisition, or the best people to hire, and their results spoke for themselves.

What they never had, that we now have, is structured data. More correctly, they had no efficient way of analyzing the comparatively tiny amount of data that they did have. Basements full of file archives were useless, because there simply wasn't the manpower to sort through all that information.

As the computer age began, we started collecting data at a rate never previously imagined, and with that we gained for the first time some inkling of what could be done with all this information. Suddenly the question of "How many hammers should I order?" became less of a gut-instinct call for an experienced manager ("Oh, we still have ten, but it's almost March and people are going to start remodeling.") and more a question of "Exactly how many did we sell last March?" Databases grew, as the value of the information therein was realized.

As databases grew, we started realizing the potential to use that growing history of data to help drive business decisions. Instead of asking "How many did we sell last March?" we started realizing the possibility of asking for a trend line, March to March, correlated with other factors, to get a fantastically accurate idea how many to order.

> ### BUSINESS INTELLIGENCE
>
> The ability to use accumulated business data to assist in making business decisions and accurately predicting their results is the core of business intelligence.

As I said in the introduction, this chapter is about the idea of BI, rather than the implementation. What you're going to read in this chapter is:

➤ **The purpose and ideas behind of business intelligence:** You'll learn what sort of information is useful and why, so that you'll have some idea what you might want to collect.

➤ **An introduction to BI concepts:** The chapter will cover how such concepts apply to databases in general, although not so much SQL Server in particular. I'll describe data modeling differences between BI, reporting-oriented OLAP systems, and the more interactive, transactional OLTP systems this book has focused on so far.

➤ **Delivering a BI solution:** Having built up some understanding of the goals and structures of BI data modeling, I'll bring the chapter to a close with a description of how one might go about delivering the final product of BI in the form of reports, dashboards, and, in general, actionable data.

BI Is Better Than the Alternative

There's a good reason so much effort has gone into creating and enhancing BI tools in the last decade or so: demand. Businesses are buying BI products and services at an encouraging rate — at least, if your career involves working in the BI space. The demand is driven, of course, by a simple concept: BI works.

The alternative is, of course, making decisions without collecting and analyzing data. Being rather literal-minded sometimes lets me categorize that kind of decision making as business ignorance. I don't want to make you think it's impossible to run a business that way — it's been done for centuries — but in a competitive environment where others are using BI, it's going to be a challenge. I'm sure some people can do it, but if your choice is between knowing and not knowing what your success drivers are, wouldn't you rather know?

Making Decisions Based on Data

Having decided, inevitably, to pursue the BI course it's necessary to decide exactly what data to collect. After all, it's not going to help anyone to collect the shoe sizes of your employees (unless, for example, you sell shoes and need internal testing), nor to simply gather every e-mail that mentions a new product. You're going to have to have some kind of selectivity and analysis before you're going to make your data collection pay off. What you present to the business owners must be not just data but information.

In most BI projects, choosing the data sources begins with a top-down approach. Business leaders, knowing that a large volume of data is accumulating in their company, want to be able to use that data for decision support. The leaders might call on you and your compatriots to build them a BI system, but it is from them and theirs that you'll discover what information is important. By speaking with the business owners and conducting a series of interviews with the potential consumers of your nascent BI project, you can begin to select the sources of data that you'll need to collect and summarize in order to provide the information they request.

INTERVIEWS

In a recent project of mine, the product owner was fond of answering the question "So, which of this data do you need?" with "I don't know . . . better keep it all." Keeping it all takes time and resources, which you'll see more clearly later in the chapter. With a little pushing back, I discovered that in fact he did know which data was most important, and usually that meant more limited scope and more focused development efforts.

Many software shops, including mine, are using agile/scrum methodology for software development. In scrum, one eschews a large, up-front requirements-gathering process in favor of iterative development and rework. Because every effort is made to preserve working software through the whole process, scrum practitioners under time pressure have the option of cutting scope rather than slipping a ship date. Thus it's important to know what the most useful data points are, so you can focus on those.

As you begin your interviews, use open questions about the purpose of the reports and the information needed, but try to focus on the end product. You can't do everything, and it's going to be the report requirements that eventually drive the limits you're going to implement around data collection. What you're not going to report, you very likely don't need to keep.

Once you know what data you need, you can begin researching where you might find it. Companies store data in databases, sure, but there are many different database products. You'll also find data in e-mails, in EDI files, and on whiteboards. Too many times you'll find that the most critical and valuable of your company's data assets are located in Excel spreadsheets owned by a few key employees in each department. Only once you know what data you need, though, can you start narrowing down which of these data sources you're going to have to locate. I'll talk a lot more about collecting data from disparate sources in Chapter 20, so for now let's categorize that data a little bit.

Structured Data

Ah, the dream. When you're first doing interviews, this is what the business owners imagine all data looks like. Structured data is stored in a database, an EDI file, a validated XML file, or in some other structure that's easily machine-readable and guarantees at least some minimal degree of data integrity. Although you'll likely still have a lot of work to do to clean this data and correlate it with other data you've collected, whenever you're looking at structured data sources you're in a comfortable space.

Unstructured and Semi-Structured Data

Unstructured data refers, broadly, to data that's exceptionally difficult to extract pieces of information from; think of a video, image, PDF file, or audio recording. Unstructured data can contain critical information, but getting at that information in a useful way is going to be a challenge.

That's not exactly a new problem, which is why tags and metadata are becoming very commonly found on data that would formerly have been purely unstructured. The use of topical tags, geospatial data, or keyword lists (among other metadata) can lend enough to an otherwise unstructured file to allow some useful categorization. When metadata is present on this type of information, what you have is semi-structured data.

Five Experts, Five Opinions

Just collecting data doesn't provide useful business intelligence. A collection of data without analysis is like a box of unsorted photographs: There could be some useful treasures in there, but it doesn't exactly tell a story.

Consider the fable of the blind men and the elephant. Each of them had current, useful, topical, accurate data, yet each comes to a different conclusion. The one feeling the elephant's ear thought the elephant was broad and flat, the one feeling the leg thought the elephant was like a tree, and so on. Until the disparate data points are brought together, they don't describe reality well. Five experts looking at uncorrelated data can reasonably produce five opinions, any or none of which might be accurate.

It's worth remembering sometimes that even if you do produce a beautiful, insightful analysis in the end, it's still going to be interpreted by people who are fallible. You can take some consolation in the fact that their decisions can easily become data points against which future decisions can be measured, so a good BI system provides a bit of a consolation prize when things go wrong.

Past Performance Predicts Future Behavior

Seems obvious, doesn't it? If there's an uptick in chocolate sales every February, for example, you're going to want to stock up in January in anticipation of this year's bump. Yet the thing that's going to keep you employed as a database developer is the limited grasp most businesses have on their past performance.

This doesn't mean they don't have the data. Again, data-wise today's business has an embarrassment of riches. What's at the core of the need you're going to fill is taking that historical data and making it clean, fast, and accessible to the right people.

Who Uses BI?

Let me save myself a lot of pages by saying, "Who doesn't?" The use of at least rudimentary BI is pervasive now. People at every level of a company make use of reports to help them make data-based decisions. Project managers look at completed tasks in the form of burn down charts. Floor managers watch work rates and absenteeism.

THOSE WHO FORGET HISTORY: THE DATA WAREHOUSE

Now that you've been introduced to the concept of business intelligence, it's time to move on to the real meat of the topic: how a BI implementation differs from a run-of-the-mill transactional implementation in Microsoft SQL Server 2012. As I mentioned, this chapter is pretty light on code, but this section has some design problems to wrap your head around. I hope you didn't let those neurons get cold.

Most of the examples you've seen up to this point have had a couple of assumptions embedded in them. To wit, most have assumed that the system you're designing requires a fair amount of concurrency — that is, many users at a time — and that the users will be performing all kinds of activities including inserts, updates, and deletes. In short, you've been quietly encouraged to think about OLTP, or OnLine Transaction Processing databases.

The thing that makes an OLTP design inadequate for most BI needs is that transactional systems have no memory. Back in Chapter 14, when you read about transactions and locks, one of the first examples I gave you to describe transactional processing was moving money from one bank account to another. The example looked something like this:

```
UPDATE checking
   SET Balance = Balance - 1000
   WHERE Account = 'Sally'
UPDATE savings
   SET Balance = Balance + 1000
   WHERE Account = 'Sally'
```

From a transactional standpoint, the job is done: Sally has moved $1,000 from checking to savings. From a BI standpoint, though, you've lost track of certain kinds of information:

➤ What was Sally's savings account balance yesterday?

➤ How many transfers were done last week, for a total of how much?

➤ What was Sally's average daily balance?

➤ Is the amount the customers are saving rising or falling?

The reason you can't answer those questions is that transactional systems tend to be very Zen, living only in the moment. There is another database you're going to read about now that's much more concerned about what's happened in the past: the data warehouse.

The Purpose of the Data Warehouse

Unlike the transactional system(s), which help a business operate moment-to-moment, the purpose of a *data warehouse* (DW) is reporting and decision support. The reporting demands on a data warehouse are frequently time-dependent, so one significant difference between the data warehouse and the transactional system is that the data warehouse should be time-sensitive. That is, it should retain not only the current image of a record (and I'll talk about what current means later on) but also what that record looked like before, or at least what the transition looked like. It should keep track of those facts for all of history (subject to archival and purging) for any report that depends on them. Anything not related to BI, that doesn't have any kind of reporting dependency, doesn't really belong in the data warehouse.

Because the information in the data warehouse is usually time-dependent, you should be able to see what happened during a particular period. The questions I posed before about Sally's account should be perfectly natural queries for a data warehouse.

> **THE DATA WAREHOUSE**
>
> The data warehouse is an online database providing quick access to either current or historical data, optimized for reporting of summary data or trend analysis.

However, when I say the DW should contain historical data, I don't want you to confuse that with things like mandatory data archival, which could just be a set of tape backups of transactional data. It's one thing to, say, keep seven years' worth of accounting system backups on tape to drag up from a dusty basement in case of an audit, and something completely different to have seven years' trending data about payment promptness from various clients. The data warehouse might not contain everything you need for an audit, and the crate full of ancient tapes does little to assist in a decision-support model.

OLTP versus OLAP

If the data models you've read about up until now have been OLTP, your data warehouse is *OLAP*: *OnLine Analytical Processing*. Just as the purposes of those two concepts are different, so are the design principles involved in their implementation.

OLTP databases are, once again, focused on multiuser access with high concurrency. Because there will be many users simultaneously reading from and writing to all parts of the database, information is stored in a highly normalized fashion; that tends to mean that updates done around different parts of the system write to different tables, preventing locking conflicts and deadlocks.

Also, because data updates are frequent, developers tend to encourage low fill-factors on indexes in OLTP environments. In fact, I'd go so far as to say I'm downright stingy with OLTP indexes — clearly many are necessary, but each one requires very careful consideration because it impacts data update speed.

Finally (for now), OLTP databases tend to have embedded within them business rules galore. Because there may be multiple ways to access the database, developers tend to introduce constraints and triggers in an attempt to prevent bad data making its way in. Furthermore, access for most users may be limited to stored procedures, so the incoming processes are all tightly controlled. OLTP databases do quite a bit of work trying to maintain a consistent state, so that any single snapshot of the database obeys all the appropriate business rules.

OLAP databases are focused on data retrieval and reporting. Concurrency is rarely an issue in the world of OLAP, because data loads tend to be done only by automated processes; human interaction with an OLAP database is typically read-only. In a read-only scenario, there aren't any lock conflicts, as any number of people can share a read lock.

Because concurrency is not as big an issue, denormalized data models are common. Data loading is handled by *ETL (extract, transform, and load)* processes that typically run on time intervals, and those processes will frequently store data in a redundant fashion that allows fast reads and minimal joins. These denormalized models are often highly indexed for fast retrieval, and index maintenance can be handled at ETL time. The indexing on an OLAP system is done with very high fill-factors resulting in compressed indexes for very fast reads.

OLAP systems are often light on business rules, sometimes even ignoring such simple structures as basic relational integrity constraints. It's important to remember that your data warehouse may source data from many systems, each of which may have a completely different set of business rules, so the data warehouse itself — your OLAP design — will want to be as business rule agnostic as you can manage. Data cleansing can be done by the ETLs, so the rules don't need to be enforced again here. The job of the OLAP design is to take as much time as needed (within limits) to store data in such a way that, at data retrieval time, the database returns information to the user quickly.

OLAP data models need not even be strictly relational data models. *MOLAP (multidimensional OLAP)* modeling is something I'll cover further in Chapter 20, when you read more about SQL Server Analysis Services and cubes. *ROLAP (relational OLAP)* is where you'll start here, as in any case it's likely to be where you start. Once you've created a ROLAP database (whether you do so from a Kimball or an Inmon perspective), you can use that to build a MOLAP system in SSAS.

Kimball versus Inmon

In the early days of electricity, Thomas Edison and Nikolai Tesla independently developed very different means of generating and distributing electricity. Edison and General Electric wanted to wire the country DC power transmission infrastructure while Tesla, backed by Westinghouse, proposed AC. Edison and Tesla were bitter rivals, and the two standards coexisted in some form even into the 1960s, but AC has finally become the accepted standard. What Tesla and Edison's "War of Currents" was to electricity, Bill Inmon and Ralph Kimball have brought to data warehouse design.

A chapter on business intelligence and data warehousing probably doesn't seem like the place you'd expect to read about dramatic ideological wars between followers within highly dogmatic sects and, largely, you'd be right. It's not nearly that divided, but this is the closest this book is likely to come to drama so I should probably make the most of it. That said, the true extent of the differences between the Inmonites and the Kimballites (no, I did not make that up) is not so severe as all that.

The Inmon Data Warehouse

Bill Inmon can accurately be described as the father of data warehousing, not only because of his early efforts in defining the very concept but also because of his continued presence in the industry as a leader. The Inmon data warehouse is a large (dare I say monolithic?) central repository for all corporate data. Data sources located anywhere in the company are tapped, their data cleaned, and the results stored in a normalized database (see Figure 17-1) that's distinct from a transactional system in a few ways:

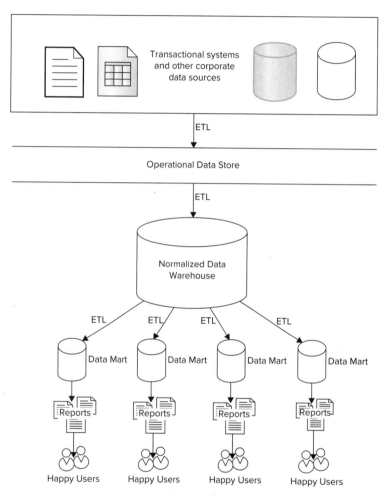

Transactional systems and other corporate data sources

ETL

Operational Data Store

ETL

Normalized Data Warehouse

ETL   ETL   ETL   ETL

Data Mart   Data Mart   Data Mart   Data Mart

Reports   Reports   Reports   Reports

Happy Users   Happy Users   Happy Users   Happy Users

FIGURE 17-1

➤ It's nonvolatile, meaning that once a record is stored it's left alone.

➤ The database is time-dependent, with each stored fact timestamped so that the flow of history can be re-created.

➤ Like data (even from different sources) is categorized similarly, so that all facts about a given topic are stored together.

Reporting directly from the central data warehouse can be cumbersome, because of the relational design. Consumption of data from an Inmon data warehouse is frequently done, instead, through localized data marts. These reporting data marts frequently use a star schema, with a centralized fact table surrounded by categorizing dimensions. There will be more on star schemas and dimensional modeling later in the chapter.

The Inmon model is can be summarized as a "top-down" approach. A large investment must be made up front to locate data from all over the company and incorporate it into the central relational model. The significance of this effort is not lost on corporate decision makers, who must decide whether the investment is likely to pay off. Once complete, the Inmon data warehouse is very flexible, because of the relational model at its core. The individual data marts can be altered and reloaded from source data with (relative) ease, and can be scaled to their individual uses. That all corporate data has been related accurately is a benefit not to be underestimated.

The Kimball Approach

So if your company doesn't have the resources to produce a global, relational corporate data warehouse, what's the alternative? Ralph Kimball's work on dimensional data warehousing has become extremely popular among data architects. One key reason is because it provides many of the positive benefits of data warehousing without the overhead of working top-down. Kimball data warehousing can deliver value in short order, although scaling up can be a bit of an issue.

Developing a Kimball data warehouse is the bottom-up approach to counter Inmon's top-down. Rather than try to model the whole of the company's data, Kimball suggests developing a dimensional data mart for each business unit that needs one (see Figure 17-2). The collection of data marts so generated constitutes, together, the corporate data warehouse.

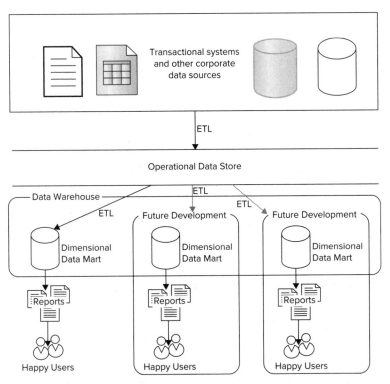

FIGURE 17-2

Kimball warehousing is far more compatible with rapid development paradigms (such as agile development) than the Inmon model, because it fits neatly into the same development pattern. Each data mart is geared toward a specific, immediate set of reporting requirements. The data sources and ETLs that load the data mart are a consequence of the desired result, and once it's done the feature is complete.

Creating a Kimball data warehouse has a relatively low cost of entry. Because small data marts are created to address specific business problems, the time it takes to solve each problem is fairly small; that's a strong bit of encouragement for the business folks who want to see the end product. What's more, it's simpler for developers to wrap their heads around, because the problem space is so much smaller than the Inmon model. Development can be done in parallel, also, allowing different groups to create their own dimensional models and generate their own results quickly.

That last is a good segue into the drawbacks of the Kimball approach. You see, one of the advantages of the Inmon model is that is facilitates *cross-domain reporting*; what I mean by that is that given the relationships defined between two areas, say Sales and Production, it's relatively easy (in an Inmon environment) to produce reporting based on the combination of related Sales and Production data. A Kimball-designed environment could easily have no discernible relationship between separately developed Sales and Production data marts, preventing any meaningful reporting across domains.

All things being equal, you're more likely to see or implement a Kimball approach before an Inmon design, but it's important that you're aware of both so that you can make a decision when the time comes.

Kinmon or Imball Warehouses

Once again I consider the folks who are learning about this, and I know there are a few ecumenical minds among you wondering why only a purist approach will do. As it happens, this is a growing trend, and the answer is simply that one approach or the other is not always right. You can plan ahead to create a Kimball-style dimensional data mart, but design it to integrate into a larger whole.

While that's mostly beyond what I'm going to try to cover in a beginning text, it's worth bringing up a couple considerations so you know they exist. The up-front development usually associated with an Inmon data warehouse is changed to a definition of corporate information standards that can be used to integrate Kimball data marts. Locate common dimensions and ensure that they share a set of common transformations (and preferably common sources). Consider the granularity of the data you're going to store, and try to make it compatible across data marts. If you plan for your data to be compatible before you start grinding it up in the ETLs, you'll have a much easier time integrating it again later.

DIMENSIONAL MODELING: WHY BE NORMAL?

In Chapter 8, you read about normalization of your data model, and you were generally pointed to the third normal form. *3NF*, to remind you, is the process of getting everything in each of your tables to rely on that table's primary key; in fact, the key phrase to remember was "the key, the whole key, and nothing but the key." Never was there a serious attack on normalization in that chapter; I presented it as an obvious decision. Clearly, you were instructed to normalize your database to 3NF. There were examples, and charts, to support this idea, and now I'm going to ask you largely to forget it.

In dimensional modeling, you have to let go of many of the tenets of a normalized database because they don't support the primary mission of OLAP: raw speed when reporting data, particularly aggregated data. OLAP databases are all about retrieval speed, and so you should be willing to pay a price of admission at ETL time — when loading the data into the model — to recover a larger amount of time when reading it back out. To that end, you're going to store redundant data so it's available wherever you want it, minimizing the number of joins that are necessary. You're going to reduce the data model's role in enforcing data consistency, leaving that to the ETL. You may likely want to store the same data in detail and in aggregate, violating even first normal form. To summarize, this is something new.

Another reason for dimensional modeling is that it's generally easier to understand when seen by those who don't make a career in databases. The reports that are delivered from a typical BI system aren't sent to database developers, but sent to all those other consumers of information within the company. While they may be good at their jobs, it's a rare CEO who can read an ER diagram. A dimensional model, however, is much simpler to comprehend: Here's the sales fact, and here are the dimensions by which it can be sliced. This allows the potential for ad hoc reporting on a much grander scale than through a standard relational model.

Measures and Metrics

That's an awful lot of talk about how you're going to want to store data without much mention of the data you're going to store. To begin work on your data warehouse, you need to know what you want to store. Let's begin, then, by breaking down the storage elements in your data warehouse. Once you know what's going in there (and where to put it), you can start working out where to get it, and you'll be well on your way.

The basic units of data storage in a dimensional model are measures. *Measures* are numeric data that accurately describe some element of your business; they could be counts of things (say, units sold or requests processed), or money, or any kind of thing you might want to add up. The real key is that measures are the aspects of your business that can be summed, added, or averaged, or in some way can have math done on them to learn information.

Metrics are closely related to measures. A *metric* is a number that's a gauge of success, or somehow an actionable indicator about the health of your business. A metric is defined by a mathematical operation on one or more measures — that just means that while a measure by itself might constitute a metric, so might a calculation using two measures. *Gross margin* is a great example of a metric: Your measures may include sales price and cost, and the gross margin metric can then be calculated as (sales price-cost)/sales price.

As I just described it, gross margin sounds like a pretty concrete metric. For each product you sell, you look at what it cost to manufacture and what you sold it for and do the math. That calculation measures something true about a real object, and could almost be justified as a measure itself. A metric does not have to be something as concrete as that, however. Metrics must be useful, but they don't necessarily have to measure something real. Let me give you an example.

In a chocolate shop (a topic close to both my heart and my wallet), a box of truffles is sold to a customer. This is a fact and will go into the data warehouse (more about facts in a moment). One measure on this fact might accurately say that 12 truffles were sold, and another that the sales price was $25. From another system comes production data: The cost per truffle was $0.90 for several batches then, because of a supplier change, the cost dropped to $0.85. The cost per truffle and the number of batches done at each cost are stored in another fact.

Sadly, there is no way to directly reconcile — in an accounting sense — the gross margin on the box of truffles you just sold. Why not? Well, to start with, the sales system doesn't store those 12 truffles separately. They don't have individual bar codes or RFID tags; they're completely interchangeable in that system. Because it doesn't differentiate, it's entirely possible that some cost 90 cents and others 85, so the gross margin on the box is unknown. But is that really a problem?

A metric is just a yardstick, or more accurately a meter stick. It's not always important to be able to track down a particular product and declare that the value of the metric is known for that and every other unit off the assembly line. Instead, it's easy enough to compute the average cost of units produced during a month (or across an arbitrary set of dimensions...more on them shortly as well), and then compute the average sales price over that same month or set of dimensions. The number you get — although it measures nothing concrete — is a perfectly useful metric. Should that number go up or down, it tells you something useful.

Which metrics your data warehouse needs to report is a decision best left to the business folks. What you'll be concerned with is where to get the measures needed to calculate such metrics and what to do with those measures once you get them. I'll talk about ETLs in a bit to resolve the first of those questions, but as for where to put it: Each measure is a fact.

Facts

Here you come to yet another chicken and egg problem. It's very difficult to describe facts without dimensions, but dimensions mean nothing without facts. Facts and dimensions are like bacon and eggs, coffee and donuts, or Han Solo and Chewbacca. Among the similarities is that one has to go first, so here you go with facts.

In dimensional modeling, you'll deal with star joins whenever possible. A *star join* is a join wherein one single table is joined to, well, as many others as you like, but each of those is joined only to the center table, as seen in Figure 17-3.

In a star join, every join is a one-to-many join, with the center table as the many side. SQL Server is very smart about performing

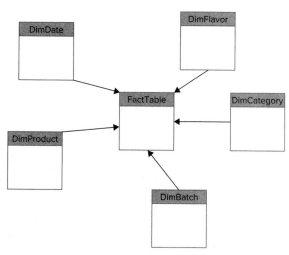

FIGURE 17-3

star joins in an optimized fashion, so reporting out of this kind of structure is pretty fast. The center table is a fact table that contains, to no one's surprise, facts.

> **WHAT ARE FACTS?**
>
> Each fact is a time-sensitive measure of business data; in fact, measures are
> sometimes referred to as facts, but I prefer the less ambiguous nomenclature.
> When you store a fact in a fact table, you are asserting that something measurable
> has happened, you've categorized it with dimensions, and you've stored the
> measurement(s) that are appropriate for calculating your metrics.

Your fact table(s) will have one or more dimension columns related to the dimension tables —
represented as the joins in Figure 17-3 — and one or more measure columns (or, sometimes,
metrics).

Facts can be stored using any level of granularity that seems appropriate, but all will fall broadly
into three types:

➤ Transactional

➤ Periodic snapshot

➤ Accumulating snapshot

Transactional Facts

This is definitely the easiest type of fact to understand. Each fact in a *transactional* fact table
represents a single, atomic entity. A row in this type of fact table might represent an activity
performed by a representative, or a line item on a sales order, or a deposit into an account. The
measures on the fact all draw from that one instance or event, and the dimensions categorize it
in as many ways as are required by your reporting needs.

As you might imagine, transactional fact tables can be both very wide — they may require many,
many dimensions and have a large number of measures — and very long. Think of the transactional
fact table that produces your phone bill every month, showing each call you made; that table has
everyone's records in it. As you go into the chapters on SQL Server Reporting Services, SQL Server
Analysis Services, and SQL Server Integration Services, remember the magnitude of this kind
of table.

Periodic Snapshots

A *periodic snapshot* table stores the state of a measure at regular intervals. By naming the interval
and taking a snapshot, rather than storing a row simply whenever an event happens to occur, you
can enable a completely different level of reporting: You can create reports that can quickly provide
aggregates and reports that can easily give information even when nothing (transactionally) has
changed.

For one example, let's stick with that phone company call log — I'm going to call it FactCalls — to
help you understand how a periodic snapshot can be used to speed aggregate reporting. If you were
to query FactCalls for the number of phone calls made in the United States this year, you'd be in for
a bit of a wait while SQL reads the hundreds of billions of rows relevant to your query. Perhaps you

want to break that information down by state, or hour, or what have you, but if you have to wade through the raw transactional data to get there it's going to take a while.

By taking a daily snapshot storing a measure — total calls — on a daily basis and storing that in a fact table, the number of rows that represent a year drops from those hundreds of billions to 365 (or 366). Nothing speeds up a query better than reducing the amount of data needed by nine orders of magnitude, take it from me.

Another way to think about time-dependent state data is with balances. An account balance wouldn't probably be directly stored in a transactional fact table; that table would more likely store each individual deposit and withdrawal. A bank manager, though, might very reasonably ask what the total balances are in the bank on the first of each month — a question that could be answered through the transactional table (by adding up all the deposits and withdrawals, and then subtracting the one from the other), but again the question is time-consuming. It's worse when you consider the manager will likely want to see those balances trend over time, so you'll have to add them up again and again for a single report.

Instead, a snapshot of all the balances can be taken daily and stored in a FactAccount table. Each day's (or month's, or year's) account statistics can then be computed quickly and efficiently.

Accumulating Snapshots

This third type of fact is less common than the others, but addresses a case that's easy to define and not nearly so easily handled using another fact type. An accumulating snapshot is used to track a data point through a fixed series of steps or state transitions, such that its progress or status can easily be reported.

One fixture of such a table is a series of one or more state transition dates or timestamps (not strictly required, but it's an exceedingly common feature). Imagine, for example, you're tracking bugs in software. Obviously you'll have precious little data to track, but humor me. Each bug, once entered into the transactional system, follows a path: It's reviewed and then either assigned or deleted; if it was assigned then a fix is coded, the bug is sent to test, and finally completed. If I were to store each of these events transactionally — that is, create a separate row in a fact table each time the bug changed status — I'd have a hard time answering the question "How many bugs currently need review?" Sure, you could do it, but it'd be a sluggish nightmare of T-SQL coding.

The more elegant solution to this kind of reporting dilemma is to store all the state transitions in an accumulating snapshot fact. Each time a state changes, the fact row for that bug is updated with the new state (and any appropriate measures). Contrast that with transactional or periodic snapshot facts, whose rows should (almost) never be updated and you see how different this structure can be. By instantiating those state transitions within each row, queries about the state at a given time, time spent in each state, and relationship between state transitions can be simply and efficiently reported.

- ➤ **Additive:** Measures that can be added across all dimensions. Most measures, such as counts or dollar totals, fall into this category.

- ➤ **Semi-Additive:** Measures that can be added across some dimensions and not across others. One example of a semi-additive measure is an account balance: You can add it across different cross-sections of account type or customer demographic, but adding it over a date dimension (my balance yesterday plus my balance today) creates a meaningless number.

➤ **Non-Additive:** Measures that cannot be added across any dimension. Percentages and ratios, for example, usually don't make sense to sum across dimensions.

Dimensions

All right, that's about enough talk about dimensions without giving you any details. Every fact is going to have at least a few dimensions, and frankly there's a reason we call this kind of OLAP data modeling *dimensional*. This next topic is, if you'll forgive me, a critical dimension to the concept of BI data modeling.

What Is a Dimension?

Conceptually, a *dimension* is some attribute along the values of which you might slice data. If the English structure there is a bit obtuse, try it in context: Perhaps the fact you're analyzing is about sales at the aforementioned chocolate shop. Knowing that the sales in the fact table add up to $100,000 is useful, perhaps, but more information is almost certainly needed. How much of that was from this month? How much from truffles, from caramels, or from chocolate sauce? What portion was wholesale versus retail? Each of these categories is one dimension of the data, and you'd like to get information about each.

In your actual, physical data model the dimensions are the spokes on your star join. Transactionally, you might think of each as a lookup table: Each will have a key (either numeric or text) and a set of useful attributes, with the fact table referring to the key. By looking at the dimensions related to each fact it's easy and intuitive to see which values the totals can be broken down by or drilled down into.

The Time Dimension

Among the most common of all dimensions in BI is time. After all, data warehouses (and fact tables, by extension) are full of time-sensitive data, so having some idea when something happened is vital to your reporting, but implementing time as an actual dimension isn't necessarily obvious. Why, you might think, shouldn't I simply put date and/or time fields on my facts and be done with it?

Making the case for a date dimension requires a brief description of what such a dimension might look like. It needs a key, obviously, which is commonly either a DATE or an INT (personally, I like using DATE, and not for nothing). In addition to the key it typically has some selection of labels (short, medium, and long date formats, for example); some attributes such as year, month, day of month, quarter, week of year, and so on; and possibly some extended information like fiscal year, day of the week, and whether a particular date is some important element to your reporting like the last Friday of a month, or a holiday.

Using an actual time dimension table is a fixture in many modern BI systems because it offers a couple advantages over just storing a date. The first is reporting consistency: The date dimension gives the same labels back every time. The attributes allow perfectly consistent categorization into quarters, fiscal years, holidays, and what have you. While a fully realized date dimension might have a lot more, see Table 17-1 for an example of a very simple date dimension.

TABLE 17-1: A Sample Date Dimension

DIMDATEKEY	YEAR	MONTH	DAY	ISWEEKEND	ISHOLIDAY
1/1/2012	2012	1	1	1	0
1/2/2012	2012	1	2	0	1
1/3/2012	2012	1	3	0	0
1/4/2012	2012	1	4	0	0
1/5/2012	2012	1	5	0	0

What's more, though, using date as a dimension lets you roll dates up into hierarchies, which (in the BI realm) are dimensions that roll up into levels of categorized dimensions. Think of a Year, which has four Quarters, which each have three Months, which have Days; now consider a report by year, and the ability to drill into each year to see its quarters, and so on. Your date dimension is key to creating this.

Finally . . . I much prefer using DATE rather than INT for the key into my date dimensions. Before the DATE type was available (in SQL 2008), I could easily have been convinced the other way; DATETIME is an 8-byte type, and INT (at 4 bytes) is more than sufficient for a key. However, converting an INT back to a date necessarily requires either using a JOIN and a lookup or else doing some kind of date math, and requiring the dates from your date keys is a common enough function, so it's not ideal. DATE lets you store the key in a 3-byte structure that requires no conversion, so I'm personally sold.

Slowly Changing Dimensions

Managing the values coming into your dimensions at ETL time isn't necessarily completely straightforward. In simple cases, such as with the date dimension, you can imagine that there may be anything from no changes ever, to perhaps the occasional insert. With others, like a product dimension, you might see important, time-sensitive changes occur: For example, what do you do when a product is discontinued, or when its suggested price changes?

For each dimension that you create, you'll have to ask yourself a couple of questions. Can your dimension values change, or is this dimension insert-only? If they can change, what kind of history do you want to keep about those changes? What you'll find is that your dimensions will typically fall into one of three buckets.

Type 0

In a type 0 dimension, values are constant. Once you populate a row in a type 0 table, you're making a contract: This row is correct, it's complete, and you're never going to touch it again.

Obviously management of type 0 dimensions is pretty simple: Just prevent updates and you're done. However, it's equally clear that a true type 0 dimension is a rare thing. One you might consider is the one you've already read about in detail: The date dimension is unusual in that it has a pretty fixed set of values that are predictable to a great extent. If your company has a habit of changing holidays, though (and if that's an element in your date table), you may not even be able to count on that one.

Type 1

When implementing *type 1 slowly changing dimensions*, I'm always reminded of George Orwell: "Oceania was at war with Eurasia: therefore Oceania had always been at war with Eurasia."

Type 1 dimensions do permit change, but the change is done in place via an update statement. No notion that the value was ever different is preserved, so the change will affect not only new rows and new reports but also history. A good example of a type 1 dimension is where the attributes on the dimension are limited purely to descriptive text; perhaps you might think of a Shippers dimension referred to by a sales fact, containing only a code (UPS, FEDEX, and so on) and a full name. Were a company to change its full name, you could simply update that row in place; the code could stay the same, and reports referring to bygone eras could display the new name without issue.

Type 2

Type 2 dimensions have history. Not in the sense that they're old and venerable — not much in the BI realm can claim that — but in the sense that they genuinely do store their historical values.

The folks who give you your data warehouse requirements, in my experience, quite frequently think of all dimensions (and all other data) as being like a type 2 dimension. They naturally think of the database as containing everything that it's ever contained, and if they ask you what things looked like last year — or even yesterday — they expect you to get it. With a type 1 dimension, you might not be able to answer, and type 0 is pretty rigid, so when you really need it all, you can implement type 2: *date-dependent values*.

The principle of a type 2 dimension is that when an attribute is updated, the old set of attributes is preserved and marked expired; the new version can then be saved and marked as active from now on, until it is in turn replaced. You can think of it as storing changes like this: From January 1 to July 3, this product was current, not on sale, and cost $9.99; from July 4 through July 31, it was current, on sale, and cost $7.99; from July 31 until the present, it is discontinued and costs $5.99.

This isn't too hard to implement, but it does have more complexity than the simpler type 1 implementation. To understand better, look at this potential implementation of the example shown in Table 17-2.

TABLE 17-2: A Type 2 Slowly Changing Dimension

DIM PRODID	PROD CODE	PROD NAME	PRICE	ISON SALE	IS CURRENT	FROM DATEKEY	TO DATEKEY
1	6PC	6-Piece Caramels	$9.99	0	1	1/1/2012	7/3/2012
2	6PT	6-Piece Truffles	$11.99	0	1	1/1/2012	7/3/2012

continues

TABLE 17-2 *(continued)*

DIM PRODID	PROD CODE	PROD NAME	PRICE	ISON SALE	IS CURRENT	FROM DATEKEY	TO DATEKEY
3	6PC	6-Piece Caramels	$7.99	1	1	7/4/2012	7/31/2012
4	6PT	6-Piece Truffles	$9.99	1	1	7/4/2012	7/31/2012
5	6PC	6-Piece Caramels	$9.99	0	0	8/1/2012	12/31/9999
6	6PT	6-Piece Truffles	$11.99	0	1	8/1/2012	12/31/9999

Observe a couple things about this dimension:

➤ **There are multiple rows for each product.** Denormalization in an OLAP system is natural — don't fear that — but it does complicate updates to the table. You have to manage updates to the table by looking up the code and the date on which you got the new data, and then comparing to see whether you need to expire the old row and insert a new one.

➤ **When saving a new fact, the appropriate dimension might be determined by the fact date.** This means that the same key-plus-date-range join is required. Fortunately that's not needed when reporting, as the DimProdID is still a natural choice for a foreign key in most cases.

While type 2 dimensions are more difficult to create and manage, the reporting implementation for history goes from, well, impossible to possible. If I want to know how much of my profit margin in July came from sale products, or how long after discontinuing a product I finally sold out of it, I can find out.

Snowflakes

When I mentioned hierarchies earlier, I did so in context of using a date dimension and seeing that it contained enough information to deduce some kind of hierarchical structure. After all, there will be many, many times when you'll want to categorize your data into such a structure — humans just seem to be wired that way.

There are tools to help you determine data hierarchy — SQL Server Analysis Services is one that will get special mention — but until you've gained some familiarity with cubes (a topic that will be covered lightly in the next chapter), it's easier to create hierarchies by building additional dimensions. When you do this — creating star joins that extend a step or two beyond the fact table — you're creating a snowflake schema like the one shown in Figure 17-4.

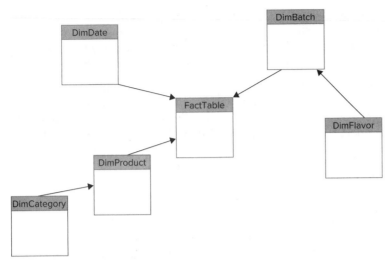

FIGURE 17-4

Snowflake designs are simple for database designers to understand, because they work the same way a similar transactional design works. Contrast this with the star schema from Figure 17-1, however, and you'll see that the joins to get a report are no longer quite so simple. Not every table links directly to the fact, which makes the query optimizer have to work that much harder.

When you find the need to create categories and subcategories like this, you might also consider a hybrid approach. You can leave the snowflaking in place to help categorize data on the way into your data warehouse, but store the foreign keys to every layer of the hierarchy in the fact. Be careful, though, with implementations like this that involve slowly changing dimensions (type 1 or 2). If later developers aren't careful, it's easy to have dimensions that roll up to one category in your fact table, and another through the snowflake.

That amounts to, in essence, three options for storing multi-level category data in a dimensional schema:

➤ **Snowflake schema with normalization:** Works like a transactional database, so is easy to understand and implement. If your snowflake dimensions are type 1 slowly changing dimensions, though, you'll lose history if a dimension changes, such as when a product changes categories. Type 2 slowly changing dimensions make history easier to capture but require a more complex lookup to store.

➤ **Denormalized star schema:** Stores all levels of the hierarchy right on the fact. For example, the `FactSales` table might contain both the `DimProductID` and the `DimProductCategoryID`. This requires passing the category in from the ETL, but history is captured in any case; if a product changes categories, rows stored before the change preserve their rollup values. Whether that's a good or a bad thing depends on your requirements, but in general I like a data warehouse that remembers what happened accurately (I'm not a big fan of revisionist history).

➤ **Hybrid approach (snowflake schema with denormalization):** Store all the keys on the fact (like in the star schema design), but also preserve the snowflake relationships to determine categorization at import time. This allows centralized control of categorization (if two source systems have the same product rolled up into different categories, the data warehouse is the arbiter), but preserves history (the links are stored on the fact).

This is where you get into more of the art of data modeling for a data warehouse, as the correct solution to this kind of problem is going to depend a lot on what you need to store and, more important, what you need to report. As with so many areas of this book, I can't tell you what's going to work best for you. Understand your options, try some proof of concept code using data that looks like your data and reports that look like your reports, and then TEST, TEST, TEST.

The NULL Dimension Value

I'm sure you can imagine any number of cases, hypothetical and otherwise, where you might not apply a dimension value to a fact. Maybe you're storing orders including a ship date, but an order hasn't shipped yet. Perhaps you'd like to keep track of the color of the products you're selling, but not every product has a relevant color. For whatever reason, you'll find in your data warehouse times where your transactional system has a nullable foreign key value, and you might think nothing of it — you can simply keep your foreign key in the data warehouse nullable, and that can be the end of it.

Your option is to keep a NULL record in your dimension tables. By storing a there-is-no-record record, you can keep your column NOT NULL and use INNER JOINs consistently. This also means, like with the labels on a date dimension, that display of the NULL record is consistent: The label that appears may be an empty string or some kind of descriptive text (such as "No Category"), but it will be the same every time rather than depend on the developers to be consistent.

Either of these approaches may work for you. Using straight NULL is certainly more intuitive for the developers, and you should never underestimate the importance of that; you're not likely to be the only one working on this. On the flip side, though, there are really only two reasons you're creating a data warehouse: to keep track of historical data that your transactional system forgets, and to produce reports against that data. The performance of those reports can get very interesting if you have a lot of OUTER JOINs, which will be required the moment you make those foreign key columns nullable.

What impact does an OUTER JOIN have on query performance? To find out, try walking through this example in the AdventureWorks data warehouse.

Your task is a simple one: Get the total of all Internet sales for products where a volume discount was not applied. Looking into the data model, you'll see the FactInternetSales fact table that's likely to help, and a DimPromotions dimension that will help you determine whether such a discount was used for a particular order. If you write the simple, INNER JOIN version of this query, it's likely to look something like this, and should return about 156 rows:

```
SELECT FIS.ProductKey, SUM(FIS.OrderQuantity) SumOrderQuantity
FROM FactInternetSales FIS
JOIN DimPromotion DPR
  ON FIS.PromotionKey = DPR.PromotionKey
```

```
    WHERE EnglishPromotionType <> 'Volume Discount'
    GROUP BY FIS.ProductKey
```

Code snippet Chap17.sql

Because performance is important, you won't want to run with that just yet, though (if I haven't said "TEST" enough times yet . . .). Take a look at the query plan for this in Figure 17-5 and you'll see that it's all scan and no seek, which should raise a red flag. It's not necessarily wrong, but it definitely suggests that you give a thought to either your query structure or your indexing strategy.

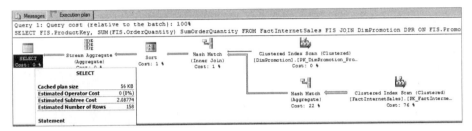

FIGURE 17-5

For this query, an index that allows you to look up the facts you need based on `PromotionKey` seems like a good idea. Take note of the query cost (in Microsoft Voodoo Units) by hovering the mouse over the `SELECT` icon in the query plan, and you'll see a cost of 2.08774 if your system matches mine; remember this as a measure of how your index performs. If you create a covering index as follows, you'll see the query plan change.

Available for
download on
Wrox.com

```
    CREATE NONCLUSTERED INDEX ixFIS_PromotionKey
    ON [dbo].[FactInternetSales] ([PromotionKey])
    INCLUDE ([ProductKey],[OrderQuantity])
```

Code snippet Chap17.sql

And the plan becomes this (see Figure 17-6), with a cost of 0.572339.

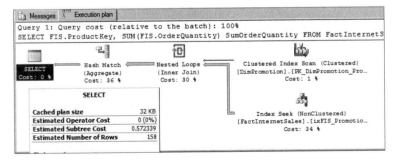

FIGURE 17-6

So that's an improvement, and because it's using the covering index you're not likely to do much better.

Remember what you're trying to discover, though — whether this query would perform any differently without the INNER JOIN. If the PromotionKey column were nullable, would that make any difference? Rewriting the query to use an OUTER JOIN requires that you handle the NULL case, and should look something like this.

Available for download on Wrox.com

```
SELECT FIS.ProductKey, SUM(FIS.OrderQuantity) SumOrderQuantity
FROM FactInternetSales FIS
LEFT JOIN DimPromotion DPR
  ON FIS.PromotionKey = DPR.PromotionKey
WHERE DPR.EnglishPromotionType <> 'Volume Discount'
  OR DPR.PromotionKey IS NULL
GROUP BY FIS.ProductKey
```

Code snippet Chap17.sql

If you test, you'll see it returns the same 156 rows that the original query returned, so that's good (in this case, there are no NULLs to find). If you check the query plan, though (in Figure 17-7), it's interesting to note that it's not quite the same.

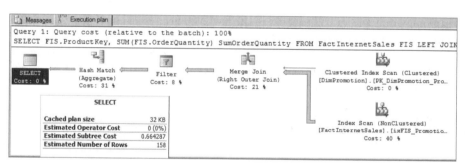

FIGURE 17-7

This query is still using your covering index, so its cost is only a bit higher — .664287, or about 15 percent higher — but that could vary depending on your data. The point is that in this case it's more expensive. Why?

Depending on how you write the OUTER JOIN, the filter is applied later in the plan (after the JOIN), because you might want rows from the left side where no row is found on the right. You've said, by way of this OUTER JOIN, that there may be rows in the left table that have no match in the right table, and that you'd be interested in those; the query can't eliminate those early . . . it can't filter until after the JOIN.

I can't stress enough that the design that work best for you will depend on the situation. Perhaps your performance difference is less than 15 percent, and you've got a cadre of junior developers with you who may not understand the NULL dimension row concept; if that's the case, you can use regular NULL rows all you want. If you find that you're using many OUTER JOINs and your performance is suffering from it, you'll want to consider using a blank row.

ETLS

In the process of designing your data warehouse, you've now done a fair amount of research. Even if you're working closest to a Kimball model, you're going to have looked into data sources that will drive at least one data mart. You'll have interviewed data owners about the rules and constraints around each data source, and you'll have talked with business folks about the reporting they'd find the most useful on the other end. You've got data sources, a destination data model, and concept reporting, but what you don't have yet is a way to move the data from the source to the destination. You're going to have to extract data from one or more places, transform it into something that fits into your dimensional model (and clean it up on the way in, perhaps), and then load the transformed data into the data warehouse. *Extract, transform, and load*, or *ETL*, is a process common to all data warehousing implementations.

Sourcing Your Data

Where does the data for your data warehouse come from? The first part of an ETL is *extract*, and SQL Server 2012 provides plenty of flexibility to extract data from a great variety of sources within SSIS (which you'll read about in Chapter 20). To recap a bit but frame things differently, I want you to think about the sources you might use as fitting into a few categories (there are so many possibilities I can't cover them all, but these are common in my experience). For each type of data in the following list, think of how clean and structured the data might be.

➤ Live sources, including

    ➤ **SQL Server.** These are either within the same instance or, much more commonly, on a different instance or server.

    ➤ **Other databases.** Examples are Oracle, Informix, DB2, and so on, which will contain structured data with at least some potential for data consistency and integrity.

    ➤ **Excel or other application file data.**

➤ Offline sources, including

    ➤ **Flat files.** These are exported from anywhere; the data quality is not enforced by the file you're receiving, so there are always questions about data integrity. When speaking of flat files, think of CSV (comma-separated values), other delimited files, fixed-length fields, or even ragged files.

    ➤ **EDI files.** These deserve special mention. These are text files whose structure depends on a set of broadly defined specifications, but the use of each field is often loosely interpreted by individual businesses, making data integrity a challenge.

    ➤ **XML files.** These can either be validated against an XSD (and therefore have some measure of data integrity) or not.

No matter where your data lives now, you want it — or a copy of it — to live in your data warehouse. That's going to mean an ETL process, even if the transformation is minimal, and extraction means you're going to be reading data that — if it's a live source — may have other users whose purposes might not perfectly coincide with yours. Concurrency, then, is one problem you have to deal with.

The level of data integrity in your source is going to have a significant impact on your ETL process. Even in highly structured databases such as SQL Server, you may not be able to guarantee that the data is properly constrained and likely to be within expected limits; outside such sources, you're in completely uncharted waters. (You're lucky if the source data maps accurately onto the expected number of fields, or the prescribed data type, and don't expect that it's going to have the right semantic meaning every time.) Data integrity is, then, another problem you have to resolve in ETLs.

Enforcing Conformity

As data rolls into your data warehouse, it would be lovely if it all lined up neatly into the facts you've designed with the dimensions (and dimension values) you expect. Not only would that be nice, but in fact it's pretty much required, and sadly you can't really expect much cooperation from your source systems on that. Even if you have only a single source system, you have to make sure that what you get conforms to what you expect, and the moment you get a second source your problems more than double. The problems don't appear to have a linear growth rate (it's more like a factorial . . . think O(n!) for you algorithm geeks), because each new system has to potentially integrate with all preexisting systems. Every time you get two systems in sync, though, you reduce the complexity by one. In short, this is worth taking some time to resolve up front.

The first rule of cleaning incoming data is not to trust that it's clean already. I've personally seen projects slip schedule because insufficient time was planned to clean incoming data, usually because cleaning wasn't thought to be necessary. "I've got the file spec . . . this is what the data will look like" should read to you a bit like a badly misspelled e-mail claiming to be from your bank and asking for your account number and password. File specs lie, and you should believe the data is clean as soon as you've started working through a reasonable sample of live data and not before.

That said, what kinds of problems you're likely to encounter depend quite a bit on the source. A structured database, for example, is almost certainly type-safe; if it says a column is of some kind of date type, you can be pretty comfortable that a date is coming through — although not necessarily that what comes will fit into a DATETIME (unless that's what it is). A DATE of 1/1/0001 is valid, but will blow up if you try to insert it into a DATETIME. An Oracle NUMBER(10) is an integer type, but a big one won't fit into an INT.

If the source is more unstructured, you can't even necessarily count on getting as many fields as you're told to expect. Even if you do, the text in a flat file where a date should be might say "no date," "null," "September the eighteenth, nineteen hundred twenty-six," or "wibble." If you do a format check (everything's got the right number of digits and slashes), you still can't rely on getting dates; 1/1/0000 fits the format, as does 16/17/18.

Dates are easy to call out here, but you can extrapolate, I'm sure. The question is what to do when you encounter dirty data. In fact, the most interesting part of that isn't about technique; there are many techniques for detecting and cleaning data, and SSIS will let you do most of them. The real question is what you want to do when you encounter some particular data error. Some errors (say, a malformed file with the wrong number of columns) might be best dealt with by aborting the extract altogether. Some fields might be optional, so that bad data might require simply storing a NULL or some other value to indicate the row was only partially imported. Other fields, more central to the purpose of the import, might require that the whole row is invalidated. Only your business rules will determine the answer for each error, but be assured you will want a strategy in place.

Resolving Conflicts by Defining Authoritative Data

If you import data from multiple sources, what do you do when they disagree? Expecting disparate sources to agree on all the particulars is a bit like trusting a file spec to accurately describe what's going to arrive, which (as I said in the last section) is something I trust up there with an e-mail titled "mAke Monney FA$T." If your sales and production systems both provide product information but you find that information in conflict, how should it be resolved?

For each piece of data entering your data warehouse, you should be able to specify which data source is the *system of record* for that data point. The system of record is the authoritative source for that data point; anything else is just hearsay.

For example, the sample dimension in Table 17-2 (earlier in the chapter) has two attributes that could have different sources: IsOnSale and IsCurrent. The Production source system, in this case, is the authoritative source for the IsCurrent field, meaning that those are the folks who know when something's been discontinued. When they move to a new revision, they know, and their data should drive that bit. The sales manager who handles the Sales source system, though, knows when a product goes on sale. Even if the Sales system contains IsCurrent data, and even if you find that in your export, you'd always defer to the Production data on that.

STORING NON-AUTHORITATIVE DATA

Storing non-authoritative data in your data warehouse, usually as a placeholder, is certainly something that's done. However, it introduces a fair bit of complexity when it comes time to (perhaps) overwrite it with "real" data that shows up later. Sometimes it's better to leave the target field NULL than to store a questionable data point; other times you may want to store both data points. Your choice should be dictated by your reporting requirements.

Two, Three, or More Stages

Once you have a set of transformations in mind, it's time to start figuring out logistically how you're going to get the data from point A to point B. ETLs can be read-intensive operations, so it's good to take a few precautions.

To begin, imagine you're in about the simplest situation I can devise, but one that I've seen several times in real life: You have a single SQL Server data source, and your data warehouse lives in the same instance of SQL Server. You'll rarely be this lucky, but even this simple case starts to illustrate some of the concerns you'll have with more complex ETLs.

If you're faced with that kind of architecture, you might shoot for a one-step ETL. A SQL Server Agent job could run each night, executing one or more stored procedures that SELECT the previous day's data, transform it using T-SQL, and INSERT the resulting rows into your data warehouse.

Just because you can, though, doesn't mean you should. ETLs are usually more complicated than that. A few common problems with a monolithic stored procedure ETL are:

➤ Long transactions will introduce locking and concurrency issues into the source system.

➤ Working outside a transaction can extract an inconsistent database state if users are working.

➤ Adding a second source system, especially one not on the same SQL Server, will be problematic. If the data from the new system has to be integrated with the SQL data before loading, "problematic" may be read as "intractable."

➤ Failure can leave you unable to recover the day's data because Zen-master transactional systems have already forgotten what the data looked like when you tried to extract it.

Resolving these issues will virtually always mean introducing multiple stages to your ETL. How many stages will depend largely on how many layers of integration and transformation you'll need to accomplish your goals.

Dealing with Concurrency During ETLs

Let's look at the concurrency issues first. Depending on when and how long your extraction runs, you might be inconveniencing some users (never a good thing, because they're often directly or indirectly responsible for your paycheck). A long extract query — especially one that reads core tables (such as `SalesOrderDetail`) — is likely to be unpopular with salespeople who are trying to write data into that table while you have it locked. If multiple extracts per day are required, a long-running ETL can cause trouble. You do, though, have to read the data, and you might have to do it in the daytime. How can you prevent blocking?

A WORD ON WITH (NOLOCK)

I've heard this in countless interviews, I kid you not. When I ask about how to prevent blocking (or deadlocking) during long queries, hopeful job-seekers immediately suggest adding this hint to the query: "Just SELECT from the table and use WITH (NOLOCK), and your blocking issues are solved." If only it were that easy. That doesn't, and I mean this sincerely, ingratiate a candidate during an interview. It's a bit like trying to speed your car up by putting jet fuel in the tank; in some cases it just might work, but usually you just end up melting the engine (also, I told you not to do either one).

NOLOCK can be very dangerous, especially at ETL time. Although it will prevent your query from locking the tables it's reading, it also stops the ETL process from respecting other locks. This means that, in a busy system, you're likely to be reading dirty data and quite possibly storing an inconsistent state in your data warehouse, where it will live forever. Don't be tempted.

Before you go to a lot of trouble to prevent blocking, look at the most simple and obvious solution: Can you simply schedule your job so that it meets your needs without inconveniencing anyone? This is a very common solution, as so many businesses do close at night. By speaking to the database administrator (if that's not you) or the system owner, you can usually identify a window of time at night that can be used for maintenance, ETLs, and any other invasive tasks you might have to do.

Should you be working on a system that's got busy worker bees (or better yet, customers) entering data 24/7, you'll want to look at other options such as database mirroring or database snapshots. I'm not going to go deep into the mechanics of these methods, as they're a bit outside the beginners' programming realm, but you should know they're out there.

Database mirroring is a way to have a live, read-only copy of your database that's kept in sync with the original through a mechanism built into SQL Server. While a mirror is often kept up as part of a high-availability environment — allowed to become the live, read-write version should the main database server fail — it can also be used to do reporting without inflicting locks on the transactional system. Transactions entered live while tables in the mirror are locked will make their way in when the lock is released.

If you don't have the resources to set up additional SQL servers just to support your ETL, you can reduce your locking footprint by creating a database snapshot. This gives you a consistent, point-in-time view of the database that's read-only and usable by you (and anyone you grant permission to) until it's dropped.

Creating a snapshot is very, very fast, because no data is copied — it's read from the same files as the live database. What happens is that any pages that are altered after the snapshot is created are stored outside the main database files and only merged back in when the snapshot is dropped; this does, as you might imagine, produce some significant overhead, but it doesn't block the users entirely. For more on the risks and benefits of snapshots, you'll need to consult a more advanced text.

Caching Your Extract — The Operational Data Store (ODS)

Because the biggest problem isn't reading the data but reading it for a long time, one easy optimization is to separate the extraction and transformation into separate steps. If your extract is fast, your concurrency issues become much easier to deal with. Furthermore, if your data has to be integrated with data from another source system, you don't want to lock both up while your business logic is applied (deciding which system is authoritative, or comparing who has newer data), or perhaps this might not even be possible; you may have to integrate flat-file data with other flat-file data, or with live data. The common solution to both these problems is to extract data first into an intermediate storage area called an Operational Data Store, or ODS (see Figures 17-1 and 17-2).

Because an ODS is used primarily as a cache, the table structure in the ODS doesn't have to conform to the dimensional model you've built for your data warehouse. Instead, it can be made to mirror the structure of your source data, so that an extract becomes very simple. Furthermore, the ODS is assumed to store data that hasn't yet been cleaned — you can do that in the next step — so constraints (including foreign keys, NULLs, and uniqueness) are frequently dispensed with. The ODS gets to receive the raw source data, quickly.

Once you place the data for one or more sources into an ODS, you no longer have to worry about concurrency. This data is yours, and you can take your time in transforming, cleaning, and analyzing it until it's ready to be loaded into either your data warehouse or, if further cleaning or integration with more systems is required, a second-stage ODS. You might even think about a database mirror or snapshot as being like a first-stage ODS, from which data is loaded into a private ODS as a second stage.

The ODS helps to resolve the last issue mentioned previously: recovering from errors. If you try to extract directly from a source system and either the extract or, much more likely, the transformation fails (due to dirty data or an unhandled exception case), a transactional database in use will have already forgotten what things looked like when you started your attempt. Further attempts will capture only later and later data, forcing you to (perhaps) work from a backup to get back in sync.

By designing the ODS to mirror the structure of the source data, you make errors on extract much more rare: No transformation and few (if any) constraints will allow not just a fast extract but a reliable one as well. At that point, if you try to transform the data and load it to the next stage, failure leaves you with a copy of your original data in the ODS, waiting for you to fix the error and try again. Once you have a verified fact load in the data warehouse, it's up to you whether to keep a copy of the data in the ODS, make a backup, or simply purge the ODS entirely.

MAKING YOUR DATA ACTIONABLE: BI REPORTING TECHNIQUES

Consider all the work you've put in to creating your data warehouse, which includes all the interviews, design sessions, and modeling; all the wrangling over every dimension, and whether it's necessary, or if it should be type 1 or type 2. Even in the relatively quick-turnaround world of a Kimball data warehouse, you'll have sunk rather a lot of your time before you finally see the data loading neatly into the system. Yet all that work comes to exactly naught if you can't produce a report from it. Reporting is the whole reason you're creating a data warehouse.

BI reporting is different from data warehousing in the same sense that data is different from information. "We sold 10,000 widgets in June" may be accurate data, but it's perfectly useless as information without some kind of context. It would be great to know whether that's better or worse than May, or how it compares to last June. You might wonder whether that keeps the business on track to hit its yearly sales goal, or how individual salespeople are tracking toward their own goals. It would be good to know which factors may have contributed to that performance, either positively or negatively. You are going to need a report, stat, that can answer the questions that are really important to your business.

Goals

Lots of business metrics can be measured against goals. The financial reports on the radio often tell of how a company's revenue measured up against "analysts' expectations," which seems to trump in importance how much the revenue grew against prior periods. Sales forecasts drive targets for bonuses, and product return rates may impact a decision to make a recall. What all these things have in common is that they are not just measures but measures as they compare to a goal set by someone in the company.

Goals are targets for performance. Comparing a metric against a goal gives context to the metric that it wouldn't otherwise have, allowing you to make a quick judgment about whether the data you get from the metric is positive or negative information.

Setting goals can't just happen at random, however. Setting goals requires some history, and that's exactly what you're providing as you create the data warehouse. By watching metric trends over time, business leaders can learn what realistic goals might look like. Those goals can then be created as entities within the data warehouse to display on the reports.

Note that goals within the data warehouse are entirely independent from the source data. Nowhere in the sales database does it tell you (necessarily) what a good target for next July's sales might be; the goals don't come in through the ETLs. Goals are something you'll need to set on your own, typically with some kind of a date range attached (similar in structure to a type 2 slowly changing dimension); you want to know what a goal was during a past period, so you can see that period measured against the goal as it existed.

Goals are also metric and dimension specific. If you declare a sales target, that target applies to a particular set of dimension values: It will almost certainly contain the time dimension (a particular month), and it could have a product dimension (if it's a product-specific goal). It might be a target for each salesperson, or for a product line, or what have you, but the goal must be measurable against the data — a measure and a set of dimensions — that you have stored in your data warehouse.

Key Performance Indicators

In the past, most cars had gauges for many aspects of the engine's operation. There was an oil pressure gauge, a fuel gauge, a tachometer to measure the engine speed, and a thermometer — each of these provided detailed information about the exact state of one of the engine's systems.

Later, the oil pressure gauge mostly disappeared and was replaced by an oil light. Temperature, too, became an on/off indicator, illuminating only in the event of a problem. Fuel gauges — not yet ready to disappear — have gained a light whose purpose is to tell you when there's only a bit of fuel left. Lots of gauges have been replaced, or enhanced, by a quick bit of information: the light that says "pay attention, there's a problem here." This is the thought behind Key Performance Indicators, or KPIs.

KPIs are simplified metrics measured against goals, and they're usually displayed as graphics such as a thermometer or a stoplight, with obvious gradients to indicate trouble. Each KPI graphic relates information about the health of your business in some area, but not in detail. The KPI is the "check engine" light of your BI reporting in that it doesn't tell you what the problem is, just that there is one, and (very broadly) where it might be. SQL Server Reporting Services provides some graphics just for this type of information: You can display it as a gauge, shown in Figure 17-8, or as an indicator, in Figure 17-9.

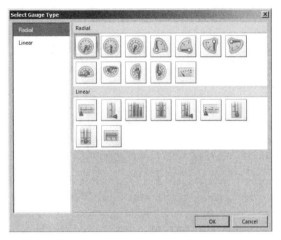

FIGURE 17-8

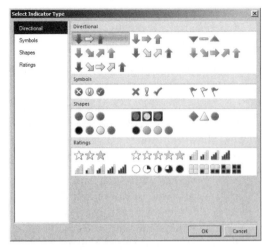

FIGURE 17-9

By defining KPIs in either SSRS or SSAS, you can provide executive-level summaries of business health and a very fast way to check for time-sensitive trouble.

Dashboards

The automobile analogy I drew for KPIs was no accident. The automotive dashboard has, for some time, been viewed as a model of information architecture. The driver, with only a fraction of his or her attention, has instant access to all the most important information about the condition of the vehicle. The simplicity and intuitiveness of this interface lets the driver pay more attention to the critical, moment-to-moment decisions about environment, traffic, and obstacles, and only calls attention to the car when there's a problem. It's no wonder that businesses have been searching for a way to model the dashboard concept to assist their management in decision making.

Dashboards contain current information about the state of the business right now. The idea behind a dashboard is that it's there to help you in the day-to-day or hour-to-hour performance of your job, rather than to help you analyze long-term performance or planning (which might require more detail or trend analysis). As you can imagine, KPIs are prime material for dashboards, but other metrics, such as those displayed in charts or those measured against goals, are regular occurrences.

Something to consider when designing a dashboard is how the immediate nature of the data required is going to mesh with your ETL strategy. A nightly ETL isn't likely to help provide up-to-the-minute reporting for your dashboards; that's going to give you once per day data, which is less compatible with the whole purpose of the dashboard.

Yet again there's no one right way to accomplish accurate, timely dashboard reporting, and there could easily be whole books on the topic — this isn't the place for a detailed discussion, but it's a fine spot for a quick nudge in the right direction. One option is to run very small, frequent ETLs to transfer a very limited amount of information — just what's needed for the metrics on your dashboard — to the data warehouse. If you can make that ETL non-intrusive, using a mirror for example, you can run it on a period of minutes rather than days and have quite current information. Another is to stop that ETL once the data is in the ODS, and do intra-day reporting directly from the ODS; this has the advantage of preventing some duplication of effort, but doesn't work well with data that's integrated from many sources. On the wild side, you can — and I have — use a messaging engine such as Microsoft Biztalk Server to pick up on changes relevant to the dashboard and bring those changes asynchronously to the data warehouse — advanced stuff, to be sure, but uniquely powerful.

Scorecards

Performance scorecards are to BI dashboards what your long-term car maintenance records are to your car's dashboard. Although the dashboard can tell you what's going on right at this moment, the scorecard — with its own KPIs, performance metrics, and goals — usually measures data trends over time, and progress toward future goals.

Scorecards fit much more neatly into the established scheme of running data into your warehouse on a nightly or longer periodic basis. In fact, given their nature, scorecards very often rely on summary tables — facts that contain aggregate, rather than atomic, values. The reason is that a scorecard is often summarizing data that could span many millions of detail rows, and calculating those totals in real time is prohibitively expensive. In short, it takes too darned long, so do it at night during your ETL and then just report on it.

Detail Reports

Where dashboards are a point-in-time summary and scorecards a long measurement over time, *detail reports* are the staple that underpins both. These are what the workers down in the trenches use when some higher-up sees a KPI go red on a dashboard and demands that somebody do something.

Of course, a KPI doesn't say what's wrong, just that something is, and broadly in what area. When sales for some product drop off unexpectedly, somebody's going to want to know why, and the reason may well be buried in all this data you're collecting. Detail reports — often filtered or grouped by a variety of dimensions — help in the investigation by showing everything that's happened, allowing some brilliant researcher to pore over the details and come up with a theory.

Detail reports are in some sense the easiest thing in the world to produce, or at least to create a first draft. Were you to create a report in SSRS and just follow the wizard, dropping a fact (of detail grain) and a few dimensions into the query designer, what you'd end up with is a great start toward a detail report.

Drill-Down

One of the most natural questions when looking at summary data is "How does that break down into categories?" Just like when you were learning about designing snowflake dimensions, the idea of a hierarchy of data is a way of looking at things that fits neatly into human thinking. By layering a summary report into a hierarchy of levels of detail (shown in Figure 17-10), you allow your users to break down large numbers into

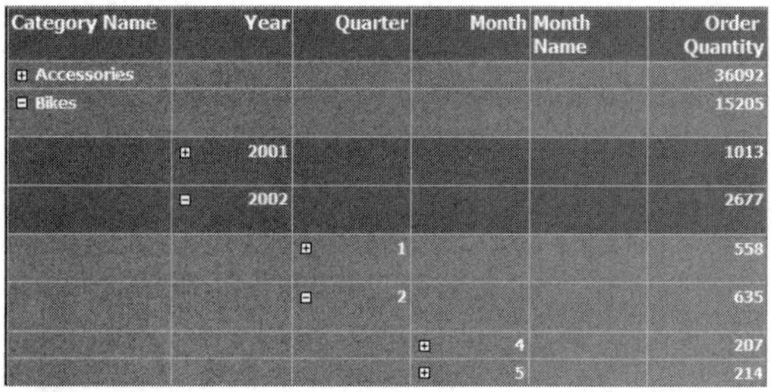

Category Name	Year	Quarter	Month	Month Name	Order Quantity
⊡ Accessories					36092
⊟ Bikes					15205
	⊟ 2001				1013
	⊟ 2002				2677
		⊟ 1			558
		⊟ 2			635
			⊡ 4		207
			⊡ 5		214

FIGURE 17-10

manageable pieces, and to compare those pieces against others to work out what's got that KPI in the red.

Expanding a summary to the next level of detail in place within a report is called *drill-down*. Creating drill-down within an SSRS report is possible from within the Report Creation wizard, simply by checking the Enable Drilldown box, as shown in Figure 17-11.

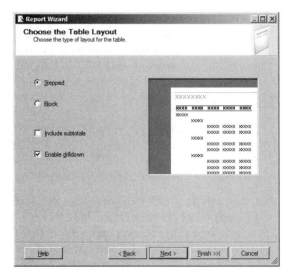

Drill-Through

Drill-through is a concept closely related to drill-down, but the implications — and the implementation — are quite different. Whereas drill-down implies seeking lower and lower levels of summarized data within the same report, *drill-through* usually results in an entirely new report containing summary or detail data about an area of interest.

FIGURE 17-11

Consider again that alarmingly red KPI that has your boss's boss (what I like to call your grand-boss) handing out tasks like candy on Halloween and calling for hourly status reports. Somewhere, underneath that KPI, there's some detail data that produced the information. There's goal data and there are facts with their measures, and those combined to create the statistic that's interrupting your day. Drill-through is the idea that, by clicking a report element (which could be a KPI, or an aggregated measure, or a bar graph, or what have you), a new report will show up displaying the summary or detail data responsible for that report element. That sort of thing can shorten your investigation precipitously.

If the KPI is part of a scorecard showing that monthly sales have failed to meet your goal, for example, the drill-through report might look like the one in Figure 17-11. Using that data, you could narrow the problem down to a particular product that's underperforming, or (with slightly more detail) to the end of a sale or a failed promotion.

Creating accurate drill-through reports can be tricky. The mechanism within SSRS that you'd use is simple enough; you can create a hyperlink on any element, and pass through parameters to match the filters on the parent report. That is to say, if your parent scorecard is showing only products in a particular category, you'd certainly want to apply that same filter to the drill-through report. What's more, if your hyperlink is on more specific data (say, the row in Figure 17-11 for Q1 2002, showing 558 units sold), you'd also want to add those filters — that you only want to drill through to Q1 of 2002 — so you'd want to pass those through as parameters as well.

Ad Hoc Reporting

Even with all that work and research users never are satisfied, are they? Someone always wants a report that's exactly like one you're providing, only different in some way critical to the way their business unit operates. That's one of the more understandable applications of Murphy's Law, because it's only after seeing the existing capabilities that they may be inspired to work up their requirements, but still it can feel a bit thankless.

However carefully you plan, you might find that giving the users what they want involves giving them a toolset to easily create what they want. For that, Microsoft has provided Report Builder with SSRS. For more information on how Report Builder, works continue on; you'll get much more detail in Chapter 19, but for now I'll mention that you'll want to create views rather than give your users direct access to the tables, and that unless you're prepared for fact-to-fact joins, you should probably not put multiple facts in the same model. Fact-to-fact joins aren't verboten, but unless you've prepared a compatible indexing strategy — that is, unless you've specifically prepared for them — they can be terrifically taxing.

SUMMARY

Business intelligence (BI) encompasses a whole realm of database application development that's at once an integral part of the SQL Server stack and a different way of thinking from the transactional model. A successful BI implementation is very challenging without an understanding of the end-to-end data flow. Data sources can be scattered across the company. By performing a series of interviews with stakeholders, you can help set expectations in line with reality. The scope of your data warehousing project will depend on whether your company wants to invest in the long-term, high-payout epic that is an Inmon data warehouse, or the much shorter cycle of a Kimball model. Understanding these well enough to guide your company's decision will help you along the way.

Once it's time to do your implementation, you're likely to use a dimensional data model involving facts surrounded by dimensions. Such a data model is rarely normalized, containing a great deal of redundant data wherever necessary to speed report output. You'll populate it with an ETL process probably driven by SQL Server Integration Services. SSIS can help to extract data from your data sources into an ODS, transform it into your dimensional model while managing change within slowly changing dimensions, and load the result into your data warehouse.

Finally, you can engage additional tools to create reports. Fixed reports in either a summary style, a dashboard, or a scorecard can be created in SQL Server Reporting Services. Those reports can be fed either directly from your data warehouse or from a SQL Server Analysis Services cube, or you can set up a report model and allow your users to create ad hoc reports using Report Builder.

A business intelligence project is a significant undertaking in any case, but the payoff is virtually always worth it.

EXERCISES

1. A business has a manufacturing process whereby products go through build, test, and shipping phases. A report is required to show the number of products in each phase of the cycle at any given time. Which fact type should be used to store this information?

2. List at least two ways of minimizing the impact of ETLs on transactional system users.

▶ WHAT YOU LEARNED IN THIS CHAPTER

TOPIC	CONCEPT
Business intelligence	The ability to use accumulated business data to assist in making business decisions and accurately predicting their results is the core of business intelligence.
Data warehouse	A database full of nonvolatile, time-sensitive facts about data needed for business intelligence. A data warehouse can be designed top-down, containing all the company's data, and reports generated from smaller data marts, as per Bill Inmon. It can also be created bottom-up, as a collection of topical data marts that together constitute the data warehouse, as per Ralph Kimball. Both approaches have merit, and hybrids are often created.
Data mart	A topical database designed for high-performance reporting and usually created with a dimensional data model.
Measures and metrics	Measures are the numeric values that make up the business data. Metrics are calculated from measures, and represent information that can be used to make decisions about some aspect of the business.
Facts	Collections of measures (and sometimes metrics) stored in the data warehouse. Each fact has its data categorized by one or more dimensions. Facts can be transactional, periodic snapshots, or accumulating snapshots.
Dimensions	Each dimension represents a way to categorize the data in a fact. Date is a very common dimension, but you can use any kind of categorization that makes sense to your business. Dimensions come in type 0, which never change; type 1, which change in place without keeping history; and type 2, which preserve history but make for more complex queries.
ETLs	Extract, transform, and load processes are part of every data warehouse project. SQL Server provides SSIS to create ETLs.
ODS (Operational Data Store)	A cache of transactional data designed to allow maximum concurrency for transactional users while allowing the ETL to take its time on transformation, integrate data from various sources, and perform error handling.
BI reporting	Reporting for business intelligence has some common themes. Goals indicate target values for metrics, and are a requirement for creating key performance indicators. KPIs are graphical, easy-to-read indicators about the health of some part of a business. KPIs, goals, and metrics combine in dashboards for current conditions, and scorecards for trends. Dashboards and scorecards might allow drill-through to detail rows.

18

BI Storage and Reporting Resources

WHAT YOU WILL LEARN IN THIS CHAPTER:

➤ The tools SQL Server provides to perform BI reporting

➤ Multidimensional querying in T-SQL using analysis functions

➤ How to create and use columnstore indexes

➤ An introduction to building a cube in SQL Server Analysis Services

➤ Methods of providing self-service reporting with different SQL Server components

Once you begin to understand the promise and structure of a business intelligence system, your mind can start to really swim with possibilities. To be perfectly honest, that's what I truly hope, because once you start to envision your BI system, you're that much closer to designing and building it — and building things is what gets people into this business in the first place. SQL Server 2012 has a wide variety of tools available to help you build a BI system, and this is the chapter where you'll actually get to do a little hands-on work with them.

With all the theory you were subjected to in the last chapter, this hands-on practice will be quite a contrast. If you've jumped straight here but haven't read Chapter 17 yet, I do strongly suggest you do so unless you're already familiar with BI concepts and structures; this chapter really does build on that one, and you'll want to be fresh on the basics.

ORDER THE BI SAMPLE PLATTER — ON US!

When I was in Atlanta for TechEd recently, my travelling compatriots and I went out for some barbecue at a local restaurant recommended by a friend. When we arrived, we knew we wanted barbecue, but didn't know exactly what the local specialties were, and the menu offered little help — everything looked good. When we jokingly shared our dilemma with the waitress, she simply smiled and asked us to wait a moment, and then she brought back a platter of samples for us to share. They were divine, and gave each of us a much better concept of exactly what we wanted to order. Needless to say, dinner was memorably delicious.

You can liken our quest for BBQ to your quest for BI; you know you want some, but you might not be sure at all what exactly you want off the menu — or even what's on the menu. This chapter is intended to be the menu and taster platter rolled into one, giving you a chance to try out a few of the tools provided by SQL Server to deliver the BI you want. Once you have an idea what you're after, you'll probably want a full order — say, books like *Professional Microsoft SQL Server 2012 Analysis Services with MDX* by Sivakumar Harinath et al., or *Professional Microsoft SQL Server 2012 Reporting Services* by Paul Turley and others, to complete your order.

BI IN T-SQL

To a man with only a hammer, every problem looks like a nail. By now you're starting to get a pretty good grasp of how to get around using T-SQL, and you might well ask why any other tool could possibly be needed to build a BI system on a SQL Server platform. While you'll certainly see me play devil's advocate later on, for the moment I'm going to go ahead and encourage that. T-SQL has plenty to offer the BI developer, and because of its familiarity it's a great place to start.

BI through T-SQL is a matter of querying dimensional models and summary tables. If that sounds simple enough, remember that you're also going to need a way to populate summary tables, and to do a variety of aggregates and other functions — and you're going to have to do all that over very large datasets, very fast. Getting your numbers right in T-SQL is (relatively) easy; getting the right numbers fast can be harder. We'll start with the easy part.

Introducing the AdventureWorks Data Warehouse

All of the examples in this chapter refer to a database called AdventureWorksDW, which is a data warehouse based on the AdventureWorks transactional database you've used throughout the text. You can download AdventureWorksDW from www.wrox.com, and I strongly recommend that you do so before continuing. Following along with the examples in this chapter is how you're really going to get a taste of what's possible in each of the tools, and each example is worth a dozen of my written pages.

Once you have downloaded it and loaded it into your SQL Server instance, you should take a few minutes to familiarize yourself a little with the AdventureWorksDW database. Start by navigating to Database Diagrams in the Object Explorer: you'll find no fewer than nine diagrams waiting there for your perusal. Take a look at each, familiarizing yourself with the star and snowflake schemas you'll find there. One you'll use several times is the Internet Sales schema, shown in Figure 18-1.

As you can see in the figure, Internet Sales uses one central fact table called (both predictably and, therefore, as a hint toward good naming practices) FactInternetSales. This table has nine dimensions arrayed around it in a snowflake schema: DimDate, DimPromotion, DimCurrency, DimProduct, DimCustomer, and DimSalesTerritory all connect directly to the fact, while DimProductSubcategory and DimProductCategory snowflake off DimProduct (making a hierarchy) as DimGeography and DimSalesTerritory do off DimCustomer. Note that the link to

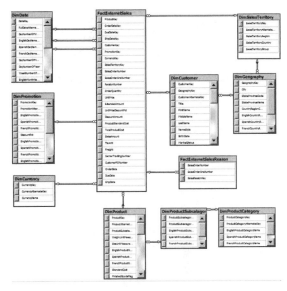

FIGURE 18-1

DimSalesTerritory occurs in two different places; this sort of denormalization is not uncommon in a data warehouse.

The other fact within this schema, FactInternetSalesReason, is used to link an order and line item (the basic units of FactInternetSales) to a sales reason, but DimSalesReason is not included in this schema. That table does exist, but the purpose of this schema display is to show the relations available to FactInternetSales; the other fact is related, but its dimension is not.

You'll use FactInternetSales as the basis for your first BI-style analysis queries done through T-SQL.

Using T-SQL Analysis Functions

The foundation of analysis in T-SQL is something you've already done, way back in Chapter 3: SELECT, particularly in combination with aggregates such as SUM or AVG and GROUP BY, will make up a very large portion of the data you'll need to report in many environments. However, there are plenty of data transformations available to do things that would be pretty difficult to accomplish — or, more accurately, accomplish with any reasonable speed — with the simplest aggregates.

PIVOT and UNPIVOT

In the FactInternetSales table, each order has an order date; this is a natural source for breaking down data into years and months, for example, to analyze trends. For example, let's say you've been asked to produce month-by-month data per year for analysis. The output needs each year broken out by month, and months should be viewable as month names (for example, "September") rather than any numeric equivalent. A reasonable start to such a query might look like this:

```
SELECT
  YEAR(OrderDate) OrderYear,
  FORMAT( OrderDate, 'MMMM', 'en-US' ) OrderMonth,
  SUM(ExtendedAmount) SumExtendedAmount
FROM FactInternetSales
GROUP BY YEAR(OrderDate), FORMAT( OrderDate, 'MMMM', 'en-US' )
ORDER BY SUM(ExtendedAmount) DESC
```

Code snippet Chap18.sql

```
OrderYear   OrderMonth   SumExtendedAmount
----------- -----------  --------------------
2004        June         1949361.11
2004        May          1878317.51
2003        December     1731787.77
2004        April        1608750.53
2004        March        1480905.18
...
2002        September     350466.9912
2002        November      335095.0887
2004        July          50840.63

(37 row(s) affected)
```

THE FORMAT FUNCTION

The FORMAT function is new with SQL Server 2012. It has two required arguments (the value to format and the target formatting) and one optional (the culture to target). FORMAT uses the set of .NET format strings that any C# or VB.NET folks reading will already know, which is pretty handy, and it's culture-aware: If you don't specify a value for the culture argument it just uses whatever your session is using. If you do, the output can change to any language you have installed. When you need to be able to produce output in any language, this is a great option.

This produces all the right data, but not in a format that's easy to read. It's difficult, for example, to get it to order correctly; ordering by month name won't work, so you'll have to add a month number column to order by and then select it out later...yuck. Besides, the real requirement (once you ask a little further) is to produce not a long column of data, but years down the left and months across the top — like a Microsoft Excel PivotTable. Fortunately, T-SQL has your back with PIVOT.

To use PIVOT, your query will have two parts.

➤ You'll query out the data values you need.

➤ You'll specify a set of data values from one column to pivot out as separate columns and a value to aggregate.

So, to convert the previous query to a `PIVOT` query, you'll first remove the aggregate (`SUM` and `GROUP BY`) from the source, add the `PIVOT` clause, and then surround the whole thing with a `SELECT` statement (whose result set is the output of the `PIVOT` expression):

Available for
download on
Wrox.com

```
SELECT PivotOrders.*
FROM (
    SELECT
        YEAR(OrderDate) OrderYear,
        FORMAT( OrderDate, 'MMMM', 'en-US' ) OrderMonth,
        ExtendedAmount
    FROM FactInternetSales
) FormattedOrders
PIVOT (
    SUM(ExtendedAmount)
    FOR OrderMonth IN (
        [January],[February],[March],[April],[May],[June],
        [July],[August],[September],[October],[November],[December]
    )
) PivotOrders
```

Code snippet Chap18.sql

When you run this query, you'll get a result set like the one shown in the table that follows:

OrderYear	January	February	March	...	October	November	December
2001	NULL	NULL	NULL	...	513329	543993	755528
2002	596747	550817	644135	...	415390	335095	577314
2003	438865	489090	485575	...	1080450	1196981	1731788
2004	1340245	1462480	1480905	...	NULL	NULL	NULL

Note that `PIVOT` is always an aggregator; you can't put detail rows into the cells in the `PIVOT` table, which becomes clear if you try to figure out what value would go where. Also take note of an important limitation: When you use `PIVOT`, you must — really must — know each and every value that you want to call out as a column. See how all the month names are listed out (in brackets) in the previous query? If you can't do that, you can't pivot. For a pivot that can handle a more general case, producing columns for an arbitrary set of values, you're going to have to write a stored procedure that produces dynamic SQL.

`UNPIVOT`, predictably, does exactly the opposite as `PIVOT`; it takes a set of columns and turns them into a set of rows. It's worth noting, though, that while the two functions are, in a very real sense, opposites, they are not reciprocals; that is, if you take a dataset and `PIVOT` it, when you `UNPIVOT` the result you're not going to get your original dataset back. Why not? Remember, `PIVOT` is an aggregator...the detail rows are gone. While you can get back your original *structure*, you cannot get back your original *data*.

PIVOT AND UNPIVOT SYNTAX

Okay, yes, I'm completely with you: The syntax for PIVOT that I showed you previously (and, likewise, the syntax for UNPIVOT) is a bit challenging to get right the first time. In fact, I still find it occasionally difficult to puzzle out when I need it, because like many of the analysis functions you're going to see here it's only needed occasionally. Any time I need to do this, I end up in Books Online, checking out the syntax once again, because I've only got so much room upstairs and frankly I need it for other things than twice-a-year UNPIVOT syntax. Don't worry if you find it challenging when you suddenly realize you need it...Books Online is there for a reason.

Using the OVER Clause to Summarize Along Varying Grains

The OVER clause has been expanded in SQL Server 2012 to apply to a much broader range of functions than before. Introduced with SQL 2005 and enhanced in each version since, OVER lets you define a window of your results over which you want to perform some kind of function. You were introduced to this in the section on "Windowing Functions" in Chapter 7; this is where you get to look at it from a different angle.

OVER can now be applied to virtually any aggregate, and has received a much longer list of modifiers than it had before. There's no way I can go through them all here in detail, so I'm going to focus on a few common problems you'll likely be asked to solve and leave the advanced solutions to arise from your mind as their requirement present themselves.

ANALYSIS PERFORMANCE

While you think about what you can do with OVER, you should also think about an area of development focus that often receives short shrift in the first pass over a set of reports or analysis functions: performance. While performance is important in all systems, oftentimes testing is done on unrealistically small datasets so performance problems aren't noticed until later. Designing your queries for speed from the beginning, then, can be difficult...but that's no reason to ignore it.

If there is one thing you always want to pay attention to when tuning a query, it's disk reads. Every time you have to go out to the disk for another page, you're spending an eternity (relatively speaking), so the more work you can do per read the better. Because OVER can be applied across more aggregates in SQL 2012, you can summarize data over different grains in a single pass. Does that mean you get all that analysis for free, though? As it happens, the answer is "probably not." Before you assume you've found an optimal solution, test, test, test!

First consider producing several distinct aggregates. When you've used aggregates before, it's always been the GROUP BY clause that determines what group each aggregate covers. Because that's no longer your only option, you can produce different aggregates together that can be compared against each other. For example, consider adding up sales by month by territory for the information in `FactInternetSales`. Easy enough? Now, imagine you want to take each number and compare it to the total sales for that territory across all months, and the total sales for that month across all territories.

Doing this in a single SQL statement would previously have involved liberal use of CTEs, subqueries, or derived tables — and of course, you could still do it that way. Instead, though, you can do it with only a single SELECT and then apply your aggregates over whatever group you'd like, as shown here.

Available for download on Wrox.com

```
SELECT DISTINCT DST.SalesTerritoryRegion,
  EOMONTH(OrderDate) OrderEndOfMonth,
  SUM(ExtendedAmount) OVER
    (PARTITION BY SalesTerritoryRegion, EOMONTH(OrderDate)) RegionMonthSales,
  SUM(ExtendedAmount) OVER
    (PARTITION BY SalesTerritoryRegion) RegionSales,
  SUM(ExtendedAmount) OVER
    (PARTITION BY EOMONTH(OrderDate)) MonthSales,
  SUM(ExtendedAmount) OVER
    (PARTITION BY SalesTerritoryRegion, EOMONTH(OrderDate)) /
    SUM(ExtendedAmount) OVER
      (PARTITION BY SalesTerritoryRegion) RegionSalesPct,
  SUM(ExtendedAmount) OVER
    (PARTITION BY SalesTerritoryRegion, EOMONTH(OrderDate)) /
    SUM(ExtendedAmount) OVER
      (PARTITION BY EOMONTH(OrderDate)) MonthSalesPct
FROM FactInternetSales FIS
JOIN DimSalesTerritory DST
  ON FIS.SalesTerritoryKey = DST.SalesTerritoryKey
ORDER BY SalesTerritoryRegion, OrderEndOfMonth
```

Code snippet Chap18.sql

When you run this query, you'll see a result set that looks like this.

Sales Territory Region	Order EndOfMonth	Region Month Sales	Region Sales	Month Sales	Region SalesPct	Month SalesPct
Australia	2001-07-31	209653	9061001	473388	0.0231	0.4428
Australia	2001-08-31	222538	9061001	506192	0.0245	0.4396
Australia	2001-09-30	173994	9061001	473943	0.0192	0.3671
Australia	2001-10-31	217993	9061001	513329	0.024	0.4246
Australia	2001-11-30	210684	9061001	543993	0.0232	0.3872

As usual, there are several interesting things to notice about this. The ones I'd like to call out are the EOMONTH() function and the DISTINCT keyword. EOMONTH() is new with SQL 2012, and is a quick way to get the last day of the month; in prior versions of SQL Server, there were a few different ways to accomplish this, but none was anything like that simple or obvious. DISTINCT is of interest here because despite each row clearly specifying an aggregate, the whole statement isn't one; that is, without the DISTINCT, you'd see one row per row in FactInternetSales (on the order of 60,000). This statement has no overall grouping (no GROUP BY clause), so it's really more of a de facto aggregate than de jure.

Among the other types of information you'll often need to produce are running sums and moving averages. These are also calculations that before SQL 2012 have been...well, problematic is an accurate description. They've been possible (heck, T-SQL is a Turing-complete language, so technically anything's *possible*), but never particularly simple until now.

To add these kinds of functions to your query, you need to tell SQL over which rows in the window (remember, the window is defined by the PARTITION BY keyword and ordered by the ORDER BY within that) you want to compute over. In this case, you can start with a CTE to do the initial aggregate, and then easily produce both a running total within each territory and a six-month moving average by telling the SUM and AVG aggregates to compute only over certain ROWS.

Available for download on Wrox.com

```
WITH MonthTerritorySales AS (
SELECT DST.SalesTerritoryRegion,
    EOMONTH(OrderDate) OrderEndOfMonth,
    SUM(ExtendedAmount) RegionMonthSales
FROM FactInternetSales FIS
JOIN DimSalesTerritory DST
  ON FIS.SalesTerritoryKey = DST.SalesTerritoryKey
GROUP BY DST.SalesTerritoryRegion, EOMONTH(OrderDate)
)
SELECT SalesTerritoryRegion, OrderEndOfMonth, RegionMonthSales,
    SUM(RegionMonthSales) OVER (
        PARTITION BY SalesTerritoryRegion
        ORDER BY OrderEndOfMonth ROWS UNBOUNDED PRECEDING) RunningTotal,
    AVG(RegionMonthSales) OVER (
        PARTITION BY SalesTerritoryRegion
        ORDER BY OrderEndOfMonth ROWS 6 PRECEDING) SixMonthMovingAverage
FROM MonthTerritorySales
```

Code snippet Chap18.sql

This query results in the running total and moving average shown below.

SalesTerritory Region	OrderEndOf Month	RegionMonth Sales	Running Total	SixMonthMoving Average
Australia	2001-07-31	209652.9046	209652.9046	209652.9046
Australia	2001-08-31	222538.2892	432191.1938	216095.5969
Australia	2001-09-30	173993.5128	606184.7066	202061.5688
Australia	2001-10-31	217993.3828	824178.0894	206044.5223
Australia	2001-11-30	210683.5628	1034861.6522	206972.3304

As you can tell, you have a lot of flexibility here.

GROUP BY ROLLUP, CUBE, and GROUPING SETS

When you're setting up a data warehouse, one thing that's helpful to remember is why you're doing it. It's generally for only one reason: reporting. That means anything that plays into making your reports simpler or faster (provided you're not having a problem with accuracy) is the way to go. To that end, at ETL time it's pretty common to roll up data into summary tables for quick reporting.

That sounds perfectly simple, but of course nothing is ever quite as easy as it sounds. Let's walk through an example to show how your dimensions can cause your summary table to grow, where that creates a problem, and what you might do to fix it. To start, the following is a sample fact table to use as a basis for this work (the code to create and populate it is available for download). I've chosen to create and use this small table to more easily demonstrate these features, because it's easier to see all the combinations here than by looking in the tens of thousands of rows in the AdventureWorksDW database.

Available for download on Wrox.com

SaleDate	Region	Product	Quantity
2012-01-10	Portland	Salted Caramels	12590
2012-01-31	Seattle	Venezuelan Truffles	1770
2012-02-10	Portland	Salted Caramels	15250
2012-02-12	Portland	Rose Caramels	5400
2012-03-08	Seattle	Salted Caramels	1310
2012-03-10	Portland	Venezuelan Truffles	180

Code snippet Chap18.sql

Given the fact shown in the previous table, you can imagine reporting requirements: sales by year, by quarter, or by month; sales by product or by region; or sales by any combination: regional sales by quarter, for example. While this fact table has only six rows, you're of course planning to report against years' worth of data comprising millions of rows, so you decide to create a summary table rather than query the fact directly. You can load the summary at ETL time, and you're all set… right? You quickly devise a summary table structure that looks like this:

Year	Quarter	EndOfMonth	Region	Product	TotalSold

And you can load all the data from your fact. However, you've still got somewhat of your problem: In the sample data, anyway, your summary table isn't doing a lot of summarizing. No two rows will even be added across all these dimensions. While that may look like a quirk of carefully created test data — because it is — when you start looking into tables with more than a few dimensions, it's a real problem. Five dimensions with 12 possible values in each makes for (in the worst case) 248832 possible dimensional combinations…you're not going to summarize well over that.

What's really trouble is that you're still stuck aggregating your aggregates. You've spent all this effort to create a summary table, but if you want to know the sales for 2012, or the sales for a particular product, you're still reading many rows.

One thing you can do is to store not only the dimensional combinations that exist in your data, but also the ones that roll data up to higher and higher levels. For example, rather than just putting the row for each region and product combination, you can also store the row for each region's or product's summary information. Choosing which combinations you're going to store will lead you to GROUP BY ROLLUP, CUBE, or GROUPING SETS.

GROUP BY ROLLUP lets you create not only the combinations that exist in your data, but also rollups within the hierarchical order you create in the ROLLUP statement. That lets you create (for example) the year, quarter, month reporting with a quick seek to "year" that doesn't have to read quarter, month, or even day. Sticking just with the date data for the moment, look at this query and what it will produce using ROLLUP.

```
SELECT YEAR(SaleDate) SaleYear,
    DATEPART(QUARTER, SaleDate) SaleQuarter,
    MONTH(SaleDate) SaleMonth,
    SUM(Quantity) TotalSold
FROM FactChocolateSales FS
GROUP BY ROLLUP (YEAR(SaleDate), DATEPART(QUARTER, SaleDate), MONTH(SaleDate))
```

Code snippet Chap18.sql

When you run this query, you'll get a result set (shown below) that contains the data aggregated across the different grains you specified.

SaleYear	SaleQuarter	SaleMonth	TotalSold
2012	1	1	14360
2012	1	2	20650
2012	1	3	1490
2012	1	NULL	36500
2012	NULL	NULL	36500
NULL	NULL	NULL	36500

If you want to find the year's total from this result (which you could store as a summary table), you simply search for 2012-NULL-NULL and you get your results from a single row. That's speed your users will appreciate. Notice, though, that there's no row for the first quarter that doesn't include a year; ROLLUP creates a hierarchy in the order the fields are specified (in this case Year, Quarter, Month). Because these dimensions are dependent in nature, you can query them ROLLUP as a hierarchy and get all the meaningful combinations.

GROUP BY CUBE is for independent dimensions, when you need all the possible rollups because there is no hierarchy. When grouping by region, product, and year, for example, you might want to select by year only, or region and year, or product only, and summarizing using CUBE will cause all of those to be instantiated. To see all the example rows I'm going to stick with just region and product for the moment; feel free to experiment by adding the year when you get to the exercises at the chapter's end.

```
SELECT Region, Product,
    SUM(Quantity) TotalSold
FROM FactChocolateSales FS
GROUP BY CUBE (Product, Region)
```

Code snippet Chap18.sql

When you run this query, the result will contain the following rows.

Region	Product	TotalSold
Portland	Rose Caramels	5400
Portland	Salted Caramels	27840
Portland	Venezuelan Truffles	180
Portland	NULL	33420
Seattle	Salted Caramels	1310
Seattle	Venezuelan Truffles	1770
Seattle	NULL	3080
NULL	NULL	36500
NULL	Rose Caramels	5400
NULL	Salted Caramels	29150
NULL	Venezuelan Truffles	1950

CUBE produces every possible combination and rollup...it even has more rows in its return set than exist in the actual fact (although that's an artifact of the artificial test data). Still, when it comes to reading the data later, nothing can be faster: Any combination of included and skipped dimensions produces a seek to the very data you need. Keep this in mind as you read on about SQL Server Analysis Services.

GROUP BY GROUPING SETS lets you specify explicitly which levels will be instantiated, so that you can store less than you might store CUBE, but still have more flexibility than ROLLUP. The syntax can get long if you have many combinations to request, but by specifying each you can finally fill in the summary table defined previously. You'll need to request a group for a total summary, one for product only, one for region only, and one for each combination of product, region, and any date granularity you want searchable. Here's a pretty good start.

```
SELECT YEAR(SaleDate) [Year], DATEPART(QUARTER, SaleDate) Quarter,
    EOMONTH(SaleDate) [EndOfMonth], Region, Product, SUM(Quantity) TotalSold
FROM FactChocolateSales
GROUP BY GROUPING SETS (
    (), --Total Summary
    (Region), --Region only
    (Product), --Product only
```

```
    (YEAR(SaleDate), Region), --Year / region combinations
    (YEAR(SaleDate), Product), --Year / Product combinations
    (YEAR(SaleDate), DATEPART(QUARTER, SaleDate), Region), --etc.
    (YEAR(SaleDate), DATEPART(QUARTER, SaleDate), Product), --etc.
    (YEAR(SaleDate), DATEPART(QUARTER, SaleDate), EOMONTH(SaleDate), Region, Product),
    (YEAR(SaleDate), DATEPART(QUARTER, SaleDate), EOMONTH(SaleDate), Region),
    (YEAR(SaleDate), DATEPART(QUARTER, SaleDate), EOMONTH(SaleDate), Product)
)
```

Code snippet Chap18.sql

Executing this query will produce the output you see here. As you can see, GROUPING SETS causes as many rollup combinations to return as you write in the query.

Year	Quarter	EndOfMonth	Region	Product	TotalSold
2012	1	2012-02-28	Portland	Rose Caramels	5400
2012	1	2012-02-28	NULL	Rose Caramels	5400
2012	1	NULL	NULL	Rose Caramels	5400
2012	NULL	NULL	NULL	Rose Caramels	5400
...					
2012	1	2012-03-31	Seattle	NULL	1310
2012	1	NULL	Seattle	NULL	3080
2012	NULL	NULL	Seattle	NULL	3080
NULL	NULL	NULL	Seattle	NULL	3080

Summarizing data in this way can make it extremely fast to retrieve, as long as you have proper indexing and well-formed queries to get the data back out, but it can take an awful lot of storage space and cost a fair amount of time during your ETLs. In general, that's a cost you'll be willing to pay in a BI solution — you want to spend ETL time to speed reporting time — but remember, all things in moderation.

Columnstore Indexes

If all that work with summarizing data along different grains sounds like a problem, that's okay; it's not the only way. When you're dealing with fact tables containing millions of rows or more, the real point is that reading all the data from all those rows takes too long, so what you need is a way to read fewer rows...preferably only what you need. Enter the *columnstore index*, which is SQL Server 2012's killer feature for BI.

A columnstore represents a fundamentally different way of arranging your data on disk. You may recall that SQL Server ordinarily stores each row as a unit, packing as many onto each page as possible (refer to Chapter 9 for a refresher on SQL Server storage if you need to). When each page of data is read, it contains all the columns in all the rows that fit on the page.

By contrast, a columnstore places the data from each column on disk contiguously. Because column data tends to be repetitive, this allows for highly compressible storage. Furthermore, it means only the columns you select are read from disk, and there is a significant benefit on buffer hits. The end result is that, when dealing with star joins and aggregates, queries run faster by orders of magnitude...sometimes as much as 1,000 times.

If you're waiting for the other shoe to drop, you're starting to read wisely. Of course, if a columnstore were nothing but good, it would be the default storage mechanism. Reconstituting the whole row from a columnstore takes time, sometimes more than from a rowstore. Also, updating data in a columnstore is challenging, so DML statements — INSERT, UPDATE, DELETE, or MERGE — are not a supported feature at this time. Do take a moment to let that sink in: Once you put a columnstore index on a table, that table becomes read-only. To update a table with a columnstore, you must drop the columnstore index, alter your data, and rebuild the index.

That's not as bad a caveat as it may seem, given the nature of most ETL solutions. In general, you'll run your ETL at night, so the drop and rebuild of the columnstore would happen as part of the process. In that rather common context, the columnstore makes perfect sense.

Building a columnstore index is very much like building any other index: You simply run a CREATE COLUMNSTORE INDEX statement, name the target table, and then list all the columns you want present in the index (up to a maximum of 1024). And if creating it is easy, using it is easier; just run your normal queries, and let the query optimizer do its work.

```
CREATE NONCLUSTERED COLUMNSTORE INDEX icol_factTable ON factTable
    (col1, col2, …, coln);
```

 NOTE *It doesn't matter in which order you list the columns when you create your columnstore index. In effect, you're only naming the columns that will be included, but since each is stored separately the index can retrieve as efficiently from the first column as the last.*

SQL SERVER ANALYSIS SERVICES, OR HOW I LEARNED TO STOP WORRYING AND LOVE THE CUBE

When it comes to industrial-strength data mining and analysis, there's a certain segment of the SQL Server community that waits for you to put down your T-SQL toys and start using the real grown-up tools. While SQL Server 2012 has expanded dramatically on what's possible in T-SQL, SQL Server Analysis Services still offers a far more complete suite of powerful tools to quickly produce any slice of data you need. SSAS comes with a learning curve, though, and books thicker than this one have been written on its use. The next few pages exist to give you some idea what you'll find in SSAS, and hopefully will provide enough information to help you figure out whether you need one of those books.

Understanding SSAS Modeling

So what, exactly, does SSAS do? I'm going to go backward this time, and hit you with the complicated part first: In a sense, the primary service provided by SSAS is the organization of metadata about various data sources into a unified semantic model for reporting. SSAS does plenty else in terms of creating structures that allow fast reporting from those data sources, but the real magic is that high-performance cross-source reporting is possible at all. The management of the metadata that defines the relationships among your data sources is a key part of the tool.

SQL Server Analysis Services can handle that metadata in two completely different ways, which is a change over prior versions. In SQL Server 2008 and earlier, SSAS used the Unified Dimensional Model to keep track of the relationships between entities, and it's been quite a successful format. UDM builds your data into cubes, permitting very fast access to data aggregated across any combination of dimensions.

Recently, though, the rise in popularity of ad hoc reporting tools has driven SSAS to support a tabular format using the Vertipaq engine (the same that powers the columnstore indexes you just read about) overlayed by a BI Semantic Model (BISM). BISM is a simpler model that can even be a transparent layer right over your source data, making ROLAP (more on this in a minute) more of a realistic option. You have to pick one of these when you install an instance of SSAS, and each has advantages in different situations.

Unified Dimensional Model (UDM)

This is how SSAS has always worked. When you create a model in the UDM, what you're really doing is giving SSAS the tools it needs to create a cube. The cube can be repopulated from the source data on a regular basis, and provides a fantastic level of speedy access to your data — provided you have the proper tools and language to deal with it. Querying the UDM doesn't happen in T-SQL, oh, no. Once you have the cubes built, you're using MultiDimensional eXpressions, or MDX, which is a more set-based language than T-SQL. Using MDX, you can quickly navigate the cube and get data aggregated across virtually any set of dimensions.

Reporting from a UDM-based SSAS installation is easy through SQL Server Reporting Services, either through report builder or with deployed reports; you can also get to this data in Excel through PowerPivot.

The BI Semantic Model (BISM)

UDM's cube is a bit heavy; it's a serious undertaking to build a cube, and it's important to do plenty of research first. BISM offers a different model, one that can be built from source tables and refreshed easily. BISM (or at least the Vertipaq engine that drives it) was really introduced under the hood with PowerPivot for SQL Server 2008, but has been updated and made more capable in SQL Server 2012.

When your analysis services installation uses tabular mode, it's configured to use BISM and Vertipaq; you can query it using MDX if you like, or you can use DAX. DAX is a query language based on Microsoft Excel formulas (there's that PowerPivot ancestry showing through), so tools that know either language can query the database. Using the Vertipaq engine, a BISM-based analysis services database scales up to billions of rows on the right hardware, although UDM is still the king of larger data sources.

As a rule of thumb, BISM is a good choice for:

➤ Rapid development

➤ End-user access

➤ Small to moderate data scope

➤ SharePoint and Excel-based access

➤ ROLAP (Relational OLAP) models with more normalization and snowflake dimensions

Whereas UDM is a better choice for:

➤ Complex models

➤ Large-scale implementations

➤ MOLAP (Multidimensional OLAP...get that star schema perfected)

In Chapter 19, when you get more deeply into Reporting Services than you will in this chapter, you'll get a chance to work with a BISM-based model. For now, since you're not going to get another crack at it, the examples will stick with the more BI-centric UDM. Besides...once you've been exposed to building a cube, you'll have a great appreciation for the simplicity of the tabular model.

BUILDING YOUR FIRST CUBE

You can get a feel for what it takes to use SSAS by building a cube based on the AdventureWorks data warehouse. Once you've had a chance to poke around there, you can take a look at some of the other ways of providing BI reporting.

> **NOTE** *For this example, you'll be working within the SQL Server Data Tools, or SSDT. Note that SSDT is entirely different from the SQL Server Management Studio that you've been mostly working with thus far. The SQL Server Data Tools is a different work area that is highly developer- (rather than administrator-) focused; indeed, it is a form of Visual Studio that just has project templates oriented around many of the "extra" services that SQL Server offers. In addition to the work you'll do with SSDT in this chapter, you will also visit it some to work with Reporting Services, Integration Services, and more Analysis Services in the chapters ahead.*

TRY IT OUT **Creating an SSAS Project in SSDT**

This is one of the most advanced examples in the book, so get ready for some fun. You'll build a cube in SSAS, which gives you high-speed multidimensional analysis capability. This one will use UDM, but you'll get a chance to use BISM in a little bit. Building your cube will require several steps: You'll need to build a data source, a data source view, some dimensions, and some measures before your cube can be realized.

Start a New Project

To build an SSAS cube, you must first start a project by following these steps:

1. Open the SQL Server Data Tools and create a new project.

2. In the New Project dialog box under Installed Templates on the left, choose Business Intelligence ⇨ Analysis Services.

3. In the main pane, select Analysis Services Multidimensional and Data Mining Project, as you can see in Figure 18-2.

4. Name your project **FirstCube** and click OK.

FIGURE 18-2

You're now presented with an empty window, which seems like a rare beginning to a project with a template; really, you have nothing to start with, so it's time to start creating. The first component you'll need is somewhere to retrieve data from: a data source.

Building a Data Source

To create the data source you'll use for your first cube, follow these steps:

1. Navigate to the Solution Explorer pane on the right, right-click Data Sources, and click New Data Source. This will bring up the Data Source Wizard, which will walk you through the creation process just as you'd expect.

2. Before you skip by the opening screen as you usually would, though, take note of what it says (just this once...you can skip it later). I won't re-type it here, but it's giving you a heads-up about the next component you'll create: the data source view.

3. Meanwhile, go ahead and click Next to continue creating your data source. In this next screen, it's time to set up a connection string.

4. If your AdventureWorksDW database is visible as a selection already, go ahead and choose it; if not, click New.

5. For your server name, enter (local), and then drop down the box labeled Select or Enter a Database Name and choose AdventureWorksDW.

6. Click OK to return to the wizard and then click Next.

7. You can now enter the user you want SSAS to impersonate when it connects to this data source. Select Use the Service Account and click Next. Using the service account (the account that runs the SQL Server Analysis Server service) is fairly common even in production, but make sure that service account has privileges to read your data source.

8. For your data source name, type **AdventureWorksDW** and then click Finish.

Building a Data Source View

Now that you've created a data source, you'll need a data source view (as the Data Source Wizard suggested). Follow these steps:

1. Right-click Data Source Views and choose New Data Source View. Predictably, up comes the Data Source View Wizard to walk you through the process. Click Next.

2. Make sure the AdventureWorksDW data source is selected and then click Next.

3. On the Select Tables and Views screen, choose FactInternetSales under Available objects and then click the right arrow to move it into the Included Objects column on the right.

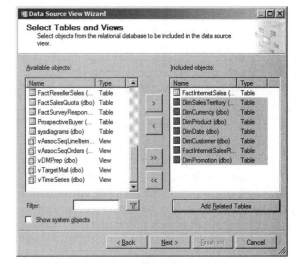

FIGURE 18-3

4. To add its related dimensions, click the Add Related Tables button as shown in Figure 18-3 and then click Next. Note that one of the related tables is a fact, not a dimension. There's no distinction made at this level. Later, you will be able to select and edit dimensions individually.

5. On the last screen, name your data source view according to its contents: **Internet Sales**.

6. Click Finish to create the Internet Sales data source view, and you'll see it in the content pane, looking something like Figure 18-4 (your exact layout may vary).

Creating Your First Cube

Now for the exciting part...you get to create your first cube.

1. Right-click Cubes in the Solution Explorer and select New Cube to bring up the Cube Wizard. This will walk you through choosing measure groups (which you currently know as fact tables), the measures within them, and your dimensions for this cube. Don't worry about the word "cube" here and think you just have to stick with three dimensions, either; cube is just a metaphor, and you can create a four-dimensional hypercube, a tesseract, or an unnamed higher-dimensional object if you want (and you're about to do so!). To begin, click Next.

2. On the Select Creation Method screen, make sure Use Existing Tables is selected, and click Next.

3. The wizard will now want you to tell it where to find measure groups. You could help it out by telling it those are in your fact tables, but never mind — it's smart enough to figure it out. If you click Suggest, it will automatically select the correct tables. Do so (the result is shown in Figure 18-5) and then click Next.

4. Now the wizard would like to know which measures from your measure groups (fact

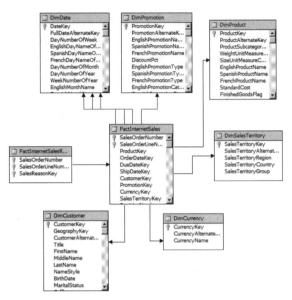

FIGURE 18-4

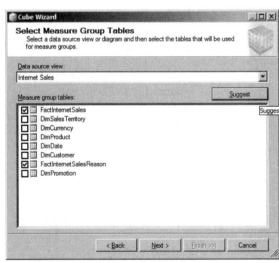

FIGURE 18-5

tables) you'd like to store in the cube. By default it's got them all selected; go ahead and accept this by clicking Next.

5. At this point, you have measures, but you still need dimensions; the wizard will select the dimension tables from your data source view and invite you to create them as new dimensions in the UDM. Again, by default they're all selected, and you can click Next.

6. The wizard is now ready to complete. Verify you have something that looks like Figure 18-6, and go back to make corrections if you need. If everything appears to be in order, click Finish.

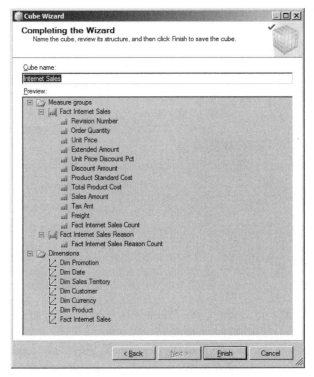

FIGURE 18-6

Making Your Cube User-Friendly

Right about now, you're probably expecting something like "congratulations, you're done!" After all, you've built up the connection, designated the measures and dimensions, and defined your cube, so it would be nifty if you could just start browsing it, but you're not quite there yet. First you'll want to make some of your dimensions a little more friendly; they're currently just defined by their keys because SSAS doesn't know which fields in your dimension tables to use as labels. Once you've settled that, you'll need to deploy and process your cube for the first time before it's ready to use.

1. In the Solution Explorer under Dimensions, double-click DimDate. The Dimension Editor will come up, allowing you to make this dimension a bit more useable.

2. To make the date attributes available, highlight all of them (except DateKey, which as you can see is already in the attribute list) and drag them to the attribute list.

3. Date, of course, is a dimension that can be naturally defined as a hierarchy (like you did quite manually in the T-SQL grouping examples). Drag Fiscal Quarter from the Attributes pane to the Hierarchies pane to start creating a hierarchy.

4. Drag Month Number of Year to the `<new level>` tag under Fiscal Quarter, and DateKey similarly below that.

5. Finally, rename the hierarchy (right-click it and choose Rename) to **Fiscal Quarter - Month**. The result should look something like Figure 18-7.

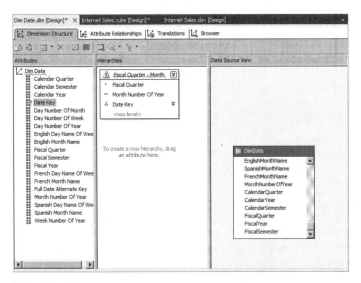

FIGURE 18-7

6. Save the DimDate dimension and close the dimension editor. You will be prompted to save changes to your cube along with the new dimension changes; do so.

7. For each of the other dimensions, don't create hierarchies for now, but bring all the interesting text columns into the Attributes pane (you can bring over all the non-key columns except for the Large Photo column in the Products table), and re-save the dimensions.

Deploying the Cube

There's more you can do to create useful hierarchies, but for now it's time to build, deploy, and process the cube. This process can be started by following these steps.

1. Select Deploy First Cube on the Build menu. You'll see a series of status messages as the cube is built, deployed, and processed for the first time. You'll receive a few warnings when you deploy FirstCube, and if they're warnings and not errors, you can safely ignore them for now.

2. When it's done and you see Deployment Completed Successfully in the lower right, your first cube is ready to browse.

 NOTE *When you set up a user in your data source view, you chose the service user — this is the user that's running the Analysis Services service. If that user doesn't have a login to your SQL Server, you're going to receive an error when you try to process your cube.*

In addition, this example bypasses a step that's important for processing hierarchies in cubes with large amounts of data: creating attribute relationships. The cube will still successfully process (though you will receive a warning), and for the data volumes in the AdventureWorksDW database it will perform adequately. For larger data volumes, you will need to address this warning. For more information on how to do that, consult the more complete SSAS text.

3. In the Solution Explorer pane, double-click the Internet Sales cube and then look in the tabs above the main editing pane for the Browser tab and click that.

4. Now you can drag and drop your measures (such as ExtendedAmount) and your dimensions and hierarchies (look for the Fiscal Quarter - Month hierarchy under the Due Date dimension) into the query pane, and voilà — your data is sliced and diced as quickly as you please.

How It Works

Whew! That was a lot of setup, but the payoff is pretty good too. What you've done is to build your first cube, and under the hood you've created a UDM-based semantic model queryable through the MDX language. This cube isn't fully complete — you'd probably want to add some aggregations, attribute relationships, and other elements, but it's an impressive start.

It started when you chose your project type. The Multidimensional project types build the UDM-based data models, whereas the Tabular Project types build your model in BISM. Because I plan to bring you through PowerPivot shortly (which is BISM-based), I led you down the UDM route here. You'll find that for basic operations the two are equally capable.

Once you had your project put together, you had a few components to create on the way to browsing your cube. Let's call a few out.

➤ **Data source:** Your data source is a connection to an individual place where data for your BI reporting can be found. While this one was a SQL Server data source, you can use any number of providers, both included and third-party. Nothing here should surprise you too much; this is a similar kind of list to what you'd find in SSIS, for example.

➤ **Data source views:** A data source view is a much more interesting animal. Using a data source, the data source view contains a set of tables or views, and defines the relationships among them. Each DSV is usually built around a business topic, and contains any tables related to that topic.

➤ **Cubes:** While the next thing you proceeded to create was a cube, the Cube Wizard went ahead and built measure groups and dimensions for you along the way. Without those, you haven't got much of a cube. The cube isn't a pass-through directly to your source data. To update the data in the cube, you must process the cube; you can do this through a regularly scheduled job with SQL Agent or, of course, manually. In this case, the wizard took care of a lot of the details for you, but you'll read more about what the cube really is in a few minutes.

Data Sources

Each cube you create must have at least one data source — otherwise it would be empty, and that's not very useful for report delivery. As it drives every decision from the start, this is the first thing you're going to create.

A *data source* is a location where you're going to retrieve some data. That means it identifies a SQL Server, for example, or maybe a text file. There are many types of data sources that SSAS has out of the box, including these (among others):

➤ SQL Server Native Client

➤ OLE DB Provider for Microsoft Directory Services

➤ Microsoft OLE DB Provider for Oracle

➤ Microsoft OLE DB Provider for Indexing Service

➤ Microsoft OLE DB Provider for Analysis Services

➤ Microsoft Office 12.0 Access Database Engine OLE DB Provider

While a data source describes where some of your data will come from, it does not describe which data will be retrieved from that location. The data source simply encapsulates the connection information, including server (and possibly database) identification and security, but it doesn't contain a field list, stored procedure call, or query. That's the job of the data source view, which you'll see next.

Having identified a connector type and a server, the data source wizard will inquire who, during a regular processing run, should be accessing this data source. You'll need to identify a user to impersonate when connecting (you don't necessarily want to connect as the user who's trying to refresh the cube, as that user may not have direct access rights to the database) and the transaction isolation level to use while reading. If you're a bit fuzzy on transaction isolation levels, take a quick gander back at Chapter 14 for a refresher.

While a cube must have at least one data source, it's not limited to only one. Part of the nifty power of a cube is that it can synthesize data from different sources if only that data is mapped together in some kind of model...which is what you're doing here. As long as the data in your different data sources is related, go ahead and tie in whatever sources are appropriate. That said, take it with a warning: Correlating data from within even a single data source can sometimes be a problem...before you start crossing data from multiple sources, do your homework and be sure everything's going to be fully compatible (or at least make a plan for what will happen when it's not).

Data Source Views

Of all the components of a cube, this may be the one that's most easy to grasp, because it falls squarely within the realm of the straight-up transactional data modeling and queries you've been practicing for more than a dozen chapters by now. The data source view defines the entities you're going to have available to your cube from your data source(s), what the relationships are between them, and how they're going to look to the user. You can think of it as a view, just like you've written, only instead of defining just a single table or query it's a view of the whole database...or at least that part of it you want to expose to the cube.

Into a data source view you can drop tables, which can be from a transactional database or a dimensional model. As you add them, noting of course that you may be adding things from various sources, feel free to provide a friendly name (easily accessible in the properties) to your tables or even your columns in order to make things a little more consistent between sources or just nicer to the end user.

You can also add *named queries* to the DSV, which is so much like creating a view in ordinary T-SQL that it makes no sense to call it anything different.

Just as in the SQL Server Management Studio interface, you can create more than one database diagram here. Each is still part of this data source view, and what's available to your cube is the sum of all the available diagrams. If it makes things easier, though, you can separate groups of tables into different diagram panes. The thing to remember is that each DSV should encapsulate one business area, so if you find yourself creating more than a couple diagrams, it's worth stepping back and examining your strategy a bit. If you have so many disparate topics mashed together, it might be useful to split into multiple DSVs.

Cubes

Within this Analysis Services model, the whole reason to create data sources and data source views is to power a cube.

The cube is described with a geometric word, which is a reasonable way to get your head around it. As I mentioned earlier, your cube isn't limited to the normal three-dimensional world, but if you cast it that way in your mind you'll have an easier time coming to grips — I know I go completely barmy when I try to imagine what a four-dimensional hypercube is shaped like. Nevertheless, each dimension you create — date, product, promotion — is one dimension on your cube. Where they meet, there you'll find the measures stored that match that combination of dimensions.

The cube aggregates all the available measures — a measure group — that relate to a set of dimensions, and it does so across every possible combination of dimensions. That means the cube is storing a great deal of redundant data, but retrieving any individual value is very fast. Because all the combinations are explicitly stored, it's the work of a moment for Analysis Services to slice data across any dimensions you choose and quickly provide your measure values.

All that aggregation has a cost, of course. Think of it a bit like an index. When you create an index on a table, you pay up-front creation cost to initially populate the index, and you have ongoing transaction costs related to maintenance whenever data changes. In return, you get a lot of fast, cheap data retrieval.

The difference between a cube and an ordinary index, with respect to this analogy, is in the maintenance schedule. Once you've defined your cube, the cube must be *processed* before it contains anything. The cube definition — what you build in SSDT — is a bit like the `CREATE INDEX` statement, but it differs in that it doesn't do the initial data population; that only happens when you process the cube. Likewise, when your source data is updated, the cube remains static until you process your data again instead of updating in real time like an index would.

The cube definition has a lot of elements that I'm going to defer to a more complete text; here, I'll cover dimensions and measure groups — the required elements — enough to get you started, but the rest of the cube's primary attributes are shown here just so you'll know what it's capable of.

Measure Groups

You may recall from the last chapter that a measure is some numeric data that, when manipulated in some way, can become a metric that tells you something useful about your business. You also read about fact tables, and how that's where you store measures. Because a typical fact table is a collection of measures, you can see why Analysis Services refers to a fact table as a measure group.

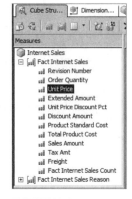

Measure groups, being the data that you're going to be reporting on, are the core of a cube structure. It shouldn't surprise you, then, to find them on the Cube Structure tab in your project. On that tab, you can add new measure groups, add new measures to an existing measure group, or edit the measures you already have. The measure groups and their measures are displayed in the Measures pane on the top left, and it should look something like Figure 18-8.

Measures are assumed to be additive by default (review Chapter 17 if you want a reminder about measure types). That means when you look at the measure across a group of dimensions, SSAS shows you the sum of the relevant values for that measure. That's not the only kind of aggregate you might want, though; some measures are best described by a count, a minimum or maximum value, or an average.

FIGURE 18-8

Try creating a measure for the average Order Quantity, which is a measure that exists in the `FactInternetSales` measure group:

1. Right-click the `FactInternetSales` measure group and select New Measure on the context menu. You'll see a list of measure columns from the table; choose Order Quantity.

2. From the Usage dropdown, select Average Over Time (your dialog box should look like Figure 18-9).

3. Click OK.

Once you've done this, you'll see a red squiggle — like a misspelled word — under the `FactInternetSales` measure group. This is telling you that you've created a time-based measure (which you have), but the cube doesn't know yet which dimension to view as time. You'll correct that in the next section.

FIGURE 18-9

You have a great deal of flexibility with your measures, and this is only the sampler plate. Feel free to experiment on your own, and if it looks like you need to take this further then it's time to get a book that specializes in SSAS.

Dimensions

Defining dimensions for your cube started out pretty easily; the wizard took care of the basics for you, providing a working cube with only your tables to go on. By looking at the schema you selected and detecting the star join that's represented there, the wizard was able to deduce which tables were facts (measure groups) and which were dimensions. Let's take it a little bit further now and see what you can do with the dimensions you have.

Changing Dimension Properties

Remember back in the last chapter when you read that dimensions are about categorizing your data? When you're looking at a dimension that's as simple as that, one that's just a straightforward category, that's going to look a lot like the dimensions that were created for you. However, there's so much more you can do.

The time dimension is a particularly useful one in virtually any cube, and it gets special treatment by many reporting tools (including Project Crescent, which you'll get a view of later in the chapter). This cube has a dimension that's got all kinds of date information, but it hasn't yet had that dimension set up to be the time dimension for the cube. Let's go ahead and do that now.

1. In the Cube Structure toolbar, click the leftmost icon to start the Add Business Intelligence Wizard.

2. After clicking past the splash screen, choose Define Dimension Intelligence from the wizard's main selection list and then click Next.

3. For your dimension of choice, choose Order Date — you can use that as the main time dimension for now, although you could easily choose others. In fact, feel free to do so once you're done with this; you can have more than one time dimension defined, and you can even do each one on a different hierarchy. For now, though, select Order Date.

4. Click Next.

5. If it's not already selected, in the next screen select Time for Dimension Type, and then you can choose which time attributes correspond to your existing dimensional attributes. For now, click Include on Year, Quarter, Month, and Date. For those selections, respectively, set the Dimension Attribute column to Calendar Year, Calendar Quarter, Month Number of Year, and Full Date Alternate Key, as shown in Figure 18-10.

6. Click Next to see a summary of the work to be done.

7. Click Finish to define the date dimension. Once this is done, the red squiggle for the `FactInternetSales` measure group should disappear, as you have a time dimension enabled.

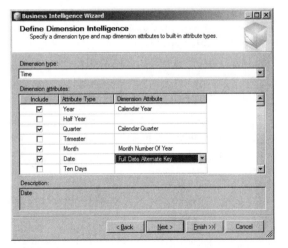

FIGURE 18-10

Hierarchies

Some dimensions naturally want to exist as a hierarchy. Time/date, geography, category-subcategory relationships...these are all ways you might want to drill through intermediate levels down to your details.

Given the denormalized nature of a data warehouse, hierarchies frequently are embedded within a single table rather than take up several as they might in an OLTP database. The geographic hierarchy of Group - Country - Region, for example, exists entirely within the `DimSalesTerritory` dimension. Time can form multiple hierarchies — such as year-month-day, year-quarter-month, year-week-day, or fiscal year - fiscal quarter - fiscal month — all from the data within `DimDate`. Although you may have only one date measure you base this on, you can report the date dimension based on any of these hierarchies.

The advantage of setting up a dimensional hierarchy (when one exists within your data and business rules) is that it allows you to easily categorize and drill down into your data. For example, if you set up a product category - subcategory - product hierarchy, it's easy to report at the category level and then break down the results into subcategories, and finally into individual products. Creating hierarchies is among the first things you'll want to do when you create a new cube.

The Rest of the Cube

Once you have your dimensions and measure groups in place, you have a cube, but there's always more you can do. The following represent advanced topics well beyond the scope of this book, but they're worth introducing so you'll know what to read about later if you need to go beyond the basics.

➤ **Calculations:** The cube's equivalent of computed columns or subqueries. Using MDX, these can be quite intricately defined. You can define a new measure based on existing measures, or compute a *named set*, which is a multidimensional data array that can be used in other calculations.

➤ **KPIs:** Also known as key performance indicators, these provide a quick stratified scale that you can display graphically to see whether a measure is in an acceptable range of values. KPIs require goals to measure against, which can be defined within the KPI structure.

➤ **Actions:** You can add these to the cube, allowing you to perform reporting, drill-through, or user-definable actions that are context-sensitive.

➤ **Partitions:** Let you split your cube's storage based on values within the cube.

➤ **Aggregations:** These are a bit like indexes in a relational model; they define specific aggregates that should be computed and stored in the cube during cube processing for quick access later.

➤ **Perspectives:** These can provide different views of your cube, limiting each to a topical area. By giving users a more limited view than the whole of your dataset, you can make things simpler and enforce security as well.

➤ **Translations:** These are exactly what they sound like: You can name your cube elements in various languages, so that the same numbers can be comprehensible to international users.

Cubes are an enormously powerful tool, and if you need to build one you'll now have some idea what you're after.

SELF-SERVICE BI: USER TOOLS

Preparing a cube, a set of reporting views, or an SSAS Tabular Model only gets you part of the way to BI. Those steps build up a data source that's intuitive, which is critical, but once that data source exists it has to be read. Your users need tools they can easily understand that can attach to the data sources you've created so that they can visualize the data, turning the raw numbers into real intelligence.

In the past, BI reporting has largely been handled through enterprise reporting tools such as SQL Server Reporting Services. A common case is for business users or analysts to design a set of reports and ask the developers to create them; the developers then do their best to generate the reports as requested, the business users refine their requirements based on what they receive, and the cycle of software development continues.

Tools they need and tools they shall have, but not everything is included in the box. SQL Server 2012 not only provides a very full-featured reporting tool in SQL Server Reporting Services — which you'll get to dive more deeply into in a couple chapters — but also interacts with both Microsoft Excel and SharePoint to deliver reporting and data manipulation in places where users may not even know they're hitting SQL Server.

Report Builder

SQL Server Reporting Services includes Report Builder 3.0 as a user-oriented tool for creating custom, ad hoc reports. While this is, again, a topic for the next chapter, for now it's a baseline to use when looking at the other reporting tools available.

Report Builder is a full-featured reporting tool, capable of everything you could do with Reporting Services in SSDT. That doesn't mean that a user has to be a full-fledged developer to use it, though. As soon as you point Report Builder to a report model rather than a lower-level data source, a simpler set of interface tools takes over that's designed to be usable by a business user rather than a software engineer.

While it can still be a bit overwhelming to a rank amateur, Report Builder has one huge advantage over the remaining tools you'll read about next: It comes with SQL Server. Report Builder is right there when you do your installation; it doesn't need SharePoint (although it can integrate if you have a SharePoint server), it doesn't need Office (although it can output to Word or Excel), it can simply live on its own within the reporting components you can install out of the box. Because it's fully a part of SQL Server, you'll get much more exposure to Report Builder in this book, but not just yet. It's covered in much more detail in Chapter 19, which focuses on Reporting Services.

PowerPivot: Lightweight BI with SharePoint and Excel

The cycle of software development is something that you might want to steer away from with BI. Surprising as it may seem, that whole "requirements-implementation-requirements evolve-repeat" pattern can be viewed as a distraction rather than a goal by people who actually want the data you've collected so they can make decisions. The trouble is that, until recently, it's been difficult to provide truly user-friendly tools that can obviate the role of the developer in the process. Reporting, it turns out, is pretty complicated, and users are intimidated by tools like Report Builder.

What users aren't intimidated by is Excel. It's one of the most commonly used data analysis tools in any office, and business analysts are, largely, comfortable with it. Its use in BI until recently has been largely confined to exports from other data sources. Excel just hasn't had the capability to deal with very large datasets, so it's been limited to dealing with small data summaries. Enter PowerPivot for Excel, giving massive data manipulation to the masses.

 NOTE *PowerPivot was made available for SQL Server 2008 R2 and Excel 2010 as a free download, and has been enhanced for SQL 2012.*

Let's start with the basics, like what exactly PowerPivot is and what it can do. PowerPivot uses the Vertipaq engine — the same one behind SSAS's tabular format and SQL Server's columnstore indexing — to do fast aggregation and analysis of large datasets within an Excel spreadsheet. By working within Excel, all the familiar Excel analysis tools are available including PivotTables, charts, graphs, and the like. What's more, PowerPivot expands the amount of data that Excel can store — up to 2GB on disk, and 4GB in memory (the disk storage is highly compressed, so 2GB on disk could be much more than 4GB worth of in-memory data).

To work with PowerPivot, first you need to install PowerPivot for Excel or PowerPivot for SharePoint. Creating a model can be done either directly through the interface in Excel or by building a tabular model with SQL Server Analysis Services; either way you'll produce a BI Semantic Model (BISM) that can be used to load data from your data source.

When you load data into a PowerPivot worksheet, it stays loaded. That means that, while the data may be sourced from any number of places including SQL Server, Excel, or other data providers, once you've loaded that data into your PowerPivot sheet it's in there to share. You can pass the sheet around and everyone, even those without access to the original data source, can see the data and create new charts or PivotTables. Those with access can refresh the data, and security can be defined at the entity level...which is to say, you can limit who can see which tables.

Sharing is nice...you can even share your PowerPivot documents on SharePoint. SharePoint and PowerPivot are fully integrated, so you can put your PowerPivot-based analysis on your SharePoint site for everyone (or everyone with rights, anyway) to see, update, and collaborate. To interact fully with PowerPivot for SharePoint requires that you install PowerPivot components within SharePoint; you'll want to fob that off on your SharePoint administrator.

PowerPivot and Analysis Services

You can load data directly into PowerPivot from your native data sources, but if you're planning a larger-scale self-service BI initiative including Report Builder, you may already be creating data models in SSAS. PowerPivot can easily ride on either a tabular or a multidimensional-based model, since all the tables, relationships, hierarchies, KPIs, and other BI elements will already be embedded in the model. In fact, a PowerPivot sheet created natively in Excel without the help of SSAS contains a tabular model as part of its nature, which can be imported as an SSAS tabular project in SSDT. By sharing such a model on SharePoint, you can access it through PowerPivot, Power View, and Report Builder; because all those will be using exactly the same model as a BI data source, the data across reports in all those platforms will agree.

DAX in PowerPivot

PowerPivot uses the DAX language under the hood to query and even define its data models. DAX is a language based on Excel formulae, and has been enhanced for SQL 2012 with new features. You don't have to know DAX to use PowerPivot; you can get a fair amount done through the UI without ever writing code, but when it comes time to create computed columns or KPIs you're going to want to start writing code.

The advantage of the tabular model here over multidimensional is a very different learning curve. Cubes are queried using MDX, which is a difficult language to learn, in much the same way that linear algebra and differential equations are kind of challenging math topics. DAX, on the other hand, has a fairly short learning curve. If you're trying to get quick results, you'll have a lot easier time picking up DAX and tabular models than you ever will with cubes and multidimensional.

Viewing SQL Server Data in PowerPivot for Excel

One of the reasons PowerPivot can process large datasets with such speed is that it works in memory. The data in the columnstore is highly compressed, and by working entirely within your main memory, PowerPivot can do remarkably fast processing on the dataset. However, that dataset is a snapshot that has to be refreshed from the source data from time to time, which isn't always ideal. If you want to keep things current, it's possible to build a tabular model that uses a pass-through to SQL Server to get your data directly when you query. Pass-through mode is available only when your data source is a single SQL Server data source, though.

 NOTE *Because PowerPivot isn't a purely SQL Server technology (it requires either Excel or SharePoint to function), I'm not going to cover it in further detail here. If you want to delve deeper into the world of PowerPivot for self-service BI, read a book like* Professional Microsoft PowerPivot for Excel and SharePoint *by Sivakumar Harinath et al. If your user base wants to do desktop, self-service BI but isn't sophisticated enough for Report Builder, this is a direction you'll want to explore.*

Power View

Consider the different users in your company who may want to use ad hoc BI. Report Builder covers the power users who want to build highly detailed reports, so you have them taken care of. PowerPivot is a great option for Excel-like data analysis, which empowers the less technical users who want to build PivotTables and charts from the raw data — think of them as the Excel set. There's a third option, Power View, which is designed for people who are less into Excel and more into PowerPoint.

Power View is a visual, point-and-click application for end-user reporting from a BISM-based model on SharePoint. SharePoint and SQL Server are both integral parts of Power View, and for that reason you're just getting an introduction and not a full course, but again you ought to know what it's like so you can decide whether you need to learn it.

What Power View does is report and render in real time. As you add data elements to your page (using an interface not entirely dissimilar to an Excel PivotTable), the data is displayed immediately. You can add many list or chart elements on each page, and when you use filters and slicers against any one, they apply to all — which keeps everything you see relevant to everything else. Clicking to highlight a slice of data, similarly, highlights that data in all related elements.

Power View can do dazzling things with only a few clicks, and the results are easy to share. You can either store your reports in SharePoint (where you have to be to create them anyway), or output them to PowerPoint to take them on the road. What's more, a PowerPoint file created by Power View can be just as interactive as it originally was if you're connected to your SharePoint server.

SUMMARY

Once you've started storing data, it's important to get at it. Sometimes it's enough just to query your transactional database, but the amount of data collected these days has led to more specialized structures and new tools for fast retrieval. SQL Server 2012 adds myriad new features designed to give fast, easy access to the data in your databases, whether they're transactional systems or data warehouses.

You can query your database using T-SQL, as you've done this whole book so far, and there are many kinds of analysis possible — even more than what's been presented here. Probably the most significant new feature is the columnstore index, which can return data orders of magnitude faster than traditional indexes in some circumstances; however, simply organizing a data warehouse and running analysis functions like GROUPING SETS against a star join can return very useful data fast.

SQL Server Analysis Services is a powerful tool for building analytical models to help you slice your data against a variety of dimensions. SSAS can operate in multidimensional (the way it always has) or tabular mode. SSAS tabular models can be made against either an OLAP or an OLTP database, and will be covered more in Chapter 19. Multidimensional models are really driven by OLAP databases, and allow you to build cubes for fast access to aggregated data.

There are three self-service BI tools that come with SQL Server, although two of them also require integration with other Microsoft technologies to work. Report Builder stands on its own, and is designed for advanced users to build ad hoc reports (this is another tool you'll use in the next chapter). PowerPivot combines the power of a tabular model with the simplicity of Excel to do quick, fast analysis even on fairly large datasets. Power View is a graphical reporting tool that allows users to easily build tables, charts, and graphs in an interactive fashion, and is designed even for novice data analysts to use.

With all the emphasis on getting the most from your business data, the focus on BI technologies in SQL Server isn't likely to diminish soon. You've only had the sampler plate after this book; now you'll know which ones you want to learn more about.

1. Write a query that retrieves sales amounts from `FactInternetSales` in the AdventureWorksDW database and returns those amounts organized by month and showing a three-month rolling average.

2. Which ad hoc reporting tool would probably be best for an executive trying to create a quick PowerPoint presentation? A mid-level business analyst?

3. (Bonus) Install PowerPivot for Excel, and import the data from your cube. Create a pivot table and observe how the slicers operate.

▶ WHAT YOU LEARNED IN THIS CHAPTER

TOPIC	CONCEPT
PIVOT and UNPIVOT	These T-SQL commands turn rows into columns and columns into rows, respectively.
ROLLUP, CUBE, and GROUPING SETS	Using these analysis functions, you can produce aggregations across virtually any combination of permutations of your dimensions.
Columnstore indexes	Columnstores can produce blindingly fast queries, especially when used in a star join scenario. However, they do not currently support updates, so when updating data the columnstore must be dropped and rebuilt.
UDM versus BISM	SQL Server Analysis Services can work in multidimensional mode, building cubes stored with the Unified Dimensional Model format, or it can work in tabular mode, storing tabular models as a BI Semantic Model. One instance of SSAS can work in only one mode, but you can install multiple instances of it.
The cube	A multidimensional structure storing data aggregated across virtually every combination of dimensions, the cube allows exceptional query performance in BI scenarios. Data is refreshed whenever the cube is processed.
Report Builder	A reporting tool geared toward power users. You'll learn more about this tool in Chapter 19.
PowerPivot	Running within Excel or SharePoint, PowerPivot can leverage the Vertipaq engine (which powers columnstore indexes and SSAS tabular models) to perform high-speed desktop data analysis.
Power View	Another end-user BI analysis tool, Power View produces beautiful, interactive reports quickly and easily from a BI Semantic Model. Power View requires SharePoint to function.

19

Reporting for Duty, Sir! A Look at Reporting Services

WHAT YOU WILL LEARN IN THIS CHAPTER:

➤ Which components of SQL Server exist to deliver reports

➤ The lifecycle of a report

➤ How to use Analysis Services with Reporting Services to deliver ad hoc reports

➤ How to use SSDT to create a report server project

➤ How to deploy reports to the report server

After all the queries have been written, after all the stored procedures have been run, there remains a rather important thing you need to do in order to make your data useful — make it available to end users.

Reporting is one of those things that seems incredibly simple, but turns out to be rather tricky. You see, you can't simply start sticking numbers in front of people's faces; the numbers must make sense and, if at all possible, capture the attention of the person for whom you're reporting. To produce reports that actually get used and, therefore, are useful, there are two things to keep in mind:

➤ **Use just the right amount of data:** You should not try to do too much in one report; nor should you do too little. A report that is a jumble of numbers is going to quickly lose a reader's attention, and you'll find that it isn't used after the first few times it is generated. Likewise, a barren report will get just a glance and get tossed without any real thought. Find a balance that makes each report both complete and concise.

➤ **Make it appealing:** Another important element in reporting is making it look nice and pleasing to the eye — something many developers just don't have a knack for, sad as it is to say. An ugly report is a dead report, so this is a skill you'll have to learn.

In this chapter, you're going to be taking a look at the Reporting Services tools that first appeared as a downloadable web add-on in SQL Server 2000, and became a core part of the product in SQL Server 2005. As this functionality has become of greater importance than ever, the coverage here has grown appropriately; still, there is simply too much to cover to get it all in one chapter of a much larger book. If you find that this "taste" whets your appetite, I recommend reading a book dedicated specifically to Reporting Services such as *Professional SQL Server 2012 Reporting Services* by Paul Turley.

REPORTING SERVICES 101

Odds are that you've already generated some reports in your day. They may have been paper reports off a printer (perhaps in something as rudimentary as Access's reporting area — which is, to me, actually one of the best parts of Access). They may have been off a rather robust reporting engine such as Crystal Reports. Even if you haven't used tools that fancy, you've run stored procedures as part of the exercises in this book, and one can argue that those are essentially very simple (and not necessarily nice-looking) reports — I would tend to agree with that argument. If anyone ever asked you for the data from your database, that was a request for a report.

The reality, however, is that managers and coworkers today expect something more. This is where Reporting Services comes in. Reporting Services really has two varieties of operation:

➤ **Reports generated in SQL Server Data Tools:** Even though SSDT looks like a full-fledged IDE (Integrated Development Environment), this doesn't necessarily mean you have to write code. You can actually create simple reports using drag-and-drop functionality — something you'll do in this chapter as an example or you can design fairly robust reports.

➤ **Reports generated from BI Semantic Models:** This is making use of a relatively simple, web-driven interface that is meant to allow end users to create their own simple reports. Creating the models relies on SQL Server Analysis Services, which you read about in Chapter 18, but what you do in this chapter is different. While I hope you read that chapter, it's not required for what you'll learn here.

Note that while your users can eventually access these reports from the same Reporting Services web host, they are based on somewhat different architectures (and, as you will see, are created in much different fashions).

REPORTING SERVICES AND ANALYSIS SERVICES

In prior versions of SQL Server, report models were a product of Reporting Services; you'd create those using a report model project in SSDT, and then deploy them to the report server for end users to build reports against in Report Builder. Starting with SQL Server 2012 and the introduction of the BI Semantic Model (BISM), the report models have been absorbed into SQL Server Analysis Services, which makes for much tighter integration between the two components. Be ready to switch context between SSRS and SSAS at a moment's notice in this chapter.

In addition, Reporting Services provides features for pre-generating reports (handy if the queries that underlie the report take a while to run), as well as distributing the report via e-mail.

UNDERSTANDING THE SSRS REPORT LIFECYCLE

Your role as a developer within the SSRS space can lead you to places you wouldn't expect. Far from being limited to simply writing T-SQL to power your reports or creating layouts and drill-throughs, your job might involve some tasks that feel more administrative in nature. Even if you're not the one who has to deal with them, you should have some idea what sort of things your administrators might be called on to do, so here's an introduction to the lifecycle of a report in SSRS from a holistic perspective. First you need to develop reports (or report models, as you'll see), and then you need to organize and secure them, and finally you'll want to see those reports delivered to end users.

Developing Reports in SSRS

SSRS report development is a lot more than just queries and layout. Sure, those things are key, but what you can give to your users is more than just *RDL* (*Report Definition Language*) files. Each RDL needs at least one data source to draw from, and each data source needs a query or a stored procedure to run. As a report developer, you may find yourself creating tabular models (using SQL Server Analysis Services) as well. An SSAS *tabular model* is a defined set of tables or views with clear relationships, from which an end user can create useful ad hoc reporting. All these come under the broad heading of report development.

> **RDL FILES**
>
> *RDL* (*Report Definition Language*) is an XML-based format that constitutes the definition of an SSRS report. An RDL file describes layout, data mapping, and all the information the report server needs to fetch data and render the report.

Managing Your Reports

Sometimes you might be able to get away with just developing reports and then standing back and allowing others to handle the rest of the work. As you work through this chapter, though, you're going to see how reports are managed by the report server for two reasons:

➤ **Quite often this will be your responsibility, so it's best to know what it's all about.**

➤ **Unless you have an assistant helping you through the examples in this chapter, there's nobody else to do it for you.** You can't get much out of a report without trying out a deployment (although you can preview, of course), and a report model is next to useless until it's deployed. The data sources you create can also be shared, and deploying those to the server is how you'll learn to manage them. In short, this is required material even if you didn't expect to do much with it.

Deploying reports to the report server is only a part of management; like you might expect, security is a feature as well. After all, not every report should be available to every user.

Delivering Reports to Users

There is one more step in the lifecycle of a report beyond its creation and deployment. Remember, that thing you deploy — the model or RDL — doesn't actually show a user anything. You can think of an RDL as a template that tells SSRS where to get data and how to lay it out once it's been retrieved, but the RDL doesn't contain any data itself. Thus, the thing you've built and deployed is really an empty container waiting to be filled.

Running a report and making the completed output available to users is the last phase. Although I'm going to focus on manual report runs here, I'll give you at least an introduction to the idea of automating report runs — making them happen on a defined schedule, and then sending the results to a subscriber list. You can also cache reports on a schedule, so that long-running queries can happen during downtime and their reports can be presented quickly on demand later. Finally, SSRS reports can be viewed through different viewers depending on how they're rendered; you can send a rendered report to Word, Excel, PDF, or its native Report Viewer format. Once this last step is done, you can be sure your job is complete.

Once you've actually loaded an instance of a report with data, rendered it, and delivered the rendered output to a user, your report lifecycle is complete. Keep this lifecycle in mind as you read through this chapter, as you'll gain insight from it while you look at different options that are available while you're working.

UNDERSTANDING THE REPORTING SERVICES ARCHITECTURE

There are a lot of moving parts to a platform like SQL Server, and Reporting Services is not just one component, it's many. If you've done a complete Reporting Services installation, you'll find several components installed that are directly part of SSRS, and each is used in one or more aspects of the reporting lifecycle. When you're reading about each, try to think of how it's going to be used in terms of development, management, and delivery.

SSDT: Report Designer

Most of the components of Reporting Services deal with managing and delivering reports, but until you have reports to deliver or manage, Reporting Services is more or less useless. The part of SQL Server that will help you create reports and report models alike is the *SQL Server Data Tools* (*SSDT*). Like Integration Services, Reporting Services and Analysis Services development uses this lightweight version of the Visual Studio IDE to provide you with the tools and wizards that you need for development, as well as integration with source code control systems and other team development tools.

The product of your report development in SSDT will be SSRS reports stored as RDL files (for the most part...there are other file types you'll read about later). When you deploy an RDL file to the report server, it gets stored in the report server database for use by the rendering engine.

SSRS Windows Service

Speaking of the rendering engine, you'll find that the rendering engine in SSRS can be found running as a Windows service called SQL Server Reporting Services (unless you're in SharePoint integrated mode, in which case it's a SharePoint service). Reporting Services is responsible for more than just rendering, though; it's also the component that handles data processing, delivery, and security. Every time you attempt to interact with a report stored on the report server, you're actually asking the service whether you have access to the report, and if so to please fetch the data (as described by the datasets and data sources referenced in the RDL) and render the report according to the layout stored there.

For all practical purposes, this is the heart of Reporting Services.

Report Manager

The Report Manager is a browser-based tool that acts as the interface to all the reports, data sources, and other user-created elements on your report server. Report Manager is where you'll navigate to do the following:

➤ Upload objects to the report server

➤ View reports

➤ Create or edit reports with the Report Builder

➤ Browse or edit data sources

➤ Set up report-level security

Pretty much any time you want to interact with content you've created, you're doing that through the Report Manager. It's not for report server configuration, but for accessing your own objects.

Report Builder

In SQL Server 2012, there's a great emphasis not only on providing reports to your users, but also on giving them the tools to build their own reports. Report Builder is one such tool, but it's pretty powerful.

Report Builder works with RDL files, so it can edit any report, even one created in SSDT. That said, it's much more accessible than SSDT, which is (with its Visual Studio pedigree) very developer-oriented. A power user could take the reins with Report Builder and, given a good semantic model to work against (you'll create one later in the chapter), create powerful reports using wizards and visual editing tools.

Report Viewer

At some point, you'll want to look at the reports you or others have created. Yeah, I know, that's crazy talk, but I'm sticking with that assertion. The Report Viewer is a control available in Visual Studio that can display a report, and even perform the rendering if needed. It can run in either remote or local processing mode; remote lets the report service do the work, whereas local will perform the rendering in the control. Which you choose depends on your situation; for example, it might depend on how much data you're slinging around the network, or whether you have local code you want to use on your report that's not available to the report server.

BUILDING SIMPLE REPORT MODELS

Although this chapter introduces itself as a Reporting Services chapter, it needs to contain Analysis Services as well to provide a full tour. The shift from natively built report models in SSRS 2008 to SSAS-built BISM models in 2012 is a seismic shift, but it brings huge benefits in terms of allowing many types of reporting to be possible from your models. Because ad hoc reporting is an important part of many companies' reporting strategies, you can try outbuilding a report model first.

SQL SERVER ANALYSIS SERVICES INSTALLATION MODES

This book doesn't deal with installation much at all, and more to the point, there aren't very many places in this book where your installation choices matter. This is one time when it does matter. Do you know what happened when your copy of SQL Server was installed? Many beginners install using all defaults, which works pretty well most of the time. In fact, it works fine here...depending on what you want to do.

To proceed with the Report Builder example in this chapter, you need an instance of SQL Server Analysis Services installed in Tabular mode. If you accepted the defaults, you're in Multidimensional mode, and I'm afraid switching modes (particularly if you went through the cube-building example in Chapter 18) is problematic. Instead, you'll want to run the SQL Server installer, choose to "Perform a new installation of SQL Server 2012," and install just the Analysis Services feature. The key difference from the default is on the Analysis Services Configuration screen, where you must change the Server Mode choice from Multidimensional mode to Tabular mode.

To create a simple model, start by opening SQL Server Data Tools. As recently as the last version of SQL Server, you created a Report Model to build the view of your data you wanted to expose to the users. Not so in SQL Server 2012, where now you'll harness the full power of SQL Server Analysis Services to create a very full-featured and powerful report model using the Vertipaq engine (the same component that drives columnstore indexes).

Creating a Project

To create a project, follow these steps:

1. Choose File ➪ New Project to bring up the dialog box shown in Figure 19-1.

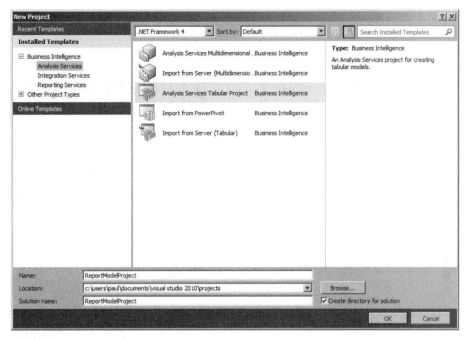

FIGURE 19-1

2. Select Analysis Services (under Business Intelligence) as the template type, and choose Analysis Services Tabular Project as your template, as shown.

3. Choose an appropriate name (I've gone with the rather descriptive **ReportModelProject**) and click OK. This brings you to what should look like an everyday, run-of-the-mill Visual Studio development environment.

 NOTE *Note that the exact appearance of the dialog box shown in Figure 19-1 may vary somewhat depending on whether you have Visual Studio installed and, if so, which specific languages and templates you've installed. The image is of the most generic SQL Server–only installation.*

Adding Data to Your Model

If your Visual Studio environment is still in its default configuration, you should see the Solution Explorer on the top-right side containing your empty BI Semantic Model, called Model.bim. What you need to do now is start adding entities to your model.

1. Right-click Model.bim and select Properties. Verify that the Workspace Server listed is your SSAS tabular mode instance. If it's not, you can set that now by typing it into the Workspace Server property in `servername\instancename` format.

2. On the Model menu, choose Import from Data Source, and you'll see the selection screen shown in Figure 19-2.

3. You're now in the Table Import Wizard, which leads you through selecting some data for your model. It probably won't surprise you that you're going to use Microsoft SQL Server for your data source; it should be selected by default.

4. Click Next to get to the start of the meaty stuff — the base configuration page of the wizard.

Although the concepts are the same as you've seen in a few other places in the book, there are one or two new things here, so let's take a look at several key elements to this dialog box:

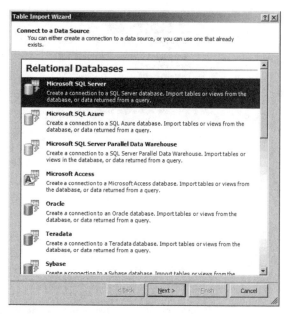

FIGURE 19-2

➤ **Friendly connection name:** This is the moniker you're going to apply to this connection going forward. It's nice to have something that describes the rest of the options, and you'll notice that the friendly connection name builds itself into something reasonably descriptive as you select the remaining options.

➤ **Server name:** This one is what it sounds like and is the same as you've seen before. Name the server you want to connect to for this connection, or, if you want to connect to the default instance of SQL Server for the local server, you can also use the aliases of local or . (a simple period). Notice that if you use the period, the friendly name above interprets that to mean localhost.

➤ **Windows/SQL Server authentication:** Choose the authentication type to connect to your server. Microsoft (and, I must admit, me too) would rather you used Windows authentication, but if your server is not in your domain or if your administrator is not granting rights directly to your Windows login, you can use an administrator-supplied SQL Server–specific username and password.

➤ **Connect to a database:** Here you can continue down the logical path of selecting a database on the server you have chosen.

5. In my case, I've selected the local server, Windows authentication, and our old friend the AdventureWorks database, as shown in Figure 19-3. Tabular models can be created easily against either normalized or dimensional databases; this example uses the OLTP version. If you're thorough — and I do encourage it — use Test Connection whenever you're on a dialog box like this to ensure you entered things correctly. Provided that works, click Next.

6. This brings up the Impersonation Information dialog box shown in Figure 19-4. Remember that in a tabular model, you're going to have to refresh data from the source system periodically. What you choose here defines who will appear to be doing that: either a specific user or the Analysis Services service user. As long as the SSAS user has access to your database, it's fine for you to use the service user for this example, but think about your business security model when doing this in real life. You're likely to have a specific user who has the minimal rights needed to do this operation, and you'll specify that user here.

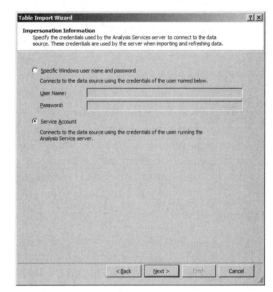

FIGURE 19-3   FIGURE 19-4

7. When you click Next from the Impersonation Information screen, you'll get a chance to decide how you'd like to grab data for this model. You can:

➤ Select from a list of tables and views to choose the data to import

➤ Write a query that will specify the data to import

8. I'd have a hard time justifying a query at this stage under any circumstances that I can imagine; if you want only part of a table, or the results of a more complex query, use a view. The sort of business logic you'd need to embed here shouldn't be hidden within a data source definition. Leave the default (a list of tables) and click Next to start choosing data to import.

9. Given your choice, the contents of the next dialog box in the Table Import Wizard probably shouldn't surprise you. You are asked to select from a list of tables and views, and Figure 19-5 shows just exactly that — a list of the tables and views in the AdventureWorks database.

10. Start by selecting `SalesOrderDetail` and notice that a friendly name — the same name, `SalesOrderDetail` — is assigned. Go ahead and insert spaces to make the name three words ("Sales Order Detail").

FRIENDLY NAMES

I've said throughout the book that objects need to be named so that the developer who follows you can understand what the name refers to. When building report models and other objects intended for consumption outside the developer space, that is, things for end users, the importance of this principle grows from "very important" to "profound."

---

11. Next, click the Select Related Tables button and see what happens. SQL Server will use the rules that it knows about the relationships between the tables (based on defined foreign keys) to figure out which tables are related to the one or more tables you have already selected. In this case, it chose `SalesOrderHeader` (the parent of your `SalesOrderDetail` table) and nothing else, so you'll need to add a couple more tables. Add the `Customer`, `Person`, and `Product` tables to finish your choices, and make sure you have friendly names specified, as shown in Figure 19-5.

12. Before you finish, highlight the Customer row as shown and click the Preview & Filter button. This gives you a chance to narrow the data you're going to import from the Customer

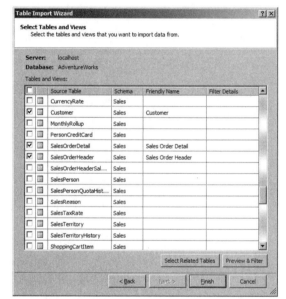

FIGURE 19-5

table. While I'd like to reiterate that using the filters you see here to perform business logic would be a bad idea, using them to skip unneeded columns is perfectly sound. For this model, deselect the `rowguid` and `ModifiedDate` columns as you see in Figure 19-6, and then click OK.

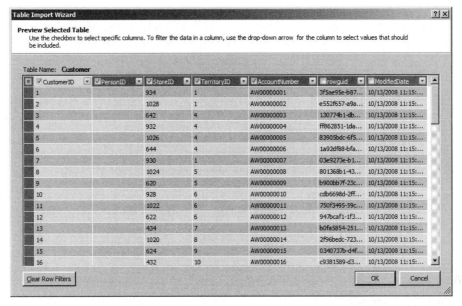

FIGURE 19-6

13. Go into the filters on the `Person` table as well and remove the following columns: `AdditionalContactInfo`, `Demographics`, `rowguid`, and `ModifiedDate`. Once you've applied your filters and returned to the Select Tables and Views dialog box, click Finish to complete the wizard.

When processing completes, you should see something very like Figure 19-7.

Did that surprise you? You may have thought you were doing purely schema work, describing a set of tables and preparing to define relationships and computations on them, and here SQL Server comes charging in and starts doing a data import. What gives?

The tabular model in SSAS is, as has been stated, based on the same Vertipaq engine that drives columnstore indexes and PowerPivot. Part of the speed of this engine is that it likes to work entirely in memory, and using the highly compressed columnstore format allows it to load a huge amount of data into a reasonably small memory footprint. Your data has been loaded from your source tables and placed into a set of in-memory columnstores, from which it can be read with blinding speed.

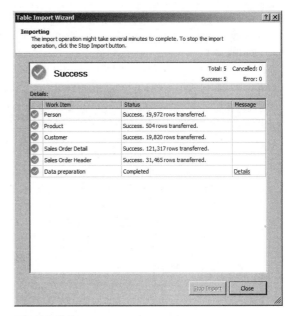

FIGURE 19-7

Close the import window, and you'll see your data on the screen, ready for the next steps. You have data in your SSAS tabular model now, and the model knows how to refresh it, so you can start adding relationships and computed measures that can be used in your reports.

The Model Designer

Now that you have a model, take a look around the designer before starting to modify it. By default you should be in Grid view, as shown in Figure 19-8. If by chance you see something more similar to Figure 19-9, you're in Diagram view.

Switching from Diagram view to Grid view is done via the pair of buttons in the bottom right; the one highlighted in Figure 19-8 selects Grid view, and the one in Figure 19-9 selects Diagram view.

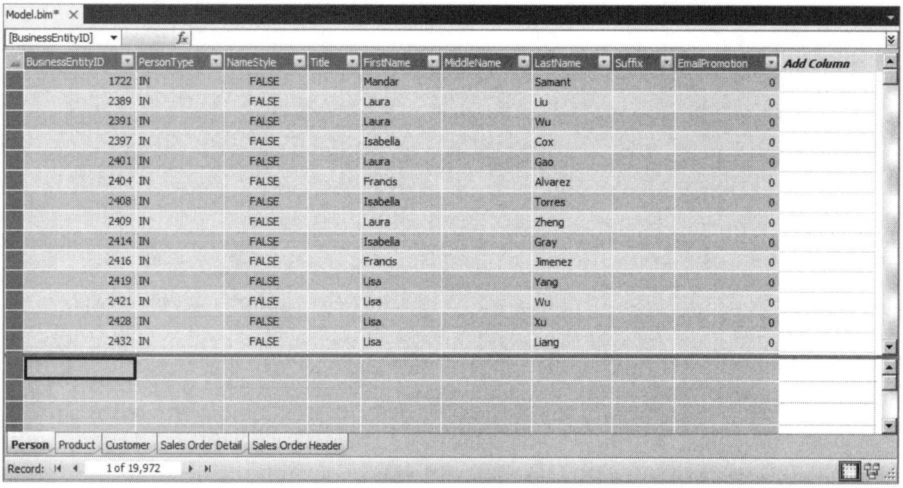

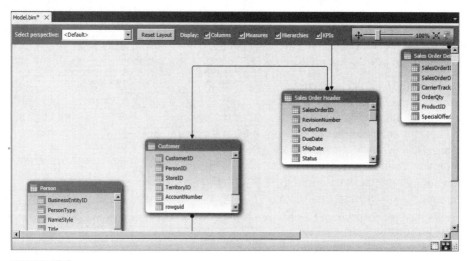

FIGURE 19-8

FIGURE 19-9

Grid View

In Grid view, you'll look at only one table at a time, and rather than a column list you can see the actual data in each of your tables. Grid view is where you can create some of those computations that you could optionally display in the Display section of Diagram view; it's where you define computed columns, measures, and KPIs. From top to bottom, here are the parts of the Grid view screen (refer back to Figure 19-8 to see the Grid view screen).

➤ **Function bar:** When you create or view any kind of computed measure, this is where the formula lives. If you've ever used Excel, this should be familiar; it works just like the Excel format bar. Formulae are entered using the *DAX* (*Data Analysis eXpressions*) language, inherited from PowerPivot for Excel and enhanced for SQL Server 2012.

➤ **Data grid:** This is your data, both what you imported and any computed columns you've defined.

  ➤ **Data columns:** Each column you imported is visible here. The dropdown menus at the top of each allow you to filter and sort each column. Each data type has a set of predefined filters. For example, while numbers can use things like equality or inequality, dates also have options like Last week, Between, or Year to date.

  ➤ **Add column:** To add a new computed column, highlight a cell in the Add Column column and type an equals sign (=) as if you were writing an Excel formula. Then complete the formula (in the formula bar) using DAX. You'll see a little of this later in the chapter.

➤ **Measure grid:** The measure grid is the (initially empty) set of cells directly beneath the data grid, and it is where you can create measures. Measures are computed values that represent aggregates. You can define these in the measure grid using DAX, or by shortcuts in the toolbar.

➤ **Table tabs:** You can see the data and measures from only one table at a time, but all your tables are on these tabs at the bottom of the window.

➤ **Row count:** Easily enough, this shows the number of rows in the currently filtered view of your table. You can see the row count underneath the table tabs.

Diagram View

Diagram view is all about manipulating tables and relationships. As you can see, it displays the tables you've imported in a format very like the one used in the diagrams you created back in Chapter 5. Each table is represented as a list of its fields and any additional table elements you've defined within the model. Relationship lines drawn between tables indicate where a foreign key relationship is defined.

You'll also notice right away that even with the few tables you've imported, there's just not enough real estate to show everything. To mitigate this, you can use the controls across the top of the window to help you filter what you see (refer back to Figure 19-9 to see the Diagram view screen).

➤ **Select perspective:** Lets you split the collection of tables you've imported into smaller sub-models that are more easily contained on the screen. Like the database diagrams you worked with before, each perspective should be made to apply to a single business area.

➤ **Reset layout:** Moves your tables into a simple shape, determined by the designer based on their relationships. This automated layout isn't always perfectly intuitive, so be prepared to do a little manual layout after you do it. Once you do this it can't be undone, so don't press this button once you've done a lot of layout work unless you really want to start fresh.

➤ **Display:** Shows four checkboxes, all checked by default, to choose what to show with each table.

➤ **Columns:** The original columns you imported, plus any computed columns you define within the model.

➤ **Measures:** Aggregates based on columns. You'll create a measure later in the chapter.

➤ **Hierarchies:** Defined on columns you want to drill into. They're very similar to the ones you defined in the last chapter when you were working on your cube.

➤ **KPIs:** Key Performance Indicators are measures with a goal range so that they can quickly display information about whether a goal is being reached. As KPIs are a bit of an advanced usage, you won't be learning to create a KPI in this book.

➤ **Zoom bar:** Use this to zoom in and out; allows you to quickly navigate around larger models. Although your models should generally be focused enough on a business area that you won't need to zoom much, some problems just take up a little more room. You'll see the zoom bar again in the next chapter when you look at the designer pane for developing SQL Server Integration Services packages.

Manipulating Relationships between Objects in Data Source Views

Although the wizard tries to put information together about the tables you've imported, it has to base its information on the column names, types, and foreign key references in the source database. Even though foreign keys are great for giving you a well-defined description of the relationship between two tables, there are relationships that don't have formal foreign keys defined on them. In the case of the semantic model you just created, you have no formal foreign key between Product and Sales Order Detail (ProductSpecialOffer joins to both, and that is the only formal way they are related). The ProductID is, however, a viable join item between the two tables, so you'll need to add that reference to the semantic model.

1. Click the Diagram View button in the bottom right (refer back to Figure 19-9 if you need). Visual Studio brings up a visual representation of the tables involved in the perspective, and, as you can see in Figure 19-10, it is unaware of the relationship between SalesOrderDetail and Product.

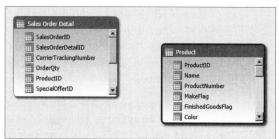

FIGURE 19-10

2. Click and drag ProductID from the SalesOrderDetail table onto the ProductID in the Product table, and SQL Server will create the relationship. The relationship should now be shown, as it is in Figure 19-11.

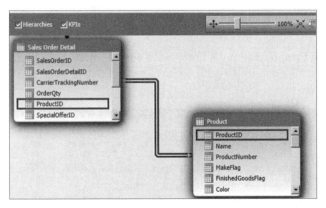

FIGURE 19-11

NOTE *Note that the click-and-drag order to relate tables is the opposite of what is used in most diagramming tools where you establish foreign keys. In most diagramming environments, you drag from the parent table to the child; the model designer works just the opposite, although if one side is a unique key then the drag order will be ignored and the key will be assumed to be the parent.*

Adding to Your Data Model

Although you could deploy and use the data model as you currently have it, there's more it can do. I've alluded several times to performing calculations in your model using the DAX language, and now you'll get a chance to try that out (but just a little...this book isn't a DAX tutorial). Just to give you a flavor of the language and some idea about how it works, here's how you can create a computed column and add a measure to your model. Once you get started with DAX, even just a smidgeon, you'll find it easy to advance using Books Online for guidance.

Adding Computed Columns

Like a computed column built on a table with T-SQL, a computed column in your tabular model has a value for every row in your table. Unlike T-SQL, though, DAX will let you reference other tables and perform some more advanced calculations in your computed column definition. For your first computed column, suppose you've been asked to report on the total dollar amount of all the discounts that have been given. You have all the components to figure this out in the SalesOrderDetail table, but the computation hasn't been done. While this could be done on each individual report, centralizing the computation in your data model prevents anyone from coming up with creative (and possibly incorrect) ways to work it out on different reports; you don't want two reports computing the same metric two different ways.

1. Click the Grid View button (in the lower right), and then click the bottom tab for the Sales Order Detail table.

2. Scroll to the right until you see the empty column marked Add Column, and click the top cell.

3. You can then enter the following formula and press Enter, with a result that — once it's finished processing — should resemble Figure 19-12.

FIGURE 19-12

```
='Sales Order Detail'[UnitPrice] * 'Sales Order Detail'[OrderQty] *
 'Sales Order Detail'[UnitPriceDiscount]
```

AUTOCOMPLETE IN DAX

Once you type that equals sign, you're in DAX, and the development environment knows it. Some of the syntactic elements, like the quote marks, will be filled in automatically depending on exactly what you type. For example, if you type =Sa (as if you had begun to type the name of your Sales Order Detail table), you'll get a dropdown menu of tables you might have meant — as well as a suggestion for each field in the table. Choose the entry containing the `UnitPrice` field, for example, and you can get those quotes and brackets right without ever typing one.

4. Right-click the column header and choose Rename to change the computed column name to Line Discount Total. Notice that the values are all filled in; these are computed when you define the column and then whenever you refresh the table data, so they're just as fast as any other column when you're retrieving data later.

5. The next computed column you'll create is a reference to another table. To add a computed column from another table (you can only create a reference to another table that's in your semantic model), click into the next empty computed column cell (a fresh column should have appeared to the right of the one you just created), and enter the following formula into the formula bar.

```
=RELATED(Product[Name])
```

NOTE *As you might remember from Chapter 17, denormalization is an easy way to speed up reporting; looking in one table is much faster than joining two. Denormalization in a tabular model is as easy as defining a computed column to get its value from a related table, and the model — because it understands the relationships and contains all the data — prevents anything from getting out of sync. The data is copied when the table is refreshed, so you never have to give it another thought.*

6. Once the column data is populated, rename the new computed column to Product Name. The result should look something like Figure 19-13.

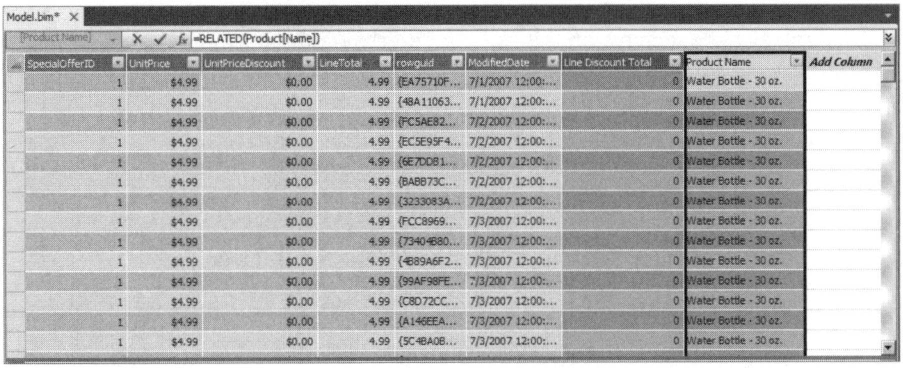

FIGURE 19-13

The RELATED function doesn't have to be the end of your statement; if you were looking up a numeric value, you could produce a computed value that used that value, combined with values from the current table and any other related table to produce whatever complex value your business logic requires.

NOTE *What would RELATED do, you might ask, if there is more than one relationship defined between the table you're looking at and the target table? DAX has a USERELATIONSHIP function that lets you resolve to the path you want to follow. Look around in the DAX dropdown syntax for ideas on other ways to compute values, or explore Books Online for more in-depth syntax.*

Adding Measures to the Measure Grid

The measure grid is the empty set of grid cells located below your table values. Its location is somewhat of a clue toward its intended purpose: This is where things like column totals go, says that bottom slot, but it's capable of a whole lot more than that.

Just like when you created the computed columns, you can try simple (and, if not complex, at least less simple) examples. And when it comes to simple measures, nothing is easier than a column sum...but there are a few things equally easy.

1. If you're not still looking at the Sales Order Detail table in Grid View, return there now, and click the column header for the LineTotal column.

2. Now look in the button bar for the Sum button and click the dropdown arrow to its right, as shown in Figure 19-14. There you can see a list of available aggregates you can perform on that column.

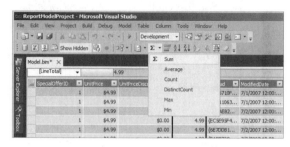

FIGURE 19-14

3. Clicking any of the items on the list will add that computation as a measure in the measure grid.

  ➤ **Sum:** Adds all the values in the column.

  ➤ **Average:** Computes the mean, which is the sum divided by the count of rows.

  ➤ **Count:** Counts all the rows, even if there are duplicates.

  ➤ **DistinctCount:** Counts all the distinct values in the column.

  ➤ **Max:** Contains the largest value in the column.

  ➤ **Min:** Contains the smallest value in the column.

4. For this example, choose Sum, and then widen the column by clicking the line separating its column header from the next column and dragging right (again, like in Excel). The result will look like Figure 19-15. Notice that the sum has already been computed over the whole set, and also take a look at what's in the formula bar.

FIGURE 19-15

If you start thinking you might be able to add a measure that includes an aggregate of values from a related table...well, you'd be right. Dividing the sum of one column by the sum of another is a great way to get a percentage measure, too. Let's combine the two to find the percentage off list price that a product is sold for, on average.

To do this, you first need to add a computed column to retrieve the related value.

1. Go ahead and add a column that gets the ListPrice column from the Product table (using `=RELATED(Product[ListPrice])`), and name that column `ListPrice`.

2. Add the measure by clicking anywhere in the measure grid and using the following formula:

```
Avg List Price Discount:=FORMAT(1-(SUM([UnitPrice]) / SUM([ListPrice])),
"Percent")
```

3. Widen the column so you can see it, and it should look like Figure 19-16.

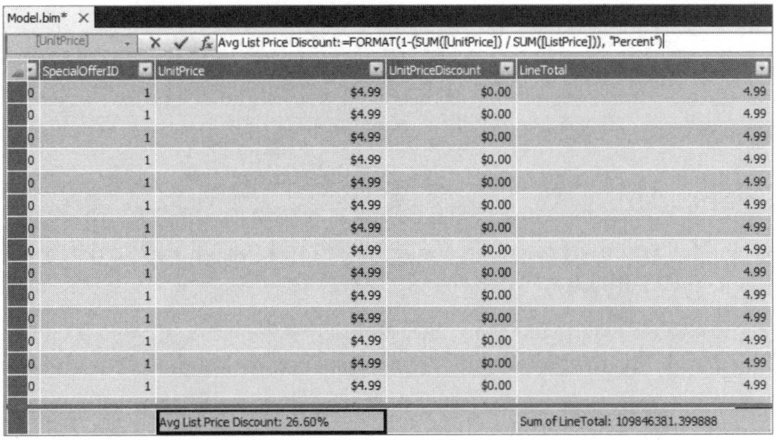

FIGURE 19-16

Once again, you might be tempted to leave this sort of computation to your report builders. Of course, any of them can sum the values in a column — or at least, if they can't, they shouldn't be building reports. However, keeping your business logic consistent across reports (or even reporting technologies like PowerPivot and Power View) is much easier if you keep it centralized in your model, and as you can see not every measure is quite as simple as a sum. Figure out which measures you want to expose when you build your model, and then have your report users access them directly.

TRY IT OUT **Measures Respond to Filters**

Now that you've created some measures, you're looking at your data in a new way (though you're just scratching the surface...there's a lot more to DAX). You might wonder, for example, whether the measures you created are going to be useful based on the data you collected. There's some browsing around you can do to explore just that.

Using the dropdown menu at the top of the SpecialOfferID column, deselect all the values by clicking on the Select All entry, and then check the box next to the value 16. What happens to your measure values?

Try some other filters and see whether you can find patterns in the data.

How It Works

The measures you create in the measure grid are sensitive to the filters you apply. By limiting your view to only those details that used a `SpecialOfferID` of 16 (which corresponds to Mountain-500 Silver Clearance Sale), you're seeing products that were given a much deeper discount than usual: On average they were sold to dealers at 80 percent off the normal list price.

Roles

There's one last element that is important to add to your model. As it turns out, the world rather likes to outfit any access to a large repository of data with some kind of security system, and SSAS provides the tools you need.

TRY IT OUT Role Security

To grant access to your model, you need to create one or more roles, assign appropriate rights to each, and then add your users to the appropriate roles.

1. On the Model menu, choose Roles, and then click New. Give your role a name (I chose Administrator Role), and then drop down the Permissions box to examine your choices. You have five:

   ➤ **None:** Predictably, grants no rights at all.

   ➤ **Read:** Lets its members read data from the model.

   ➤ **Read and Process:** Allows read access and the right to process the model to reload fresh data.

   ➤ **Process:** Doesn't allow reading, but lets the user refresh data. This might be useful for a service account.

   ➤ **Administrator:** Grants read (without any data restrictions) and process access, as well as the ability to modify the schema.

2. Set up an Administrator Role by choosing Administrator, and then supplying an appropriate description. Your result should look something like Figure 19-17.

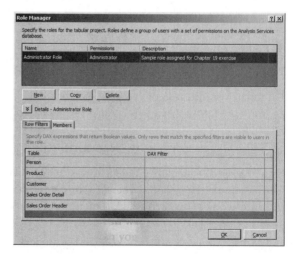

FIGURE 19-17

3. Click over to the Members tab and add yourself. Go on, you deserve it.

How It Works

By default, no user has access to the data contained in your model. Access is granted to the roles you create, and the users who are members of those roles can see any rows to which the role has access.

In this example, you created a role with administrative rights. This role can view any data in the model. Advanced security is an advanced concept, so I'm not going to delve too deeply into it, but unrestricted use is clearly not the end of the story. You have no control over what data an administrative user can browse.

If you were to use a role with Read or Read and Process permissions, you have much more control over the data each user can see: You can write a filter in DAX for each entity and store it right in the role definition. That way, when users with that role accesses the data, that user can see only what you've allowed them to see.

A user can be a member of any number of roles. A user who is a member of multiple roles will find the rights to be additive. That is, if one role allows only row X, and another only row Y, the user who is a member of both roles can see both X and Y.

Note that role security is based on which rows the user can see, rather than which columns. You can't hide whole columns through security.

Building and Deploying Your Data Model

Building a BI Semantic Model is all well and good, but if no one can get at it, it serves little purpose (much like designing a stored procedure, but never actually adding it to your database). To make your model usable to end users, you must *deploy* it.

Fortunately, deploying your model couldn't get much easier.

Indeed, the hard part is knowing that you need to and then finding the command to do so. To deploy, simply drop down the Build menu and choose Deploy. You can watch its progress in the Deploy window that pops up (shown in Figure 19-18).

The tabular model is now deployed to your tabular-mode instance of SQL Server Analysis Services. To find it, open SQL Server Management Studio and connect to that instance of Analysis Services. If you browse the databases there (assuming your project is still open in SSDT), you'll see something like Figure 19-19.

You can see one database called ReportModelProject, which is what you were working on, but there's a second one that has a GUID of some kind attached to it. Where did that come from?

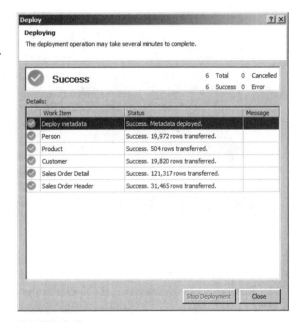

FIGURE 19-18

FIGURE 19-19

The project you have open in SSDT is using SSAS for all that fast processing of tabular data. That's not a function of Visual Studio — not even the BI-specific version you're using. SSDT is creating that SSAS database behind the scenes and using it to process all the data you're working with. Once you close your project (or simply close SSDT — go ahead, as you're done with it for the moment) that unfortunately-named second database will vanish.

Report Creation

Your newly deployed tabular model is, of course, not a completed report. Instead, it merely facilitates reports; however, considering there are lots of business-type people who understand reports but not databases, facilitating reports can be a powerful thing. Now that it is deployed, you can generate many reports from just the one model.

To see and generate reports, you need to leave the SQL Server Data Tools and actually visit the reporting user interface, which is basically just a website. Navigate to http://<your reporting server host>/reports — in my case, I have it right on my local system, so I can get there by navigating to http://localhost/reports, as shown in Figure 19-20. The URL will redirect to a slightly longer path, as seen in the figure.

NOTE *Depending on your server configuration, you may need to run Internet Explorer with elevated permissions to see the Report Server interface. The error you will receive will be to the effect of "User does not have required permissions. Verify that sufficient permissions have been granted and Windows User Account Control (UAC) restrictions have been addressed." If you see that error, close your browser, right-click the IE icon and choose Run as Administrator for elevated permissions.*

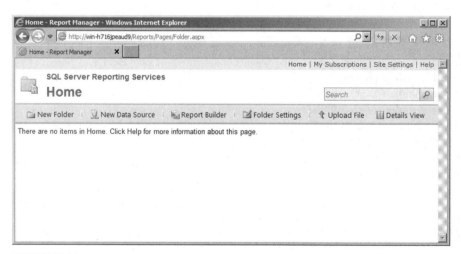

FIGURE 19-20

This is essentially the home page for user reports and such. By "and such," among other things, I'm referring to data sources like the model you just created, but naturally that's not on your page yet. What you're going to want to do now is add your model to the report server so that reports can access it.

But first, let's take a quick tour:

➤ **New Folder:** Lets you create folders to build up a regular hierarchical structure within the report server.

➤ **New Data Source:** Lets you either create a data source or add one you've already created (such as ReportModelProject).

➤ **Report Builder:** An application that you can launch from within the report server. It allows you to create new reports or edit existing ones, with almost the same flexibility as you can find in SSDT. It's a great tool for a report developer. When your end users want to create their own reports (and they're not interested in PowerPivot or Power View), this is their tool as well.

➤ **Folder Settings:** Lets you set security permissions on your current folder.

➤ **Upload File:** Lets you add existing reports, data sources, or other report server entities from a file on disk.

➤ **Details View:** Changes the folder view from large icons to a small icon list, showing more information about each object.

Adding a Data Source

Go ahead and add your data source by clicking on New Data Source. You'll immediately get a barrage of text entry cells to fill out, but most are fairly self-explanatory. Use Figure 19-21 as a guide to help you if you're not sure. The important sections are:

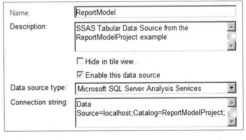

FIGURE 19-21

➤ **Name:** An arbitrary, user-friendly name for this report data source. This can be made available to end users (not just developers), so make it readable.

➤ **Description:** A longer description, also for the consumption of end users.

➤ **Data source type:** Which data source type you want to retrieve data from. You can choose from a fairly long list of types supported by Reporting Services.

➤ **Connection string:** The address of your data source. Each data source type has different requirements.

The rest of the screen is about security. When a report tries to get access to the data through this data source, which credentials should it use? You have a few choices.

➤ **Credentials supplied by the user running the report:** Your users are asked to enter a username and password whenever they try to access the data source.

➤ **Credentials stored securely in the report server:** You should choose this option when you have a dedicated user who has the rights to run this report.

> ➤ **Windows integrated security:** Allows each user to access the data source using his or her Windows credentials.

> ➤ **Credentials are not required:** Your data source is completely unsecured, and if that doesn't give you chills then I've taught you nothing. This can be used for things like file data sources, although even those may need to live in secure locations that require a credential to access.

For this data source, use integrated security; you're a member of the administrative role you created for your model, so that should provide all the rights you need. To be sure, click Test Connection; if you get a green success message, click OK to continue.

Creating a Report with the Report Builder

Now that you have a data source, you have everything you need to start delivering reports to your end users. From this point on, keep in mind that the tool you're about to use is geared not only for developers, but also for advanced users. Where you see the results of the choices you made in building the model (such as object names), consider what an end user would need to see in order to make good choices.

Go ahead and click Report Builder to get started, and you'll see the startup screen shown in Figure 19-22.

 NOTE *The Report Builder relies on a small applet that will try to install itself on your system the first time you navigate to the Report Builder. You must accept the installation of the applet if you want to use the Report Builder.*

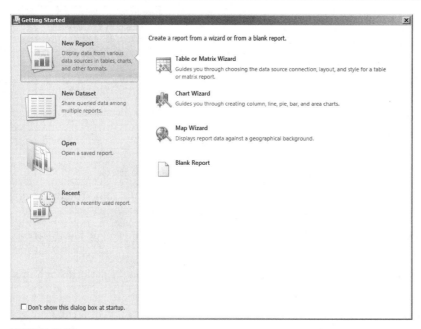

FIGURE 19-22

Right away, you'll see that Report Builder is designed to be friendly; notice the large, colorful buttons and long text descriptions. Don't be fooled...this is a powerful tool, and you're only scratching the surface.

NOTE *Here's a little foreshadowing for later in the chapter. The most interesting option on this screen that you're not going to use right now is New Dataset. This lets you define a complete query against a database and share that query between any number of reports. You'll see a great application for this when you start on report server projects in the next section; shared datasets are great for common parameters.*

You're going to stick with a table report (the default as it happens) and build a relatively simple report listing all orders that paid with some method other than a credit card.

To begin, follow these steps:

1. Start up the Table or Matrix Wizard by clicking it. You are first invited to either select or create a dataset.

NOTE *Don't confuse a dataset with a data source; a dataset is a specific query, whereas a data source is a whole collection of tables.*

2. Because you haven't created any shared datasets, you'll want to create a new one by selecting Create a dataset and clicking Next.

3. In the next dialog box, you are asked to select the source of your report data. Here, you can create a new data source by clicking the New button or search your report server's folders with Browse. For this project, click Browse and you should see what you need. Go ahead and select the model you just created, and click Test Connection to verify it works from there.

4. Click Next to get to the data selection page, shown in Figure 19-23.

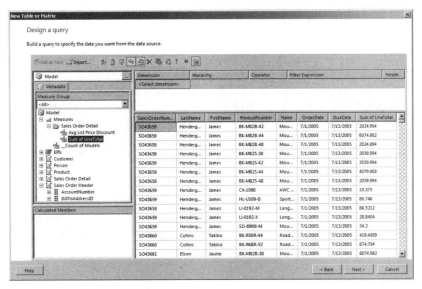

FIGURE 19-23

5. Within the Measure Group pane, navigate to each table and drag the relevant columns into the grid on the bottom right:

- ➤ SalesOrderHeader.SalesOrderNumber
- ➤ Person.LastName
- ➤ Person.FirstName
- ➤ Product.ProductNumber
- ➤ Product.Name
- ➤ SalesOrderHeader.OrderDate
- ➤ SalesOrderHeader.DueDate
- ➤ Measures.Sales Order Detail.Sum of Line Total

Remember that this was to be a report of orders that paid with something other than a credit card; next, you'll add a filter to the report to limit it to just those orders.

6. To add a filter, drag the SalesOrderHeader.CreditCardID field up to the filter area (at the top, where it says "Select Dimension"). This sets you up to use the Credit Card ID as a filter.

7. You still need to set the exact filter criteria. The default comparison operator is `equal`, which meets your need, so click the Filter Expression dropdown and select Blank. After a quick recalculation, you have your filtered data. Go ahead and click Next.

8. Now you get to choose which axis you want to use for each value. Row Groups arrange themselves vertically down the left side of the report, and Column Groups arrange horizontally across the top. Where they intersect, the fields you drop in the Values box will be aggregated and displayed (in general, think of dimensions in the row and column groups and measures in the Values group). For the simple *table report* that you're doing, you can skip the column groups (including both row and column groups produces a *matrix report*). Drop all the fields except Sum of Line Total into the row groups box, and then drop Sum of Line Total into the Values box.

> **NOTE** *Notice that when you drop your measure in Values, it switches to Sum (Sum of Line Total). Measures in this section will be aggregated, and sum is the default aggregate operator. If you prefer a different type of aggregate, click the down arrow on the right side of the measure in the box and select something else. There's a surprisingly long menu to choose from.*

At this point, only two more screens separate you from the full Report Designer. The next screen asks you to make some choices about the report layout. Once you have the report up in the designer you'll be able to make all kinds of changes, but it's worth it to use the wizard to get as close to the layout you want as possible. Figure 19-24 shows your options.

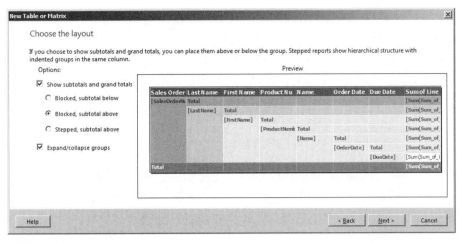

FIGURE 19-24

9. You can click each option to get a sample of what each might look like in the preview pane, using this handy guide as a reference. Choose whatever you like from the following:

> **Show subtotals and grand totals:** Tells the wizard to automatically add both group and report level total fields. These will use the same aggregates you chose for your Values fields.

>> **Blocked:** Shows each dimension in its own column.

>> **Stepped:** Uses a single column with values indented to their level in the hierarchy.

>> **Subtotal Placement:** Choose to place the subtotals above or below their groups.

> **Expanded or Collapsed:** Expands and collapses groups interactively. If you deselect this, all your groups will be displayed in their entirety.

10. The last screen brings you to the most critical choice you're going to have to make about your report: What color do you want it to be? There are only a few options, and they haven't changed noticeably in years, but there is a whole screen in the wizard offering you a choice. Don't worry...you can customize the colors once you're in the designer if you don't like any of the default schemes.

11. Finally, you're through the report wizard. Click Finish to bring up the Report Designer. This is a fairly robust drag-and-drop design environment that will let you perform just about any level of editing you want to do, from a complete redesign to subtle tweaks.

12. Let's finish by making a few small changes in the Report Designer. Go ahead and click in the title area to add the title, Non Credit Card Orders. When you're done, you should wind up with something that looks like Figure 19-25 (note that I've resized columns a bit to help them fit on a page; feel free to do the same if you wish).

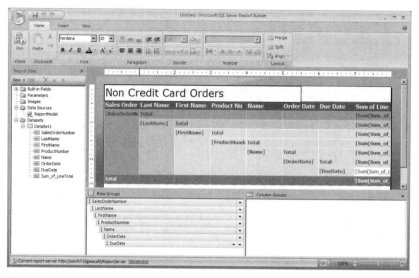

FIGURE 19-25

 NOTE *Depending on how your report server is configured, you may be able to run the report with just what you've put in thus far. For some systems, however, there is likely to be a restriction that requires you to filter your results in some manner (to avoid excessive loads) before executing the report. This report is filtered already at the query level, so no further filtering is likely to be required.*

When you're ready, click Run, and you'll see the fruits of your labor, as shown in Figure 19-26.

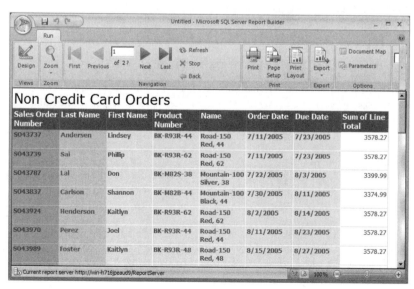

FIGURE 19-26

You, do, however, have a minor problem — the report has quite a few pages (it will not show how many for sure until you navigate to the end) and the information isn't very useful the way it is currently sorted. No problem! The Report Builder enables you to easily enable interactive sorting on any column.

1. Click the Design button in the upper left to return to the Report Designer.

2. Next, right-click on the column header for Sales Order Number and choose Text Box Properties from the context menu. There's plenty in here, so feel free to browse around some of the options before you continue.

3. When your curiosity is satisfied, click Interactive Sorting, and then set it up like you see in Figure 19-27. You need to sort groups (because your data is collected into row groups), you want to sort by Sales Order Number (because that's which header you're editing), and you want to apply the sort to everything in the dataset. When you're done, click OK to return.

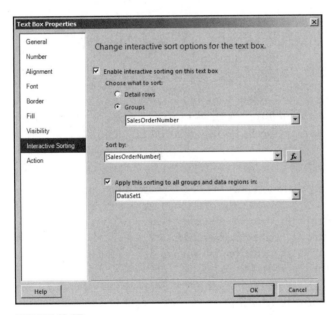

FIGURE 19-27

Try to do the same to the LastName header. There's one thing you'll find that's not perfectly intuitive, though: When you choose whether to sort detail rows or groups you'll still choose groups, but you also still want to choose the SalesOrderHeader group. Why? Because that's the outermost group on your row, and you want to sort everything under that.

Once you've finished, run your report again. You can try out the interactive sort by simply clicking the up/down arrows next to the columns of the report that you've enabled for sorting. In my case, I'm going to sort based on the person's last name, as shown in Figure 19-28. Notice how the report is automatically grouped where it makes sense (avoiding repeating values).

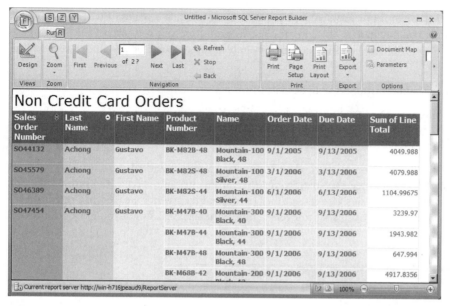

FIGURE 19-28

Play around with the report and you'll find that you can easily resort the result in other ways. Note that you also could have defined a default sort order — for example, sorting those with the soonest due date — by setting it in the Sort and Group dialog box (next to Filter in the toolbar).

Deploying from Report Builder

This report currently lives entirely within Report Builder. If you want to share it with anyone, you need to publish it to the report server. Fortunately, that's a perfectly simple proposition. Because Report Builder is an integral part of the report server, all you need to do is to save the report. The directory structure you'll be offered is the one in the report server itself, and once you've saved the report (presumably in the root, because you haven't created any new folders yet) it will be visible to those with sufficient rights on the report server.

A Few Last Words on BI Semantic Models

BISM is certainly not the be-all, end-all of reporting. It is, however, a very cool feature in the sense that you can expose data to your end users in a somewhat controlled fashion (they don't see any more than you put in the data source, and access to the data source is secured such that you can control which users see which data sources), but still allow them to create specific reports of their own. What's more, when you grant access to a BISM data source, it allows your users to use Report Builder, PowerPivot, or Power View all against the same data. Reports generated in any of those tools will balance, as they're drawing from the exact same data store. BISM is a great way to enable ad hoc reporting, and also to develop in-house reports.

Finally, keep in mind that you generated only one very simple report for just the most simplistic of layouts. Report Builder, and the other tools that access BISM, allow for basic graphing and matrix reporting as well.

REPORT SERVER PROJECTS

Report Models can be considered to be "scratching the surface" of things; Reporting Services has much more to offer than that. (Indeed, there are entire books covering just Reporting Services; there is that much to it.) In addition to what you've already seen, the SQL Server Data Tools allow you to create report server projects.

As I mentioned, there are entire books on just this subject, so I am going to give you a little taste of the possibilities through another simple example. (You're just going to do the same example using the project method.)

Building a Report Server Project

At this point, you should be fairly comfortable with several of the concepts you're going to use here, so I'll spare you the copious screenshots such as those you've already endured and get to the nitty-gritty of what needs to be done to get you up to the new stuff:

1. Open a new project using the Report Server Project template in SQL Server Data Tools (note that this is different from the Analysis Services project you used earlier). No project wizard for you this time; you get to do things manually.

2. Create a new data source against your AdventureWorks database. (Right-click the Shared Data Sources folder and fill in the dialog box — use the Edit button if you want a helpful dialog box to build your connection string.) Note that to deploy this new data source, you need to name it something other than the name you used earlier in the chapter (assuming you did that example).

3. Right-click the Reports folder and choose Add New Report. This takes you to the Report Wizard — click Next to move on to the Data Source Selection screen. Select the data source you just created. Then click Next.

   This should bring you to the query dialog box shown in Figure 19-29.

4. You can type this query as shown; it should roughly duplicate the report you built in the Report Model section, including the filter to remove credit card orders. You could also enter the query using the query builder and, while in the builder, even execute the query to verify that it returns the expected data. Note that you also could have executed a stored procedure at this point or retrieved data directly from a specific table.

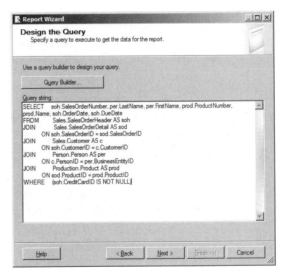

FIGURE 19-29

5. Click Next and accept the Tabular report type; now you come to the Table Design Wizard shown in Figure 19-30.

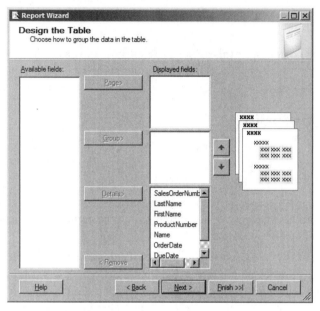

FIGURE 19-30

6. Because the query has already trimmed things down to just the columns you need (and, as it happens, even grabbed them in proper order, although you could reorder things if you wanted to), you can just select and move everything into the details box.

> **NOTE** *The Page and Group fields here allow you to set up sort hierarchies. For example, if you wanted everything to go on to separate pages based on individual customers (say, for the sales people to understand the status of their particular customers) you could move Company Name up to the Page level. Likewise, you might instead do groupings (instead of pages) based on product name so that your people pulling the orders from inventory can grab all the product needed to fill all outstanding orders in one trip.*

7. Again, click Next, and you are presented with a Table Style dialog box. Choose whatever is to your liking (I'm just going to stick with Slate) and again click Next to be greeted with the summary of what your report selections were. Change the name to **Non Credit Card Orders** and click Finish to create the report definition, as shown in Figure 19-31 (yours may look a tad different if you chose a different style than I did).

NOTE *The Toolbox and Report Data panes may be located slightly differently depending on your particular configuration of Visual Studio. Both have been made visible and docked here for demonstration purposes.*

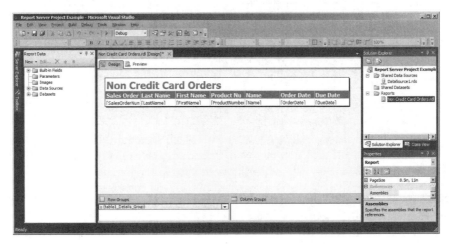

FIGURE 19-31

If you're familiar with other Report Designers, this will seem familiar, as the WYSIWYG editor you're presented with here is somewhat standard fare for Report Designers (certainly some are more robust, but the presentation of the basics is pretty typical). Notice, however, that the name you selected for the report became the report's default header.

8. If you go ahead and click the Preview tab for the report, you'll find that it is largely the same as the one you generated using the Report Builder. There are, however, some formatting areas where the defaults of Report Builder are perhaps a tad better than you have here — in particular, it makes no sense for you to report the time as part of the date if the time is always going to be midnight. With that in mind, let's make some alterations to the wizard-generated report.

TRY IT OUT **Altering Report Projects**

You have a really great start to your report, generated in seconds by the wizard. It is not, however, perfect. Let's get your dates formatted more appropriately.

1. Right-click the first date field (Order Date) and select Text Box Properties to bring up the dialog box shown in Figure 19-32.

2. Click the function button (fx) to indicate that you want to change the output to a function result. This brings up a function dialog box, as shown in Figure 19-33.

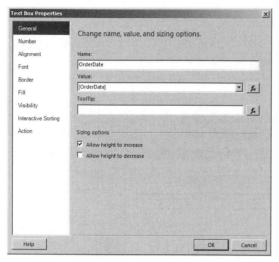

FIGURE 19-32

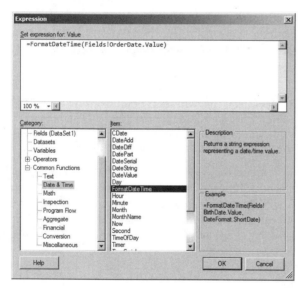

FIGURE 19-33

3.   Add the use of the FormatDateTime function. Note that I've expanded the function helper down below. You can double-click functions to insert the base function name into the window above. It will provide context-sensitive tooltips similar to other parts of Visual Studio as you are filling in the function. Also note that this particular function has an optional parameter that allows you to specify a particular date representation style (say, European or Japanese), but you're going to allow the function to format based on whatever the localized settings are on the server.

4.   Click OK, and move to the Alignment tab. Change the Horizontal option to Right to cause the field to be right justified (typical for most reports).

5. Click OK, and repeat the process for DueDate.

6. Preview the report again; it should look something like Figure 19-34. Note that I've played around with column sizes a bit (try it!) to use the page efficiently.

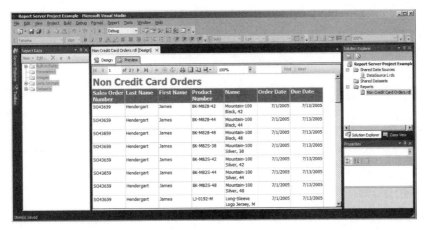

FIGURE 19-34

How It Works

Under the covers, the Report Designer is manipulating an RDL file (remember that RDL, Report Definition Language, is actually an XML implementation). As you make your changes in the Report Designer, the content of the RDL file is changed so the report generator will know what to do.

To see what the RDL looks like, right-click the report in the Solution Explorer and choose View Code. It's wordy stuff, but here's an excerpt from one of the fields you just edited in the report:

```
<TablixCell>
 <CellContents>
  <Textbox Name="OrderDate">
   <CanGrow>true</CanGrow>
   <KeepTogether>true</KeepTogether>
   <Paragraphs>
    <Paragraph>
     <TextRuns>
      <TextRun>
       <Value>=FormatDateTime(Fields!OrderDate.Value)</Value>
       <Style>
        <FontFamily>Tahoma</FontFamily>
       </Style>
      </TextRun>
     </TextRuns>
     <Style>
      <TextAlign>Right</TextAlign>
     </Style>
    </Paragraph>
   </Paragraphs>
```

```
  <rd:DefaultName>OrderDate</rd:DefaultName>
  <Style>
   <Border>
    <Color>LightGrey</Color>
    <Style>Solid</Style>
   </Border>
   <PaddingLeft>2pt</PaddingLeft>
   <PaddingRight>2pt</PaddingRight>
   <PaddingTop>2pt</PaddingTop>
   <PaddingBottom>2pt</PaddingBottom>
  </Style>
 </Textbox>
 </CellContents>
</TablixCell>
```

Were you to become an expert, you could, if desired, edit the RDL directly.

Deploying the Report

The only thing left to do is to deploy the report. With Report Builder, you were able to simply save your report directly into the report server. Here, saving just puts the RDL file onto disk (and in your project file, and hopefully into some kind of source control solution). To deploy, you can right-click the report in the Solution Explorer and choose Deploy. There is, however, a minor catch: You need to define the target to deploy to in the project definition.

1.   Right-click the Report Server Project and choose Properties.

2.   In the TargetServerURL field, enter the URL of your report server. In my case, this is as simple as `http://localhost/ReportServer`, but the server name could be any server you have appropriate rights to deploy to. (The Virtual Directory may also be something other than `ReportServer` if you defined it that way at install.)

 NOTE *Depending on your server configuration, you may not be able to deploy unless you are running SSDT with enhanced privileges. If you see an error indicating you do not have sufficient rights to deploy the report, simply close SSDT and reopen it by right-clicking its icon and choosing Run as Administrator. Retry the steps above, and your report should deploy.*

After you've deployed, you'll want to view the report. Navigate to your report server (if on the local host and using the default directory, it would be `http://localhost/Reports`, just as it was for the Report Model examples). Click on your report project, and choose your Non Credit Card Orders report. It will take a bit to come up the first time you load it. (If you navigate back to it again, the report definition will be cached and thus come up more quickly.) You should see your report just as you defined it in your project.

SUMMARY

Reporting Services has had a major impact on many SQL Server installations. For many companies, having a relatively robust reporting server built right into their central data store has been liberating, making it much easier to disseminate information to data consumers. For other organizations, Reporting Services has provided an adequate solution to replace long-standing reporting packages such as Crystal Reports. SQL Server 2012 made ad hoc reporting a priority, greatly enhancing your ability to deliver reporting capabilities — instead of just reports — to your end users.

In this chapter, I've really only scratched the surface of what's possible. You can parameterize reports, embed charts, integrate reports with other products (such as Microsoft SharePoint Services or Microsoft Office SharePoint Services), drill through from one report to another, and even embed reports inside of other reports.

For more information on reporting, I suggest a book specific to Reporting Services such as *Professional SQL Server 2012 Reporting Services* by Paul Turley.

EXERCISES

1. Add the Production.ProductSubCategory table to your semantic model and place the SubCategoryName in a computed column on the Sales Order Detail table. Do the same with Sales.SalesTerritory and TerritoryName. Hint: To add new tables to your existing model, go to the Model menu and choose Existing Connection.

2. Using Report Builder, create a report using the Sum of Line Total measure as the value and the two new dimensions you just added in Exercise 1 as the dimensions. You may try this as either a table or a matrix. Hint: For a matrix report, place one dimension in the Row Groups and the other in the Column Groups.

▶ **WHAT YOU LEARNED IN THIS CHAPTER**

TOPIC	CONCEPT
Report lifecycle	Your reports will begin with the development phase, where you'll work against business requirements to develop a query and a layout that can respond accurately to a business problem. Once developed, the reports are managed by the report server, which handles organization and security. Finally, the reports are delivered to the end user, either through the Report Manager or the Report Viewer control.
Reporting Services architecture	The Report Server service is the heart of SQL Server Reporting Services (SSRS), and is responsible for communicating with the database and rendering reports from RDL files. Reports are developed in SQL Server Data Tools (SSDT) or in Report Builder and organized on the report server by Report Manager. Report Manager also handles security, subscriptions, and scheduling, and can render reports for viewing. Reports can be viewed using the Report Viewer control as well.
SSAS tabular models	Using SQL Server Analysis Services (SSAS) in tabular mode, you can create BI Semantic Models to permit developer- or user-created reports. These models can be deployed to a tabular instance of SSAS and referenced by data sources stored on the report server for consumption by SSRS. The same models can also be used as a base for PowerPivot or Power View reporting.
RDL	Report Definition Language (RDL) is the XML-based descriptive language used to store the reports you develop. It is shared by both report server project reports and by Report Builder reports, and each can edit the other's objects.
Report Builder	Report Builder is a full-featured GUI for building reports that is less developer-centric than SSDT. Report Builder is available through the Report Manager for users to create or edit reports.
Report server projects	For a more integrated development experience, you can create report server projects in SSDT. These projects allow full integration with other Visual Studio projects, including access to source control tools. After you identify a target server, you can deploy these projects from the development environment directly to a report server to use in Report Manager.

20

Getting Integrated with Integration Services

WHAT YOU WILL LEARN IN THIS CHAPTER:

➤ Your first exposure to the concepts of Extract, Transform, and Load procedures

➤ Using a wizard to create your first SQL Server Integration Services package

➤ How to navigate in the SSIS development environment within SQL Server Data Tools

➤ How to execute and deploy SSIS packages

 NOTE *If you're running a mixed environment with SQL Server 2005 or 2008 (or migrating from one of those versions), do not fear. SQL Server 2012 Integration Services still supports older SSIS packages. Use the Integration Services Project Conversion Wizard within SSDT to help upgrade older SSIS packages to SSIS 2012 format.*

In the previous chapter, you got your first serious taste of the SQL Server Data Tools (also sometimes referred to as SSDT). In case you skipped that chapter, SSDT is the Visual Studio development environment with some special SQL Server–oriented project templates and

tools. The very different ways you can use that environment for just SQL Server development gives something of a taste for just how flexible the Visual Studio development environment is — as you'll see, Integration Services has a pretty different feel than Reporting Services does.

In this chapter, you'll be looking at how to utilize SQL Server Integration Services (often simply called SSIS) to perform basic import and export of data, and I'll briefly discuss some of the other things possible with tools like Integration Services.

UNDERSTANDING THE PROBLEM

The problems being addressed by Integration Services exist in at least some form in a large percentage of systems — how to get data into or out of your system from or to foreign data sources. It can be things like importing data from the old system into the new, or a list of available items from a vendor — or who knows what. The common thread in all of it, however, is that you need to get data that doesn't necessarily fit your tables into them anyway.

What you need is a tool that lets you *Extract*, *Transform*, and *Load* data into your database — a tool that does this is usually referred to simply as an *ETL* tool. Just how complex of a problem this kind of tool can handle varies, but Integration Services can handle nearly every kind of situation you may have.

 NOTE *This may bring about the question "Well, why doesn't everybody use it then since it's built-in?" The answer is one of how intuitive it is in a cross-platform environment. There are third-party packages out there that are much more seamless and have fancier UI environments. These are really meant to allow unsophisticated users to move data around relatively easily — they are also outrageously expensive. In general, the choice of an ETL tool, which can be anything from in-house custom scripting to SSIS to a six-figure third-party tool, depends on lots of factors. SSIS strikes a very good balance between ease of use and power, which makes it extremely popular.*

USING THE IMPORT/EXPORT WIZARD TO GENERATE BASIC PACKAGES

An SSIS package is essentially the SSIS equivalent to a program. It bundles a set of instructions (potentially including limited conditional branch logic) such that it can be moved around, cloned, edited, and so on. The Import/Export Wizard is a tool to automate building such a package for a relatively simple import or export.

Starting the Wizard

To use the Import/Export Wizard, follow these steps:

1. Start the SQL Server Data Tools from the programs menu on your system, and start a new Integration Services project (as shown in Figure 20-1). As you can see, I've named this project `Chapter20Project`.

FIGURE 20-1

2. On the far right (assuming you haven't moved any of the dockable windows around), you should find a node in the Solution Explorer called SSIS Packages. Right-click this and choose the SSIS Import and Export Wizard, as shown in Figure 20-2.

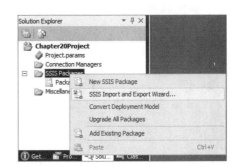

Choosing Your Data Sources

3. This brings up an introduction dialog box that is pretty useless (that same Welcome dialog box you probably grew tired of in the chapter on Reporting Services), but click Next and you move on to a far more fundamental dialog box to help you set up a connection to a data source. (See Figure 20-3.)

FIGURE 20-2

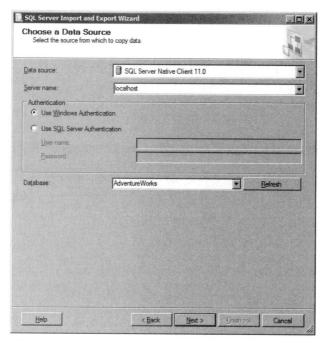

FIGURE 20-3

NOTE *Microsoft continues to make the mistake of using the same term — data source — in two different ways in this dialog box. The first is the overarching concept of a source of data — complete with all of the information that goes into making a connection string (server, authentication, database, and the like). The second way is a sub-element of the first — the data source as an OLE DB driver type.*

4.   For now, leave the actual Data Source dropdown box as SQL Native Client — this is generally the preferred method for accessing SQL Server. From there, set up your authentication information (I've used Windows Authentication in the preceding example) and choose AdventureWorks as your database.

5.   You're now ready to click Next, where you'll see what is, at first glance, essentially the same dialog box. This time, however, you're going to make a bit of a change in things. Change the Destination field to be Flat File Destination and, as shown in Figure 20-4, the rest of the options change to something more suitable to a file system–based destination instead of a table in your SQL Server.

FIGURE 20-4

As you can see, I've chosen to name my output file `TextExport.csv` (be sure to place the file somewhere you have write privileges), and filled out the other information in a manner appropriate for a typical comma-delimited file.

> **WARNING** *Let me digress long enough to warn you to be very careful about using comma-delimited files. While this is something of a "tried and true" method of exporting and importing data, consider your delimiter very carefully — does your data potentially already have commas in it? What is that going to do to your exported (or imported) data? What's more, this is a plain text output format; if you have security or privacy requirements you need to comply with, you're opening a dangerous hole with a CSV file. Just something to keep in mind when you're deciding on formats (if the choice is yours — most of the time it won't be).*

I'm not going to go into real detail on this, because the options available will vary widely depending on the particular OLE DB data source you've selected. Indeed, the real point of the moment is just that SSIS alters the dialog box to give you contextual choices that are relevant to the particular OLE DB data source you're using. In the preceding example, I've simply entered my filename (the Column names in the first data row option is checked by default), and it's time to click Next again. This takes you to choices for selecting what data you want out of your source database. You have two choices here:

➤ **Copy data from one or more tables or views:** This performs a straight copy out of a table or view. The data from a view is treated exactly as if it were a table, but with all the joins and filtering encapsulated within the view intact.

➤ **Write a query to specify the data to transfer:** This allows you to select out of pretty much any operation that's going to yield a result set. You can use any kind of T-SQL statement, even calls to stored procedures or table-valued functions.

Let's start by taking a look at the Query option. If you choose this option and click Next, you get yet another dialog box; this one pretty boring in the sense that all it does is give you a box where you can enter the text of your query. (See Figure 20-5.)

FIGURE 20-5

In my example here, I've shown where you could be setting up to export a list of employees that you hired in the first month of 2004. If you want to test this, you can type the query, and then try testing it with the Parse button to make sure that the query you want to run is syntactically valid, or you can copy it into a query window in the Management Studio and test it there. Then click Next to get to the dialog box shown in Figure 20-6.

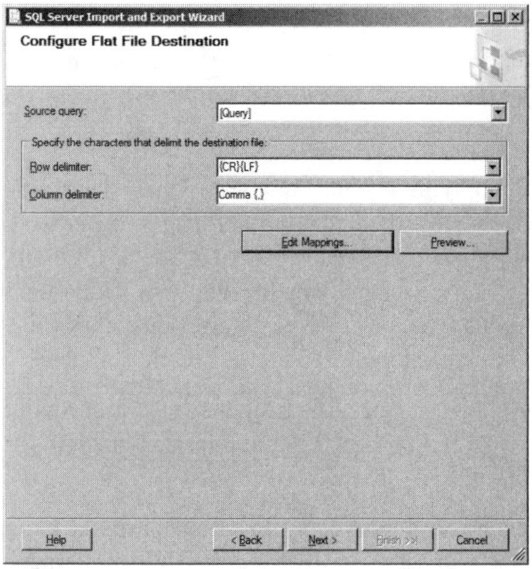

FIGURE 20-6

For starters, this sets you up to decide what you want your flat file to look like. You can easily change the row delimiter. (For example, if you're exporting for use in a Linux- or UNIX-based system, you may want to choose just a line feed rather than the line feed/carriage return option.) You can click Preview to see whether your query looks like it's going to return the data that you expect. (See Figure 20-7.)

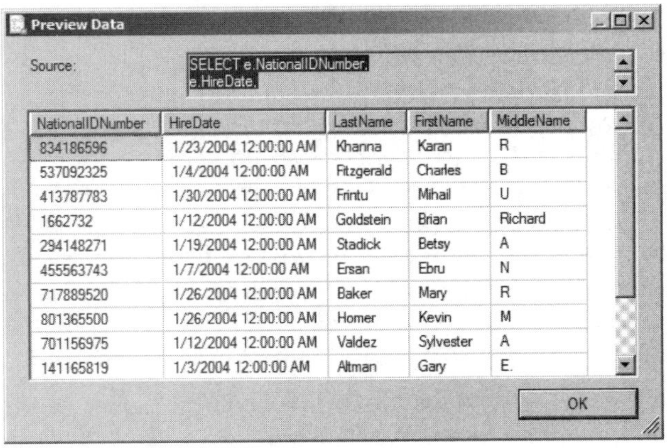

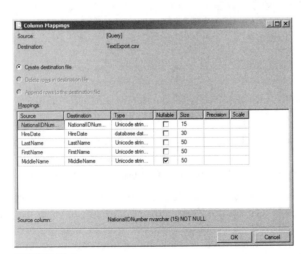

FIGURE 20-7

Completing the Wizard

After you're done determining these options, follow these steps to finish the Wizard process:

1. Click OK, and you're back to the Configure Flat File dialog box.

2. Click the Edit Mappings button, which takes you to the dialog box shown in Figure 20-8.

FIGURE 20-8

At first, things will probably appear pretty mundane here, but, actually, things are getting a lot more interesting.

3. Click any of the Destination column values. You'll see a dropdown option appear, and that will include the option to ignore that column, essentially omitting a source column from the destination when you output the file.

> **NOTE** *This should bring up the question of "Why would I have even put the column in the original query if I was just going to ignore it at output?" The reasons are multifold. First, you may have wanted the column there primarily for preview purposes to verify that the data is what you expected — for example, including the names to verify that it seems like the right people when you only intend to output the EmployeeID. Also, you may be using a query that is copied from some other source and want to avoid editing it (for example, if it is particularly complex), or you may be executing a function or stored procedure that you don't even want to consider editing for this purpose.*
>
> *One other point: This dialog box is shared with the direct table choice. (Back when you chose Query, you had the option of a table, remember?) So the option is even more applicable in direct table copy scenarios, where there may be many columns in the table that you don't want in the end output.*

4. Click the Type column values, and you'll see a number of choices.

> **NOTE** *I highly recommend resizing the columns in this dialog box so you can see what the Type column is really trying to show you. Just hover your mouse over the right side of the column header much as you would if you were using Excel, and then click and drag the column divider to the right to enlarge the column.*

➤ Most of the time you'll stick with whatever the default conversion was, based on the source data type.

➤ Sometimes you may want to change the output type in some way, for example, treating integer data as a string to deal with some expectation of the end destination of your data. (Not all systems treat what is seemingly the same data the same way.)

➤ You can mess with the nullability and scale/precision of your data. It's pretty rare that you would want to do this, and it's something of an advanced concept, but suffice to say that if you were to use more advanced transformations (instead of the default Import/Export Wizard), this might be an interesting option to facilitate error trapping of data that isn't going to successfully go into your destination system. In most cases, however, you would want to do that with WHERE clauses in your original query.

5. Because you didn't make any substantive changes here, click Cancel to go back to the Configure Flat File dialog box, and then click Next to move on to the next dialog box.

At this point, you'll get a simple confirmation dialog box. It will synopsize all the things that you've asked the wizard to do — in this case:

➤ Copy rows from [Query] to `TextExport.csv`.

➤ The new target table will be created.

➤ The package will be saved to the package file `c:\users\username\documents\ visual studio 2010\projects\Chapter20Project\Chapter20Project\ Package1.dtsx`. The package will not be run immediately.

6. Click Finish, and your package is created.

A little more about the confirmation dialog box. Most of this is self-explanatory, but I want to stress a couple of things:

➤ **It will create the file for you with the name specified.** If, when you designed the package, the file had been detected as already existing, you would have been given some options on whether to overwrite the existing file or just append the data onto the end of it.

➤ **Perhaps more important, notice that a *package* is being created for you.** This package is what amounts to an SSIS program. You can have SSIS execute that package over and over again (including scheduling it), and it will perform the defined export for you each time.

➤ **Note that it says that your package will *not* be run immediately.** You need to either execute this package manually or schedule it to run.

 NOTE *Let me stress again that this is just something of a preparation step; your package has not run, and your data is not yet exported. You still need to execute or schedule the package to get your actual exported file. That side of things — the execution of the package — is the same for all SSIS packages though, and isn't Import/Export Wizard-specific, so I'll hold that side of things until the next section.*

The Import/Export Wizard can, with the information you provide through its dialog boxes, create a package for you to do a simple import or export even if you don't have the first idea what to do in SSIS when faced with a blank canvas.

EXAMINING PACKAGE BASICS

Fully examining all the parts of an SSIS package and the uses of each piece can fill up the entire book on its own. (Indeed, there are many books dedicated to the subject.) But understanding at least the fundamentals is important to make even the most basic use of Integration Services, so let's take a look at the package that the Import/Export Wizard just created for you.

Assuming you still have the Data Tools open (including the package you just created — if not, open that back up), you should have a fairly standard looking Visual Studio window up similar to Figure 20-9, with the exception of having some fairly Integration Services–oriented stuff in the main pane (as well as in the Connection Managers pane just below the main pane).

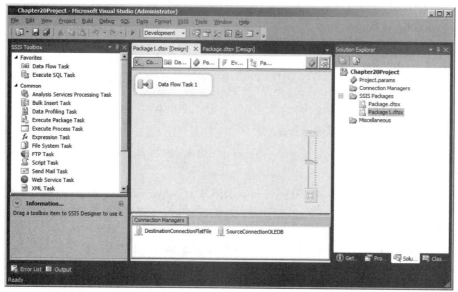

FIGURE 20-9

Before you explore the Integration Services panes, focus first on the standard Visual Studio Solutions Explorer pane. By default, it's in the upper right. It was what you right-clicked to start the Import/Export Wizard). You should see two packages there. The first — simply titled `Package.dtsx` — was a default package created when you first chose the Integration Services template when you created your new project. It should be empty, and can be deleted. `Package1.dtsx` will be the one you want to select (you can rename it if you choose) in order to follow the remaining discussion in this section. If you've stepped through things right with the text, it will already be in front of you.

With that out of the way, let's look at a few of the key panes...

Connection Managers

> **NOTE** I know...I know.... You expected me to go top down! Well, that's not just my natural resistance to conformity; I have a more logical reason to get the Connection Managers pane out of the way first: It's simple, and you'll be a while on the main pane, so let's get it out of the way.

By this point, you may well already have a solid idea as to what the Connection Managers pane (featured in Figure 20-10) is all about. It's about allowing you quick access to all the connections, both sources and destinations, that are used in your package.

FIGURE 20-10

If you double-click either of the two connection managers, you should see a dialog box that looks pretty similar to the dialog boxes that you worked with earlier in the previous section. (Refer back to Figures 20-3 and 20-4.) Notice, however, that they are not quite the same. Indeed, the FlatFileConnection Manager has a lot of the same information, but has a somewhat different editing format. For example, Figure 20-11 shows the part of the dialog box oriented around editing the data types you want to output.

That said, there really isn't anything new here. The connection managers area is just a path to allow you to edit your connection information (for both input and output) after you've exited the wizard.

Project Connections

FIGURE 20-11

While you're currently working with just a single package (in fact, you may have already deleted the default `Package.dtsk`), you might be thinking purely within the package you're writing now. For just a moment, though, I want to expand your perception to a wider application and imagine that this isn't just the package you're creating, but the *first* package you're creating.

In that context, the Connection Manager you just created could easily have broader applicability, by which I mean you might need to use it in multiple packages. Rather than re-create it for each, you can share this Connection Manager with every package in your project by promoting it to a Project Connection.

TRY IT OUT   Creating a Project Connection

You've already created (through the Import/Export Wizard) two Connection Managers within `Package1`. Let's turn the source, which contains an OLE DB connection to your local server and a query selecting some employee information, into a project connection usable by every package within the current project.

Looking at the Connection Managers pane (refer back to Figure 20-10 if you wish), right-click on `SourceConnectionOLEDB` and select Convert to Project Connection from the context menu. Visually, this will give you two cues when it's done: In the Connection Managers pane `SourceConnectionOLEDB` is now `SourceConnectionOLEDB 1` and appears in boldface, and in the Solution Explorer pane you'll see `SourceConnectionOLEDB 1.conmgr` under Project Connections.

How It Works

The Project Connection you've just created is now shared among all the packages you create within this project. If you change anything — say, you add a field to the query, or parameterize the target server for deployment — every package that utilizes that Project Connection sees the change. Instead of having to maintain the same information in several places, you've now centralized it.

The Package Editor Pane

This is something of the "meat and potatoes" section of the package. While you obviously couldn't move much data around without the connections discussed in the previous section, you'll find that the connection side of things won't look all that different from package to package. The actual flow and handler side of things will, however, often vary a great deal.

As you can see along the top of Figure 20-12, the package editor has five tabs to it, so let's explore each of these in turn.

First, though, notice the slider bar in the lower right corner: This controls the zoom level for your package layout, and is seen in several of the tabs. Complex package layouts can span a great deal of real estate, and this feature (new for SQL Server 2012) drew great applause from experienced SSIS developers at TechEd. You'll be happy it's there.

Control Flow

This does pretty much what its title would indicate. It controls flow between different logical constructs, or "tasks," in your package. In Package1, you have only one task defined, the Data Flow Task visible in Figure 20-12, but if you select that task (as I have in Figure 20-13), you'll see that it shows an arrow coming out of it.

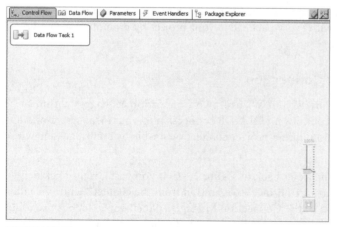

FIGURE 20-12

FIGURE 20-13

The arrow is representative of possible flow. You could, for example, add an FTP or external process task to your package to deal with elements of your Extract, Transform, and Load processes that can't be handled within the one data flow task that you have. This control flow aspect is critical to many packages in several ways:

- **Precedence:** The flow outlined in this part of the package establishes precedence. Think about this for a moment: If you need to FTP your data export to some external system after you've created it, you need to be sure that the FTP process does not fire until the export portion of the package is complete (or, more specifically, successful); control of flow is what lets you do this.

- **Multitasking:** If multiple tasks are available that do not have dependencies on earlier tasks (or are dependent on the same task), the package can allow the tasks to branch and run simultaneously.

- **Branching:** Further branching can take place depending on specific return conditions from the previous task. For example, retrieving a file if your FTP succeeds, but notifying an operator if it doesn't.

What, exactly, there is to potentially edit varies widely depending on the specific type of task you have. It might range from things as complex as connection and login information (as would be needed in something like the FTP task mentioned earlier) to something as simple as there being nothing to edit at all. (Indeed, were you to edit your data flow task, it would actually take you to the Data Flow tab, with nothing specific to control flow.)

Data Flow

Well, because the example is based around a data flow task, it's probably not surprising to find a little bit more meat in this area. You can edit the data flow by either double-clicking your data flow task in the Control Flow tab, or selecting the Data Flow tab, and then selecting the data flow you're interested in from the dropdown in the top of the pane (as shown in Figure 20-14).

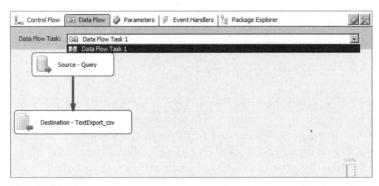

FIGURE 20-14

The wizard you ran has populated these data flow items for you, but let's take a quick look inside so you can relate to the various pieces; either double-click the Source — Query flow item, or right-click it and choose Edit. This brings up the OLE DB Source Editor shown in

Figure 20-15. The default option for editing is called the Connection Manager, but notice that, while there is overlap, there are several differences versus the dialog box that you looked at earlier. If you were using a parameterized query, this would be where you could edit the properties of those parameters.

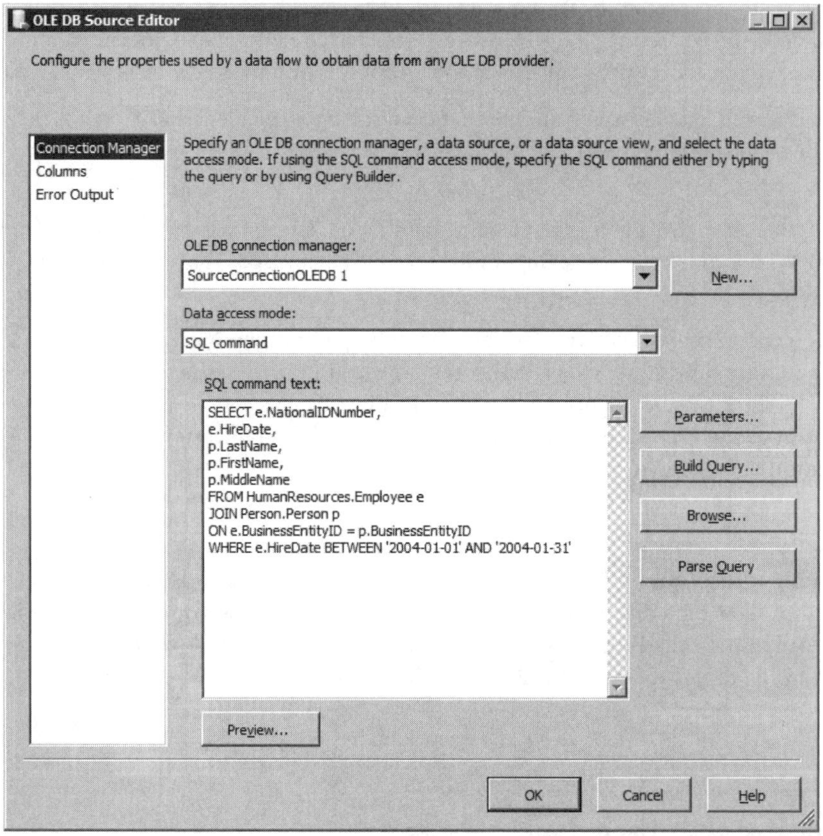

FIGURE 20-15

Before you leave the Data Flow section, select the Error Output option for this dialog box, as shown in Figure 20-16. The key thing to draw out of this dialog box is that you have different options for handling data flow errors. For this simple wizard-generated data flow item, all errors are considered fatal for the package, and the package will close with a fail returning to whatever called the flow item. (In this case, the data flow task in the control flow area, which will in turn pass the failure on and cause the package to terminate.) Other options would include ignoring the error (and skipping the row) or redirecting the row (perhaps to a holding table where the row can be manually or programmatically repaired before reattempting to import). Consider these options as you graduate into more advanced packages.

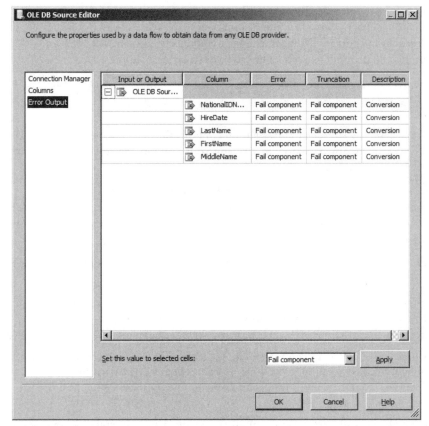

FIGURE 20-16

Cancel out of all the dialog boxes to leave things as they were when you completed the wizard.

Mapping Fields

The wizard has handled quite a number of tasks for you, including mapping source columns to destination columns. Let's take a look at how what you asked for in the wizard was implemented, because you'll likely need to do this manually at some point.

To begin with, remember that your destination connection manager has columns defined. Even though in this case it's a flat file, meaning that it's an empty text file to start with, SSIS has a set of columns and a file layout in mind, stored in the destination connection manager. The wizard first set that up (see Figure 20-11 again if you want to see it), and then built a set of column mappings (visible in Figure 20-8) that directed the output of selected columns from your source data into the defined output columns.

If you want to change that later, though, it's relatively easy. From within the Data Flow that you're already looking at, double-click the Destination — TextExport_csv task and select Mappings on the left side. You'll be presented with a table view of the source and destination columns with lines between. The lines are doing exactly what you might think: showing which source columns deposit their data in which destination columns. You can change mappings by clicking the lines and deleting them, and/or by dragging and dropping source columns to destination columns.

Once you've had a moment to try this out, click Cancel so that your changes aren't saved.

Resolving References

In the wizard's construct here, the source and destination columns line up quite neatly. I want to take a quick diversion from the happy path now to give you your first look at how to fix problems when everything isn't quite so naively idyllic.

Sometimes changes can have unexpected consequences, and tracking those down is a pretty significant part of a developer's job. ("The first step is putting the bugs in, the second is taking them out.") Let's make a change to your source that's not compatible with your destination and see how SSIS handles it, and how you can handle it when SSIS doesn't do it for you.

1. From the data flow task (Data Flow Task 1), open the source again by double-clicking Source - Query and selecting the Columns node on the left.

2. In the grid at the bottom, change the output column NationalIDNumber to just IDNumber. The mapping created between the source and destination by the wizard had NationalIDNumber mapped to NationalIDNumber. So what happens when you click OK?

   The result is that you've left SSIS completely unfazed. In prior versions you might have caused a problem, because mapping was done by name, but in 2012 it's a little smarter about handling IDs. That's nice, but it doesn't give you much practice in handling adversity.

3. Check the mappings in your destination again if you want to see, but you'll do something a little different now so you can tell what it would look like if there were an error.

4. Go back into your source columns and this time, in the table at the top, uncheck the box next to MiddleName. This prevents that column from being sent to the next component in the data flow task.

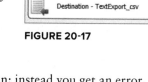

5. When you click OK this time, you'll see something new, visible in Figure 20-17.

   The red X on the green (success) output from the source indicates a mapping error. Your destination is expecting five columns, but it's receiving only four. It certainly isn't going to assume anything about what should go into the missing column; instead you get an error, and the package won't run until it's fixed.

FIGURE 20-17

6. If you double-click the error path, you'll get a dialog box like the one in Figure 20-18, giving you the opportunity to fix the missing references.

What you do here depends on the nature of the problem; one thing this dialog box won't let you do is add new source columns (you'd have to do that where you removed the column in the first place).

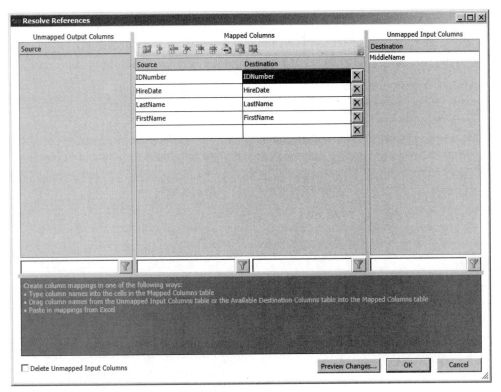

FIGURE 20-18

What you can do is either map an existing source column to the unmapped destination (you can see the unmapped destination on the top-right) or simply delete the unmapped input columns using the checkbox on the bottom-left. Don't do either for now; instead just cancel out, and go back into the source and add the MiddleName column again by checking the box next to it. The column will re-map automatically.

Parameters

Parameters in SSIS are used exactly like parameters in T-SQL stored procedures or functions. What might surprise you is that, until this version, there was no such thing as parameters in SSIS. Instead, there were variables, and using them was edging toward advanced material. Parameters work a lot more simply.

The Parameters tab is used to track the parameters that exist for this package only. Like Connection Managers, you can also have project-level parameters, although promoting them isn't as easy; you have to create them as project parameters rather than package parameters. Let's stick with a package parameter for this example.

Using Parameters

Let's make it so that a custom header can be added to the output file based on the parameter value.

1. Go to the Parameters tab and click the Add Parameter button on the top-left.

2. Fill in the values as follows:

COLUMN	VALUE
Name	DestinationHeader
Data Type	String
Value	*** Header - Default ***
Sensitive	False
Required	False
Description	Header to tack on to the destination file

3. The next two steps apply the parameter you just created to the Header property of the destination file. Return to the Control Flow tab and right-click the Data Flow task. Click Parameterize.

4. Set the property at the top as shown in Figure 20-19, and use the existing parameter you just created. Note that you could create a new parameter from within this dialog box, but you can also choose any existing package-level or project-level parameter.

That's it...now whatever you set as the value of that parameter will be output as a file header on your destination. Later in the chapter, you'll learn how to set runtime values on parameters when it's time to execute the package.

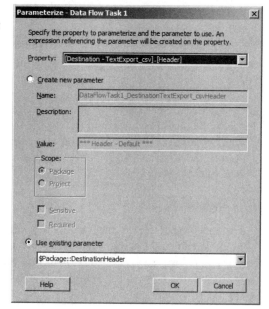

FIGURE 20-19

Project Parameters

There's not much to say about project parameters that wasn't already said about project connections. If you create parameters at the project level, they'll be shared by every package in your project (even if they're not used by the package). Be careful not to create mandatory project parameters that aren't mandatory for every package.

Event Handlers

Moving over to the Event Handlers tab, you can see the many events that we can supply code for. Activate the dropdown (as I have in Figure 20-20). While the default is `OnError`, you can deal with a very wide range of scenarios. Let's examine how a few of these might be used:

➤ `OnError`: Well, I would hope that this is the most obvious one. As you would expect, this event is fired in the event an error is detected. It allows you to address the error in some fashion.

➤ `OnWarning`: Basically the same as `OnError`, but it allows you to examine and possibly address warnings too.

➤ `OnProgress`: For long-running processes, this can be handy for updating some form of progress indicator (perhaps a status table somewhere).

➤ `OnPreExecute`: Allows for things like preparation code to run prior to starting the main part of the task.

And this is, of course, just a taste. What events to use will vary by need. When you create an event handler you can use the canvas just like the control flow canvas, so you can utilize the full range of SSIS functionality to handle the event however you wish.

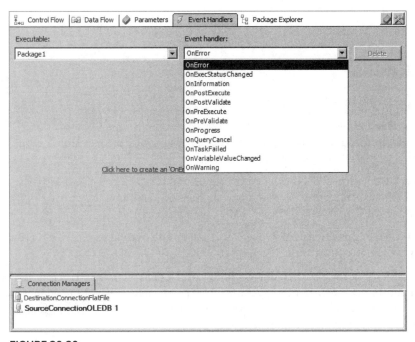

FIGURE 20-20

Package Explorer

This is, again, one of those things that is what it sounds like. Much like Windows Explorer is a way to explore your file system in a folder-based paradigm, the Package Explorer allows you to explore the package in a similar paradigm. This can be useful if your package grows a bit large and unwieldy, and you're searching for a particular component. In Figure 20-21, I've expanded a few of the folders to give you a feel of the Package Explorer.

FIGURE 20-21

EXECUTING PACKAGES

There are a few ways to execute an SSIS package:

➤ **From within the Development Studio:** The SQL Server Data Tools, just like any other instance of Visual Studio, allows for the idea of you running your packages from within the development environment (you gotta be able to debug!).

➤ **The Execute Package Utility:** This is essentially an executable where you can specify the package you want to execute, set up any required parameters, and have the utility run it for you on demand.

➤ **From SQL Server Management Studio:** Once you've deployed your package to a server, you can locate and execute it from within SSMS.

➤ **As a scheduled task using the SQL Server Agent:** I'll talk more about the SQL Server Agent in Chapter 21, but for now, realize that executing an SSIS package is one of the many types of jobs that the agent understands. You can specify a package name and time and frequency to run it in, and the SQL Server Agent takes care of it.

➤ **From within a program:** There is an entire object model supporting the notion of instantiating SSIS objects within your programs, setting properties for the packages, and executing them.

 NOTE *Instantiating SSIS objects is fairly detailed stuff — so much so that Wrox has an entire book on the subject (Professional SQL Server 2012 Integration Services by Knight et al., Wiley 2012). As such, it's outside the scope of this book. It's there for advanced study when you're ready.*

Executing a Package inside the Development Studio

This works just like debugging most any Visual Studio project. Simply press F5, click the green arrow on the toolbar, or choose Start Debugging from the Debug menu. As it builds (assuming it builds successfully), you should see the Data Flow Task (Data Flow Task 1) first display an amber spinner, and then a green check (indicating it ran successfully). If there were multiple steps to your package, you would see each task fire in turn (sometimes many at once) until the overall package was complete.

Go ahead and run the package this way, and then check out the produced text file. (Its exact location will depend on whether you specified a full path in your file definition or how Visual Studio is configured.) If your package fails, shown by a red X icon on the task, it's possible you're trying to write the file where you don't have write privileges; change the destination path if you have trouble.

Executing within SSMS

Once you've successfully run the package in debug mode and satisfied yourself that it's the package you want to go with, you can pack it up and deploy it to your SQL Server. A package thus deployed can easily be found within SSMS and executed, so let's give that a go.

Deploying SSIS Packages

The first thing you're going to have to do is deploy the package. In prior versions of SSIS, this could be a bit of a chore, but in 2012 you've got a much easier time.

 NOTE *If you're already familiar with the older method, or have infrastructure already built up around doing things the old way, you can right-click the project and select Convert to Legacy Deployment Model.*

Using the SSIS 2012 deployment wizard requires that your database instance be primed to receive packages into a special database: the Integration Services catalog. Because this catalog doesn't exist by default, you should create it now.

1. Open SSMS and connect the Object Explorer to your destination server if it's not open already.

2. Navigate to the Integration Services node, right-click, and choose Create Catalog.

3. In the dialog box, click Enable CLR Integration, and then enter a password to encrypt the SSIS catalog (do not lose this). Click OK.

4. Now you can see the SSISDB node under Integration Services. Right-click that and select New Folder, name it Chapter 20, and click OK. You now have a location you can deploy to.

5. To deploy your package, return to SSDT. Right-click the project and choose Deploy. The deployment wizard launches, beginning with yet another purely descriptive introduction screen.

6. Clicking Next brings you to a dialog box shown in Figure 20-22. It asks what exactly you'd like to deploy. Leave Project Deployment file selected. The filename you see (ending in `.ispac`) is what your `.dtsx` package will compile to.

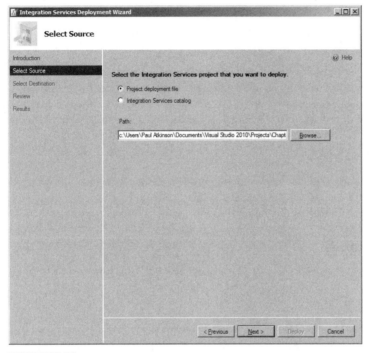

FIGURE 20-22

7. Clicking Next brings you to a dialog box where you select the server you'd like to deploy to. You can enter the server name or, like virtually anywhere you're entering a server name, you can use `(local)` or `.` to indicate the default instance on the local machine.

8. For the path, drill down to `Chapter 20`, select it, and click Next to view the review screen.

9. Once you're satisfied with the choices, go ahead and click Deploy and then Close after the progress completes.

Congratulations, you've deployed your project!

> **NOTE** *You don't have to deploy with SSDT, however, if you don't want to. Your `.ispac` file can be deployed to an Integration Services catalog through SSMS. Simply drill into the catalog down to the Projects node, right-click that node, and choose Deploy Project to invoke the Deployment Wizard. On the Select Source page of the wizard, choose to deploy a Project deployment file and provide the path to your `.ispac`. Using this method, you can deploy to servers outside your development arena.*

Executing the Package

Now that you've deployed the package, you can execute it by drilling into the SSISDB node in Management Studio down to your package, seen in Figure 20-23.

When you select Execute, you'll get a dialog box showing the parameter you created, which allows you to override the default value for this run. Go ahead and set it to whatever you'd like before running the package; this is the text you'll see at the head of the export file.

Execution of your package in this context is fully asynchronous; the package is being run by the SSIS service in the background, and you simply receive notification that you have successfully started the run. If you'd like, you can look at the Overview Report (shown in Figure 20-24) — one of many built-in SSIS-related reports that detail the status of all the activity on your SSIS instance.

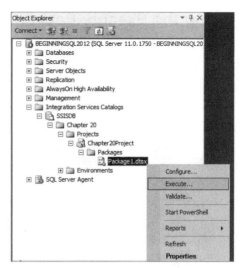

FIGURE 20-23

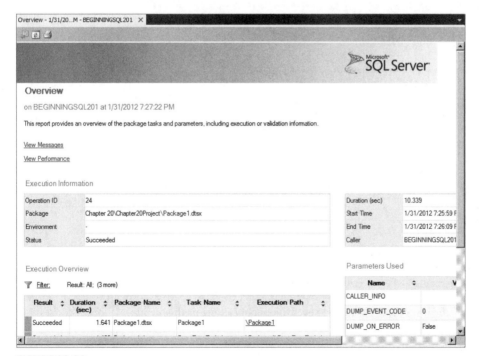

FIGURE 20-24

This package should run in less time than it takes for you to click through, so it will be complete by the time you look at the report (if you choose to do so). Once it's done, you can look for the output file in the directory you chose for it, and inside you will see the output along with your parameterized header.

Using the Execute Package Utility

The Execute Package Utility comes in two forms: a UI-driven application by the name of DTExecUI.exe, and a command-line version simply called DTExec.exe. For the exploration here, you'll fire up DTExecUI.exe. You can also navigate using Windows Explorer and find a package in the file system (they end in .DTSX) and then double-click it to execute it. Do that to your original export package, and you should get the execute dialog box shown in Figure 20-25.

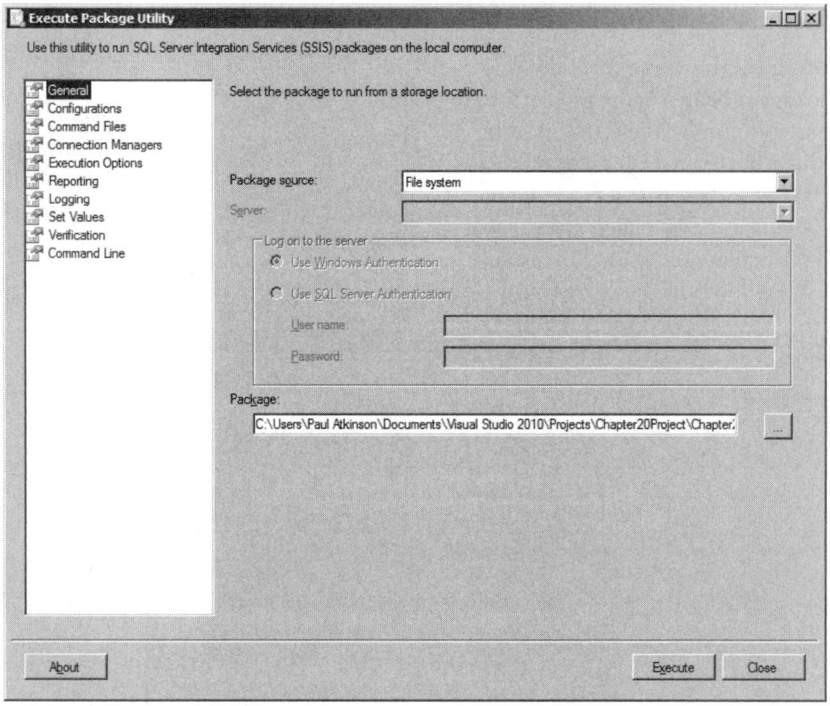

FIGURE 20-25

This is quite different from the dialog box you got when you executed the package from within SSMS. As you can see, there are a number of pages within this dialog box that you can select by clicking the various options to the left. Coverage of this could take up a book all to itself, but let's look at a few of the important things on several key pages within this utility.

General

Many fields on this first dialog box are fairly self-explanatory, but let's pay particular attention to the Package Source field. You can store SSIS packages in one of three places:

➤ **The File System:** This is what you did using the Import/Export Wizard package. This option is really nice for mobility; you can easily save the package off and move it to another system.

> ➤ **SQL Server:** This model stores the package in SQL Server. Using this approach, your package will be backed up whenever you back up your MSDB database (which is a system database in every SQL Server installation).

> ➤ **SSIS Package Store:** This storage model provides the idea of an organized set of "folders" where you can store your package along with other packages of the same general type or purpose. The folders can be stored in either MSDB or the file system. Note that in SQL Server 2012 Integration Services, this is secured; if you haven't been explicitly granted rights, you can't use this option. (As with many things in Windows, if you are able to run DTExecUI as Administrator, you can bypass the security warning.)

Configurations

SSIS allows you to define configurations for your packages. These are essentially a collection of settings to be used, and you can actually combine more than one of them into a suite of settings.

Command Files

These are batch files that you want to run as part of your package. You can use these to do system-level things such as copying files around to places you need them. (They run under whatever account the Integration Services Service is running under, so any required access on your network need to be granted to that account.)

Connection Managers

This is a bit of a misnomer. This isn't so much a list of connection managers as it is a list of package connections. By taking a look at the Description column, you'll see many of the key properties for each connection your package uses. Notice that in the example package, you have two connections, but one is project-level. If you look, you'll see how only the one that relates to file information (for your connection to the flat file you're using) is there, and the other that specifically relates to SQL Server (the export source connection) isn't shown here.

Execution Options

Do not underestimate the importance of this one. Not only does it allow you to specify how, at a high level, you want things to happen if something goes wrong (if there's an error), but it also allows you to establish checkpoint tracking — making it easy to see when and where your package is getting to different execution points. This can be critical in performance tuning and debugging.

Reporting

This one is all about letting you know what is happening. You can set up for feedback: exactly how much feedback is based on which events you decide to track and the level of information you establish.

Logging

This one is fairly complex to set up and get going, but has a very high "coolness" factor in terms of giving you a very flexible architecture of tracking even the most complex of packages.

Using this area, you can configure your package to write log information to a number of preconfigured "providers" (essentially, well-understood destinations for your log data). In addition to the preinstalled providers such as text files and even a SQL Server table, you can even create your own custom providers (not for the faint of heart). You can log at the package level, or you can get very detailed levels of granularity and write to different locations for different tasks within your package.

Set Values

This establishes the starting value of any runtime properties your package uses. (There are none in the simple package in this chapter.) The runtime parameters you can create and set in the 2012 version may make this useful only for legacy packages.

Verification

Totally different packages can have the same filename (just be in a different spot in the file system, for example). In addition, packages have the ability to retain different versions of themselves within the same file or package store. The Verification dialog box is all about filtering or verifying which package/version you want to execute.

Command Line

You can execute SSIS packages from the command line (handy when, for example, you're trying to run DTS packages out of a batch file). This option within the SSIS Package Execution Utility is about specifying parameters you would have used if you had run the package from the command line.

The utility establishes most of this for you; the option here is just to allow you to perform something of an override on the options used when you tell the utility to execute.

Executing the Package

If you simply click Execute in the Package Execution Utility, your package will be off and running. After it runs, you should find a text file in whatever location you told your package to store it; open it up, take a look, and verify that it is what you expected.

Executing Using the SQL Server Agent

I haven't really discussed the SQL Server Agent up to this point, but, from an SSIS point of view, think of the SQL Server Agent as a job scheduler that allows you to do the same thing as running DTExec.exe, but on a specific time and frequency basis with very robust job- and task-scheduling systems to integrate your package into a larger set of system jobs.

I will discuss the agent in a bit more detail in Chapter 21.

Executing a Package from within a Program

SQL Server offers a very rich object model that is usable from within any .NET language. The programmability object model is well beyond the scope of this book, but suffice to say that you can programmatically execute packages and dynamically build packages to meet a certain need before executing them.

A FINAL WORD ON PACKAGES

I want to take a moment and reiterate that this chapter has only touched the surface of what's possible. As I've said before, there are entire books (rather large ones actually) written around Integration Services as the sole topic.

The package you focused on here was generated by the Import/Export Wizard, but the end product was a typical SSIS package. Not only can you edit it, but you could well have built it from scratch yourself. You can easily add other tasks to deal with things like "scrubbing" data after importing it to some form of "staging" area and then perform additional tasks. You can add complex branching to deal with errors or perform several tasks in parallel; the possibilities go on and on.

In the next chapter's section on using ETLs in a business intelligence/data warehousing context, you'll read about a conceptual framework for building out robust ETLs that move data through multiple stages. Refer back to this chapter if you need to, and you'll see how these concepts apply to that real-world application.

SUMMARY

SQL Server Integration Services is a robust Extract, Transform, and Load tool. You can utilize Integration Services to provide one-off or repeated import and export of data to and from your databases — mixing a variety of data sources while you're at it.

While becoming expert in all that Integration Services has to offer is a positively huge undertaking, getting basic imports and exports up and running is a relative piece of cake. I encourage you to start out simple, and then add to it as you go. As you push yourself further and further with what SSIS can do, take a look at other books that are specific to what SSIS has to offer.

EXERCISES

1. Using the Import/Export Wizard, create a package that imports data from the file you exported during this chapter into a new table called `TestExport`. Do not forget to drop this table once you're done with Exercise 2.

2. Deploy the package you just created and run it from the management studio. Hint: If you use the existing project from this chapter and you see a deployment warning that this project already exists, it's safe to continue.

▶ WHAT YOU LEARNED IN THIS CHAPTER

TOPIC	CONCEPT
ETL	Extract, Transform, and Load processes broadly encompass the whole range of times that you want to either retrieve data from some kind of foreign data source and save it in your own database, or vice-versa. The tool provided with SQL Server to accomplish ETL is SQL Server Integration Services.
Packages	A package is a single SSIS program. Each package consists of a control flow, which is a series of tasks, each of which can execute as soon as all its prerequisites have completed.
Import/Export Wizard	The simplest way to create a useful SSIS package, this wizard walks you through creating a source and destination for your data and mapping one to the other. The end product of the wizard is not an actual data import or export, but a package capable of performing one.
Executing packages	Packages can be run from within SSDT for debugging, as well as through SSMS or SQL Agent once they've been deployed. You can also execute them from the command line using the DTSExecUI utility, or programmatically.
Deploying packages	To deploy packages to SQL Server, you must first build the SSISDB catalog and create a destination for your packages. Once the catalog exists, you can deploy using a wizard within SSDT.

21

Playing Administrator

WHAT YOU WILL LEARN IN THIS CHAPTER:

➤ Running repetitive jobs in off hours

➤ Setting login and user security

➤ Understanding the backup and recovery process

➤ Using maintenance scripts to run backup and recovery

➤ Using PowerShell to automate administration tasks

And so, here you are. You've read about so many aspects of creating a database (and I do hope you're looking forward to putting that learning into practice), that you probably feel like you're at the end of the road for now, but there's one thing left. Someone's eventually going to have to use that database you've developed, so it's time to talk a bit about maintenance and administration.

As a developer, I can just hear it now: "Isn't that the database administrator's job?" If you did indeed say something like that, step back, and smack yourself — *hard* (and no, I'm not kidding). If there is anything I hope to instill in you in your database development efforts, it's to avoid the "Hey, I just build 'em, now it's your problem" attitude that is all too common out there.

A database-driven application is a wildly different animal than most standalone applications. Most standalone applications are either self-maintaining, or deal with single files that are relatively easy for a user to copy somewhere for backup purposes. Likewise, they usually have no "maintenance" issues the way that a database does.

That thing you create, when you put all this to work, broadly falls into what's called the *persistence layer* — the part of the application that persists, or hangs around. While the application code sits unaltered run after run, everything that's saved into the database stays...and has to, or else you've got big problems. You must ensure that the information in your database persists, even beyond the immediate user experience.

This chapter looks at some of the tasks that are necessary to ensure that your end users can not only recover from problems and disasters, but also perform some basic maintenance that helps things keep running smoothly.

Among the things this chapter touches on are:

➤ Scheduling jobs

➤ Security

➤ Backing up and restoring

➤ Performing basic defragmentation and index rebuilding

➤ Using alerts

➤ Using Policy Based Management

➤ Automated administration

➤ Archiving

Although these are far from the only administration tasks available, these do represent something of a minimum set of plans you should expect to address in your application's overall deployment plan.

For purposes of this book, I largely stay with the GUI tools that are included in SQL Server Management Studio (I will touch very briefly on Policy Based Management and PowerShell). Be aware, however, that there are more robust options available for the more advanced user that allow you to programmatically control many of the administration features via the SQL Server Management Objects (SMO) object model. Those options are geared more toward the career DBA, so I'm just letting you know they're out there.

SCHEDULING JOBS

Many of the tasks that you'll learn about in the remainder of the chapter can be *scheduled*. Scheduling jobs allows you to run tasks that place a load on the system at off-peak hours. Scheduling also ensures that you don't forget to take care of things. From index rebuilds to backups, you'll hear of horror stories over and over about shops that "forgot" to do that, or thought they had set up a scheduled job but never checked on it.

 NOTE *If your background is in Windows Server, and you have scheduled other jobs using the Windows Scheduler service, you could utilize that scheduling engine to support SQL Server. Doing things all in the Windows Scheduler allows you to have everything in one place, but SQL Server has some more robust branching options.*

There are basically two terms to think about: Jobs and Steps.

➤ **Steps:** Single processes that will execute or a batch of commands that will run. Steps are not independent. They exist only as members of jobs.

➤ **Jobs:** A grouping of one or more steps that should be run together. You can, however, set up dependencies and branching depending on the success or failure of individual steps. (For example, Step A runs if the previous step succeeds, but Step B runs if the previous step fails.)

Jobs can be scheduled based on the following criteria:

➤ Daily, weekly, or monthly basis

➤ A specific time of the day

➤ A specific frequency (say, every 10 minutes, or every hour)

➤ When the CPU becomes idle for a period of time

➤ When the SQL Server Agent starts

➤ In response to an alert

Steps are run by virtue of being part of a job and based on the branching rules you define for your job. Just because a job runs doesn't mean that all the steps that are part of that job will run; some may execute and others may not, depending on the success or failure of previous steps in the job and what *branching rules* you have established. SQL Server not only allows one step to fire automatically when another finishes but also allows for doing something entirely different (such as running some sort of recovery step) if the current step fails.

In addition to branching you can, depending on what happens, also tell SQL Server to perform the following:

➤ Provide notification of the success or failure of a job to an operator. You're allowed to send a separate notification for a network message (which would pop up on users' and screens as long as they are logged in), a pager, and an e-mail address to one operator each.

➤ Write the information to the event log.

➤ Automatically delete the job (to prevent executing it later and generally "clean up").

What does it mean to notify an operator? Let's take a quick look at how to create operators in Management Studio.

Creating an Operator

If you're going to make use of the notification features of the SQL Agent, you must have an operator set up to define the specifics about who is notified. This side of things — the creation of operators — isn't typically done through any kind of automated process or as part of the developed code; these are usually created manually by the DBA. You'll take a rather brief look at it here just to understand how it works in relation to the scheduling of tasks.

Creating an Operator Using Management Studio

To create an operator using Management Studio, you need to navigate to the SQL Server Agent node of the server for which you're creating the operator. Expand the SQL Server Agent node, right-click the Operators member, and choose New Operator.

 NOTE Be aware that, depending on your particular installation, the SQL Server Agent Service may not start automatically by default. If you run into any issues or if you notice the SQL Server Agent icon in Management Studio has a little red square in it, the service is probably set to manual or even disabled; you will probably want to change the service to start automatically. Regardless, make sure that it is running for the examples, Try It Out, and Exercises found in this chapter. You can do this by right-clicking the Agent node and selecting Start.

You should be presented with the dialog box shown in Figure 21-1. (Mine is partially filled in.)

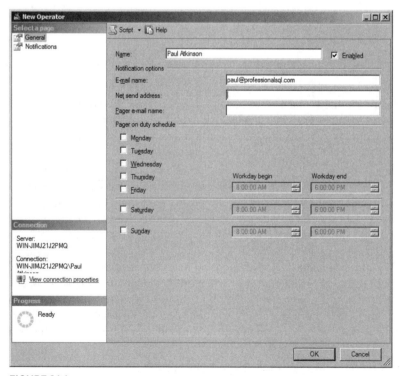

FIGURE 21-1

You can then fill out a schedule indicating what times this operator is to receive e-mail notifications for certain kinds of errors that you'll see on the Notifications tab.

Speaking of that Notifications tab, go ahead and click over to it. It should appear as in Figure 21-2.

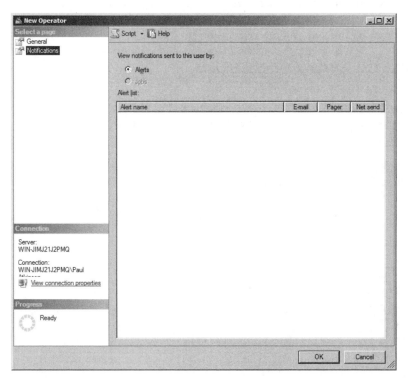

FIGURE 21-2

Until you have more alerts in your system (I'll get to those later in this chapter), this page may not make a lot of sense. What it is about is setting up which notifications you want this operator to receive depending on which defined alerts are triggered. Again, it's harder to understand this concept before you've gotten to alerts, but suffice to say that alerts are triggered when certain things happen in your database, and this page defines which alerts this particular operator receives.

Creating Jobs and Steps

As mentioned earlier, jobs are a collection of one or more steps. A step is a logical unit of work, such as backing up one database or running a T-SQL script to meet a specific need such as rebuilding all your indexes or updating statistics for the query optimizer.

Even though a job can contain several steps, this is no guarantee that every step in a job will run. They will either run or not run depending on the success or failure of other steps in the job and what you've defined to be the response for each case of success or failure. For example, you might cancel the remainder of the job if one of the steps fails, but failure of another step might simply write a message to the Windows Event Log and move on to another step in the job.

Just like operators, jobs can be created in Management Studio, as well as through programmatic constructs. For purposes of this book, you'll stick to the Management Studio method. (Even among highly advanced SQL Server developers, programmatic construction of jobs and tasks is relatively rare, although I know some programmers who are very proficient with it.)

Creating Jobs and Tasks Using Management Studio

SQL Server Management Studio makes it very easy to create scheduled jobs. Just navigate to the SQL Server Agent node of your server, and then right-click the Jobs member and select New Job. You should get a multimode dialog box, shown in Figure 21-3, which helps you build the job one step at a time.

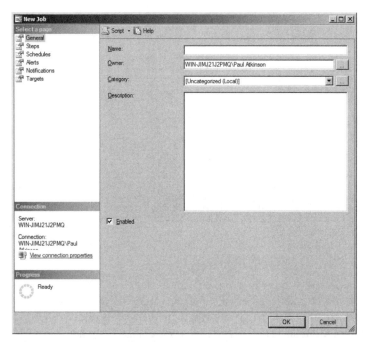

FIGURE 21-3

The name can be whatever you like as long as it adheres to the SQL Server rules for naming as discussed early in the book.

Most of the rest of the information is, again, self-explanatory with the exception of Category, which is just one way of grouping jobs. Many of your jobs that are specific to your application are going to be uncategorized, although you will probably on occasion run into instances where you want to create Database Maintenance, Full Text, or Replication jobs; those each go into their own category for easy identification.

NOTE *If you're feeling especially organized, you can create your own custom job categories from within SSMS. Under the SQL Server Agent node, right-click Jobs and select Manage Job Categories; the rest is pretty self-explanatory.*

You can then move on to Steps, as shown in Figure 21-4. This is the place where you tell SQL Server to start creating your new steps that will be part of this job.

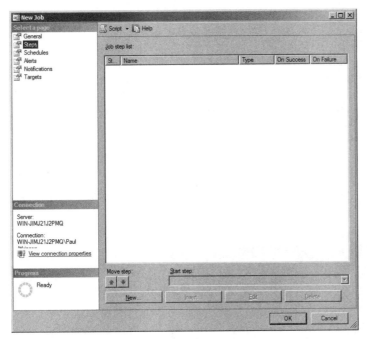

FIGURE 21-4

To add a new step to your job, follow these steps:

1. Click the New button in Figure 21-4 and fill in the new dialog box, shown in Figure 21-5 under the General tab. If you want to follow along with the text (and I do suggest it if you're going through this the first time), use a T-SQL statement to raise a bogus error just so you can see that things are really happening when you schedule this job.

NOTE *Note, however, that there is an Open button to the left of the command box; you can use this to import SQL scripts that you have saved in files.*

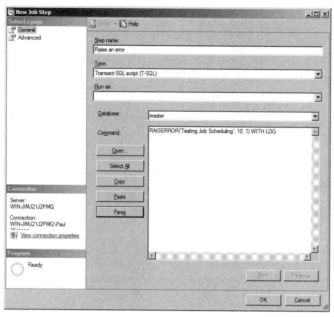

FIGURE 21-5

2. Click the Advanced tab to reveal the dialog box shown in Figure 21-6; it's here that you really start to see some of the cool functionality that the job scheduler offers.

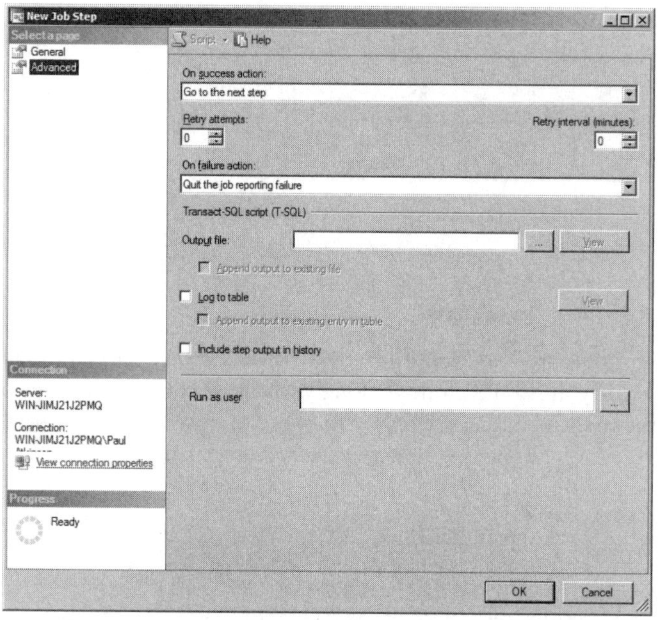

FIGURE 21-6

Notice several things in this dialog box. You can:

➤ Automatically set the job to retry at a specific interval if the task fails.

➤ Choose what to do if the job succeeds or fails. For each result (success or failure), you can: quit reporting success, quit reporting failure, or move on to the next step.

➤ Output results to a file. (This is very nice for auditing.)

➤ Impersonate another user (for rights purposes).

 NOTE *Note that to impersonate a user, you have to have the rights for that user. If you're logged in as a sysadmin, you can run the job as the dbo or just about anyone. The average users would probably only have the guest account available (unless they were the dbo) but, hey, in most cases general users shouldn't be scheduling their own jobs this way anyway. (Let your client application provide that functionality.)*

3. Okay, so there's little chance that your RAISERROR statement is going to fail, so go ahead and take the default of Quit the Job Reporting Failure for the On Failure Action. (You'll see other possibilities later in the chapter when you come to backups.)

4. That moves you back to the main New Job dialog box, and you're now ready to move on to the Schedules node, shown in Figure 21-7.

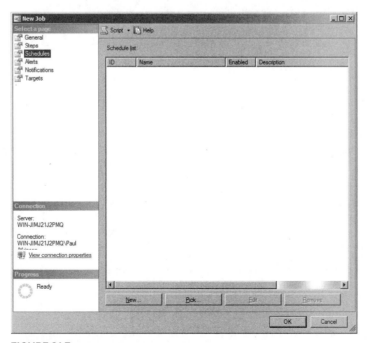

FIGURE 21-7

In this dialog box, you can manage one or more scheduled times for this job to run. To actually create a new scheduled time for the job to run, you click the New button. That brings up yet another dialog box, shown in Figure 21-8.

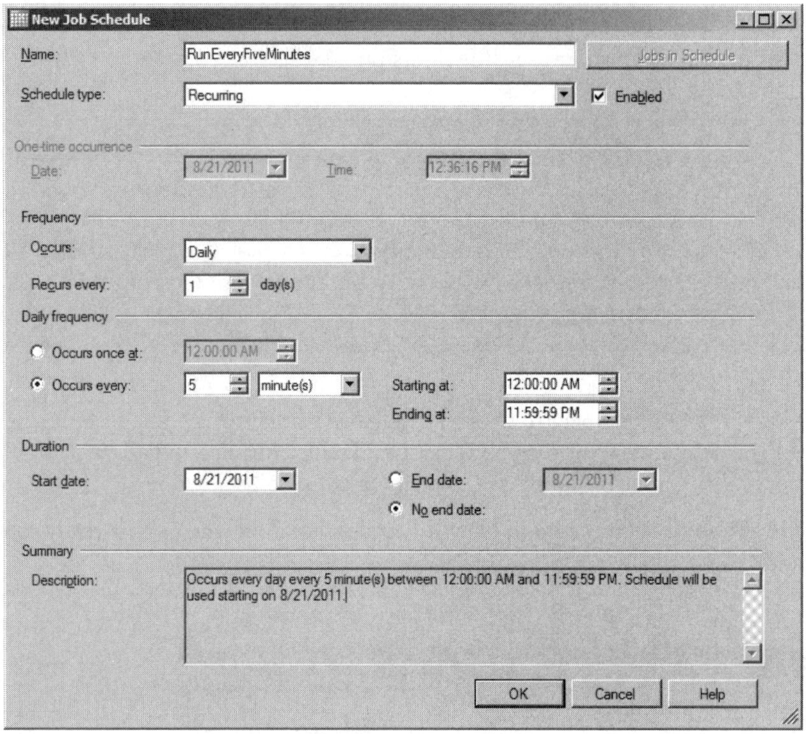

FIGURE 21-8

5. I've largely filled this one out already (lest you get buried in a sea of screenshots), but it is from this dialog box that you create a new schedule for this job. Recurrence and frequency are set here.

The frequency side of things can be a bit confusing because of the funny way that they've worded things. If you want something to run at multiple times every day, you need to set the job to Occur Daily Every 1 Day. This seems like it would run only once a day, but then you also have the option of setting whether it runs once or at an interval. In our case, you want to set your job to run every 5 minutes.

6. Now you're ready to move on to the next node of the job properties — alerts, shown in Figure 21-9.

FIGURE 21-9

From here, you can select which alerts you want to make depending on what happens. Choose Add and you get yet another rich dialog box, shown in Figure 21-10. This dialog box has the following nodes:

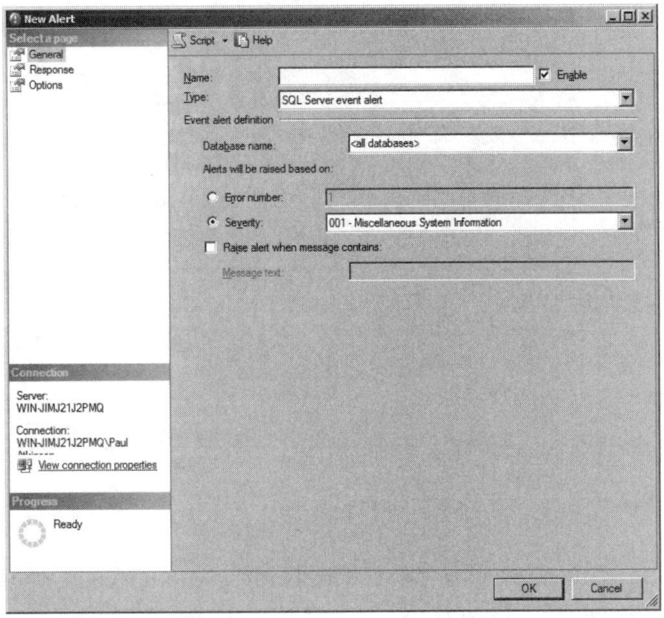

FIGURE 21-10

➤ **General:** Here, you fill out some of the basics. You can, for example, limit this notification to one particular database. You can also define just how severe the condition needs to be before the alert will fire (in terms of severity of the error).

➤ **Response:** This is shown in Figure 21-11.

 NOTE *Notice that you can choose the operator that you created earlier in the chapter. It is through the definitions of these operators that the SQL Server Agent knows what e-mail address or net send address to make the notification to. Also notice that you have control, on the right side, over how your operator is notified.*

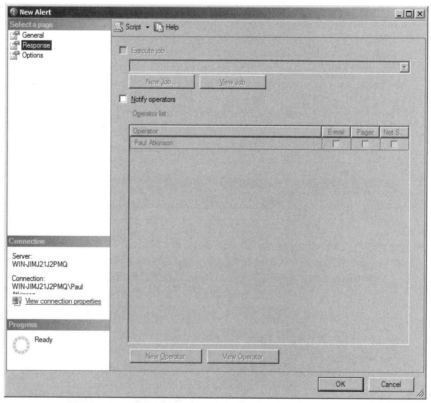

FIGURE 21-11

➤ **Options:** This is shown in Figure 21-12. This is where you can choose how to notify the operator you chose in the last step.

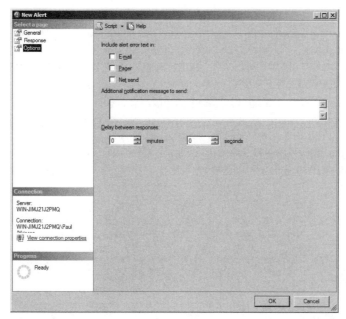

FIGURE 21-12

7. Go back to the Notifications node of the main New Job dialog box, shown in Figure 21-13. This window lets you bypass the older alerts model and define a response that is specific to this one job; just stick with what you already have for now, although you could define specific additional notifications in this dialog box.

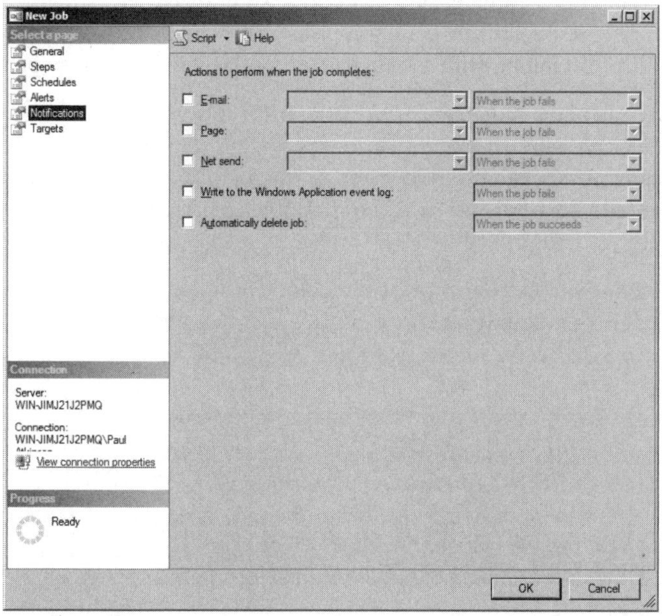

FIGURE 21-13

8. The last node in the list is the Targets node. This one generally falls in both the administrator and the advanced realms, as it is based on the idea of one SQL Server scheduling jobs onto other SQL Servers. Be aware that it's there for special needs, but a detailed description of Targets belongs in either an advanced or an administrator text, rather than this beginning programmer book.

9. At this point, you are ready to choose OK and exit the dialog box. You'll need to wait a few minutes before the task fires, but you should start to see log entries appear every five minutes in the Windows Event Log. You can look at this by navigating to Start ⇨ Programs ⇨ Administrative Tools ⇨ Event Viewer. You'll need to switch the view to use the Application Log rather than the default System Log.

> **NOTE** *Don't forget that, if you're going to be running scheduled tasks like this one, you need to have the SQL Server Agent running for them to be executed. You can check the status of the SQL Server Agent by running the SQL Server Configuration Manager and selecting the SQL Server Agent service, or by navigating to the SQL Server Agent node of the Object Explorer in Management Studio.*
>
> *Also, don't forget to disable this job. (Right-click the job in Management Studio after you've seen that it's working the way you expect. Otherwise, it will just continue to sit there and create entries in your Application Log; eventually, the Application Log will fill up and you can have problems with your system!)*

LOGINS AND USERS

Although SQL Server security is a matter of some depth and critical importance, it is not a topic I'm going to cover deeply in a beginning programmer book. If I don't skim the surface a bit, though, you may end up out of your depth on a few relatively common tasks that have more to do with application design than server administration. Beginning with a little background, then, here's a primer.

In general, we think of security as being a matter of authentication and permission. Authentication is the part where the system decides whether you are who you say you are (passwords are the most obvious mechanism out of many possible), and permission is whether, now that the system accepts that it's you, you have the rights to do what you're asking to do; whether you can read from a particular table or run a specific stored procedure.

Principals are the basic unit of authentication. A principal can be atomic, like a user, or it can be a group; either way, the principal is the requesting entity. SQL Server can recognize Windows domain users, domain groups, or native SQL Server logins and roles.

> **NOTE** *To see the principals that exist for any given database, you can query the* `sys.database_principals` *table from within that database in SQL Server Management Studio. For server principals (whether they have rights within the database or not), use* `sys.server_principals`.

Security Modes

When you install a new instance of SQL Server, you're asked to select the security mode and must choose between Windows Integrated security and Mixed Mode. Speaking as an application developer this is sometimes chosen for you, leaving you simply to respond to the server's configuration as-is, but often you'll get a choice. Obviously if you're going to be involved in the decision you ought to know what your criteria might be.

SQL Server can always recognize Windows domain users and groups as principals. The choice is between that alone, and that plus allowing you to create native SQL Server logins that don't relate directly to Windows users. To select domain users and groups only, choose Windows Integrated security; to allow native logins as well, choose Mixed Mode.

In either case, SQL will create a superuser account named sa ("System Administrator") as a native-mode login. Choosing Mixed Mode will require a password for the sa user, whereas choosing Windows authentication will create the account in a disabled state. Of critical importance, though, is that this user is common to all SQL instances. That means that attackers know about it, so always, always, *always* keep it disabled or secured with a well-protected password.

There are many issues to consider when choosing between modes, but I'm just going to hit on a couple (as in many places in this chapter, advanced knowledge here really is in the DBA realm). In general, Windows authentication is preferred because:

➤ **It is more secure.** It uses the built-in Kerberos authentication.

➤ **Managing users and groups is easier.** There's only one list (in Active Directory) to maintain.

➤ **The sa login is disabled.** This closes one avenue of attack.

However, many installations still use Mixed Mode. Among the considerations that may lead you there are when you're:

➤ Operating in a heterogeneous environment where not every user can have a domain login

➤ Operating across untrusted domains

Whichever mode you find your server running, it is possible to change it — but make sure your choice works with the IT administrators who will have to maintain it in the long term.

Creating Logins and Users

Logins and Users can be thought of as broadly corresponding to the two aspects of security: authentication and permission. Logins identify which principals are recognized by SQL Server; domain users or groups without a SQL Server login never get checked for object permissions, and this is where native SQL logins are defined for authentication. Users, which are associated with a login, are granted permission to perform actions against a database.

Logins are created at the server level, not the database level. To create a login through SQL Server Management Studio, follow these steps:

1. Drill down from the server into the Security node, and then right-click Logins and select New Login. You'll receive a multimode dialog box like the one in Figure 21-14.

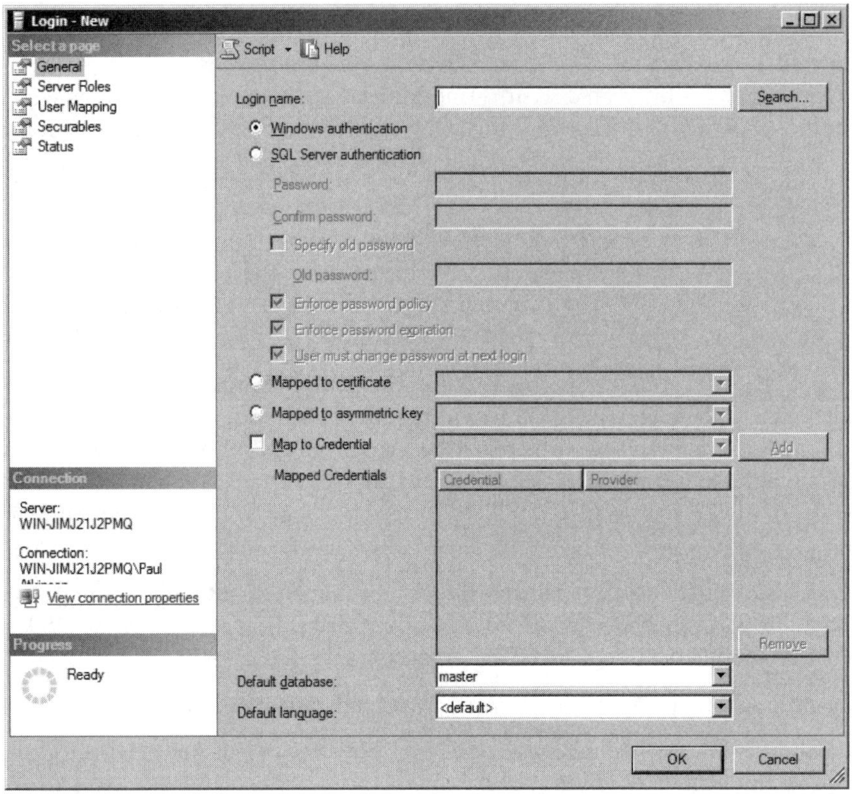

FIGURE 21-14

While there's a lot more in this dialog box than belongs in this book, creating a simple login — the common case — is very easy.

2. The login needs a name, and if you're using Windows Integrated security, it already has one. You can enter the Active Directory domain login here, including the domain (in the common DOMAIN\Username format) and that's enough. If you're in Mixed Mode that works as well, but you may also select SQL Server Authentication and enter both a username and a password.

3. You can create one or more users for this login right away by choosing User Mapping in the left side of the dialog box. This allows you to map this login to new (or existing) usernames in each database you have rights to on your system, as you can see in Figure 21-15.

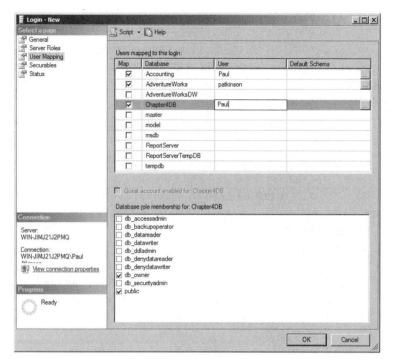

FIGURE 21-15

4. If you find you need to learn more about users and logins — and well you might — start by consulting your friendly local DBA, who lives and breathes this stuff the way you do T-SQL. Meanwhile, let's talk about how you might make use of the users who have been created by you or by the DBA.

Rights and Ownership

Creating a user doesn't quite get you all the way there, you see. By itself, the user is just a container for a set of permissions, and if it's empty it can't do much. Like any proper security system, SQL Server assumes you can't do anything by default and allows you the right to perform operations only through explicit permission.

There's one set of permissions for each database that's complete, whose user can do anything: dbo, the database owner. A database can have only one owner, but that user can do anything — read any table, run any procedure, create or delete any object, and even grant or deny permissions to existing or new principals. By default the user who creates a database is dbo. (Way back in Chapter 5 you read about schemas and ownership...if you're fuzzy on those issues, now would be a fine time to skim that chapter again.)

Besides ownership, any user can be given rights to do just about anything. Roles can be created to package up sets of rights to grant as a block to users, or else individual rights (for example, the right to execute a specific sproc, or read from a particular table, or update that table) can be granted by the dbo.

BACKUP AND RECOVERY

No database-driven application should ever be deployed or sold to a customer without a mechanism for dealing with backup and recovery. As I've probably told people at least 1,000 times: You would truly be amazed at the percentage of database operations that I've gone into that do not have any kind of reliable backup. In a word: EEEeeeeeek!

There are two simple rules to follow regarding backups. First, do them early and often, and second, an untested backup isn't a backup.

The follow-up to the first rule to not just back up to a file on the same disk and forget it; you need to make sure that a copy moves to a completely separate place (ideally off-site) to be sure that it's safe. I've heard a firsthand account of a server actually catching fire. (The stench was terrible, he said, as he dealt with the freaked out staff.) You don't want to find out that your backups went up in the same smoke that your original data did.

The second rule is far too often ignored. Once a backup goes on disk (or tape, or wherever it goes), you're not done. Until you know for sure that the backup can be restored, you're at risk. In a traditional backup scenario, where a backup goes to disk, and then to tape, and then the tapes are kept safe off-site, you must remember to regularly retrieve a tape and do a restore onto a test server to ensure the backups are, in fact, backups, not just landfill.

> **NOTE** *In my first-ever gig as a DBA, I found servers—SQL Server and otherwise—all running without backups I took care of that first thing, and actually needed one less than a week later. However, some months after that we needed to retrieve a different server backup (not one of mine, for which I'm eternally thankful) from one of the tapes, and found that the tape backup had been failing silently for a very long time. Without delving into the complex ways in which that can come about, the lesson is as I've already said—test your backups, or you don't have backups.*

For applications being done by the relative beginner, you'll probably stick with referring the customer or onsite administrator to SQL Server's own backup and recovery tools, but, even if you do, you should be prepared to support them as they come up to speed in their use. In addition, there is no excuse for not understanding what it is the customer needs to do.

Creating a Backup

Creating a backup file of a given database is actually pretty easy.

1. Navigate in Object Explorer to the database you're interested in, and right-click.

2. Choose Tasks ➪ Back Up, as shown in Figure 21-16.

You'll get a dialog box that lets you define pretty much all of the backup process, as shown in Figure 21-17.

3. The first setting here is pretty self-explanatory — what database you want to back up. From there, however, things get a bit trickier.

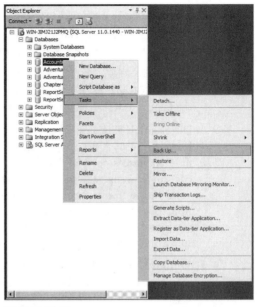

Getting into the items that may not yet make sense, first up is the recovery model. The Recovery Model field here is just notifying you what the database you've selected for backup is set to; it is actually a database-level setting. I'm going to defer discussion of what this is for a bit; I'll get to it in the next section when you read about backing up transaction logs.

Now, those are the simple parts, but let's break down some of the other options that are available.

FIGURE 21-16

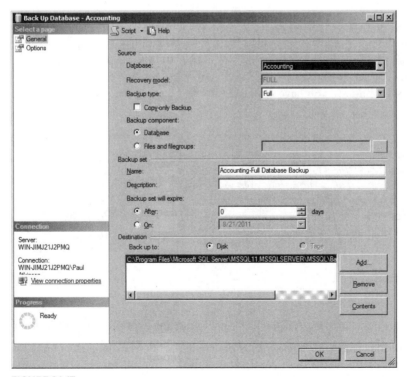

FIGURE 21-17

Backup Type

First of the choices you need to make is the backup type. Depending on the recovery model for your database (again, be patient with me, I'll get there on what this is), you'll have either two or three types of backups available:

> **Full:** This is just what it sounds like: a full backup of your actual database file as it was as of the last transaction that was committed prior to your issuing the Backup command.

> **Differential:** This might be referred to as a "backup since." When you take a differential backup, it only writes out a copy of the extents (see Chapter 9 if you've forgotten) that have changed since you did the last full backup. These typically run much faster than a full backup does and will take up less space. How much less? Well, that depends on how much your data actually changes. For very large databases where backups can take a very long time to run, it is very common to have a strategy where you take a full backup only once a week or even only once a month, and then take differential backups in between to save both space and time.

> **Transaction Log:** This is again just as it sounds: a copy of the transaction log. This option shows up only if your database is set to Full or Bulk logging (meaning this option is hidden if you are using simple logging). Again, full discussion of what these are is coming up shortly.

A subtopic of the backup type is the backup component, which applies only to full and differential backups.

For purposes of this book, discussion focuses on backing up the whole database. That said, you'll notice another option titled Files and Filegroups. Back in the chapters on database objects and creating databases, I touched briefly on the idea of filegroups and individual files for data to be stored in. This option lets you select just one file or filegroup to participate in this backup; I highly recommend avoiding this option until you have graduated to the "expert" class of SQL Server user.

 NOTE Again, I want to stress that you should avoid this particular option until you've got yourself something just short of a doctorate in SQL Server backups. The option is for special use, designed to help with very large database installations (figure terabytes) that are in high-availability scenarios. There are major consistency issues to be considered when taking and restoring from this style of backup, and they are not for the faint of heart.

Backup Set

A backup set is basically a single name used to refer to one or more destinations for your backup.

SQL Server allows for the idea that your backup may be particularly large or that you may otherwise have reason to back up across multiple devices — be it drives or tapes. When you do this, however, you need to have all the devices you used as a destination available to recover from any of them — that is, they are a "set." The backup set essentially holds the definition of what destinations were involved in your particular backup. In addition, a backup set contains some property information for your backup. You can, for example, identify an expiration date for the backup.

Destination

This is where your data is going to be backed up to. Here is where you define one or more destinations to be utilized for one backup set. For most installations this is a file location (which later is moved to tape), but you can also define a backup device that would let you go directly to tape or similar backup device.

Compression

Since SQL Server 2008, you can specify whether to have SQL compress backup files as they're written. Because backing up is virtually always a disk-bound (instead of CPU-bound) activity, compression provides not only smaller backup files but vastly faster backups for large databases. There's a server default setting that specifies whether SQL compresses backups by default or not, and the setting in this dialog box defaults to Use the Server Default Setting, but you can override that here if you want.

Options

In addition to those items just covered from the General node of the dialog box, you also have a node that lets you set other miscellaneous options. Most of these are fairly self-describing. Of particular note, however, is the Transaction Log area.

Schedule

With all this setup, wouldn't it be nice to set up a job to run this backup on a regular basis? Well, the Script button up at the top of the dialog box provides a means to do just that. Click it, and you'll get a list of options. Choose the Script Action to Job option. This brings up the Job Schedule dialog box you saw earlier in the chapter, but with the job steps already completed (including all the options you've specified). You can then define a regular schedule to run the backup you just defined by selecting the Schedules tab and filling it out as you desire.

 NOTE *Note that there are several more options for backups that are only addressable via issuing actual T-SQL commands or using the .NET programmability object model SMO. These are fairly advanced, so further coverage of them isn't warranted in this beginner text.*

Recovery Models

Well, I spent most of the last section promising that I would discuss them, so it's time to ask: What is a recovery model?

Well, back in the chapter on transactions (see Chapter 14), you learned about the transaction log. In addition to keeping track of transactions to deal with transaction rollback and atomicity of data, transaction logs are also critical to recovering data right up to the point of system failure.

Imagine for a moment that you're running a bank. Let's say you've been taking deposits and withdrawals for the last six hours — the time since your last full backup was done. Now, if your system went down, I'm guessing you're not going to like the idea of going to last night's backup and losing track of all the money that went out the door or came in during the interim. See where I'm going here? You really need every moment's worth of data.

Keeping the transaction log around gives you the ability to "roll forward" any transactions that happened since the last full or differential backup was done. Assuming both the data backup *and* the transaction logs are available, you should be able to recover right up to the point of failure.

The recovery model determines what type of log records are kept, and for how long; there are three options:

➤ **Full:** This is what it says; everything is logged. Under this model, you should have no data loss in the event of system failure assuming you had a backup of the data available and have all transaction logs since that backup. If you are missing a log or have one that is damaged, you'll be able to recover all data up through the last intact log you have available. Keep in mind, however, that as keeping everything suggests, this can take up a fair amount of space in a system that receives a lot of changes or new data.

➤ **Bulk-Logged:** This is like "full recovery light." Under this option, regular transactions are logged just as they are with the full recovery method, but bulk operations are not (so the name isn't exactly intuitive...it's more like "Bulk-Not-Logged"). The result is that, in the event of system failure, a restored backup contains any changes to data pages that did not participate in bulk operations (bulk import of data or index creation, for example), but any bulk operations must be redone. The good news about this one is that bulk operations perform *much* better. This performance comes with risk attached, so your mileage may vary.

➤ **Simple:** Under this model, the transaction log essentially exists merely to support transactions as they happen. The transaction log is regularly truncated, with any completed or rolled back transactions essentially being removed from the log (not quite that simple, but that is the effect). This gives you a nice tight log that is smaller and performs better, but the log is of zero use for recovery from system failure.

NOTE *One common use of Simple mode is to facilitate large data changes. If you have to do a large insert or update (but aren't using bulk loading), sometimes a Full-mode log can grow to an unmanageable size (if the log fills the disk, that can cause trouble). By switching the database to Simple mode, you can perform your update (managing your own safety using backups) and then return to Full mode when you're done.*

For most installations, full recovery is going to be what you want to have for a production-level database. End of story.

Recovery

This is something of the reverse of the backup side of things. You've done your first backup, you've scheduled a job so your backups are done religiously, and now you want to restore one, to test your backups, for recovery purposes, or merely to make a copy of a database somewhere.

Once you have a backup of your database, it's fairly easy to restore it to the original location. To get started, it works much as it did for backup: Navigate to the database you want to restore to and right-click; then select Tasks ⇨ Restore. Up comes the Restore dialog box, as shown in Figure 21-18.

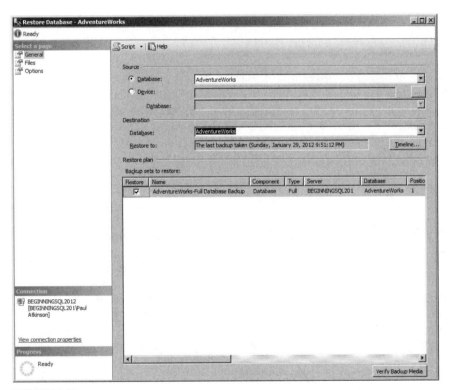

FIGURE 21-18

As long as you just want to take your old backup and slam it over the top of the new backup database, this is pretty straightforward; simply choose OK, and it should restore for you without issue.

Restoring to a Different Location

Things get tricky when you want to change something about where you're restoring to. As part of the backup process, the backup knows what the name of the database that was backed up, and, perhaps more important, it knows the path(s) to the physical files that it was supposed to be using.

Changing the destination database name is right there — no biggie — the problem is that changing the destination database name does nothing to change which physical files (the MDF and LDF files) it's going to try to store to. To deal with this, go to the Files node of the Restore dialog box.

You can accept SQL Server's help in relocating files, or do each manually. If you choose the Relocate All Files to Folder option, you have only to specify a folder each for the data and log files, and SQL does the rest. If you want to relocate each file manually, notice the Restore As column. In this part of the dialog box, you can replace every original file's destination location and name. Either way, SQL Server provides you with the way to deal with restoring multiple copies of a database to the same server (perhaps for test purposes) or installing your database to a new volume or even a new system.

Recovery Status

This one is merely about the state you want to have the database be in when you are done with this restore. This has particular relevance when you are restoring a database and still have logs or differential backups to apply to the database later.

If you go with the default option (which translates to using the WITH RECOVERY option if you were using T-SQL), the database would immediately be in a full online status when the restore operation is complete. If, for example, you wanted to restore logs after your initial restore was done, you would want to select one of the two other options. Both of these prevent updates from happening to the database, and leave it in a state where more recovery can be done; the difference is merely one of whether users are allowed to access the database in a "read-only" mode or whether the database should be appear as still being offline.

 NOTE *The issue of availability is a larger one than you probably think it is. As big of a deal as I'm sure it already seems, it's really amazing how quickly users will find their way into your system when the restore operation suddenly marks the database as available. Quite often, even if you know that you will be "done" after the current restore is completed, you'd like a chance to look over the database prior to actual users being in there; once they start making changes, things get more complicated. If this is the case, be sure and use the* NO RECOVERY *method of restoring. You can later run a restore that is purely for a* WITH RECOVERY *option and get the database fully back online once you're certain you have things just as you want them.*

INDEX MAINTENANCE

Back in Chapter 9, you learned about the issue of how indexes can become fragmented (remember page splits?). This can become a major impediment to the performance of your database over time, and you need to have a strategy in place to deal with this issue. Fortunately, SQL Server has commands that reorganize your data and indexes to clean things up. Couple that with the job scheduling, and you can automate routine defragmentation.

NOTE *You may still run into maintenance scripts that use the old* DBCC DBREINDEX *or* DBCC INDEXDEFRAG *commands. Both of these have been replaced by functionality within the* ALTER INDEX *command. The older* DBCC *commands are still supported for backward compatibility, but Microsoft may remove them at any time, so you should be proactive about updating those scripts should you come across any.*

ALTER INDEX is the workhorse of database maintenance. Most of this was covered lightly back in Chapter 9, but let's revisit this one, and then look at how to get it scheduled.

ALTER INDEX

The command ALTER INDEX is somewhat deceptive in what it does. Although most ALTER commands are about changing the definition of an object — you ALTER tables to add or disable constraints and columns, for example — ALTER INDEX is different; it is all about maintenance and zero about structure. If you need to change the makeup of your index, either you still need to DROP and CREATE it or you need to CREATE and use the DROP_EXISTING=ON option.

An abbreviated version of the ALTER INDEX syntax looks like this:

```
ALTER INDEX { <name of index> | ALL }
    ON <table or view name>
    { REBUILD
        [ [ WITH ( <rebuild index option> [ ,...n ] ) ]
            | [ PARTITION = <partition number>
                [ WITH ( <partition rebuild index option>
                    [ ,...n ] ) ] ] ]
    | DISABLE
    | REORGANIZE
        [ PARTITION = <partition number> ]
        [ WITH ( LOB_COMPACTION = { ON | OFF } ) ]
    | SET ( <set_index_option> [ ,...n ] )
    }
    [ ; ]
```

A fair amount on this is fairly detailed "realm of the advanced DBA" stuff — typically used on an ad hoc basis to deal with very specific problems, but there are some core elements here that should be part of your regular maintenance planning. Let's start by looking at a couple of top parameters and then look at the options that will be part of your larger maintenance planning needs.

➤ **Index Name:** You can name a specific index if you want to maintain one specific index, or use ALL to indicate that you want to perform this maintenance on every index associated with the named table.

➤ **Table or View Name:** Pretty much just as it sounds: the name of the specific object (table or view) that you want to perform the maintenance on. Note that it needs to be one specific table. (You can't feed it a list and say, "Do all of these please!")

REBUILD

This is the "industrial strength" approach to fixing an index. If you run ALTER INDEX with this option, the old index is completely thrown away and reconstructed from scratch. The result is a truly optimized index, where every page in both the leaf and non-leaf levels of the index have been reconstructed as you have defined them, either the defaults, or using switches to change things like the fill factor.

> **NOTE** *Careful with this one. By default, as soon as you kick off a REBUILD, the index you are working on is essentially gone until the rebuild is complete. Any queries that relied on that index may become exceptionally slow (potentially by orders of magnitude). This is the sort of thing you want to test on an offline system first to have an idea how long it's going to take, and then schedule to run in off hours, preferably with someone monitoring it to be sure it's back online when peak hours come along.*

The Enterprise version of SQL Server does include a special ONLINE version of this option that keeps the index alive and builds the new one parallel to the old. However, realize that non-Enterprise versions do not have that option, and, even if they do, the creation of the index will be a significant load on the system; tread carefully when rebuilding. In general, treat this one as though it can have major side effects while it runs, and leave its use squarely in the domain of the database administrator.

DISABLE

This one does what it says, only in somewhat drastic fashion. It would be nice if all this command did was take your index offline until you decided what you want to do, but instead it essentially marks the index as unusable. Once an index is disabled, it must be rebuilt (not reorganized, but rebuilt; the option you just read about with the "here be dragons" type warning on it) before it will be active again.

This is one you're very, very rarely going to do yourself. (You would more likely just drop the index.) It is far more likely to happen during a SQL Server upgrade or some other oddball situation.

> **WARNING** *Yet another BE CAREFUL warning with this one. If you disable the clustered index for your table, it has the effect of disabling the table. The data remains, but is inaccessible to all indexes because all indexes depend on the clustered index — the entire table is effectively offline until you rebuild the clustered index.*

REORGANIZE

BINGO!!! from the developer perspective. With REORGANIZE you hit a happy medium in life. When you reorganize your index, you get a slightly less complete optimization than with a full rebuild, but one that occurs online. (Users can still utilize the index.)

This should, if you're paying attention, bring about the question "What exactly do you mean by '*slightly* less complete'?" Well, REORGANIZE works only on the leaf level of your index; non-leaf levels of the index go untouched. This means that you're not quite getting a full optimization, but, for the lion's share of indexes, that is not where your real cost of fragmentation is, although it can happen and your mileage may vary.

Given its much lower impact on users, this is usually the tool you'll want to use as part of your regular maintenance plan; let's take a look at running an index reorganization command.

TRY IT OUT **Index Reorganization**

To run this through its paces, you'll do a reorg on a table in the AdventureWorks database. The Production.TransactionHistory table is an excellent example of a table that is likely to have many rows inserted over time and then have rows purged back out of it as the transactions become old enough to delete. In this case, you'll reorganize all the indexes on the table in one simple command:

```
ALTER INDEX ALL
ON Production.TransactionHistory
REORGANIZE;
```

You should get back essentially nothing from the database — just a simple message: Command(s) completed successfully.

How It Works

The ALTER INDEX command sees that ALL was supplied instead of a specific index name and looks up which indexes are available for the Production.TransactionHistory table (leaving out any that are disabled because a reorganization will do nothing for them). It then enumerates each index behind the scenes and performs the reorganization on each, reorganizing just the leaf level of each index (including reorganizing the actual data because the clustered index on this table will also be reorganized).

Archiving Data

Ooh — here's a tricky one. There are as many ways of archiving data as there are database engineers. If you're building an OLAP database, for example, to utilize with Analysis Services, that often addresses what you need to know as far as archiving for long-term reporting goes. Regardless of how you're making sure the data you need long term is available, there will likely come a day when you need to deal with the issue of your data becoming simply too voluminous for your system to perform well.

As I said, there are just too many ways to go about archiving because every database is a little bit different. The key is to think about archiving needs at the time that you create your database. Realize that, as you start to delete records, you'll hit referential integrity constraints and/or orphaning records; design in a logical path to delete or move records at archive time. Here are some things to think about as you write your archive scripts:

➤ **Is the data in an OLAP database?** If you already have the data in an OLAP database, you probably don't need to worry about saving it anywhere else; talk to your boss and your attorney about that one.

➤ **How often is the data really used? Is it worth keeping?** Human beings are natural-born pack rats — just a bit larger than the rodent version. Simply put, we hate giving things up; that includes data. If you're only worried about legal requirements, think about just saving a copy of never or rarely used data to tape (I'd suggest multiple backups for archive data) and reducing the amount of data you have online; your users will love you for it when they see improved performance.

➤ **Don't leave orphans.** As you start deleting data, your referential integrity constraints should keep you from leaving that many orphans, but you'll wind up with some where referential integrity didn't apply. This situation can lead to serious system errors.

➤ **Realize that your archive program will probably need a long time to run.** The length of time it runs and the number of rows affected may create concurrency issues with the data your online users are trying to get at; plan on running it at a time where your system will have not be used.

➤ TEST! TEST! TEST!

POLICY BASED MANAGEMENT

This is a relatively advanced feature that was introduced with SQL Server 2008. The idea is fairly simple: Modern relational systems are all about proactive management of your data — why not proactively manage the objects and rules applied to the server?

With Policy Based Management, you establish a set of rules to govern your server or even all servers in your domain. There is a wide list of items that can have policies attached to them, for example:

➤ **Object names:** Want to enforce that all stored procedures begin with `sp`? No problem. You can establish such a rule using Policy Based Management.

➤ **ANSI `ARITHABORT` options:** All databases should have the ANSI `ARITHABORT` option set to `true` by default.

How exactly these are enforced is set by rule — treatment options include:

➤ **On Demand:** Check for violations of policy only when an administrator has specifically requested the policy audit.

➤ **Scheduled:** Run an audit of policy violations according to some schedule (creating a list of violations, but not changing anything).

➤ **On Change: Prevent:** This proactively prevents the policy violation from being allowed. Using the earlier example, any stored procedure that didn't start with `sp` would fail during creation.

➤ **On Change: Log:** This notes the violation, but simply logs it (facilitating later reporting).

Most installations do not need the power behind Policy Based Management, but it is a tremendous leap forward in manageability for larger, multi-server environments.

AUTOMATING ADMINISTRATION TASKS WITH POWERSHELL

Although the tools within Management Studio and T-SQL for creating and scheduling jobs are powerful, flexible, and easy, sometimes tasks come up that require just a little more. The SSMS options are fairly complete when it comes to dealing with SQL Server itself, but what if your administrative tasks require complex interaction with programs outside of SQL Server? For those uncommon cases, you can use Windows PowerShell.

What Is PowerShell?

PowerShell v2.0 is a Windows scripting environment that ships natively with Windows Server 2008 R2 (which is what I expect many if not most of you are using at the time of this writing). PowerShell is different from prior command shells that shipped with Windows (such as cmd.exe or, for us really old folks, COMMAND.COM) in that it isn't simply a text utility; it's managed code that's fully integrated with the .NET Framework.

So what does that mean for you? It means:

➤ Scripts written in PowerShell can pass objects around.

➤ You have integration with the Windows security model.

➤ You can dig into the .NET libraries and interrogate or make use of existing objects.

➤ You can manage local or remote servers.

➤ You can do all of that (in this context) in concert with managing your SQL Servers, so that information from across your domain can be integrated into the actions taken by your management scripts.

Let's say you want to regularly back up your databases, for example, because — and I want to be absolutely crystal clear about this — you do. Most of the time, you'll be happy to set up a scheduled backup job within the SQL Agent context you read about above and that's that: The backups land somewhere on disk, and now they're out of your hands.

If you've got to follow them a bit further down the road than that, however, you may want to consider PowerShell. Although you can easily create and restore backups using PowerShell (and I'll show you how in a minute), you can also move the files to a network location, invoke a tape backup process, and even monitor application status in conjunction with your system maintenance, because PowerShell can invoke the .NET components on your system.

This is about as advanced as I'm going to get in this book, but again it's better to know it's out there, and I can't imagine you'd get the idea of what's possible out there without getting your hands dirty.

Installing and Enabling PowerShell

This is the easiest thing in the world with SQL Server 2012, because if you have SQL installed then you have PowerShell. For the first time, PowerShell is required to complete a SQL Server installation; conveniently, it's installed by default with Windows Server 2008 R2 and Windows 7. If you're trying to install SQL Server on another version of Windows, the SQL installer directs you to the PowerShell installation instructions.

Cmdlets and Modules

PowerShell has several kinds of functions, but many of the most useful are *cmdlets* (pronounced like commandlets). With a verb-noun-naming convention — for example, `Get-Command` or `Backup-SqlDatabase` — they're pretty easy to read, and you can always use `Get-Help <cmdlet>` if you're stuck...yep, that's another cmdlet.

There are far too many cmdlets to list here, and I'm not even going to try. However, that also means there are too many to show on your screen when you're searching for just the right one. To help organize, PowerShell lets you group cmdlets into modules. One module that you're likely to become familiar with contains the SQL Server–related functionality, and that's called Sqlps.

Sqlps

Sqlps is the SQL Server PowerShell module that encapsulates the SQL-related functionality you're going to be after. Obviously PowerShell can do a lot more than what's in this module, but as a SQL developer this is going to be your home. You can start a PowerShell session and shortcut straight to Sqlps by right-clicking any object in SSMS and choosing Start PowerShell.

Again, try to avoid thinking of PowerShell as a command-based utility (such as sqlcmd). The functions and cmdlets you invoke within the shell aren't returning text (necessarily), they're returning full-fledged .NET objects, including arrays of objects. That means if you invoke a cmdlet to return a SQL Server, for example, you should be careful whether you're returning the name, or a handle to the server itself.

For now, let's focus on some of the simpler functionality; after all, this is supposed to be a beginner book. Once you try this yourself, you can decide how much further you want to take it on your own.

TRY IT OUT **Writing a PowerShell Script**

For your first PowerShell script (if, in fact, that's what this is), you'll do something you've already done earlier through the SSMS interface: back up a database. Follow these steps:

1. Open Notepad and enter the following PowerShell script:

```
$dbName = "AdventureWorks"
$date = Get-Date
$bakFileName = $dbName + "_" + $date.Year + $date.Month + $date.Day + ".bak"
Backup-SqlDatabase -database $dbName -BackupFile $bakFileName
```

Code snippet Chap21.txt

2. Save this file somewhere easily accessible; for this example, I suggest `C:\scripts\BackupAdventureWorks.ps1`. The ps1 extension is standard for PowerShell scripts.

3. Open a PowerShell session by right-clicking the AdventureWorks database node in the Object Explorer and choosing Start PowerShell. This opens what looks like an old DOS command prompt, if that means anything to you. Notice in Figure 21-19 that the path in the command line broadly echoes the object hierarchy in the Object Explorer.

4. To run the script file you just saved, simply enter its fully qualified name (`C:\scripts\ BackupAdventureWorks.ps1`) at the command prompt.

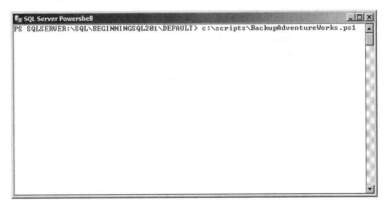

FIGURE 21-19

Watch as the backup commences. You'll see a status bar appear within the PowerShell window.

5. When the backup is all done, look in your default backup location — probably `C:\Program Files\ Microsoft SQL Server\MSSQL11.MSSQLSERVER\MSSQL\Backup\` — and you'll see the backup in place with today's date on it. You can use this script again and again to create dated backup files.

How It Works

Let's go through this script line by line. The script begins with a variable assignment, putting the string "`AdventureWorks`" into a variable called `$dbName`. From this, you can infer that no variable declaration is required, and if you guessed that variables are denoted simply by a `$` character, you'd be right. What's less obvious is that a variable used in this way can be any type at all...not just primitive types like `int`, Boolean, or character, and not just an extended set including strings, but anything. I could have assigned that any .NET object there is, including a database connection, an array, a dictionary, or something from one of my own class libraries (if I loaded the assembly, which is beyond what you're doing here). Regardless of the advanced possibilities, this is a simple variable assignment.

The next line is also a variable declaration, assigning the return value of the cmdlet `Get-Date` to the `$date` variable. That return value isn't a date string, though, or even a SQL DATE or DATETIME data type; it's a fully fleshed-out .NET `datetime` type, with all the methods available that implies. That means that to use it in a string, some formatting methods are required.

The third line just does string concatenation, putting together a filename that includes the date. That `$date` variable contains time information, too, if you want it.

Finally you call the `Backup-SqlDatabase` cmdlet, passing it a couple simple parameters: the database to back up and the target file. Because there's no directory specified, it uses SQL Server's current default location.

Deployment and Execution

Although there are many ways to deploy a PowerShell script, I'm going to focus on one that'll fit easily with the rest of the work you've been doing: running your PowerShell scripts via a SQL Agent job. (For more options, find a PowerShell book. This is the T-SQL book.)

When you're creating a job step, like you did earlier in the chapter, you may not have taken note of the Type selection on the Job Step Properties dialog box (if not, look back at Figure 21-5). What you did with that before, when you left it at its default value, was to enter T-SQL. As it happens, another choice you have there is PowerShell.

Using the knowledge you have already, it's almost a no-brainer to create a job to run the script you've just written. However, if you create the job step with type PowerShell and use the command C:\scripts\BackupAdventureWorks.ps1, and then run the job, well...you won't get errors (or not obvious ones), but you won't get results.

To troubleshoot, look at the Advanced tab of your step, and notice that for PowerShell you've got options to save the output. Try it like you see in Figure 21-20, and then rerun the script and look in the log file.

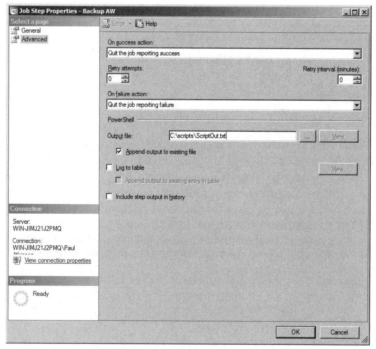

FIGURE 21-20

When you look in the ScriptOut.txt file, you'll see something like this:

```
The job script encountered the following errors. These errors did not
stop the script:
```

```
A job step received an error at line 5 in a PowerShell script. The
corresponding line is 'Backup-SqlDatabase -database $dbName -BackupFile
$bakFileName'. Correct the script and reschedule the job. The error
information returned by PowerShell is: 'Failed to resolve the path
`SQLSERVER:\' to an object of type 'Microsoft.SqlServer.Management.Smo.Server'.
Either set your location to the proper context, or use the -Path parameter
to specify the location.
```

The highlighted error gives you a clue as to the problem. When you tested your script, you did so having invoked PowerShell from within a context menu in SSMS; it was already directed to your database instance. When run through SQL Agent, PowerShell is invoked at what can be thought of as the root node. To fix the problem, simply add some context to your script, like this:

```
$dbName = "AdventureWorks"
$date = Get-Date
$bakFileName = $dbName + "_" + $date.Year + $date.Month + $date.Day + ".bak"
Set-Location \SQL\SERVERNAME\DEFAULT\
Backup-SqlDatabase -database $dbName -BackupFile $bakFileName
```

Code snippet Chap21.txt

Replace *SERVERNAME* with your server name, and *DEFAULT* with your instance name if you're not using the default SQL instance. Save the `.ps1` file again and kick off the job. Voilà — automatic, dated backups, courtesy of PowerShell!

SUMMARY

Well, that gives you a few things to think about. It's really easy to, as a developer, think about many administrative tasks and establish what the increasingly inaccurately named *Hitchhiker's Guide to the Galaxy* trilogy called an "SEP field." That's something that makes things like administration seem invisible because it's "somebody else's problem." Don't go there!

> **NOTE** *A project I've heard about from several years ago is a great example of taking responsibility for what can happen. A wonderful system was developed for a non-profit group that operates in the northwestern United States. After the company was in operation for about eight months, an emergency call was placed to the company that developed the software (it was a custom job). After some discussion, it was determined that the database had somehow become corrupted, and it was recommended to the customer that the database be restored from a backup. The response? "Backup?" The development company in question missed something very important. It knew it had an inexperienced customer who would have no administration staff—who was going to tell the customer to do backups and help set it up if the development company didn't? I'm happy to say that the development company in question learned from that experience, and so should you.*

NOTE *Intelligence is the ability to learn from your mistakes. Wisdom is the ability to learn from the mistakes of others. Go forth and be wise!*

Think about administration issues as you're doing your design and especially in your deployment plan. If you plan ahead to simplify the administration of your system, you'll find that your system is much more successful; that usually translates into rewards for the developer (that is, you!).

EXERCISES

1. Take the command that you made to reorganize your `Production.TransactionHistory` table, and schedule it to run as a weekend job Sunday mornings at 2AM.

2. Perform a full backup of the AdventureWorks database. Save the backup to `C:\MyBackup.bak` (or alter slightly if you don't have enough disk space on that volume).

3. Restore the backup you created in Exercise 2 to a new database name — NewAdventures.

► **WHAT YOU LEARNED IN THIS CHAPTER**

TOPIC	CONCEPT
Responsibility for administration	Because databases exist in the persistence layer, your work is going to require maintenance. Maintenance plans aren't just the DBA's responsibility, but the developer's as well.
SQL Server Agent	SQL Agent is a component of SQL Server that can create jobs with steps and branching, and then schedule those jobs to run.
Logins and users	You can install SQL using Windows Authentication or Mixed Mode. Logins can be either Windows logins from Active Directory or native SQL logins if you're using Mixed Mode. Users are the logins who are granted access to a particular database.
Backup and recovery	You can accomplish backups either through the SSMS interface or by executing T-SQL backup commands; same thing with restores. Backups can be full (the whole database), differential (all the extents modified since the last backup), or transaction log only. Backups are only as good as the last tested restore.
Index maintenance	You can use SQL Agent to invoke index rebuilds or reorganization. Rebuilding is more complete than reorganization, but more difficult to do while keeping the database online for users.
PowerShell	Windows Server 2008 includes a powerful scripting language called PowerShell, and SQL Server 2012 contains cmdlets (PowerShell commands) that can help to manage your SQL Server through scripting.

Answers to Exercises

This appendix provides the solutions for the end-of-chapter exercises located in Chapters 1–21.

CHAPTER 1

Answer to Question 1

The `master` database contains system tables that keep track of all the objects in the system, including the `master` database itself.

Answer to Question 2

`datetime` stores times to a precision of 3/100 sec and fits into eight bytes. `datetime2` stores times in anywhere from seconds (`datetime2(0)`) to 100 nanoseconds (`datetime2(7)`), and takes from six to eight bytes.

CHAPTER 2

Answer to Question 1

Reporting Services, Analysis Services, and Integration Services all have their programming interface in SSDT. If you have the full version of Visual Studio, the SQL 2012 development tools also permit T-SQL development there.

Answer to Question 2

You can see the predicted plan using the Show Estimated Execution Plan button or menu item. To see the actual plan, use Show Actual Execution Plan, and then run the query.

CHAPTER 3

Answer to Question 1

```
SELECT * FROM Production.Product
```

Answer to Question 2

```
SELECT * FROM Production.Product WHERE ProductSubcategoryID IS NULL
```

Answer to Question 3

```
INSERT INTO Production.Location
    (Name, CostRate, Availability, ModifiedDate)
VALUES ('Test', 0.00, 0.00, '20110901')
```

Answer to Question 4

```
DELETE Production.Location WHERE Name = 'Test'
```

CHAPTER 4

Answer to Question 1

```
SELECT P.LastName AS Name
FROM Person.Person P
JOIN HumanResources.Employee E
    ON P.BusinessEntityID = E.BusinessEntityID
WHERE E.NationalIDNumber = '112457891'
```

 NOTE *The name returned should be Walters.*

Answer to Question 2

```
--Option 1 (Union)
SELECT P.ProductID, P.Name
FROM Production.Product P
LEFT JOIN Sales.SpecialOfferProduct SOP
    ON P.ProductID = SOP.ProductID
WHERE SOP.SpecialOfferID IS NULL
UNION
```

```
SELECT P.ProductID, P.Name
FROM Production.Product P
JOIN Sales.SpecialOfferProduct SOP
    ON P.ProductID = SOP.ProductID
JOIN Sales.SpecialOffer SO
    ON SO.SpecialOfferID = SOP.SpecialOfferID
WHERE SO.Description = 'No Discount'

--Option 2 (Outer Joins)
SELECT P.ProductID, P.Name
FROM Production.Product P
LEFT JOIN Sales.SpecialOfferProduct SOP
    ON P.ProductID = SOP.ProductID
LEFT JOIN Sales.SpecialOffer SO
    ON SO.SpecialOfferID = SOP.SpecialOfferID
WHERE SO.Description = 'No Discount' OR SOP.SpecialOfferID IS NULL
```

CHAPTER 5

Answer to Question 1

Perform the following steps:

1. In the Object Explorer window, right-click the AdventureWorks folder, and click Tasks ⇨ Generate Scripts, as shown in Figure A-1.

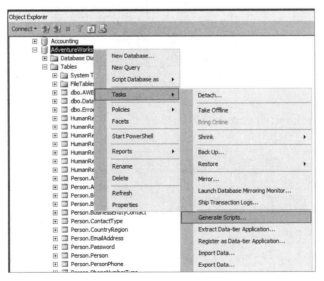

FIGURE A-1

2. Click Next on the Introduction screen if it appears.

3. Check both the `HumanResources.Employee` and `Sales.Customer` tables, as partially shown in Figure A-2.

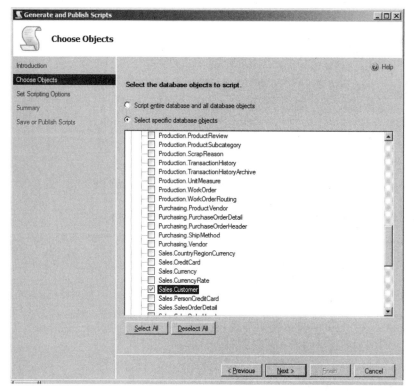

FIGURE A-2

4. Proceed through the rest of the wizard and click Finish.

Answer to Question 2

```
CREATE DATABASE MyDB
ON
  (NAME = 'MyDB',
   FILENAME = 'C:\Program Files\Microsoft SQL Server\MSSQL11.MSSQLSERVER\
MSSQL\DATA\MyDBData.mdf',
   SIZE = 17MB,
   FILEGROWTH = 5MB)
LOG ON
  (NAME = 'MyDBLog',
   FILENAME = 'C:\Program Files\Microsoft SQL Server\MSSQL11.MSSQLSERVER\
```

```
      MSSQL\DATA\MyDBLog.ldf',
        SIZE = 5MB,
        FILEGROWTH = 5MB);
```

Answer to Question 3

```
CREATE TABLE Foo (Col1 VARCHAR(50));
```

CHAPTER 6

Answer to Question 1

```
ALTER TABLE Customers ADD CONSTRAINT AKCustmersFedIDNo UNIQUE (FedIDNo);
```

Answer to Question 2

```
--Good
ALTER TABLE Employees ADD CONSTRAINT NotOwnManager
CHECK (EmployeeID <> ManagerEmpID)
--Better
ALTER TABLE Employees WITH NOCHECK ADD CONSTRAINT NotOwnManager
CHECK (EmployeeID <> ManagerEmpID)
--Best
ALTER TABLE Employees WITH NOCHECK ADD CONSTRAINT NotOwnManager
CHECK (EmployeeID <> ISNULL(ManagerEmpID, EmployeeID-1))
```

This last option has the advantage of working even when ManagerEmpID is null. Without the ISNULL function, this would fail on a NULL (because any comparison to NULL is false, even <>), so you can catch that case and compare to EmployeeID - 1 (which will never equal EmployeeID).

CHAPTER 7

Answer to Question 1

```
SELECT CONVERT(VARCHAR(10), HireDate, 1) AS HireDateMMDDYY
FROM HumanResources.Employee
```

Answer to Question 2

```
SELECT DISTINCT P.BusinessEntityID, P.LastName, P.MiddleName, P.FirstName
FROM Person.Person P
LEFT JOIN Sales.Customer C
    ON P.BusinessEntityID = C.PersonID
LEFT JOIN Sales.SalesOrderHeader H
    ON C.CustomerID = H.CustomerID
WHERE H.SalesOrderID IS NULL

SELECT DISTINCT P.BusinessEntityID, P.LastName, P.MiddleName, P.FirstName
FROM Person.Person P
WHERE P.BusinessEntityID NOT IN (
```

```
    SELECT C.PersonID
    FROM Sales.Customer C
    JOIN Sales.SalesOrderHeader H
        ON C.CustomerID = H.CustomerID
);

WITH ActiveCustomers (BusinessEntityID)
AS (
    SELECT DISTINCT C.PersonID
    FROM Sales.Customer C
    JOIN Sales.SalesOrderHeader H
        ON C.CustomerID = H.CustomerID
)
SELECT DISTINCT P.BusinessEntityID, P.LastName, P.MiddleName, P.FirstName
FROM Person.Person P
LEFT JOIN ActiveCustomers A
    ON A.BusinessEntityID = P.BusinessEntityID
WHERE A.BusinessEntityID IS NULL;

SELECT DISTINCT P.BusinessEntityID, P.LastName, P.MiddleName, P.FirstName
FROM Person.Person P
WHERE NOT EXISTS (
    SELECT *
    FROM Sales.Customer C
    JOIN Sales.SalesOrderHeader H
        ON C.CustomerID = H.CustomerID
    WHERE C.PersonID = P.BusinessEntityID
```

Answer to Question 3

```
WITH BigSpenders AS (
    SELECT CustomerID
    FROM Sales.SalesOrderHeader H
    GROUP BY CustomerID
    HAVING SUM(TotalDue) > 70000
), TopOrders AS (
SELECT H.CustomerID, H.SalesOrderID, H.OrderDate, H.TotalDue, ROW_NUMBER()
  OVER (PARTITION BY H.CustomerID ORDER BY OrderDate DESC) OrderRow
FROM Sales.SalesOrderHeader H
JOIN BigSpenders S
    ON H.CustomerID = S.CustomerID
)
SELECT CustomerID, SalesOrderID, OrderDate, TotalDue
FROM TopOrders
WHERE OrderRow <= 5
ORDER BY CustomerID, OrderRow
```

CHAPTER 8

Answer to Question 1

Patient (PatientID, PatientName, SSN)

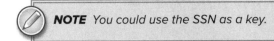

NOTE *You could use the SSN as a key.*

Physician (PhysicianID, Physician Name)

Hospital (HospitalID, Hospital Name)

Treatment (TreatmentID, Treatment Name)

Visit (PatientID, PhysicianID, HospitalID, TreatmentID, AdmitDate, ReleaseDate)

CHAPTER 9

Answer to Question 1

You could use `sys.dm_db_index_physical_stats`; you could drill down under the table's Indexes node in Object Explorer; or you could query `sys.indexes`.

Answer to Question 2

```
CREATE NONCLUSTERED INDEX ie_ProductModel_ModifiedDate
ON Production.ProductModel (ModifiedDate);
```

Answer to Question 3

```
DROP INDEX ie_ProductModel_ModifiedDate
ON Production.ProductModel
```

CHAPTER 10

Answer to Question 1

```
CREATE VIEW Sales.PersonSales
AS
SELECT C.CustomerID, P.LastName + ', ' + P.FirstName PersonName,
    SUM(TotalDue) SumTotalDue
FROM Person.Person P
JOIN Sales.Customer C
    ON P.BusinessEntityID = C.PersonID
JOIN Sales.SalesOrderHeader H
    ON C.CustomerID = H.CustomerID
GROUP BY C.CustomerID, P.LastName + ', ' + P.FirstName

GO
```

Answer to Question 2

```
ALTER VIEW Sales.PersonSales
WITH ENCRYPTION
AS
```

```
SELECT C.CustomerID, P.LastName + ', ' + P.FirstName PersonName,
    SUM(TotalDue) SumTotalDue
FROM Person.Person P
JOIN Sales.Customer C
    ON P.BusinessEntityID = C.PersonID
JOIN Sales.SalesOrderHeader H
    ON C.CustomerID = H.CustomerID
GROUP BY C.CustomerID, P.LastName + ', ' + P.FirstName
```

Answer to Question 3

```
GO

ALTER VIEW Sales.PersonSales
WITH ENCRYPTION, SCHEMABINDING
AS
SELECT C.CustomerID, P.LastName + ', ' + P.FirstName PersonName,
    SUM(TotalDue) SumTotalDue, COUNT_BIG(*) RecordCt
FROM Person.Person P
JOIN Sales.Customer C
    ON P.BusinessEntityID = C.PersonID
JOIN Sales.SalesOrderHeader H
    ON C.CustomerID = H.CustomerID
GROUP BY C.CustomerID, P.LastName + ', ' + P.FirstName

GO
```

CHAPTER 11

Answer to Question 1

```
DECLARE @Var1 INT = 2, @Var2 INT = 4;
SELECT @Var1 + @Var2 AS VarSum;
```

Answer to Question 2

```
DECLARE @MinOrder MONEY;

SELECT @MinOrder =  MIN(LineTotal)
FROM Sales.SalesOrderHeader H
JOIN Sales.SalesOrderDetail D
    ON D.SalesOrderID = H.SalesOrderID
WHERE H.CustomerID = 29506

SELECT @MinOrder MinOrder;
```

Answer to Question 3

```
sqlcmd -E -d AdventureWorks -Q "SELECT COUNT(*) FROM Sales.Customer"
```

CHAPTER 12

Answer to Question 1

```
ALTER PROC [dbo].[spTriangular]
@ValueIn int,
@ValueOut int OUTPUT
AS
DECLARE @InWorking int;
DECLARE @OutWorking int;
IF @ValueIn >= 32
BEGIN
    RAISERROR ('Error: spTriangular has a max input of 32, and was called with
%d.',16,1, @ValueIn);
    RETURN -1;
END
IF @ValueIn != 1
BEGIN
        SELECT @InWorking = @ValueIn - 1;


        EXEC spTriangular @InWorking, @OutWorking OUTPUT;

        SELECT @ValueOut = @ValueIn + @OutWorking;
END
ELSE
BEGIN
        SELECT @ValueOut = 1;
END
```

Answer to Question 2A breakpoint should be set on IF @Valuein != 1, with a condition of @ValueIn = 1 / Is True.

One way to do this is:

1. Set a breakpoint on the IF @Valuein != 1 line using F9 or a mouse click in the left margin.

2. Right-click on the breakpoint and select Condition.

3. Enter the value @ValueIn = 1 and set the evaluation criteria to True.

CHAPTER 13

Answer to Question 1

```
CREATE FUNCTION [dbo].[fnTriangular] (
    @ValueIn int)
RETURNS int
AS
BEGIN
    DECLARE @ValueOut int;
```

```
        IF @ValueIn > 32
        BEGIN
            SET @ValueOut = NULL;
        END;
        ELSE IF @ValueIn > 1
        BEGIN
            SET @ValueOut = @ValueIn + [dbo].[fnTriangular] (@ValueIn - 1);
        END;
        ELSE
        BEGIN
            SELECT @ValueOut = 1;
        END;

        RETURN @ValueOut;
    END
```

Answer to Question 2

```
    CREATE FUNCTION dbo.LineItemCurrencyExchange (
        @SalesOrderID INT,
        @TargetCurrencyCode nchar(3),
        @CurrencyRateDate DATETIME
    )
    RETURNS @OutTable TABLE (
        SalesOrderDetailID INT,
        OrderQty SMALLINT,
        ProductID INT,
        UnitPrice MONEY,
        UnitPriceConverted MONEY
    )
    AS
    BEGIN

        DECLARE @EndOfDayRate MONEY;

        SELECT @EndOfDayRate = EndOfDayRate
        FROM Sales.CurrencyRate
        WHERE CurrencyRateDate = @CurrencyRateDate
        AND ToCurrencyCode = @TargetCurrencyCode;

        INSERT @OutTable

        SELECT SalesOrderDetailID,
            OrderQty,
            ProductID,
            UnitPrice,
            UnitPrice * @EndOfDayRate
        FROM Sales.SalesOrderDetail
        WHERE SalesOrderID = @SalesOrderID

        RETURN;
    END

    GO
```

```
SELECT *
FROM dbo.LineItemCurrencyExchange (
    43659,
    'EUR',
    '2005-07-05 00:00:00.000'
)
```

CHAPTER 14

Answer to Question 1

To create a deadlock, you will need to open two connections. In SSMS, each query window has its own connection, so opening two query windows will suffice for that condition. If you place the code that follows into each window and run it in pieces as specified, you can generate a deadlock.

QUERY WINDOW 1

```
BEGIN TRANSACTION

    UPDATE HumanResources.Employee
    SET BirthDate = BirthDate
    WHERE BusinessEntityID = 1;

    -- Step 1: Run to here --

    UPDATE Person.Person
    SET PersonType = 'EM'
    WHERE BusinessEntityID = 1;

    --Step 3: Run to here (Deadlock occurs) --

ROLLBACK
```

QUERY WINDOW 2

```
BEGIN TRANSACTION

    UPDATE Person.Person
    SET PersonType = 'EM'
    WHERE BusinessEntityID = 1;

    UPDATE HumanResources.Employee
    SET BirthDate = BirthDate
    WHERE BusinessEntityID = 1;

    --Step 2: Run to here (system will wait) --

ROLLBACK
```

CHAPTER 15

Answer to Question 1

```
CREATE TRIGGER [Production].[trgLimitPriceChanges]
ON [Production].[Product]
FOR UPDATE
AS
    IF EXISTS
        (
         SELECT *
         FROM inserted i
         JOIN deleted d
            ON i.ProductID = d.ProductID
         WHERE i.ListPrice > (d.ListPrice * 1.15)
        )
    BEGIN
        RAISERROR('Price increase may not be greater than 15 percent.
                   Transaction Failed.',16,1)
        ROLLBACK TRAN
    END

GO
```

Answer to Question 2

```
ALTER TRIGGER [Production].[trgLimitPriceChanges]
ON [Production].[Product]
FOR UPDATE
AS
    IF UPDATE(ListPrice)
    BEGIN
        IF EXISTS
        (
            SELECT *
            FROM inserted i
            JOIN deleted d
               ON i.ProductID = d.ProductID
            WHERE i.ListPrice > (d.ListPrice * 1.15)
        )
        BEGIN
            RAISERROR('Price increase may not be greater than 15 percent.
                       Transaction Failed.',16,1)
            ROLLBACK TRAN
        END
    END
GO
```

CHAPTER 16

Answer to Question 1

```
DECLARE @SalesOrder XML ([dbo].[SalesOrderXML])
```

Answer to Question 2

XML is case-sensitive: The `<from>` tag is not closed correctly (it's "closed" as `<From>`).

CHAPTER 17

Answer to Question 1

Accumulating snapshot should be used.

Answer to Question 2

➤ Scheduling the ETL during maintenance windows

➤ Using a database mirror

➤ Using a snapshot (or snapshot isolation)

➤ Using `NOLOCK` (which is extremely risky, by the way)

CHAPTER 18

Answer to Question 1

```
WITH MonthSales AS (
SELECT EOMONTH(OrderDate) OrderEndOfMonth,
    SUM(ExtendedAmount) RegionMonthSales
FROM FactInternetSales FIS
GROUP BY EOMONTH(OrderDate)
)
SELECT OrderEndOfMonth, RegionMonthSales,
    AVG(RegionMonthSales) OVER (
        ORDER BY OrderEndOfMonth ROWS 3 PRECEDING) ThreeMonthMovingAverage
FROM MonthSales
```

Answer to Question 2

Power View is for executive analysis and quick production of graphical content, and can directly produce PowerPoint files.

PowerPivot is designed for mid-level analysts who excel, hrrm, at Excel.

Answer to Bonus Question

To import data from your cube into PowerPivot for Excel, follow these steps:

1. In Excel, click the PowerPivot menu and open the PowerPivot window.

2. Click From Database ⇨ From Analysis Services or PowerPivot. This starts the Table Import Wizard.

3. Select your cube data source (be sure to select your UDM mode SSAS instance). Click Next.

4. Rather than typing in an MDX query, click Design.

5. Drag at least one measure and at least two dimensions (your choice) into the selection area. When you see the data you want to analyze, click OK.

6. Click Finish to complete the Table import Wizard.

CHAPTER 19

Answer to Question 1

To add the `Production.ProductSubCategory` table to your semantic model, and place the `SubCategoryName` in a computed column on the Sales Order Detail table (and to do the same with `Sales.SalesTerritory` and `TerritoryName`), open your model project in SSDT and follow these steps:

1. Click Model ⇨ Existing Connections. Your connection should be selected by default.

2. Click Open.

3. Choose Select from a list of tables and views to choose the data to import, and click Next.

4. Select `Production.ProductSubCategory` and `Sales.SalesTerritory`.

5. Click Finish.

6. In Diagram view, do the following:

    1. Create the Customer.TerritoryID ⇨ SalesTerritory.TerritoryID Relationship by dragging SalesTerritory.TerritoryID onto Customer.TerritoryID.

    2. Create the ProductSubcategoryID Relationship by dragging ProductSubcategory .ProductSubcategoryID onto Product.ProductSubCategoryID.

7. In Tabular view, do the following:

    1. Add computed column `ProductSubcategoryName` with the formula `=RELATED(ProductSubcategory[Name])`.

    2. Add computed column `SalesTerritoryName` with the formula `=RELATED(SalesTerritory[Name])`.

8. Deploy your model by choosing Deploy ReportModelProject on the Build menu.

Answer to Question 2

To create a report using the Sum of LineTotal measure as the value, and the two new dimensions you just added as the dimensions using Report Builder, follow these steps:

1. From Report Manager, run Report Builder. This opens the Table or Matric Report wizard.

2. Step through the wizard. Choose the existing data model, and either place both dimensions in the Row Groups or place one there and the other in Column Groups.

3. Place the Sum of LineTotal measure in the Values box. The remaining options are up to you.

CHAPTER 20

Answer to Question 1

To create a package that imports data from the file you exported in Chapter 20 and into a new table (using the Import/Export Wizard), follow these steps:

1. Working in an SSIS project in SSDT, find a node in the Solution Explorer called SSIS Packages.

2. Right-click this, and choose the SSIS Import and Export Wizard.

3. Click through the introduction screen and fill in a data source as shown in Figure A-3.

4. For your destination, choose AdventureWorks, as shown in Figure A-4. Figure A-5 shows your source and destination selections.

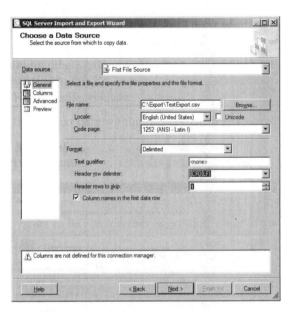

FIGURE A-3

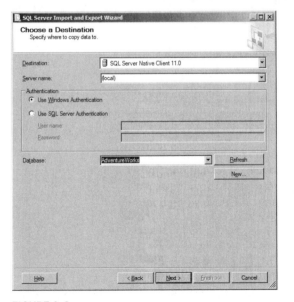

FIGURE A-4

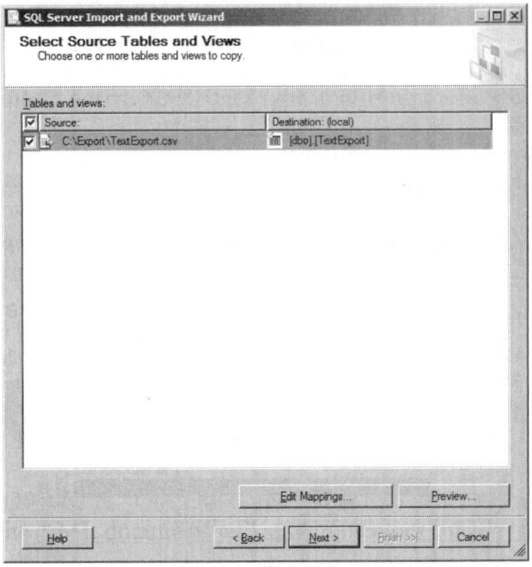

FIGURE A-5

5. Finish the wizard, and you'll be left with a package that looks like Figure A-6.

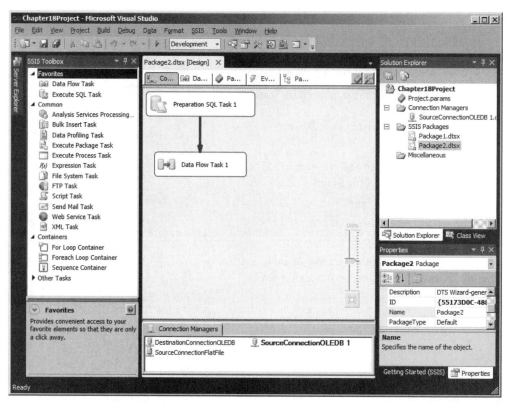

FIGURE A-6

Answer to Question 2

To deploy the package you created in question 1 and run it from the management studio, follow these steps:

1. Right-click the project and choose Deploy to launch the deployment wizard, and proceed to the Select Source screen shown in Figure A-7.

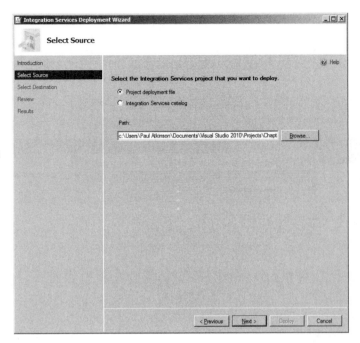

FIGURE A-7

2. Set your destination path to /SSISDB/Chapter 20/Chapter20Project, as you see in Figure A-8. Figure A-9 shows the review screen at the end of the wizard.

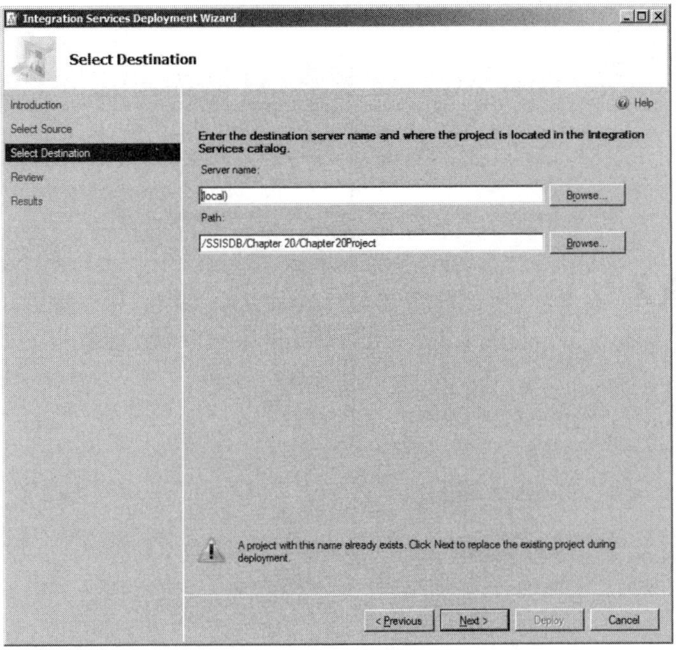

FIGURE A-8

3. Click Deploy to finish.

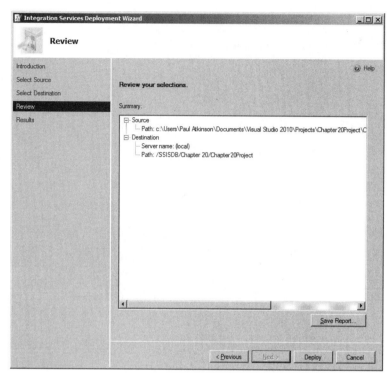

FIGURE A-9

4. Having deployed your package, launch it from the Object Explorer in SSMS, as shown in Figure A-10.

CHAPTER 21

Answer to Question 1

To take the command that you made to reorganize your `Production.TransactionHistory` table and schedule it to run as a weekend job Sunday mornings at 2AM, follow these steps:

1. Create a new job from the Object Explorer in SQL Management Studio and give it a descriptive name, such as what you see in Figure A-11.

FIGURE A-10

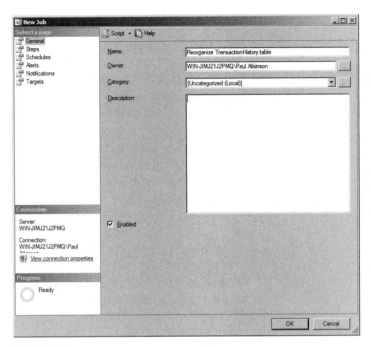

FIGURE A-11

2. Add a new step to the job, giving it a name and the command shown in Figure A-12.

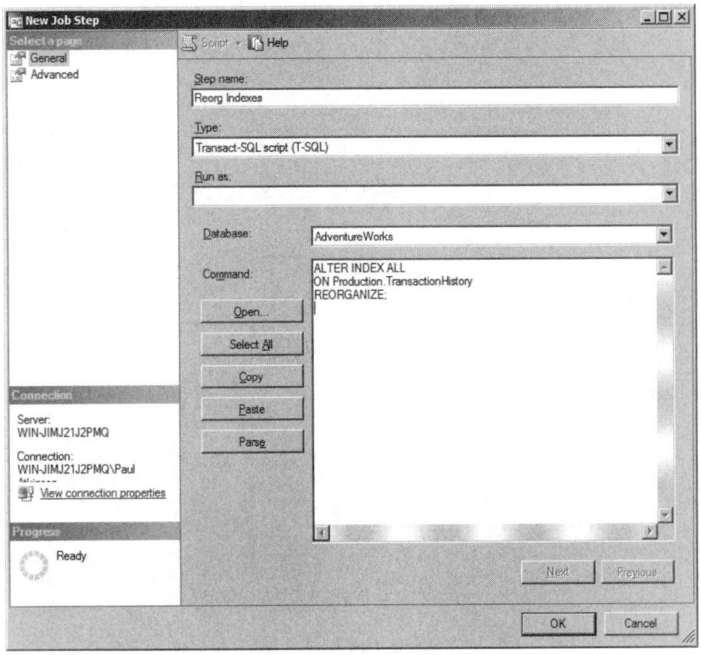

FIGURE A-12

3.   Figure A-13 shows how to set up the schedule to run the job on Sundays at 2AM.

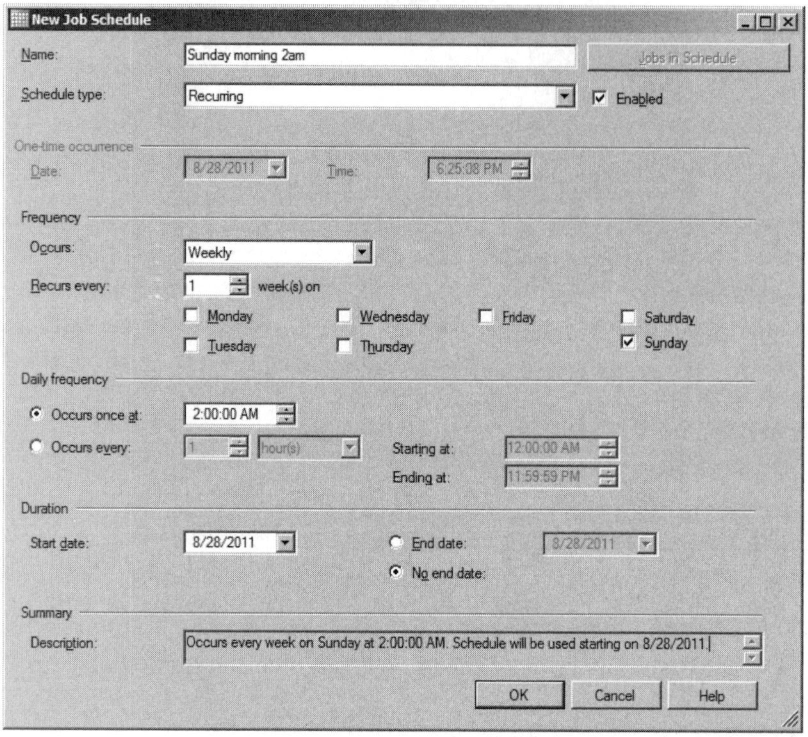

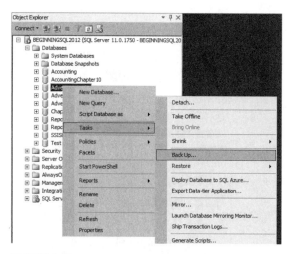

FIGURE A-13

Answer to Question 2

There are two ways to do this: through the interface, or with a SQL script.

To use the UI dialogs, follow these steps:

1.   Start with the Object Explorer.

2.   Right-click AdventureWorks and select Tasks ⇨ Back Up (see Figure A-14).

3.   On the Backup dialog box, select an appropriate backup location as shown in Figure A-15.

FIGURE A-14

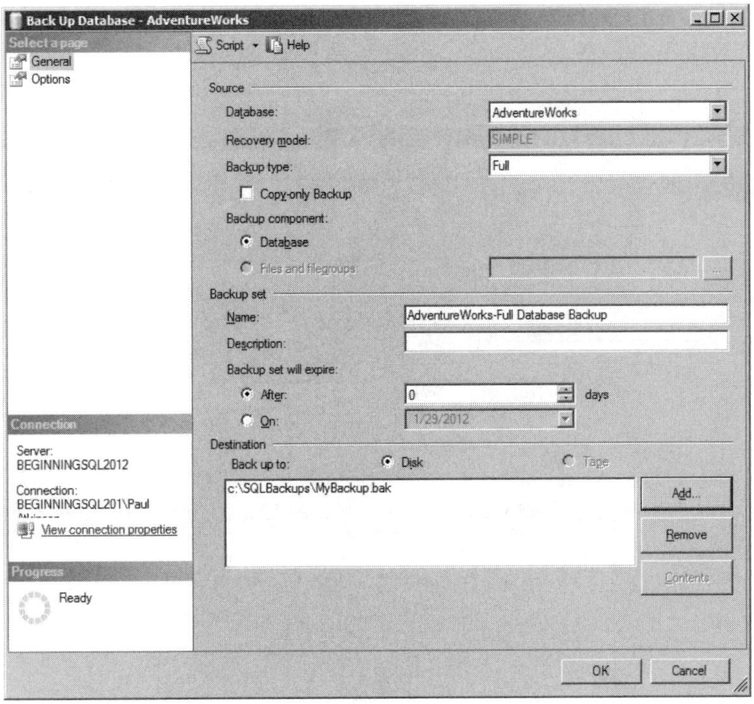

FIGURE A-15

Alternatively, you could use something similar to the following SQL script:

```
BACKUP DATABASE [AdventureWorks] TO  DISK = N'c:\SQLBackups\MyBackup.bak'
WITH NOFORMAT,
NOINIT,  NAME = N'AdventureWorks-Full Database Backup', SKIP, NOREWIND, NOUNLOAD,
STATS = 10
```

Answer to Question 3

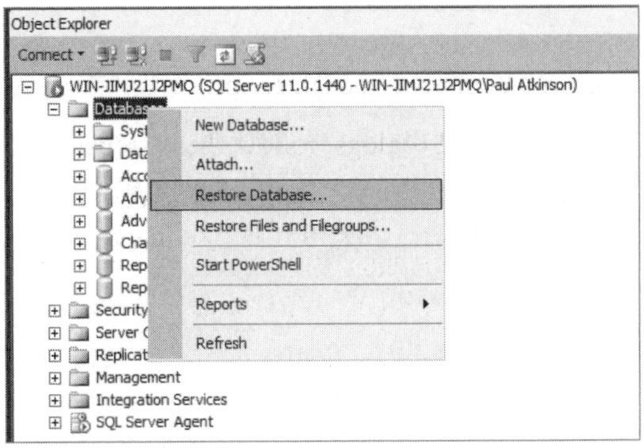

There are two ways to do this: through the interface, or with a SQL script.

To use the UI dialogs, follow these steps:

1. Start with the Object Explorer.

2. Right-click Databases and select Restore Database (see Figure A-16).

3. Fill in the Restore dialog box with the device (the backup file you just created)

FIGURE A-16

and the target, NewAdventures. Don't forget to check the box next to the database at the bottom, as shown in Figure A-17.

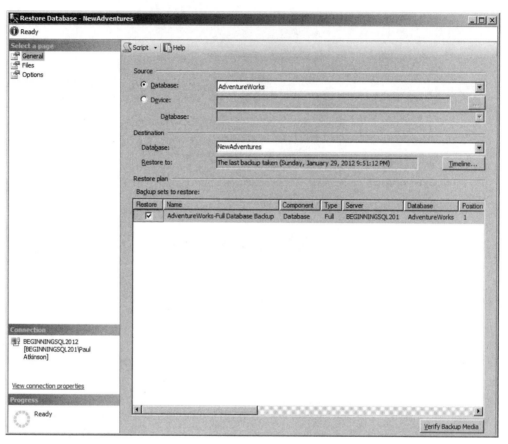

FIGURE A-17

4. (Optional) On the Files tab, shown in Figure A-18, you can move the destination files to a new location if you want.

5. When you're finished, you can click OK to start the restore.

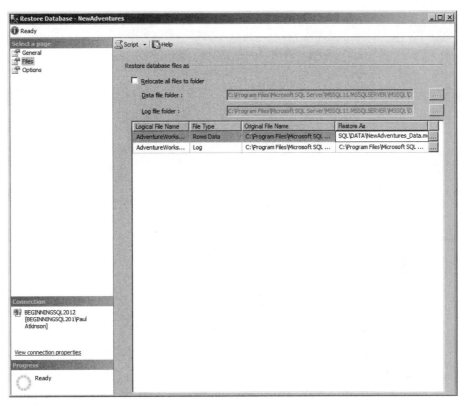

FIGURE A-18

Alternatively, you could use something similar to the following SQL script:

```
USE [master]
RESTORE DATABASE [NewAdventures] FROM  DISK = N'C:\Export\MyBackup.bak'
WITH  FILE = 1,
MOVE N'AdventureWorks_Data' TO N'C:\SQL_Data\NewAdventures_Data.mdf',
MOVE N'AdventureWorks_Log' TO N'C:\SQL_Logs\NewAdventures_log.ldf',
NOUNLOAD,  STATS = 5
```

INDEX

G

O

Q

S